Defining and Classifying Children in N

The Library of Essays in Child Welfare and Development
Series Editor: Michael Little

Defining and Classifying Children in Need

Edited by

Nick Axford

Dartington Social Research Unit, UK

ASHGATE

Published by
Ashgate Publishing Limited
Wey Court East
Union Road
Farnham
Surrey GU9 7PT
England

Ashgate Publishing Company
Suite 420
101 Cherry Street
Burlington, VT 05401-4405
USA

Ashgate website: http://www.ashgate.com

British Library Cataloguing in Publication Data
Defining and Classifying Children in Need. – (The Library
   of Essays in Child Welfare and Development)
   1. Child welfare 2. Family assessment 3. Children –
   services for
   I. Axford, Nick
   362.7

Library of Congress Cataloging-in-Publication Data
Defining and Classifying Children in Need / edited by Nick Axford.
   p. cm.
Includes index.
1. Child Welfare. 2. Family assessment. 3. Children–Services for. I. Axford, Nick.

HV715. D445 2008
362.7–dc22

2008002373

ISBN:978-0-7546-2556-8

Mixed Sources
Product group from well-managed
forests and other controlled sources
www.fsc.org Cert no. SGS-COC-2482
© 1996 Forest Stewardship Council

Printed and bound in Great Britain by
TJ International Ltd, Padstow, Cornwall

Contents

PART IV   MEASURING THE NEEDS OF CHILD POPULATIONS

PART V   TOWARDS MEETING CHILDREN'S NEEDS

Acknowledgements

The editor and publishers wish to thank the following for permission to use copyright material.

American Psychological Association for the essay: A.H. Maslow (1943), 'A Theory of Human Motivation', *Psychological Review*, **50**, pp. 370–96. Copyright © 1943 American Psychological Association.

BAAF Publications for the essay: Dora Black (1990), 'What Do Children Need from Parents?', *Adoption & Fostering*, **14**, pp. 43–51. Copyright © 1990 BAAF Publications.

Baywood Publishing for the essay: Ian Gough and Theo Thomas (1994), 'Why Do Levels of Human Welfare Vary Among Nations?', *International Journal of Health Services*, **24**, pp. 715–48. Copyright © 1994 Baywood Publishing Co., Inc.

Blackwell Publishing for the essays: Raymond Plant (1985), 'Welfare and the Value of Liberty', *Government and Opposition*, **20**, pp. 297–314. Copyright © 1985 Blackwell Publishing Ltd; Robert E. Goodin (1985), 'The Priority of Needs', *Philosophy and Phenomenological Research*, **45**, pp. 615–25. Copyright © 1985 Blackwell Publishing Ltd; Michael Rutter (1989), 'Pathways from Childhood to Adult Life', *Journal of Child Psychology and Psychiatry*, **30**, pp. 23–51. Copyright © 1989 Association for Child Psychology and Psychiatry, published by Blackwell Publishing Ltd and reproduced with permission; Gordon Jack (1997), 'An Ecological Approach to Social Work with Children and Families', *Child and Family Social Work*, **2**, pp. 109–20. Copyright © 1997 Blackwell Publishing Ltd; Robert Goodman (1997), 'The Strengths and Difficulties Questionnaire: A Research Note', *Journal of Child Psychology and Psychiatry*, **38**, pp. 581–85. Copyright © 1997 Association for Child Psychology and Psychiatry, published by Blackwell Publishing Ltd and reproduced with permission; Dennis P. Cantwell (1996), 'Classification of Child and Adolescent Psychopathology', *Journal of Child Psychology and Psychiatry*, **37**, pp. 3–12. Copyright © 1996 Blackwell Publishing Ltd; Roy Parker (1998), 'Reflections on the Assessment of Outcomes in Child Care', *Children & Society*, **12**, pp. 192–201. Copyright © 1998 Blackwell Publishing Ltd; Michael Little (1999), 'Prevention and Early Intervention with Children in Need: Definitions, Principles and Examples of Good Practice', *Children & Society*, **13**, pp. 304–16. Copyright © 1999 Blackwell Publishing Ltd.

Cambridge University Press for the essay: Conduct Problems Prevention Research Group (1992), 'A Developmental and Clinical Model for the Prevention of Conduct Disorder: The FAST Track Program', *Development and Psychopathology*, **4**, pp. 509–27. Copyright © 1992 Cambridge University Press.

Series Preface

This series of books crosses rarely traversed academic and disciplinary boundaries. There are many experts in child development, but few who understand the law or the provision of effective interventions. Few leading thinkers on the law bother much with questions of child development, or the way the law is put into practice by children's services. Those that pioneer prevention generally know little about safety nets to catch the impoverished whose impairments are so significant that the state becomes the parent. Most of the writing and thinking on these subjects comes from Europe, North America and Australasia, ignoring the development of the majority of children who live in what is now called the economic South.

This series of books brings together thinking from across these fields of interest. In so doing, it provides an ecology of evidence on how the state responds to children, effectively and ineffectively.

The starting point is the volume by Barbara Maughan and Michael Little, *Child Development*. In the last quarter of a century understanding about the causes and consequences of impairments to children's health and development has transformed. More is known about the relative contribution of genetics and the environment. The way in which the brain re-wires itself at critical points in a child's development is now clearer. The interplay of environmental influences such as poverty, neighbourhood and family with the individual characteristics of the child is beginning to come into view.

There is a considerable distance, however, between knowing why problems occur and doing something about them. There are other influences on society's response such as the relative merits of children's and parents' rights, the relationship between state and parent in deciding what should be done, as well as questions of resource and priority. Nick Axford's volume *Defining and Classifying Children in Need* explains the benefits of a single theoretical framework for dealing with these and other questions.

This theme is taken forward by Emily Buss and Mavis Maclean in their volume *The Law and Child Development*. They helpfully contrast the situation in the US and the UK explaining how the former has placed greater emphasis on the parents' and children's rights to autonomy, while the latter has made more progress in articulating and protecting children's needs.

The hinterland between these worlds is state care for extremely poor children suffering significant impairments to their health and development. Here the state has to decide who is in need, and why and how to intervene. Mark Courtney and June Thoburn's volume *Children in State Care* shows how, when it is responsible, the state struggles to get right even the basic elements of child development, for example, the stability of living situations.

Michael Little and Barbara Maughan take a much more expansive and optimistic view of children's services in their volume *Effective Interventions for Children in Need*. But very little of what is known about what works, for whom, when and why – a reasonable proportion of which is summarised in their volume – is put into mainstream practice.

Is it worse still in poorer parts of the planet? As Dwan Kaoukji and Najat M'Jid demonstrate in their volume *Children's Services in the Developing World*, fortunes are mixed. Catastrophe, war and poverty produce risks that children in the economically developed world can hardly contemplate. Yet most children do not succumb to these risks, and the ability of civil society to respond to those that do often puts children's services in the economic North to shame.

As well as providing a sound body of evidence for students of child development and children's services, it is hoped this *Library of Essays in Child Welfare and Development* series will encourage the inquiring mind to exploit the potential for understanding what follows from straying across academic and disciplinary borders.

MICHAEL LITTLE

Series Editor

Chapin Hall Center for Research at the University of Chicago, USA

and Social Research Unit at Dartington, UK

Introduction

Over a decade ago, Bradshaw described need as 'too imprecise, too complex, too contentious to be a target for policy ... [it] leaves a lot to be desired both as an epidemiological identifier and also as a basis for evaluating the performance of policies' (1994, p. 45). He is not alone in those views. Need as a concept has been subject to much discussion, with commentators interpreting it variously as dressed-up preferences (Goodin, 1988) or wants manufactured by capitalism (Illich, 1999). Others, however, advocate need as universal basis for the distribution of welfare (Doyal and Gough, 1991; Plant, 1991). Indeed, recent years have witnessed a revival in the popularity of measuring need in developing, but primarily in developed, countries as a precursor to distributing health, education, housing, social security and social care resources (Percy-Smith, 1996; Stewart, 1996; Axford, 2008a).

In children's services, policy reforms in this direction have been driven by at least three influences. First is the expectation that agencies should achieve maximum benefit from limited means. This increases the pressure to chart need before allocating resources. Second is the growing realization among academics, practitioners and policy-makers that children's problems are best understood if viewed from several perspectives; need as a concept encourages such a holistic approach. Third, public disquiet about social inequalities – notably the way in which people with similar needs are treated differently – has focused more attention on service consistency.

The results are evident in the attention given to identifying and providing services to meet children's needs. The Looking After Children initiative, for example, provides a method for measuring needs, making plans and assessing outcomes for children cared for away from home (Parker *et al.*, 1991). It has been adapted and implemented in Western and Eastern Europe, Australia and Canada (for example, Jones *et al.*, 1998; Kufeldt *et al.*, 2000; Wise, 2003; Champion and Burke, 2004). Similarly, the *Framework for the Assessment of Children in Need and their Families* (DoH *et al.*, 2000; Sinclair, 2000; Gray, 2002) has been implemented in England and Wales (Cleaver *et al.*, 2004) and piloted in Australia, Canada, Ireland and Sweden (see, for example, Fernandez and Romeo, 2003; Buckley *et al.*, 2007). Meanwhile, the *Matching Needs and Services* method for developing needs-led, evidence-based services has been used in numerous locations in Europe and North America (Little, Bullock, Madge and Arruabarrena, 2002; Melamid and Brodbar, 2003; Taylor, 2005).

Geographically the concept of needs-led services clearly has a far reach. That said, it is important to note that it has particular purchase in England and Wales where local authorities are legally required to identify and to assist 'children in need'. According to the Children Act 1989, these are children whose health or development is actually impaired or likely to become so without remedial help (Part III, s. 17(10)). More recent legislation and guidance reinforce this focus, referring to children with 'additional needs', defined as those at risk of poor outcomes, and encouraging local agencies to measure the level of need locally and use the results as the basis for planning services (DfES, 2003; Children Act 2004; HM Government, 2005).

The result over the last two decades in England and Wales has been a concerted effort to develop more sophisticated approaches to assessing need at the individual level (Parker *et al.*, 1991; DoH *et al.*, 2000; Horwath, 2001; DfES, 2006a, 2006b) and a proliferation of research into 'children in need' at an aggregate level – both national and local (see, for example, Ward and Peel, 2002; DoH, 2001; DoH, 2000; DfES and National Statistics, 2006; Axford *et al.* 2008). Although this focus necessarily affects the balance of this book, much of this work has had a wider impact internationally (as indicated earlier), and the broad messages apply across different contexts.

One common factor is that those charged with defining and classifying children in need admit to finding the task difficult. Much of the research just referred to has conceptual weaknesses, and each measure has its own idiosyncrasies. The resulting inconsistencies are perhaps not surprising given such complications (see McCrystal, 2000). Thus, attempts to measure need in relation to children have variously looked at the cause or context of need, its manifestations or symptoms, the responses of service providers to need and individuals' perceptions of what they need (Sinclair and Carr-Hill, 1996; Sinclair, 2001). Ironically, 'children in need' often get lost amidst these impostors.

Culyer wrote of need that 'the idea won't do – but we need it' (Chapter 5, p. 83). In a similar vein, others have suggested that, while it is difficult to make need work theoretically, it has resonance empirically and is useful in policy and practice (Doyal and Gough, Chapter 3, this volume). It seems that the idea will not go away; indeed, in the absence of a better alternative, identifying and meeting the needs of children and their families will continue to be perennial tasks for children's services agencies. This volume seeks to help those charged with such responsibilities. It was not possible to give a comprehensive survey of the field. Instead, essays were chosen to illustrate some of the main theoretical, methodological and practical developments in recent years and because they were deemed to be interesting and useful for those working with individual children or in service planning. Several academic disciplines are represented, including political philosophy, social policy, social work, psychology and prevention science. Collectively, contributions also cover a range of needs and professions – education, health, social care, youth justice and so on – but, given the intended readership, the focus is primarily on conceptualizing and measuring need at a generic or 'global' level. The purpose of this Introduction, which follows the order of the book, is to explain the significance and context of the selected essays and link them to the broader context and literature on the subject of defining and classifying children in need.

The Theory of Need

A scrutiny of the more philosophical works on the subject in recent decades reveals that need is a complex concept that resists definition (see, for example, Miller, 1976, 1999; Fitzgerald, 1977; Ignatieff, 1985; Braybrooke, 1987; Moon, 1991; Sheppard, 2007). Even so, there have been various attempts to spell out what 'need' comprises and to operationalize the concept by developing lists of needs. Not surprisingly, these efforts have been criticized on various grounds, but robust counter-critiques have been formulated, defending the notion of 'universal needs' that apply in any country at any time. It is argued here, therefore, that need continues to be a helpful concept for informing decisions about if and how the state should intervene in the lives of children and families and for guiding the allocation of welfare resources in society. An important rider to this contention is that the way in which need is conceptualized affects how it is met, or at least the nature of strategies designed to meet it. Essays have been selected for this volume to elucidate these points.

Debates about the nature of need occur primarily in the context of philosophical discussions concerning social justice and the distribution of welfare goods. In Chapter 1 Raymond Plant outlines the New Right critique of a welfare state committed to meeting its citizens' needs. He notes that critics argue that it acts as a brake on economic growth and that it tends to grow because needs are open-ended or 'elastic'. Critics also contend that a needs-based welfare state cannot be claimed – as it frequently is – to concern enhancing freedom or rectifying injustice since 'economic outcomes [of markets] are unintentional and unforeseeable and therefore cannot produce coercion or injustice' (p. 10).

In the course of his rebuttal, Plant defends and elaborates the notion of basic needs (see also Plant *et al.* 1981; Plant, 1991). His first counterargument is that the economic outcomes *are* foreseeable insofar as 'those who enter a market with least, will end up with least' (p. 11), suggesting responsibility, if not intentionality. In addition, he stresses that 'there is *some* connection between liberty and ability' (p. 12, original emphasis) in that it is unreasonable to claim that someone is free to do something that they cannot do (for example, afford to go on a round-the-world cruise). In other words, if liberty is to have any value, then individuals must satisfy some basic needs in order to act at all. These basic needs are defined as well-being (more than physical survival) and the ability to act effectively (which also requires psychological resources). Plant acknowledges that such basic goods need to be 'cashed' in terms of specific goods and that the way in which this happens will be culture-dependent, but argues that they 'should be distributed equally just because there are no a priori moral reasons for any other sort of distribution' (p. 15). He further defends the notion of needs-based claims and the obligation to provide welfare on the grounds that '[t]he worst-off members of society do suffer a constraint on the value of liberty and they do suffer injustice given that there are alternatives' (p. 18).

Also coming from the perspective of political philosophy, Robert Goodin makes a similar argument in Chapter 2 in that he begins by attacking the concept of need and ends up defending it. Initially, he queries the value of need, particularly the claim that satisfying needs should take priority over satisfying desires. His argument critques propositions typically used to buttress the concept and the view that it deserves priority over other claims. Thus, he points out that the notion of meeting need, as it is commonly used, can be as much about providing unnecessary benefits as about avoiding harm. He also claims that the contention that something is a need when the harm that will ensue if it is not satisfied is outside the person's control is easily undermined, and notes that some needs are non-urgent, just as some desires (non-needs) are urgent. In sum, there is only an imperfect correlation between need and harm-avoidance, involuntariness and urgency, and so need cannot be used to justify priority *on these grounds*.

Instead, Goodin argues that '[t]he most plausible analysis of needs ... construes them as Rawlsian[1] "primary goods". These are defined as the goods – or, in the case of needs,

---

[1]   In his seminal book *A Theory of Justice* (1971) John Rawls argued that '[a]ll social primary goods – liberty and opportunity, income and wealth, and the bases of self respect – are to be distributed equally unless an unequal distribution of any or all of these goods is to the advantage of the least favoured' (p. 303).

conditions or circumstances more generally – that are necessary instruments to any and all particular ends which one might pursue' (p. 27). This perspective clearly resonates with the view advanced by Plant in Chapter 2. Further, Goodin suggests that one of the advantages of need-satisfaction defined in this sense is that it is 'non-committal'; there is no need to judge whether a particular end is valuable and, on that basis, to judge whether X (to do Y) is a valid need, since satisfying the need is indispensable to a variety of ends.

It will be apparent from the two essays discussed above that there has traditionally been considerable doubt and wrangling among academics about the concept of need. In Chapter 3, and writing in this contentious context, Len Doyal and Ian Gough seek to reformulate the concept rigorously and operationalize it so that it can have practical use for social policy. Their arguments, originally put forward in 1984, were later developed elsewhere, most clearly in their seminal publication *A Theory of Human Need* (1991; see also Doyal, 1988; Gough, 2000 for a summary). They start by acknowledging the critiques of need as being relative (or subjective) and enabling experts or vested interests to impose their own 'top-down' beliefs on vulnerable groups. Their response is to identify two universal goals, or 'basic needs', that must be achieved in order for a given individual to act (in the sense of perform an action), irrespective of the morality of that action or the cultural, geographic or historical context in which it takes place: these are *physical health* and *personal autonomy*. Failure to satisfy these needs, they argue, will always cause an individual to suffer harm. They refer briefly to the 'intermediate goals' such as food, shelter and clothing that are necessary to achieve the main goals, later developed into a list of 11 intermediate needs – the properties of goods, services, activities and relationships that enhance physical health and autonomy in all cultures (Doyal and Gough, 1991, pp. 191–221). Further, and responding to accusations of paternalism, their essay argues for maximum participation in defining and implementing need-based policies.

The publication of *A Theory of Human Need* (*THN*) fuelled the debate on defining and measuring need, with several alternative views being expressed (see, for example, Hewitt, 1992, 1993; Drover and Kerans, 1993; Wetherly, 1996; Tao and Drover, 1997). Chapter 4 reproduces Kate Soper's critique because it captures the essence of some of these discussions. She observes that theories of need veer between being so abstract and uncontroversial as to be interesting but ultimately uninformative and being so precise and culturally relative that robust universal statements become impossible. She argues that *THN* successfully bridges this 'thin–thick' divide. In particular, she praises its emphasis on the dual discernment of needs by experts and welfare claimants and its helpful distinction between what is fundamental to human well-being (needs) and what may be considered to contribute to further flourishing (wants).

Others have also articulated this distinction, suggesting that a person can need something they do not want (food in the case of an anorexic teenager) and want something they do not need (a millionaire's umpteenth car) (Ware and Goodin, 1990), and that whereas a person is always impoverished when their needs are not met, the denial of subjective preferences rarely has such drastic effects (Wiggins, 1985). Soper also applauds Doyal's and Gough's attack on the prevailing cultural relativism at the time. It may be true at one level that needs are relative to an individual's physical circumstances – one is unlikely to need a winter coat in Dubai or a swimsuit in Antarctica – and what others in society have and do, but harm nearly always ensues if some human purposes are not fulfilled – for example, minimum calorific intake is largely absolute and fixed by nature (Goodin, 1990). Thus, *THN* argues that the 'satisfiers' to meet universal needs *are* culturally variable – for example, the need for nutrition and protection from the elements can be met from a potentially infinite variety of cuisines and forms of dwelling. However, Soper questions aspects of the *THN*, arguing in particular that it is more ethnocentric than it claims (see also Tao and Drover, 1997), that need-satisfaction at the level advocated may be ecologically unsustainable and that there are problems surrounding the definition of and focus on 'basic' needs – which she regards as somewhat puritanical. It is not necessary here to rehearse responses to these criticisms (see Gough, 2000 for a discussion), but the debate about what level of well-being might realistically be attainable and how far this incorporates the satisfaction of wants is increasingly salient in children's services (Jordan, 2006).

The final two essays in Part I descend from the somewhat lofty heights of abstraction scaled in the earlier chapters and discuss the application of the concept of need in policy and practice. In Chapter 5 Tony Culyer proposes a set of conditions that must be met for the term 'need' to be of practical use in allocating health-care resources efficiently and equitably. Two general points have particular salience for children's services. The first is that ascribing to someone a need is more than saying that they have a particular deficit or impairment.[2] Rather, it is bound up with issues concerning the value of changing that individual's circumstances, the availability of resources and knowledge to address the deficit and improve the circumstances, the capacity of the individual concerned to benefit from any intervention and the fair and equitable distribution of resources more widely (see Sheppard and Woodcock, 1999). Second, the use of need in service settings is most useful when it is articulated with a high degree of specificity and when there is consistency of response: that is, there should be clarity about the objectives (or desired outcomes) and about what exactly will be provided to whom, and there should be an attempt to ensure that individuals with similar needs get similar services (with those having different needs receiving different services) (see Little and Sinclair, 2005).

Jonathan Bradshaw's aim in Chapter 6 is to clarify for those working in social welfare services what is meant by social need and how to identify it. He suggests that it tends to be identified by asking individuals what they want (*felt* need), by calculating the demand for services (*expressed* need), by extrapolating the sociodemographic characteristics of service-users for the whole community (*comparative* need) and by ascertaining levels of expert-defined need (*normative* need). His essay shows how these definitions relate to one another so that policy-makers and practitioners can decide what constitutes the 'real need' that it is appropriate for services to meet. The hypothetical example given of determining the housing needs of the elderly illustrates some of the dilemmas requiring consideration. Although the focus of the previous chapters has mostly been on normative need, later chapters will show that this is where there has been least work in children's services.

The Needs of Children

There are various ways of categorizing what children need, depending in part on the underpinning theory and empirical evidence. Notwithstanding these differences and critiques of a need perspective, there is broad agreement about children's main needs and general

---

[2]   'Impairment refers to the absence of normal health development – that is, when a condition usually interferes with daily social functioning and performance' (Hill, 2002, p. 511).

acceptance of the value of an ecological perspective in which the needs of an individual child are best understood in the context of his or her family and wider environment. Over the last two decades these ideas have taken hold in children's services in Western developed countries and, as later chapters demonstrate, they inform both individual assessment and service planning. It is also important to note, however, that while need has a prescriptive force that makes it a useful guide to allocating resources, recent developments in research into child psychopathology suggest that child development is more complex than this approach assumes. The resulting, more sophisticated, understanding of what children need has the potential to promote more effective interventions. The essays chosen for Part II discuss these points in more depth.

The tendency for researchers to formulate lists of what people need has already been highlighted (Doyal and Gough, 1991; Nussbaum, 2000). One of the best-known lists, described in Chapter 7 by Abraham Maslow, covers physiological needs, safety, love, esteem and self-actualization, and is ordered in a (not rigid) hierarchy of 'relative prepotency' so that the latter or 'higher' needs generally emerge only once the earlier, more basic, ones are satisfied (see also Maslow, 1970). Maslow's theory is designed to help explain what drives, or motivates, human behaviour and is based primarily on clinical experience and the observation that the thwarting of basic needs produces psychopathological results. In relation to safety, for example, he argues that children need an organized world characterized by routine or rhythm because they show signs of anxiety and distress when confronted with, say, family quarrelling or separation from parents. To some degree this is a life-span model, in the sense that self-actualization is not considered to be attained until adulthood, but arguably it is better to see needs as occurring at the same time – intertwining, rather than forming a progression (Hill and Tisdall, 1997). Indeed, several other authors have taken a developmental perspective and sought to articulate the fundamental requirements of healthy child development, or, put another way, the conditions that are statistically associated with good outcomes (for a review see Seden, 2001).

Thus, Dora Black, in Chapter 8, lists both basic needs for children, including physical care, affection, guidance and control, and independence, and the consequences of these not being met, including deprivation and demanding behaviour (pp. 132–33). This perspective derives explicitly from research into 'normal' child development and the causes and consequences of deviation from the norm (p. 136). Drawing on Bowlby (1951) and others, for instance, she notes the short- and long-term effects on children of poor attachment and stresses the need for intimacy and opportunities for forming close, loving relationships with responsive people. Kellmer-Pringle (1975) adopts the same approach in *The Needs of Children*, which had a considerable currency in the 1970s, where she takes for granted the satisfaction of children's physiological and safety needs and focuses on their needs for love and security, new experiences, praise and recognition, and responsibility (see also Towle, 1987). In a similar vein, Brazelton and Greenspan (2000, p. ix) identify 'the very most basic needs, the kinds of care without which children cannot grow, learn, and thrive', including physical protection, safety and regulation, and developmentally appropriate experiences. Their list of 'irreducible needs' is based partly on research showing how residents of Romanian orphanages who were denied warm nurturing or stimulating interaction developed severe physical, intellectual and social deficits.

These portrayals of children's needs within developmental psychology have been criticized on two main counts (see Woodhead, 1997). First, the need perspective is accused of presenting childhood as a period of dependency on adults, when in reality children shape their own environment (see also Mayall, 2002). This is certainly a danger, but it can be countered in two ways. The balance and precise form of children's needs change as they grow older, but their broad needs remain the same as adults. This much is apparent from standard child development texts (for example, Dworetzky, 1996; see also Waldfogel, 2006). Thus, a need perspective renders children no more dependent than it does adults. Most approaches today also give considerable prominence to the notion of *autonomy* – an evolving capacity to make informed choices about what should be done and how to go about it. So, for an infant it might mean deciding which toys to play with or contributing to a family discussion about where to go for a day out, whereas for a teenager it might involve choosing a college course or set of friends, or campaigning on a particular social or political issue.

The second critique concerns *content*, in that need lists give an air of spurious certainty when in fact there is disagreement about what constitutes children's best interests. Some items are considered to be particularly value-laden or ethnocentric – for example, the emphasis on individual responsibility is considered to reflect Western individualistic thinking. In response, it might be argued that this is more apparent than real and that there is flexibility in most lists because of the separation of needs from satisfiers (Maslow, in Chapter 7, also encourages a search for the unity behind cultural specificity). As part of the same critique, it is inferred that expert-defined needs may be out of kilter with children's views of what they need, although, to state the counterargument, evidence for this is scant; indeed, several studies asking children what they want from parents have produced results that resonate strongly with the aforementioned lists – wanting to be loved, understood, cared for, supervised, appreciated and so on (see Hill and Tisdall, 1997). All this said, the notion of definitive sets of needs must be balanced with the fact that there are multiple pathways through childhood to adulthood.

Michael Rutter makes this point strongly in Chapter 9 where he demonstrates that understanding development from childhood to adulthood involves analysing 'a quite complicated set of linkages over time [and] … is not simply a matter of determining the level of correlation for particular behaviours from one age to some later age' (p. 144). His essay concentrates on exploring the interplay over time between intrinsic and extrinsic factors that impact on individual development and, as such, highlights significant developments in understanding since earlier work. He notes that Bowlby's (1951) argument that maternal deprivation in infancy leads to permanent, irreversible damage (indicating continuity) has been undermined by research – including his own *Maternal Deprivation Reassessed* (Rutter, 1981) – showing that individuals can recover from early adverse experiences (indicating discontinuity) – for example, if they subsequently experience a positive rearing environment. Contending that reality is 'a rather complex mix of both continuities and discontinuities' (p. 141), he sets out a series of principles and concepts that can help with understanding both normal development and psychopathology, including risk and protective factors, causal mechanisms and the salience of how individuals interpret and negotiate given stressors. Using such devices to trace and reflect on complex interactions in a given child's life makes it easier to state accurately what that child needs in order to achieve healthy (unimpaired) development (see Little *et al.*, 2004).

Further, in a deliberately incomplete review of long-term longitudinal studies, Rutter identifies a 'reasonably representative' (p. 155) set of patterns showing that links in chains of adversity are not inevitable but, rather, that there are contingencies which, if not met, may result in adaptive routes. For example, not every child admitted to a residential institution will return to a discordant family and end up leaving home early and marrying a deviant spouse. The last part of the essay sketches out various mechanisms that might help to explain the patterns identified, ranging from genetic and biological factors to how individuals process cognitively what is happening to them and how they cope with difficulties (see also Rutter, 1999). Underpinning the perspective offered is the view that basic research into child development of the kind described has significant potential to inform prevention and treatment activities for vulnerable children – a point revisited in more depth in Part V of this volume.

The developmental approach to the provision of children's services, embodied by the previous contributions, has been fuelled by an ecological perspective, as elaborated by Gordon Jack in Chapter 10. This approach is underpinned by research showing that children's physical and psychological well-being is related to parents' levels of social support and their wider environment, whether directly or indirectly via a 'buffering' effect in the context of stressors. Jack focuses on the effects of social support networks on parenting and levels of child maltreatment; the implications for determining children's needs of other connections between (i) environment (including housing, income and community resources), (ii) parental capacity and care-giving and (iii) child development are explored in more depth elsewhere (for example, Jack, 2001; Seden, 2002; Barnes *et al.*, 2006; Chaskin, 2006).

It is easy to take this approach for granted today but Jack's essay is helpful for drawing attention to an earlier preoccupation with investigating allegations regarding abuse and what he characterizes as a 'discourse of child protection' (p. 174) focused on pathological family interactions. He praises attempts to move things forward in the shape of a more phenomenological approach that views abusive incidents in the context of other factors and likely long-term effects (see DoH, 1995). At the same time he criticizes a tendency in the field to seek solutions by changing social work practice and management rather than influencing broader sociopolitical factors. Policy and practice developments in the decade since arguably reflect the more holistic perspective advocated. Drawing on international research, they often entail multi-agency efforts intended to tackle risk factors at several levels in order to break the causal chains referred to above (e.g. Sanders, 1999; Webster-Stratton *et al.*, 2001; DfES, 2003; Little and Abunimah, 2007; Zappone, 2007). Attempts to articulate children's needs, then, have helped to shift the debate away from concerns with scandals and processes and disabused false dichotomies (environment versus psychology). Instead they have focused attention on what can be done practically to meet children's needs and improve child well-being. Any intervention with this end in mind must start with good assessment, the subject of Part III.

Assessing the Needs of Individual Children

The purpose of assessing the needs of an individual child is to decide whether and how to intervene in his or her life. It involves ascertaining the nature and causes of the difficulties faced and designing a service capable of improving the child's well-being and, ideally, meeting the identified need. There are various approaches to need assessment, including a large number of psychiatric and psychological measures focused on specific health, behavioural and emotional difficulties (see Verhulst and Van der Ende, 2002; Tiffin and Richardson, 2006) and educational assessments of children's intellectual capacity and attainment (Tymms, 1999). Different instruments also have different functions – early screening, more in-depth profiling and ongoing monitoring (Edmunds and Stewart-Brown, 2003) – and whereas some are primarily concerned with diagnosis, others are explicitly to help with service planning. There is overlap between these categories, of course, as will be seen.

The focus in Part III of the book is on the more generic assessment measures in children's services, some of which have been evaluated (see the introductory section of this chapter). Some of these emerged in recent years partly as a response to child abuse scandals where failures to record accurately the child's situation and share that information with relevant agencies have been blamed for the poor service response. These approaches mark valuable progress relative to much that went before. In particular, the ecological framework tends to be embedded, so that practitioners are encouraged to be more systematic and consistent in what they record. However, weaknesses remain, notably: forms being filled out incorrectly or patchily; a tendency to collect too much information and not do enough with it; a reliance predominantly on tools that are questionable in terms of validity or reliability; a reluctance to use taxonomical formulations that can inform prognoses and identifying intervention that work the best; limited aggregation of the data gathered for planning purposes; and a failure to exploit the information to help track outcomes. The essays have been selected for this volume in order to illuminate these issues and show what is possible.

In Chapter 11 Robert Goodman describes the development and testing of the Strengths and Difficulties Questionnaire (SDQ) – a screening instrument designed to uncover problems with behaviour, emotions and relationships among children aged 4–16 years.[3] It is elegant in its simplicity. Containing only 25 items and fitting easily on one side of paper, it can be completed by parents or teachers in as little as two minutes (a self-report version is also available for older children). It generates results that correlate highly with those produced by longer, proven instruments and performs as well as these more complex measures in its ability to discriminate effectively between normal and clinical cases. Subsequent work in various countries has provided further evidence of its validity and reliability and identified cut-off scores for 'abnormal' or 'high need' cases that are closely associated with clinical diagnosis of disorder (see, for example, Smedje *et al.*, 1999; Goodman *et al.*, 2000; Klasen *et al.*, 2000; Goodman, 2001; Muris *et al.*, 2003; Hawes and Dadds, 2004).

Numerous other generic instruments for assessing psychopathology have been developed in different countries (see, for example, Smith and Brun, 2006). Most of them cover similar content, are user-friendly and have evidence of validity and reliability, but the choice of the scale will depend on the purpose of the exercise and the resources available. Skevington and Gillison (2006), for example, describe the KIDSCREEN instrument, which was developed and tested by a European consortium and which assesses quality of life from the child's perspective in terms of physical, mental and social well-being (Ravens-Sieberer *et al.*, 2005). While such measures should not be used in isolation when making practice decisions, as professional judgement remains vital, they invariably offer important benefits, notably: good validity (they measure objectively what they say they measure); good reliability (they produce

---

[3]   The measure is considered more robust for children aged 11–16 years.

consistent scores – both between individual professionals but also over time for the person applying them); and norm data against which individuals can be compared. Thus, it is known that any child scoring 7 or more out of 10 for the SDQ 'hyperactivity' subscale is highly likely to have a clinical hyper-kinetic disorder (e.g. ADHD) and to require intervention.

Goodman's essay raises the issue of classification. It places some children in a category marked 'normal' and determines that others are 'abnormal'. (These are statements of fact, not value judgements.) Most branches of science rest on some form of taxonomy. Chemistry, for example, has the periodic table charting the structure of the elements and their relationship to one another; Linnaeus set out a way of grouping together plants; and medicine has several classifications of diseases. Taxonomy can be defined as 'a way of applying a logical and comprehensive structure to describe characteristics and the way in which these are inter-related to form identifiable groups' (Sinclair and Little, 2002, p. 128). In Chapter 12 Dennis Cantwell discusses the conceptual and empirical issues regarding taxonomical formulations as they apply to child and adolescent psychopathology (see also Rutter and Taylor, 2002a, 2002b; Taylor and Rutter, 2008). Elsewhere in children's services, Packman and colleagues (1985) have written about children entering the care system in terms of 'the victims, the volunteered and the villains' and Moffitt (1993) distinguished between life-course persistent and adolescence-limited offenders. As part of their statistical returns, governments may require children's services agencies to allocate each child they deal with to a preordained 'need group' related to the *cause* of the child's need (see, for example, DoH, 2000). So the idea of taxonomy is not new in the field, but it remains controversial and Cantwell provides helpful pointers that will apply in various contexts.

He starts by acknowledging common objections to classification, notably the fear of stigma and labelling, before tackling the main conceptual issues, such as whether taxonomies should be based on categories (where a person does or does not meet the criteria) or dimensions (which allow for capturing multiple symptom patterns in an individual). The major official international classifications of disease (ICD-10)[4] and psychiatric disorder (DSM-IV)[5] are categorical. If such systems are to be useful when making diagnoses, it is important that they demonstrate good inter-rater and test–retest reliability. This is likely to be boosted when those applying such tools in assessment contexts do not simply have a list of symptoms, but also follow a procedure regarding where, how and in what order to source relevant data. Validity is even more crucial. One test is response to intervention: '[i]f certain clinical syndromes respond differentially to the same type of intervention the first assumption might be that the clinically defined syndrome is heterogeneous in nature' (p. 193). Another test of validity is association with certain psychosocial factors; the fact that, say, family dysfunction and parental discord are more associated with disruptive behaviour disorders than with anxiety and mood disorders suggests that it makes sense diagnostically to separate out the two broad classes of disorder. A further factor to take into account when determining validity is the temporal nature of the

---

[4]   The *International Classification of Diseases*, 10th edition, came into use in WHO member states in 1994 and is used to classify diseases and other health problems recorded on many types of health and vital records, including death certificates and hospital records. It enables the storage and retrieval of diagnostic information for clinical and epidemiological purposes and provides the basis for compiling national mortality and morbidity statistics.

[5]   The *Diagnostic and Statistical Manual of Mental Disorders*, 4th edition, is published by the American Psychiatric Association and includes all currently recognized mental health disorders.

condition. A disorder that persists into adult life, for example, may be phenomenologically similar to one that is seen only in childhood but be fundamentally different aetiologically. Cantwell also notes that the classification of children in need will evolve with new knowledge, particularly from the field of genetics. One wonders how well the taxonomies embedded in several assessment tools currently used in children's services would fare if subjected to such scrutiny. There has been little investigation of this, although the evidence from one such analysis does not offer grounds for optimism (Forrester *et al.*, 2007).

So the critical question is why is taxonomy useful in the context of children in need? Cantwell's observations illustrate three potential uses (see also Sinclair and Little, 2002). First, a taxonomy provides a conceptual structure for understanding what Sinclair (2001, p. 131) describes as 'the multiplicity, the complexity, and the compounding nature' of children's needs. All children are unique, but some are more similar than others and some share a similar constellation of need. A better understanding of such patterns can help explain the causes of need and predict with greater accuracy the likely outcome from a specific intervention. Second, taxonomy encourages practitioners, policy-makers and researchers to discuss children's needs using a common language – an important consideration given the wide variation in understanding (see, for example, Sinclair and Carr-Hill, 1996; Carr-Hill *et al.*, 1997, 1999). Third, taxonomy can serve as a practical mechanism to link individual and collective planning in children's services – a theme developed in Chapter 13.

At face value it might seem strange to include an essay on outcomes in a book about defining and classifying children in need. Yet Roy Parker's reflections in Chapter 13 offer several reasons why the connection between need and outcome is obvious and helpful – albeit neglected. First, assessments of need and outcomes are both to do with matters that concern ordinary parents about their children, however they are categorized. Second, while it is important to disaggregate the notions of need and outcome to reveal differential development in different areas of children's lives, there is also a case for general assessment. Thus, a global measure of impairment to development can provide a useful estimate outcome as well as helping to decide whether a child is in need and requiring a service (Little *et al.*, 2003). Third, the prediction of outcomes can also inform decisions about the appropriate allocation of scarce resources. The concept of need implies both a requirement to prioritize demands on children's services and an assumption that something can be done to address the problem in question, so analyses to estimate the likelihood of success of a certain course of action should affect who gets what help. Fourth, Parker calls for a different type of social accountancy characterized by 'more child-centred types of aggregated data' (p. 202). He contrasts the information traditionally collected at the planning level – concerned with administrative indicators, inputs and costs and subjected to considerable comparison with similar agencies – with that collected at the individual child level – personalized and rarely used comparatively – and argues that the two need to be linked. Both types of data, of course, are used for the purposes of need assessment *and* outcome measurement. (Part IV of this volume develops this theme.) Fifth, the information that is gathered in (need) assessments can be used in evaluation (of outcomes) – for example, as a baseline against which to compare data collected at a later stage (which, of course, may essentially be further need assessments).

In Chapter 14 Brian Sheldon continues the theme of using need data for evaluation purposes in his discussion of SCEDs (Single Case Experimental Designs). He argues that this approach to evaluation and its attendant assessment requirements are rigorous but also attuned to individual problems, and advocates it as a response to 'social work's acceptance of subjectivity, unbridled eclecticism, exclusively verbal and qualitative assessment and evaluation, and "open-plan" (unstructured, blank-sheet) case recording' (p. 211). As an evaluation technique, SCEDs essentially involve the systematic introduction and withdrawal of an intervention with a child or family while monitoring progress on selected variables (see, for example, Kazi and Wilson, 1996; Dillenburger, 1998). The assessment requires there to be clarity about the issue in question and that discrete goals and related indicators be spelt out; hazy objectives, psychopathological labelling and complex case formulations are unhelpful. Sheldon describes several applications of SCEDs – for example, with regard to school discipline techniques and modified parenting methods respectively.

Recent analyses of assessment and case-recording in children's services highlight a number of problems, including a lack of consistency and standardization within and between departments, poor focus in some instances and a disconnection between identified difficulties and what case file data suggest is actually provided in terms of services (Horwath, 2001; see also Tunstill and Aldgate, 2000; Walker *et al.*, 2003). These studies suggest that the introduction of a more quantitative element, which is what Sheldon advocates here, would help with making succinct and accurate diagnoses and prognoses. Although SCEDs are rarely used in social care, partly because of the perceived conflict with therapeutic objectives, practitioners report their usefulness, not least in the powerful demonstration-effect for parents (see, for example, Slonim-Nevo and Ziv, 1998). The practices described in the previous paragraph can be developed through professional supervision and by ensuring that clinical assessment forms have space for the systematic recording of outcomes. This need only be in relatively simple terms, such as whether the child's needs have been met. Clinical practice tools can be used in this work, particularly when used in consultation with colleagues and supervisors (Little, 2002; Little and Mount, 2003).

Measuring the Needs of Child Populations

The methodological and empirical literature on measuring the needs of child populations is sparse relative to the volume of material on assessing the needs of individual children. Yet such needs assessments serve important functions: guiding the allocation of scarce resources; informing service development; and providing useful data to help detect if the resources invested are having the desired effect. The essays selected for Part IV show how need may be measured at national, agency (and inter-agency) and area levels. They also cover the felt, expressed, comparative and normative categories in Bradshaw's taxonomy (see Chapter 6). Together, they point towards the need to develop more sophisticated approaches that have strong theoretical underpinnings, link data from different sources, use epidemiological methods, aggregate data on individuals, use taxonomies and feed directly into service design.

In Chapter 15 Ian Gough and Theo Thomas examine several possible explanations of variation between countries in levels of human welfare, including the level of economic development, the political orientation of a society (capitalist or socialist) and the extent of democracy (see also Gough and Thomas, 1994). The measures of human welfare selected are based on Doyal's and Gough's *Theory of Human Need*, so that they are cross-culturally valid and apply to the 128 nation-states in the world with a population at the time of more than 1 million. They also rely on valid and reliable indicators compiled by international agencies for c.1990; for example, low birth weight is used to capture 'health' and primary school completion rate as a measure of 'education'. Although the data are often inadequate, particularly in poorer countries, the approach shows how *normative* need can be operationalized and creates a useful by-product in that it 'tentatively confirms' the notion that satisfaction of intermediate needs predicts fulfilment of basic needs; it offers some empirical validation of the *THN*.

Even so, a local children's services planner requires something more grounded. In Chapter 16 Janie Percy-Smith discusses operationalizing the *THN* for a community audit in a large conurbation. For example, there were questions about stress and depression (relating to the *basic* need for autonomy) and about the quality of diets (concerning the *intermediate* need for adequate nutritional food and water) (Percy-Smith and Sanderson, 1992). Of 4600 randomly selected adults, one-third responded to a postal survey, giving a sample of 10 per cent of the overall adult population (ca. 16 000). The study combined a measure of felt need with information about normative need; thus, respondents' assessments of whether they ate healthily (felt need) were complemented by data on the incidence of food poisoning and doctors' evaluations of levels of cholesterol in patients' diets (normative need). Percy-Smith argues for the value of joining together information about several kinds of need in this way, although this appears to be rare, as is assessing felt need in this systematic way. A more common approach is to hold disparate focus groups and user consultation sessions which, with their emphasis on inclusion and ownership, have the advantage of better representing the views of families; their major drawback, however, is the likelihood of small non-representative samples and giving disproportionate weight to the views of the strongest contributors (Axford *et al.*, 2008).

Percy-Smith's essay also makes important points regarding the purpose of population needs assessments (see also Hawtin *et al.*, 1995). Such studies provide critical information for hard decisions about allocating scarce resources as they measure the shortfall between need and resources (or existing services) and so help with setting priorities and justifying decisions. They also inform the evaluation of policy and thereby strengthen public accountability by providing baseline data against which to assess the effectiveness of services. Moreover, if significant unmet needs remain, population needs assessments may suggest that alternative strategies need to be considered.

Despite these benefits, children's services agencies in Western developed countries have consistently struggled to identify children in need in their area and provide services accordingly – at least in any systematic way. Why is this? Michael Preston-Shoot and Veronica Wigley offer some answers in Chapter 17. Staff are often reluctant to participate in needs assessments because of heavy workloads or because they are wary of ensuing organizational change – a product of studies not always being properly linked to planning and provision. A lack of inter-agency collaboration, particularly with regard to information-sharing, and the use of different thresholds can make it difficult to compare data from several sources. Furthermore, those expected to undertake the task may lack the relevant experience and knowledge to do this. These observations are based in part on a needs assessment undertaken by the authors in one jurisdiction involving social care, education, health and the police. This is described in the essay, showing what *is* possible. Proformas were completed for each child on caseloads during one calendar month, with 7 per cent of children in the area found to be 'in need' when the results were aggregated. As such, the focus was on *expressed* need.

Other tried-and-tested methods for measuring expressed need involve gathering quantitative (e.g. Little, Axford and Morpeth, 2002) or qualitative (e.g. Little *et al.*, 1999) data from case files and grouping the children together according to the similarity of their needs. Such methods have been applied in numerous countries in Europe and several states in the United States (Little and Madge, 1998; Tunnard, 2002; Melamid and Brodbar, 2003; Johnson and Sawbridge, 2004; Taylor, 2005; Boendermaker, 2006; for alternative approaches see Colton *et al.*, 1995, Ward and Peel, 2002). Much earlier, Packman (1968) calculated what she called the 'total childcare problem' by adding together, for one day in 1960, the numbers of children in one country receiving specified forms of social care provision.[6] Cruder methods for establishing the level of expressed need also exist: children's services agencies often calculate the extent of child need by summing the numbers of children at risk of maltreatment, with special needs, in care or locked-up, and in England and Wales the official estimate of children in need is the number known to social services departments at any one time (DoH, 2000; DfES and National Statistics, 2006).

To a large extent, these methods are creatures of their time and represent attempts to get evidence into decision-making in social services. Their strength is that they exploit routinely collected data on individual children in the context of service provision (see previous section). Much work has been done in this area using the Looking After Children assessment tools (for example, Ward *et al.*, 2002; Sempik *et al.*, 2008) but there is considerable potential for further aggregation of data from more generic assessment tools (Utting, 2008). The well-documented weaknesses of case file data can be addressed by improving the quality of the instruments used for individual child assessment (see chapters in Part III) but also by collecting data direct from children and families (see below). The other obvious drawback with audits of expressed need is that they tie need to service receipt: however, not every child who receives a service is in need, just as some children will be in need without coming into contact with a service provider (Axford, 2008a). A different approach, then, is to ascertain the prevalence in the wider community of the sociodemographic characteristics of service recipients (*comparative* need). In Chapter 18 Andrew Bebbington and John Miles report a survey of 2500 children entering care over a specified six-month period. For each child they recorded socioeconomic factors widely associated with being 'in need' – benefit-dependency, mother under 21 years, minority ethnic group status and so forth. Where all such factors hold, the probability of that child entering care is 1 in 10 (compared with 1 in 7000 where none applies). The authors constructed an index from the selected variables and used it to rank electoral wards by severity of need.

In the same vein, David Gordon and Frank Loughran (Chapter 19) developed a child deprivation index to guide the allocation of resources amongst social services childcare teams in a rural area (see also Noble and Smith, 1994). The method was based on the empirical fact that childcare clients originate predominantly from families in poverty (see also Bennett, 2005). A similar index has been used as part of the formula for determining how central governments allocate funding to local jurisdictions (see, for example, Carr-Hill *et al.*, 1997). It comprises four risk factors associated with relatively intensive interventions or being at risk

---

[6]   This included children who were: awaiting adoption; in residential care or approved schools; supervised under child protection legislation (in private foster homes and nurseries); and maintained in local authority boarding schools or hostels on account of maladjustment.

of maltreatment: lone-parent household, rented accommodation, household receiving basic social assistance and household with priority housing need.

Although the comparative approach to measuring need is arguably more meaningful than allocating resources according to population size or existing provision (demand), important weaknesses remain. Estimates of need that are based on existing provision are intrinsically conservative, especially since they invariably focus on a subset of services (see Rowlands, 1997). The number of children who receive a particular intervention is also determined by factors other than need – the mix and availability of services, eligibility criteria, decision-making processes, how agencies are organized and so on. And although there is a link between low household income and children having disabilities or emotional, conduct or hyperkinetic disorders, most deprived children develop reasonably well (Gordon, 2000; ONS, 2000; Little and Mount, 1999). Moreover, estimates of area need are often based on indicators such as economic development and may not give due weight to other factors associated with child need (see, for example, Hall, 2000, pp. 67–68).

A potential solution to these difficulties is to measure normative or expert-defined need using quantitative social survey techniques (see Bryman, 2004). This might apply to a neighbourhood or city, using data collected from parents via a household survey or from children using online questionnaires in school settings. The population may typically be sampled using random or quasi-random methods, focusing either on all children aged 0–17 or, depending on the purpose, a particular subset, such as the under 5s. Measures tend to cover different aspects of children's and families' lives and the level and nature of service use, and often include a mixture of standardized and bespoke questions. Such studies have been rare to date in children's services, certainly relative to the number of small-scale qualitative analyses of what service-users feel they need (Axford *et al.*, 2008), but they are becoming more popular in Western developed countries and, arguably, increasingly sophisticated (see, for example, Beinart *et al.*, 2002;[7] Buchanan and Ritchie, 2004; Bhabra *et al.*, 2006a, 2006b; Hobbs *et al.*, 2007; Axford and Whear, 2008; Kiernan, 2008). Contrary to common perception (Preston-Shoot and Wigley, this volume, p. 279), population surveys *do* include families with significant difficulties and need *not* entail complex and time-consuming questionnaires. As much as the approach draws on community profiling in social care, it also resembles public health epidemiology, translating the study of how often diseases occur in different groups of people and why (Coggon, *et al.*, 1993; Detels, 2004) into the study of the prevalence and aetiology of childhood developmental impairment (see, for example, Frombonne, 2002; Morisky, 2004). Applied at regular intervals, such studies can chart trends in child well-being which, as indicated above, is critical to the task of monitoring policy effectiveness (see, for example, Collishaw *et al.*, 2004).

The final essay in Part IV, by Nick Axford and colleagues (Chapter 20), illustrates how information about children's needs drawn from different sources can be used to help provide a basis for service development. The study described focuses on one geographical area with a total population of 121 000 and links together visually data from single- and inter-agency audits, a community household survey and administrative records. In doing so it demonstrates, for example, the extent to which some children in need do not receive services (and vice

---

[7]   The survey instrument used for the national study is also used by Communities that Care at the neighbourhood level.

versa), the importance of agencies besides social services in meeting children's needs and the tiny number of children on whom much children's services resource is concentrated. Such information can be used by planners to determine where and how to make new investments, which services should be decommissioned and whether thresholds for gaining access to services might require adjustment. But how? It is common for need audits to be completed with much enthusiasm and then for the report to gather dust on the shelf.

This essay therefore provides pointers about how to act on the results, specifically describing practice tools that can be applied at the individual and aggregate levels to help with tasks such as determining the seriousness of a child's need and designing needs-led services. Other chapters in Part IV similarly connect needs assessment and service development. For instance, we read how need analyses can inform the allocation of budgets, not only geographically (Gordon and Loughran, this volume, Chapter 19), but also with regard to the nature of services. Similarly, an analysis that moves from charting factors associated with need to explaining such associations provides important clues about the preventive activity required (Bebbington and Miles, this volume, Chapter 18). The final Part of this volume develops these ideas.

Towards Meeting Children's Needs

The gap between the assessment of need and the interventions provided is well documented (see, for example, Parker 1971; DoH, 1995; Percy, 2000). Too often, population needs assessments are conducted badly, on an ad hoc basis or for the wrong reasons – to satisfy personal curiosity, to use an underspent budget, to placate inspectors. The individuals involved then struggle to engage the critical mass of colleagues needed to act on the findings, or are unable to feed the results meaningfully into a service development process. Other stimuli then fill the gap (Little, Bullock, Madge and Arruabarrena, 2002). For example, services are sometimes fashioned in response to scandals. Yet money can be spent unwisely on stopping something that rarely occurs. Services also emerge when well-meaning people meet to brainstorm a response to an observed problem, such as when curfews are applied to 'crack down' on anti-social behaviour. But such efforts rarely tackle the underlying problem. Further, it is tempting for planners to be supply-led rather than needs-led in their thinking (Audit Commission, 1994), for example to provide 100 care foster places simply because that is what was required in the previous year. The result is service provision where the broad objectives may be clear – to protect children from harm and help them achieve their potential – but where more specific objectives and means of attaining them are somewhat vague (Utting *et al.*, 2001). The essays included in Part V, therefore, demonstrate practical ways of using high quality data to develop needs-led, evidence-based services.

In Chapter 21 Karin Janzon and Ruth Sinclair show how routinely collected data can be better utilized to inform strategic planning. Drawing on various readily available data sources (including census and administrative records), they demonstrate why, in one social services department, expenditure consistently overran the budget by a significant margin: the budget for services had not kept pace with increased need. In particular, the size of the child population had increased by a fifth in under ten years, with a corresponding growth in numbers of children looked after and changes in local policy regarding entry to and leaving care that had increased the activity around placements. The fact that 'most of the findings were surprising and, sometimes, a revelation, to senior staff' (p. 334) illustrates the untapped potential of strengthening the link between evidence of need and decisions about resource allocation (see also Gordon and Loughran, this volume, Chapter 19; Noble and Smith, 1994; Gould, 2001; Pinnock and Garnett, 2002). More precise estimates of the pattern of need, the services received by children and families and the level of unmet need – actual or likely impairment to health or development in the absence of service contact – can be obtained through epidemiological research, in what is an area of growing interest (Ford, 2008; Rutter and Stevenson, 2008).

Population needs assessments can also inform service development in other ways. Specifically, they can shift attention beyond the macro-issues of how much is provided, where and to whom to the micro-details of *what* services should comprise. In Chapter 22 the Conduct Problems Prevention Research Group in the USA describes the evolution and proposed features of a programme to prevent conduct disorder. It cites epidemiological studies charting the prevalence of conduct disorder (4 –10 per cent) and identifying the underlying risk factors and causal mechanisms – family stress, inconsistent parenting, child non-compliance and so on. The authors conclude that there are two strategic points for intervention – school entry and transition to middle school – and that the goals should include helping children to control their anger, promoting more positive and less punitive parenting and supporting teachers with classroom management. Thus, the 'developmental model' outlined informs a theory of change or logic model about what should be done, which is then elaborated in terms of a 'clinical model' comprising five components. Many previous attempts to address conduct disorder have floundered because they failed adequately to analyse need and therefore to recognize the value of a comprehensive, long-term and multi-stage design.

The essay proceeds to describe in some detail what the then-proposed FAST Track (Families and Schools Together) programme should involve, covering target group, duration, frequency of contact, location, referral processes and so on. Such specificity is rare in children's services (Little and Sinclair, 2005) but it is possible here and in similar ventures (see, for example, Barker, 1991; Olds and Kitzman, 1990; Greenberg *et al.*, 1998; PRC, 2004) because the epidemiological analysis helps show how to break the underlying chain of effects.[8] It might also be argued that this degree of detail is a prerequisite to meaningful evaluation because it clarifies what precisely is being tested (Axford *et al.*, 2006). Not surprisingly, given the strength of its theory of change, FAST Track was shown in an evaluation by randomized controlled trial to 'work', with moderate and sustained positive effects on key outcome variables (CPPRG, 1999a, 1999b, 2007).

Several more formalised 'operating systems' for service development have emerged in recent years (Renshaw, 2008) and have helped integrate needs assessment into the planning process. An operating system describes a method to help communities, agencies or local authorities develop or choose effective prevention, early intervention and treatment models

---

[8]   For reviews of similar programmes see: Carr (2002); Little and Mount (1999); also the following databases:

Blueprints: http://www.colorado.edu/cspv/blueprints/
Promising Practices (RAND): http://www.promisingpractices.net/programs.asp
SAMSHA: http://www.samhsa.gov/Campaigns_programs/campaigns_alpha.aspx
Penn Prevention: http://www.prevention.psu.edu/projects/index.html
Campbell Collaboration: http://www.campbellcollaboration.org/
Cochrane Collboration: http://www.cochrane.org

(Fagan *et al.*, 2008). It may be likened to a computer system such as Microsoft Vista, while models like Nurse Family Partnership or Incredible Years are analogous to computer programmes such as Microsoft Word or PowerPoint. Among the better known approaches are Communities that Care (Hawkins and Catalano, 1992; Utting and Fairnington, 2004), Getting to Outcomes (Chinman *et al.*, 2004), PROSPER (Spoth *et al.*, 2004), Results-Based Accountability (Friedman, 2005; Friedman *et al.*, 2005) and Common Language (Little *et al.*, 2009). Most represent attempts to connect prevention science and community engagement (Weissberg and Greenberg, 1998; Spoth and Greenberg, 2005; see also Parker and Heapy, 2006), in other words to harness the evidence yielded by scientific methods – in this case epidemiological research – and enable innovative professionals and laypeople to use that evidence in a structured process to design new interventions, or adapt existing models, and develop a sense of ownership of the resulting services. The aforementioned methods usually require an analysis of need early on in the process, and some stipulate that this be done by way of a scientific survey of the prevalence of different risk and protective factors among children in the community (Utting, 2008).

Michael Little outlines a prototype of one such approach in his discussion of prevention and early intervention with children in need (Chapter 23). The method is intended for use by children's services practitioners and users and involves identifying children with similar need profiles before agreeing the desired outcomes and drawing on evidence to design services that might logically achieve those outcomes. Little describes its use in a rural district to develop a service for children found by an inter-agency need audit to have minor social, emotional or learning difficulties thought likely to lead to school exclusion, youth crime and strained family and social relationships (for other examples see Little *et al.*, 2002). His concern to encourage structured service design techniques such as this is informed by the conclusions of an extensive review of the literature (Little and Mount, 1999) that effective prevention and early intervention relies on 'well-defined activity on behalf of well-defined groups of children' (p. 364) and 'clear evidence about the likely causes of children's problems' (p. 365).

The final essay by Nick Axford and Vashti Berry (Chapter 24) shows how strategies for measuring children's well-being at the individual, agency and community levels were used to chart need in one jurisdiction[9] and then to develop and evaluate the impact of new services. In doing so it demonstrates in practice three important connections encouraged earlier in this Introduction. The first is between individual and aggregate data; the use of screening instruments and succinct and structured case records makes it easier to undertake single and inter-agency need audits because the data are gathered more consistently. The second connection is between need and outcomes; undertaken periodically, individual and group needs assessments help with monitoring trends and provide some indication of the impact of services. The third connection is between need and service; a structured service design process allows need data from agency audits and community surveys to be used alongside other information (from local consultations and the international 'what works' evidence) to develop new interventions. The brief case study is imperfect, but it illustrates what is possible.

---

[9]   The chapter concerns the district focused on in Chapter 21.

Where Next?

This Introduction opened by noting the ambivalence, even scepticism, often expressed about the concept of need. Yet the essays selected illustrate the extensive use of need in charting child well-being and analysing such data to inform the planning of children's services at the individual and group levels. That said, it is clear that in practice this has proved difficult to do well. As Doyal and Gough remark in Chapter 3, 'One is left then with a paradox: the concept of human needs is continually if confusingly used at the level of social welfare practice by the most varied groups, but is either dismissed or elided at the level of theory' (p. 35). So what are some of the key messages and areas for further research emerging from this volume? These concluding comments fall into three areas.

First, contributions suggest that the concept of need is robust enough to be useful in the context of children's services for determining which children require what in order to ensure that they can enjoy healthy development. In particular, it serves the helpful function of translating the complex interplay of risk and protective factors in children's lives into statements of action, and can be harnessed to set a threshold for intervention defined in terms of levels of impairment to children's health and development.

There are several important avenues for further study, however. One concerns what level of child well-being is realistically attainable given scant resources and how far this incorporates the satisfaction of wants as well as needs (Jordan, 2006). Critiques of the dominant deficit-based developmental model in favour of a more strengths-based approach suggest that assessment and intervention should concentrate increasingly on promoting positive development rather than simply on preventing problems (Lopez *et al.*, 2003; Moore and Keyes, 2003; Seligman, 2005). Related to this is the question of whether need offers the most suitable rubric for determining the allocation of resources and evaluating the impact of services: for example, is it necessarily congruent with efforts to promote children's rights (Axford, 2008a) and does it help or hinder the cause of social justice (Craig *et al.*, 2008)? The understanding of children's needs and how best to meet those needs will also be furthered by research into the pathways from childhood to adulthood, in particular the mechanisms by which risk 'gets into the body' (Rutter, 1996; Maughan and Rutter, 2008) and the influence of neighbourhood and family risks on child development (Barnes *et al.*, 2006).

Second, selected chapters show that it is possible to measure children's needs well at both the individual and population levels, but that there is significant room for improvement within children's services in order to bring common practice up to the standard of the best. In particular, there is scope for the greater use of standardised measures and quantitative evidence relative to more qualitative and opinion-based assessments, and for more community-based epidemiological studies to balance the plethora of administrative audits. When they are being used to help plan services at an agency or local authority level, studies would ideally: adopt a multi-dimensional perspective of need; cover several domains of child well-being; gather data on representative samples of children in the community – where possible directly from the children; use tried-and-tested measures; and be repeated at regular intervals to help with monitoring trends over time (Axford *et al.*, 2008).

A major challenge in this area is to improve the quality of routine recording about children's needs in case files so that the data it generates can be used for the purposes of aggregation and evaluation. Concerted efforts in recent years to do this have arguably had limited success, so this remains something of a holy grail, not least because it is bound up with a range of complex issues, including for example training and the diversity of experience in this respect amongst the children's services workforce (Morpeth, 2004). There is also the need to develop and test taxonomical formulations that demonstrate strong reliability and validity and that can be used to help guide policy and practice decisions about the allocation of resources (Forrester *et al.*, 2007; Taylor and Rutter, 2008).

Third, there are now several methods available for strengthening the link between high quality population needs assessments and rigorous service development. These offer the potential for reducing the likelihood of such studies being consigned to a cupboard and forgotten about. The problem is that their use is the exception; it needs to be the exception for these methods *not* to be used. At the same time, these methods, or 'operating systems', are relatively new and there is much to learn about how they can best be used. In particular, there is a need to work out how the methods can ensure that the programmes designed or selected using them are implemented with quality and in a sustainable way (Bumbarger and Perkins, 2008; Fagan *et al.*, 2008).

Writing when he did, Bradshaw (1994) was probably right about the problems with using the concept of need in a policy context. In children's services, different people meant different things by the term 'need' without necessarily being aware of this, and what is essentially a description of the state of children's health and development had become confused with an administrative threshold. The concept of need and the way it was operationalised had become unnecessarily imprecise and confusing. With exceptions, some of which are described in this volume, it would have been difficult to use it to determine resource allocation or help formulate evidence-based services. Since then, however, as several of the essays in this volume demonstrate, the concept of normative need has been formulated more carefully and attempts to operationalise it have led to greater accuracy of measurement. There has been no revolution, and no-one would dare suggest that everything is perfect. But some of the instruments now used in the context of epidemiological studies are much more sophisticated than those in common use even a few years ago, and they offer a reasonable hope of monitoring the performance of policy and practice.

One might justifiably ask how central the concept of need is to some of these developments, to which one response, evident in several of the contributions in this volume, is that it provides a bridge between the worlds of science on the one hand and policy and practice on the other. It translates the language of risk and protective factors into statements indicating the actions required to ensure healthy development. A fuller response is required, but for now it may be contended that a corner has been turned. The next decade will determine how serious we are about developing needs-led children's services, which in turn will be apparent by how willing we are to exploit, test and develop emerging methods of measuring and meeting children's needs. The essays in this volume will hopefully inspire some readers to travel the distance.

References

Audit Commission (1994), *Seen But Not Heard: Co-ordinating Community Child Health and Social Services for Children in Need: Detailed Evidence and Guidelines for Managers and Practitioners*, London: HMSO.

Axford, N. (2008a), *Exploring Concepts of Child Well-Being: Implications for Children's Services*, Bristol: Policy Press.

Axford, N. (2008b), 'Conducting Needs Assessments in Children's Services', *British Journal of Social Work*, Advance Access, doi: 10.1093/bjsw/bcn103.

Axford, N., Green, V., Kalsbeek, A., Morpeth, L. and Palmer, C. (2008), 'Measuring Children's Needs: How are we Doing?', *Child and Family Social Work*, Advance Access, doi: 10.1111/j.1365-2206.2008.00591.x.

Axford, N., Berry, V. and Little, M. (2006), 'Enhancing Service Evaluability: Lessons from a Programme for Disaffected Young People', *Children & Society*, **20**(4), pp. 287–98.

Axford, N., Little, M. And Morpeth, L. (2003), *Children Supported and Unsupported in the Community*, Report submitted to the Department of Health, Dartington: Dartington Social Research Unit.

Axford, N. and Whear, R. (2008), 'Measuring and Meeting the Needs of Children in the Community: A Survey of Parents on a Housing Estate in Dublin, Ireland', *Child Care in Practice*, **14**(4), pp. 331–53.

Barker, W.E. (1991), 'Empowering Parents: The Evolution, Expansion and Evaluation of a Program', *Zero to Three*, 8–15April, Arlington, TX: National Center for Clinical Infant Programs See also: http://web.ukonline.co.uk/oaw/publications.htm.

Barnes, J., Katz, I., Korbin, J.E. and O'Brien, M. (2006), *Children and Families in Communites: Theory, Research, Policy and Practice*, Chichester: John Wiley and Sons.

Beinart, S., Anderson, B., Lee, S. and Utting, D. (2002), *Youth at Risk? A National Survey of Risk Factors, Protective Factors and Problem Behaviour among Young People in England, Scotland and Wales*, London: Communities that Care.

Bennett, F. (2005), 'Promoting the Health and Well-Being of Children: Evidence of Need in the UK', in J. Scott and H. Ward (eds), *Safeguarding and Promoting the Well-Being of Children, Families and Communities*, London: Jessica Kingsley Publishers.

Bhabra, S., Dinos, S. and Ghate, D. (2006a), *Young People, Risk and Protection: A Major Survey of Primary Schools in On Track Areas*, Report to the Department for Education and Skills, London: Policy Research Bureau.

Bhabra, S., Dinos, S. and Ghate, D. (2006b), *Young People, Risk and Protection: A Major Survey of Secondary Schools in On Track Areas*, Report to the Department for Education and Skills, London: Policy Research Bureau.

Boendermaker, L. (2006), 'Crisis Admissions in Dutch Juvenile Justice Institutions: Finding a Solution', *Journal Of Children's Services*, **1**(4), pp. 61–69.

Bowlby, J. (1951), *Maternal Care and Mental Health*, Geneva: World Health Organization.

Bradshaw, J. (1994), 'The Conceptualization and Measurement of Need: A Social Policy Perspective', in J. Popay and G. Williams (eds), *Researching the People's Health*, London: Routledge.

Braybrooke, D. (1987), *Meeting Needs*, Princeton, NJ: Princeton University Press.

Brazelton, T.B. and Greenspan, S.I. (2000), *The Irreducible Needs of Children: What Every Child Must Have to Grow, Learn, and Flourish*, Cambridge, MA: Perseus Books Group.

Bryman, A. (2004), *Social Research Methods*, Oxford: Oxford University Press.

Buchanan, A. and Ritchie, C. (2004), 'Using Standardized Measures to Prioritize Services for Children and Families in Need', *Journal of Social Work*, **4**(2), pp. 167–78.

Buckley, H., Whelan, S., Murphy, C. and Horwath, J. (2007), 'Using an Assessment Framework: Outcomes from a Pilot Study', *Journal of Children's Services*, **2**(1), pp. 37–47.

Bumbarger, B. K. and Perkins, D. F. (2008), 'After Randomised Trials: Issues Related to the Dissemination of Evidence-based Interventions', *Journal of Children's Services*, **3**(2), pp. 55–64.

Carr, A. (ed.) (2002), *Prevention: What Works with Children and Adolescents? A Critical Review of Psychological Prevention Programmes for Children, Adolescents and their Families*, Hove: Brunner-Routledge.

Carr-Hill, R.A., Dixon, P., Mannion, R., Rice, N., Rudat, K., Sinclair, R. and Smith, P. (1997), *A Model of the Determinants of Expenditure on Children's Personal Social Services*, York: University of York.

Carr-Hill, R.A., Rice, N. and Smith, P.C. (1999), 'The Determinants of Expenditure on Children's Personal Social Services', *British Journal of Social Work*, **29**, pp. 679–706.

Champion, R. and Burke, G. (2004), 'Implementing Looking after Children (LAC) as a Collaborative Practice and Policy Framework in Victoria, Australia', Paper Presented to the Sixth International Looking After Children Conference and Fifth National Child Welfare Symposium, Ottawa, 16–19 August at: http://office-for-children.vic.gov.au/__data/assets/pdf_file/0010/16885/lac_conference_paper.pdf (accessed 6 November 2007).

Chaskin, R. (2006), 'Family Support as Community-Based Practice: Considering a Community Capacity Framework for Family Support Provision', in P. Dolan, J. Canavan and J. Pinkerton (eds), *Family Support as Reflective Practice*, London: Jessica Kingsley Publishers.

Cleaver, H., Walker, S. and Meadows, P. (2004), *Assessing Children's Needs and Circumstances: The Impact of the Assessment Framework*, London: Jessica Kingsley Publishers.

Chinman, M., Imm, P. and Wandersman, A. (2004), *Getting to Outcomes 2004: Promoting Accountability Through Methods and Tools for Planning, Implementation and Evaluation*, Santa Monica, CA: RAND Corporation.

Coggon, D., Rose, G. and Barker, D.J.P. (1993), *Epidemiology for the Uninitiated* (3rd edn), London: BMJ Publishing.

Collishaw, S., Maughan, B., Goodman, R. and Pickles, A. (2004), 'Time Trends in Adolescent Mental Health', *Journal of Child Psychology and Psychiatry*, **45**(8), pp. 1350–62.

Colton, M., Drury, C. and Williams, M. (1995), 'Children in Need: Definition, Identification and Support', *British Journal of Social Work*, **25**, pp. 711–28.

CPPRG (Conduct Problems Prevention Research Group) (1999a), 'Initial Impact of the Fast Track Prevention Trial for Conduct Problems I: The High-Risk Sample', *Journal of Consulting and Clinical Psychology*, **67**, pp. 631–47.

CPPRG (1999b), 'Initial Impact of the Fast Track Prevention Trial for Conduct Problems II: Classroom Effects', *Journal of Consulting and Clinical Psychology*, **67**, pp. 648–57.

CPPRG (2007), 'Fast Track Randomized Controlled Trial to Prevent Externalizing Psychiatric Disorders: Findings from Grades 3 to 9', *Journal of the American Academy of Child and Adolescent Psychiatry*, **46**(10), pp. 1250–262.

Craig, G., Burchardt, T. and Gordon, D. (eds) (2008), *Social Justice and Public Policy: Seeking Fairness in Diverse Societies*, Bristol: The Policy Press.

Detels, R. (2004), 'Epidemiology: The Foundation of Public Health', in R. Detels, J. McEwen, R. Beaglehole and H. Tanaka (eds), *Oxford Textbook of Public Health* (4th edn), Oxford: Oxford University Press.

DfES (Department for Education and Skills) (2003), *Every Child Matters*, Cm. 5860, London: The Stationery Office.

DfES (2006a), *Common Assessment Framework for Children and Young People: Managers' Guide*, London: DfES.

DfES (2006b), *Common Assessment Framework for Children and Young People: Practitioners' Guide*, London: DfES.

DfES and National Statistics (2006), *Children in Need in England: Results of a Survey of Activity and Expenditure as Reported by Local Authority Social Services' Children and Families Teams for a Survey Week in February 2005: Local Authority Tables and Further National Analysis*, at: www.dfes.gov.uk/rsgateway/DB/VOL/V000647/vweb02-2006.pdf (accessed 16 November 2006).

Dillenburger, K. (1998), 'Evidencing Effectiveness: The Use of Single-Case Designs in Child Care Work', in D. Iwaniec and J. Pinkerton (eds), *Making Research Work: Research Policy and Practice in Child Care*, Chichester: John Wiley and Sons.

DoH (Department of Health) (1995), *Child Protection: Messages from Research*, London: HMSO.

DoH (2000), *Children in Need in England: First Results of a Survey of Activity and Expenditure as Reported by Local Authority Social Services' Children and Families Teams for a Survey Week in February 2000*, London: Department of Health.

DoH (2001), *The Children Act Report 2000*, London: Department of Health.

DoH, Department for Education and Employment and Home Office (2000), *Framework for the Assessment of Children in Need and their Families*, London: The Stationery Office.

Doyal, L. (1988), 'Basic Human Need and Objective Well-Being', *Revue de Sociologie Internationale*, **2**, pp. 133–89.

Doyal, L. and Gough, I. (1991), *A Theory of Human Need*, Basingstoke: Macmillan.

Drover, G. and Kerans, P. (1993), *New Approaches to Welfare Theory*, Aldershot: Edward Elgar.

Dworetzky, J.P. (1996), *Introduction to Child Development*, St Paul's, MN: West Publishers.

Edmunds, L. and Stewart-Brown S. (2003), *Assessing Emotional and Social Competence in Primary School and Early Years Settings: A Review of Instruments and Approaches*, London: Department for Education and Skills.

Fagan, A.A., Hanson, K., Hawkins, D.J. and Arthur, M.W. (2008), 'Bridging Science to Practice: Achieving Prevention Program Implementation Fidelity in the Community Youth Development Study', *American Journal of Community Psychology*, **41**, pp. 235–49.

Fernandez, E. and Romeo, R. (2003), *Implementation of the Framework for the Assessment of Children and their Families: The Experience of Barnardos Australia*, Report to the UK Department of Health, Australia: University Of New South Wales.

Fitzgerald, R. (ed.) (1977), *Human Needs and Politics*, Rushcutters Bay, NSW: Pergamon.

Ford, T. (2008), 'Practitioner Review: How Can Epidemology Help Us Plan and Deliver Effective Child and Adolescent Mental Health Services?', *Journal of Child Psychology and Psychiatry*, **49**(9), pp. 900-914.

Forrester, D., Fairtlough, A. and Bennet, Y. (2007), 'Describing the Needs of Children Presenting to Children's Services: Issues of Reliability and Validity', *Journal of Children's Services*, **2**(2), pp. 48–59.

Friedman, M. (2005), *Trying Hard is Not Good Enough: How to Produce Measurable Improvements for Customers and Communities, Victoria*, Canada: Trafford Publishing.

Friedman, M., Garnett, L. and Pinnock, M. (2005), 'Dude, Where's My Outcomes? Partnership Working and Outcome-Based Accountability in the UK', in J. Scott and H. Ward (eds), *Safeguarding and Promoting the Well-being of Children, Families and Communities*, London: Jessica Kingsley Publishers.

Frombonne, E. (2002), 'Case Identification in an Epidemiological Context', in M. Rutter and E. Taylor (eds), *Child and Adolescent Psychiatry* (4th edn), Oxford: Blackwell.

Goodin, R.E. (1988), *Reasons for Welfare: The Political Theory of the Welfare State*, Princeton, NJ: Princeton University Press.

Goodin, R.E. (1990), 'Relative Needs', in A. Ware and R.E. Goodin (eds), *Needs and Welfare*, London: Sage.

Goodman, R. (2001), 'Psychometric Properties of the Strengths and Difficulties Questionnaire (SDQ)', *Journal of the American Academy of Child and Adolescent Psychiatry*, **40**, pp. 1337–45.

Goodman, R., Ford, T., Simmons, H., Gatward, R. and Meltzer, H. (2000), 'Using the Strengths and Difficulties Questionnaire (SDQ) to Screen for Child Psychiatric Disorders in a Community Sample', *British Journal of Psychiatry*, **177**, pp. 534–39.

Gordon, D. (2000), 'Inequalities in Income, Wealth and Standard of Living in Britain', in D. Gordon and C. Pantazis (eds), *Tackling Inequalities: Where Are We Now and What Should Be Done?*, Bristol: The Policy Press.

Gough, I. (2000), 'The Needs of Capital and the Needs of People: Can the Welfare State Reconcile the Two?', in I. Gough (ed.), *Global Capital, Human Needs and Social Policies: Selected Essays, 1994–1999*, Basingstoke: Palgrave.

Gough, I. and Thomas, T. (1994), 'Need Satisfaction and Welfare Outcomes: Theory and Explanations', *Social Policy and Administration*, **28**(1), pp. 33–56.

Gould, N. (2001), 'Developing an Approach to Population Needs Assessment in English Social Services', *Social Work and Social Sciences Review*, **9**(1), pp. 22–35.

Gray, J. (2002), 'National Policy on the Assessment of Children in Need and their Families', in H. Ward and W. Rose (eds), *Approaches to Needs Assessment in Children's Services*, London: Jessica Kingsley Publishers.

Greenberg, M.T., Kusché, C. and Mihalic, S.F. (1998), *Promoting Alternative Thinking Strategies (PATHS): Blueprints for Violence Prevention, Book Ten: Blueprints for Violence Prevention Series*, D.S. Elliott, Series Editor, Boulder, CO: Center for the Study and Prevention of Violence, Institute of Behavioral Science, University of Colorado.

Hall, C. (2000), *Organisation and Outcome in Personal Social Services for Children and Families*, Report submitted to the Department of Health, Dartington: Dartington Social Research Unit.

Hawes, D.J. and Dadds, M.R. (2004), 'Australian Data and Psychometric Properties of the Strengths and Difficulties Questionnaire', *Australian and New Zealand Journal of Psychiatry*, **38**, pp. 644–51.

Hawkins, J.D. and Catalano, R.F. (1992), *Communities that Care: Action for Drug Abuse Prevention*, San Francisco, Jossey Bass.

Hawtin, M., Hughes, G. and Percy-Smith, J. (1995), *Community Profiling: Auditing Social Needs*, Buckingham: Open University Press.

Hewitt, M. (1992), *Welfare, Ideology and Need*, Hemel Hempstead: Harvester Wheatsheaf.

Hewitt, M. (1993), 'Social Movements and Social Need', *Critical Social Policy*, **13**(1), pp. 52–74.

Hill, M. and Tisdall, K. (1997), *Children and Society*, London: Longman.

Hill, P. (2002), 'Adjustment Disorders', in M. Rutter and E. Taylor (eds), *Child and Adolescent Psychiatry* (4th edn), Oxford: Blackwell.

HM Government (2005), *Guidance on the Children and Young People's Plan*, London: Department for Education and Skills.

Hobbs, T., Little, M. and Kaoukji, D. (2007), 'Using the Strengths and Difficulties Questionnaire (SDQ) to Measure the Behaviour and Emotional Health of Children in Schools in the United Kingdom', *International Journal of Child and Family Welfare*, **10**(3-4), pp. 150–64.

Horwath, J. (2001), 'Assessing the World of the Child in Need: Background and Context', in K. Horwath (ed.), *The Child's World: Assessing Children in Need*, London: Jessica Kingsley Publishers.

Ignatieff, M. (1985), *The Needs of Strangers*, New York: Viking.

Illich, I. (1999), 'Needs', in W. Sachs (ed.), *The Development Dictionary: A Guide to Knowledge as Power*, London: Zed Books.

Jack, G. (2001), 'Ecological Perspectives in Assessing Children and Families', in J. Horwath (ed.), *The Child's World: Assessing Children in Need*, London: Jessica Kingsley Publishers.

Johnson, R. and Sawbridge, P. (2004), 'Family Placements: Matching Needs and Services', in V. White and J. Harris (eds), *Developing Good Practice in Children's Services*, London: Jessica Kingsley Publishers.

Jones, H., Clark, R., Kufeldt, K. and Norman, M. (1998), 'Looking After Children: Assessing Outcomes in Childcare. The Experience of Implementation', *Children & Society*, **12**(3), 212–22.

Jordan, B. (2006), 'Well-Being: The Next Revolution in Children's Services?', *Journal of Children's Services*, **1**(1), pp. 41–50.

Kazi, M.A.F. and Wilson, J. (1996), 'Applying Single-Case Evaluation in Social Work', *British Journal of Social Work*, **26**(5), pp. 699–717.

Kellmer-Pringle, M. (1975), *The Needs of Children*, London: Hutchinson.

Kiernan, G., Axford, N., Little, M., Murphy, C., Greene, S. and Gormley, M. (2008), 'The School Readiness of Children Living in a Disadvantaged Area in Ireland', *Journal of Early Childhood Research*, **6**(2), pp. 119–44.

Klasen, H., Woerner, W., Wolke, D., Meyer, R., Overmeyer, S., Kaschnitz, W., Rothenberger, A. and Goodman, R. (2000), 'Comparing the German Versions of the Strengths and Difficulties Questionnaire (SDQ-Deu) and the Child Behavior Checklist', *European Child and Adolescent Psychiatry*, **9**, pp. 271–76.

Kufeldt, K., Simard, M. and Vachon, J., with Baker, J. and Andrews, T-L. (2000), *Looking After Children in Canada*, Final Report submitted to the Social Development Partnerships of Human Resources Development, Fredericton: University of New Brunswick at: http://www.unbf.ca/arts/CFVR/documents/Looking-After-Children.pdf (accessed 6 November 2007).

Little, M. (2002), *Prediction: Perspectives on Diagnosis, Prognosis and Interventions for Children in Need*, Dartington: Warren House Press.

Little, M. and Abunimah, A. (2007), 'Improving Outcomes for Children in the Island of Ireland: The Role of Philanthropic Investment', *Journal of Children's Services*, **2**(2), pp. 60–67.

Little, M., Axford, N. and Morpeth, L. (2002), *Aggregating Data: Better Management Information and Planning in Children's Services*, Dartington: Warren House Press.

Little, M., Axford, N. and Morpeth, L. (2003), *Threshold: Determining the Extent of Impairment to Children's Development*, Dartington: Warren House Press.

Little, M., Axford, N. and Morpeth, L. (2004), 'Risk and Protection in the Context of Services for Children in Need', *Child and Family Social Work*, **9**(1), pp. 105–18.

Little, M., Axford, N., Morpeth, L. and Hobbs, T. (2009), *Service Design in Children's Services*, Dartington: Warren House Press.

Little, M., Bullock, R., Madge, J. and Arruabarrena, I. (2002), 'How to Develop Needs-Led Evidence-Based Services', *MCC Building Knowledge for Integrated Care*, **10**(3), pp. 28–32.

Little, M. and Madge, J. (1998), *Inter-Agency Assessment of Need in Child Protection*, Dartington: Dartington Social Research Unit.

Little, M., Madge, J., Mount, K., Ryan, M. and Tunnard, J. (1999), *Matching Needs and Services* (2nd edn), Dartington: Dartington Academic Press.

Little, M. and Mount, K. (1999), *Prevention and Early Intervention with Children in Need*, Aldershot: Ashgate.

Little, M. and Mount, K. (2003), *Paperwork: The Clinical Assessment of Children in Need*, Dartington: Warren House Press.

Little, M. and Sinclair, R. (2005), 'The Evolution of Family Support', in N. Axford, V. Berry, M. Little and L. Morpeth (eds), *Forty Years of Research, Policy and Practice in Children's Services: A Festschrift for Roger Bullock*, Chichester: Wiley.

Lopez, S.J., Snyder, C.R. and Rasmussen, H.J. (2003), 'Striking a Vital Balance: Developing a Complementary Focus on Human Weakness and Strength Through Positive Psychological Assessment', in S.J. Lopez and C.R. Snyder (eds), *Positive Psychological Assessment: A Handbook of Models and Measures*, Washington DC: American Psychological Association.

McCrystal, P. (2000), 'Operationalising the Definition of Children in Need from UK Child Care Legislation', in D. Iwaniec and M. Hill (eds), *Child Welfare Policy and Practice*, London: Jessica Kingsley Publishers.

Maslow, A. (1970), *Motivation and Personality*, New York: Harper and Row.

Maughan, B. and Rutter, M. (2008), 'Development and Psychopathology: A Life Course Perspective', in M. Rutter, D. Bishop, D. Pine, S. Scott, J. Stevenson, E. Taylor and A. Thapar (eds), *Rutter's Child and Adolescent Psychiatry* (5th edn), Oxford: Blackwell Publishing.

Mayall, B. (2002), *Towards a Sociology for Childhood: Thinking from Children's Lives*, Buckingham: Open University Press.

Melamid, E. and Brodbar, G. (2003), 'Matching Needs and Services: An Assessment Tool for Community-Based Service Systems', *Child Welfare*, **82**(4), pp. 397–412.

Miller, D. (1976), *Social Justice*, Oxford: Clarendon.

Miller, D. (1999), *Principles of Social Justice*, Cambridge, MA: Harvard University Press.

Moffitt, T. (1993), 'Adolescent-Limited and Life-Course-Persistent Anti-Social Behaviour: A Developmental Taxonomy', *Psychological Review*, **110**, pp. 674–701.

Moon, B. (1991), *The Political Economy of Basic Human Needs*, Ithaca, NY: Cornell University Press.

Moore, K.A. and Keyes, C.L.M. (2003), 'A Brief History of the Study of Child Well-being in Children and Adults', in M.H. Bornstein, L. Davidson, C.L.M. Keyes and K.A. Moore (eds), *Well-being: Positive Development Across the Life-Course*, Mahwah, NJ: Lawrence Erlbaum Associates.

Morisky, D.E. (2004), 'Community Assessment of Behaviour', in R. Detels, J. McEwen, R. Beaglehole, and H. Tanaka (eds), *Oxford Textbook of Public Health* (4th edn), Oxford: Oxford University Press.

Morpeth, L. (2004), *Organisation and Outcomes in Children's Services*, Unpublished PhD Thesis, University of Exeter.

Muris, P., Meesters, C. and van den Berg, F. (2003), The Strengths and Difficulties Questionnaire (SDQ): Further Evidence for its Reliability and Validity in a Community Sample of Dutch Children and Adolescents, *European Child and Adolescent Psychiatry*, **12**, pp. 1–8.

Noble, M. and Smith, T. (1994), '"Children in Need": Using Geographical Information Systems to Inform Strategic Planning for Social Service Provision', *Children & Society*, **8**(4), pp. 360–76.

Nussbaum, M.C. (2000), *Women and Human Development: The Capabilities Approach*, Cambridge: Cambridge University Press.

Olds, D. and Kitzman, H. (1990), 'Can Home Visitation Improve the Health of Women and Children at Environmental Risk?', *Pediatrics*, **86**, pp. 108–15.

ONS (Office for National Statistics) (2000), *Social Inequalities: 2000 Edition*, London: Stationery Office.

Packman, J. (1968), *Child Care: Needs and Numbers*, London: Allen and Unwin.

Packman, J., Randall, J. and Jacques, N. (1985), *Who Needs Care?*, Oxford: Blackwell.

Parker, R.A. (1971), *Planning for Deprived Children*, London: National Children's Home.

Parker, R., Ward, H., Jackson, S., Aldgate, J. and Wedge, P. (eds) (1991), *Looking After Children: Assessing Outcomes in Childcare*, London: HMSO.

Parker, S. and Heapy, J. (2006), *The Journey to the Interface: How Public Service Design Can Connect Users to Reform*, London: Demos/Engine.

Percy, A. (2000), 'Needs-Based Planning for Family and Child Care Services in Northern Ireland: Problems and Possibilities', in D. Iwaniec and M. Hill (eds), *Child Welfare Policy and Practice*, London: Jessica Kingsley Publishers.

Percy-Smith, J. (1996), 'Introduction: Assessing Needs – Theory and Practice', in J. Percy-Smith (ed) *Needs Assessments in Public Policy*, Buckingham: Open University Press.

Percy-Smith, J. and Sanderson, I. (1992), *Understanding Local Needs*, London: Institute for Public Policy Research.

Pinnock, M. and Garnett, L. (2002), 'Needs-Led or Needs-Must? The Use of Needs-Based Information in Planning Children's Services', in H. Ward and W. Rose (eds), *Approaches to Needs Assessment in Children's Services*, London: Jessica Kingsley Publishers.

Plant, R. (1991), *Modern Political Thought*, Oxford: Blackwell.

Plant, R., Lesser, H. and Taylor-Gooby, P. (1981), *Political Philosophy and Social Welfare*, London: Routledge & Kegan Paul.

PRC (Prevention Research Center) (2004), *Generacion Diez*, at: http://www.prevention.psu.edu/projects/middle.html (accessed 13 August 2004).

Ravens-Sieberer, U., Gosch, A., Rajmil, L., Erhart, M., Bruil, J., Duer, W. *et al.* (2005), 'KIDSCREEN-52 Quality of Life Measure for Children and Adolescents', *Expert Review of Pharmacoeconomics and Outcomes Research*, **5**(3), pp. 353–64.

Rawls, John (1971), *A Theory Of Justice*, Cambridge, MA: Harvard University Press.

Renshaw, J. (2008), *Tools for Improving Outcomes and Performance: Comparing Six Different Approaches*, London: IdEA.

Rowlands, J. (1997), 'A Better Way to Define Needs', *Children's Services News*, July, p. 4.

Rutter, M. (1981), *Maternal Deprivation Reassessed*, Harmondsworth: Penguin.

Rutter, M. (1996) 'Stress research: accomplishments and tasks ahead', in R.J. Haggerty, L.R. Sherrod, N. Garmezy and M. Rutter (eds), *Stress, Risk and Resilience in Children and Adolescents: Processes, Mechanisms and Interventions*, Cambridge: Cambridge University Press.

Rutter, M. (1999), 'Psychosocial Adversity and Child Psychopathology', *British Journal of Psychiatry*, **174**, pp. 480–93.

Rutter, M. and Stevenson, J. (2008), 'Using Epidemiology to Plan Services: A Conceptual Approach', in M. Rutter, D. Bishop, D. Pine, S. Scott, J. Stevenson, E. Taylor and A. Thapar (eds), *Rutter's Child and Adolescent Psychiatry* (5th edn), Oxford: Blackwell Publishing.

Rutter, M. and Taylor, E. (2002a), 'Clinical Assessment and Diagnostic Formulation', in M. Rutter and E. Taylor (eds), *Child and Adolescent Psychiatry* (4th edn), Oxford: Blackwell.

Rutter, M. and Taylor, E. (2002b), 'Classification: Conceptual Issues and Substantive Findings', in M. Rutter and E. Taylor (eds), *Child and Adolescent Psychiatry* (4th edn), Oxford: Blackwell.

Sanders, M.R. (1999), 'The Triple P Positive Parenting Program: Towards an Empirically Validated Multilevel Parenting and Family Support Strategy for the Prevention of Behavior and Emotional Problems in Children', *Clinical Child and Family Psychology Review*, **2**(2), pp. 71–90.

Seden, J. (2001), 'Assessment of Children in Need and their Families: A Literature Review', in Department of Health (ed.), *Studies Informing the Framework for the Assessment of Children in Need and their Families*, London: The Stationery Office, pp. 3–80.

Seden, J. (2002), 'Underpinning Theories for the Assessment of Children's Needs', in H. Ward and W. Rose (eds), *Approaches to Needs Assessment in Children's Services*, London: Jessica Kingsley Publishers.

Seligman, M.E.P. (2005), 'Positive Psychology, Positive Prevention, and Positive Therapy', in C.R. Snyder and S.J. Lopez (eds), *Handbook of Positive Psychology*, Oxford: Oxford University Press.

Sempik, J., Ward, H. and Darker, I. (2008), 'Emotional and Behavioural Difficulties of Children and Young People at Entry into Care', *Clinical Child Psychology and Psychiatry*, **13**(2), pp. 221–33.

Sheppard, M. (2007), *The Idea of Practice: Social Work and Social Exclusion*, Aldershot: Ashgate.

Sheppard, M. and Woodcock, J. (1999), 'Need as an Operating Concept: The Case of Social Work with Children and Families', *Child and Family Social Work*, **4**(1), pp. 67–76.

Sinclair, R. (2000), 'Framework for the Assessment of Children in Need', *Child Care in Practice*, **6**(2), pp. 174–81.

Sinclair, R. (2001), 'The Language of Need: Social Workers Describing the Needs of Children', in Department of Health (ed.), *Studies Informing the Framework for the Assessment of Children in Need and their Families*, London: The Stationery Office.

Sinclair, R. and Carr-Hill, R.A. (1996), *The Categorisation of Children in Need*, London: National Children's Bureau.

Sinclair, R. and Little, M. (2002), 'Developing a Taxonomy for Children in Need', in H. Ward and W. Rose (eds), *Approaches to Needs Assessment in Children's Services*, London: Jessica Kingsley Publishers.

Skevington, S.M. and Gillison, F.B. (2006), 'Assessing Children's Quality of Life in Health and Social Services: Meeting Challenges and Adding Value', *Journal of Children's Services*, **1**(2), pp. 41–50.

Slonim-Nevo, V. and Ziv, E. (1998), 'Training Social Workers to Evaluate Practice', *International Social Work*, **41**, pp. 431–42.

Smedje H., Broman, J-E., Hetta, J., and von Knorring, A-L. (1999), 'Psychometric Properties of a Swedish Version of the "Strengths and Difficulties Questionnaire"', *European Child and Adolescent Psychiatry*, **8**, pp. 63–70.

Smith, M. K. and Brun, C. F. (2006), 'An Analysis of Selected Measures of Child Well-being for Use at School- and Community-based Family Resource Centers', *Child Welfare*, **85**(6), pp. 985–1010.

Spoth, R.L. and Greenberg, M.T. (2005), 'Toward a Comprehensive Strategy for Effective Practitioner-Scientist Partnerships and Larger-Scale Community Health and Well-Being', *American Journal of Community Psychology*, **35**(3-4), pp. 107–26.

Spoth, R., Greenberg, M., Bierman, K. and Redmond, C. (2004), 'PROSPER Community-University Partnerships Model for Public Education Systems: Capacity-Building for Evidence-Based, Competence-Building Prevention', *Prevention Science*, **5**(1), pp. 31–39.

Stewart, F. (1996), 'Basic Needs, Capabilities, and Human Development', in A. Offer (ed.), *In Pursuit of the Quality of Life*, Oxford: Oxford University Press.

Tao, J. and Drover, G. (1997), 'Chinese and Western Notions of Need', *Critical Social Policy*, **50**, pp. 5–25.

Taylor, E. and Rutter, M. (2008), 'Classification', in M. Rutter, D. Bishop, D. Pine, S. Scott, J. Stevenson, E. Taylor and A. Thapar (eds), *Rutter's Child and Adolescent Psychiatry* (5th edn), Oxford: Blackwell Publishing.

Taylor, K. (2005), 'Understanding Communities Today: Using Matching Needs and Services to Assess Community Needs and Design Community-Based Services', *Child Welfare*, **84**(2), pp. 251–64.

Tiffin, P.A. and Richardson, G. (2006), 'Appendix 1: The Use of Structured Instruments in the Assessment of Violence Risk', in A. Hagell and R. Jeyarajah-Dent (eds), *Children Who Commit Acts of Serious Interpersonal Violence: Messages for Best Practice*, London: Jessica Kingsley Publishers.

Towle, C. (1987), *Common Human Needs*, London: NASW Press.

Tunnard, J. (2002), 'Matching Needs and Services: Emerging Themes from its Application in Different Social Care Settings ', in H. Ward and W. Rose (eds), *Approaches to Needs Assessment in Children's Services*, London: Jessica Kingsley Publishers.

Tunstill, J. and Aldgate, J. (2000), *Services for Children in Need: From Policy to Practice*, London: The Stationery Office.

Tymms, P. (1999), *Baseline Assessment and Monitoring in Primary Schools: Achievements, Attitudes and Added-value Indicators*, London: David Fulton Publishers.

Utting, D. (2008), *Assessing and Meeting the Need for Parenting Support Services: A Literature Review*, London: National Academy for Parenting Practioners.

Utting, D., Rose, W. and Pugh, G. (2001), *Better Results for Children and Families: Involving Communities in Planning Services Based on Outcomes*, London: NCVCCO.

Utting, D. and Fairnington, A. (2004), *Communities that Care: A Guidebook*, London: Communities that Care.

Verhulst, F. and Van der Ende, J. (2002), 'Rating Scales', in M. Rutter and E. Taylor (eds), *Child and Adolescent Psychiatry*, Oxford: Blackwell.

Waldfogel, J. (2006), *What Children Need*, Cambridge, MA: Harvard University Press.

Walker, S., Shemmings, D. and Cleaver, H. (2003), *Write Enough: Effective Recording in Children's Services*, at: www.writeenough.org.uk (accessed 18 July 2003).

Ward, H., Jones, H., Lynch, M. and Skuse, T. (2002), 'Issues Concerning the Health of Looked After Children', *Adoption and Fostering*, **26**, pp. 1–11.

Ward, H. and Peel, M. (2002), 'An Inter-Agency Approach to Needs Assessment', in H. Ward and W. Rose (eds), *Approaches to Needs Assessment in Children's Services*, London: Jessica Kingsley Publishers.

Ware, A. and Goodin, R.E. (1990), 'Introduction', in A. Ware and R.E. Goodin (eds), *Needs And Welfare*, London: Sage.

Weissberg, R. and Greenberg, M.T. (1998), *Community and School Prevention, in* I. Siegel and A. Renninger (eds), *Child Psychology in Practice, Volume 4, Handbook of Child Psychology* (5th edn), New York: John Wiley.

Wetherly, P. (1996), 'Basic Needs and Social Policies', *Critical Social Policy*, **16**(1), pp. 45–65.

Wise, S. (2003), 'An Evalution of a Trial of Looking After Children in The State of Victoria, Australia', *Children and Society*, **17**(1), pp. 3–17.

Webster-Stratton, C., Reid, J.M. and Hammond, M. (2001), 'Preventing Conduct Problems, Promoting Social Competence: A Parent and Teacher Training Partnership in Head Start', *Journal of Clinical Child Psychology*, **30**, pp. 238–302.

Woodhead, M. (1997), 'Psychology and the Cultural Construction of Children's Needs', in A. James and A. Prout (eds), *Constructing and Reconstructing Childhood: Contemporary Issues in the Sociological Study of Childhood* (2nd edn), London: Falmer.

Zappone, K. (2007), 'Freedom and Prevention: Developing Effective Children's Services in Tallaght, Ireland', *Journal of Children's Services*, **2**(3), pp. 64–73.

Part I
The Theory of Need

[1]

Welfare and the Value of Liberty*

Raymond Plant

THE IDEA OF THE WELFARE STATE IS CURRENTLY TREATED with more scepticism across the political spectrum than at any time during its development. Insofar as the institutions of the welfare state were consolidated during the period of Butskellite consensus which lasted until the late 1960s, in the more polarized political climate of today it is now seen on both the Right and the Left to embody many of the failures implicit in that consensus. It was assumed, so it was argued, that the fiscal dividends of growth could be used to increase welfare in a relatively painless way by maintaining the absolute position of the better off and using the dividends of growth via public expenditure on health, education and welfare to improve the relative standing of the worst-off members of society.[1] In this way it was thought that the social and economic rights of citizenship could be extended within a market economy without putting excessive strain on that economy. Obviously there were sharp disagreements between the political parties about how far these social and economic welfare rights should go and how far the welfare state should be seen as a vehicle of redistribution, but nevertheless, the existence of such a state, which would go well beyond a residual welfare state attempting to prevent destitution, was not seriously questioned. Indeed the degree of consensus over these matters, part of what has been called 'the end of ideology' effectively marginalized the writings and warnings of critics. Many of the basic ideas of contemporary neo-liberal critics of the redistributive welfare state such as Hayek and Friedman were published during this period[2] but

* An earlier version of this paper was given at All Souls College, Oxford. The author would particularly like to thank Ronald Dworkin, Steven Lukes, Alan Ryan, David Miller and Anthony Honoré for their helpful comments.

[1] C. A. R. Crosland, *Social Democracy in Europe*, Fabian Society, 1975.

[2] F. Hayek, *The Constitution of Liberty*, London, Routledge & Kegan Paul, 1960; M. Friedman, *Capitalism and Freedom*, Chicago, University of Chicago Press, 1962.

they did not make a very wide impact and they were often thought of as eccentrics who were attempting to stand in the face of the tide in history because many, particularly convergence theorists,[3] saw the development of the welfare state and the entrenching of social and economic rights of citizenship as a necessary concomitant of the development of a complex urban industrial society. Of course, there were those, as much on the Left as on the Right, who pointed out that the welfare state, committed to meeting *needs* was in principle profoundly anti-capitalist. The welfare rights of the citizen gave him a standing and status based upon the need which was independent of his performance in the market[4] but even those who saw this point seem to have dismissed it on the ground that the apparently limitless potential for economic growth within the mixed economy, and fine tuning by Keynesian demand management, could cope with this implicit contradiction.

What then has led to the disenchantment and to the growth in importance of the neo-liberal critique of the welfare state developed by writers such as Hayek and Friedman?

THE ECONOMIC CONSTRAINTS

First there is undoubtedly the more constrained economic environment within which both Labour and Conservative governments have had to operate, particularly since 1974. This has had the effect, so it is argued, of throwing into relief the problem of providing the resources for the extension of welfare rights within, broadly speaking, a capitalist economy. Many defenders of the welfare state had previously argued that the welfare state was necessary to secure the legitimacy of capitalism because it dealt with the inevitable side-effects of unconstrained capitalism such as poverty and an illegitimate extent of inequality which, if allowed to continue unchecked, would produce degrees of envy and resentment which might well threaten the maintenance of such an economy. On this view, the welfare state, while it embodied uncapitalist or even anti-capitalist assumptions was nevertheless a 'necessary evil' which

[3] C. Kerr, *Industrialism and Industrial Man*, London, Heinemann, 1962.

[4] D. Thompson, 'The Welfare State', *The New Reasoner*, Vol. 1, No. 4, 1958, pp. 44–62.

could be financed out of fiscal dividends of growth. However, the difficulties in sustaining growth and the deep seated difficulties in securing increased productivity in the British economy led many to see the welfare state as a brake on economic development and to confront what O'Connor[5] from the Marxist Left has called 'the fiscal crisis of the state'. The fiscal crisis lies in the fact that in a constrained economy with a welfare state the government has two contradictory imperatives. The first is welfare expenditure, seemingly necessary to secure legitimacy, the second is to secure the conditions of capital accumulation necessary for capitalist development. High rates of incremental growth might allow both of these imperatives to be pursued at once, a constrained economy on the other hand would make this balancing act difficult to sustain. Faced with contradictory pressures the right-wing formation which has come to be called the New Right is prepared to cut back welfare provision in order to secure the possibility of capital accumulation. This strategy, if it were to be successful, would involve more than attacks on 'waste' and would involve substantial cuts in that range of public expenditure which was directed to securing welfare rights.

However, this strategy does not necessarily imply a lack of concern with the plight of the worst-off members of society because, if it is combined with a vigorous defence of capitalism as found for example in the writings of Hayek and Friedman, then it could be argued that in fact the poor would get relatively richer by a trickle-down or echelon advance process whereby, in a relatively unconstrained market, what the rich consume today will trickle down to the poor who will be able to consume these things eventually.[6] Greater inequality might well, on this view, make society as a whole richer, including the worst off. A very minimal residual welfare safety-net might be needed to meet the requirements of the few with special needs and to prevent absolute poverty and destitution, but this would have very little in common with a redistributive welfare state acting as a transfer branch of government.

Coupled with this view is the argument that if not tightly constrained the welfare state has an inbuilt tendency to grow.

---

[5] J. O'Connor, *The Fiscal Crisis of the State*, New York, St Martin's Press, 1973.
[6] F. Hayek, *The Constitution of Liberty*, p. 44.

The critic rejects the view that there is a definite range of needs for the welfare state to meet at a definite level, which could then mean that it could reach a plateau of level funding. Needs are open-ended and if they are seen as the basis of welfare rights there is no intrinsic limit to the extent of such rights and the claims on the resources of the state which such rights embody. Consequently, welfare demands on the state are not clearly limited and, as Enoch Powell[7] has argued, if these needs are supposed to be satisfied at no cost to the individual at the point of delivery, then the demand is infinite.

The state is under enormous pressure to meet such needs, particularly in the sphere of health. But the state has no resources of its own; it derives its income from taxation, but increasing taxation is likely to have an effect on incentives and thus on economic performance, and borrowing is likely to increase inflation or push up interest rates which again have effects upon economic performance. On this view a good deal of thinking about welfare is a victim of what Samuel Brittan[8] has called the 'Wenceslas myth' — that welfare provision is a matter of generosity or stinginess on the part of the state, whereas the reality is, of course, that welfare provision comes out of taxation and borrowing and we cannot detach this from economic growth.

This problem about the insatiability of need is linked to another feature of the welfare state which the New Right regards as both central and baneful — the connection between the welfare state and pressure groups. The elastic idea of welfare needs encourages the formation of pressure groups which seek to secure government funding to meet the 'needs' which they have identified. This pressure group activity, including producer groups of services such as doctors, nurses, teachers and social workers, is unregulated and leads to important and deleterious economic consequences for government in the sense that the political parties in a welfare society are subject to electoral pressure continually to promise to increase the provision of welfare resources.

This is, broadly speaking, the political and economic case developed by the New Right against the welfare state as it

[7] E. Powell, *Medicine and Politics*, London, Pitman, 1966.
[8] S. Brittan, *The Role and Limits of Government*, London, Temple Smith, 1983.

has developed in Britain since the war. The difficulties in implementing any kind of plan to cut back the growth of welfare in the interests of the productivity of the private sector of the economy are clear enough in the current British political context. Despite the apparent support of the then Chancellor for the Central Policy Review Staff's paper to the Cabinet on reducing public expenditure on welfare services including the NHS, the outcry was widespread enough, across the political spectrum, to make Mrs Thatcher say during the general election campaign in 1983 that the NHS was safe in Conservative hands. The cutbacks which have been made, which are very marginal in terms of radical surgery which the neo-liberal, New Right diagnosis would require, have been met by widespread opposition not just by the producer interest groups concerned but also in the country at large.

However, there is in addition, a moral case made by the New Right which has to be taken account of in any serious attempt to develop a defence of the welfare state and this is particularly associated with the influential writings of Hayek. This attack is an attempt to confront some of the values on which the welfare state might be thought to be based. The remainder of the article will be concerned with this fundamental critique and an attempt to answer its main points.

THE VALUES CALLED IN QUESTION

The argument which is often brought into play when defending the welfare state is that left to its own devices the economic market will limit freedom and cause injustice. On this view an unconstrained market will produce large inequalities and those at the bottom of the resultant stratification will not have the resources to make their demand effective in the market and thus their freedom will be diminished. Similarly, those who are at the bottom and suffer poverty and relative deprivation are the victims of injustice. Thus the argument is that a welfare state which seeks some measure of redistribution is an attempt to increase the freedom of the worst off and to rectify the injustices in distribution which the market creates.

Hayek decisively rejects the points about coercion in relation to the outcomes of economic markets. Such outcomes are not coercive in Hayek's view because coercion depends crucially upon intention. As he says in *The Constitution of Liberty*:

... we presuppose a human agent if we say that we have been coerced ... Coercion occurs when one man's actions are made to serve another man's will, not for his own but for the other's purpose ... Coercion implies both the threat of inflicting harm and the intention thereby to bring about certain conduct.[9]

Coercion is a strongly intentional concept but in Hayek's view economic transactions in the market do not share this degree of intentionality. In the market innumerable individuals make small decisions to buy and sell in the light of their necessarily restricted knowledge and in the light of their own view of their own interests. In a complex economy some will no doubt suffer as the result of the aggregate of individual decisions which are made but these outcomes were not intended and not foreseen by the individuals concerned. Any harm or limitation on resources which changes a person's opportunities is an unintended, remote and unforeseen consequence of individual decisions taken for all sorts of different, limited reasons. The lack of individualized intention and the unforeseeable nature of economic outcomes make it impossible to describe economic processes as coercive.

Hayek is able to make the same case by concentrating upon freedom as well as coercion. In *The Constitution of Liberty* Hayek adopts a strongly negative view of liberty in which to be free is to be free from the intentional coercion of another. In this connection it is perhaps useful to look at his rejection of the view that liberty involves having powers, capacities and abilities. There are two reasons why Hayek rejects freedom as ability. The first is that it assimilates freedom to omnipotence:

Once this identification of freedom with power is admitted, there is no limit to the sophisms by which the attractions of the word 'liberty' can be used to support measures which destroy individual freedom.[10]

The second is that to equate liberty with power or capacity means that:

it is only too easy to pass from defining liberty as the absence of restraint to defining it as the 'absence of obstacles to the realisation of our desires'

[9] F. Hayek, *The Constitution of Liberty*, p. 133.
[10] ibid, p. 16.

or even more generally 'the absence of external impediment'. This is equivalent to interpreting it as the effective power to do what we want.[11]

Given this conception of negative liberty as freedom from intentional coercion ('presupposing the action of a restraining human agent') Hayek is able to claim that in general the outcomes of markets do not decrease freedom. In the first place, because of the lack of foreseeability and intentionality, any impediments to action are not the result of the action of a restraining human agent; secondly even if I suffer economic deprivation as the result of markets, because there is no link between liberty and power and capacity, my lack of resources to enable me to pursue my desires is not coercive. If we put these points together, therefore, they underpin the rejection of the view that redistribution via a welfare state is important to liberty.[12] Thus, the freedom of the worst off is not diminished by their lack of resources.

Similarly they do not suffer from injustice. Injustices equally are only caused by intentional actions. Therefore there is no moral basis for a critique of the market in terms of its injustice. The suffering which may be caused by the operation of the market is not to be rectified by claims to rights, justice and equality. The provision of a welfare safety-net whether by voluntary or political action is a gift to be bestowed not a right to be claimed. There might be good pragmatic goals for the provision of a residual welfare safety-net but this is not a response to a moral imperative and certainly the provision of welfare for redistributive purposes has no moral legitimacy.

Hayek makes this point as follows in the context of a discussion of justice:

It has of course to be admitted that the manner in which benefits and burdens are allocated by the market mechanism would in many instances have to be regarded as very unjust if it were the result of a deliberate allocation to particular people. But this is not the case. These shares are the outcome of a process the effect of which on particular people was neither intended nor foreseen. To demand justice from such a process is clearly absurd, and to single out some people in such a society as entitled to a particular share evidently unjust.[13]

[11] ibid, p. 16.

[12] ibid.

[13] F. Hayek, *Law, Legislation and Liberty, Vol. II: The Mirage of Social Justice*, London, Routledge & Kegan Paul, 1976, p. 64.

This argument about justice is backed up by a claim that in a morally pluralistic society there are no agreed criteria of distributive justice which could guide the allocative decisions of the state and that for the state to pursue redistributive welfare policies in such circumstances is deeply illiberal. In a liberal society the state should not pursue some particular view of the good life, because people will disagree about what the good life consists in; but if, granted the range of moral disagreement, the state seeks to impose *one* view of distributive justice, as opposed to another, then it cannot treat its citizens as equals.[14] A redistributive welfare state, founded upon the pursuit of social justice will be incompatible with the moral divergence of a modern society. To try to implement one conception of justice as opposed to another is not to treat this divergence with the respect that it deserves. On this view, despite often cited claims to the contrary, a redistributive welfare state does not treat its citizens with equal respect.

These two arguments about liberty and justice make a radical strike at the normative basis of the welfare state which has frequently been stated in terms of increasing liberty or rectifying injustice and any defender of the welfare state who seeks to portray it as a more than pragmatic phenomenon – to buy off social discontent, or to create a reasonably healthy workforce – will have to come to terms with this critique because he will not be able to trump pragmatic claims in favour of diminishing the welfare state with claims about freedom and justice.

THE MEANING OF LIBERTY

Obviously in the context of both freedom and justice Hayek's argument depends crucially upon his claim that economic outcomes are unintentional and unforeseeable and therefore cannot produce coercion or injustice which depend upon coercers and distributors being identified as specific human agents. However, these claims need to be disentangled a little. In the case of foreseeability we need to go back to the passage from Volume II of *Law Legislation and Liberty* cited above. In that passage the

---

[14] For a forceful statement of this view see J. Gray, 'Classical Liberalism, Positional Goods and the Politicisation of Poverty', in K. Kumar and A. Ellis (eds), *Dilemmas of Liberal Democracies*, London, Tavistock, 1983, pp. 181–82.

unforeseeability involved is in relation to individuals – 'These shares are the outcome of a process the effect of which on particular people was neither intended nor foreseen'. However, it is not clear that the moral critique of the market in relation to the lack of freedom of the worst off has ever been made on individual cases. Usually the argument has been in terms of groups – that as a general rule those who enter a market with least, will end up with least. *If* this can be foreseen as a rule of thumb, and I believe that it can, then Hayek's argument about foreseeability loses much of its power. As it stands it presents a criticism of a view which few, if any, critics of the market have ever held. However, as such this point does not make much of a dent in Hayek's armour, although it will be seen to be important later, because he can still call upon the points about intentionality as well as the fundamental point about the difference between freedom and power/ability/capacity.

Even if the outcomes of markets could be foreseen for the worst off as a general category, this would still not in Hayek's view limit their freedom because freedom does not consist in having the power or the resources to satisfy desires; it consists in freedom from intentional coercion. However, the sharp distinction which Hayek draws here is dubious even in the context of his own work. In his discussion of coercion in Chapter IX of *The Constitution of Liberty* Hayek makes the wholly sensible point that a monopolist could be regarded as exercising coercion if he controls what Hayek calls an 'essential commodity' or an 'indispensable supply'. But it is not at all clear why this should be regarded as coercive unless there is some conceptual link between such basic goods and the exercise of liberty. Unless there was this analytical connection between certain basic goods and liberty, we might regard the actions of the monopolist as being unpleasant and morally abhorrent in various ways but *not* coercive. The point can be made in a more general way about coercion. If on Hayek's own view of coercion, a coercive restraint is removed on my conduct, then I am enabled to do something which I was not realistically able to choose before. Of course in my new found freedom I may choose not to do it but nevertheless the limitation on coercion is an *enabling* factor. Alternatively the imposition of coercion may make me realistically unable to do what I was able to do before. Before the gun was held to my head I was able to walk through the door, now realistically I am unable to do so. On these grounds therefore there is a basis for saying that there is *some* connection between liberty and ability.

The second reason why there could be thought to be a connection between freedom and ability is to take up another theme in Hayek's work, namely the value of liberty. Hayek rests his case for the value of negative freedom on the basis of our ignorance:

> If there were omniscient men, if we could know not only all that affects the attainment of our present wishes but also our future wants and desires there would be little use for liberty . . . Liberty is essential in order to leave room for the unforeseeable and unpredictable; we want it because we have learned to expect from it the opportunity of realising may of our aims.[15]

Now of course this is very important and has to be preserved in a full account of the value of liberty, but as Hayek himself makes clear in this passage liberty is an opportunity-related concept. He clearly wants to restrict the idea of opportunity here to mean the opportunity to capitalize upon the accidental and the unforeseeable which is important for human progress and this is fair enough; but surely this is too restricted a view of opportunity, it also means that I value negative liberty because of the private space it offers me to do what I want. I value liberty because freedom enables me to advance my ends and purposes and it is surely the case that to do this means that I need resources, powers and opportunities of a more substantial kind than merely the openings which my ignorance reveals. This point is central to Rawls, for example, when he speaks about the value of liberty:

> . . . the worth of liberty is not the same for everyone. Some have greater authority and wealth and therefore greater means to achieve their aims.[16]

This is not to say that their *liberty* is unequal, only that the *value* of freedom varies in relation to their powers and opportunities. This is, I believe, the fundamental idea behind the proposal by MacCallum[17] in which freedom is defined as the

---

[15] F. Hayek, *The Constitution of Liberty*, p. 29.
[16] J. Rawls, *A Theory of Justice*, Oxford, Oxford University Press, 1972, p. 204.
[17] G. MacCallum, 'Negative and Positive Liberty', *Philosophical Review*, 1967, pp. 312–34.

freedom of x from y to do or become z. The opportunity to do or become z is what makes the absence of constraint (y) valuable to us; it is that in which the work of liberty resides and as such requires powers and abilities as well as Hayek's opportunities to exploit ignorance.

On these views, therefore, there are strong reasons for rejecting Hayek's account of liberty as having nothing to do with abilities. However, even if we have given reasons for seeking to link ability with freedom, at least in explaining in an intelligible way why liberty is precious, we still have to respond to Hayek's point that if we make this connection then one gets into the absurd position of not being able to distinguish between the value of freedom and omnipotence. There are two issues here. The first is an account of the abilities/powers/capabilities which are important to the value of liberty. We have to put some restriction on this list otherwise we fall foul of Hayek's strictures. The second is to say something about the relationship between the list of basic powers/capacities/abilities on one side and freedom on the other because not all the restrictions on my abilities can be said to lower the value of liberty.

Hayek's argument is that if we link freedom and ability in the way I have done, then the value of my liberty declines in proportion to my abilities, and this is absurd because there are many things which I am unable to do which have no bearing upon the value of freedom — I cannot be in two places at once, I cannot prove Golbach's conjecture, I am unable to run a four-minute mile, I cannot afford to go on a round-the-world cruise, and all these differently based inabilities lower the value of liberty. If this argument is to be rebutted, because as it stands it is quite powerful, we need some idea of which abilities/powers/capacities relate most directly to the value of liberty. The most plausible answer to this problem is to say that these are the powers and capacities which bear most directly on the possibility of agency. My capacity for agency clearly must have a bearing upon the value of any liberty. If I am unable to act at all, not for this or that particular purpose, but at all, then negative liberty will be of no value to me.

So, are there any basic needs which an agent has to satisfy in order to act at all? If there are, then this will answer Hayek's criticism, because we could then distinguish those basic goods/

powers/opportunities which an agent would need to make liberty valuable from those other powers and abilities the lack of which it would be absurd to regard as restrictions on the value of freedom — such as my inability to run a four-minute mile. In his discussion of monopoly Hayek has already conceded that there are certain necessary goods or indispensable conditions for human beings to be free and it can be argued that the most obvious way of characterizing these goods is in terms of the necessary conditions of agency.

What are these goods? At the most basic level it seems clear that physical survival is a necessary condition of agency and that, as such, survival is a basic human good — this good of course has to be cashed in terms of specific goods such as health care and the minimum economic conditions of survival. This type of argument has been developed by a number of writers in a range of places.[18] The terminology of these arguments differs and does reveal different conceptions of the issues involved as well as different philosophical assumptions.[19] Nevertheless, for the purposes of this article, the thrust of the argument is very similar, and is quite close to Hayek's own views about necessary goods in the context of monopoly coercion. However, the basic good of physical survival and the specific ways in which this is cashed in terms of health care and income maintenance is fairly minimal as it stands and would not take the defence of the welfare state in terms of the values of freedom much beyond the idea of the welfare state as a residual institution (although this is useful in defending the welfare state against libertarians such as Nozick[20] who really see no role for it at all, even at a residual level, and against neo-liberals such as Hayek and Acton[21] who see a residual welfare state as justifiable only on pragmatic and not on moral grounds).

Nevertheless one can go beyond this minimalist idea towards a more comprehensive view by arguing that sheer physical

18 R. Plant, H. Lesser and P. Taylor-Gooby, *Political Philosophy and Social Welfare*, London, Routledge & Kegan Paul, 1981; J. Rawls, op. cit; A. Gewirth, *Reason and Morality*, Chicago, University of Chicago Press, 1978; L. Doyal and I. Gough, 'A Theory of Human Needs', *Journal of Critical and Social Policy*, 10, 1984, pp. 6–38.

19 See A. K. Sen, *Choice, Welfare and Measurement*, Oxford, Blackwell, 1982.

20 R. Nozick, *Anarchy, State and Utopia*, Oxford, Blackwell, 1974.

21 H. B. Acton, *The Morals of Markets*, London, Longman, 1971.

survival is not the only generic good relating to agency and thus to the value of liberty. One has to think also in terms of *well-being*. Sheer survival is a necessary condition of agency but it is clearly not a sufficient one because someone can literally survive on a respirator but clearly the possibility of purpose fulfilment requires more than this. What it in fact requires cannot be specified except in a culture-dependent way, but in our society the ability to act as an agent is going to require, first of all, negative liberty but, more than this, to be able also to act *effectively*. For liberty to be valuable, a person is going to require possession of resources both material and psychological and these will specify various sorts of welfare goods such as education etc. In order to make negative liberty effective and valuable these resources, however they are defined in a particular society, which comprise the power to act at all in an effective manner are going to be basic goods of agency.

However, while this argument defines a class of basic goods and basic needs in relation to such goods, it does not of itself say anything about distribution. The link with the idea of the value of liberty, however, gives us the clue for a distributive principle. If we accept liberal assumptions about equality of respect, together with the kind of view to be found in Hayek that we lack criteria for saying that one person is more deserving than another, then there are no moral grounds for saying that some people deserve to have a greater value of freedom than others, or, to put it another way, that some people deserve to have more effective basic liberty. In these circumstances, therefore, those welfare goods which define the conditions of effective agency and the value of liberty should be distributed equally just because there are no a priori moral reasons for any other sort of distribution.

There is a difficulty here which has been explained in a recent paper by Amartya Sen in which he argues that the basic goods approach borders on fetishism and that we should be concerned more with the ways in which people are differently capable of transforming such goods.[22] However, as Sen clearly recognises, there are problems of indexing these basic transformations of goods into capabilities and, of course, producing

[22] A. K. Sen, op. cit., p. 368.

interpersonal comparisons between different agents' possibilities of transforming a bundle of goods necessary for agency into equal capacities. I am certain that Sen is right here, but I regard at least the second of these issues as insoluble and that in the absence of a scientific basis for making interpersonal comparisons, we have to opt for an initial equal distribution of the basic conditions of agency as the closest we can get at the political level for equalizing basic capacities, despite the inequalities in effective powers which would follow from the truth of Sen's point made above.

THE DEGREES AND KINDS OF COERCION

So far the argument has been couched in terms of the value of liberty but there is a second strand to the argument which has to be deployed in order fully to meet the neo-liberal argument that can be mounted in terms of liberty, namely in relation to coercion. It will be remembered that part of Hayek's argument is that the outcomes of markets are non-coercive because they are neither intended nor foreseen in relation to individuals. I have already argued that the point about foreseeability is irrelevant in relation to individuals and that it is possible to argue that for the worst-off groups it is foreseeable that in entering the market with least, they will broadly end up with least. This does not, of course, show that these outcomes were intended, but is this sufficient to show that the worst off are not coerced? This problem poses at a macro-level the problem of double effect posed by moral philosophers at the micro-level. If, for example, as a doctor I prescribe a massive dose of a pain killing drug to stop the pain of a weak, terminally ill patient and it kills that person and that this is foreseeable but unintended is this sufficient to discount moral responsibility? Clearly there are arguments both ways but, if we say that as a matter of routine my intended actions produced a foreseeable but unintended outcome for another person, then it is going to be disingenuous to argue at some stage that I am not responsible for the foreseeable but unintended consequences of my action. Indeed, if this were not so, there would be a strong incentive continually to narrow down the characterization of intention so that it does not include the foreseeable consequences. In these circumstances there are good reasons for saying that you are responsible for the routine foreseeable consequences of an action, the intention of which is described in a different way. If we apply this to the market context we could then argue that *if* as an empirical fact those who enter the market with least will tend to end up with least and *if* this affects the capacity for agency, and *if* this is known to be the case as a foreseeable general outcome, even though it is not intended, and *if* there is an alternative course of action available, namely a market constrained by a redistributive welfare state, then we can argue the market is coercive. This is to say, in my intentional activity in buying and selling in an unconstrained market I have no intention to act coercively, nevertheless if as a routine consequence of my exercising my freedom in this way, some persons are put in the position of lacking the conditions for effective agency, then I am by my action, although not my intention, supporting a system which lowers the value of liberty for others and this is coercive.

Having made and defended some of these distinctions, we are now in a position to deal with the neo-liberal strictures on social or distributive justice. It is central to Hayek's argument here that the outcomes of markets which adversely affect the position of an individual do not result in injustice. Of course the person may be poorer, he may suffer but he does not suffer injustice. The difference is crucial for only if he suffered an injustice would this generate a moral claim on the resources of the state to rectify that injustice. The key to this argument is that considerations of justice are irrelevant because the outcomes of the market were not willed or intended by anyone and maldistribution or expertise can occur only where there is a distributor intentionally making a maldistribution. However, this degree of intentionality is lacking in the case of markets and thus injustice cannot arise.

However, first of all, it is not clear that injustice is *only* a matter of how a particular outcome came about or arose, but rather is as much a matter of our response to the outcome. Certainly someone who was born with a severe handicap does not suffer an injustice because of the genetic lottery, but where justice and injustice come in is in our response to his position. If we fail to compensate him when we could have done so, at no damaging cost to ourselves, then this is where injustice lies.

In addition though, the argument deployed in the context of

freedom becomes relevant here. In a sense Hayek's own argument about justice parallels the case of freedom as turning upon intentionality. Because there is no intentionality there is no injustice. However, as we have seen, the situation in respect of intentionality is much more complex than Hayek allows. Although my intention in the market is to buy and sell for my own particular reasons, nevertheless if it is a foreseeable outcome that individuals will do badly in the acquisition of basic or general goods which bear upon the value of freedom, then that outcome is unjust given that there is an alternative available — a redistributive welfare state.

So far then, I have argued that there is a defensible view of the obligation to provide welfare both in terms of freedom and justice. The worst-off members of society do suffer a constraint on the value of liberty and they do suffer injustice given that there are alternatives. However this last phrase brings us back to some of the more practical considerations discussed in the earlier part of the article because, of course, the argument at that point was that the alternative actually produced major problems of its own, particularly its cost and the welfare state's relation to the rest of the economy. While it may be that there are strong moral arguments in favour of the welfare state, if there are great practical and economic difficulties they may tend to override the moral considerations. One of these practical objections relates to the ambiguity and indeterminacy of welfare. It will be remembered that part of the neo-liberal critique is that because the claims of welfare are indeterminate, the welfare state has an inbuilt tendency to grow. There is no plateau to be found, new needs are constantly being discovered (invented?) and being put on the political agenda, requiring an expansion of the welfare state. Because needs are politicized in this way[23] the welfare state becomes like a financial bottomless pit with no clear limit to the resources it can claim.

In my own argument about the generic goods of welfare as basic needs, I conceded the case that such goods are culturally relative and that there will therefore be disputes expressed in political ways about what would satisfy such needs and it does seem to me that there can indeed be no alternative to this.

[23] J. Gray, op cit.

There can be no context-independent, purely conceptual answer to the question of how extensive basic goods should be and to this extent the basis of the neo-liberal case is conceded. However, the search for a non-politicized answer to this question is fruitless; but it does seem to me that there are some limits and constraints which make sense even within a welfarist perspective. The first and most basic one is that there is no obligation to provide for the basic needs of some individuals if this puts at risk the satisfaction of similar needs of others. This principle certainly works at the level of personal morality. Similarly there can be no obligation on society to meet basic needs if to do so would imply a comparable cost or risk. In this case the onus would be on the critic of welfare to show that providing for well-being would be likely to put at severe risk the economic resources necessary to continue to provide for the well-being of all citizens. The second constraint would be the Rawlsian one. There is no duty to continue to try to equalize well-being if in fact the economic consequences of so doing would actually mean that there would be fewer resources for well-being. That is to say there might be a level of provision of welfare which falls short of equal provision, because an attempt to go beyond that towards equality would be likely to make everyone, including the professed beneficiaries of more equal treatment, worse off. On this view, it would be irrational, if our concern is with well-being, to prefer a system of strict equality of well-being if this actually lowered the level of welfare to everyone including those whom the egalitarian was most trying to help.

In addition, most neo-liberals, unlike libertarians such as Nozick, do in fact concede a minimal safety-net welfare state and it is clear that such a view has to depend upon a clearly defined concept of absolute poverty, but it is of course notoriously difficult to define poverty in such non-relative terms, and to concede a residual welfare state without a clearly *limited* notion of poverty which is publicly acceptable is to open up their own conception of the welfare state for the same kind of expansion for which they criticize 'welfarists'.

CONCLUSIONS

In this article I have offered a defence of a redistributive welfare state in reply to neo-liberal critics and this has very largely been predicated upon freedom and justice. However, this is not to say that such a stance would provide much of a defence of the welfare state as it actually exists in Britain. Indeed it is sadly lacking in both the dimensions of freedom and justice. Its record in terms of distributive justice has been rather poor[24] with the middle classes being the greatest beneficiaries of a great deal of welfare spending. Its bureaucratic organization and the role of the personal social services quite frequently seem to be paternalistic and to threaten personal liberty. Because of these factors, which cannot be adequately rehearsed here, there seem to me to be good grounds for seeing the welfare state in many respects as dealing with the consequences of a maldistribution or unjust distribution of income and that the central welfare demand, whether in terms of justice or of welfare, would therefore be on the lines of such a redistribution of income, subject to the two constraints of comparable risk and the Rawlsian difference principle which I have already discussed.

[24] J. le Grand, *The Strategy of Equality*, London, Allen & Unwin, 1982.

[2]

The Priority of Needs

ROBERT E. GOODIN
University of Essex

1. Supposing, as we ordinarily do, that satisfying needs takes priority over satisfying mere desires, it is small wonder that we should strive to cloak our claims in the language of necessity. Sometimes we overreach ourselves. Harry Frankfurt shows that the Principle of Precedence breaks down when the putative needs are just desires at one remove — when they are, in his terminology, merely 'volitional needs'.[1] But bracketing out these counterfeit claims will not, as Frankfurt hopes, suffice to save the Principle of Precedence. At most, needs correlate in only a rough and ready way with various other factors which do deserve priority consideration. The priority we often seem to accord needs is thus purely epiphenomenal. Furthermore, the purposes we wish the Principle of Precedence to serve could usually be better furthered through other avenues.

2. Frankfurt writes, "All necessities are . . . conditional: nothing is needed except in virtue of being an indispensable condition for the attainment of a certain end" (p. 3). In the case of volitional needs, we need X for Y, and we desire Y. In the case of nonvolitional needs, we need X for Y, and we need Y. But for what? All necessities are conditional. We cannot 'need Y' simpliciter. We can only need Y for some further end.

With volitional needs, desires underlie needs. There is no more reason for us to provide people with what they need, in this sense, than there is for us to satisfy people's desires themselves. That is why Frankfurt thinks volitional needs claims are so weak. That is why they should enjoy no precedence over desires.

But much the same is true of nonvolitional needs as well. What underlies them is not desires but rather the 'further end' for which the needed

---

[1] Harry G. Frankfurt, "Necessity and Desire," *Philosophy and Phenomenological Research* 45 (September 1984): 1-13; subsequent citations to this article are indicated by page numbers in the text.

need is an 'indispensable condition'. Just as there is no more reason to satisfy people's volitional needs than there is to satisfy the desires that underlie them, however, so too is there no more reason to satisfy people's nonvolitional needs than there is to promote the 'further ends' that underlie
them. Nonvolitional needs, by an argument perfectly paralleling Frankfurt's own, must enjoy no precedence over the 'further ends' underlying
them.

Whether nonvolitional needs deserve to enjoy systematic priority over
mere desires thus reduces to the question of whether the 'further ends'
they serve should systematically take precedence over mere desires. I can
find only one plausible reason for thinking they should. Notice that nonvolitional needs, by definition, promote ends that are unconnected with
the bearer's own desires. Promoting those ends, if valuable at all, must
therefore be objectively valuable. This is in contrast to the subjective values served by satisfying people's desires. Perhaps, then, we give nonvolitional needs priority over mere desires because we think that promoting
objective values takes priority over promoting subjective ones.

That argument may or may not go through. But if it does, it goes
through in too strong a form to be of any use to defenders of the Principle
of Precedence as we know it. The difference between objective and subjective values is a difference of kind. If that difference makes a moral difference at all, then it must make more of a difference than the mere
'difference of degree' that is embodied in the Principle of Precedence. As
Frankfurt describes it, that Principle "attributes to needs only a quite minimal moral superiority over desires. It maintains no more than that when
there is a competition between a desire and a need for the same thing, the
need starts with a certain moral edge. . . . Meeting A's need is *prima
facie* morally preferable to satisfying B's desire" (p. 3), but like all *prima
facie* demands this one is liable to be overridden.[2] That is simply not the
sort of strong priority that the sharp distinction between objective and
subjective values would lead us to adopt.

3. Frankfurt himself offers two grounds for the Principle of Precedence.
The first is that "allocating resources to meeting needs takes precedence

---

[2] Frankfurt has not misdescribed the Principle of Precedence, either. In the paradigm cases
of nonvolitional needs, what is needed is needed in order to promote the objective good
of sustaining life itself. But we do not give that objective good complete priority over subjective desires. We allow people, in pursuit of purely subjective ends, to do all sorts of
things that cost people's lives (either their own or those of others; either directly or indirectly; either probabilistically or with utter certainty; etc.).

over allocating them to fulfilling mere desires" because "the former aims at avoiding harm, while the latter aims only at providing unneeded benefits" (p. 7).

The first step in this argument is to define harms and benefits. "Being harmed," in Frankfurt's terms, "has to do with becoming worse off than one was, while failing to obtain a benefit is more a matter of not becoming better off than before" (p. 6). To that definition is added, as an ethical postulate, the proposition that "making things better is, for a moral point of view, less important (measure for measure) than keeping them from getting worse" (p. 7).

All of that I happily concede. But that alone is not enough to derive the Principle of Precedence. For that, Frankfurt has to equate 'meeting needs' with 'avoiding harm' and 'fulfilling mere desires' with 'providing benefits'. Then, and only then, will the postulated priority of avoiding harm take him to the desired priority of needs.

The equation is legitimate, however, only in a very particular set of circumstances. Given his definitions, the pairing presupposes a state of the world in which (a) our (nonvolitional) needs are presently being met and (b) our 'mere desires' are not presently being met. Then and only then will not meeting our needs make us worse off than we are at present.[3] Then and only then will not satisfying our desires merely fail to make us better off than we are at present.

Imagine now a different state of the world. Suppose some of my (mere) desires are presently being satisfied. In that situation, your failing to provide me with whatever I (volitionally) need to continue satisfying those desires would make me worse off than I am at present. On Frankfurt's ethical postulate that not making people worse off should enjoy priority, the continued satisfaction of my mere desire should enjoy exactly the same priority as meeting anyone's real (nonvolitional) needs. There is no reason to suppose that Frankfurt (or anyone else) would care to embrace this bizarre and viciously conservative implication of his analysis. But that is where his argument inevitably leads.

---

[3] That is true on Frankfurt's official definition of harm, at least. Later he enters the caveat that "the life of a person whose condition is bad becomes worse and worse as long as his condition does not improve, simply because more of a bad thing is worse than less of it" (p. 7). That allows him to say that a person is being made worse off by the continuing failure to meet his needs, and not just by a cessation of meeting his needs. But the use of 'bad' in this caveat begs the question of what is wrong with not meeting people's needs; yet the use of that term is crucial in preventing the same principle from indicating a continuing failure to satisfy someone's mere desires as a 'harm' done to him.

4. Frankfurt's second and rather more promising argument for the Principle of Precedence is that, with nonvolitional needs, "whether or not the harm ensues is outside the person's voluntary control." Mere desires and the volitional needs that flow from them, in contrast, "are voluntary, which means that the person need not have the needs at all" (p. 7).

'Voluntariness' in this context might mean either (or both) of two things. One is that the desires were voluntarily adopted in the first place. The other is that the desires can be voluntarily renounced. Usually — but not always — desires are voluntary in both senses and needs in neither.

A focus on voluntariness-in-the-first-instance would surely be misplaced. Consider the case of someone suffering kidney failure owing to his own previous voluntary actions — a botched suicide attempt, say, or a drug overdose. That person's need for renal dialysis must surely count as a paradigm case of a nonvolitional need. He needs the dialysis machine to meet a need, not merely to satisfy a desire. The voluntariness of the previous acts that led him to need the machine does nothing to make his need for it any less of a need now.

Of course, we may well think that such a person's claim to scarce kidney dialysis units is less strong than that of someone who is not to blame for his own plight. We may want to give priority to satisfying claims with no voluntary aspects to their histories. The point here, however, is that that does not track perfectly with a rule to accord priority to satisfying needs. Some perfectly nonvolitional needs may indeed have just such a voluntary aspect to their histories.

'Voluntariness' can, alternatively, be understood as 'alterability'. This seems to be Frankfurt's preferred interpretation. When discussing 'constrained volitional needs' — ones which deserve nearly as much priority as nonvolitional ones — Frankfurt grounds their priority in the fact that they are "ineradicably persistent" (p. 9). The point, made by Rawls and Charles Taylor in addition to Frankfurt, is that if your mere desires are being disappointed there is something you can do to protect yourself from this disappointment, viz., alter your desires.[4] Nonvolitional needs, by definition, are beyond any such volitional control. And since there is no opportunity for people to protect themselves in this way where genuine needs are concerned, the social obligation to satisfy such claims is stronger than the social obligation to satisfy people's mere desires.

---

[4] John Rawls, "Social Unity and Primary Goods," *Utilitarianism and Beyond*, ed. A. Sen and B. Williams (Cambridge: Cambridge University Press, 1982), pp. 159-86. Charles Taylor, "Responsibility for Self," *The Identities of Persons*, ed. A. O. Rorty (Berkeley: University of California Press, 1976), pp. 281-99.

Again, we may well think it is more important for us to protect people the less able they are to protect themselves. But this translates only very imperfectly into a priority for needs over mere desires. It is simply not true that all nonvolitional needs are such that people cannot take any steps to protect themselves. True, they cannot protect themselves in the one particular way Frankfurt picks out, i.e., they cannot alter their needs in the way they can alter their mere desires. But altering them is only one of many possible ways of protecting oneself from the harm one would suffer. And it surely is the inability to protect oneself, rather than the inability to protect oneself in any particular way, that matters morally.

Consider the case of a particularly talented medical technician suffering kidney failure. Let us suppose that he could easily build himself a kidney dialysis machine and operate it all by himself. The fact that he could protect himself does not make his need for kidney dialysis any less of a nonvolitional need. What it does show is that not all nonvolitional needs are beyond our control to protect ourselves from, and entitled to special priority on those grounds.

Or, again, consider the case of a desire that has given rise to a purely volitional need that the agent cannot now alter. I am a keen mountaineer, let us suppose. My desire to climb mountains gives rise to purely-volitional needs for ropes and spikes. But once my desires have taken me onto the icy ledges of Everest, I can no longer revise my desires and extinguish my need for ropes and spikes. One's inability to renounce one's volitional needs may, once again, make one more entitled to social assistance. But what it does not do is make volitional needs into nonvolitional ones. Thus, according priority to inalterable claims here too fails to track perfectly with a rule according priority to nonvolitional needs.

The previous arguments suggest that nonvolitional needs are not 'involuntary' in either of the two possible senses, taken singly. Neither are nonvolitional needs necessarily involuntary in both senses taken together. A talented medical technician who needs kidney dialysis because of his own botched suicide attempt would have a perfectly nonvolitional need for such a machine, though it would be one which was involuntary in neither of the two senses identified above.

In short, we may want to accord priority to claims that count as involuntary in either or both of the senses identified here. But that does not translate into a rule according priority to needs over mere desires, since needs are not necessarily involuntary and mere desires are not necessarily voluntary in either (or both) of those senses. If we are going to have a priority rule here, it should cue on things that matter (voluntariness) rather than on things that correlate only imperfectly with them (needs/desires).

5. Various other imperfect correlates also contribute to the illusion that needs deserve priority over mere wants. Among these is the relative urgency of the two types of claims. Relatively urgent claims are those which will be of substantially less value (and, in the limiting case, none at all) if met later rather than if met now. Relatively nonurgent claims are those which will be of approximately the same value if satisfied later as if satisfied now.[5]

Claims that are relatively urgent in this sense command a certain measure of priority over ones that are not. Failing to meet the former promptly means forsaking them forever; failing to meet the latter now means merely postponing them. This priority is far from absolute. One and the same resource might be required urgently to serve a perfectly trivial end, or nonurgently to serve a tremendously important one. Then we may well prefer to serve the more important end and forsake the trivial one forever. (We will be particularly inclined to do so if we suppose this a common occurrence, so the important would be infinitely postponed if we were to give priority to the urgent in each such instance.) But at the very least, urgent claims command a *ceteris paribus* priority over nonurgent ones, and that priority probably persists to some extent even where the importance of the ends served is not strictly equal.

That might seem to translate into a priority for needs over mere wants. In the paradigm cases that come most easily to mind, needs are more urgent than wants. One's needs for food, water or shelter are of a 'now or never' sort. It is pointless to postpone the claims of famine victims. If they are not fed this year, they will not be around next year to benefit from a food aid program.

But again, there is only a rough and ready correlation between urgency and needs. Some desires that are indisputably 'mere desires' are every bit as urgent as needs. My desire to hear Pavarotti's farewell performance next week is one such urgent desire. And on the other side, some needs are relatively nonurgent. The need of the cataract patient for treatment sometime over the next five years is one example. But the waiting lists of the U.K. National Health Service hospitals are full of other examples: they would not be eligible for NHS treatment unless there were a genuine need present, but they would not be on the waiting list unless theirs were nonurgent needs.

---

[5] Cf. T. M. Scanlon, "Preference and Urgency," *Journal of Philosophy* 77 (1975): 655-69.

6. The most plausible general analysis of needs, in my view, construes them as Rawlsian 'primary goods.' These are defined as goods — or, in the case of needs, conditions or circumstances more generally — that are necessary instruments to any and all particular ends which one might pursue.[6]

Now, needs defined as necessary instruments inevitably have a kind of logical-cum-temporal priority over mere wants. By definition, you cannot get what you want until you have what you need: that is just what it means for something to be a 'necessary instrument.' But that in itself is not enough to explain why needs enjoy the sort of social priority they ordinarily do.

To say that it is necessary to satisfy needs *before* wants is not to say that needs should be satisfied *instead* of wants. Jack's needs must, *ex hypothesi*, be satisfied before Jack's wants can be satisfied; but that provides no good reason for thinking that Jack's needs should be satisfied before, much less instead of, Jill's wants. Temporal priority does not translate automatically into value priority. The necessity of satisfying needs before wants can be satisfied does not imply that it is more important to satisfy needs than wants.

On the contrary, the value of instruments — however necessary they may be — cannot possibly exceed the value of the ends which they serve. If the value of needs is purely instrumental, then the satisfaction of Jack's needs cannot be any more valuable to Jack (or anyone else, by extension) than is the satisfaction of the desires or other ends for which those needs are necessary instruments. The value of need-satisfaction, where needs are construed merely as necessary instruments, is thus wholly derivative from the value of want-satisfaction. The former cannot therefore take priority over the latter. Or at least it cannot claim priority on those grounds, anyway.

To make out a case for the priority of needs over wants, what we must emphasize is not their role as necessary instruments but rather the *wide variety* of ends for which they are necessary instruments. That is what is so

---

[6] For related though not identical arguments see: David Miller, *Social Justice* (Oxford: Clarendon Press, 1976), chap. 3; Henry Shue, *Basic Rights* (Princeton: Princeton University Press, 1980); and Norman Daniels, "Health-Care Needs and Distributive Justice," *Philosophy & Public Affairs* 10 (1981): 146-79. Talk of 'necessary instruments', incidentally, explains why people can be said to need some things without wanting them: on this analysis, that just means that they have not realized that (or readjusted their wants in light of the realization that) some particular instrument is necessary in order to accomplish what they want.

distinctive about primary goods. That, likewise, is what is so distinctive about needs-cum-primary goods.

As a first approximation, the argument for the priority of needs as primary goods would go like this. Granted, needs are no more than necessary instruments. Granted, the value of satisfying them is wholly derivative from the value of the ends which they are instrumental in producing. All this said, however, it may nonetheless be true that the value of satisfying any particular need always exceeds the value of satisfying any particular want because of all the other wants which satisfying that need also helps us to satisfy.

That argument as stated will not quite do. It confuses being a necessary instrument to any ends with being a necessary instrument to all ends. Some (perhaps most) resources, even if they are primary goods, will diminish with use. Although the resource may well be a necessary instrument for attaining a wide variety of ends, once it is committed to the pursuit of any one of them it becomes unavailable for pursuit of any of the others. Money is a prime example. You need it for any of various purposes: to buy a house, or a car, or a yacht, or a color television. But the dollar spent on buying a house ceases to be available to you for buying a car. In such cases, it is simply incorrect to say that the value of the dollar to you is a function of its value in buying you a house *and* a car and so on. Instead, it is a function of the dollar's value to you in buying you a house *or* a car or so on.

The argument for the priority of needs over wants would fail were the reference to resources that are nonreusable in this sense. If a resource can be used to promote any of a variety of ends, but only one of them, then its value is wholly derivative from the value of that one end. It may be valuable to have more options rather than less where we are (temporarily) uncertain as to the relative value of the various ends which we may be asked to choose between in our use of the resource.[7] But that sort of uncertainty-based option value aside, the fact that the needed resource could have been used for any of a variety of other purposes does nothing to enhance its value, since at the end of the day it can only be used to pursue one of them.

Not all resources are like that, however. Perhaps the paradigm case of a reusable resource is health. It is a necessary instrument for the accomplishment of a great variety of goals. But unlike money it does not (ordi-

---

[7] I say 'temporarily' because, if the uncertainty is not resolved or at least diminished by the time we are ultimately forced to choose which way to exercise the option, then we will have been no better off with the option than without it. The value of options is thus derivative from the value of postponement: their value is just the value of buying time.

narily, anyway) diminish with use. Exceptional goals like scaling Everest aside, health functions rather like a chemical catalyst that enters into a reaction but then emerges at the end unchanged, available for reuse in exactly the same form and quantity as before.

Where need-statements refer to reusable resources of this sort, a certain measure of priority of needs over wants is justified. Of course, the value of satisfying needs is still purely instrumental and entirely derivative from the value of the various wants which those instruments help us satisfy. So it is inconceivable that needs, even of this sort, should take priority over the set of all wants taken as a whole. But needs for reusable resources might take priority over any *particular* want, because they are instrumental in (and hence derive value from their role in) satisfying various other wants as well as that one.[8]

This argument gives rise to a Principle of Precedence, but one which is doubly qualified. Firstly, priority is granted only if (and only insofar as) the needed resource is both *multipurpose* and *reusable*. If a resource is required for a single purpose, or exhausted with a single use, there is no reason on this argument to suppose that satisfying the need for that resource is any more important than satisfying the desire for that purpose to be accomplished. Secondly, this Principle of Precedence is qualified in the extent of priority it accords such needs over desires. Whereas any particular such need might enjoy priority over any particular desire, no such need (nor such needs taken as a whole) may enjoy priority over all desires taken as a whole.

Thus, even this best possible argument for the priority of needs over desires is qualified in important respects. Most importantly, it extends only to certain classes of need-claims and accords them priority, once again, on the basis of features (reusability; serving multiple purposes) that are only contingently and imperfectly connected to the notion of a 'need' per se.

7. All of the arguments considered so far argue for the priority of needs over mere desires on the grounds that satisfying the former is, in some

---

[8] This also explains why Frankfurt's 'nonvolitional' needs enjoy priority over 'volitional' ones. The problem is not, as Frankfurt (p. 7) supposes, that the latter "have too little necessity in them." The problem is instead that they do not have enough satisfaction in them. Volitional needs may be necessary instruments, all right; but they are instruments to the satisfaction of only one particular desire. Hence they can claim no priority over the desire from which their own value is derived. Nonvolitional needs, being necessary instruments to the satisfaction of many different desires, can claim priority over any one of them by appealing to value they derive from their role in satisfying all the others.

sense or another, *more valuable* than satisfying the latter. Another way of arguing for the Principle of Precedence takes precisely the opposite tack. Suppose we have no acceptable theory of value, or anyway none we would feel justified in imposing on others through social choices. Under those circumstances, need-satisfaction would once again prove to be preferable to want-satisfaction. This is not because it is seen to be more valuable. Without a theory of value, we can hardly claim that. It is instead because need-satisfaction is *more noncommittal*. In order to justify satisfying any particular desire, we require a theory of value guaranteeing that it is valuable to satisfy that desire. Since needs are indispensable instruments to a wide variety of ends, we do not have to be able to show that any one of them is particularly valuable in order to suppose that satisfying the need is nonetheless valuable.

That argument is probably truer to the phenomenology of the situation. A large part of the appeal of notions of needs in liberal democracies surely lies in the fact that, both politically and morally, they constitute a kind of least common denominator which proves enormously useful in building coalitions among diverse interests. Needs, like ambiguous phraseology, allow us to fudge all sorts of problems.

Like all fudges, however, this does not solve the problem but merely shifts it. While pretending to justify need-satisfaction without reference to any theory of value, this solution in fact inevitably appeals to just such a theory in a slightly different way. Arguments for need-satisfaction successfully avoid having to claim that any particular end is desirable. Since needs serve a wide variety of ends, we do not have to be able to show that any particular one of those ends is valuable in order to suppose that satisfying the need might be valuable. But we do have to have good reasons for believing that at least *some* of those ends are valuable. If needed resource R is instrumental to any and all of a hundred ends, but all of those ends are worthless, then the instrumental value of R itself is inevitably nil.

8. A sharp demarcation between needs and mere desires is, politically, a double-edged sword. Some hope it will serve egalitarian purposes: needs take precedence over mere desires, provided only we can distinguish the two sharply enough; so the demarcation exercise, if successful, will guarantee that the worst-off get first claim on social resources. But, of course, the demarcation exercise serves inegalitarian impulses as well: by circumscribing people's needs tightly enough, we can honor their claims easily and have lots left over to allocate to others on the basis of mere desire. The Reagan 'safety net', like the Elizabethan Poor Law, is clearly a strategy for reducing allocation to the poor by focusing exclusively on their needs-based claims.

624 ROBERT E. GOODIN

If what we want are more egalitarian outcomes, we may be well advised to shift all the argument over into terms of 'mere desire'. Then we will obviously have to offer some further argument as to why we should satisfy desires equally, and indeed what it might mean to do so. None of that is easy or straightforward. But at least that approach avoids artificial thresholds. The price of a priority rule (favoring needs, or anyone or anything else for that matter) is that the rule is plausible only so long as the claims are modest; yet once the claims have been satisfied those prior considerations can legitimately be dropped out of our subsequent reckoning altogether. An egalitarian argument couched purely in terms of mere desires has the strength of being able to keep the claims of the disadvantaged ever-present in a way that needs-based arguments cannot.

[3]

A theory of human needs*

LEN DOYAL and IAN GOUGH

Abstract

This paper challenges the view that the concept of human needs is essentially subjective by exploring the individual and social prerequisites for any successful human action. Also, it shows the goal of progress in meeting human need to be both rational and practicable, provided that further communicational, constitutional and ecological prerequisites are met. At the heart of the analysis is the belief that without a viable conception of human need, socialist theory and practice – especially concerning questions about social welfare – loose their moral and political coherence.

1. INTRODUCTION: THE PROBLEM

It is time either to defend and refine the concept of human needs or to banish it entirely from our vocabulary. Our goals in this paper are, first, to argue for the absolute centrality of the notion of human needs to any meaningful discussion of human welfare and human suffering, and, second, to reformulate the concept in a rigorous way to facilitate its application to a wide range of contemporary problems.

We maintain that a concept of human needs is an essential component in formulating a feasible socialist vision of what the future could be like. We believe that such a vision is a crucial counter-weight to the revived individualism of the New Right. Though much of what follows is of a philosophical character, we think that it has direct political relevance in showing where socialists should be heading. However, the question of concrete political *strategy* – how to get from here to there – is not explicitly dealt with in this paper.

Put more precisely, the idea of human needs, and the related distinction between *needs* and *wants*, is central to (at least) two important areas of contemporary debate: that concerning social policy and the future of the welfare state and that concerning the possibility of alternative forms of human society. Yet in both contexts there exists a curious ambivalence about the notion of needs. When confronted head-on, many commentators will express doubt about the philosophical validity of *any* concept of human needs. But,

---

* We would like to express our gratitude to Lesley Doyal without whose labour this paper would not be in its present form. We also thank: David Barker, Bernard Burgoyne, Ruth Elkan, Jeff Evans, Norman Geras, Margaret Jones, John Lea, Philippe van Parijs, Jonathan Rée, Peter Taylor-Gooby, Peter Townsend and especially Grenville Wall.

A THEORY OF HUMAN NEEDS

in their everyday lives, and implicitly in much of their writing, they continue to use something very much like it! Theoretically denied an existence, human needs in practice, it seems, just will not go away. Before elaborating on our theory, it will help if we briefly consider this contemporary ambivalence.

In debates on *social policy*, the 'welfare state' is often defined by writers of a Fabian or reformist persuasion as the collective recognition by society of certain human needs, and the organisation of mechanisms to meet those needs. Yet, whenever the meaning of the term 'need' is *theoretically* probed, it is almost always rejected as 'socially-relative' or 'subjective' by writers across the political spectrum:

> 'The word "need" ought to be banished from discussion of public policy.'[1]
> (A. Culyer, et al)
> 'The idea of "need" is subjective, transient, fleeting and based on value judgements.'[2]
> (P. Armstrong)
> 'As in all other contexts of use, to speak of "a need" or being "in need" presupposes a standard or norm, and different norms will create different "needs".'[3]
> (R. Fitzgerald)

Phenomenological research suggests that 'needs' are constructed by the providers of state services according to the dictates of welfare ideologies, specific management practices and the constraints within which particular agencies operate.[4] Economists claim that only the concepts of preferences and demand have sufficient 'objectivity' to be used as the criteria for allocating goods and services under conditions of scarcity.[5] Many Marxists argue that needs are merely social constructions internal to any particular society.[6]

Nor is it just the epistemological status of the concept that is under attack; so are its political implications. In particular, there is widespread criticism of the use of need as a criterion for defining welfare priorities and for justifying the redistribution of resources. Critics on the right argue that it leads at best to state paternalism, and at worst to political despotism.[7] Critics on the left argue that the discourse of needs provides a convenient rationale for the rationing of scarce welfare resources in capitalist society, and that it legitimates apparently benevolent policies which actually serve quite different ends.[8]

Yet, this barrage of criticism and disapproval seems to have little relevance for those involved in the *concrete* problems of articulating and defending particular social policies, where 'need' remains a part of everyday discourse. Whether a social worker is asked to explain the allocation of a home-help to a particular elderly person, or a social planner is asked to justify the payment of higher welfare benefits to larger families, some notion of 'need' will lie at the heart of their answer. This is not to say that practitioners and policy-minded writers are unaware of the potential ambiguities of the concept. Bradshaw, for example, has distinguished between (a) 'normative' need defined by 'experts' and practitioners of various kinds; (b) 'felt' need self-defined by individuals when asked; (c) 'expressed' need, or felt need translated into a demand for a particular service; and (d) 'comparative' need, or deficiencies in the delivery of a service to a particular population group when compared with another group with the same characteristics.[9] But however useful such a taxonomy of needs may be, it cannot reconcile the conflicts

CRITICAL SOCIAL POLICY

between these definitions, nor do any of them attain a rigorous form of objectivity.[10]

A researcher like Townsend, who has consistently attempted to reconcile notions of 'objective' and 'socially relative' need, reveals the resulting ambivalence. He distinguishes objective need from conventionally-acknowledged needs (usually those defined by government agencies) and individual subjective needs.[11] His life's work has been devoted to operationalising the first, objective standard of need, for instance in his major study of poverty in Britain.[12] But in the process, he has been accused of smuggling in cultural standards and idiosyncrasies of taste which undermine the very objectivity to which he aspires.[13] There can be no doubt that at times, he is ambiguous. Thus at one point he states: 'The concepts of absolute and relative needs are, as conventionally interpreted, incompatible, and indeed the concept of "absolute" need deserves to be abandoned.'[14] While elsewhere he argues that objective needs *can* be distinguished from conventionally acknowledged needs according to their properties of 'detachment, quantifiable measurement, reproducibility, systematic comparison and validation.'[15]

The ambiguity is not just Townsend's. Clearly scientific standards of the preceding kind are important if 'need' stands any chance of being rigorously formulated. Yet some have argued that such standards can themselves represent vested interests and that there is another danger of tipping over into an 'expert' definition of need influenced by the values, knowledge and ideology of particular *professions*. This tendency for researchers to impose their own 'top-down' beliefs about human needs has been challenged in recent years by social movements representing numerous groups and communities, such as the homeless, single parents, the disabled, tenants, and battered women. They are concerned with articulating their own view of their specific needs, often by means of a collective dialogue. It is in this context that they often condemn existing welfare provision and try to justify *their* preferred alternatives. One is left then with a paradox: the concept of human needs is continually if confusingly used at the level of social welfare practice by the most varied groups, but is either dismissed or elided at the level of theory.

The situation is remarkably similar in debates about alternative forms of society. Whether one considers the libertarian vision of Illich, the 'green' socialism of Bahro, the asceticism of Gandhi or the communism of Marx and Engels, somewhere there will be a reference to a society that meets human needs better than that of the present day. It is almost self-evident that, without some vision of humankind bettering itself through discovering more and more about its basic needs and about how to satisfy them most effectively, there would be little point to any form of socialist or liberational struggle. Certainly, as regards Marxism itself, there would be little left other than perhaps a purely *descriptive* analysis of different modes of production and/or an account of the dysfunctional relationships between the institutions of capitalism.

Yet, there is a marked reluctance to face up to this fact. Soper, for example, argues that even in Marx's writings, potentially a rich source of ideas on human needs, there exists a fundamental dichotomy.[16] On the one hand, there is a pluralist view which explicitly abandons any notion of a fixed human nature and stresses the open-ended character of needs and the extent to which their conscious perception is always socially mediated. Alongside this there exists his humanist perspective which claims that there is a variety of needs that bridge social formations and are better served by some societies than others. Though Geras has demonstrated that Soper is wrong in claiming the existence of this duality in Marx's own thought, it certainly exists within contemporary Marxism.[17] Thus, those who wish to retain the idea of an essential human nature and associated human needs usually refer to the Frankfurt school and, in particular, to Marcuse's distinction between true and false needs.[18] However, the majority of Marxists now favour the pluralist, open-ended view – and for good political reasons. Just as some conservatives and liberals detect a potentially despotic tendency in discourse about human need, many on the left glimpse the totalitarian spectre of Stalinism. But the dilemma remains. In practice, if not in theory, Marxists seemingly must use some idea of human need in order to demonstrate the oppression, inequality and injustice of capitalist society. Unless there is some yardstick – some common denominator which all people share – which can be employed to assess the success of particular social practices, then any notion of social progress is itself thrown into question.

A failure to come to terms with this fact has recently led to attacks on Marxism by some of those need-orientated political groups and social movements to which we have already referred. By far the most important of these is the feminist movement, which argues that Marxism has not recognised women as a social group in their own right. Hence, it is argued, most Marxists have ignored women's specific needs or attempted to incorporate them within traditional Marxist categories.

Similar criticisms could be made by other groups such as blacks, the elderly, single parent families, or the homeless. This recognition has helped to generate the political 'fragments' of recent years which focus on the group-specific needs of their members traditionally blurred over by a purely class analysis.[19] The same is true of the green movement and the peace movement, which focus on capitalism's development of the forces of *destruction* through the uninhibited evolution of that very technology which was once seen by socialists as the key to the future progress and liberation of humanity. In short, one of the things unifying these new social movements is their rejection of the 'productivist' side of Marx's thought and an interest in his humanist perspective where the notion of human need does play a central role.[20] They are also at one in questioning definitions of need imposed by the state and in counterposing their own collectively derived definitions. Thus, political developments concerned both with the welfare state and with the broader goals of a future society *implicitly* utilise a concept of universal human needs. In so doing, they have made a coherent, rigorous – and above all explicit – theory of need all the more urgent.

2. A SUMMARY OF OUR ARGUMENT

We begin in Section Three by illustrating how arguments about the distinction between needs and wants usually collapse into the subjectivism which we wish to attack. In Section Four we argue that this can be overcome by defining

CRITICAL SOCIAL POLICY

basic individual needs as those goals which must be achieved if any individual is to achieve any other goal – however idiosyncratic or culturally specific those other goals are. We suggest that these basic individual needs fall into two pairs: survival/health and autonomy/learning. The rest of the paper develops this conception of basic needs in three stages. Since humans are social animals we specify in Section Five a set of four social pre-conditions or basic *societal* needs without which individuals cannot satisfy their basic individual needs. These are production, reproduction, culture/communication and political authority. By this stage we will have outlined the abstract pre-conditions for individual and social life to be minimally viable. It then becomes necessary to take the crucial step of dynamising this system so that it engages with contemporary debates about social policy and human welfare.

In Section Six we do this by linking the notion of historical progress with the *optimisation* of basic individual needs, and by arguing that it is possible rationally to assess strategies for such optimisation, irrespective of culture or historical location. In other words, we specify a need for human *liberation* – the goal of maximising individual or collective *choice* in meeting basic needs through an awareness of the potential of contemporary theoretical and practical understanding. It will be argued that this potential can be communicated in ways which are, in principle, universalisable, so that relativistic arguments which erect conceptual barriers between cultures or classes are both arbitrary and politically dangerous. Lastly in Section Seven we return to the social pre-conditions of individual activity and articulate *communicational* and *constitutional* needs which are the necessary educational and democratic conditions for basic individual needs to be optimised. We also briefly introduce ecological needs which take into account the global constraints within which all attempts to optimise individual needs must necessarily operate.

Our general theory and the stages in our argument can be summarised in the following diagram.

	Abstract Universal Needs		**The Optimisation of Universal Needs through History**
Individual Needs	1. Survival/health Autonomy/learning	⟶	3. Human liberation
Societal Needs	2. Production Reproduction Culture/Communication Political authority	⟶	4. Communicational, constitutional and ecological pre-requisites for human liberation

It will be noted that our theory embraces both individual and societal needs and argues that the two are dependent on each other for overall success. Thus, we reject individualist conceptions of human need which abstract people from their social and historical location and impose upon them a static conception of 'human essence'. At the same time we attack functionalist accounts which reify arbitrary moments of history and result in relativistic conceptions of need. Unlike Maslow's well-known hierarchy of individual

A THEORY OF HUMAN NEEDS

needs, in which the most basic needs must be satisfied before higher needs can be met, we therefore argue that human needs are systematic or interwoven like a web.[21] Crucially, however, they are systematic in a dynamic way. Our postulated need to optimise – to open up choices about the most fundamental aspects of human life through debate – ensures that the system we endorse would remain open in character.

Our aim in this paper is to outline the appropriate grammar of discussion for debate about needs to take place. At this stage our theory cannot determine the precise nature of *specific* needs; it cannot for instance spell out what policies would best meet the needs of the elderly in Britain today. In future work, we shall operationalise our theory so that it can gain a purchase on the sorts of debates which are mentioned in the introduction. We believe that it provides a powerful mechanism for defining the specific needs of individuals and groups, for evaluating their level of need-satisfaction, and for devising and assessing appropriate strategies for improving these levels. But for the moment our goal in this paper is to enable debates about needs to be rigorously formulated and to be distinguished from debates concerning wants or specific interests.[22] The paper is long and parts of it are not easy, but we felt it essential to return to fundamental philosophy before we could really make sense of debates about more concrete needs in the here and now.

3. NEEDS, WANTS AND RELATIVISM

There can be no doubt that our common-sense understanding of what sorts of things needs are, is often confused and ambiguous. This is due in part to the fact that the word 'need' is employed in such diverse ways. Probably the most common uses fall into two categories which are sometimes kept separate and sometimes conflated. First, 'need' is used to refer to a particular category of *goals* which in common parlance are believed to apply to *all* people. These are often referred to as human needs, or basic needs. Examples would be 'this person needs more protein' or 'this child needs more physical contact'. Such needs are commonly contrasted with 'wants' which are goals or desires derived from an individual's preferences or her/his social and cultural environment. The contrast between need as goal and want as goal is often recognised in everyday discourse as in, for example, 'I want a cigarette but I really need to stop smoking'. Secondly, 'need' can refer to *strategies* which are believed to provide successful routes for the achievement of *any* goal – whether these goals are regarded as needs or wants in the first sense. Examples of this usage would be 'This person needs to see a doctor' or 'I need a new hi-fi' or even 'This car needs a new brake system' and 'Britain needs to spend more on defence'. Let us consider these different meanings in more detail.

We have observed that *aims* or *goals* are classified as needs if they are believed to be applicable to all persons or to all people in specific groups. This is because it is thought that under specified circumstances, if a human remains without the relevant satisfier(s) then damage of some sort will be done – in much the same sense that a biologist or botanist would argue that if the physical needs of an animal or plant went unmet they too would be damaged.[23] Put more positively, when people ordinarily speak of needs, they

11

CRITICAL SOCIAL POLICY

usually have some idea of the sorts of things that are required for a person basically to 'get by' as a person. Such ideas will in turn be based upon some, usually ill-defined, conception of *human nature*: of those physiological or emotional gaps which, again, it is 'unnatural' or 'abnormal' not to try to fill.[24] For example, it is often argued that everyone needs a given standard of health and that it would be unthinkable to try for less in any 'progressive' social policy. Hence, everyone needs specific amounts of food, shelter and clothing because those are the intermediate goals which are necessary to achieve the general one. So, implicit in ordinary discourse and explicit in many writings on the subject, is the view that if a set of general or intermediate goals count as needs, it is because they are *universalisable*. It will be in the interest of all humans in the same circumstances to try to achieve them.

Conversely, when goals are described as 'wants', it is precisely because they are *not* regarded as universalisable in the way we have just described. That is to say, they are not linked directly to the achievement or maintenance of some aspect of the human condition which is accepted as normal and necessary for everyone. Of course, the human capacity to conceptualise goals in unlimited ways means that the range of what are seen as 'wants' far exceeds that of 'needs'. Wants in this sense fall into two categories: those which are satisfiers of accepted needs and those which are not. For example, I may want Mac-Donald's hamburgers because I am hungry and need food. Yet my choice of MacDonald's would not itself be classified as a need since it is idiosyncratic to a particular taste or culture. Since all food falls into this category, it is necessary to distinguish between nutrients and the culturally specific ways in which they are combined. Similar points can also be made about items such as clothing, or shelter.[25]

Unlike needs, wants are always thought of as *perceived* goals which are justified by reasons which have little to do with more general beliefs about the human condition. So it will be accepted that someone can quite legitimately want say, to, watch a certain film while recognising that they will be hard pushed to justify their need for it even if they try. However, the fact that they might try indicates that people can be mistaken about what they need – that perceived needs are not necessarily real needs. Here again, to the extent that people bother to make such a distinction (and most do in one way or another!) decisions about which are which will depend on what is deemed necessary to maintain the individual in an 'acceptable' state. Thus, to use a hackneyed example, the diabetic may want sugar so badly that their perception is one of need. They may well feel that they cannot 'go on' without it. But what they *need* is insulin – even if they have never heard of it and do not have the capacity to conceptualise it as a choice. Similarly, the taste for MacDonalds may well subside once it is learned how much fat they contain and that too much fat, like cigarettes, can damage your health.[26]

We have seen, however, that 'needs' can also be used to refer to *strategies* for attaining goals which in themselves might be regarded as either needs or wants in the senses already described. So when it is argued that a way of attaining X – whether X is viewed as a want or a need – is doing Y, then Y is referred to as a need. For example, someone might say that to obtain a goal commonly accepted as a need (eg for physical warmth) it is necessary to do

12

certain sorts of things (eg dress appropriately for the weather). Equally, how-ever, someone might refer to a strategy as a need if it is directed towards an obvious want (eg to buy a video-machine to watch certain films on tele-vision). In these cases, the only thing that determines whether or not the strat-egy is classified as a need is its potential empirical success in achieving the goal in question. Of course, what in some circumstances may be referred to as goals will in others be described as strategies, and this can be another source of confusion and ambiguity in discourse about needs. Food, shelter or cloth-ing for example, can clearly be described in either way and this is because des-criptions of needs and wants are hierarchical in character. Beginning from some overall goal viewed as desirable or 'natural', the *means* by which it is sought can be thought of as an end in its own right if its strategic relation to the overall goal remains in the background. The same can be said of strategies for the attainment of this *intermediate* goal and so on. So just as clothing may be described as either a goal or a strategy, the same can be said, say, of specific types of clothes and of the money necessary to buy them.[27]

Of course, the preceding characterisation of the ways in which needs are spoken of and written about, raises as many questions as it answers. While the problem of empirically assessing strategies for the achievement of specific aims cannot be under-estimated, the sorts of debates which we are addressing here concern needs viewed as *goals*. In this respect, all that we have shown so far is that there is a commonly employed distinction between needs and wants and that it is rooted in the belief that there are some goals which are naturally linked to the human condition which it will always be appropriate to try to satisfy, whilst there are other goals about which the same cannot be said. Thus, the coherence of the distinction between needs and wants – and of the belief that it can be made in any sort of 'objective' way – is totally predicated on some agreement about the human condition and about those goals which it is necessary to attain if people are to reach or to maintain some generally acceptable standard.

But what if there is no such agreement? First of all. there is much dispute about whether or not some needs (eg those related to sexuality) 'naturally' exist or not. Second, even if it is accepted – as presumably it must be – that there are certain needs (eg food, water) which must be met for humans to sur-vive, it can still be argued that there are so many ways of meeting them that in practice the distinction between needs and wants tells us more about those who make it than it does about humans generally. According to this argu-ment the distinction between needs and wants is essentially *normative* and if agreement about values does not exist, there seems to be no further grounds for arbitration.[28] For example, if different groups set nutritional standards at different levels, then there seems to be no 'higher' or 'universal' standard to which appeal can be made. Indeed, it has been argued that this is why so many debates about social policy go in circles.[29] In short, what began as a relatively clear distinction in ordinary discourse – that between needs and wants – becomes extremely muddled when its basis is challenged. For if there is no rational way of resolving disputes about what is and is not generalisable about the human condition or about specific groups of humans, then what are needs for some can be said to be merely wants for others – and vice versa.

13

CRITICAL SOCIAL POLICY

How then can *rational* decisions about production, consumption or resource allocation be made under socialism – or any other system?

4. PERSONS: SURVIVAL/HEALTH, AUTONOMY/LEARNING

There can be no question that on the face of it, relativists who believe in the essential subjectivity of human need have a case. People do have strong feelings about what they need and these feelings do vary enormously between cultures and over time. Indeed, as Runciman has shown, groups which are viewed by others as deprived may not agree and may even resent the suggestion that they are.[30] Yet, there is also evidence that a consensus exists in Britain at present about the range of necessities which form a social poverty line below which no one should be allowed to fall.[31] Such conflicting evidence suggests that perception as such is not a reliable guide for the determination of those basic needs which, as we have argued, are either explicitly or implicitly referred to in much of the contemporary literature on social welfare. It also suggests that the reliability of perception should itself be somehow evaluated, and that by definition this cannot be done with reference to any given consensus about the character and limitation of human need. Again, if *any* distinction is coherently to be drawn between wants and needs, a non-subjective demarcation criterion must be found. Both Galtung and Plant et al – among others – have recently suggested an alternative approach which we hope to elaborate and improve.[32]

They argue that analyses of need are integrally related to ideas about what is necessary for persons to be capable of *any* successful action – irrespective of the aim of the action or the perceptions or culture of the actor. Such necessary conditions thus delineate basic individual needs. We argue that they fall into two categories: *conceptual* conditions which stipulate what sorts of things basic needs are in principle and *empirical* conditions which do the same in practice. They are, as it were, opposite sides of the same ontological coin: *personhood*. The former concerns what characteristics a being must possess if it can intelligibly be said to be a person rather than, say, an animal or plant. For example, being a recognisably successful actor in this sense minimally entails possessing the attribute of *life* and of *distinguishability* in one's action from others who might perform the same act. In this respect, 'survival' and 'personal identity' are attributes which all persons need – in a purely formal sense – in order to be classified as persons at all.

Of course, however successful we might be in elaborating such formal attributes, our analysis will cut little ice unless it also has some purchase on the sorts of things which people *empirically* require to be successful actors. To know this will be to understand basic individual needs as the practical prerequisites for achieving those characteristics of personhood laid down by conceptual analysis. For example, in order to survive, all persons (who are *homo sapiens*) have several physical requirements which must obviously be met. In what follows, we shall see that similar considerations apply to the development and maintenance of personal identity. While much of our analysis will be theoretical – how best to conceptualise human needs – we shall not lose sight of what this entails in practical terms. Again, in reality, concepts

14

A THEORY OF HUMAN NEEDS

and practice always go hand in hand and can only be separated for analytical purposes. Suffice it to say that even moderate success in elaborating universalisable needs from either perspective will deal a severe blow to any relativistic interpretation of need.[33]

Kant was the first writer systematically to develop the type of 'transcendental' analysis which emphasises the fact that certain conditions have to be met in order for distinctively human actions to be a possibility. Although he was not concerned with elaborating a theory of human need, he did articulate many concepts and arguments relevant to such theorisation. He reasoned that if we agree that people can be held responsible for their actions, their 'egos' must be assumed to possess autonomy – to be free and to be capable of rational deliberation.[34] In this respect, Kant continued the tradition of dualism in Western thought begun by Descartes, and also foreshadowed the distinction in modern analytical writing between 'action' and 'behaviour'. Neo-Kantians like Weber later argued along similar lines that the behaviour of someone's body had to be distinguished from the action that 'accompanied it'. Thus, the body of someone running down the road may be moving in ways explicable with reference to causes – as construed by a physiologist or biochemist. But however much observational evidence is gathered, we will be no closer to identifying and explaining what the runner is doing. Running for a bus, escaping from a tormentor or jogging are only three of many possible interpretations. Identifying the specific action in question will require knowledge of the *reason* for it – the aims and beliefs which prompted the decision to act in one way rather than another.[35]

The implications of this conception of action and its understanding for the identification of basic human needs are as follows. While it *may* be true that all human goals are specific to particular cultures, in order to achieve these goals people have to *act*. Furthermore, it follows that there are certain preconditions for such actions to be undertaken – people must have the mental ability to deliberate and to choose, and the physical capacity to follow through on their decisions. To put this another way, in order to act successfully, people again need physically to survive and need enough sense of their own identity or autonomy to initiate actions on the basis of their deliberations. Survival and autonomy are therefore basic needs: they are both conceptual and empirical preconditions for the achievement of *other* goals. This is so irrespective of the degree of physical or mental freedom individuals may perceive themselves as possessing.[36] People may live in an authoritarian society based on force, or they may for other reasons conceive themselves as having little influence over their personal destiny (eg because of their religious beliefs). But in both instances, their freedom of *agency* will be unimpaired to the extent that their constrained actions are still believed (by them and by others) to be done *by* them instead of *to* them.[37] Without the imputation of such responsibility, it would make no sense to encourage victims of physical or ideological oppression to liberate themselves. Therefore, viewed as the basic needs of all agents – those attributes without which any action is impossible – survival and autonomy seem to provide a sort of abstract bridge between radically different cultures.

The reader might respond at this stage with, 'Yes, but so what?'. For to call

15

CRITICAL SOCIAL POLICY

survival a human need seems tautologous – as indeed it is if this is where we stop. Physical survival on its own cannot do justice to Kant's theorisation of personhood. This is easily demonstrated by the victim of a motor accident who survives on a life support system but cannot act independently. Indeed, whether or not the victim is believed to be capable of any action in the future – a question answered with reference to the probability of the mental preconditions for action being regained – will eventually determine her/his fate. The same applies to incurable mental damage – irrespective of cause. Those who have been in long term catatonic states will at some point be presumed to be almost as incapable of any ordinary human action as the person/body on the life support sytem. Were it possible to decide with absolute certainty that they would not recover, then similar ethical questions concerning the artificiality of their survival might be raised. Indeed, it might well be argued that the appalling conditions of many chronic wards in mental hospitals is testimony to the fact that 'moral' questions of this kind have not been taken seriously enough.

So, it is *health* rather than survival – both physical and mental health – which is the most basic human need and the one which it will be in the interest of individuals to satisfy before any others.[38] As far as *physical* health is concerned, this entails the recognition that there is a minimal empirical point beyond which the capacity for successful actions is so reduced that the actor will be regarded by others as abnormal – however the abnormality may be culturally regarded. This same notion of a base is also applicable to *mental* ill-health, although here the deciding factor is the incapacity to perform some tasks culturally regarded as normal without the excuse of a physical handicap, old age or poor physical health. We now know that physical health will always require a minimum level of nutrition and liquid, varying amounts of sleep, exercise, warmth and so on. Mental health will similarly require an empirical minimum of human contact, emotional support, opportunity for emotional expression and privacy.[39] Since the capacity for successful actions will be proportional to the satisfaction of health needs of both kinds, they can be ranked. Thus in all cultures, people will be regarded as *more or less* 'healthy' – whatever the culture under consideration and however 'health' is conceptualised. Of course, as already indicated, the subjectivist might respond by claiming that the existence of minimal needs like the above is obvious and solves no interesting problems about why they are conceptualised in such diverse ways.[40] Yet, even at this early stage of the argument, such admissions implicitly endorse the existence of basic needs, their difference from wants and the dangers likely to arise if they are not met.

The second set of basic needs which must be met for actions to be successful relates to individual identity or autonomy – the private and public sense of 'self'. In order for actions to be identified as such, they must be *initiated* by individual persons. Returning to our discussion of Kant, 'initiate' is a crucial word here, because a person who initiates an action is presumed to do so in a fundamentally different way than a machine (eg a robot) might appear to do. The machine is understood with reference to its mechanism and nomological regularities. Yet, people consist of more than the relationships between their bodily components. They acquire their autonomy as individuals with reference

A THEORY OF HUMAN NEEDS

to their capacity to formulate aims and beliefs and to put them into practice.[41] Again, this must be the case both in principle and in fact. Hence, all things being equal, we hold individuals practically and morally responsible for their actions but we do not do the same for machines.

Of course, in different cultures beliefs will vary about how much control individuals have over their destiny, as will associated codes of morality.[42] Yet, in all known cultures, responsibility will and must be allocated on a day to day basis in order for actors to be *individuated* from each other. This, among other reasons, is why individuals in all societies are given personal *names*. Were such individuation not possible, we would be unable to link actions with their initiators while actors would equally be unable to link themselves with the actions they perform. Such a situation – the absence of autonomy – would spell disaster in any society. Among other things it would mean that all individual learning would cease. What would be the point? Similarly, actors could never develop the confidence to act or to recognise their successes in so doing. Thus our second basic need for autonomy translates into the basic need for *creative consciousness* – the ability in theory to formulate both goals and strategies for achieving them.

For this need to be met in practice, *teachers* will be required who already possess their own autonomous identities and the physical and mental skills which go with them. People do not teach themselves to act – they have to *learn*, and this is a further individual need which goes hand in hand with autonomy. To be sure which skills are learned will vary from culture to culture, but they are not totally variable. Again, there is a universal empirical base line defining what individuals must do to meet their needs for health and autonomy. For example, children have to learn to interact socially in minimally acceptable ways, irrespective of the specific cultural rules they follow in the process. Persistently lying to, or punching, one's fellows will never be a recipe for successful social interaction. Similarly, in all cultures, language skills are necessary as the medium through which actors learn conceptually to order their world and to deliberate about what to do in it.[43] In this sense, consciousness is essentially social – the by-product of educational interaction with others. To the extent that consciousness is partly linguistic, then it is obviously social. As Wittgenstein has shown, just as there can be no such thing as a purely private language, so there can be no such thing as a purely private person. To the extent that consciousness is directed towards particular motor skills, then as with language it must also be learned in a series of highly complex social interactions.[44] The problem with the Robinson Crusoe myth is that he already knew how to be so industrious (and racist!) because he had already been taught. It is not, as the song goes, that 'people who need people are the luckiest people in the world'. Everyone needs people to be anyone.

Yet again, from the perspective of capacity for successful activity, some forms of learned consciousness will be regarded as more appropriate than others. This will depend both on *what* is taught and on the purpose for which it is taught. Focusing for now on the former, to be, say, a good carpenter, cook or whatever, you need to learn certain specific skills. However, success will also depend on the actor's learned sense of self and self potential, which in turn depends on *how* (s)he is taught. For example, if you are taught that

CRITICAL SOCIAL POLICY

you are shiftless and incapable then your perception of the extent of your autonomy – your confidence – will be impaired. This applies not just to individuals but to groups.[45]

But how can this *social* process of education be reconciled with our emphasis on the formal need for *individual* autonomy? Does not the process of socialisation necessarily restrict the expression of such autonomy? To see that this is not the case, it is essential to recognise that actors are socialised into following *rules* – expressions of collectively held and enforced aims and beliefs. These will range from the obviously public (eg how to exchange one set of goods for another) to those which seem essentially private (eg bathing, toilet etiquette, etc). Such rules constitute the parameters of our sense of self and of others – our individual vision of what (formally) is and is not privately and publicly possible. Yet the autonomy necessary for successful action to occur is not compromised by the necessity to follow rules – quite the opposite! This is easily seen by differentiating between rules and individual interpretations of them. People are identified and identify themselves as playing chess with reference to the appropriate set of rules. But their autonomy as players is secure because there are so many different ways that they might individually select to play. Their perception of their quality as players – much less their ability to play at all – is dependent on those with whom they interact. So, successful *individual* action is always predicated on some form of present or past *social* interaction and therefore on the minimally healthy and autonomous existence of others. This will be the case in all cultures, whatever their particular social definition of the scope and limits of individuality.[46]

5. SOCIETAL NEEDS: PRODUCTION, REPRODUCTION, COMMUNICATION, AUTHORITY

Thus far in our consideration of individual needs, we have simply assumed that it was possible for health and autonomy through education to be achieved. However, since learning is a social process, it necessarily involves individuals interacting in social *groups*. This means that certain pre-requisites must be met for any such groups or for society as a whole to function with any degree of long term success. Individuals therefore have basic *societal needs* – those social preconditions for the achievement of the individual needs we have just described. These can be conceptually and empirically analysed in four categories.[47]

The first concerns material production. In any society activity must obviously be directed toward material production. In all cultures, it is necessary somehow to create the food, liquid, clothing and shelter required for a minimal level of health to be collectively achieved. Such activities constitute the material base of the culture. Of course, they will vary between cultures, especially when these are radically different. Nomadic, hunter-gatherer, agricultural and industrial societies all approach their respective material tasks in different ways. Yet they all share the common problems of trying to make nature do their bidding and all face obstacles about which, as we shall see, they can agree despite cultural differences.[48] Since Marx and Durkheim it has become a commonplace that material production is essentially social.

18

Humans are not genetically endowed with the physiology or mentality to enable them to survive on their own – much less in any sense to 'prosper'. Group interaction in the form of a division of labour is thus required, with the character and complexity of component rules differing with specific cultures and types of production. The material surplus that such interaction makes possible is also necessary for *traditions* of problem solving to develop, thus enabling productive skills to be socially remembered and handed down and individuals to be taught to produce.

The sphere of material production, however, is broader than the process of people interacting with nature to produce goods. It encompasses, as Marx argued, the related processes of exchange, distribution and consumption – the whole set of activities from planting the seed to eating the meal.[49] Once there is any division of labour, exchange becomes a necessity and the question of distributing the produce must be solved. It is a truism that the mechanisms of effecting exchange and distribution vary widely between cultures but there can be no doubt that it is necessary for all societies to adopt *some* such mechanism. The mechanisms may of course result in labourers receiving less than is necessary to meet their basic individuals needs, but this does not invalidate the argument that there is a universal societal need to distribute goods generated in the process of production.

The second formal requirement for the survival of any culture is successful reproduction – the process 'which begins with ovulation and ends when the child is no longer dependent on others for necessities of survival'.[50] It thus includes two separate elements: biological reproduction and infant care and socialisation. It may seem strange to regard the former as intrinsically social, once the truism is accepted that immaculate conception is impossible. However, mating and childbirth always occur against the background of specific rules (eg those of kinship and confinement) and consistently successful childbirth requires a material environment adequate to basic pre- and post-natal health needs. Of course, the societal need for biological reproduction will often conflict with other individual needs – particularly those of women.[51] The extent to which this is so will be examined later. However, for now it is necessary only to recognise that everyone in a particular culture needs that level of biological reproduction necessary to sustain the social division of labour that materially provides for them. A further component of the division of labour will also be required for infant care and socialisation. These tasks will usually be carried out by the same people – often groups of women – although in ways which will vary between cultures. Historically, the mechanism for fulfilling both types of reproductive need has been some form of family structure, though with a wide variation of kinship patterns. To say this, is not, of course, to endorse any particular set of social relations.[52] It is simply to underline the societal need for certain types of technical and communicational practices – for example midwifery and the learning of basic principles of infant care.

The third formal requirement for the success of any social system concerns communication. Actors are not born with an understanding of theories and practices relevant to the modes of production and reproduction of their society. Nor will they necessarily be pre-disposed to accept the particular

CRITICAL SOCIAL POLICY

system of allocation and distribution which typifies it. As we have seen, such understanding and acceptance has to be learned through the use of language and formal and informal education. This will in turn be predicated on an already existing *culture* – a body of rules which partly defines the form of life of the society involved. Such rules enable social goals to be achieved because through their linguistic expression they constitute the medium by which aims and beliefs are individually and collectively acted upon. The resulting *communication* obviously takes many forms, but two are vital for our purposes here, since they are crucial to the achievement of socially-defined goals.[53]

The first concerns *technique*. Each culture will possess a collective memory of how its previous members learned to tackle their most important productive and reproductive tasks. Unless the society in question maintains this collective memory, it will suffer disastrous consequences which would impinge on all its individual members. Secondly, each society will require rules to *legitimate* acquisition, exchange and distribution in ways which conceptually link different types and amounts of labour with what people receive for their work. For individuals to be able to plan to meet their material needs, they must know and accept that they will be allocated goods and services in return for their labour according to certain rules. The absence of sustained conflict in a society suggests that aspects of its distributional system have been internalised irrespective of its (probably) hierarchical character and the 'ideological' nature of many of its rules. Consider, for example, the web of beliefs which convince people within capitalist societies that the market is a natural and fair mechanism for the organisation of production, consumption, exchange and distribution. You do not have to be a Marxist to see that without the acceptance of such principles, capitalism would have great difficulty surviving.[54]

Finally, it is clear that the mere existence of sets of rules – of a culture in our sense – will not guarantee their perpetuation or implementation. There must be some system of *political authority* – ultimately backed up by sanctions – which will ensure that they will be taught, learned and correctly followed. The exact character of such authority will vary enormously, depending on the size, complexity and equity of different societies. Yet, however centralised or dispersed the authority may be, it must be effective in its own terms if the society in question is to survive – much less in any sense to flourish.[55] One does not have to believe in Hobbes' 'war of all against all' to accept this. It is a consequence of the importance which we have already shown attaches to rules as the social cement which ensures the possibility of social and therefore of individual survival. Since individuals will not always perceive it to be in their immediate interests either to follow the rules or to teach others to do so, some system for ensuring that they do is essential.

Indeed, the further one moves from Durkheim's vision of traditional society towards the 'organic solidarity' of industrial nations, the more important this becomes – especially if part of its legitimation emphasises the privacy of the individual and the moral acceptability of the pursuit of self-interest. In this context, as Hegel so clearly recognised, some form of central authority is unavoidable – a 'state' which through its institutional structure ensures that the key rules of the culture are both taught and enforced.[56] The

A THEORY OF HUMAN NEEDS

material manifestation of political authority will always be some form of government, a system of justice and some social mechanism for law enforcement.[57] Again, it is important to stress that one does *not* have to approve of the legal 'super-structure' of any particular social system to recognise that if its most fundamental rules are consistently broken without retribution, then it and its members will either perish or be incorporated into another system where their basic individual needs stand a greater chance of being met.

In general then, these four societal needs – production, reproduction, cultural communication and political authority – constitute the structural properties which any minimally successful mode of social organisation must embody.[58] The degree to which individual needs are met will depend *in principle* on such success, which will in turn depend on individuals who are healthy, autonomous and educated enough to know what is expected of them, how to do it and what will happen if they do not. This interdependence between individual and societal needs should make it clear that we are not adopting the sort of abstract individualism which, for example, is so often attributed to utilitarian writers.[59] Yet, it should be equally clear that we do not accept forms of functionalism which presuppose that individual actors simply mirror the structural properties of their social environment.[60] *The only criterion for evaluating social systems which we are advocating thus far is: how far do they enable individual basic needs to be met?* This makes it clear that we are conceptualising basic individual needs in a way that is independent of any particular social environment. And just because a society is in principle capable of meeting such needs, does not of course entail that they *will* be met. Some of the most developed societies in the world fail to meet the most minimal individual needs of many of their members. To take an extreme case, South Africa does not meet even the minimum nutritional needs of a large part of its population.

6. OPTIMISING BASIC NEED SATISFACTION AND HUMAN LIBERATION

It should now be clear that there are certain pre-conditions which are necessary for successful human actions to be intelligible and to occur in any culture. Through equating these pre-conditions with individual and societal needs, we have apparently found a way round the problems of ethnocentricity with which we began. Yet it could still be argued that while our analysis has succeeded in stipulating such needs in conceptual and empirically minimal terms, it does little or nothing to show how they should be specified in concrete social situations. This will inevitably be the case for notions of human need which begin and end in a transcendental vein. For as we have seen, once we move beyond points about which even few relativists would disagree (eg the human need for oxygen), the cultural symbolism through which needs are expressed can vary so radically as to suggest little possibility of cross-cultural agreement or comparison.[61]

Interestingly, Hegel made a similar point in connection with Kant's transcendental analysis of moral judgement. He argued that Kant's conception of the ego was only given real meaning by the historical circumstances in which

21

CRITICAL SOCIAL POLICY

it found concrete expression. Thus conceptions like freedom, reason and autonomy when divorced from particular circumstances are mere abstractions.[62] For example, bravery in one culture may be perceived as stupidity in another. In this way, relativism once again raises its head, for if actual perceptions of basic individual and societal needs are predicated on the cultural and historical location of the perceiver, then the distinction between needs and wants remains blurred.

In order to get beyond this impasse we have to move away from an abstract and static notion of need, which is geared simply to the conditions under which successful action can occur. Instead we require a dynamic conception of how to *optimise* basic need satisfaction given the *best understanding* but *without* engaging in cultural imperialism or the dogmatic imposition of expertise. The importance for socialism of such a conception is clear. Only in this way can the basic goal of human liberation – optimising individual and societal need satisfaction for all – be coherently expressed. Without such a concept there would be little point in trying to change any society, and especially one which more or less met the *perceived* needs of its members. Thus, if demands for such changes are to be rationally defended, it must be on the basis of a set of evaluative criteria. That such criteria cannot simply be based on individual preference is equally clear.[63] Indeed, arguments which conflate needs with wants are both morally and philosophically problematic. Let us consider each in turn.

From a *moral* point of view, what could it mean, for instance, to claim that people in the Third World, suffering from a characteristic disease of under-development that could be cured or prevented by the application of Western medical technology (or facing agricultural problems that could also be solved with Western techniques) do not *need* to take advantage of such knowledge? In what *sense* could they not need to? The only justification we can see is the one which the relativist would opt for – people cannot 'need' what they do not want. Yet we have already shown this argument to be incorrect. Hence, the argument that people who are unhealthy (admittedly here against the background of 'Western' conceptions of prevention and cure) need to do something about it, mean that they need to learn how to do so and how to translate their understanding into practice. To restrict the quality or quantity of basic needs to fit in with a particular level of cultural perception is need-lessly and immorally to close-off the consciousness and practice of some groups from others. It is to deny as impossible that very expression of human consciousness on basic practical issues which human history has repeatedly shown to be possible. At each stage of what we would now consider to be pro-gress – however defined – people were constrained by the conceptual bound-aries of their culture. Had these boundaries stopped their learning one could not account for the possibility of this paper, the improved health patterns of most of its readers or the intellectual formulation of the specific issues which it is discussing.[64] It is this process of learning and the ability to translate it into practice that we shall define as human *liberation*. From now on we shall argue that such liberation (wherever it is possible) constitutes a fundamental human need.

But in saying this, it might seem that we are simply reiterating the basic

A THEORY OF HUMAN NEEDS

need for education – albeit on a cultural rather than individual level – which we have already discussed. The concrete question still remains as to *what* should be optimised in the pursuit of liberational needs. After all, any product of human labour (eg nuclear weapons) might be created in greater numbers with absurd consequences. As we have hinted in the introduction, conceptions of liberation as a generalisable goal have traditionally been interpreted either as unlimited material *production* or the expansion of individual *choice*. Both approaches have representatives in socialist thought and reflect an unresolved tension in Marx's writing. For our purposes, the first formulation is problematic because it is now clear that for a variety of social, economic and ecological reasons the dream of unrestrained production has for many turned into a nightmare of Taylorism, unemployment, pollution, corporate imperialism, the fear of nuclear destruction and the exhaustion of global resources.[65] This has in turn focused attention on the 'quality of life', again highlighting the importance of the distinction between wants and needs. Thus, the second approach to theorising liberational needs – optimising the satisfaction of basic individual needs in principle and in practice – seems more promising if it can be shown to be conceptually and strategically coherent.

Philosophically, the link between choice – the freedom *from* unnecessary impediments to the satisfaction of basic needs and the freedom *to* maximise self-discovery – and liberation has a long history. Indeed, it was an essential part of the Hegelian background both to Marxism and to various forms of liberal thought. However, the key difference between these two approaches has been their conception of the social and economic context within which such freedoms could best express themselves: individually through the market, or collectively within a more centrally planned society.[66] Arguably applicable in either case, Hegel's view seems to us still to be the most fruitful, when he maintains that the more we learn about what we are capable of doing, the more we learn about ourselves. In this process, we discover what is *arbitrary* about the social and natural world (eg slavery or super-naturalistic accounts of killer diseases) and what is *not arbitrary* (eg the need for literacy to have access to different cultural traditions, or the necessity to drink unpolluted water to stay healthy). Hegel also accepted that such learning is essentially social and argued that it has its own characteristic patterns of historical development.[67] In some of his writings, Marx develops similar ideas – again focusing on the unnatural, arbitrary constraints which prevent humanity achieving all that it is capable of. The key difference between the two is that Marx argues that there exists a programme of political action to remove such constraints. He claims that people are potentially in charge of their own destinies rather than, as Hegel suggests, swept along by a river of history which they might understand but can do little about. And if they do possess the power potentially to alter certain historical outcomes, then they inevitably must *select* between two or more such outcomes.

So for Marx, and for socialism generally, what is optimised when human liberation occurs is the ability to select *options* to meet individual and societal needs – options which have emerged as a by-product of mental and manual labour down the ages.[68] To regard the capacity for such choice as a basic human need is not to succumb to cultural imperialism – to claim, for example,

CRITICAL SOCIAL POLICY

that the Rest should mimic the West. It is simply to insist that those denied such choices are disadvantaged compared to those who are not, and that this is the case for contingent, alterable reasons. Of course, what choices individuals in groups will make if they develop the requisite intellectual and material capacity must remain an open question.

We have argued that the *maximisation* of creative choice about ways of satisfying health and autonomy needs – the ability to select 'life-chances' unencumbered by arbitrary, cultural constraints – is itself a basic human need. This will enable us to be much more concrete and less abstract about how to measure progress in meeting the other basic needs which have already been introduced. For as Hegel argues, we must judge what such maximisation entails in terms of those real choices which *already exist* in principle and which the broad span of contemporary theoretical and practical understanding makes possible.[69]

So much for the principle. What about the practice? Here we run into difficulties for three reasons. The first is that what is scientifically and technologically correct or incorrect can be a matter of some dispute. Yet the problem with the sorts of attacks on positivism and scientism that often characterise the anti-science/technology movement is that they risk throwing out the baby with the bath water. Some scientifically-based technologies just do indisputably work, are useful in the pursuit of basic needs and are better than others.[70] However, other technologies are more dubious in this respect (for example those associated with the Green Revolution or genetic engineering) and require much debate for their liberational potential (or lack of it) to be understood. The question of appraisal is therefore shifted, from questions about whether or not the technology works to how it should be designed, how extensively it should be employed, who should control it . . . and so on.[71] Without this sort of understanding, the use value of the technology will be either unrealised or misappropriated.

Second, disputes also rage over the appropriate social arrangements or practices for optimising the satisfaction of basic needs. Examples from our society include the role of preventive and curative strategies in improving health levels, the nature and organisation of education, the system of housing the elderly, the merits of different forms of childbirth, and the techniques of redistributing resources in society. Again, over some practices there is little dispute, for example that the ability to read and write enhances the autonomy of children whilst exposure to arbitrary physical violence inhibits it. However, in many areas there is an important ongoing debate, for example over the merits of home versus hospital delivery of babies. As we shall see, even where social practices are hotly contested, it is implicitly assumed by the disputants that it is possible in principle to distinguish between correct and incorrect solutions.

Third, even if ways of rationally resolving these issues are found, others will materialise concerning resource constraints. For again, a technology or a social practice which is 'appropriate' in the best sense of the word may exist but there may not be enough resources for it to be distributed universally. Some technologies or social practices will influence the basic needs of everyone (eg effective medicines, more successful agricultural methods, suitable

24

housing, environmental regulation). Others will be relevant to specific groups (eg educational techniques for infants or special housing facilities for the elderly). In both cases, however, political and economic issues will be raised.[72] These issues cannot be resolved without reconsidering our four societal needs from a liberational perspective – the social pre-conditions for optimising basic individual need satisfaction.

7. OPTIMISING THE SATISFACTION OF BASIC NEEDS: THE SOCIAL AND ECOLOGICAL CONTEXTS

The question of how to maximise need oriented understanding must be answered through the articulations of two final sets of needs – *communicational* and *constitutional*. We have repeatedly seen that all need satisfaction is social in character – including the need for the progressive optimisation of choice. It follows that an important necessary condition for such maximisation is a framework of negotiations within which the most rational solutions to problems of technique and scarcity can be debated and decided. In his theory of critical communication, Habermas has implicitly argued that there are three necessary conditions for an 'ideal speech situation' within which such negotiations can occur.[73]

First, participants should possess the best available understanding concerning the technical issues raised by whatever problems they are trying to solve. In many cases, such knowledge will not itself be in dispute and the focal point of this stage of negotiation will be primarily educational. Second, if there is such a dispute and participants are debating the correctness of a particular mode of understanding, then they will require specific methodological skills. If the understanding is technical, then established procedures of experimental assessment will be crucial. For example, whether or not a particular chemical causes a specific side effect or whether a particular organisational system will be cost efficient can only be effectively established in this way. Conversely, if the issue to be decided is itself communicational, or in Habermas' terms 'practical' in character, then a different set of hermeneutic methods will be appropriate in order correctly to understand the meaning of actions. The third condition for optimising the success of critical communication is to minimise the influence of vested interests which place unwarranted constraints on the direction and content of relevant debate. In this sense, the normative structure of the debate itself is just as important as correct information and relevant methodology. All of those who have the capacity usefully to contribute must be encouraged to do so, and all of those who would attempt to distort the course of the debate for purely contingent reasons must similarly be discouraged.

Hence, to summarise, if discussion concerns technique (eg the need for a new technology) then questions of workability will be paramount. If it concerns scarcity (eg the need for the wider availability of a new technology) then availability of resources and productive and distributional potential will be crucial issues. If it concerns communication (eg the reasons why people find it hard to understand the uses/dangers of a new procedure) then problems about meaning and consciousness will be to the fore. In all cases, however,

25

CRITICAL SOCIAL POLICY

the belief must be that there is a rational solution to be achieved through a critical process rather than through arbitrary domination.

Habermas is not suggesting that negotiations about human needs, or what he calls 'generalisable interests', are now conducted in accord with this idealisation.[74] Rather his point is that, to the extent that they are not, the solutions which are reached lack the generalisability which only an 'ideal speech situation' devoid of vested interest can ultimately provide. Habermas sees education and democracy as the only counters to the irrationality of such interests. As regards the former, participants must develop 'communicative competence' or, roughly, the ability successfully to understand and interact with others in terms of a complicated set of linguistic and social norms. Among other things, this will entail an appreciation of the rules of argument and a willingness to allow them – rather than, say, force – to determine its outcome. Concerning the latter, individuals must all have an opportunity to participate in debates to which they can potentially make a contribution. This is important because there is no way of determining who will have the information or the creative imagination that is relevant to formulating the most rational solution.[75]

Some critics have argued that such a view of rationality is hopelessly idealistic, since all known speech situations are dominated by the contingencies of power, and that it is difficult under existing modes of social organisation to see how this could be otherwise.[76] Habermas' response – which we endorse – is that his ideal is admittedly counterfactual but nonetheless implicit in the methods and content of arguments which currently do take place. There would be little point in ever arguing if we did not believe that rational deliberation is better than brute force. To the extent that one can rationally trust any mode of understanding, it will be because it is the outcome of extensive argument according to rules one also trusts.[77] In short, now that we have established what sorts of things human and social needs are, the discovery of how to improve our capacity to satisfy them (or to understand why and when we cannot) requires rigorous democratic debate situated in the context of available technical and practical choices and insulated from the irrationality that dominates other aspects of social life.

The criticisms of Habermas' idealism which do bite, concern the lack of a clear political direction in his work. It is fine, for example, to draw analogies – as he does – between effective democratic communication and the aims of writers like Freud and Marx. To the extent that they too advocated communicational techniques for stripping appearance from reality, and for revealing the individual or social contingency of false perceptions, then their aims are similar to his (and our) own. Yet he has little to say on the question of how to mobilise politically to achieve such aims.[78]

Implicitly, however, his message is clear enough. For the optimisation of basic need-satisfaction to be meaningfully and democratically negotiated – for liberation to be a *practical proposition* – individuals must have the *right* and the *capacity* to so negotiate. That is to say, humans also have *constitutional* needs which stipulate the social rules by which these rights and capacities will be guaranteed – irrespective of whatever other social rules they may happen to follow. So, for example, there can be little doubt that the capitalist mode of production is riddled with 'arbitrary' interests competing for dominance, and that were the articulation and implementation of social policy to be determined totally by them, little would result but much confusion and few resources. Yet, there can equally be no doubt that the centralism of most existing communist societies is equally liable to suppress rational debate about such policies. Indeed, in the light of the notorious crises of underproduction of such countries – even when compared with similar crises of overproduction under capitalism – it is an *open* question how much private enterprise and how much central planning are necessary for efficient production oriented towards need-satisfaction. Basic questions about individual constitutional needs – what individuals are entitled to as a matter of right – cannot be decided by any simple reference to existing capitalist or socialist modes of production and reproduction.

With this question in mind, there has recently been a resurgence of interest in Rawls' theory of justice.[79] He poses the problem of constitutional needs through a theory of individual needs and related rights which resembles our own. Beginning with the question of subjectivity, he asks whether there is any way in which the intuitive principle of justice as *fairness* might be made more explicit without resorting to utilitarian dictates of taste or to self interest. Pursuing this question, he rejects the unregulated market as the sole appropriate mechanism for determining a just allocation of goods and services related to basic need satisfaction. For a variety of reasons it has in practice led to inequitable distribution which in turn has placed recipients in unequal competitive positions, thus generating even more inequality. Rawls envisages a hypothetical negotiation (very like Habermas' ideal speech situation) about the provision of 'primary goods' – a concept similar to, though broader than, our preceding account of basic needs.[80] A group of individuals all share similar and relevant technical understanding and have to opt for specific principles of justice in the form of a constitution for a society in which they will then have to live. They do not know what their own social or economic position will be and therefore cannot judge how they will fare when the principles are put into practice. Under these circumstances, Rawls argues that they would most rationally opt for a system of distributional rules which would maximise their life chances, again irrespective of the position in which they eventually found themselves. The situation is analogous to that of a child told to slice a cake fairly and ensuring that this happens as rationally as possible by ensuring that s/he will not know in advance which piece s/he will receive.[81]

Rawls claims that the constitutional results of such deliberations would have three key characteristics. First, *basic liberties* (eg freedom of speech, freedom of assembly, etc) would be protected ensuring a democratic mode of political organisation. Only in this way would putative violations of individual rights be publicly debated and the other communicational advantages of democracy be put into practice. Second, *social inequality* would only be tolerated to the extent that it benefited the least well off through expanded production. In other words, Rawls does not deny that inequality may foster improvements in productivity, but he leaves to those who would so argue the burden of proof and the task of formulating workable policies to ensure an equitable distribution. Third, *equality of opportunity* would be instituted.

27

CRITICAL SOCIAL POLICY

Since Rawls argues that inequality can (and can only) be legitimised if it results in increased productivity, the third principle ensures that the competition for places in the resulting social hierarchy would be efficient and fair.[82]

Only if all three principles are met will primary goods be maximised in quantity and justly distributed. Since basic freedoms are guaranteed, opportunity for the rational expansion of creative choice on an individual or collective basis would be maximised. In practice, this would mean recognising the value of accumulated civil, political and social rights achieved in Western countries, but at the same time recognising their limits and inadequacies, for example in the fields of official secrets and the right to privacy. Since inequality is tolerated only to the extent that it can be seen to serve the interests of the least advantaged, the society envisaged is as progressive as is socially and materially possible. In practice, this would mean that income differentials themselves would have to be costed and justified. And since equality of opportunity is guaranteed, the development of self perpetuating elites, who might attempt to control critical discourse, is denied. In practice again this would involve moving beyond current policies to provide every person with the optimum access to educational, health and other welfare resources, whilst at the same time denying others the right to inherit property. It would also justify certain policies of positive discrimination in favour of disadvantaged groups.

Thus, to the extent that they can be put into practice, Rawls' three principles presuppose that people can collectively understand *what* is materially required to guarantee equality of opportunity. They thus embody some conception of basic needs similar to our own. Without an understanding of health and educational needs, along with an acceptance that they should in principle be optimally satisfied, the formulation of a coherent strategy for distributive justice would be impossible. Any other socialist criterion of redistribution will inevitably presuppose such understanding and acceptance if it stands any chance of success. On the other hand, people with special skills and attitudes will be necessary to develop and implement such strategies. And they will only emerge in sufficient numbers as a product of the very process of constitutional redistribution which they can then help to accelerate.

We end up with an apparent paradox: that some type of central state responsibility, control and provision is a necessary prerequisite for the redistributive policies which are in turn preconditions for basic individual needs to be met in practice. Only through the provision of effective social welfare (amongst other things) can a way be found out of an otherwise crippling and vicious circle of inequality and its consequences for further inequality. Indeed, Gutmann adds 'welfare rights' – including rights to the satisfaction of our individual needs – to the basic liberties which, problematically, Rawls argues have priority over his other two principles.[83] Only in this way can one avoid the claim that his position reduces to yet another ideological plea for abstract liberties which in practice cannot be realised. Thus, in principle, the human need for liberation and the societal need for political authority are in no way incompatible. The question is not whether or not there should be a state. It is what sort of state it should be, and how it could meet the needs and rights of those it should serve rather than dominate.

28

A THEORY OF HUMAN NEEDS

In placing so much emphasis on Rawls' conception of constitutional needs, we are not denying that there are problems with his view. Indeed, the critical literature here is so vast that we can hardly do it justice. The most important criticisms have revolved around the argument that Rawls' own development of his position is too closely wedded to existing capitalist forms and thereby begs a range of questions concerning scarcity, production, and redistribution.[84] The problem, however, with these arguments is that they often do not acknowledge that such questions should remain open to continual debate. Rather, they move in the opposite direction, simply claiming that under socialism there would be no problem of scarcity and hence, no necessity for a mechanism of redistribution. But, of course, this equally begs the question of what is and is not possible. The respective contribution of planning and the market mechanism in solving problems of production and distribution is currently a matter of heated debate among socialists from the Greater London Council to the Chinese government in Peking.[85] It is, again, an open question – just as open as the degree to which democratic debate, with its communicational requirements and liberational potential, is compatible with extensive state ownership and control. Surely, the experience of four decades of 'actually existing socialism' can no longer be ignored here, though one must always bear in mind the pernicious impact of a hostile world capitalist environment on this experience. At this level of analysis our theory cannot directly provide the answer to these questions, but it can help in clarifying the goal. This is the vision of healthy, educated individuals struggling equally together to look after themselves and each other in ways which fairly maximise their creative potential. We would argue that this vision is the essence of the most constructive interpretation of Rawls' position – and of forms of socialism which take individual rights seriously.[86]

Nevertheless, if the arguments against Rawls outlined above are in our view unfounded, there do remain several inadequacies and lacunae in his work which need rectifying. The first of these concerns the relative lack of attention paid to citizen *participation* in his work. It would appear that a Rawlsian constitution is possible which yields a society of benign bureaucrats with little popular political participation. Given our emphasis on the necessity for maximum participation in defining and implementing need-based policies, this absence is of obvious importance. Gutmann rehearses four arguments for maximising and equalising participatory opportunities: to protect oneself and one's group against tyranny by others, to produce better policies through involving in the decision making process those who are directly affected by the decisions, to encourage self-development and a capacity for political judgement, and lastly to guarantee the equal dignity of all citizens. She suggests that these are strong arguments for adding, so to speak, a fourth constitutional principle to Rawls' three: to diffuse political power to the maximum extent consistent with his principle of distributive justice.[87]

This 'participatory principle' must remain subordinate to his distributive principle since the latter is a precondition for the former. Thus, Gutmann argues that attempts to extend participatory opportunities in the context of a grossly unjust and inegalitarian society – the development of community control over schools in the USA in the late 1960's, for example – vividly illustrate

29

CRITICAL SOCIAL POLICY

how this may actually widen inequality from both a substantive and partici-patory perspective.[68] Again, this is another way of saying that the *image* of freedom and democracy may be just that: if struggles for more equal repre-sentation do not challenge the unfairness of the political and economic sys-tem, then they will inevitably fail to achieve what should be their real ultimate goal – the meeting of human needs. But, having agreed on the primacy of dis-tributive norms, Gutmann's argument would support measures such as industrial democracy, the decentralisation of much policy-making to the local level, and public accountability over bureaucracies and professional groups. It thus extends the previous constitutional prerequisites for com-municative competence.

Another notable absence in Rawls' work concerns the sphere of reproduc-tion, one of our basic societal needs noted above. Though at one point he questions the necessity of the family, on the whole it is taken for granted in his work. This absence raises two sets of issues: first, those associated with bio-logical reproduction and in particular the specific interests of women in this process; and second those associated with social reproduction and the specific interests of children and child-carers in that process. Applying his principles of social justice to the first, one can justify certain fundamental women's rights, including the right to free contraception and abortion on demand. No woman can be said to possess autonomy as regards choice of pos-sible life chances if this right is removed.[89] But the sphere of social reproduc-tion raises perhaps more difficult questions. On the one hand, the physical, mental and moral immaturity of children (leaving aside the thorny question of the age at which they cease to be children) would justify the need for specific *rights* for them, and the need to *protect* them against impediments to their development as healthy and autonomous adults. On the other hand, the spec-ific needs of the mother – or the primary carer of a child – imply that the maxi-mum freedom to experiment in alternative child-care arrangements should be encouraged. The necessity here, as elsewhere, is to stimulate choice by remov-ing social regulations and other normative constraints which institutionalise restricted forms of child care. Yet this must be done within bounds set by the guarantee of specific rights for all children linked to their basic needs.[90]

With additions such as these to Rawls' constitutional needs, it will be apparent that the four societal pre-conditions for meeting individual needs have been covered. In each case, we have outlined in abstract terms some con-ditions for optimising the societal needs for production, reproduction, cul-ture/communication and political authority in order that they foster the optimisations of choice about the individual needs which were the starting point of our theory.

However, one final point remains to be made concerning the ecological constraints on the limits of economic production. It is not possible to improve the satisfaction of basic individual needs or the social pre-conditions for these unless sufficient material resources are available. The whole of our argument is premised on this, yet there can be few who doubt that there are *some* natural limits to human production in a world of rapidly increasing population and industrialisation. Given that such limits exist, then the optimisation of individual need-satisfactions will not only be constrained by

A THEORY OF HUMAN NEEDS

the extent of human knowledge and the mode of its communication. Ulti-mately human needs have to be defined as those levels of health and auton-omy which are generalisable to *all* people in *all* societies, given present levels of resources and potential levels in the not-too-distant future. Thus it is important to stress that the logic of the politics of human need is irrepressably global in scope: no group of humans can have their basic needs excluded from consideration.

This being said – and we recognise its utopian ring – three points are in order. First, ecological strategies for conserving and protecting the environ-ment from needless waste and pollution may have such immediate and dram-atic consequences for basic individual needs that they will quickly become incorporated into debates about wider political issues. This is at present beginning to happen, for example, with struggles concerning the toxic conse-quences of many industrial processes. Thus ecological needs do not simply concern the *availability* of natural resources; they also relate to what is done with them and why. Perhaps nothing more dramatically illustrates the dis-tinction between needs and wants – and the ways in which it can be moulded to serve arbitrary interests – than public demand for commodities which are known to be manufactured in ways which pollute the environment.[91] Second, the conflicts of economic and other interests which plague attempts to protect the environment on a national level, are exponentially compounded when one moves to the international arena. As a result most ecological struggles are at present restricted to those societies where the political process – at least in principle – gives them some chance of making an impact and where a minimal level of basic need satisfaction has already been achieved. Yet this situation runs the severe risk that the environmental needs of the developed countries could well be met at the expense of the basic needs of the rest of the world.[92] Clearly we cannot spell out policy implications in any detail here, but a third point can be made. It is that, if they are to be success-ful, international strategies for satisfying basic needs (eg those recently sug-gested by the ILO and the Brandt Report, among others) must conform to the same communicational and constitutional norms which we have argued are necessary for the success of national strategies.[93] In particular, enormous constraints would have to be placed on the vested interests of the developed nations and of powerful groups within them. The political possibility of achieving such constraints and the circumstances under which it could be done is another open question. Indeed, at the moment, any effective answer seems almost inconceivable; but what is even more inconceivable is to stop trying to reach one – to relinquish the goal of human liberation on a global scale.

We conclude, then, with a second generalisability criterion for defining human needs. The first, introduced early on in this paper, distinguished needs from wants by reference to those things which all human beings have in common. The second, with which we end our paper, *limits* the optimisation of need-satisfactions on the first criterion according to the quantity and quality of natural resources of the earth, and dictates that the contingency of history cannot justify the lack of equity with which they are at present con-sumed. It follows that all other things being equal, *global redistribution* should

31

CRITICAL SOCIAL POLICY

have priority over national redistribution – though the two are not necessarily incompatible. It is again unclear what this would mean in terms of immediate strategy, since the politics of need will continue to be practised primarily on a national level – where it is practised at all. What is even more unclear is the implication of our position for protecting the environment in the generalisable interests of all *future* individuals. Struggles over the dumping of high level radioactive and other highly toxic waste provide a concrete example of this extremely important issue. But what is clear is that the Baconian vision of nature as an unending store house and an unfillable cistern is over. In the long term – if there is to be one – awareness of the delicacy of the biosphere must go hand in hand with democratically planned production for human need.[94]

CONCLUSION

In this paper, we have shown that the concept of basic human need is crucial for the coherence of socialist theory and practice, and for other debates on policies about human welfare. We believe that our conceptualisation of basic needs is not ethnocentric and illustrates the incorrectness and immorality of relativist arguments to the contrary. (Consider, for example, the health and autonomy necessary for subjectivists to argue their case with the force they often do!). We have also shown that it is pointless to abstract the determination of health and autonomy needs from the social and environmental context on which they are predicated. Finally, relativist arguments again to the contrary, we have demonstrated that progress has occurred in the discovery of new and more successful ways of satisfying basic needs which apply to all humans. Universal human liberation has thus been shown to be a cogent though open ended concept. It has this character because the struggle for liberation is an essentially collective quest. If it is to succeed, it will entail critical and democratic communication which is directed toward this end and no other. For this in turn to be possible – for vested interests to be curtailed and the health and education necessary for effective participation in such debates to be ensured – a constitution must be created which is specifically devoted to these ends and enforced by a state authority similarly so devoted. Such an authority cannot ultimately be restricted to nation states, regardless of how difficult it is at present to imagine what this would mean in theory or in practice.

We realise that many of these arguments have raised a range of theoretical and practical issues which are highly contentious. First, much contemporary socialist discourse does not place the same degree of emphasis on the individual, on the ahistorical character of some basic needs, and on the importance of democratic institutions in ensuring that their expanded satisfaction is as widespread and as morally responsible as possible. We recognise that we have not, for example, explicitly reconciled our views with such interpretations of Marx's writing. Second, we recognise that many of our arguments have been highly abstract and that we might be accused of self-indulgence by those primarily interested in tactical and pragmatic questions. How, they may ask,

A THEORY OF HUMAN NEEDS

can we convincingly talk of health and learning as basic needs without being much more specific about how these concepts are to be operationalised and how they are to be put into everyday practice? Problems raised here, for example, include specifying acceptable 'satisfiers' of basic needs and negotiating those levels of health and education which are consistent with universalisable programmes of redistribution. Third, and here is where we sense a veritable chorus of potential criticism, it could be argued that despite our still abstract discussion of constitutional needs, we have never really come to grips with the structural constraints on doing the things we suggest which are imposed by existing monopolies of power. Nor have we recognised the depth of the divisions within, and conflicts of interest between, those groupings which are separately struggling against such monopolies. In short, theorising is all well and good. What is our political strategy for putting our theory into practice?

Our anticipation of these questions is disconcerting and frustrating for we believe that we are developing answers to all of them. For this reason, we are at present writing a book which explores these issues in more detail. In the meantime, we would be grateful for critical comment. It little behoves us to argue that meeting human needs in the best possible ways is an essentially social task . . . and then not to ask for help.

Len Doyal is Senior Lecturer in Philosophy, Middlesex Polytechnic and Ian Gough, is Senior Lecturer in Social Administration, Manchester University. Their book, A Theory of Human Needs, *will be published by Macmillan in 1985.*

References

1 Culyer A.J., Lavers, R.J. and Williams A. 'Health indicators', in Shonfield A. and Shaw S. (eds.), *Social Indicators and Social Policy*, London, 1972, p.114

2 Armstrong, P. 'The myth of meeting needs in adult education and community development', *Critical Social Policy*, Vol.2, No.2, 1982, p.29

3 Fitzgerald, R. 'The ambiguity and rhetoric of "need"', in Fitzgerald R. (ed), *Human Needs and Politics*, Sydney, 1977 p.209

4 Smith, G. *Social Need: Policy, Practice and Research*. London, 1980

5 Nevitt, D. 'Demand and need', in Heisler, H. (ed), *Foundations of Social Administration*, London, 1977

6 Armstrong, *op. cit.* p.26

7 Flew, A.G.N. 'Wants or needs, choices or commands', in Fitzgerald, R. (ed), *op. cit.*

8 Taylor-Gooby, P. and Dale, J. *Social Theory and Social Welfare* London, 1981, p.23; however see Chapter 8 for another interpretation closer to our own, for example p.223

9 Bradshaw, J. 'The concept of social need', *New Society*, 30 March, 1972

10 For an elaboration and critical discussion of Bradshaw's work which ultimately suffers from the same fault see: Clayton, S. 'Social need revisited', *Journal of Social Policy*, 12, 2, 1983.

11 For example, see his: 'The needs of the elderly and the planning of hospitals' in Canvin, R. and Pearson, N. (eds), *Needs of the Elderly for Health and Welfare Services*, Exeter, 1972, p.48; 'Everyone his own home' in Townsend, P. *Sociology and Social Policy* Harmondsworth, 1976, p.89

12 Townsend, P. *Poverty in the United Kingdom*, Harmondsworth, 1979, Chapter 6

13 For example, see Piachaud, D. 'Peter Townsend and the Holy Grail', *New Society*, 10 September, 1981

14 Townsend, P. *An Alternative Concept of Poverty*, Paper prepared for the Division for the Study of Development, UNESCO, Paris, 1981, p.21

15 Townsend, P. in Canvin and Pearson (eds), *op cit.* p.48

16 Soper, K. *On Human Needs*, Sussex, 1981, Chapters 2-7

17 Geras, N. *Marx and Human Nature*, London, 1983. Geras does not explicitly refer to Soper's book but his analysis is directly relevant to it. Note particularly his list of those writers who in one way or another question the applicability of the concept of need in Marx: pp.49-54

18 Marcuse, H. *One Dimensional Man*, London, 1964, p.6; see also Chapters 9 and 10. For a contemporary

CRITICAL SOCIAL POLICY

Marxist who supports Marcuse's distinction, see C. Bay, *Strategies of Political Emancipation*, London, 1981, p.94. Cf. P. Springborg, *The Problem of Human Needs and the Critique of Civilisation*, London, 1981, Chapter 9

19 For detailed discussion of related issues see: Rowbotham, S., Segal, L., Wainwright, H. *Beyond the Fragments*, London, 1979; Barrett, M. *Womens Oppression Today*, London, 1980, Chapter 1; Hartmann, H. 'The unhappy marriage of Marxism and feminism: towards a more progressive union', in Sargent, L. *The Unhappy Marriage of Marxism and Feminism*, London, 1981

20 For example, this is the thrust of much of Leiss, W. *The Limits of Satisfaction*, London, 1978. Cf. Springborg, *op. cit*, Chapter 12. For an excellent summary of related issues, see: Soper, K. *op. cit*, chapter 9

21 First put forward in Maslow, A. 'A theory of human motivation', *Psychological Review*, London, 1943, pp.370-396

22 There is a close relationship between the concept of 'need' and that of 'interest' and similar debates have occurred about the latter – particularly in economic and political theory. Thus, for example, in *On Liberty*, Mill classically argues that each person is the best judge of her/his own interests. Yet if choice *per se* is taken to be the key criterion of interest, then as in the case of need, the idea becomes essentially subjectivist. For attempts to escape from the web of subjectivism which do not quite succeed, see Barry, B. 'The public interest' in Connolly, W. (ed) *The Bias of Pluralism*, New York, 1969; Balbus, D. 'The concept of interest in Marxian and pluralist analysis', *Politics and Society*, Vol.1. 1971, pp. 151-77; and Connolly, W. 'On "interests" in politics', *Politics and Society*, Vol.II, 1972, pp.459-77. For an excellent analysis of why their attempts fail, see: Wall, G. 'The concept of interest in politics', *Politics and Society*, Vol.5, 1975, pp.487-510. Wall also makes the point that there must be a sense in which interests are objectively determinable if the concept is to be employed for the purposes of criticising social, economic and political arrangements.

23 This is much the way Bay, C. defines 'needs' in his classic paper: 'Needs, wants, and political legitimacy', *Canadian Journal of Political Science*, September, 1968, pp.242-246. For an extension of this analysis, see his, *op. cit.*, Chapter 4. Here, among other things, he explains what he thinks is *wrong* with Marcuse's distinction between true and false needs

24 For examples of different academic approaches to linking needs with human nature, see: Renshon, S. 'Human needs and political analysis: an examination of a framework', and Smith M.B. 'Metapsychology, politics, and human needs' in Fitzgerald, R. (ed) *op. cit.*, Chapters 4 and 7. Clearly what 'human nature' might mean in this context is a complex issue. It can encompass anything from physiological pre-requisites for survival, to 'drives' thought to be totally instinctive to 'motives' considered to be more open-ended. For an excellent discussion of the relationship between humans and animals in these respects, see: Midgley, M. *Beast and Man*, Hassocks, 1978, Chapters 1-3

25 Galtung, J. 'The basic needs approach', in Lederer, K. (ed), *Human Needs*, Cambridge, Mass. 1980, pp.59-60

26 For a similar analysis in more detail, see: Plant, R. Lesser, H. and Taylor-Gooby, P. *Political Philosophy and Social Welfare*, London, 1980, pp.25-33

27 *Ibid*. pp.28-29

28 This subjectivist conclusion is extensively discussed in: Fitzgerald, R. (ed) *op. cit*. Cf. Plant, Lesser and Taylor-Gooby, *op. cit*. pp.33-36

29 Plant et al argue that Gallie's concept of 'essential contestability' is useful here and discuss the issue in these terms. Cf. Gallie, W. 'Essentially contested concepts', *Aristotelian Society*, 1955-6

30 Runciman, W. *Relative Deprivation and Social Justice*, London, 1966, Chapters 8-11

31 See the suggestive findings of a recent MORI poll: Lansley, S. and Weir, S. 'Towards a popular view of poverty', *New Society*, 25 August, 1983

32 Galtung, *op. cit*. pp.58-62; Plant, Lesser and Taylor-Gooby, *op. cit*. pp.37-38

33 Debates about the relationship between the conceptual and experiential dimensions of understanding have a history as old as philosophy itself. For our purposes, what is important is the recognition that the two cannot be completely separated – the one concerning questions of definition and the other concerning questions of fact – in the way that until recently was accepted as legitimate by most Anglo-Saxon thought. Neither should both be isolated from the practical dimensions of understanding. For a rigorous discussion of why this is the case and an accompanying analysis of 'constitutive activities' which reinforces the arguments in this paper for a non-subjectivist theory of human need, see: Doyal, L. and Harris, R. 'The practical foundation of human understanding', *New Left Review*, No.139, 1983, pp.59-78. Further, note that the emphasis here is on the *person*. In abstraction, there are many other necessary conditions for successful action which are *impersonal*. We shall discuss these as the paper progresses.

34 Kant, I. *Critique of Practical Reason*, trans. Abbott, T. London, 1963, pp.188-9; Kant, E. *Fundamental Principles of the Metaphysic of Morals*, trans. Abbott, T. London, 1963, pp.52-59.

35 The literature on the distinction between action and behaviour is immense. For the early neo-Kantians, see: Bauman, Z. *Hermeneutics and Social Science*, London, 1978, Chapter 1. For Weber, see: Giddens, A. *Studies in Social and Political Theory*, London, 1977, Chapter 4. For a review of the more recent philosophical literature, see: Bernstein, R. *The Restructuring of Social and Political Theory*, London, 1979, Part II.

A THEORY OF HUMAN NEEDS

Cf. Doyal, L. and Harris, R. *Empiricism Explanation and Rationality*, forthcoming. Some of the examples employed to illustrate related points have been developed through this collaboration

36 Plant, Lesser and Taylor-Gooby, *op. cit*. chapter 3

37 For related discussions of freedom, see: MacCullum, G. 'Negative and positive freedom', in Laslett, P. Runciman W. and Skinner, Q. (eds), *Philosophy, Politics and Society*, Series 4, Oxford, 1972, pp.174-93; Radcliffe Richards J. *The Sceptical Feminist*, London, 1980, Chapter 3; Doyal and Harris, *op. cit*.

38 Plant et al. *op. cit*. make this point (pp.49-50) but do not really develop it. Presumably because of their concern for the essential contestability argument, they continue throughout their book to focus on *minimal* standards. For this reason the potential force of their argumentative approach is never quite achieved. Indeed, as regards such minima, at one point they even suggest: 'the level of health required in order to be able to operate may vary from individual to individual, and from society to society: it may well be the case that people in poorer societies, as a result of custom, actually need somewhat less food than people in wealthier ones, and also can keep going when in a less healthy state' (pp.49-50). Even though they then deny that this makes 'the actual concept of physical health variable' (p.50), it is never made clear why and what the consequences are for the range of debates within social policy concerning the subjectivity of specific needs.

39 The problem of operationalising mental health even in minimal terms might seem more problematic than that of physical health. Certainly this has been argued by, among others, Hirst, P. and Woolley, P. *Social Relations and Human Attributes*, London, 1982, chapters 4-5. However, there are many who disagree. For example, a 1973 WHO study, World Health Organisation, *The International Pilot Study of Schizophenia*, Vol.1, Geneva, 1973, suggests that there is much cross-cultural agreement about indicators of mental illness and by implication mental health. For a relevant discussion of Maslow's attempt to identify minimal psychological needs, see: Fitzgerald, R. 'Abraham Maslow's hierarchy of needs – an exposition and evaluation', in Fitzgerald, R. (ed), *op. cit*., chapter 3

40 Rist, G. 'Basic questions about basic human needs', in Lederer, K. *Human Needs*, Cambridge, Mass. 1980, pp.235-38

41 Plant, R. Lesser, H. and Taylor-Gooby, P. *op. cit*. pp.46-51. Also see Weale, A. *Political Theory and Social Policy*, London, 1983, Chapter 3

42 For examples, see: Hirst, P. and Woolley, P. *op. cit*. chapter 2

43 A speculative account of some of these educational universals can be found in: White, J. *Towards a Compulsory Curriculum*, London, 1973, chapters 3-4. Also see: T. McCarthy's discussion of J. Habermas' account of 'universal pragmatics', in *The Critical Theory of Jurgen Habermas*, London, 1978, pp.272-82. It should now be clear that when we refer to 'teachers' or 'education' we are using the terms in their broadest sense, and not just referring to the agents or processes of formal schooling

44 Wittgenstein, L. *Philosophical Investigation*, Oxford, 1972, p.91. For a useful summary, see: Rubinstein, D. *Marx and Wittgenstein*, London, 1981, chapter 9

45 For lots of examples, see W. Ryan's classic: *Blaming the Victim*, New York, 1971

46 On the importance of the concept of rules in bridging the gap between the individual and society, and of the dangers of taking the analogy between games and social rules too far, see: Giddens, A. *Central Problems in Social Theory*, London, 1979, Chapter 2. Cf. for example, Macdonald G. and Pettit, P. *Semantics and Social Science*, London, 1981, who state (pp.138-9): 'The patriot, the freedom fighter and the socialist are not possible in any social world deprived of appropriate conceptual resources. There is no patriot who lacks the concept of nation, tradition and independence, no freedom fighter who is without the ideas of liberty, oppression and respect, no socialist who is unfamiliar with the notions of class, exploitation and equality. And yet the concepts required for the fashioning of the corresponding beliefs and desires come to individuals only by grace of the community to which they belong.' These arguments are further explained in: Doyal, L. and Harris, R. *op. cit*.

47 We are heavily indebted in this section to Williams, R. particularly his *The Long Revolution*, Harmondsworth, 1965, Chapters 2-3, and *Politics and Letters*, London, 1979, Chapter II. 3. While we differ on some details, we feel that we are all making similar points about the social context of successful individual activity. Much the same can be said of Barrington Moore, J. *Injustice*, London, 1979, Chapter 1

48 For a demonstration that this must be so, see: Doyal, L. and Harris, R. 'The practical foundation of human understanding', *op. cit*.

49 Marx, K. *Grundrisse*, trans. Nicolaus, M. Harmondsworth, 1973, introduction, especially pp.88-100

50 O'Brien, M. *The Politics of Reproduction*, London, 1981, p.16

51 Firestone, S. *The Dialectic of Sex: The Case for Feminist Revolution*, London, 1971. Cf. Rose, H. and Hamner, J. 'Women's liberation, reproduction and the technological fix', in Leonard Barker, D. and Allen, S. *Sexual Divisions and Society: Process and Change*, London, 1976, pp.199-223

52 Barrett, M. *op. cit*. chapter 6

53 Willaims, R. in his book *Communications*, Harmondsworth, 1973, p.18, stresses their importance: 'The emphasis on communications asserts, as a matter of experience, that men and societies are not confined to relationships of power, property and production. Their relationships, in describing, learning, persuading and exchanging experiences are seen as equally fundamental.' Also see: Williams, R. *The Long Revolution*, Harmondsworth, 1965, chapters 2-3

CRITICAL SOCIAL POLICY

54 Williams, R. *Problems in Materialism and Culture*, London, 1980, pp.31-49. For a more general discussion of Marxist theories of ideology see: Larrain, J. *Marxism and Ideology*, London, 1983, especially Chapter 5. For an analysis of the extent to which communicational and cultural patterns are dependent upon the *practical* foundations of social life, including production and reproduction, see Doyal, L. and Harris, R. *op. cit.* 1983.

55 See, for example, Giddens, A. *Central Problems in Social Theory*, London, 1979, p.108 and generally chapter 3. Cf. Barrington Moore, *op. cit.* pp.15-31

56 We believe that the best introduction to Hegel in this respect is: Avineri, S. *Hegel's Theory of the Modern State*, Cambridge, 1972, chapters 7-9. Cf. Taylor, C. *Hegel*, Cambridge, 1975, chapters 14-16

57 This view is incompatible with Marx's and some Marxist writing. According to both, a truly communist society would have no need for concepts of 'rights', or 'justice', much less an associated legal system or method of policing to back it up. With no scarcity, private property and associated individual greed, what would be the point? For an expansion of this position and a critique which in many respects reinforces our position, see: Buchanan, A. *Marx and Justice*, London, 1982. Cf. Campbell, T. *The Left and Rights*, London, 1983

58 This indeed is the grain of truth in traditional functionalist analysis – whatever its other problems

59 For a powerful attack on this entire tradition, see: Lukes, S. *Individualism*, Oxford, 1973

60 For related arguments which focus on Parsons' classic formulation, see: Gouldner, A. *The Coming Crisis of Western Sociology*, London, 1971, pp.218-25. For a similar critique of 'structuralist' formulations, see: Giddens, A. *op. cit.* chapter 1

61 For example: Roy, R. 'Human needs and freedom: liberal, Marxist, and Gandhian perspectives', in Lederer, K. (ed), *op. cit.* p.202. This difficulty continues to emerge in Plant et al's. analysis although they are clearly aware of it in the way in which they formulate their overall approach. Galtung (eg pp.62-71) goes into more detail in this respect but without convincing philosophical justification. It was this, among other things, which prompted us to expand and modify their approaches

62 Hegel, *Philosophy of Right*, trans. Knox, T. Oxford, 1967, pp.86-104

63 Many writers would make this obvious point. For a balanced view, see: Watt, E. 'Human needs, human wants, and political consequences', *Political Studies*, Vol.XXX, No.4. For a devastating attack on those who would argue that Marx thought anything to the contrary, see Geras, N. *op. cit.* Part III

64 For an example of the type of argument we are attacking, see: Rist, G. 'Basic questions about basic human needs', in Lederer, K. *op. cit.* pp.233-53. At best, there is a tension in much of the literature on underdevelopment between the obvious applicability of some Western technology and what is believed to be the danger of cultural imperialism and/or its use for exploitative purposes. For the potential elitism that this can give rise to, see: Horton, R. 'Lévy-Bruhl, Durkheim and the scientific revolution', in Horton, R. and Finnegan, R. (eds), *Modes of Thought*, London, 1973, pp.249-305. To illustrate the opposite side of the coin – how multi-national corporations can use subjectivists' arguments to their advantage – consider the following from Melrose, D. *Bitter Pills*, Oxford, 1982, p.80, in a discussion of drug misinformation in the Third World: 'But Glaxo did respond to an earlier query we raised about their promotion of Calci-Ostelin syrup as a general tonic in another developing country, when not only does Glaxo not do this in Britain, but the *British National Formulary* describes this use as having no justification. Glaxo's Senior Medical Adviser responded then by stressing that 'different countries' have very 'different concepts of medical practice'.

65 Soper, K. *op. cit*; Leiss, W. *op. cit.* pp.107-14

66 For a discussion of these two dimensions of freedom and their political background, see: Gutmann, A. *Liberal Equality*, Cambridge, 1980, Chapter 1. Cf. Plant, R. Lesser, H. and Taylor-Gooby, P. *op. cit.* pp.175-79

67 Norman, R. *Hegel's Phenomenology*, London, 1976, chapters 5-6; Cf. Taylor, C. *op. cit.* chapter 15

68 Bernstein, R. *Praxis and Action*, London, 1972, Part I. Cf. Walton, P. and Gamble, A. *From Alienation to Surplus Value*, London, 1972, chapter 1

69 This is the germ of political truth in his contention that: 'The Owl of Minerva spreads its wings only with the falling of dusk.' Hegel, *op. cit.* p.13

70 For detailed argument, see: Doyal, L. and Harris, R. *op. cit.* Cf. also Doyal, L. and Doyal, L. 'Western scientific medicine: a philosophical and political prognosis', in Byrke, L. and Silvertown, J. *Radical Biology*, London, 1984

71 For a useful review of related issues, see: Griffiths, D. Irvine, J. and Miles, I. 'Social statistics: towards a radical science' in Irvine, J. Miles, I. and Evans, J. *Demystifying Social Statistics*, London, 1979, pp.339-381.

72 The literature just on underdevelopment in this respect is immense. Two books which give useful summaries of the complex physical and social factors involved are: MacPherson, S. *Social Policy in the Third World*, Hassocks, 1982; Eckholm, E. *Down to Earth*, London, 1982. For questions specifically related to health, see: Doyal, L. *The Political Economy of Health*, London, 1979, chapters 3, 7. For those specifically related to education, see: Entwistle, H. *Antonio Gramsci*, London, 1979, chapter 1. Cf. Freire, P. *Pedagogy of the Oppressed*, London, 1972.

73 Habermas' analysis of this issue is extremely complex and all that we can do here is offer a rational

A THEORY OF HUMAN NEEDS

reconstruction which attempts to capture the spirit of what he is getting at. The best and most detailed guide through his relevant writings is: McCarthy, T. *op. cit.* chapter 4. For an excellent introduction to Habermas' general theories, see: Bernstein, R. *The Restructuring of Social and Political Theory*, London, 1976, Part IV. For Habermas himself, see for example: *Legitimation Crisis*, trans. McCarthy, T. London, 1976, pp.102-117

74 Habermas, J. *op. cit.* pp.111-117. Cf. McCarthy, T. *op. cit.* pp.314-15; Geuss, R. *The Idea of a Critical Theory*, Cambridge, 1981, Chapter 2

75 Habermas summarises his position about democracy as follows: 'If under these conditions a consensus about the recommendation to accept a norm arises argumentatively, that is, on the basis of hypothetically proposed alternative justifications, then this consensus expresses the "rational will". Since all those affected have, in principle, at least the chance to participate in the practical deliberation, the "rationality" of the discursively formed will consists in the fact that the reciprocal behavioural expectations raised to formal status afford validity to a *common* interest ascertained *without deception*. The interest is common because the constraint-free consensus permits only what *all* can want, it is free of deception because even the interpretation of needs in which *each individual* must be able to recognize what he wants becomes the object of discursive will-formation. The discursively formed will may be called "rational" because the formal properties of discourse and of the deliberative situation sufficiently guarantee that a consensus can arise only through appropriately interpreted generalizable interests, by which I mean, needs that can be communicatively shared.' Habermas, J. *op. cit.* p.108

76 For example, see: Lukes, S. 'Of gods and demons: Habermas and practical reason', in Thompson, J. and Held, D. (eds), *Habermas*, London, 1982, chapter 7. Cf. Keat, R. *The Politics of Social Theory*, Oxford, 1981, pp.180-90

77 Habermas, *op. cit.* pp.111-117. Also see: McCarthy, T. *op. cit.* pp.310-317

78 For example, see: Bernstein, R. *op. cit.*, pp.223-5. Cf. Lukes, S. *ibid*

79 After the publication of Rawls' *Theory of Justice* in 1972, a wide range of critical reviews of his work was published. Indeed, there was a veritable industry of them – some focusing on philosophy, others on politics and still others on specific aspects of the one or the other. For an example of the first, see: Barry, B. *The Liberal Theory of Justice*, Oxford, 1973. For the second, see: MacPherson, C.B. *Democratic Theory*, Oxford, 1973, pp.87-94; Miller, R. 'Rawls and Marxism', in Daniels, N. (ed), *Reading Rawls*, Oxford, 1975, pp.206-30. For the third, see the other papers in the Daniels collection. A useful summary of key points from these different perspectives is in: Plant, R. Lesser, H. and Taylor-Gooby, P. *op. cit.* pp.124-31. Recently, however, the importance of Rawls' views for socialist theory has been re-evaluated. This is partly due to the publication of Gutmann, A. *op. cit*; Tucker, D. *Marxism and Individualism*, Oxford, 1980; and Buchanan, A. *op. cit.* Our views have been particularly influenced by Gutmann

80 Rawls, J. *Theory of Justice*, Oxford, 1972, p.62 and pp.90-95. Rawls defines primary goods as follows: 'As a first step, suppose that the basic structure of society distributes certain primary goods, that is, things that every rational man is presumed to want. These goods normally have a use whatever a person's rational plan of life (p.62). He goes on to divide primary goods into two categories: 'social primary goods' such as 'rights and liberties, powers and opportunities, income and wealth'; and 'natural' primary goods such as 'health and vigor' (and) 'intelligence and imagination'. Where we differ from Rawls concerns the priority which he places on social primary goods. Rights and liberties will be of little use until, in our terms, the basic needs for health and vigour have been at least marginally met. Cf. Gutmann, A. *op. cit.* pp.125-6. Also, see his discussion of the 'thin theory of the good', pp.395-99.

81 Rawls, J. *op. cit.* pp.17-22 and pp.137-42. Cf. Dworkin, R. 'The original position', in Daniels, N. *op. cit.* pp.16-53. For an interesting and detailed criticism of Rawls' formulation which attacks the abstract character of his conception of personhood, see: Sandel, M. *Liberalism and the Limits of Justice*, Cambridge, 1982. For reasons which we have hinted at but which we cannot explore here in depth, we believe that it is possible successfully to combine a sympathetic interpretation of Rawls' approach with a richer conception of personhood which recognises its social parameters.

82 Rawls, J. *op. cit.* pp.60-65

83 Gutmann, A. *op. cit.* pp.122-40

84 For example, see: MacPherson, C.B. *op. cit.* pp.89-90; Miller, R. *op. cit.* pp.175-80

85 The most notable recent contribution to this debate is surely, Nove, A. *The Economics of Feasible Socialism*, London, 1983. Cf. Shalom, S. (ed), *Socialist Visions*, London, 1983 Section VI. See also the discussion of Nove in Anderson, P. *In the Tracks of Historical Materialism*, London, 1983, Chapter 4

86 For a powerful argument to this effect, along with responses to Rawls' libertarian critics from the right, see: Gutmann, A. *op. cit.* chapter 6. Cf. Tucker, D. *op. cit.* pp.189-97. For a related attempt to translate Rawls' principles into a more naturalistically conceived theory of individual rights, see: Dworkin, R. *Taking Rights Seriously*, London, 1981, chapter 6. Cf. Buchanan, A. *op. cit.* chapters 6-7. For a fascinating description of what can happen when individual rights are not taken seriously, see: Fedor, F. Heller, A. and Markus, G. *Dictatorship Over Needs*, Oxford, 1983. All three are political exiles from Hungary and the book is about Russia and Eastern Europe.

87 Gutmann, A. *op. cit.* pp.178-181, 197-203

CRITICAL SOCIAL POLICY

88 Gutmann, A. *op. cit.* pp.191-97. Cf. Gutmann, A. 'What's the use of going to school', in Sen, A. and Williams, B. *Utilitarianism and Beyond*, Cambridge, 1982, Chapter 14

89 For a recent careful argument of this case see Radcliffe Richards, J. *The Sceptical Feminist: A Philosophical Enquiry*, Harmondsworth, 1980, Chapters 4 and 8

90 These issues are discussed in Barrett, M. and McIntosh, M. *The Anti-Social Family*, London, 1982, chapter 4, especially pp.140-142, 156-158. On children's rights see Freeman, M.F.A. *The Rights and Wongs of Children*, London, 1983, chapters 1 and 2

91 Leiss, W. *op. cit.* Part Two

92 Cf. Castleman, B.I. 'The export of hazardous factories to developing nations', in Navarro, V. and Berman, D.M. (eds), *Health and Work Under Capitalism: An International Perspective*, Farmingdale, 1983

93 Cf. ILO, conclusions of the 1976 World Employment Conference, *Meeting Basic Needs: Strategies for Eradicating Mass Poverty and Unemployment*, Geneva, 1977; Independent Commission on International Development Issues (the Brandt Report), *North-South: a Programme for Survival*, London, 1980.

94 Enzensberger, H. 'A critique of political ecology', in *Raids and Reconstruction*, London, 1976, pp.253-95. He concludes by saying: 'If ecology's hypotheses are valid, then capitalist societies have probably thrown away the chance of realising Marx's project for the reconciliation of man and nature. The productive forces which bourgeois society has unleashed have been caught up with and over-taken by the destructive powers released at the same time. The highly industralised countries of the west will not be alone in paying the price for the revolution that never happened. The fight against want is an inheritance they leave to all mankind, even in those areas where mankind survives the catastrophe. Socialism, which was once a promise of liberation, has become a question of survival. If the ecological equilibrium is broken, then the rule of freedom will be further off than ever.

[4]

A Theory of Human Need

Kate Soper

The higher the level of abstraction at which any argument for universal needs is cast, the less controversial it is likely to prove, but the more open it becomes to the charge of being vacuously uninformative as a guide to specific welfare provision. Not even the most committed cultural relativist on needs is likely to disagree with Aristotle when he remarks in *Metaphysics* that, 'when life or existence are impossible (or when the good cannot be attained) without certain conditions, these conditions are "necessary", and this cause is itself a kind of necessity'.[1] If, that is, we construe this as an argument to the effect that all human beings have a need for whatever is essential to the maintenance of life and the provision of the 'good', then few will dissent from it.

Had Aristotle, however, proceeded to define human 'existence' and the 'good' in more precise terms, or to specify the conditions required for their realization (a task of discrimination in which, being Aristotle, he might well have felt obliged to distinguish between the good meat, wine, leisure and democratic institutions 'needed' by the male citizen, and the 'needs' of women and slaves), then clearly his argument would have become instantly vulnerable to the objections of the cultural relativists. For, from their perspective, his 'universally applicable' discourse on needs is exposed as all too patently ethnocentric and gender-biased.

The more, then, a theory of universal needs confines itself to stating the basic goals to be attained (Aristotle's 'existence' and the 'good', or the rather more precise, but still quite abstract, ends argued for by Len Doyal and Ian Gough in *A Theory of Human Need*[2] the less it will offend the relativists, but the further removed it must be from any pretension to assist in policy-making. For what relativists primarily object to is not claims to the effect that we all need the 'good' rather than the 'bad', or even to the effect that everyone has a need to avoid serious physical or mental harm,[3] but rather to the idea that we can

---

[1] Aristotle, *Metaphysics*, ed. D. Ross, London 1956, p. 10.
[2] Len Doyal, Ian Gough, *A Theory of Human Need*, Macmillan, London 1991.
[3] I am a little unclear as to how far Doyal and Gough would accept the general point I am making here. In their Introduction and in Chapter 1 of their book, they tend to present 'relativists' of all complexions as united in their rejection of common human needs, without much discussion of the degree of consent there would be among them to claims about universal needs of the most formal and minimalist kind. At a somewhat later stage in their argument, however, they do suggest that 'even the most staunch relativist would presumably not question the universality of the need for life-preserving quantities of water, oxygen and calorific intake. Neither, hopefully, would they dispute that without some learning and emotional support in childhood, all

say more exactly in what such needs consist, or can prescribe the
'universal satisfiers' which would guarantee their being met. Actual
needs, they will insist, together with their particular 'satisfiers', are
always culturally and historically conditioned, and anyone who argues
otherwise is guilty of generalising from an ethnocentric and temporally local conception of human nature and its needs.[4] No one, therefore, who proposes to define 'basic' or universal needs at anything less
than the most abstract level, can hope to avoid the problem that the
more empirical content they inject into their argument, thus gaining it
an essential degree of political relevance, the more at risk they are of
positing as 'objective needs' what are, in reality, culturally conditioned perceptions of the 'good'.

Arguments Against Relativism

This brings me more directly to the scrupulous and sophisticated case
set forth for the ascription of universal needs by Doyal and Gough,
since the great strength of this, so it seems to me, lies in the fact that
it is both fully aware of the dilemma I have sketched and boldly prepared to grapple with it. As they themselves recognise, the key issue is
how to chart basic need satisfaction, or 'objective welfare' without
'either embracing relativism or working at such a level of generality
that the relevance of our theory for specific problems concerning
social policy is lost' (p. 156). What is important and original (and
doubtless in the eyes of some, presumptuous) about their project is
that it not only tells us what our basic needs are (those of health and
autonomy), but offers empirical criteria for the meeting of these goals
—and is hence prepared to specify the 'universal satisfier characteristics' (or 'intermediate needs', as Doyal and Gough term them),
essential to their realization. Thus while they readily concede that the
specific *form* taken by the satisfiers of 'intermediate needs' will be
culturally divergent, the 'intermediate needs' themselves are common
to all cultures at all times, providing a standard by reference to which
levels of deprivation within particular groupings can be charted and
specific welfare strategies be defended as objectively grounded rather
than ethnocentrically motivated. Abstractly, this standard is defined
at two levels: (1) that of the 'participation optimum' (the health and

---

[3] (*cont.*)
individuals will find it impossible to join in the activities of their peers' (p. 69). But
given how close this comes to allowing relativists to agree to the existence of some basic
needs for health and autonomy, it is difficult not to feel that Doyal and Gough may, in
the earlier stage of their argument, have set up a straw-man relativism, when what was
really needed—as the above quotation appears to recognise—was an engagement with
relativist objections to the attempt to make any but fairly general claims about our
common needs. Many of the relativists cited by Doyal and Gough, I suspect, might
want to argue that their objections to a universalist theory were only intended to come
into play at a fairly low level of abstraction.

[4] One may compare here Marx's dictum that 'hunger is hunger, but the hunger gratified by cooked meat eaten with a knife and fork is a different hunger from that which
bolts down raw meat with the aid of hand, nail and tooth'. (*Grundrisse*, Harmondsworth, 1973, p. 92). If one interprets Marx here, as I think we should (cf. K. Soper, *On
Human Needs*, Brighton 1981, pp. 14–15, 88–9) as claiming that these 'different' hungers
are different in kind, rather than forms of a common content, then it constitutes a
relativist claim. This is not to dispute the tension in Marx's writing between universalist and relativist ideas on need to which Doyal and Gough draw attention (p. 27).

autonomy needed such that individuals can 'choose the activities in which they will take part within their culture', possess the cognitive, emotional and social capacities to do so and have access to the means by which these capacities can be acquired' (p. 160);[5] (2) that of the 'critical optimum' (the health and autonomy needed such that individuals can 'formulate the aims and beliefs necessary to question their form of life, to participate in a political process directed towards this end and/or to join another culture altogether') (*ibid.*). Concrete indices of this standard are provided by reference to a wide range of statistical data on the objective welfare of groups of nations in the First, Second and Third Worlds. This allows Sweden to be singled out as the average best performer, and its level of welfare provision established as 'the only logical and moral criterion that can be applied to judge need-satisfaction in the long term' (p. 161).

Now any attempt to operationalize a theory of needs to this degree is clearly fraught with problems, and it is to some of these to which I wish to turn in what follows. But I hope I have already said enough to indicate the value and importance of Doyal and Gough's project, which is all the more to be applauded given the prevailing relativism of current approaches to issues of human consumption and life-style. Indeed, whatever specific objections their argument may be open to, it is their theoretical project rather than the relativists' punctilious respect for cultural difference, which I would defend as the more politically progressive. For however well intentioned the 'difference' theorists may be, it is their admonitions against the 'cultural imperialism' of any attempt to speak to the needs of 'others' rather than Doyal and Gough's defence of universal needs, that will be most readily seized upon by all those seeking to clothe a naked disregard for the deprivation of others with the mantle of theoretical legitimacy. While cultural relativism, therefore, by presenting all intervention in the affairs of others as a potentially totalitarian distraint on their autonomy, may all too easily licence political inactivity, the argument of Doyal and Gough tends in the opposite direction by refusing to allow appeals to cultural difference to obscure objective deprivations. It is motivated, that is, by a wholly commendable sense that overcoming scepticism about the universal and objective quality of human needs may be an essential first move towards the implementation of those global welfare programmes of most practical import to the preservation of life, and promotion of cultural diversity, among the most deprived.[6]

That said, I now want to focus on what I find to be the more problematic aspects of their argument, all of which are inter-related, but which for purposes of exposition I shall deal with under the following

---

[5] There are evident parallels here with the human capabilities approach to needs and welfare theory developed by Amartya Sen (*Poverty and Famines*, Oxford, 1981; *Resources, Values and Development*, Oxford, 1984; *Commodities and Capabilities*, Amsterdam, 1985), and Doyal and Gough acknowledge its influence on their own work.

[6] For a lively staging of the issues involved in cultural relativist versus universalist approaches, and a powerful defence of the latter, see Martha Nussbaum, 'Human Functioning and Social Justice: in Defence of Aristotelian Essentialism', *Political Theory*, Vol. 20, no. 2, May 1992.

headings: 1) The conceptualization of need; 2) Autonomy and political oppression; 3) Intermediate needs; 4) The basic and the non-basic; 5) Ecology and human needs.

The Conceptualization of Need

Anyone offering a theory of basic human needs confronts the dual task, firstly of defining needs and secondly of specifying those which are 'basic'. Doyal and Gough's essential argument here is that needs are distinguished from wants in being goals which all human beings have to achieve if they are to avoid 'serious harm', this latter being defined in terms of the maintenance of physical health and autonomy. They recognise that this presupposes a consensus as to what constitutes the human condition when it is 'normal, flourishing and unharmed', but plead that any denial that such a consensus exists 'goes against deep moral convictions throughout the world. If need were simply a function of cultural or individual preference, then we would find nothing wrong with Huxley's *Brave New World*, where a diet of drugs, sex and ignorance produces a subjective contentment which is as uniform as it is awful' (p. 44).

Needs, then, according to Gough and Doyal, are to be differentiated from wants and subjective preferences in terms of their possibly unconscious status. Unlike our wants, our needs are such that we may be unaware of them and thus incapable of naming them. Experienced and articulated as they often are, it is not essential to the ascription of a need that it be subjectively apprehended.

Now, it is this issue of the experienced (or experienceable) status of need which, so it seems to me, lies at the heart of the debate between universalist and relativist approaches to needs and is central to a distinction developed in recent welfare theory between 'thin' and 'thick' theoretical approaches to need.[7] Thus, whereas a 'thin' theory is said to aim at what is universally needed independently of cultural content and subjective report, a 'thick' theory is particularist, focusing on 'needs' as these are experienced and named within a specific culture. From a 'thick' theory perspective, in fact, needs, so far from being ascribable despite the subject's knowledge of them, can only be said to exist insofar as they are consciously felt and given some expression on the part of those possessing them.

Advocates of 'thick' theory approaches may seem to be on the side of the angels in that they wish to pay attention to welfare claimants' statements of their own needs—though I think it would be mistaken to assume that anyone defending the idea of objective (and hence in principle unexperienced) needs is committed to the view that knowledge of these is the privileged province of 'experts'. Certainly, this is

---

[7] See Nancy Fraser, *Unruly Practices: Power, Discourse and Gender in Contemporary Social Theory*, Minnesota 1989, pp. 161–7; Patrick Kerans, 'Welfare and Need' (Presentation to the Fifth Conference of Social Welfare Policy, Bishop's University, Lennoxville, Quebec, August 25–7, 1991); Patrick Kerans and Glenn Drover, 'Foundations of Welfare: A Social Action Perspective', paper presented to Seminar on Theory of Welfare, Quebec, September 25–27, 1992 (forthcoming in collection of seminar papers to be published by Edward Elgar).

not the view of Doyal and Gough, who make it clear that 'experts' and those they are speaking on behalf of can be equally fallible in this respect. Hence the weight they place on the participation of both parties in the discernment of needs. I will return to this approach in my section on 'Autonomy' since I think there are some unresolved tensions in their treatment.

But whether or not the 'thick' theorists are too quick to assume that in defending the objectivity of needs, one is licensing an overweaning welfare paternalism, I think their position is open to the objection that it offers no satisfactory discrimination between needs and subjective preferences. At any rate, I am unclear on what basis the multiple (and, so it is argued, ever multiplying)[8] aspirations of groups and individuals are being defined as 'needs'. If 'needs' are inherently expansionary—their fulfilment generating the ever-new needs of the 'well-seeking' person—then any distinction between that which is needed because it is indispensable to life, and that which is desirable because life-enhancing, would seem to have been eroded.

In this respect, Doyal and Gough's approach (whether or not correctly described as 'thin')[9] has for me the definite advantage that it offers a clear set of criteria for demarcating between what is fundamental to human well-being and what we may lay claim to as a condition of further flourishing. As I hope to show in the final section of this review, such a distinction is of some considerable moral and practical importance in a world of very unequally-distributed and limited resources.

All the same, I think the issue of the cognized or cognizable status of 'need' is extremely complex, and that this may not The sufficiently recognised by Doyal and Gough. In order to bring out some of the difficulties here I shall focus on the implication of their argument that human beings may want but cannot need to engage in activities harmful to their health and survival, even though such damaging practices might be justified in terms of the 'avoidance of harm' which constitutes the procurement of pleasure (enjoyable self-indulgence), or in terms of the avoidance of suffering (the suicide who cannot endure the pain of continued existence, or the volunteer for euthanasia). I do not bring this issue up because it represents any major objection to Doyal and Gough's argument. I agree with them that for most human beings most of the time the avoidance of 'serious harm', construed as the avoidance of death/severe damage to mental and physical health, is so over-riding a priority as to justify defining it as both universal and objective, despite some individual exceptions to it. My purpose

---

[8] Patrick Kerans, for example, argues in 'Welfare and Need' (p. 2) that 'A key reason for developing a thick notion of need is to highlight the unending dynamism of human agency. People challenge institutional patterns and basic cultural orientations when they experience these as constraints to their filling ever newly discovered needs'. He also speaks in this connection of needs as self-expanding and generating needs, referring us to the Marxian notion of persons 'rich in needs', who 'the more they meet their needs, discover further needs, needs which are more evidently personal and incommensurate with those of others'.

[9] Drover and Kerans refer to Doyal and Gough's theory as 'thin' while arguing that it avoids most of the shortcomings of a 'thin' approach. I am not sure how far Doyal and Gough would go along with this description.

here is not to contest the needed status of physical health, but rather to point to what is specific about a need in respect of its cognitive status. For while it belongs to the logic of need that needs can be ascribed to persons even where they are ignorant of them (as in the case of Doyal and Gough's example of the diabetic's need for insulin), it is also important to recognize that needs are properties of subjects rather than biological organisms. They must thus be differentiated not only from wants, but also from instinctual urges and biological drives. Doyal and Gough do, in fact, acknowledge the importance of discrimination between needs and drives (pp. 35–39) and hence argue that what is at issue in determining our needs is a question 'about what *we* —as opposed to our genes—should do with our lives'. But I am uncertain how far this is consistent with the overall implication of their argument that individuals can never 'need' to engage in self-destructive acts. Thus, to take the extreme case of suicide, if Doyal and Gough grant, as I think they must, that there may be cases where individuals opt for death even where, according to their indices, basic needs for health and autonomy have been met, it might seem that the grounds on which it is argued that such individuals still have a need for survival come close to eliding a need for survival with an instinct for life.

Such an elision, however, surely fails sufficiently to respect differences between needs and instincts both in the ways in which these are experienced by the subject, and in the degree to which they can be over-ridden, and to that degree 'dispensed' with. Instincts for survival are uncontrollable, and manifest in involuntary reflexes for protection of the organism even where this is being destroyed by the subject itself; a need for survival is arguably not of this order insofar as it can be systematically denied (as to a greater or lesser degree it is in all forms of self-destructive behaviour). This is not to deny that the organism requires food even if the subject chooses to fast, but it is to highlight the ambiguous status of the concept of need which operates, as it were, at the juncture between what is organically determined and what is subjectively experienced; between the objective dictates of biology/psychology and human perceptions of what constitutes serious harm: perceptions which these dictates condition but do not finally determine. To point this out is not to deny the basis for ascribing universal needs, but it does emphasise the fact that the grounds for this ascription do indeed lie in a collective agreement about what constitutes serious harm for human beings, rather than in some supposedly wholly objective facts of our nature.[10]

In this connection, I cannot help feeling that Doyal and Gough pay too little attention to the implications for their theory of forms of behaviour which conflict with the satisfaction of the basic need for health. For given the extent to which human beings in all cultures have privileged the pleasures afforded by some forms of consumption

---

[10] One might argue in this connection that insofar as needs *can* be ascribed to persons with no experience or knowledge of them, it is by virtue of their 'genes': it is by reason of biological determination that we can say, for example, that diabetics have a need for insulin whether or not they have ever heard of the substance. However, insofar as we acknowledge that human needs do not reduce to drives of the human organism, we must grant them something more in the way of a subjectively apprehended status.

over the preservation of health, one is inclined to wonder how far the avoidance of 'serious harm'[11] can be defined without reference to a 'hedonist' need. In other words, in restricting human goals to those of physical health and autonomy, Doyal and Gough may be committed to a somewhat puritanical and limited conception of our fundamental motivations: a conception in which the quest for pleasures other than those which directly enhance health or autonomy would seem to be 'unneeded', even irrational, despite the very extensive option for them within the human community.

The role of collective agreement in grounding 'need' can be approached from a somewhat different angle by considering the potential conflicts which can arise between the satisfaction of Doyal and Gough's two basic needs. For it is difficult not to feel that in the case, for example, of the hunger striker, or of one who chooses death rather than surrender to political oppression, what is motivating their denial of their basic need for health and survival is a need to over-ride a need. Doyal and Gough will doubtless agree to this, and claim that this is precisely why they specify that both health and autonomy are equally needed. But given the extent of the differences in the choices which human beings make when faced with these conflicts of need, I think they can offer this line of argument only by raising a question about how far these are equally universal (i.e. agreed to be equally essential to the avoidance of serious harm). In other words, while there may be a consensus that deprivation of either health or autonomy causes severe damage, there may yet be extensive disagreement across cultures and between individuals within any given culture as to which 'harm' is the more serious—which need the more basic when it comes to a conflict between them. If the grounds for attributing universal needs reside in a collective agreement on what constitutes serious harm, lack of an agreement on which is the lesser evil in respect of basic need satisfaction, may put a question mark over the extent to which Doyal and Gough can claim their two needs to be on a par, both equally 'basic'.

Autonomy

One reason I have drawn attention to the question of the experienced or cognisable status of needs lies in the bearing it has for their defence of 'autonomy' as a basic need. For here, as I suggested earlier, I think there are some difficulties in reconciling their theoretical arguments for autonomy with their readiness to assume the capacity of specific

---

[11] The emphasis of my argument is on the *collective* nature of the disposition to minor forms of health impairing, but otherwise pleasurable, consumption. Doyal and Gough cite the argument of G. Thompson (*Needs*, London 1987, pp. 13–14) to the effect that the drive to consume lots of alcohol 'is not linked to preventing serious harm in some universalisable manner, even if harm can accrue in the individual if it remains unsatisfied' (p. 36). This is true. My point concerns the extent to which we might describe as 'needed' (as they often are!) those much commoner forms of pleasure-seeking (moderate consumption of alcohol or stimulants, risky sports and so forth) which although not health promoting, might bespeak a more complex sense of what is collectively deemed to constitute 'avoiding serious harm' than is registered in the specification of health and autonomy as sole conditions of this.

groups to bespeak their needs. Thus even though they argue that the more any group is denied autonomy the less able it will be to appreciate its real needs or question its forms of life, they also on several occasions insist that oppressed groups—they particularly single out women here—will 'know their requirements best'. They therefore seem to allow for a kind of spontaneous or 'gut' knowledge of need among the oppressed even as they analyse the condition of oppression as one which deprives individuals of the 'critical autonomy' essential to arriving at an understanding of their objective needs. They are understandably loath, in their discussion of women's needs, to offend against the feminist sense that these are not the province of 'scientific experts', but it is not clear that this wariness is entirely consistent with their analysis of autonomy or their claim that group interests must not be allowed 'to trump the best available codified knowledge concerning need satisfaction' (p. 309).[12] Or perhaps it would be fairer to suggest that while Doyal and Gough are fully aware of how problematic it can be to analyse what might be called 'political' needs, or the need for emancipation of oppressed groups, as if these were of the same order as the need for salt or serum which a doctor ascribes to a patient, their own approach to these difficulties is at times quite equivocal.

A related issue concerns Doyal and Gough's argument that we should measure the critical optimum levels of health and autonomy by reference to the standards achieved by those nations with the highest overall basic need satisfaction, since this assumes that social groupings or nations with the best records in this respect will be the best placed to criticize their mode of life. But it is not clear that this is empirically borne out. It is true that democratic institutions enjoyed by Western industrial nations have enhanced personal freedom of agency in ways denied under totalitarian regimes and political dictatorships. But it is less clear that they have generated the forms of questioning of their life-style which Doyal and Gough see as desirable. Indeed, it could be said that those nations which have provided most autonomy—the liberal democracies of the West—have also engendered the most complacency about their 'form of life', and certainly have not encouraged the critique of their modes of consumption which would seem essential to promoting the basic need satisfaction of other, less affluent, nations.

What, of course, is at issue here in a profound sense, though any treatment of it must be beyond the scope of this review, is the definition of 'political oppression' itself, and the extent to which this is analysed in terms of directly coercive constraints on personal freedom as opposed to a more covert manufacture of consensus or manipulation of needs and desires. Doyal and Gough allow that the development of 'critical autonomy' is not an automatic function of the provision of a Swedish level of satisfaction of basic need; yet it is not clear how this insight is to be accommodated within the terms of their model of needs. At one

---

[12] I think, too, Doyal and Gough may be a little too ready to assume a collective agreement among women as to their needs given the very diverse aspirations they express, and the very different interpretations which feminists bring to the idea of female emancipation. Nor am I entirely happy with the treatment of the need for safe contraception and child-bearing as if this were specific to women.

point, for example, in elaboration of their claim that autonomy requires the capacity to make 'significant' choices, they argue that 'the choice of a brand of soap powder which is really no different from all the others has more to do with a dimunition of autonomy than its expansion' (p. 66). But they do not argue through the grounds on which they are making these adjudications. If a Swedish citizen, who on their own argument would be benefiting from optimum levels of basic need satisfaction, were to experience the choice between soap powders as 'significant', on what basis is this sense of significance to be dismissed, and how would Doyal and Gough want to explain the loss of autonomy which they claim it would reflect?

These questions bear very directly on the degree to which Doyal and Gough can be said to have established a succcessful case for treating 'autonomy' as a basic need. My own sense here is that while they make out a very strong case for cross-cultural need for 'autonomy' conceived as a capacity to participate in any 'form of life', they are less persuasive when it comes to defending the universality of the need for any more enhanced degree of 'autonomy'—such as would constitute their 'critical optimum'—from the charge of relativism. The problem here, as always, is that the more 'elaborate' the need is conceived as being (or the more the theory 'elaborates' on the need), the harder it is to defend it as basic. Thus, the case for 'autonomy' conceived as a capacity for 'participation' is convincing precisely because its conditions are specified in such minimal terms. They can be said to be satisfied wherever and whenever any individual is possessed of the sanity, cognitive skills, and opportunities to function as a human agent: 'to do, and be held responsible for doing, anything' (p. 53). In this minimal sense, then, even the slave possesses autonomy provided he or she is capable of understanding and carrying out the master's orders. In other words, any person, however restricted their life circumstances, has satisfied the basic need for 'autonomy' at this level provided their physical and mental health has not been so severely impaired as to prevent them performing in the way they otherwise would within their culture. Now this, I think, we can accept. But can the attempt to endow 'critical autonomy' with the same objectivity be rescued from the charge that its standard is evaluative? Surely it has been arrived at in the light of what is *desirable* for all human beings; or, if preferred, in the light of a particular political and moral assessment of what is 'appropriate' to human consumption? Thus, while I understand—and indeed subscribe to—Doyal and Gough's sense that successful participation in a 'form of life' may be consistent with loss of 'critical autonomy'—they cite 'mindless' television watching as a case in point (p. 189)—I am less confident about defending the objectivity of my judgments in this respect. Some may believe, with Arnold, that 'mankind must be compelled to relish the sublime'. But can they justify this as a need? I think Doyal and Gough, in other words, may only be able to convince us of the objectivity of their claims about 'critical autonomy' if they can defend the idea that what they deem to be 'mindless' consumption or 'insignificant' choice entails serious harm. But can they do this in any non-circular way?

Intermediate Needs

Some similar difficulties arguably re-present themselves in respect of what Doyal and Gough term 'intermediate needs' (those needs which must be satisfied for all of us as a condition of health and autonomy). For here, too, I feel they may be only partially successful in securing their argument against the objections of cultural relativism.

Intermediate needs are listed as: nutritional food and clean water; protective housing; a non-hazardous work environment; a non-hazardous physical environment; appropriate health care; security in childhood; significant primary relationships; physical security; economic security; appropriate education; safe birth control and child-bearing.

Lists of this kind, as they admit, are always at risk of being somewhat arbitrary in their selection, though they defend theirs against this charge on the ground that it includes only what is required by their theory of basic needs. As I hope to show, I think this is debatable. But in the first instance, I want to focus on what might be termed the 'differentially normative status' of the items on their list, by which I mean the differing degree to which they can be operationalized (or formulated in terms which would respect differences in individual need while still providing an absolute standard of consumption). Thus, for example, a need for nutritional food can be specified in terms of the requirement for any individual expending a certain amount of energy to consume a certain number of calories, quantum of protein, etc.; and we can allow, I think, that similar formulae are possible for a number of other items on the list. But for some others ('appropriate education', 'significant primary relations', 'economic security') it is much less clear how, in the absence of cross-cultural indices for translating the norms of the 'appropriate', the 'significant' and the 'secure' into common 'contents' of consumption, they provide meaningful guides for welfare provision.

Indeed, some might argue that phrases such as 'economic security', 'significant primary relations', and the like, are so redolent of contemporary, Western perceptions of the 'good' that they very clearly reveal the ethnocentric bias that has been at work in their determination as 'universal'. Doyal and Gough, I imagine, might grant this, but still argue that in the absence of what is regarded in Western industrial societies (though, of course, we must always ask by whom) as constituting an 'appropriate' education or 'significant' primary relationship, individuals of earlier cultures or elsewhere today in the globe, have suffered, or do suffer, from serious impairment of health and autonomy. But they can respond in this way only by making themselves that much more vulnerable to the charge that their basic needs have themselves been defined in culturally relative terms—or, what amounts to the same thing, too purely analytically in terms of whatever is enhanced by an 'appropriate' level of education or a 'significant' primary relationship.

In other words, I am not convinced that Doyal and Gough do manage here to steer their desired path through the Scylla of relativism, on the one hand, and the Charybdis of politically ineffective generality, on the other. For it would seem that at least in the case of some of their cited intermediate needs, either we claim these to be common to all cultures, but only by remaining wholly non-specific as to their content, or we give them sufficient content to guide social policy, but only at the cost of acknowledging the culturally conditioned interpretations we are bringing to these.

Turning now to the point raised earlier concerning the possibly 'arbitrary' character of the list of intermediate needs, let me here simply mention in passing two candidates which, consistently with their theory, should arguably have been included. The first is 'mobility' (or 'appropriate means of transport') given how essential this is if any other intermediate needs are to be met. It may be objected that since 'mobility' is implicitly included within other items, this is a quibble. But it is a quibble which can become quite nagging in that it invites us to consider how much else we are to understand as 'implicitly' included. To cite but one instance of what I have in mind here: are we to understand aesthetic needs as definitely not 'intermediate'—as not essential to basic needs—or as implicitly included in the category of 'appropriate education'? More problematic, perhaps, is the exclusion of sexual relations—a candidate which is considered, but ruled out on the grounds that celibacy is compatible with the maintenance of physical health and autonomy. This one may concede (although it is not clear how we could ever be sure that health or autonomy had not been impaired for lack of sexual contact with others). What cannot, however, be conceded is that individuals, however celibate themselves, do not need sexual relations in virtue of their dependence for the provision of their basic needs on the continual reproduction of the species. In this 'collective' sense, sex must surely qualify as an intermediate need (quite apart from the extent to which it might qualify on the 'hedonist' grounds to which I earlier drew attention).

The Basic and the Non-basic

In this and my final section, I want to address some complex and inter-connected issues concerning the concept of a 'basic' need, the implementation of a 'basic' need programme, and the implications of such a project for our understanding of human gratification. My remarks here will be very general, and have import, I believe, for all theories of need and welfare provision, universalist and relativist, 'thin' and 'thick'.

Doyal and Gough have persuaded me of the political importance of a concept of 'basic' need, but as away into the issues I want to discuss here, it may be worth my stating very briefly the reasons which inclined me in my initial work on the theory of needs, to be wary of the idea of a 'basic' need.[13] One problem I had was that this concept implied a capacity to discriminate not only between needs and wants (or, relatedly, between needed and luxury items of consumption), but also between basic and non-basic needs, on the one hand, and non-basic needs and wants, or luxuries, on the other. The concept, that is, relies on a distinction within the concept of need itself between that which is absolutely indispensable, and that which, relative to what is basic, is dispensable, yet relative to the merely preferred, objectively essential.

Such discriminations seemed to me to be highly problematic, and all the more so, if in defining 'basic' needs as those more determined by a common human nature than culturally conditioned, we overlooked the fact that considerations of cultural relativism apply to any and every form of human consumption, however indispensable to the preservation of life. After all, even if we do grant some needs to be more needed than others, not only do these diverge between individuals, they are also only provided for today over extensive areas of the globe in virtue of a highly complex industrial infrastructure. In this sense, 'basic' need satisfaction is only achieved as a consequence of a very developed system of production and distribution whose various products and services (machinery, transport, communications) can hardly be claimed to be 'basically' needed except at the cost of allowing almost anything to be constituted as such.

Conversely an argument can always be made out for considering even the most profligate and luxurious consumption as no more than a 'specific form' in which a primary need (for food, shelter, and the like) is being met. Rather apposite here is King Lear's remarks on his daughter's clothing:

> Thou art a lady;
> If only to go warm were gorgeous.
> Why, nature needs not what thou gorgeous wear'st,
> Which scarcely keeps thee warm.[14]

Quite apart from the interesting questions Lear raises about the status of the urge to be 'gorgeous' (is it mere want or need, and if need, how basic?), he clearly targets here the problem of the 'cut-off' point between basic and non-consumption. Given that a 'basic' need for warmth requires the donning of some apparel, on what criteria exactly would we decide that any item of clothing employed had ceased to be 'appropriate' to the gratification of this need and had begun to function as the satisfier of a non-basic need or mere want?

These remarks should not be construed as implying that Doyal and Gough have not seen the difficulties here. They will defend their book as precisely offering a solution to them by providing the necessary and sufficient conditions for something to count as a 'basic' need. I raise these points, rather, because they highlight what may be a problem with Doyal's and Gough's relative disregard of the issue of *non*-basic needs or wants, and with the political neutrality, as it were, of their tendency simply to accept that the *specific form* taken by the satisfiers of intermediate needs will be culturally relative and highly divergent. In this sense, an emphasis on our common need for protection from the elements, while important, does not engage with those highly charged discriminations which must also be made between the needed or less-than-needed status of the specific products (the specific kinds of clothing or housing) with which our basic need is being satisfied.

---

[13] I am referring here primarily to *On Human Needs*, *op. cit.*, though some of the considerations I raise here are further elaborated in my review of Michael Ignatieff's *The Needs of Strangers* in *New Left Review* 152 (reprinted in *Troubled Pleasures*, Verso 1990, pp. 77–86), and in 'Who Needs Socialism?' (*Troubled Pleasures*, pp. 45–70).
[14] *King Lear*, Act II, scene 4, 264–7.

Or to put this point rather differently: I have always feared that in focusing too exclusively on needs that can be said to be common to human well-being, we overlooked the critical role of the form taken by the specific satisfiers of these common needs in the affluent and 'best performing' nations in creating basic need deprivation elsewhere in the globe. For what has to be targeted by a politics of need, so it seems to me, is not only what we share in the way of basic needs, but the causal relationship between the forms in which some are meeting these needs and the forms in which others are being deprived. Thus, to cite but one indicator of the very considerable problems raised in this area, which although acknowledged by Doyal and Gough, perhaps deserved more attention: Sweden, as we have seen, emerges statistically as the 'average best performer' in meeting needs and is looked to by Doyal and Gough as providing a moral yardstick for need satisfaction in the long term. But Sweden's per capita energy consumption is one of the highest in the world (see Table 13.1, p. 289), and certainly not one it seems automatically moral and logical to attempt to universalize—particularly when considered from the point of view of future generations.

Ecology and Human Needs

This brings me to some considerations about the generalizability of the basic needs model provided by Doyal and Gough. This is a vast and ramified subject, and I here do not propose to engage with the economic and political obstacles which currently stand in the way of any practical implementation of a basic needs satisfaction programme for all. I agree with Doyal and Gough that the obstacles here are almost all traceable to the dynamics of global capitalism; and I am also in substantial agreement with their analysis of the possible political forces and agencies which might tend to their removal (even if I am far from sanguine about the likelihood of mobilizing an effective opposition at this level). But the 'politics of need' in this sense raises huge questions which cannot be done justice to in the space of a brief review, and I shall therefore not pursue them here.

What, however, I do want to raise is a set of rather more abstract issues which arise in virtue of our current ecological situation. Doyal and Gough are quite aware of the bearing of ecological considerations on their argument, and discuss them at various points in their book. But I find their treatment unsatisfactory on a number of fairly minor points of detail,[15] and for the more general reason that it does not

---

[15] For example, I have some difficulties with their advocacy of a 'needs tax', insofar as this presumes a continuation of the differential growth rates between First, Second and Third Worlds. No doubt it is pragmatically correct to assume this, and idealistic to suppose that global policy on needs could be directed to anything more than the alleviation of the effects of poverty, at least in the immediate future. But the trouble with the tax idea is that it is corrective of the symptoms of inequity rather than directly addressed to its causes. In a general way, I think there is a problem about the Rawlsian presumption of social inequality which underlies Doyal and Gough's arguments in this area, since it suggests that deficiencies in basic need satisfaction are to be made good at the level of redistribution, rather than requiring fundamental alterations at the level of production. A related difficulty is their tendency to view economic development as threatened by pollution (see p. 143), since I think this represents an inversion of priorities: it is

sufficiently attend to the question of the need satisfaction for all which is practically consistent with indefinite ecological sustainability—particularly as this concerns the 'basic'/'non-basic' discrimination.

Let me here, for purposes of bringing out what is at stake, proffer the (all too purely academic) hypothesis that all directly economic and political obstacles to the universalization and equalization of basic need satisfaction have been removed. The question then arises, as to what common standard of living would be ecologically viable (consistent with future generations enjoying the same level of environmental consumption in perpetuo)?

Clearly (as Doyal and Gough imply in their discussion of ecological sustainability pp. 242–6), this question is almost imponderable, given the number of over-determining variables of which any projected assessment would need to take acount (for example, rate of population growth, and the impact on its decline of any improvement in need satisfaction among the most deprived global communities; levels of available resources, and technical potential for continuously enhancing the efficiency of their use; the rate and extent of pollution control and of new resources development, and so forth). All the same, I think we may at least entertain the possibility that even with the best will in the world, and the most equitable and efficient use of resources, we might not manage to attain indefinitely to anything more than an optimal (Swedish level) satisfaction of basic needs. But, allowing this hypothesis, what then becomes of their designation as 'basic'? If all that we might be able to achieve consistently with ecological sustainability is to universalize in practice, now and for future generations, what Doyal and Gough theorize as universal needs, then what are we to make of the idea that these needs are 'basic' because they are the primary requirements which must be met as a condition of any further human gratification and self-fulfilment?

Doyal and Gough might well consider this to be itself a somewhat luxurious speculation, as in a sense it is. For it certainly seems quite sufficiently utopian for our times to offer the prospect that all now, and in the future, might have access to even half of what Sweden is able to provide for its citizens! But I want to conclude by offering this 'indulgent' speculation up for consideration because of the bearing it has for the conceptualization of certain needs as 'basic', and hence on the whole issue of human gratification. For if it is true, as I am surmising it might be, that Doyal and Gough's 'basic' needs are the most we can hope to realize globally over time, then have we not in a sense surreptitiously subverted the idea of their being 'basic'? Has not their current theoretical designation as basic exposed a certain, culturally specific, apperception of human potentialities at its heart which should give us pause for thought? For if 'basic' needs can only be met for all at the cost of reneging on 'wants' (or even on that other class of

---

[15] (cont.)
economic expansion which is the problem because it generates pollution. Finally, I think more recognition should be given to the ecological problems of applying anything like a Swedish model of consumption to Third World countries, not just in resource terms, but in terms of its effects on global warming and ozone depletion.

'non-basic' needs which is implied but not discussed by Doyal and Gough) should we not morally condemn any encouragement of the view that there is something more to which we should aspire than physical health and autonomy? Relatedly, should we not submit ourselves to the rather sobering thought that it is an awareness, however subliminal it may be, that a more egalitarian global culture will cut off the prospects of any human 'flourishing' beyond that provided through basic need satisfaction, that underlies the nonchalance of affluent governments, and many of their citizens, in regard to matters of social justice and ecological sustainability? Better, says the voice of affluence, that some should flourish, even at the cost of the survival of others, than that all should manage little more than to live 'by bread alone'.

Now, it might be said in response to these speculations that they are themselves altogether too conservative in their conception of what constitutes a distinctively human 'flourishing'. That they have force, only if we assume that not living 'by bread alone' always means, shall we say, 'eating cake', that is to say, would always involve a refinement and sophistication—a luxurification—of our material needs. Thus, it will be said, it is only if we unthinkingly adopt a 'materialist-consumerist' conception of what it means to 'flourish' or expand on 'basic' need satisfaction, that we shall concern ourselves with these standard, liberal-economic, anxieties about the 'stagnating' effects of an essentially stable and reproductive provision of basic needs for all. If we cut loose from the idea of an 'improved living standard' engendered by a materialist culture, then we need no longer think of 'wants' or 'non-basic' needs always as extensions of, or ever more baroque—and resource-hungry—constructions upon primary physical needs, but as an altogether less materially encumbered, and encumbering self-development and exploration.

By and large, I am in agreement with the spirit of this line of response, with its suggestion that a 'decent and humane' standard of living for all is quite compatible with the extension in gratification of 'wants' provided these cease to be so fixated on tangible goods, and more directed to so-called 'spiritual' pleasures. Indeed, I would even claim that in restraining our material consumption we shall expand other dimensions of human enjoyment insofar as these are reliant on the less tangible goods of free time, space, safety, a non-polluted atmosphere, and so forth. If, however, these rather general arguments are in any sense valid, then what they indicate, I think, is the importance of complementing any theory of 'basic' need with an altered 'imaginary' of human wants: with what I have elsewhere referred to as a new 'erotics of consumption'.[16] For if it is true that the more affluent peoples of the world need to reduce their material *wants* if there is to be anything approaching to a universal extension of their level of basic *need* satisfaction, then it is surely equally true that a condition of the emergence of a will to sobriety in their material consumption will be the fostering of an altered conception of their pleasures. In this sense, being realist about needs may require us to be utopian about

[16] See 'Re-thinking Ourselves' in Dan Smith and E.P. Thompson (eds) *Prospectus for a Habitable Planet*, Penguin 1985 (re-printed in *Troubled Pleasures*, pp. 23–43).

wants, and the political force of any theory of basic needs prove dependant on the imagining of a new hedonist vision.

Let me only add finally, that if the primary reference of these rather general remarks on ecological sustainability and human gratification has been to Doyal and Gough's argument, it is not because I regard this as specially open to the criticism that it neglects or abstracts from these issues. On the contrary, I would argue that it is a relativist emphasis on the importance of understanding and meeting culturally generated and situated needs which may be more properly charged with being nonchalant about the future human and ecological consequences of promoting its particular conception of human flourishing. Certainly, from this point of view I find the 'thick' theory perspective on needs highly problematic given its reliance on a kind of Marxian conception of needs as ever more richly developed and indefinitely developing.[17] At any rate, it seems to be important that anyone invoking the goal of persons 'rich in need'[18] and the idea of a never ending discovery of new needs, should address the issue of the inherently limited (and currently very unevenly distributed) resources available for the realization of such a pluralist utopia of need satisfaction—and also the issue of its compatibility with the 'well-seeking' of future generations. The populist and democratic impulses of a 'thick' theory approach are of critical importance to the avoidance of paternalistic and bureaucratic approaches to welfare provision. But it would be inconsistent to concern ourselves only with respecting the subjectively authenticated needs of specific groups within particular cultural settings, without considering the democratic implications of meeting these welfare demands on the need-fulfilment of others elsewhere and in the future. In this respect, Doyal and Gough's emphasis on 'basic' needs, and their commitment to a theory which observes the logical distinction between the 'needed' and 'wanted' or 'subjectively preferred', has for me the very considerable value of allowing us to see how and why a theory of welfare will need to be placed within this broader framework of social and ecological considerations.

---

[17] Cf. note 6.

[18] My objection is not to this concept in itself or to Marxian notions about the 'rich development of individuality' and the dynamic of needs, but rather to their abstraction. Unless and until we specify more precisely what kinds of needs and consumption we are talking about, it is impossible to assess the desirability or practicality of the goals they express. I take it we are not here aspiring to persons 'rich in needs' for second homes, private aeroplanes and motor-cruisers. But if not, what criterion of need is being employed here, and will not any such criterion presume 'objective' rights of discrimination between competing claims?

[5]

NEED: THE IDEA WON'T DO—BUT WE STILL NEED IT

A. J. Culyer

If 'need' is to be a practical idea, useful in particular in helping people to allocate health care resources more efficiently and equitably, it has to have particular characteristics, the absence of any one of which makes it virtually useless. Unfortunately, in the common contexts in which the term has been taken seriously (political slogan-mongering and—on quite a different plane—philosophical discourse) at least one of these necessary conditions is always absent. The conditions proposed are these:

1. that its value-content be up-front and easily interpretable;
2. that it be directly derived from the objective(s) of the health care system;
3. that it be capable of empirical application in issues of horizontal and vertical distribution;
4. that it should be service and person specific;
5. that it should enable a straightforward link to be made to resources;
6. that it should not, if acted upon as a distributional principle, produce manifestly inequitable results.

Even when each of these conditions is met, 'need' turns out to be at best an incomplete criterion for choosing between different distributions of resources *on grounds of equity*. This seems odd, as nearly everyone thinks of 'need' as something closely bound up with equity (compared, say, with efficiency).

That 'need' is value-laden should be self-evident. The values embodied in various usages are, however, all too often obscure. The difficulty is understandable, for nearly every usage implies both a factual or positive statement (such as 'if person A does not receive entity X, then person A will have demonstrably different characteristics') and a value-laden or normative statement (such as "if the need is met, the demonstrably different characteristics are better than those if it is not met"). Recognizing that these two aspects are inherent in the idea of 'need' is the first step towards creating a workable concept. 'Demonstrably' is added on the grounds that changes in people's characteristics that are not observable (or that could not become observable through the creation of appropriate instruments to make them so) are not interesting factual statements.

While anyone is free to inject their own values into an idea of 'need', embodying what seem to be the driving values of health services (which will doubtless differ from culture to culture) seems a better way forward if the aim is to create a workable concept that people can actually use (people who, for example, are contractually committed as managers or health professionals to deliver on goals set for them by the system in which they are employed). This turns needs-talk away from *advocacy* (where the writer is essentially urging his or her own values) into *consultancy* (where the writer accepts what are perceived to be the values of his or her clients).

Horizontal equity means treating the same those who are the same in a relevant respect (such as having the same 'need'). Vertical equity means treating differently those who are different in relevant respects (such as having different 'need'). Neither type of equity is operational if the concept of 'need' is not sufficiently quantifiable for judgments of sameness or difference to be made with acceptable precision for the purposes in hand.

For service and person-specificity one must add prepositions: something (like a specific medical act) has to be 'needed' (is necessary) *for* something else to be accomplished. We must ask also *for what* it is 'needed' (necessary). And we must also ask *for whom* it is 'needed' (necessary). The first requirement is crucial in health care, for it directs attention towards the crucial question of whether *in fact* (or whether it is *probable that*) the act in question will have the effects (for the better) expected. Since so much in medical (and health) care is of unknown effectiveness (or is even of known ineffectiveness), directing attention in this way alerts one to the possibility that someone may even be seriously ill without there being any reasonable prospect (reasonable in the eyes of those who have examined the matter via, say, randomized controlled trials, overviews or meta-analyses) of medical care effectively changing their characteristics for the better. In such cases, whatever else they 'need', they do not 'need' the sort of health or medical services that might be available. Too many unsubstantiated assertions of 'need' *assume*, rather than *enquire* whether, the acts in question really are *necessary* .

Editorial

One should ask *for what* it is 'needed' because there ought to be some more ultimate good from which the 'need' in question derives its moral force (for example, health is 'needed' in order that one may 'flourish').

It should be person-specific or, at the planning and management level, group-specific since one must be able to identify who it is that 'needs' whatever is asserted to be 'needed'. One can trivialize these requirements. The statement 'surgeons need manual dexterity' is hardly elucidated by asking 'why?', for the answer may be that 'surgeons need manual dexterity in order to be surgeons'. Nor is the statement 'I need open-heart surgery' much elucidated by the justification 'if I am to live'. However, the statement 'I need prophylactic ligno-caine following my heart attack' may be false if I fear the risk of early mortality more than I value the prevention of arrhythmias. And the statement "I need gastric freezing for my ulcer" is plain false, for gastric freezing will do me no good at all and may do me harm.

The link to resources is there as a necessary condition on the ground that the context in which we most urgently need a workable concept of 'need' is to resolve (or at least inform) questions of resource distribution. While the logic in a statement like 'A needs to be healthy if she is to flourish' might meet the first two requirements, it may fail the third and fourth. One can grant a 'need' for health without granting a 'need' for medical care. A particular ground for denying the second 'need' might be because all known medical care is also known to be ineffective in the case in point. There may be other derivative 'needs' arising from the first claim (such as need for palliative care, or for more research into effective medicine) but, in the state of knowledge as it is, today, these 'needs' may coexist with the absence of 'need' for medical care.

One may as well go further: in many cases it may be possible to argue that there is more than one way of meeting a 'need'. Which one, then, is *really* 'needed'? The answer to this is that it is the one that is most cost-effective. A procedure that is less cost-effective than another cannot be held to be more needed. And even if one is to think of it as equally needed, we may as well try to be *efficient* in the way we meet 'needs' and so commit ourselves to the idea that the procedures that may be 'needed' are those that are the most cost-effective at meeting the 'need' in question. If there should turn out to be more than one of these, then we shall be indifferent between them (if there are no other grounds for preferring one to the other)—the 'need' might be met equally well through either means.

One idea of 'need' that nearly meets the requirements laid down is that of "capacity to benefit". Its value content can be made clear by elucidating the idea of 'benefit'. If an objective of the health care system is to increase 'health gain' (as it is in Britain),

then interpreting 'benefit' in terms of some acceptable measure of health gives the definition the contextual relevance insisted on by the second requirement. If health gain is sufficiently quantifiable for one to be able to identify potential gains as 'more', 'less' or 'same', then the third requirement is met. Moreover, the concept distinguishes between ill health (which may or may not imply a 'need' for health) and a 'need' for medical care (when medical care really is necessary). However, it falls at the fourth hurdle (and also would fail the fifth). If one can identify both the procedures that would (with a sufficient probability of success) generate the benefit and the sorts of patients (actual or potential) who will (probably) benefit, then that is fine, but the idea of 'need' is now becoming subtly transformed from capacity to benefit to a 'need' *for* person and service specific resources. This may seem a trivial distinction, but it can easily be shown to have major consequences for resource distributions—especially if one is seeking equity in distribution—as will shortly be seen.

A much better definition is this: a need for health care is the minimum amount of resources required *to exhaust a person's capacity to benefit*. This definition has all the good elements of the capacity to benefit notion. It also quantifies the resources that are needed (the inverted commas now being dropped) and hence meets the fourth and fifth requirements. At the planning and managerial level, it may for most purposes be adequate (at least in the National Health Service) to treat capacity to benefit as potential health gain. At more personal levels of application (which would have to be fed into more macro decision-making) the idea of capacity to benefit will often have to take account of more complex dimensions of benefit. For example, my need for surgery for my cancer of the larynx may be inadequately assessed in terms of, say, the probability that I shall live longer having the surgery rather than having irradiation alone. But I may say that I need irradiation rather than surgery on the grounds that I prefer the probability of a shorter life with a more usable voice than a longer life without one. Since some patients undoubtedly do prefer this, the planning and management system should provide for sufficient flexibility to alow me to exercise my choice (assuming, of course, that the values embodied in the health care system include sufficient weight on individual preferences of this sort), hence the importance of feedback into macro decision-making about resource distributions.

It is immediately apparent that all needs to not have to met. The purpose of the concept is, indeed, to enable people to choose on grounds of equity how resources ought to be distributed *given that there are not enough to go round to meet all needs*. Moreover, since there are needs for things that are not health services, so to distribute resources to health care as to eliminate all need for it would be inefficient (leaving lost of more important needs, even of the same people, unmet elsewhere) and inequitable (one would be meeting the trivial needs of those needing health care while leaving those of people needing other things unaddressed—and one may even be worsening the distribution of the unmet needs too).

The potentially important difference between the implications of distributing according to need, to capacity to benefit, or to ill health can be illustrated by the following two examples (each assuming that there are insufficient resources to eliminate all need).

Max and Moritz have equal (ill-)health. Suppose that they also have the same need—the amount of resources required to eliminate the capacity of each to benefit is the same. However, their capacities to benefit differ: whereas Max can be restored to full health with the available technology and within health service global resources, Moritz's health can be improved only up to a limit. Even if all resources are used that are effective, he remains chair-bound. In terms of need, we have a horizontal equity issue and, if resources are to be allocated in proportion to need, each ought to receive the same. However, since Max's capacity to benefit is higher than Moritz's he will receive a larger increment of health. Since the two started off with the same (ill-)health, the result of distributing resources equitably (and in this case equally) according to need is that the final distribution of health is unequal (in Max's favour). Suppose that resources were allocated to the capacity to benefit equity principle (in this case, an issue in vertical equity). Since Max has the higher capacity, he will receive more than under the need principle, so the resulting distribution of health will not only be unequal but even more unequal than that which results from the application of the needs principle.

In the case just discussed, the two started off with equal (ill-)health. Suppose Ollie is iller than Stan. Let them have the same capacity to benefit. But suppose also that Ollie, though iller, can have his capacity to benefit fully achieved with fewer resources than Stan, so Stan's need is greater. Distributing resources according to initial health state requires for (vertical) equity that Ollie receives more than Stan. Since they have equal capacities to benefit, Ollie will have a larger health gain. Whether it is sufficiently larger to result in a reversal of the health distribution after compared to before will depend on whether the vertical equity principle involves proportional or more than proportional discrimination in favour of the worse off individual. Distributing resources according to capacity to benefit requires that each receive the same (horizontal equity), so they will end up as unequal as they started. Distributing resources according to need (vertical equity) will require more resources to be awarded to Stan (his need being greater). Stan will therefore still end with better health than Ollie since their capacities to benefit are the same.

There are three points to be emphasized from these examples. One is that *choice of distributive equity rule matters*. First, choice of equity rule makes, in general, a difference both to the amount of resource each ought to receive and to the outcome distribution of health. So one must choose one's preferred rule. Second, using one rule rather than another can turn a horizontal equity problem into a vertical equity problem, and vice versa. Third, none of the rules has explicit regard to the *resultant, post hoc*, distribution of health (nor, if health is a necessary condition for an even more ultimate good, such as 'flourishing', does it have regard to the distribution of that more ultimate good). Distribution according to initial health accords an oddly asymmetrical priority to health (or ill-health) today rather than tomorrow. Capacity to benefit, even though it may be egalitarian in giving a 'unit' of health equal weight whoever receives it, can increase inequality in the distribution of health after health care has been allocated 'equitably'. Distribution of resources according to need can produce similar (though not usually the same) unequal distribution of health (which may be more unequal than it initially was).

What you make of these implications will doubtless depend in part on the view taken of the importance for fairness of achieving greater equality in the distribution of health itself. If greater equality *in that* were the requirement, then none of the three rules discussed is sure to achieve it, and each may, given an appropriate configuration of initial distributions of health, capacities to benefit, and needs, actually make things less rather than more equal. Since all fairness rules have something to do with equality, one needs therefore to answer the fundamental question: *equality of what?*

If one goes for greater equality in the distribution of health, then each of the rules, including distribution according to need, is flawed. Distribution ought to be made according to a judgement of the ways in which alternative patterns will promote greater equality of heath. The judgement will need to be informed by information about the current states of ill-health of populations, groups and individuals, about capacities to benefit, and about needs. But it will be the evaluated interplay between them that will determine who gets what. In practical terms, collective purchasers of health care (like British health authorities) must become sufficiently well-briefed as to the prevailing distribution of illness, the epidemiological evidence on effectiveness of preventive and therapeutic care, and the economic evidence on cost-effectiveness, for them to be able to make informed judgements for achieving greater equity on their patches.

Need remains, however, a slightly special case. Although it is insufficient as a distributional principle on its own, having a need remains a necessary condition for receiving anything at all. And to establish whether needs exist one must determine capacities to benefit for, as has been seen, absence of capacity to benefit implies no need at all. So needs and capacities to benefit must be assessed. For them to be assessed requires that *access* to initial assessment (diagnostic) procedures be as cheap as it can be made. As cheap, *not as equal*, as possible. Indeed, for some individuals, positive inducements might be necessary for them to make the initial contact with the health service. Here seems to be a fundamental case (given the values assumed) for having universal, zero (possibly even negative) price access to health care. Once that access has been achieved, however, no general equality in 'treatment' is implied. Indeed, what is implied is the basic equity of whatever *inequality in the distribution of health case* is required

to make the maximum reduction in the *inequality of the distribution of health*.

Finally, should the ethical focus indeed fall ultimately on the *post hoc* distribution of health, the question will arise as to whether the needs that should be searched out are needs only for medical care (or indeed for medical care at all). The quest then stretches out beyond the medical services into the wider realm of th determinants of health, the cost-effectiveness of policies that might affect health through these alternative pathways, and the possibility arises that equity in health is best achieved through entirely different routes from medical care. But that is entirely another editorial, as well as another approach to health policy.

[6]

A taxonomy of social need

JONATHAN BRADSHAW

One of the most crucial problems facing the social services is how to identify social need. This article attempts to provide a framework for clearer thinking about need.

The concept of social need is inherent in the idea of social service. The history of the social services is the story of the recognition of needs and the organization of society to meet them. The Seebohm Report (1) was deeply concerned with the concept of need, though it never succeeded in defining it. It saw that 'The Personal Social Services are large scale experiments in ways of helping those in need'.

Despite this interest it is often not clear in a particular situation what is meant by social need. When a statement is made to the effect that a person or group of persons are in need of a given service, what is the quality that differentiates them—what definition of social need is being used?

The concept of social need is of particular interest to economists. They have a clearcut measure of 'effective demand': demand is 'effective' when people are prepared to back it by pecuniary allocation and ineffective or non-existent when they are not. This measure will not do for the social services, because there is normally no link between service and payment (though some economists think there ought to be). If the social services are trying to cope with need without limiting it by the ability to pay, how is it actually assessed?

In practice, four separate definitions are used by administrators and research workers.

I. NORMATIVE NEED

Normative need is that which the expert or professional, administrator or social scientist defines as need in any given situation. A 'desirable' standard is laid down and is compared with the standard that actually exists—if an individual or group falls short of the desirable standard then they are identified as being in need. Thus the BMA's nutritional standard is used as a normative measure of the adequacy of a diet (2). The Incapacity Scale developed by Townsend (3) and the measure of social isolation used by Tunstall (4) are also examples of normative standards used as a basis of need. A normative definition of need is in no sense absolute. It may not correspond with need established by other definitions. It may be tainted with a charge of paternalism— i.e. the use of middle-class norms to assess need in a working-class context—though where the aspirations are to middle-class standards this may be reasonable. A further difficulty with the normative definition of need is that there may well be different and possibly conflicting standards laid down by different experts. The decision about what is desirable is not made in a vacuum. As Walton (5) has pointed out, the statement 'X is in need' is often taken as an empirical fact. This is not so. It is a value-judgement entailing the following propositions: X is in a state Y, Y is incompatible with the values held in society Z. Therefore Y state should be changed. So the normative definition of need may be different according to the value orientation of the expert—on his judgements about the amount of resources that should be devoted to meeting the need or whether or not the available skills can solve the problem. Normative standards change

A taxonomy of social need 73

in time both as a result of developments in knowledge, and the changing values of society.

II. FELT NEED

Here need is equated with want. When assessing need for a service, the population is asked whether they feel they need it. In a democracy it could be imagined that felt need would be an important component of any definition of need, but a felt need measure seems to only be used regularly in studies of the elderly and in community development. Felt need is, by itself, an inadequate measure of 'real need'. It is limited by the perceptions of the individual—whether they know there is a service available, as well as a reluctance in many situations to confess a loss of independence. On the other hand, it is thought to be inflated by those who ask for help without 'really needing it'.

III. EXPRESSED NEED

Expressed need or demand is felt need turned into action. Under this definition total need is defined as those people who demand a service. One does not demand a service unless one feels a need, but on the other hand, it is common for felt need not to be expressed by demand. Expressed need is commonly used in the health services where waiting-lists are taken as a measure of unmet need. Waiting-lists are generally accepted as a poor definition of 'real need'—especially for presymptomatic cases.

IV. COMPARATIVE NEED

By this definition a measure of need is obtained by studying the characteristics of the population in receipt of a service. If there are people with similar characteristics not in receipt of a service, then they are in need. This definition has been used to assess needs both of individuals and areas. Bleddyn Davies (6) has identified the community-wide factors which

indicate a high incidence of pathology in one area which are
not present in another. Need established by this method is
the gap between what services exist in one area and what
services exist in another, weighted to take account of the
difference in pathology. This is an attempt to standardize
provision, but provision may still not correspond with need.
The question still has to be asked—supply at what level?
The statement that one area A is in need in comparison with
another area B does not necessarily imply that area B is still
not in need.

Comparative need used to define individuals in need can
be illustrated by the following statements: 'this person X is
in receipt of a service because he has the characteristics
A–N. This person Z has also the characteristics A–N but
is not receiving the service. Therefore Z is in need.' The
difficulty in this situation is to define the significant characteristics. The method has been used by some local health
authorities to compile a risk register of babies in need of
special attention from the preventive services. Conditions
which in the past have been associated with handicap such
as forceps delivery, birth trauma, birth to older mothers,
etc., are used as indicators to babies in special need. The
definition is more commonly used in an *ad-hoc* way—a crude
rule of precedence to assess eligibility for selective services
provided by the personal social services.

Fig. 3.1 demonstrates diagramatically the interrelation of
the four definitions. Plus (+) and minus (−) denote the
presence or absence of need by each of the foregoing
definitions, i.e. + − − + is a need that is accepted as such
by the experts, but which is neither felt nor demanded by
the individual despite the fact that he has the same characteristics as those already being supplied with the service.
Other examples of the twelve possible combinations are
given. It will be noted that none of the circles in Fig. 3.1 are
coterminous and the problem the policymaker has to face,
is deciding what part of the total is 'real need'—that is need
it is appropriate to try to meet.

A taxonomy of social need　　75

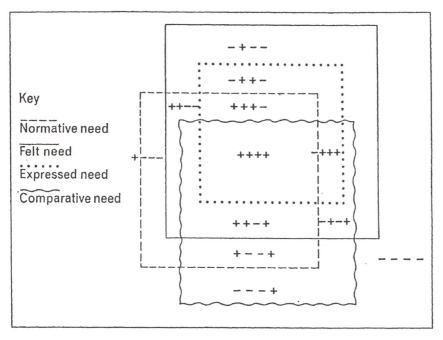

FIGURE 3.1

I. + + + +

This is the area where all definitions overlap, or (using an analogy from studies of intelligence tests) the 'g' factor of need. An individual is in need by all definitions and so this is the least controversial part of need.

2. + + − +

Demand is limited by difficulties of access to a service. Although the individual is in need by all other definitions he has not wanted to, or been able to, express his need. Difficulties of access may be due to a stigma attached to the receipt of a service, geographical distances that make it difficult to claim, charges which are a disincentive to take up, administrative procedures that deter claimants or merely ignorance about the availability of the service. Demand must also vary according to how intense is the felt need.

Two examples of need of this type, are the non-take-up of means-tested benefits, and the under-utilization of fair rent machinery.

3. + + − −

Here need is accepted as such by the expert and is felt by the individual but there is no demand as well as, and possibly because of, the absence of supply. Examples may be need for family planning facilities for unmarried girls, free nursery education, and need for chiropody services for the elderly.

4. − + + +

Here the need is not postulated by the pundits, but is felt, demanded, and supplied. The less-essential types of cosmetic surgery are examples. Also some of the work of the GP, it is often thought could come into this category, i.e. the prescribing of 'clinically unnecessary' drugs. The pundits may suggest that a compassionate label for this category could be 'inappropriate need'. On the other hand, the pundits may be exercising inappropriate value-judgements.

5. + + + −

A need that is postulated, felt, and demanded but not supplied. These needs represent likely growth areas in the social services. An example would be the need for a fatherless families allowance or adequate wage-related pensions. Resources are usually the limiting factor in this category.

6. + − − +

Here the need is postulated by the experts and similar persons are being supplied with the service, but the need is neither felt nor demanded by the individual. Some of the work of the probation officer, or the health visitors' post-natal visits (when they are not wanted) are examples of meeting this kind of need. Another example is the unwanted supply of expensive central-heating plant in public sector housing.

7. + − − −

Here need is postulated by the pundits or professionals. Examples could be found in the area of preventive medicine. To the layman the need is probably obscure, technical, and new. The need to provide fluoride in the water supplies was accepted as such by the public health experts long before it was felt, demanded, or supplied.

8. − − − +

Here a service is supplied despite the absence of need as assessed by the other definitions. This could be called a service-oriented service. Examples can be found in the many small and outdated charities to which the charity commissioners are striving to apply the doctrine of *cy prés*, i.e. paying electricity bills instead of buying farthing candles for old ladies at Michaelmas.

9. − + + −

This is need which is not appreciated by the experts and is not supplied, but which is felt and demanded. Prescriptions for bandages requested from the GP may be an example of this. Another example is the need for improved services—the need for improved educational maintenance allowances.

10. − + − −

This represents felt needs which are not within the ambit of the social services to meet. Perhaps loneliness—or the need for love/company is an example of this. A need for wealth or fame are certainly examples.

11. — + — +

A need that is not postulated by the experts but is felt, not expressed, but is supplied. People feel a need to make contributions for social benefits and the need is met by insurance stamps, but many experts feel it would be simpler to finance these benefits wholly through taxation.

12. — — — —

Absence of need by all definitions.

To illustrate how this could be used by research-workers and policymakers it might be useful to outline a hypothetical situation. The taxonomy will be discussed in relation to housing need, but there is no significance in this choice—the discussion is equally relevant to any other area of need. A local housing authority is concerned about the housing position of the elderly in their area. They wish to have assessment of the need for public sector housing for this age-group. A research-worker is therefore commissioned to do a study of the housing need. The first problem the research-worker has to face is the question of what constitutes housing need? He can either make a decision as to what he himself believes housing need to be, or he can produce information on the amount of need under each section of the taxonomy and allow the policymaker to decide what part of the total they regard as 'real need'. The research-worker decides to take the latter course of action. This will provide the maximum information with the minimum number of value-judgements. In order to produce a figure for each section of the taxonomy, he must first decide on the amount of need under each of the four separate definitions.

Normative need. It has already been pointed out that there is no one definition of normative need. Let us assume that the local housing authority are laying down the norms in this situation and they would agree that old persons living in homes lacking any of the basic amenities and old persons living in overcrowded accommodation are in need by their standards. An estimate of the number of persons in this situation could be obtained by a sample survey.

Felt need. An estimate of the degree of felt need can be obtained by means of the same sample survey by asking the respondents whether they are satisfied with their present housing and if not whether they would like to move. Ignoring the problems inherent in exploring people's attitudes on such a delicate question and remembering that their attitudes will be affected by their knowledge of alternative housing opportunities, as well as their fears about the upheaval of the move, another measure of need is obtained.

Expressed need. The local housing authority's waiting-lists provide the measure of expressed need in this context. It is at the same time the easiest measure of need to obtain and the most inadequate. On the one hand the list may be inflated by persons who have resolved their housing problem since they applied for the housing and yet who have not withdrawn their application, and on the other hand the list may underestimate expressed need if certain categories are excluded from the waiting-list; there may be a residence qualification, applications from owner-occupiers may not be accepted unless they are overcrowded, and persons who have refused the first offer may also be excluded. All these exclusions mean that the waiting-list is not an adequate measure of expressed need but because it is the only one available, it is used as another measure of need.

Comparative need. The measure of comparative need is more difficult to obtain. It would entail investigating the characteristics of elderly persons already in public sector housing and then through a sample survey obtaining an estimate of the number of persons in the community (not in public sector housing) who have similar characteristics. As the local housing authority's norms have been taken for the measure of normative need, and as the local housing authority is responsible for choosing their tenants, it is likely that in this example the characteristics of tenants will be similar to those norms and thus the measure of comparative need will be very similar (though not necessarily identical) to the measure of normative need.

The research-worker has now produced four separate but interrelated measures of need. By sorting he is able to put a figure against each of the permutations of the four measures. For instance:

+ + − + This will consist of persons whose houses are overcrowded or lack basic amenities, who want to move but who are not on the council waiting-list and yet who are 'as deserving as' other residents in council accommodation.

− + − − This will consist of persons whose housing is considered satisfactory by local authority standards, who are not on the council waiting-list, and are not in need when compared with other residents in council property and yet who want to move.

So now the policymaker is presented with a picture of 'total need' for public sector housing in their area. He is now able to use the taxonomy to clarify his decision-making. Instead of housing being allocated on the basis of either first come first served, or whether the old person is articulate, energetic, and knowledgeable enough to get on the housing waiting-list, it can now be allocated on the basis of explicit priorities. No longer is the local authority providing houses 'to meet need' but rather providing houses to meet certain specific conditions of need.

Thus the policymaker can do one of two things. Either he can decide that certain categories of the total (say + + + +, + + − +, + − − +, − + + +, + + + −) constitute 'real need' and plan to provide enough housing for the numbers in these groups, or secondly if it is found that need is very large and his resources are limited, he can decide that certain categories of need should be given priority. For instance, he may decide that category + + − + : those in need who have not applied for help (the iceberg below the waterline) should be given priority over category − + + + : those in need on all bases except that they are already adequately housed on a normative measure.

The policymaker can now return to the research-worker. Having made his priorities explicit he could ask the research worker to carry out a detailed study of the 'real need' categories to ascertain their aetiology so that in future they may be more easily identified and the services explicitly designed to get at and help them. The research worker could also use the taxonomy as a framework for monitoring the effects on need of technical advances, demographic change, changes in the standard of living, and improvements in the services.

This taxonomy may provide a way forward in an area where precise thinking is needed for both theoretical and practical reasons. Without some further classification much social policy must remain a matter of political hunches and academic guesswork. The taxonomy provides no easy solutions either for the research-worker or the policymaker. The research-worker is still faced with difficult methodological problems and the policymaker has still to make complex decisions about which categories of need should be given priority. But the taxonomy may help to clarify and make explicit what is being done when those concerned with the social services are studying or planning to meet social need.

REFERENCES

1. SEEBOHM REPORT (1968). *Report of the Committee on Local Authority and Allied Personal Services*, Cmnd. 3703 (London: HMSO).

2. LAMBERT, ROYSTON (1964). *Nutrition in Britain 1950–60*, Occasional Papers in Social Administration no. 6 (London: Bell).

3. TOWNSEND, PETER, and WEDDERBURN, DOROTHY (1965). *The Aged in the Welfare State*, Occasional Papers in Social Administration no. 14 (London: Bell).

82   *A taxonomy of social need*

4. TUNSTALL, J. (1966). *Old and Alone* (London: Routledge & Kegan Paul).

5. WALTON, RONALD (1969). 'Need: A central concept', *Social Service Quarterly*, **43**, no. 1, 13-17.

6. DAVIES, BLEDDYN (1968). *Social Needs and Resources in Local Services* (London: Michael Joseph).

Part II
The Needs of Children

[7]

A THEORY OF HUMAN MOTIVATION

BY A. H. MASLOW

Brooklyn College

I. INTRODUCTION

In a previous paper (13) various propositions were presented which would have to be included in any theory of human motivation that could lay claim to being definitive. These conclusions may be briefly summarized as follows:

1. The integrated wholeness of the organism must be one of the foundation stones of motivation theory.

2. The hunger drive (or any other physiological drive) was rejected as a centering point or model for a definitive theory of motivation. Any drive that is somatically based and localizable was shown to be atypical rather than typical in human motivation.

3. Such a theory should stress and center itself upon ultimate or basic goals rather than partial or superficial ones, upon ends rather than means to these ends. Such a stress would imply a more central place for unconscious than for conscious motivations.

4. There are usually available various cultural paths to the same goal. Therefore conscious, specific, local-cultural desires are not as fundamental in motivation theory as the more basic, unconscious goals.

5. Any motivated behavior, either preparatory or consummatory, must be understood to be a channel through which many basic needs may be simultaneously expressed or satisfied. Typically an act has *more* than one motivation.

6. Practically all organismic states are to be understood as motivated and as motivating.

7. Human needs arrange themselves in hierarchies of prepotency. That is to say, the appearance of one need usually rests on the prior satisfaction of another, more pre-potent need. Man is a perpetually wanting animal. Also no need or drive can be treated as if it were isolated or discrete; every drive is related to the state of satisfaction or dissatisfaction of other drives.

8. *Lists* of drives will get us nowhere for various theoretical and practical reasons. Furthermore any classification of motivations

must deal with the problem of levels of specificity or generalization of the motives to be classified.

9. Classifications of motivations must be based upon goals rather than upon instigating drives or motivated behavior.

10. Motivation theory should be human-centered rather than animal-centered.

11. The situation or the field in which the organism reacts must be taken into account but the field alone can rarely serve as an exclusive explanation for behavior. Furthermore the field itself must be interpreted in terms of the organism. Field theory cannot be a substitute for motivation theory.

12. Not only the integration of the organism must be taken into account, but also the possibility of isolated, specific, partial or segmental reactions.

It has since become necessary to add to these another affirmation.

13. Motivation theory is not synonymous with behavior theory. The motivations are only one class of determinants of behavior. While behavior is almost always motivated, it is also almost always biologically, culturally and situationally determined as well.

The present paper is an attempt to formulate a positive theory of motivation which will satisfy these theoretical demands and at the same time conform to the known facts, clinical and observational as well as experimental. It derives most directly, however, from clinical experience. This theory is, I think, in the functionalist tradition of James and Dewey, and is fused with the holism of Wertheimer (19), Goldstein (6), and Gestalt Psychology, and with the dynamicism of Freud (4) and Adler (1). This fusion or synthesis may arbitrarily be called a 'general-dynamic' theory.

It is far easier to perceive and to criticize the aspects in motivation theory than to remedy them. Mostly this is because of the very serious lack of sound data in this area. I conceive this lack of sound facts to be due primarily to the absence of a valid theory of motivation. The present theory then must be considered to be a suggested program or framework for future research and must stand or fall, not so much on facts available or evidence presented, as upon researches yet to be done, researches suggested perhaps, by the questions raised in this paper.

372 A. H. MASLOW

II. The Basic Needs

The 'physiological' needs.—The needs that are usually taken as the starting point for motivation theory are the so-called physiological drives. Two recent lines of research make it necessary to revise our customary notions about these needs, first, the development of the concept of homeostasis, and second, the finding that appetites (preferential choices among foods) are a fairly efficient indication of actual needs or lacks in the body.

Homeostasis refers to the body's automatic efforts to maintain a constant, normal state of the blood stream. Cannon (2) has described this process for (1) the water content of the blood, (2) salt content, (3) sugar content, (4) protein content, (5) fat content, (6) calcium content, (7) oxygen content, (8) constant hydrogen-ion level (acid-base balance) and (9) constant temperature of the blood. Obviously this list can be extended to include other minerals, the hormones, vitamins, etc.

Young in a recent article (21) has summarized the work on appetite in its relation to body needs. If the body lacks some chemical, the individual will tend to develop a specific appetite or partial hunger for that food element.

Thus it seems impossible as well as useless to make any list of fundamental physiological needs for they can come to almost any number one might wish, depending on the degree of specificity of description. We can not identify all physiological needs as homeostatic. That sexual desire, sleepiness, sheer activity and maternal behavior in animals, are homeostatic, has not yet been demonstrated. Furthermore, this list would not include the various sensory pleasures (tastes, smells, tickling, stroking) which are probably physiological and which may become the goals of motivated behavior.

In a previous paper (13) it has been pointed out that these physiological drives or needs are to be considered unusual rather than typical because they are isolable, and because they are localizable somatically. That is to say, they are relatively independent of each other, of other motivations and of the organism as a whole, and secondly, in many cases, it is possible to demonstrate a localized, underlying somatic base for the drive.   This is true less generally than has been thought (exceptions are fatigue, sleepiness, maternal responses) but it is still true in the classic instances of hunger, sex, and thirst.

It should be pointed out again that any of the physiological needs and the consummatory behavior involved with them serve as channels for all sorts of other needs as well. That is to say, the person who thinks he is hungry may actually be seeking more for comfort, or dependence, than for vitamins or proteins.   Conversely, it is possible to satisfy the hunger need in part by other activities such as drinking water or smoking cigarettes.   In other words, relatively isolable as these physiological needs are, they are not completely so.

Undoubtedly these physiological needs are the most prepotent of all needs.   What this means specifically is, that in the human being who is missing everything in life in an extreme fashion, it is most likely that the major motivation would be the physiological needs rather than any others.   A person who is lacking food, safety, love, and esteem would most probably hunger for food more strongly than for anything else.

If all the needs are unsatisfied, and the organism is then dominated by the physiological needs, all other needs may become simply non-existent or be pushed into the background. It is then fair to characterize the whole organism by saying simply that it is hungry, for consciousness is almost completely preempted by hunger.   All capacities are put into the service of hunger-satisfaction, and the organization of these capacities is almost entirely determined by the one purpose of satisfying hunger.   The receptors and effectors, the intelligence, memory, habits, all may now be defined simply as hunger-gratifying tools.   Capacities that are not useful for this purpose lie dormant, or are pushed into the background. The urge to write poetry, the desire to acquire an automobile, the interest in American history, the desire for a new pair of shoes are, in the extreme case, forgotten or become of secondary importance. For the man who is extremely and dangerously hungry, no other interests exist but food. He dreams food, he remembers food, he thinks about food, he emotes only about food, he perceives only food and he wants only food. The more subtle determinants that ordinarily fuse with the physiological drives in organizing even feeding, drinking or sexual behavior, may now be so completely overwhelmed as to allow us to speak at this time (but *only* at this time) of pure hunger drive and behavior, with the one unqualified aim of relief.

Another peculiar characteristic of the human organism when it is dominated by a certain need is that the whole philosophy of the future tends also to change. For our chronically and extremely hungry man, Utopia can be defined very simply as a place where there is plenty of food. He tends to think that, if only he is guaranteed food for the rest of his life, he will be perfectly happy and will never want anything more. Life itself tends to be defined in terms of eating. Anything else will be defined as unimportant. Freedom, love, community feeling, respect, philosophy, may all be waved aside as fripperies which are useless since they fail to fill the stomach. Such a man may fairly be said to live by bread alone.

It cannot possibly be denied that such things are true but their *generality* can be denied. Emergency conditions are, almost by definition, rare in the normally functioning peaceful society. That this truism can be forgotten is due mainly to two reasons. First, rats have few motivations other than physiological ones, and since so much of the research upon motivation has been made with these animals, it is easy to carry the rat-picture over to the human being. Secondly, it is too often not realized that culture itself is an adaptive tool, one of whose main functions is to make the physiological emergencies come less and less often. In most of the known societies, chronic extreme hunger of the emergency type is rare, rather than common. In any case, this is still true in the United States. The average American citizen is experiencing appetite rather than hunger when he says "I am hungry." He is apt to experience sheer life-and-death hunger only by accident and then only a few times through his entire life.

Obviously a good way to obscure the 'higher' motivations, and to get a lopsided view of human capacities and human nature, is to make the organism extremely and chronically hungry or thirsty. Anyone who attempts to make an emergency picture into a typical one, and who will measure all of man's goals and desires by his behavior during extreme physiological deprivation is certainly being blind to many things. It is quite true that man lives by bread alone—when there is no bread. But what happens to man's desires when there *is* plenty of bread and when his belly is chronically filled?

At once other (and 'higher') needs emerge and these, rather than physiological hungers, dominate the organism. And when these in turn are satisfied, again new (and still 'higher') needs emerge and so on. This is what we mean by saying that the basic human needs are organized into a hierarchy of relative prepotency.

One main implication of this phrasing is that gratification becomes as important a concept as deprivation in motivation theory, for it releases the organism from the domination of a relatively more physiological need, permitting thereby the emergence of other more social goals. The physiological needs, along with their partial goals, when chronically gratified cease to exist as active determinants or organizers of behavior. They now exist only in a potential fashion in the sense that they may emerge again to dominate the organism if they are thwarted. But a want that is satisfied is no longer a want. The organism is dominated and its behavior organized only by unsatisfied needs. If hunger is satisfied, it becomes unimportant in the current dynamics of the individual.

This statement is somewhat qualified by a hypothesis to be discussed more fully later, namely that it is precisely those individuals in whom a certain need has always been satisfied who are best equipped to tolerate deprivation of that need in the future, and that furthermore, those who have been de-

A. H. MASLOW

prived in the past will react differently to current satisfactions than the one who has never been deprived.

The safety needs.—If the physiological needs are relatively well gratified, there then emerges a new set of needs, which we may categorize roughly as the safety needs. All that has been said of the physiological needs is equally true, although in lesser degree, of these desires. The organism may equally well be wholly dominated by them. They may serve as the almost exclusive organizers of behavior, recruiting all the capacities of the organism in their service, and we may then fairly describe the whole organism as a safety-seeking mechanism. Again we may say of the receptors, the effectors, of the intellect and the other capacities that they are primarily safety-seeking tools. Again, as in the hungry man, we find that the dominating goal is a strong determinant not only of his current world-outlook and philosophy but also of his philosophy of the future. Practically everything looks less important than safety, (even sometimes the physiological needs which being satisfied, are now underestimated). A man, in this state, if it is extreme enough and chronic enough, may be characterized as living almost for safety alone.

Although in this paper we are interested primarily in the needs of the adult, we can approach an understanding of his safety needs perhaps more efficiently by observation of infants and children, in whom these needs are much more simple and obvious. One reason for the clearer appearance of the threat or danger reaction in infants, is that they do not inhibit this reaction at all, whereas adults in our society have been taught to inhibit it at all costs. Thus even when adults do feel their safety to be threatened we may not be able to see this on the surface. Infants will react in a total fashion and as if they were endangered, if they are disturbed or dropped suddenly, startled by loud noises, flashing light, or other unusual sensory stimulation, by rough handling, by general loss of support in the mother's arms, or by inadequate support.[1]

[1] As the child grows up, sheer knowledge and familiarity as well as better motor development make these 'dangers' less and less dangerous and more and more man-

In infants we can also see a much more direct reaction to bodily illnesses of various kinds. Sometimes these illnesses seem to be immediately and *per se* threatening and seem to make the child feel unsafe. For instance, vomiting, colic or other sharp pains seem to make the child look at the whole world in a different way. At such a moment of pain, it may be postulated that, for the child, the appearance of the whole world suddenly changes from sunniness to darkness, so to speak, and becomes a place in which anything at all might happen, in which previously stable things have suddenly become unstable. Thus a child who because of some bad food is taken ill may, for a day or two, develop fear, nightmares, and a need for protection and reassurance never seen in him before his illness.

Another indication of the child's need for safety is his preference for some kind of undisrupted routine or rhythm. He seems to want a predictable, orderly world. For instance, injustice, unfairness, or inconsistency in the parents seems to make a child feel anxious and unsafe. This attitude may be not so much because of the injustice *per se* or any particular pains involved, but rather because this treatment threatens to make the world look unreliable, or unsafe, or unpredictable. Young children seem to thrive better under a system which has at least a skeletal outline of rigidity, in which there is a schedule of a kind, some sort of routine, something that can be counted upon, not only for the present but also far into the future. Perhaps one could express this more accurately by saying that the child needs an organized world rather than an unorganized or unstructured one.

The central role of the parents and the normal family setup are indisputable. Quarreling, physical assault, separation, divorce or death within the family may be particularly terrifying. Also parental outbursts of rage or threats of punishment directed to the child, calling him names, speaking to him harshly, shaking him, handling him roughly, or actual

ageable. Throughout life it may be said that one of the main conative functions of education is this neutralizing of apparent dangers through knowledge, *e.g.*, I am not afraid of thunder because I know something about it.

physical punishment sometimes elicit such total panic and terror in the child that we must assume more is involved than the physical pain alone.   While it is true that in some children this terror may represent also a fear of loss of parental love, it can also occur in completely rejected children, who seem to cling to the hating parents more for sheer safety and protection than because of hope of love.

Confronting the average child with new, unfamiliar, strange, unmanageable stimuli or situations will too frequently elicit the danger or terror reaction, as for example, getting lost or even being separated from the parents for a short time, being confronted with new faces, new situations or new tasks, the sight of strange, unfamiliar or uncontrollable objects, illness or death.   Particularly at such times, the child's frantic clinging to his parents is eloquent testimony to their role as protectors (quite apart from their roles as food-givers and love-givers).

From these and similar observations, we may generalize and say that the average child in our society generally prefers a safe, orderly, predictable, organized world, which he can count on, and in which unexpected, unmanageable or other dangerous things do not happen, and in which, in any case, he has all-powerful parents who protect and shield him from harm.

That these reactions may so easily be observed in children is in a way a proof of the fact that children in our society, feel too unsafe (or, in a word, are badly brought up).   Children who are reared in an unthreatening, loving family do *not* ordinarily react as we have described above (17).   In such children the danger reactions are apt to come mostly to objects or situations that adults too would consider dangerous.[2]

The healthy, normal, fortunate adult in our culture is largely satisfied in his safety needs.   The peaceful, smoothly

[2] A 'test battery' for safety might be confronting the child with a small exploding firecracker, or with a bewhiskered face, having the mother leave the room, putting him upon a high ladder, a hypodermic injection, having a mouse crawl up to him, etc. Of course I cannot seriously recommend the deliberate use of such 'tests' for they might very well harm the child being tested.   But these and similar situations come up by the score in the child's ordinary day-to-day living and may be observed.   There is no reason why these stimuli should not be used with, for example, young chimpanzees.

running, 'good' society ordinarily makes its members feel safe enough from wild animals, extremes of temperature, criminals, assault and murder, tyranny, etc. Therefore, in a very real sense, he no longer has any safety needs as active motivators. Just as a sated man no longer feels hungry, a safe man no longer feels endangered. If we wish to see these needs directly and clearly we must turn to neurotic or near-neurotic individuals, and to the economic and social under-dogs. In between these extremes, we can perceive the expressions of safety needs only in such phenomena as, for instance, the common preference for a job with tenure and protection, the desire for a savings account, and for insurance of various kinds (medical, dental, unemployment, disability, old age).

Other broader aspects of the attempt to seek safety and stability in the world are seen in the very common preference for familiar rather than unfamiliar things, or for the known rather than the unknown. The tendency to have some religion or world-philosophy that organizes the universe and the men in it into some sort of satisfactorily coherent, meaningful whole is also in part motivated by safety-seeking. Here too we may list science and philosophy in general as partially motivated by the safety needs (we shall see later that there are also other motivations to scientific, philosophical or religious endeavor).

Otherwise the need for safety is seen as an active and dominant mobilizer of the organism's resources only in emergencies, *e.g.*, war, disease, natural catastrophes, crime waves, societal disorganization, neurosis, brain injury, chronically bad situation.

Some neurotic adults in our society are, in many ways, like the unsafe child in their desire for safety, although in the former it takes on a somewhat special appearance. Their reaction is often to unknown, psychological dangers in a world that is perceived to be hostile, overwhelming and threatening. Such a person behaves as if a great catastrophe were almost always impending, *i.e.*, he is usually responding as if to an emergency. His safety needs often find specific expression in a search for a protector, or a stronger person on whom he may depend, or perhaps, a Fuehrer.

The neurotic individual may be described in a slightly different way with some usefulness as a grown-up person who retains his childish attitudes toward the world. That is to say, a neurotic adult may be said to behave 'as if' he were actually afraid of a spanking, or of his mother's disapproval, or of being abandoned by his parents, or having his food taken away from him. It is as if his childish attitudes of fear and threat reaction to a dangerous world had gone underground, and untouched by the growing up and learning processes, were now ready to be called out by any stimulus that would make a child feel endangered and threatened.[3]

The neurosis in which the search for safety takes its clearest form is in the compulsive-obsessive neurosis. Compulsive-obsessives try frantically to order and stabilize the world so that no unmanageable, unexpected or unfamiliar dangers will ever appear (14). They hedge themselves about with all sorts of ceremonials, rules and formulas so that every possible contingency may be provided for and so that no new contingencies may appear. They are much like the brain injured cases, described by Goldstein (6), who manage to maintain their equilibrium by avoiding everything unfamiliar and strange and by ordering their restricted world in such a neat, disciplined, orderly fashion that everything in the world can be counted upon. They try to arrange the world so that anything unexpected (dangers) cannot possibly occur. If, through no fault of their own, something unexpected does occur, they go into a panic reaction as if this unexpected occurrence constituted a grave danger. What we can see only as a none-too-strong preference in the healthy person, *e.g.*, preference for the familiar, becomes a life-and-death necessity in abnormal cases.

The love needs.—If both the physiological and the safety needs are fairly well gratified, then there will emerge the love and affection and belongingness needs, and the whole cycle

---

[3] Not all neurotic individuals feel unsafe. Neurosis may have at its core a thwarting of the affection and esteem needs in a person who is generally safe.

already described will repeat itself with this new center. Now the person will feel keenly, as never before, the absence of friends, or a sweetheart, or a wife, or children. He will hunger for affectionate relations with people in general, namely, for a place in his group, and he will strive with great intensity to achieve this goal. He will want to attain such a place more than anything else in the world and may even forget that once, when he was hungry, he sneered at love.

In our society the thwarting of these needs is the most commonly found core in cases of maladjustment and more severe psychopathology. Love and affection, as well as their possible expression in sexuality, are generally looked upon with ambivalence and are customarily hedged about with many restrictions and inhibitions. Practically all theorists of psychopathology have stressed thwarting of the love needs as basic in the picture of maladjustment. Many clinical studies have therefore been made of this need and we know more about it perhaps than any of the other needs except the physiological ones (14).

One thing that must be stressed at this point is that love is not synonymous with sex. Sex may be studied as a purely physiological need. Ordinarily sexual behavior is multi-determined, that is to say, determined not only by sexual but also by other needs, chief among which are the love and affection needs. Also not to be overlooked is the fact that the love needs involve both giving *and* receiving love.[4]

The esteem needs.—All people in our society (with a few pathological exceptions) have a need or desire for a stable, firmly based, (usually) high evaluation of themselves, for self-respect, or self-esteem, and for the esteem of others. By firmly based self-esteem, we mean that which is soundly based upon real capacity, achievement and respect from others. These needs may be classified into two subsidiary sets. These are, first, the desire for strength, for achievement, for adequacy, for confidence in the face of the world, and for independence and freedom.[5] Secondly, we have what

---

[4] For further details see (12) and (16, Chap. 5).

[5] Whether or not this particular desire is universal we do not know. The crucial question, especially important today, is "Will men who are enslaved and dominated,

we may call the desire for reputation or prestige (defining it as respect or esteem from other people), recognition, attention, importance or appreciation.[6] These needs have been relatively stressed by Alfred Adler and his followers, and have been relatively neglected by Freud and the psychoanalysts. More and more today however there is appearing widespread appreciation of their central importance.

Satisfaction of the self-esteem need leads to feelings of self-confidence, worth, strength, capability and adequacy of being useful and necessary in the world. But thwarting of these needs produces feelings of inferiority, of weakness and of helplessness. These feelings in turn give rise to either basic discouragement or else compensatory or neurotic trends. An appreciation of the necessity of basic self-confidence and an understanding of how helpless people are without it, can be easily gained from a study of severe traumatic neurosis (8).[7]

The need for self-actualization.—Even if all these needs are satisfied, we may still often (if not always) expect that a new discontent and restlessness will soon develop, unless the individual is doing what he is fitted for. A musician must make music, an artist must paint, a poet must write, if he is to be ultimately happy. What a man *can* be, he *must* be. This need we may call self-actualization.

This term, first coined by Kurt Goldstein, is being used in this paper in a much more specific and limited fashion. It refers to the desire for self-fulfillment, namely, to the tendency for him to become actualized in what he is potentially. This tendency might be phrased as the desire to become more and more what one is, to become everything that one is capable of becoming.

inevitably feel dissatisfied and rebellious?" We may assume on the basis of commonly known clinical data that a man who has known true freedom (not paid for by giving up safety and security but rather built on the basis of adequate safety and security) will not willingly or easily allow his freedom to be taken away from him. But we do not know that this is true for the person born into slavery. The events of the next decade should give us our answer. See discussion of this problem in (5).

[6] Perhaps the desire for prestige and respect from others is subsidiary to the desire for self-esteem or confidence in oneself. Observation of children seems to indicate that this is so, but clinical data give no clear support for such a conclusion.

[7] For more extensive discussion of normal self-esteem, as well as for reports of various researches, see (11).

The specific form that these needs will take will of course vary greatly from person to person. In one individual it may take the form of the desire to be an ideal mother, in another it may be expressed athletically, and in still another it may be expressed in painting pictures or in inventions. It is not necessarily a creative urge although in people who have any capacities for creation it will take this form.

The clear emergence of these needs rests upon prior satisfaction of the physiological, safety, love and esteem needs. We shall call people who are satisfied in these needs, basically satisfied people, and it is from these that we may expect the fullest (and healthiest) creativeness.[8] Since, in our society, basically satisfied people are the exception, we do not know much about self-actualization, either experimentally or clinically. It remains a challenging problem for research.

The preconditions for the basic need satisfactions.—There are certain conditions which are immediate prerequisites for the basic need satisfactions. Danger to these is reacted to almost as if it were a direct danger to the basic needs themselves. Such conditions as freedom to speak, freedom to do what one wishes so long as no harm is done to others, freedom to express one's self, freedom to investigate and seek for information, freedom to defend one's self, justice, fairness, honesty, orderliness in the group are examples of such preconditions for basic need satisfactions. Thwarting in these freedoms will be reacted to with a threat or emergency response. These conditions are not ends in themselves but they are *almost* so since they are so closely related to the basic needs, which are apparently the only ends in themselves. These conditions are defended because without them the basic satisfactions are quite impossible, or at least, very severely endangered.

---

[8] Clearly creative behavior, like painting, is like any other behavior in having multiple determinants. It may be seen in 'innately creative' people whether they are satisfied or not, happy or unhappy, hungry or sated. Also it is clear that creative activity may be compensatory, ameliorative or purely economic. It is my impression (as yet unconfirmed) that it is possible to distinguish the artistic and intellectual products of basically satisfied people from those of basically unsatisfied people by inspection alone. In any case, here too we must distinguish, in a dynamic fashion, the overt behavior itself from its various motivations or purposes.

A. H. MASLOW

If we remember that the cognitive capacities (perceptual, intellectual, learning) are a set of adjustive tools, which have, among other functions, that of satisfaction of our basic needs, then it is clear that any danger to them, any deprivation or blocking of their free use, must also be indirectly threatening to the basic needs themselves. Such a statement is a partial solution of the general problems of curiosity, the search for knowledge, truth and wisdom, and the ever-persistent urge to solve the cosmic mysteries.

We must therefore introduce another hypothesis and speak of degrees of closeness to the basic needs, for we have already pointed out that *any* conscious desires (partial goals) are more or less important as they are more or less close to the basic needs. The same statement may be made for various behavior acts. An act is psychologically important if it contributes directly to satisfaction of basic needs. The less directly it so contributes, or the weaker this contribution is, the less important this act must be conceived to be from the point of view of dynamic psychology. A similar statement may be made for the various defense or coping mechanisms. Some are very directly related to the protection or attainment of the basic needs, others are only weakly and distantly related. Indeed if we wished, we could speak of more basic and less basic defense mechanisms, and then affirm that danger to the more basic defenses is more threatening than danger to less basic defenses (always remembering that this is so only because of their relationship to the basic needs).

The desires to know and to understand.—So far, we have mentioned the cognitive needs only in passing. Acquiring knowledge and systematizing the universe have been considered as, in part, techniques for the achievement of basic safety in the world, or, for the intelligent man, expressions of self-actualization. Also freedom of inquiry and expression have been discussed as preconditions of satisfactions of the basic needs. True though these formulations may be, they do not constitute definitive answers to the question as to the motivation role of curiosity, learning, philosophizing, experimenting, etc. They are, at best, no more than partial answers.

A THEORY OF HUMAN MOTIVATION   385

This question is especially difficult because we know so little about the facts. Curiosity, exploration, desire for the facts, desire to know may certainly be observed easily enough. The fact that they often are pursued even at great cost to the individual's safety is an earnest of the partial character of our previous discussion. In addition, the writer must admit that, though he has sufficient clinical evidence to postulate the desire to know as a very strong drive in intelligent people, no data are available for unintelligent people. It may then be largely a function of relatively high intelligence. Rather tentatively, then, and largely in the hope of stimulating discussion and research, we shall postulate a basic desire to know, to be aware of reality, to get the facts, to satisfy curiosity, or as Wertheimer phrases it, to see rather than to be blind.

This postulation, however, is not enough. Even after we know, we are impelled to know more and more minutely and microscopically on the one hand, and on the other, more and more extensively in the direction of a world philosophy, religion, etc. The facts that we acquire, if they are isolated or atomistic, inevitably get theorized about, and either analyzed or organized or both. This process has been phrased by some as the search for 'meaning.' We shall then postulate a desire to understand, to systematize, to organize, to analyze, to look for relations and meanings.

Once these desires are accepted for discussion, we see that they too form themselves into a small hierarchy in which the desire to know is prepotent over the desire to understand. All the characteristics of a hierarchy of prepotency that we have described above, seem to hold for this one as well.

We must guard ourselves against the too easy tendency to separate these desires from the basic needs we have discussed above, *i.e.*, to make a sharp dichotomy between 'cognitive' and 'conative' needs. The desire to know and to understand are themselves conative, *i.e.*, have a striving character, and are as much personality needs as the 'basic needs' we have already discussed (**19**).

III. Further Characteristics of the Basic Needs

The degree of fixity of the hierarchy of basic needs.—We have spoken so far as if this hierarchy were a fixed order but actually it is not nearly as rigid as we may have implied. It is true that most of the people with whom we have worked have seemed to have these basic needs in about the order that has been indicated. However, there have been a number of exceptions.

(1) There are some people in whom, for instance, self-esteem seems to be more important than love. This most common reversal in the hierarchy is usually due to the development of the notion that the person who is most likely to be loved is a strong or powerful person, one who inspires respect or fear, and who is self confident or aggressive. Therefore such people who lack love and seek it, may try hard to put on a front of aggressive, confident behavior. But essentially they seek high self-esteem and its behavior expressions more as a means-to-an-end than for its own sake; they seek self-assertion for the sake of love rather than for self-esteem itself.

(2) There are other, apparently innately creative people in whom the drive to creativeness seems to be more important than any other counter-determinant. Their creativeness might appear not as self-actualization released by basic satisfaction, but in spite of lack of basic satisfaction.

(3) In certain people the level of aspiration may be permanently deadened or lowered. That is to say, the less prepotent goals may simply be lost, and may disappear forever, so that the person who has experienced life at a very low level, *i.e.*, chronic unemployment, may continue to be satisfied for the rest of his life if only he can get enough food.

(4) The so-called 'psychopathic personality' is another example of permanent loss of the love needs. These are people who, according to the best data available (9), have been starved for love in the earliest months of their lives and have simply lost forever the desire and the ability to give and to receive affection (as animals lose sucking or pecking reflexes that are not exercised soon enough after birth).

(5) Another cause of reversal of the hierarchy is that when a need has been satisfied for a long time, this need may be underevaluated. People who have never experienced chronic hunger are apt to underestimate its effects and to look upon food as a rather unimportant thing. If they are dominated by a higher need, this higher need will seem to be the most important of all. It then becomes possible, and indeed does actually happen, that they may, for the sake of this higher need, put themselves into the position of being deprived in a more basic need. We may expect that after a long-time deprivation of the more basic need there will be a tendency to reevaluate both needs so that the more pre-potent need will actually become consciously prepotent for the individual who may have given it up very lightly. Thus, a man who has given up his job rather than lose his self-respect, and who then starves for six months or so, may be willing to take his job back even at the price of losing his self-respect.

(6) Another partial explanation of *apparent* reversals is seen in the fact that we have been talking about the hierarchy of prepotency in terms of consciously felt wants or desires rather than of behavior. Looking at behavior itself may give us the wrong impression. What we have claimed is that the person will *want* the more basic of two needs when deprived in both. There is no necessary implication here that he will act upon his desires. Let us say again that there are many determinants of behavior other than the needs and desires.

(7) Perhaps more important than all these exceptions are the ones that involve ideals, high social standards, high values and the like. With such values people become martyrs; they will give up everything for the sake of a particular ideal, or value. These people may be understood, at least in part, by reference to one basic concept (or hypothesis) which may be called 'increased frustration-tolerance through early gratification.' People who have been satisfied in their basic needs throughout their lives, particularly in their earlier years, seem to develop exceptional power to withstand present or future thwarting of these needs simply because they have strong,

healthy character structure as a result of basic satisfaction. They are the 'strong' people who can easily weather disagreement or opposition, who can swim against the stream of public opinion and who can stand up for the truth at great personal cost. It is just the ones who have loved and been well loved, and who have had many deep friendships who can hold out against hatred, rejection or persecution.

I say all this in spite of the fact that there is a certain amount of sheer habituation which is also involved in any full discussion of frustration tolerance. For instance, it is likely that those persons who have been accustomed to relative starvation for a long time, are partially enabled thereby to withstand food deprivation. What sort of balance must be made between these two tendencies, of habituation on the one hand, and of past satisfaction breeding present frustration tolerance on the other hand, remains to be worked out by further research. Meanwhile we may assume that they are both operative, side by side, since they do not contradict each other. In respect to this phenomenon of increased frustration tolerance, it seems probable that the most important gratifications come in the first two years of life. That is to say, people who have been made secure and strong in the earliest years, tend to remain secure and strong thereafter in the face of whatever threatens.

Degrees of relative satisfaction.—So far, our theoretical discussion may have given the impression that these five sets of needs are somehow in a step-wise, all-or-none relationships to each other. We have spoken in such terms as the following: "If one need is satisfied, then another emerges." This statement might give the false impression that a need must be satisfied 100 per cent before the next need emerges. In actual fact, most members of our society who are normal, are partially satisfied in all their basic needs and partially unsatisfied in all their basic needs at the same time. A more realistic description of the hierarchy would be in terms of decreasing percentages of satisfaction as we go up the hierarchy of prepotency. For instance, if I may assign arbitrary figures for the sake of illustration, it is as if the average citizen is satisfied perhaps 85 per cent in his physiological needs, 70 per cent in his safety needs, 50 per cent in his love needs, 40 per cent in his self-esteem needs, and 10 per cent in his self-actualization needs.

As for the concept of emergence of a new need after satisfaction of the prepotent need, this emergence is not a sudden, saltatory phenomenon but rather a gradual emergence by slow degrees from nothingness. For instance, if prepotent need A is satisfied only 10 per cent then need B may not be visible at all. However, as this need A becomes satisfied 25 per cent, need B may emerge 5 per cent, as need A becomes satisfied 75 per cent need B may emerge 90 per cent, and so on.

Unconscious character of needs.—These needs are neither necessarily conscious nor unconscious. On the whole, however, in the average person, they are more often unconscious rather than conscious. It is not necessary at this point to overhaul the tremendous mass of evidence which indicates the crucial importance of unconscious motivation. It would by now be expected, on a priori grounds alone, that unconscious motivations would on the whole be rather more important than the conscious motivations. What we have called the basic needs are very often largely unconscious although they may, with suitable techniques, and with sophisticated people become conscious.

Cultural specificity and generality of needs.—This classification of basic needs makes some attempt to take account of the relative unity behind the superficial differences in specific desires from one culture to another. Certainly in any particular culture an individual's conscious motivational content will usually be extremely different from the conscious motivational content of an individual in another society. However, it is the common experience of anthropologists that people, even in different societies, are much more alike than we would think from our first contact with them, and that as we know them better we seem to find more and more of this commonness. We then recognize the most startling differences to be superficial rather than basic, *e.g.*, differences in style of hairdress, clothes, tastes in food, etc. Our classification of basic needs is in part an attempt to account for this unity behind the apparent diversity from culture to culture. No claim is made that it is ultimate or universal for all cultures. The claim is made only that it is relatively *more* ultimate, more universal, more basic, than the superficial conscious desires from culture to culture, and makes a somewhat closer approach to common-human characteristics. Basic needs are *more* common-human than superficial desires or behaviors.

Multiple motivations of behavior.—These needs must be understood *not* to be *exclusive* or single determiners of certain kinds of behavior. An example may be found in any behavior that seems to be physiologically motivated, such as eating, or sexual play or the like. The clinical psychologists have long since found that any behavior may be a channel through which flow various determinants. Or to say it in another way, most behavior is multi-motivated. Within the sphere of motivational determinants any behavior tends to be determined by several or *all* of the basic needs simultaneously rather than by only one of them. The latter would be more an exception than the former. Eating may be partially for the sake of filling the stomach, and partially for the sake of comfort and amelioration of other needs. One may make love not only for pure sexual release, but also to convince one's self of one's masculinity, or to make a conquest, to feel powerful, or to win more basic affection. As an illustration, I may point out that it would be possible (theoretically if not practically) to analyze a single act of an individual and see in it the expression of his physiological needs, his safety needs, his love needs, his esteem needs and self-actualization. This contrasts sharply with the more naive brand of trait psychology in which one trait or one motive accounts for a certain kind of act, *i.e.*, an aggressive act is traced solely to a trait of aggressiveness.

Multiple determinants of behavior.—Not all behavior is determined by the basic needs. We might even say that not all behavior is motivated. There are many determinants of behavior other than motives.[9] For instance, one other im-

[9] I am aware that many psychologists and psychoanalysts use the term 'motivated' and 'determined' synonymously, *e.g.*, Freud. But I consider this an ob-

portant class of determinants is the so-called 'field' determinants. Theoretically, at least, behavior may be determined completely by the field, or even by specific isolated external stimuli, as in association of ideas, or certain conditioned reflexes. If in response to the stimulus word 'table,' I immediately perceive a memory image of a table, this response certainly has nothing to do with my basic needs.

Secondly, we may call attention again to the concept of 'degree of closeness to the basic needs' or 'degree of motivation.' Some behavior is highly motivated, other behavior is only weakly motivated. Some is not motivated at all (but all behavior is determined).

Another important point [10] is that there is a basic difference between expressive behavior and coping behavior (functional striving, purposive goal seeking). An expressive behavior does not try to do anything; it is simply a reflection of the personality. A stupid man behaves stupidly, not because he wants to, or tries to, or is motivated to, but simply because he *is* what he is. The same is true when I speak in a bass voice rather than tenor or soprano. The random movements of a healthy child, the smile on the face of a happy man even when he is alone, the springiness of the healthy man's walk, and the erectness of his carriage are other examples of expressive, non-functional behavior. Also the *style* in which a man carries out almost all his behavior, motivated as well as unmotivated, is often expressive.

We may then ask, is *all* behavior expressive or reflective of the character structure? The answer is 'No.' Rote, habitual, automatized, or conventional behavior may or may not be expressive. The same is true for most 'stimulus-bound' behaviors.

It is finally necessary to stress that expressiveness of behavior, and goal-directedness of behavior are not mutually exclusive categories. Average behavior is usually both.

Goals as centering principle in motivation theory.—It will be observed that the basic principle in our classification has

fuscating usage. Sharp distinctions are necessary for clarity of thought, and precision in experimentation.

[10] To be discussed fully in a subsequent publication.

been neither the instigation nor the motivated behavior but rather the functions, effects, purposes, or goals of the behavior. It has been proven sufficiently by various people that this is the most suitable point for centering in any motivation theory.[11]

Animal- and human-centering.—This theory starts with the human being rather than any lower and presumably 'simpler' animal. Too many of the findings that have been made in animals have been proven to be true for animals but not for the human being. There is no reason whatsoever why we should start with animals in order to study human motivation. The logic or rather illogic behind this general fallacy of 'pseudo-simplicity' has been exposed often enough by philosophers and logicians as well as by scientists in each of the various fields. It is no more necessary to study animals before one can study man than it is to study mathematics before one can study geology or psychology or biology.

We may also reject the old, naive, behaviorism which assumed that it was somehow necessary, or at least more 'scientific' to judge human beings by animal standards. One consequence of this belief was that the whole notion of purpose and goal was excluded from motivational psychology simply because one could not ask a white rat about his purposes. Tolman (18) has long since proven in animal studies themselves that this exclusion was not necessary.

Motivation and the theory of psychopathogenesis.—The conscious motivational content of everyday life has, according to the foregoing, been conceived to be relatively important or unimportant accordingly as it is more or less closely related to the basic goals. A desire for an ice cream cone might actually be an indirect expression of a desire for love. If it is, then this desire for the ice cream cone becomes extremely important motivation. If however the ice cream is simply something to cool the mouth with, or a casual appetitive reaction, then the desire is relatively unimportant. Everyday conscious desires are to be regarded as symptoms, as

[11] The interested reader is referred to the very excellent discussion of this point in Murray's *Explorations in Personality* (15).

surface indicators of more basic needs. If we were to take these superficial desires at their face value we would find ourselves in a state of complete confusion which could never be resolved, since we would be dealing seriously with symptoms rather than with what lay behind the symptoms.

Thwarting of unimportant desires produces no psychopathological results; thwarting of a basically important need does produce such results. Any theory of psychopathogenesis must then be based on a sound theory of motivation. A conflict or a frustration is not necessarily pathogenic. It becomes so only when it threatens or thwarts the basic needs, or partial needs that are closely related to the basic needs (10).

The role of gratified needs.—It has been pointed out above several times that our needs usually emerge only when more prepotent needs have been gratified. Thus gratification has an important role in motivation theory. Apart from this, however, needs cease to play an active determining or organizing role as soon as they are gratified.

What this means is that, *e.g.*, a basically satisfied person no longer has the needs for esteem, love, safety, etc. The only sense in which he might be said to have them is in the almost metaphysical sense that a sated man has hunger, or a filled bottle has emptiness. If we are interested in what *actually* motivates us, and not in what has, will, or might motivate us, then a satisfied need is not a motivator. It must be considered for all practical purposes simply not to exist, to have disappeared. This point should be emphasized because it has been either overlooked or contradicted in every theory of motivation I know.[12] The perfectly healthy, normal, fortunate man has no sex needs or hunger needs, or needs for safety, or for love, or for prestige, or self-esteem, except in stray moments of quickly passing threat. If we were to say otherwise, we should also have to aver that every man had all the pathological reflexes, *e.g.*, Babinski, etc., because if his nervous system were damaged, these would appear.

It is such considerations as these that suggest the bold

[12] Note that acceptance of this theory necessitates basic revision of the Freudian theory.

postulation that a man who is thwarted in any of his basic needs may fairly be envisaged simply as a sick man. This is a fair parallel to our designation as 'sick' of the man who lacks vitamins or minerals. Who is to say that a lack of love is less important than a lack of vitamins? Since we know the pathogenic effects of love starvation, who is to say that we are invoking value-questions in an unscientific or illegitimate way, any more than the physician does who diagnoses and treats pellagra or scurvy? If I were permitted this usage, I should then say simply that a healthy man is primarily motivated by his needs to develop and actualize his fullest potentialities and capacities. If a man has any other basic needs in any active, chronic sense, then he is simply an unhealthy man. He is as surely sick as if he had suddenly developed a strong salt-hunger or calcium hunger.[13]

If this statement seems unusual or paradoxical the reader may be assured that this is only one among many such paradoxes that will appear as we revise our ways of looking at man's deeper motivations. When we ask what man wants of life, we deal with his very essence.

IV. Summary

(1) There are at least five sets of goals, which we may call basic needs. These are briefly physiological, safety, love, esteem, and self-actualization. In addition, we are motivated by the desire to achieve or maintain the various conditions upon which these basic satisfactions rest and by certain more intellectual desires.

(2) These basic goals are related to each other, being arranged in a hierarchy of prepotency. This means that the most prepotent goal will monopolize consciousness and will tend of itself to organize the recruitment of the various capacities of the organism. The less prepotent needs are

[13] If we were to use the word 'sick' in this way, we should then also have to face squarely the relations of man to his society. One clear implication of our definition would be that (1) since a man is to be called sick who is basically thwarted, and (2) since such basic thwarting is made possible ultimately only by forces outside the individual, then (3) sickness in the individual must come ultimately from a sickness in the society. The 'good' or healthy society would then be defined as one that permitted man's highest purposes to emerge by satisfying all his prepotent basic needs.

minimized, even forgotten or denied. But when a need is fairly well satisfied, the next prepotent ('higher') need emerges, in turn to dominate the conscious life and to serve as the center of organization of behavior, since gratified needs are not active motivators.

Thus man is a perpetually wanting animal. Ordinarily the satisfaction of these wants is not altogether mutually exclusive, but only tends to be. The average member of our society is most often partially satisfied and partially unsatisfied in all of his wants. The hierarchy principle is usually empirically observed in terms of increasing percentages of non-satisfaction as we go up the hierarchy. Reversals of the average order of the hierarchy are sometimes observed. Also it has been observed that an individual may permanently lose the higher wants in the hierarchy under special conditions. There are not only ordinarily multiple motivations for usual behavior, but in addition many determinants other than motives.

(3) Any thwarting or possibility of thwarting of these basic human goals, or danger to the defenses which protect them, or to the conditions upon which they rest, is considered to be a psychological threat. With a few exceptions, all psychopathology may be partially traced to such threats. A basically thwarted man may actually be defined as a 'sick' man, if we wish.

(4) It is such basic threats which bring about the general emergency reactions.

(5) Certain other basic problems have not been dealt with because of limitations of space. Among these are (*a*) the problem of values in any definitive motivation theory, (*b*) the relation between appetites, desires, needs and what is 'good' for the organism, (*c*) the etiology of the basic needs and their possible derivation in early childhood, (*d*) redefinition of motivational concepts, *i.e.*, drive, desire, wish, need, goal, (*e*) implication of our theory for hedonistic theory, (*f*) the nature of the uncompleted act, of success and failure, and of aspiration-level, (*g*) the role of association, habit and conditioning, (*h*) relation to the

theory of inter-personal relations, (*i*) implications for psy-chotherapy, (*j*) implication for theory of society, (*k*) the theory of selfishness, (*l*) the relation between needs and cultural patterns, (*m*) the relation between this theory and Allport's theory of functional autonomy. These as well as certain other less important questions must be considered as motivation theory attempts to become definitive.

REFERENCES

1. ADLER, A.   *Social interest*, London: Faber & Faber, 1938.
2. CANNON, W. B.   *Wisdom of the body*.   New York: Norton, 1932.
3. FREUD, A.   *The ego and the mechanisms of defense*.   London: Hogarth, 1937.
4. FREUD, S.   *New introductory lectures on psychoanalysis*.   New York: Norton, 1933.
5. FROMM, E.   *Escape from freedom*.   New York: Farrar and Rinehart, 1941.
6. GOLDSTEIN, K.   *The organism*.   New York: American Book Co., 1939.
7. HORNEY, K.   *The neurotic personality of our time*.   New York: Norton, 1937.
8. KARDINER, A.   *The traumatic neuroses of war*.   New York: Hoeber, 1941.
9. LEVY, D. M.   Primary affect hunger.   *Amer. J. Psychiat.*, 1937, **94**, 643–652.
10. MASLOW, A. H.   Conflict, frustration, and the theory of threat.   *J. abnorm. (soc.) Psychol.*, 1943, **38**, 81–86.
11. ——.   Dominance, personality and social behavior in women.   *J. soc. Psychol.*, 1939, **10**, 3–39.
12. ——.   The dynamics of psychological security-insecurity.   *Character & Pers.*, 1942, **10**, 331–344.
13. ——.   A preface to motivation theory.   *Psychosomatic Med.*, 1943, **5**, 85–92.
14. ——, & MITTELMANN, B.   *Principles of abnormal psychology*.   New York: Harper & Bros., 1941.
15. MURRAY, H. A., *et al.*   *Explorations in personality*.   New York: Oxford University Press, 1938.
16. PLANT, J.   *Personality and the cultural pattern*.   New York: Commonwealth Fund, 1937.
17. SHIRLEY, M.   Children's adjustments to a strange situation.   *J. abnorm. (soc.) Psychol.*, 1942, **37**, 201–217.
18. TOLMAN, E. C.   *Purposive behavior in animals and men*.   New York: Century, 1932.
19. WERTHEIMER, M.   Unpublished lectures at the New School for Social Research.
20. YOUNG, P. T.   *Motivation of behavior*.   New York: John Wiley & Sons, 1936.
21. ——.   The experimental analysis of appetite.   *Psychol. Bull.*, 1941, **38**, 129–164.

[8]

What do children need from parents?

Dr Dora Black

is Consultant Child and Adolescent Psy-
chiatrist at the Royal Free Hospital, London.
This is the text of the 22nd Hilda Lewis
Memorial Lecture which she delivered at the
BAAF Medical Group AGM in October 1989.
The views expressed are those of Dr Black and
do not necessarily reflect the views of BAAF.

Introduction

Dr. Hilda Lewis, whom we are honouring
today, devoted her professional life to the
needs of children deprived of their natural
family.

As psychiatrist to the Caldecott community
and the Children's Society and as Chairman to
the Standing Conference of Societies Registered for Adoption, (the precursor of BAAF),
her pioneering work ensured that the medical
community were kept apprised of the research
basis for decision-making in this field.

It would not be an exaggeration to say that
she was among the first to recognise the
crippling effect on a child of institutional care
and she strove to promote and improve the
alternatives for children, in particular
adoption.

Her obituarist in 1966 wrote, 'At no time
were emotional factors allowed to dominate
facts and it was this attention to scientific
proof which made Hilda's work so valuable,
though it has been recognised by so few, for
she found little time to write...'. Another
obituarist wrote 'Lady Lewis showed an
insight, a forbearance and an ability to view
the whole social field of the insecure child with
a balance and perception and objectivity to
which we are all indebted'.

That tradition of scientific evaluation of
evidence is one which we as doctors strive to
adhere to and use every day in our clinical
work. The same should be true of those who

bear the responsibility for making decisions about other people's children, that is lawyers and social workers. Sadly that is not always the case. Lawyers, and particularly judges are of course trained to evaluate evidence but they have rarely had a scientific education and, especially on matters which are not strictly forensic, may be swayed by persuasive argument not necessarily supported by research. It is not the tradition in this country, and the opportunity is rarely given, for judges to follow up the outcome of their judgements and they do not commission research into the relative efficacy of different sentences.

Social work practice governed by fashionable theories

Social work has only recently become a profession. It began with the voluntary distribution of alms — hence the name almoner. There was little time to train social workers in scientific methods on the short one- and two-year courses which were hastily created to provide the increase in numbers needed in the 70s after the Seebohm Report, let alone time to give them experience of the joys and pitfalls of research at first hand. The results are predictable. Social work practice is too often subject to the vagaries of whatever theory is fashionable at the time and the casualties as always are the children. A recent study of social work decision-making in child care (Vernon and Fruin 1986) found that even when it was clear from the outset that a child would be unlikely to return home, proper permanency planning was not initiated early and the child drifted on in temporary placement.

A recent case is a good example of how a political ideology influenced the local authority social services department, the High Court and the Court of Appeal to make a decision which went against child care principles established by good quality research.

A 17-month-old boy of mixed race who had been 'temporarily' fostered by a white family from birth, because of his mother's admission to a mental hospital and his father's absence in prison, was removed to a black adoptive home on the *sole* grounds that a black family could equip him better to deal in due course with society's institutionalised racism. The child and the foster family were well and mutually

attached and the only 'fault' found with them was that the colour of their skins did not match (*The Guardian* 1989). The research evidence is either flimsy or entirely lacking for the presence of 'institutionalised racism' in British society, for the inability of white parents to help equip a black child to deal with racism, and for the extent and permanence of the damage to such children (Gill and Jackson 1983, Harris 1985). On the other hand, the research evidence for the effect on a baby and on the child and adult he becomes, of abrupt and permanent removal from his only attachment figures is extensive and unmistakable (Ainsworth 1982).

Rutter (1989) stressing a developmental perspective says, 'Thus very young infants are protected from separation experiences because they have yet to develop strong attachments; older children are protected because they have learned to maintain relationships over time and space, but toddlers are most at risk because attachments are first becoming established at that age and because they lack the cognitive skills required to maintain relationships during an absence'.

Wolkind (1984) is uncompromising on this point. 'Removing a child from its main caretaker between the ages of six months and three years should be done only in the most extreme circumstances and with great caution. There will certainly be short-term effects and... under certain circumstances, long-term consequences.'

What are these consequences and what mechanism brings them about? Bowlby's theory of attachment (Bowlby 1969) has been now shown in an elegant series of studies (summarised in Bretherton and Waters 1985) to be a major contribution to our understanding of human and indeed all primate development. The short-term effects of disruption of attachment in this age group are, as Rutter (1981) says, the syndrome of distress — the familiar triad of protest, despair and detachment. The child, bewildered by the sudden disappearance of those caretakers whom he has come to know, to trust and to depend upon, becomes sad and withdrawn. He pines, he rejects the substitute carers, is unbiddable and rages against them for not being his parents. His grief and anger may affect his bodily functioning — he goes off his food, cannot settle at night, loses control of bowels and bladder, even loss of temperature regulation and loss of resistance to infection may occur. Depending on the stage of language development and his experience, he may construct theories to explain his loss — 'I did something bad' is the most usual one in a child at the egocentric stage of development. The effect this has is to damage his self-esteem, damage his belief in a benevolent world which has hitherto met his needs, and it may cause him to test out new caretakers to the point of destruction. It would take exceptional people to be able to understand these primitive thought processes, and withstand the rejection and battering such a child might give them. If they cannot cope, they may return the child to the local authority, thus causing yet another loss for the child and (if much time has passed) the original foster parents may not be able to cope with the child's rage either, should he be returned to them. The processes then may be set in train whereby the child becomes unadoptable and is destined to foul up whatever nest he occupies. Then, only skilled, prolonged, expensive and not universally available psychiatric treatment *may* help that child to adjust to family life (Boston and Szur 1983). If it fails or is not on offer, the consequences for the child, the adult he becomes, any family he creates, and for society — you and me, are well documented and dire. Delinquency, criminality, personality disorder, marital breakdown, child abuse and mental illness are all much more common in those who have had significant breaks in the continuity of care (Rutter 1980).

Of course the child may be lucky — his new parents may be exceptional, they may have the support they need to ride the storm, the child may have inherited a sturdy constitution and be resilient. He may have unusual qualities of character. But was knowledge of all this available to the judge and social workers who made the decision that present security was to be put at risk for possible future gains? The arguments, put by BAAF in their practice note in favour of *placing* black children with black parents are not based on adequate evidence (BAAF 1989), and surely should not apply when the child is bonded already with parents of another colour so that removing him will disrupt those bonds. Recent research has shown (Chambers 1989) that black children wait longer for placement than white ones and that in most cases young children (under five) wait between six months and 30 months for black parents.

Ladner (1977) a black American sociologist in her study of 136 trans-racially adopted children was forced reluctantly to conclude that the children had *not* acquired racial ambivalence and that many whites can rear emotionally healthy black children.

We know the child under discussion is the product of a mentally ill mother and a criminal father. He may have therefore the possibility of a genetic predisposition to two serious disorders (Rutter 1989). Such children are *less* resilient than those of sturdier stock and it therefore behoves the state as guardian to take *fewer* risks with their stability (Neuchterlein 1986). One cannot help thinking that the adverse experiences in care of a few articulate and vociferous black people (Association of Black Social Workers and Allied Professions 1983) have influenced unduly those who have perhaps lacked the training to consider the *scientific* evidence dispassionately and apply these findings in each case with compassion, discretion and judgement. It was the ability of Hilda Lewis to stand out against the crowd which enabled her to recognise the good when she saw it, evaluate the evidence when she found it and campaign so effectively for the welfare of children deprived of their natural parents.

What do children need from parents or from parent substitutes? To understand what children need to develop full potential and to lead happy and productive lives we must turn to history and research.

The history of parent-child relationships

It may be hard for us to appreciate today how much worse things were for children in previous times. De Mause (1976), the American historian, has documented the casual and cruel way in which most children were reared until relatively recently. He writes, 'The history of childhood is a nightmare from which we have only recently begun to awaken. The further back in history one goes, the lower the level of child care, and the more likely children are to be killed, abandoned, beaten, terrorised and sexually abused'. Often the cruelty was 'justified'. 'Spare the rod and spoil the child', for instance.

Infanticide was common in antiquity and was described by Thomas Coram in 18th century London. The sight of babies being abandoned on dunghills inspired him to build the Foundling Hospital in 1741. Children were deliberately mutilated so that they could beg more effectively or so they could sing more sweetly (castrato). They were bought and sold and abandoned with impunity. Few children were carefully reared up to the 18th century. 'The average child of wealthy parents spent his earliest years in the home of a wet-nurse, returned home to the care of other servants, was sent out to service, apprenticeship or school by age seven, so that the amount of time parents of means actually spent raising their children was minimal' (De Mause 1976). Many children of poor families grew up unparented on the streets, as many children still do in South America and India (see for example the film *Salaam Bombay*), exposed to death, danger, starvation and exploitation. Of course, there were many parents who cared, but their beliefs about original sin and their different concept of childhood made their practices seem cruel to us today (Wolff 1989). Even devoted parents used practices we now abhor: swaddling; foot-binding, physical and sexual abuse. As late as the 19th century, children as young as ten were working 12 hours a day down the pits. Concerted and consistent efforts were made to protect children only comparatively recently. The year of the new Children's Act sees also the centenary of the passing of the law to protect children from cruelty. Since then, and often in response to scandalous cases of child cruelty and neglect, a spate of legislation has been generated. The 1948, 1963 and 1975 Children's Acts arose specifically from public concern about childhood maltreatment. Will the new Children Act extend child protection or compromise it?

I will return to that question later.

The needs of children

In spite of its many shortcomings, the family has not been bettered yet as a matrix for rearing children. The Israeli kibbutzim were

created, following Freud, as a way of minimising what was seen by the pioneers as the inevitable adverse effect of neurotic parents on offspring. Nevertheless, most outcome studies have found that the child, reared by well trained nursery nurses and teachers, tends nevertheless to replicate parental personality traits and neuroses (Bettelheim 1969).

Cooper (1985) in her chapter on 'good-enough' parenting in Adcock & White's valuable booklet summarises the child's basic needs as follows:

Physical care — warmth, shelter, food and rest, grooming and hygiene and protection from danger.

Affection — contact, holding, stroking, admiration, delight, tenderness, patience, time, making allowances for annoying behaviour, general companionship and approval.

Security — which involves continuity of care and the expectation of continuing in the stable family unit.

Stimulation of innate potential — by praise, by encouraging curiosity and exploratory behaviour, by developing skills through responsiveness to questions and to play, by promoting educational opportunities.

Guidance and control — to teach adequate social behaviour which includes discipline within the child's understanding and capacity, and which requires patience and a model for the child to copy, for example in honesty and concern and kindness to others.

Responsibility — for small things at first such as self-care, tidying play things or taking dishes to the kitchen, and gradually elaborating the decision-making the child has to learn in order to function adequately, gaining experience through his mistakes as well as his successes, and receiving praise and encouragement to strive and do better.

Independence — to make his own decisions, first about small things, but increasingly about the various aspects of his life within the confines of the family and society's codes. Parents use fine judgement in encouraging independence, and in letting the child see and feel the outcome of his own poor judgement and mistakes, but within the compass of his capacity. Protection is needed, but over-protection is as bad as responsibility and independence too early.

Cooper is helpful in pointing out the danger signs that these needs are not being met, and the consequences, the 11 'D's:

- death
- damage
- deprivation
- disturbance in personality development
- delay in language and speech development
- distorted perceptions of people and relationships
- demanding behaviour
- dependency
- delinquency
- detachment

One might quarrel with her emphases but not her main conclusions.

Winnicott's oft repeated and arresting statement, 'There's no such thing as a baby', (Winnicott 1964) brought home to me early the concept that the mother/child unit should be a unity indivisible, and that we as a society had to care for the parents if children were to be reared decently. But what happens when, despite all our efforts, parenting fails?

We need to be able to assess when parenting is good enough; we need to have tools to predict parents who are at high risk of failure and we need effective techniques of intervention. Finally, we need to be able to assess when parenting is not good enough and act swiftly to protect the child and find new parent-substitutes.

Predicting parenting failure

Frommer's (Frommer and Shea 1973), and later Lynch's work (1982) helped us to identify some predictive factors and more recently Clarkson and colleagues (Clarkson et al 1988) have devised a questionnaire *to use pre-natally* which predicts future parenting problems accurately. Leventhal and his colleagues' study (Leventhal et al 1989) demonstrates that clinicians can correctly identify newborns who are at high risk of child maltreatment (abuse or neglect).

Quinton and Rutter's (1988) research looking at inter-generational continuities in parenting breakdown, in parents who had been in care themselves, showed that there is an association between a girl being in care and failing to rear her own children, but that the association is modified by positive and rewarding experiences in childhood enhancing her self-concept and by the acquisition of a supportive spouse. They make important recommendations about the practical application of their findings.

Assessing parenting skills

Parents, of course, may be good enough at rearing some children but fail with others. The temperamentally difficult child, the handicapped or chronically ill child or the child who evokes rage because she sparks off some association in the parent which he or she cannot get in touch with and deal with may be at great risk in some families, even though her siblings thrive.

Assessment is therefore always a contextual exercise. For example, more stringent criteria may be used in assessing prospective foster or adoptive parents than assessing birth parents, so that the child of a mentally ill mother may not be removed unless the mother is very neglectful, frightening or abusive, while a less mentally ill prospective *adoptive* mother would be unacceptable.

What should the social worker, or child psychiatrist look for when assessing whether *these* parents can meet the needs of *this* child? I am now talking about birth parents or children already living in a foster or adoptive home where abuse or neglect may have occurred. The assessment of prospective foster or adoptive parents is not within the scope of this paper.

There is an extensive literature on the assessment of parenting skills. Bentovim and Bingley (1985) working in a child psychiatric department outline a systems-based assessment programme. Oates (1984), approaches the task from the stance of an adult psychiatrist assessing psychiatric disorder in the abusive parent. Jenner, (1988) a clinical psychologist, uses a three-pronged approach assessing current levels of parenting, measuring the parents' potential for change and training the parent using the Parent-Child game described by Forehand and McMahon (1981) and assessing the change that results. The Department of Health has produced a guide for social workers undertaking a comprehensive assessment for long-term planning in child abuse cases (Department of Health 1988). My colleagues Drs Wolkind, Harris-Hendricks and I (Black et al 1989) writing on this subject suggest that it is desirable to see parents together, separately and with the children. 'Parents who are reasonable apart may be quite destructive together and be unable to protect the children from their hostilities'. We stress the necessity for obtaining reports from other professionals about the family members over time to supplement our cross-sectional assessment. The relationship of parents to other adults is important — a single parent living with a supportive grandparent for example may be able to care for a child while another, lacking this support, may not. A parent who likes and trusts a social worker may cope better than one who is suspicious and hostile. We feel that assessment interviews should always aim to be therapeutic. The use of positive statements and genuine empathy for a parent who cares *about* but cannot care *for* a child can help that parent to accept a recommendation which is painful, particularly if help can be given to the parent on how to cope with family or community condemnation if she gives up her child.

For the child psychiatrist, the core of the assessment process is the detailed observation of the parent-child and parent-parent interaction. Do the parents view the child age-appropriately or are their expectations unrealistic? Can they tolerate immature behaviour (wetting, crying, demanding)? Do they demand parenting from the child (reversal of roles)? Can they demonstrate empathy with their child? Are their discipline, guidance and comfort techniques appropriate and effective? Do they use distance controls too freely with young children (shouting commands rather than physical removal or distraction). Are they aware of what can be expected of their child? Can they understand and tolerate normal attachment behaviour? Do they prepare the child for their departure? Do they enjoy the child's company, her development and achievements? Can they meet the child's needs before their own?

Is the child thriving physically and emotionally? Or is she physically and cognitively impaired, fearful, frozen, withdrawn or sustainedly sad, anxious or destructive? When stressed, to whom does she turn for comfort?

Of course it may be that the parent is good with her baby — tender, warm, attentive but cannot look after toddlers. Assessment must take into account past behaviour too.

For example, I was asked to see a 30-year-old woman of limited intellectual ability who was pregnant with her fifth child. The previous four, ranging in age from 12 down to five were in care, having at various times been severely neglected and repeatedly sexually abused by their mother's male partners. The mother had a long history of alcohol abuse. Since losing her children, she had attended a service for alcohol abusers and was abstinent. Before I could see her, she delivered. The case conference which had decided to involve me had only convened a week or so before her delivery date, having already decided that there were not sufficient grounds to remove this baby when it was born. I was unhappy with this decision to which I was not party. The evidence from the past was that the mother had been good with babies but had only limited capacity for protecting them when mobile, was inclined to pick violent men as drinking and sexual partners and had few family and social supports. I felt that by the time the child was a toddler she would be attached to her mother and removing her then would be more damaging than removing her at birth. I felt the likelihood of a therapeutic programme being successful for the mother was not great. However, one was set up. Her social worker made a good relationship with her — she continued to visit her alcohol programme, agreed not to have men visiting and agreed to a literacy programme. All went well at first. Slowly she became more evasive and withdrew from the programmes. She was discovered to be living with the man she claimed to be the father and finally they both abandoned the baby — now one year old — outside a pub, one night after they had been drinking.

The child is now in care but having to cope with the distress of losing the mother to whom she was securely attached. Could this have been prevented? The warning signs were there. Four children had suffered unimaginable hurts because she was unable to protect them. Sadly, her personality was too damaged and her cognitive ability too low to respond to the most intense and skilled help. Hope springs eternal in the human breast. The result of 'giving mother another chance' is that the child's security has been imperilled. The study of Tizard's late adopted children (1977) has now reached 16 years. Recent findings are that even after 12 or more years with good adoptive parents, there are differences detectable compared with a matched control group. They were more orientated to adult attention, had more difficulties with peers and fewer close relationships indicating some long-term effects of their early institutional and separation experiences (Hodges and Tizard 1989 — see page 17).

I want to mention two other cases where the interests of the child was sacrificed to those of the parent.

I first saw Sonny (not his real name), when at the age of 12 he had been out of school one year. His single mother had had several admissions with schizophrenia in the past but now was functioning with no florid symptoms thanks to regular medication given by the community psychiatric nurse. She had a new baby. Sonny stayed home to look after his sister because his mother was very passive and poor at guarding her from danger, and he was worried. In any case his new school was less protective and caring than primary school where he had been well-nurtured, although he had acquired few skills in reading, writing and mathematics. As he was a ward of court, permission had to be obtained for him to see a psychiatrist, a process which took a year because the local authority's lawyers were overstretched and only dealing with life and death issues. Sonny now attends our hospital school and is doing well. But without a parent who would fight for him, or a state who cared, he has had little education, has difficulty in coping with everyday stresses, is prey to numerous fears and anxieties and has had no childhood, having to care for himself and now his sister. What kind of an adult will he become?

Recently, I was consulted about a boy born two months earlier to a mother who had killed her four-year-old child and had received a hospital order. The mother had been separated at seven years of age from her parent-substitutes, with whom she had lived since soon after she was born, and taken to a new

country to join her birth parents who had had another baby whom they preferred to her. She developed elective mutism which was treated unsuccessfully at the local child guidance clinic. Her present psychiatrist was able to convince the Judge that her personality disorder was now treated successfully and, against the opposition of the social services, the new baby went to live with her. Only as an afterthought and late in the proceedings was a guardian *ad litem* appointed to represent the baby's interests. After all, the pregnancy of the mother was known about eight months previously. A GAL appointed then would have been able to obtain a second psychiatric opinion on the mother, and an assessment of parenting capacity, which would hopefully have given the Judge more information on which to base a decision which may have life-threatening implications for this baby. The Children Act 1989 will not remedy this deficiency, nor help the two children whose cases I described earlier. In each case, the mother's needs were in practice placed above the child's. It was felt to be unjust that she should lose her child — a punishment to her when she was ill, or incapable.

Will the new Children Act aid us in our prime task — to ensure that tomorrow's citizens fulfil their potential? I fear not.

Whilst on the whole it is to be welcomed as carrying out the reforms outlined in the 1987 White Paper, it does not build in the legal representation of the child as a right; the restriction in the use of wardship is in my view a retrograde step (Section 100), and at times it seems that the rights of parents are given more weight than those of children, even though Section 1 establishes the general principle that the child's welfare is paramount. Parents have more rights to challenge decisions about access at any stage and they will share rights with the local authority when children are in care. This may lead to parents having power to ruin their child's life without their having motivation to change (Adcock 1989).

One new concept in the Act is the concept of 'significant harm'. 'Harm' means ill-treatment or the impairment of health or development. Before making a care or supervision order the court has to be satisfied that the child has suffered or is likely to suffer significant harm and that the harm is attributable to the standard of care. One of the problems it seems to me in interpreting this concept is, can we make the prediction that the child is likely to suffer harm?

The best predictor of future behaviour is past behaviour. In all the cases I have described the evidence was there but it was ignored by the court and the social services. Will the new Act strengthen our hand? It is only as strong as we choose to make it. There is an opportunity here for us to protect children. Will we take it?

As Wolff (1987) says: 'almost all parents want to do the best for their children... the trouble is that some parents cannot manage this... it does not help parents to be allowed to spoil their children's lives', and again, 'one of the most important judgements in each individual case is whether the determinants of a breakdown of relationships are likely to be transient or permanent. It helps no-one to expect improvement when this is not likely to come about, or to invest inordinate efforts to keep children at home when there is no realistic hope for betterment'.

One person's experience must of necessity be limited. Even the most wise and experienced professional person has not seen enough children or followed them through enough of their life-span to be able to predict what will happen in an individual case. We need to turn to well conducted research to aid us. Some of this research I have referred to, but we are only at the beginning. Unless social workers and lawyers join with psychologists and psychiatrists in evaluative studies, the rich vein of our experience cannot be mined. I would like to finish with an example of missed opportunity.

Fifty years ago a massive social experiment took place. Three and a half million children were evacuated, mostly without parents, from Britain's cities, to be billeted haphazardly on more or less willing, more or less able, more or less kindly foster parents. No one studied the process and outcome, no one documented the results — (except for novelists — see Waugh (1942) and Bawden (1974) for example). Yet the upheaval had profound effects, for good or ill, on nearly half the population (Wicks 1988).

Conclusion

I want to leave you with five main points.

1 Attachment bonds should be protected in early childhood. The state should not be able to disrupt well-functioning caretaker-child (and sibling-child) bonds, no matter how great the future gains might be thought to be.

2 A child's sense of time differs according to age and must be taken into account.

3 It may be a form of racism to make black children wait an unacceptably long and damaging period of time to obtain a perfect racial parental match.

4 Wherever possible decisions about children should be based on research findings tempered by experience and common sense and when the research is not available, it should be commissioned.

5 As children's doctors, we have access to research findings, a knowledge of normal development and its deviations, the skills to demonstrate compassion and empathy for parents whilst putting children's needs first. We know where to go to obtain effective treatment for families and who can benefit from it and we have the training to make painful yet necessary decisions without flinching. In my view we must encourage social services and the courts to consult us at an earlier stage than they have hitherto.

References

Adcock M, 'Child care and the state', Lecture given at Institute of Family Therapy Conference, June, 1989.

Ainsworth M D S, 'Attachment: retrospect and prospect' in *The place of attachment in human behaviour,* (ed) Parkes C M and Stevenson-Hinde J, Tavistock, London, 1982.

Association of Black Social Workers and Allied Professions, *Black children in care: evidence to House of Commons, Social Services Committee,* London, 1983.

BAAF, *The placement needs of black children*, Practice Note 13, 1989.

Bawden N, *Carrie's war*, Penguin, Harmondsworth, 1974.

Bentovim A and Bingley L, 'Parenting and parenting failure' in *Good enough parenting* (ed) Adcock M and White R, *op cit*, 1985.

Bettelheim B, *Children of the dream*, Thames and Hudson, London, 1969.

Black D, Wolkind S and Harris-Hendricks J (eds), 'Assessing parenting capacity' in *Child psychiatry and the law,* Gaskell, Royal College of Psychiatrists, London, 1989.

Boston M and Szur R (eds), *Psychotherapy with severely deprived children,* Routledge, London, 1983.

Bowlby J, *Attachment,* Hogarth Press, London, 1969.

Bretherton I and Waters E (eds), *Growing points of attachment — theory and research,* U. Chicago Press, Chicago, 1985.

Chambers H, 'Cutting through the dogma', *Social Work Today* 5 Oct., 14 – 15, 1989.

Clarkson J E, Monaghan S M, Gilmore R J, Muir R C, Crooks T J and Egan T G, 'Predicting and preventing parenting problems', *New Zealand Medical Journal,* 101 (838): 12 – 14, 1988.

Cooper C, '"Good-enough", borderline and "bad-enough" parenting' in *Good-enough parenting* (eds) Adcock M and White R, BAAF, London, 1985.

De Mause L (ed), *The history of childhood,* Souvenir Press, London, 1976.

D.O.H., *Protecting children,* HMSO, London, 1988.

Forehand R and McMahon R, *A clinician's guide to parent training,* Guildford Press, N.Y., 1981.

Frommer E A and O'Shea G, 'Antenatal identification of women liable to have problems managing their infants', British Journal of Psychiatry, 123, 149 – 156, 1973.

Gill, O and Jackson B, *Adoption and race,* Batsford, London, 1983.

Guardian Law Report — 'Adoption of a child of mixed race', 8 September p 39, 1989.

Harris K, *Trans-racial adoption,* BAAF, 1985.

Hodges J and Tizard B, 'Social and family relationships of ex-institutional adolescents', *Journal of Child Psychology and Psychiatry,* 30:1, 77 – 98, 1989.

Jenner S The assessment and treatment of parenting skills, paper presented at The Child Abuse Conference, Institute of Psychiatry, 1988.

Ladner J, *Mixed families,* Doubleday Anchor N.Y., 1977.

Leventhal J M, Garber R B and Brady C A, 'Identification during post partum period of infants who are at high risk of child maltreatment', *Journal of Paediatrics,* 114(3):481 – 79, 1989.

Lynch M A and Roberts J, *Consequences of child abuse,* Academic Press, London, 1982.

Nuechterlein K H, 'Childhood precursors of adult schizophrenia', in *Journal of Child Psychology and Psychiatry,* 24, 297 – 300, 1986.

Oates M, 'Assessing fitness to parent' in *Taking a stand,* BAAF, 1984.

Obituary *British Medical Journal,* 5th November, 1966.

Quinton D and Rutter M, *Parenting breakdown,* Avebury, 1988.

Rutter M, 'Attachment and the development of social relationships' in M Rutter (ed) *Scientific foundations of developmental psychiatry,* Heinemann, London, 1980.

Rutter M, *Maternal deprivation reassessed,* (2nd Edition) Penguin, 1981.

Rutter M, 'Pathways from childhood to adult life', *Journal of Child Psychology and Psychiatry,* 30.1, 23 – 51, 1989.

Tizard B, *Adoption: a second chance,* Open Books, London, 1977.

Vernon J and Fruin D, *In care: a study of social work decision making,* National Children's Bureau, London, 1986.

Waugh E, *Put out more flags,* Penguin, 1942.

Wicks B, *No time to wave goodbye,* Bloomsbury, London, 1988.

Winnicott D, *The child, the family, the outside world,* Penguin, 1964.

Wolff S, 'Prediction in child care', *Adoption and Fostering,* 11 *1,* 11 – 17, 1987.

Wolff S, *Childhood and human nature,* Routledge, London, 1989.

Wolkind S, 'The child psychiatrist in court: using the contributions of developmental psychology' in *Taking a stand,* BAAF, 1984.

Acknowledgements

With thanks to Dr Jean Harris-Hendricks and Mrs Judith Bevan for constructive comments on earlier drafts.

[9]

Pathways from Childhood to Adult Life[*]

Michael Rutter[†]

Abstract—Principles and concepts of development are reviewed in relation to life-span issues noting the need to consider: development in its social context; timing of experiences; intrinsic and experiential factors; continuities and discontinuities; parallels and differences between normal and abnormal development; heterotypic and homotypic continuities; key life transitions; risk and protective factors; indirect chain affects; mediating mechanisms; age as an index of maturational and experiential factors. Developmental findings from childhood to adult longitudinal studies are reviewed for possible mediating factors. These include: genetic mechanisms; the (non-genetic) biological substrate; shaping of the environment; cognitive and social skills; self-esteem and self-efficacy; habits, cognitive sets and coping styles; links between experiences.

Keywords: Life-span development, developmental continuities/discontinuities, turning points in development, personality development

Introduction

Throughout his highly productive life, Jack Tizard was strongly committed to the application of research methods in psychology to issues of relevance for social policy and practice (see Clarke & Tizard, 1983). However, he was equally committed to the need for basic research that is focused on the elucidation of the processes and mechanisms underlying normal and abnormal development. In his letter to the Chief Scientist outlining the philosophy of the Thomas Coram Research Unit, he was forthright in arguing that it was essential to combine both approaches. Research must bring forth new ideas and fresh knowledge so that patterns of practice may be improved in the future; it is not enough simply to assess the best of what is being done today.

My own debt to Jack is enormous; not only in gaining an appreciation of how research and policy interact but, more particularly, in learning how epidemiological and longitudinal research methods may be used in this connection. Our collaboration in the Isle of Wight studies (Rutter, Tizard & Whitmore, 1970; Rutter, Tizard, Yule, Graham & Whitmore, 1976) was an exciting learning experience for me. Jack was an extremely generous as well as immensely stimulating teacher, whose combination of unwavering methodological rigour and intellectual openness provided a model that

---

Accepted manuscript received 12 *August* 1988

[*]Jack Tizard Memorial Lecture. Delivered on 1 July 1988 at the Association for Child Psychology and Psychiatry Annual Conference, London.
[†]Honorary Director, MRC Child Psychiatry Unit, Institute of Psychiatry, University of London, U.K.
Requests for reprints to: Professor M. Rutter, Department of Child and Adolescent Psychiatry, Institute of Psychiatry, De Crespigny Park, Denmark Hill, London SE5 8AF, U.K.

all of us who worked with him strove to follow. The longitudinal element in the Isle of Wight studies, four years, was relatively short, but it served to alert me to the importance of understanding how developmental processes served to bring about both stability and change. This elucidation of the mechanisms underlying continuities and discontinuities of development over the life-span is crucial if we are to devise improved means of intervening to bring about long term gains for children suffering intrinsic or extrinsic hazards during their growing years.

It has to be said that Jack was always sceptical of claims that short term experiences could have long term effects and that permanent change should be the goal of treatment. In his presidential address to the British Psychological Society (Tizard, 1976), he argued for the importance of the immediate environment as the main influence on a person's behaviour, and he urged that we should abandon notions about the long term value of preventive interventions such as Headstart, and that instead we should examine the characteristics of the environment that contribute to immediate happiness and well being. Those cautions remain apposite today, and both of the first two Jack Tizard lectures—by Alan Clarke (Clarke & Clarke, 1984) and by Ron Clarke (1985)—developed these themes well and showed their importance.

On the other hand, Jack was well aware that, in some circumstances, adverse experiences could have long term sequelae, as he demonstrated in his own collaborative research on the development of children who suffered the combination of malnutrition and psychosocial privation (Hertzig, Birch, Richardson & Tizard, 1972; see also Tizard, 1975). His point was *not* that continuities did not occur, but rather that simplistic concepts of immutable effects needed to be put aside and replaced by more dynamic notions of the continuing interplay over time between intrinsic and extrinsic influences on individual development. This is the theme that I seek to explore in this paper.

Over the last three decades there have been major changes in the ways in which the developmental process has been conceptualized. During the 1950s beliefs in the consistency of personality and in the lack of major changes after the first few years of life held sway (see Kelly, 1955). Longitudinal studies sought to chart this early stabilization of personality (see Moss & Susman, 1980), and it was urged that maternal deprivation in infancy led to permanent, irreversible damage (Bowlby, 1951). However, longitudinal studies failed to show high temporal stability and the claims on maternal deprivation were subjected to severe academic criticism (e.g. O'Connor, 1956; Orlansky, 1949; Yarrow, 1961). It became clear that people changed a good deal over the course of development and that the outcome following early adversities was quite diverse, with long-term effects heavily dependent on the nature of subsequent life experiences (Clarke & Clarke, 1976). Even markedly adverse experiences in infancy carry few risks for later development if the subsequent rearing environment is a good one (Rutter, 1981).

The pendulum swung and it came to be argued that there was little continuity in psychological development, such continuity as there was being dependent on people's interpretation of their experiences (Kagan, 1984). Mischel (1968, 1969) challenged the very notion of personality traits and argued that much behaviour was highly situation-specific. These claims gave rise to equally vigorous dispute on both the concepts and the empirical findings (Block, 1979; Epstein, 1979; Epstein & O'Brien,

1985; Hinde, 1987; Hinde & Bateson, 1984; McCall 1977; Magnusson, 1988; Nesselroade, 1988; Olweus, 1979).

In recent years there has been a limited swinging back of the pendulum, as investigators have been faced with evidence demonstrating a rather complex mix of both continuities and discontinuities (Rutter, 1987a). That mix applies to all phases in the developmental process, but my focus today is on the longer time span of connections between childhood and adult life.

Principles and concepts of development

Before proceeding to consider some of the key findings from several major longitudinal studies, it may be useful first to outline some of the principles and concepts of development that derive from research findings both on normal development (Rutter, 1987a) and on psychopathology (Rutter, 1984a,b; Rutter, 1988).

The first point is that a life-span perspective is necessary (Rutter, 1984b). That is because *Homo sapiens* is a social animal and because social development occurs in relation to a person's interactions and transactions with his or her social environment (Erikson, 1963; Bronfenbrenner, 1979; Hinde, 1987; Hinde & Stevenson-Hinde, 1988). Because key social experiences such as marriage or childbearing tend not to occur during the childhood years, social development needs to be extended into adult life. A related point is that development includes the *content* of emotions and social relationships as well as *capacities* in these areas of functioning. Maccoby (1984) made the point that, although there are important universals in development, social development follows more than one pathway and has more than one endpoint— hence the plural of pathways in the title of this paper.

A related issue is that the *timing,* as well as the nature, of experiences is likely to influence their impact. The importance of timing arises for several different reasons. First, the effects on neural structure and functioning will be affected by what is happening at the time in neural development. This is illustrated by the effects of prenatal androgens on both brain organization and sexually dimorphic behaviours in later life (Mayer-Bahlburg, Ehrhardt & Feldman, 1986), by the varying effects of brain damage at different ages (Goodman, 1987; Rutter, 1982) and by the effects on binocular vision of uncorrected strabismus in infancy. Secondly, the effects will also be influenced by sensitivities and vulnerabilities deriving from the psychological processes that are emerging at the time. Thus, very young infants are protected from separation experiences because they have yet to develop strong attachments; older children are protected because they have learned to maintain relationships over time and space; but toddlers are most at risk because attachments are first becoming established at that age and because they lack the cognitive skills required to maintain relationships during an absence (Rutter, 1981, 1987a). Thirdly, timing may be important because experiences may be felt differently, or give rise to different societal responses, if they arise at non-normative times. For example, this may apply to the links between teenage pregnancy and difficulties in parenting (Hayes, 1987), to those between early marriage and an increased risk of divorce (Otto, 1979), to the differences in effects between redundancy in middle life and retirement in old age (Warr, 1987) and to the psychological consequences of unusually early puberty (Graham & Rutter, 1985).

A biological perspective, of course, requires an emphasis on both intrinsic and experiential influences on development. Genetic factors will play a part in shaping not only individual differences in psychological characteristics but also their developmental course (Plomin, 1986; Plomin & Thompson, 1988). In addition, it is likely that physiological transitions such as puberty, which involve major changes in hormonal output and in bodily configuration, will have a psychosocial impact (Petersen, 1988; Rutter, in press a). However, development is also affected by environmental factors that are not accompanied by somatic alteration. Experiences within and outside the home have been shown to make an impact on intellectual (Rutter, 1985a) and behavioural development (Rutter, 1985b).

A fourth consideration, also stemming from a biological perspective, is that both continuities and discontinuities are to be expected (Hinde, 1988; Hinde & Bateson, 1984; Rutter, 1987a). The process of development is concerned with change and it is not reasonable to suppose that the pattern will be set in early life. Physiological alterations, as at puberty, and new experiences will both serve to shape psychological functioning. However, continuities will occur because children carry with them the results of earlier learning and of earlier structural and functional change. This does not necessarily mean that a person's characteristics at one age will predict the degree or type of *change* over a later time period, but it does mean that it is likely to predict later *levels* of functioning, because they will incorporate earlier levels. The importance of this distinction is well shown in the excellent recent study of primary school effectiveness undertaken by Mortimore, Sammons, Stoll, Lewis and Etab (1988). Final attainment level was strongly correlated with family background and with the child's level of skills at school entry, but *progress* between 7 and 11 yrs was most strongly associated with school characteristics. The importance of differentiating between progress and final attainment level is also shown in Tizard, Blatchford, Burk, Farquahar and Plewis' (1988) important longitudinal study of children attending inner city infant schools.

The next issue is that there can be no presupposition that normal and abnormal development do, or do not, involve the same mechanisms or do, or do not, share the same qualities; rather there must be a concern empirically to test for similarities and dissimilarities (Rutter & Sandberg, 1985; Rutter, 1988). It is clear that both occur. Thus, it may well be that the features associated with the development of a pattern of heavy drinking in the general population parallel those that play a role in the emergence of alcoholism; by contrast it is possible that the pathways leading to schizophrenia or bipolar affective disorder include elements that do not constitute any part of normal development.

A sixth consideration is that there must be a search for heterotypic as well as homotypic continuities. In other words, we must recognize that behaviours may change in *form* whilst still reflecting the same basic *process*. There are, however, methodological hazards that must be avoided in any consideration of heterotypic continuity. The mere finding that behaviour X at one age is correlated with behaviour Y at a later age provides no basis for assuming continuity. In any complex statistical analysis, many such correlations are bound to arise by chance. To infer continuity it is important either to show that both behaviours, although different in form, function similarly in their association with risk factors and/or consequences, or to replicate the longitudinal correlation in another sample (or preferably both). Nevertheless, it is clear that there are heterotypic continuities that have withstood these tests. For example, there is continuity between social isolation, peer rejection, odd unpredictable behaviour and attention deficits in childhood and schizophrenic psychosis in adult life (Nuechterlein, 1986; Rutter, 1984a). It has also been found that conduct disorder in childhood leads not only to antisocial personality disorders in adult life, but also to a broader range of social malfunctions associated with an increased risk of depressive disorder—the former pathway being more common in males and the latter in females (Robins, 1986; Quinton, Rutter & Gulliver, in press; Zeitlin, 1986).

A life-span perspective requires attention to the variety of transitions that occur during the course of development, such as leaving the parental home, starting work, getting married and becoming a parent. However, it also brings a further consideration—the need to focus on the process of *negotiation* of life transitions, and not just their occurrence or the behavioural outcome that follows. Thus, the fact of getting married at a particular age is one thing, but it is equally important to consider why and how the decision was taken when it was, as well as the social context of the decision and the characteristics of the spouse.

An eighth consideration is the need to take into account individual differences in the meaning of, and response to, such transitions. Thus, parenthood that arises unwanted at the age of 15 yrs will not be the same as a wanted child being born to a young adult in the context of a happy marriage, and both will differ from the experience of having a first child after a decade's unsuccessful attempts to conceive associated with multiple treatments for infertility. All three will differ yet again from parenthood as a result of artificial insemination by donor or adoption or fostering.

A ninth issue is that an emphasis is needed on both risk *and* protective factors, together with interactions between them (Rutter, 1983; in press a). Both good and bad experiences influence development. However, it is also crucial that some experiences that seem negative at the time may nevertheless be protective. Just as a resistance to infection stems from ''successful'' encounters with the infective agent in a modified or attentuated form (the basis of immunization), perhaps too resistance to psychosocial adversity is fostered by successful copying with earlier stressful experiences. Elder's (1974, 1979) example of the strengthening effect of older children having to take on family responsibilities during the great economic depression is a case in point.

A related issue is the need to recognize the importance of indirect chain and strand effects in the developmental process (Brown, 1988), as well as direct influences. In other words, the impact of some factor in childhood may lie less in the immediate behavioural change it brings about than in the fact that it sets in motion a chain reaction in which one ''bad'' thing leads to another or, conversely, that a good experience makes it more likely that another one will be encountered. For example, academic success at school is likely to increase the chance of a well-paid job in adult life and better living conditions—not because passing exams alters personality but simply because academic credentials open the doors to career advancement which in turn is associated with a range of social advantages in adult life.

28   M. Rutter

The penultimate principle is that there must be a concern to elucidate the processes and mechanisms involved in such indirect and direct effects. It is, of course, important to determine the various factors associated with an adaptive psychosocial outcome. Thus, it has been useful that research has shown that these are more likely if the child has positive characteristics such as high self-esteem and a positive social orientation; if the family shows warmth, harmony and cohesion; and if adequate social supports are available (Masten & Garmezy, 1985). However, if we are to use this information to develop effective means of fostering normal development and of preventing mental disorder, we must go on to ask *how* self-esteem develops, which experiences or biological qualities are likely to foster it, and by which mechanisms does it operate.

Finally, in studying these processes and mechanisms, it is necessary to appreciate that age is an ambiguous variable; the finding that some psychological function increases as children grow older does not, in itself, provide an answer as to why or how this happens (Rutter, in press b). It may occur as a result of physiological maturation (but, if so, there is the further question of which aspect of maturity is crucial; thus, cognitive and endocrinological maturity do not necessarily proceed hand in hand). Equally, however, the psychological advance may derive from the cumulative effect of certain sorts of experiences or from the occurrence of particular types of experiences that usually arise only later in childhood or adolescence.

In short, the investigation of pathways from childhood to adult life requires an analysis of a quite complicated set of linkages over time. It is not simply a matter of determining the level of correlation for particular behaviours from one age to some later age.

Some childhood to adult life longitudinal studies

With these considerations as a background, let me turn to the empirical evidence on pathways from childhood to adult life. I will not dwell on the findings on correlations over time for particular psychological characteristics, as these have been extensively reviewed previously (see e.g. Moss & Sussman, 1980; Rutter, 1987a). Suffice it to say that the correlations between early or middle childhood and adult life for most psychological features are general positive, but quite low. There is some tendency for children's behaviour to predict adult behaviour, but the correlations are too weak for much useful prediction at the individual level.

Psychopathological continuities

That conclusion, however, applies to normally distributed characteristics as assessed in the general population. The situation with respect to psychopathological features is somewhat different in that some types of disorder, especially conduct disturbances, do exhibit substantial continuity between childhood and adult life. Robins (1978) showed that antisocial personality disorder in adulthood was almost always preceded by conduct disturbance in childhood, so that continuity looking backwards is very strong indeed. However, because conduct disturbance in the childhood years is very common, and because only about a third persist into adulthood, continuity looking forwards is less impressive. This finding raises several important issues. First, there is the question of whether the apparent reduction in conduct problems is real or whether, rather, the form of disturbance has changed but the disorder nevertheless continues—the issue of heterotypic continuity. As already noted, conduct problems do indeed lead on to a broader range of adult disorders. Using the ECA retrospective data, Robins (1986) reported that when women had had three or more conduct problems in childhood, 85% had some form of psychiatric disorder in adult life compared with 41% of the remainder. The relative risk (a four-fold increase) was greatest for drugs, alcohol and antisocial problems, but there was also a two-fold increase for emotional disorders.

The second issue is what features differentiate the individuals who are most likely to show persistence of disorder into adult life. The Stockholm longitudinal study (Magnusson, 1988) showed that the risk was particularly great for boys who exhibited the combination of aggression, hyperactivity and poor peer relationships. Compared with well-adjusted boys, the risk of having adult criminality *and* alcohol abuse *and* psychiatric disorder was 20 times higher and, compared with the total population rate, it was still more than seven times higher! The children with multiproblem patterns were few in number but they accounted for much of the persistence.

The findings from the Cambridge longitudinal study of working class London boys confirm the markedly increased risk for persistent adult criminality associated with both hyperactivity and conduct disturbance in childhood. In that longitudinal study of 411 boys, only 24 had as many as six convictions by their 26th birthday. Twenty of these 24 men had shown hyperactivity and/or conduct disturbance at 8–10 yrs; a ten-fold increase in risk that accounted for 83% of chronic adult offenders (Farrington, Loeber & Van Kammen, in press).

Parker and Asher's (1987) excellent recent review of the association between poor peer relationships in childhood and adult disorder emphasizes the importance of both low peer acceptance and aggressiveness as predictors of school dropout, adult criminality and probably also other types of adult problems. Shyness/withdrawal does not seem to carry the same risks. As Parker and Asher point out, many issues remain to be resolved. Thus, it is not clear whether the risk stems from lack of social skills, lack of social ties or negative socially disapproved behaviour. Moreover, it remains uncertain whether low peer acceptance is merely an incidental correlate of persisting psychopathological disturbance or whether it plays a causal role in continuities over time because it predisposes to deviant socialization experiences and opportunities. Nevertheless, the evidence from longitudinal studies that have examined hyperactivity, conduct disturbance and poor peer relationships is that when present in marked pervasive form they carry a markedly increased risk for adult disorder of one kind or another.

This does not necessarily mean that the continuities stem from intrinsic psychological processes. It could be that the persistence of disorder simply reflects the continuation of the psychosocial risk factors that gave rise to the children's problems in the first place. This is a very real possibility because conduct disorders are particularly associated with types of family discord and disorganization and of parental deviance that tend to be very persistent (Rutter, 1985b). We need to focus on circumstances where children's environments have changed markedly for the better in order to see if this is accompanied by parellel improvements in the children's conduct disturbance. Richman, Stevenson and Graham (1982), in their longitudinal study from age 3–8 yrs, found that a reduction in marital disharmony made no difference to the likelihood that children's problems would remit; however, improved parent–child relationships (as reflected in increased parental warmth and reduced criticisms) were associated with benefits for the children. It seems that the specifics of children's interpersonal interactions may be more important in continuity than the overall family circumstances.

A more dramatic change in children's circumstances was investigated by Hodges and Tizard (1989 a,b) in their follow-up to age 16 yrs of children reared in residential nurseries until at least age 2 yrs and then adopted or restored to their biological parents at some time between 2 and 7 yrs (Tizard & Hodges, 1978). The restored group, whose families tended to be disturbed and disadvantaged, showed a high rate of antisocial behaviour, with almost all having had contact with the police and/or psychiatric services. The adoptees, most of whom were in stable harmonious homes, were much less likely to show this pattern, but tended to be more worried, unhappy and fearful than the comparison group children. These differences would seem to reflect their current circumstances more than their early institutional experiences. However, both the adoptees and restored children were very similar to each other, and different from controls, in being more oriented towards adult attention and in having more difficulties with peers and fewer close peer relationships. As the experiences of the adoptees and of the restored children were so different over the decade preceding the 16 yr follow-up, it must be inferred that the institutional upbringing for the first few years of life had left some social sequelae that were somewhat resistant to later influences, at least up to the age of 16 yrs. Nevertheless, it is notable that this persistence in terms of subtle qualities of peer relationships stands out as different from the pattern exhibited by other behaviours.

A further possibility that has to be considered is that the children's behaviour, as a result of its impact on other people, makes later stressful environments more likely. It is clear that both conduct disturbance and poor peer relationships, the two types of psychopathology most likely to persist, carry that potential. Thus, Robins (1986) reported that the ECA data showed that women aged 30–49 yrs who showed three or more conduct problems in childhood had a two-fold increased risk of job loss during the 6 mths before interview, a two-fold increased risk of break-up with a spouse or lover and a four-fold increased risk of break-up with a best friend during the same time period. These retrospective data require confirmation from longitudinal studies, but the strong implication is that behavioural disturbance predisposes to an increased likelihood of adverse psychosocial experiences or life events in adult life. Kandel and Davies (1986), using longitudinal questionnaire data, similarly showed that adolescent depression was associated with an increased risk of certain kinds of social stress situations in early adult life.

Psychosocial pathways

With that possibility in mind, let me turn to a few of the long term longitudinal studies that have attempted to chart the various steps that might be involved in

Pathways from childhood to adult life 31

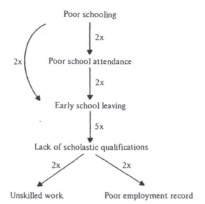

Fig. 1. Simplified pathway from poor schooling to poor job success (Gray
et al., 1980).

pathways from childhood to adult life. The first investigation to mention is our follow-up of inner London children from age 10 yrs to one year after leaving school (Gray, Smith & Rutter, 1980). Figure 1 summarizes the pathways leading from poor schooling to poor job success. We found no effect of schooling that was independent of later circumstances, but the indirect continuities were quite strong. The children who went to less effective schools were twice as likely as other children to show poor school attendance; poor attenders were twice as likely to leave school early without sitting national examinations—necessarily this meant that all left without scholastic qualifications, compared with only a fifth of other pupils; those without qualifications were in turn twice as likely to go into unskilled work and were twice as likely to have a poor employment record as shown by their getting dismissed from jobs. These continuities were still evident after controlling for other variables such as the individual's measured intelligence and social circumstances.

Of course, the chain of adversity was far from inevitable, in that each link was open to other influences that could break (or strengthen) the chain. For example, black girls were particularly likely to have a good attendance record and to stay on at school beyond the period of compulsory education (Maughan, Dunn & Rutter, 1985a; Maughan & Rutter, 1986). As a result of their unusual educational persistence they left school with exam qualifications that were substantially better than might have been expected on the basis of their reading skills on entering secondary school or the quality of the schools they attended. Conversely, boys with poor reading skills tended to leave school without exam qualifications, not so much because their academic limitations meant that they failed exams, but rather because their conduct problems tended to be associated with leaving school early without sitting any exams (Maughan, Gray & Rutter, 1985b).

The second study to mention is the follow-up of institution-reared children undertaken by David Quinton and myself, together with colleagues (Quinton & Rutter, 1988). The young people were interviewed in depth in their mid 20s and comparable data were obtained for a general population sample, reared at home by their biological parents, and followed up over a comparable time period. The findings showed a chain by which parenting breakdown in one generation *sometimes* led to parenting breakdown

32 M. Rutter

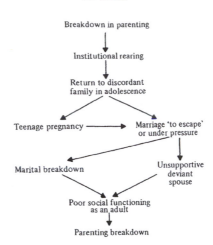

Fig. 2. Simplified model of intergenerational transmission of parenting breakdown (Quinton & Rutter, 1988).

in the next. Not surprisingly, perhaps, the adult outcome of the institution-reared girls was significantly worse than that of the comparison group, and overt parenting breakdown was found only in the institutional sample, occuring in a third of cases. Numerous statistical analyses were undertaken to determine the possible mechanisms underlying the heterogeneity in outcome.

Figure 2 presents a selection of the findings in terms of the intervening steps leading to eventual parenting breakdown. The story begins with a variety of psychosocial problems in the girls' parents; these problems were associated with parenting difficulties and with lack of social support, which in turn led to the girls' admission to residential nurseries or Group Homes where they remained off and on, or continuously, until adolescence. On leaving the institutions, many of the girls either had no family to which to go or they returned to the same discordant families from which they had been 'rescued' when young. Faced with these stressful circumstances, many married hastily to 'escape' or under pressure as a result of a teenage pregnancy. An institutional upbringing led many of the girls to feel that they could not control their lives and they tended not to plan ahead with either work or marriage. As one might have expected, these impulsive marriages undertaken for negative reasons were often to deviant men from similarly disadvantaged backgrounds and many of the marriages broke down. Alternatively, the women were left unsupported in a conflictful, unrewarding marital relationship. These adult circumstances were then associated with a markedly increased risk of poor social functioning in adult life which, in turn, was accompanied by an increased risk of parenting breakdown.

It will be appreciated that this chain of adversities is made up of a series of contingencies which, if not met, are likely to result in different consequences. Figure 3 provides one example of how a more adaptive chain of circumstances could arise. The girls who were admitted to the institution after the age of 2 yrs, not having experienced early disruptions of parenting, were much more likely to return to a harmonious family on leaving the Children's Home in adolescence. The presence

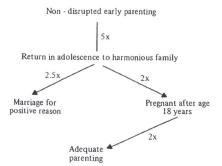

Fig. 3. Simplified adaptive chain of circumstances in institution-reared women (1) (Quinton & Rutter, 1988).

of such a harmonious home at that time made it more than twice as likely that the girls would marry for positive reasons (i.e. not under pressure or to escape) and that they would not become pregnant until age 19 or later. Both these circumstances increased the likelihood of adequate or good parenting.

Fig. 4. Simplified adaptive chain of circumstances in institution-reared women (2) (Quinton & Rutter, 1988).

In a sense, that chain involved a series of partially interconnected social circumstances. However, some risk pathways were turned into more adaptive routes as a result of adventitious happenings. Thus, for example, it was a policy of the Children's Homes to distribute the children among many different schools in order to avoid an undue weighting of institutional children in any one school, which could lead to adverse labelling. As a consequence, some children had much more positive school experiences than others. Those who had good experiences were three times as likely to show planning in their choice of careers and of marriage partner. This meant that they were much more likely to marry for positive reasons which, in turn, much increased the likelihood that they would marry a non-deviant man with whom they developed a warm confiding relationship. The presence of such marital support

34   M. Rutter

greatly increased the likelihood that they would show good social functioning and good parenting as a young adult. This chain of connections remained after controlling for other variables, such as the girls' non-deviant behaviour in childhood and adolescence.

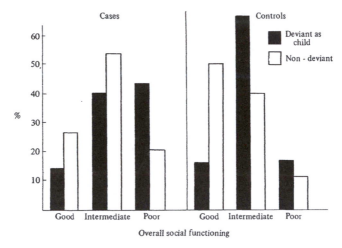

Fig. 5. Childhood deviance and adult outcome (males) (based on Rutter, Quinton & Hill, in press).

Nevertheless, deviant behaviour was itself associated with outcome, and this statistical relationship was substantially stronger in males than in females (Rutter, Quinton & Hill, in press). The findings for males showed that childhood deviance was significantly associated with poor overall social functioning in adult life, there being a two-fold increase in risk. However, among those showing childhood deviance, an institutional rearing was still associated with a two-fold increase in poor social functioning. In other words, there was a pathway involving childhood deviance, but also one or more that involved other features.

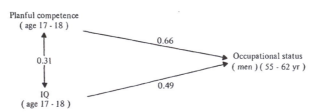

Fig. 6. Berkeley longitudinal studies: the role of planful competence (Clausen, 1986).

Our data suggested the important role of planning as a factor associated with good adult outcomes. However, we had to measure planning retrospectively, with all the uncertainties that retrospective measurement involves. The Berkeley longitudinal studies (Clausen, 1986) provided the opportunity to assess the same effect prospectively. What was termed 'planful competence' was measured at age 17–18 yrs, when there was also an assessment of IQ. The two measures intercorrelated only modestly at the 0.31 level. Strikingly, planful competence correlated 0.66 with occupational status in late middle life, at age 55–62 yrs, a stronger correlation than that found with IQ.

Table 1. Number of marriages according to Senior High School level of planful competence (percentage distribution) (men)

| | Planful competence | | |
	High	Inter.	Low
Total	100	100	100
None	—	5	—
One	82	75	55
Two	18	15	32
Three or more	—	5	14
Number of subjects	28	20	22

(Data from Clausen, 1986)

As in our institution-reared sample, a lack of planful competence was also associated with an increased risk of marital breakdown. Nearly half (46%) of those who lacked such planning had two or more marriages, compared with 18% of those with high planning. The comparable figures for females (based on a slightly different measure) were 46% versus 6%. It is evident that characteristics shown in adolescence were quite strongly predictive of marital and occupational circumstances in middle life, some 40 yrs later. Note, however, that what is evident is *not* unchanging behaviour over time, but rather a style of dealing with life circumstances that increased the chances of things turning out less well.

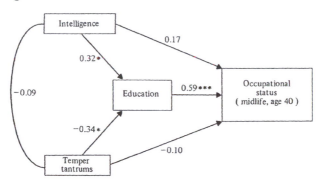

Fig. 7. Temper tantrums in childhood and occupational status in adult life (based on Caspi, Elder & Herbener, in press).

The Berkeley and Oakland studies were also used as a data-base by Caspi, Elder and Herbener (in press). Once again, a variety of chain reactions are to be seen. Figure 7 summarizes the consequences of a pattern of frequent temper tantrums in childhood. This type of 'explosive' behaviour made it significantly more likely that there would be an early exit from school and hence less likely that the person would

36   M. Rutter

end up with good educational attainments in early adult life. Poor attainments were, in turn, associated with lower occupational status in mid life. The childhood behaviour had no direct effect on occupational level, but it had an important indirect effect via its impact on scholastic attainment.

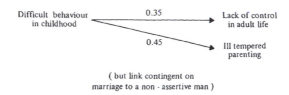

Fig. 8. **Longitudinal study of Berkeley women: adult sequelae of difficult behaviour in childhood (Caspi & Elder, 1988).**

Difficult behaviour in childhood was also associated with an increased risk of ill-tempered parenting and of poor social control in adult life in women (Caspi & Elder, 1988). Interestingly, however, this outcome was contingent on marriage to a non-assertive man. Difficult behaviour made it significantly more likely that the women *would* marry men with these characteristics and, if they did, they were more likely to show poor social control in mid life. If they did not, however, there was *no* such tendency.

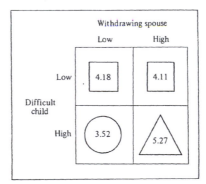

Fig. 9. **The behavioural consequences of difficult girls' mate-selection patterns. Dependent variable: women's undercontrolled behaviour at midlife (1 = low, 9 = high) (Caspi & Elder, 1988).**

The findings are summarized in Fig. 9. The score in the triangle in the bottom right hand corner shows the lack of adult control score when there was the combination of difficult childhood behaviour in the women and unassertive withdrawal in the spouse. The rate of poor control is significantly higher than that in all other cells. Caspi and Elder (1988) concluded that the continuities reside in interactional styles that operate in two ways: firstly, through selection of environments and relationships (as shown by the effect on choice of spouse); secondly, through elicitation of interactions that bring out maladaptive behaviours (the interactive effect shown in Fig. 9).

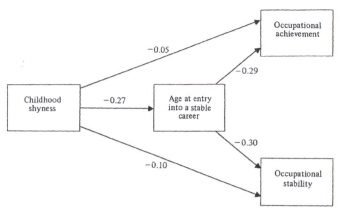

Fig. 10. Adult sequelae of childhood shyness (based on Caspi, Edler & Herbener, in press).

Childhood shyness, another early manifest characteristic, showed a rather different causal chain. It was accompanied by an increased likelihood of late entry into a stable occupational career; late entry was then associated with a lower level of occupational achievement and greater occupational instability. It seemed as if career entry at an atypically late point meant a lesser investment in career skills and benefits and hence an increased career vulnerability.

However, it should not be assumed that people who undergo key life transitions unusually late are always thereby disadvantaged. Elder (1986) showed that, in some circumstances, it could be protective if the late transitions opened up new opportunities. In the Berkeley Guidance Study, low achieving youths from a deprived background who, in adolescence, scored low on measures of social competence tended to join the Armed Forces unusually early, often dropping out from high school to do so (this was in the late 1940s during a period of conscription). Military service was associated with a prolongation of education (the great majority took up schooling again in the Army) and with a delay in both marriage and the starting of careers. For these deprived youths, military service proved to be an important turning point that enabled them to acquire scholastic and occupational skills that they would not have had otherwise; also their later marriage meant that they were marrying at a time when they were more self-sufficient and part of a better functioning social group. Follow-up into middle life showed that this was accompanied by a beneficial change in life trajectory; their outcome was significantly better than expected on the basis of their background and their functioning in adolescence. Of course, in the population as a whole, military service was not likely to have this beneficial effect and it is not argued that it should be recommended as a solution to deprivation. Rather, the point is that even experiences with many negative aspects can be helpful if they serve to provide adaptive opportunities that would not otherwise have been available.

The importance of timing is evident in another longitudinal project, the Stockholm study reported by Magnusson (1988). Unusually early puberty in girls, a menarché under the age of 11 yrs, was associated with a marked increase in drunkenness and in other forms of norm-breaking in mid adolescence. It was found that this increase was a function of a greater tendency to be part of an older peer group. The early maturing girls who did not mix with older teenagers did not exhibit any increase in norm-breaking. It seemed that the stimulus was physiological but the mechanism was psychosocial (Magnusson, Stattin & Allen, 1986). However, later follow-up in the mid 20s showed that early maturity was no longer associated with an increase in norm-breaking. It was inferred that the early maturing girls had adopted an older adolescent style of behaviour that was evanescent, because as peer groups changed so the influences on behaviour altered; hence there was no long term persistence.

The early maturing girls were also more likely to drop out of school, again following the pattern of older girls. However, unlike the school leaving of older girls who had completed their education, the premature drop-out of the early maturers meant that they left with lower educational attainments. This outcome was persistent; probably because to reverse it would have required a return to education at a later age. Although this was possible, it required a major step that few took. The continuity stemmed from a closing down of opportunities rather than from any intrinsic personality change as such. Similarly, leaving school meant that many turned to marriage and home making. As a consequence, the early maturers had significantly more children at age 26 yrs than the remainder of the sample. Again, this was a continuity that lay in the consequences of early behaviour rather than in internal change in the women themselves.

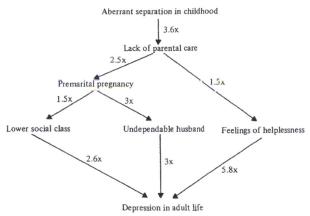

Fig. 11. Simplified model of the links between aberrant separation in childhood and depression in adult life (based on data from Brown *et al.*, 1986).

Several of the studies that have been discussed have drawn attention to pregnancy, marriage and choice of occupation as important turning points in people's lives. The importance of these life transitions is shown again in the study of adult women by Brown and his colleagues (Brown, Harris & Bifulco, 1986; Harris, Brown & Bifulco, 1986, 1987). Figure 11 summarizes some of the main findings. The pathway starts with aberrant separations from parents in childhood (sometimes leading to institutional admission). This was associated with an increased risk (3.6 ×) that parental care would be poor. Poor parental care was then associated with a 2.5 times increase in the likelihood of a premarital pregnancy. Such a pregnancy increased the risk that the girl would land up with an undependable husband and also it made it more likely that the girl would not rise in social class. Lack of parental care separately increased the probability of the woman showing feelings of helplessness. Each of these three strands (i.e. to a lower social class, to a poor marriage and to feelings of helplessness) was associated with an increased vulnerability to depression in adult life. It was notable, as in the other studies, that each link in the chain was contingent on how the life transitions were negotiated. Thus, parental separation carried no risk if it did not lead to poor parental care. Similarly, if the premarital pregnancy was coped with well it did not have the ill-effects noted in Fig. 11.

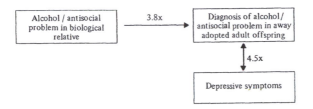

Fig. 12. **Simplified model of links between genetic risk factor for alcohol/antisocial problems and occurrence of depression (Cadoret *et al.*, in press).**

Another pathway that requires mention is that through genetic influences. In their investigation of children who were adopted in early life and therefore not reared by their biological parents, Cadoret, Troughton, Morens and Whitters (in press) found both direct and indirect genetic effects. They found that alcohol or antisocial problems in biological relatives were associated with a 3.8 times risk of similar problems in the away-adopted adult offspring—a direct genetic effect. These problems in the biological family were not associated with any direct effect on depression in the offspring. On the other hand, individuals with alcohol or antisocial problems were over four times as likely to show depressive symptoms—a substantial indirect genetic effect. It remains uncertain just why antisocial disorder is associated with an increased risk of depression, but many studies have shown that it is. One explanation is probably that the deviant behaviour leads to both stressful interpersonal interactions and social disadvantage (cf. Robins, 1986), both of which in turn predispose to depression.

My account of long-term longitudinal studies has been deliberately incomplete. The pattern of findings in the studies cited is more complex than I have been able to indicate and, of course, there are many other studies that could have been considered. Nevertheless, the overall patterns that I have presented are, I think, reasonably representative of those reported in the literature and, as I have shown, many of the key patterns have been replicated across studies. These patterns fall far short of anything approaching a complete explanation of developmental connections. Nevertheless, they do point to some of the ways in which chain effects may arise. It remains to bring the findings together in a consideration of the various processes and mechanisms that might underlie these continuities (and discontinuities) between childhood and adult life (see Maughan & Champion, in press; Rutter, 1984c).

Possible mediating factors for continuities and discontinuities

Genetic mechanisms

The first possibility is that both continuities and change may be mediated genetically. This may occur in several different ways. Thus, the persistence of a disorder from childhood to adult life may be a function of the intrinsic qualities of a genetically determined condition; this may apply to autism where there seems to be a strong genetic component (Folstein & Rutter, 1987; Smalley, Asarnow & Spence, 1988). Less obviously, however, genetic factors need to be considered in relation to the continuity between conduct disorder in childhood and personality disorder in adult life. Although the broad run of conduct problems and of delinquent behaviour in childhood seems to have only a weak genetic component, the evidence suggests that genetic factors may well be more important in the subgroup that persist into adult life (Rutter, MacDonald, Le Couteur, Harrington, Bolton & Bailey, submitted). Equally, however, genetic mechanisms may play a part in the continuities between two different forms of behaviour. Thus, this may apply to the connections between social oddities and attentional deficits in childhood and schizophrenic psychoses in adult life (Nuechterlein, 1986; Gottesman & Shields, 1976) and to depression in early adult life as a precursor of Huntington's disease in middle age (Folstein, Franz, Jensen, Chase & Folstein, 1983).

In addition, however, genetic factors may also operate indirectly in leading to types of psychopathology that then are associated with an increased vulnerability to other forms of psychiatric disorder. Thus, the study of Cadoret *et al.* (in press) showed that this probably occurred with genetic mechanisms in relation to antisocial disorders which were, in turn, associated with an increased risk of depressive symptomatology.

Biological substrate

Secondly, mediation may lie in aspects of the biological substrate that are not genetically determined. For example, several investigations have shown statistical associations between pregnancy and birth complications and schizophrenia in adult life (Lewis & Murray, 1987; Murray *et al.*, in press; Parnas, Schulsinger, Teasdale, Schulsinger, Feldman & Mednick, 1982). The mechanisms involved in this association remain uncertain but it may be that the later maturation of brain systems linked with schizophrenia, possibly dopaminergic neural systems, activates the mental disorder because the relevant brain structures were damaged at birth (Weinberger, 1987). The brain pathology as such is not progressive, but the effects are not manifest until much later because the brain systems associated with schizophrenia have yet to develop. The suggestion remains speculative so far as schizophrenia is concerned but there are well-established medical examples of similar late effects or of changing manifestations with age. Thus, there is the link between encephalitis lethargica (or brain damage from boxing) in early adult life and the later development of Parkinsonism. Similarly, there are the well established associations between viral infections and the development of various forms of cancer some decades later. The association between high alcohol exposure *in utero* and attentional deficits in childhood provides an example of a prenatal effect (Porter, O'Conner & Whelan, 1984); the adult sequelae are as yet unknown.

However, the mediation does not necessarily have to involve organic brain damage. For example, the animal experiments of Levine and others (Hennessy & Levine, 1979; Hunt, 1979) showed that physical stress in infancy led to both enlarged adrenal glands and increased resistance to later stressors. Also, the administration of prenatal adrenogens is associated with an increased tendency for females to show tomboyish behaviour (Mayer-Bahlberg *et al.*, 1986). Adequate sensory experiences are necessary for the development of the related neural systems. This has been well demonstrated for vision, but the sensory deprivation of non-visual stimuli has also been shown to have effects on brain structure and function (Greenough, Black & Wallace, 1987; Rosenzweig & Bennett, 1977).

Shaping of environment

A third mediating mechanism is to be found in the ways in which a person's behaviour or experiences in childhood serve to shape the environment experienced in adult life. This is seen most obviously in the connections between eduational achievement and later occupational status, as shown in several of the longitudinal studies discussed. It is important to emphasize that the link is *not* just a secondary consequence of individual qualities such as IQ. The Stockholm Study (Magnusson, 1988; Magnusson *et al.*, 1986) showed how early puberty in girls could lead to drop-out from education; our own longitudinal studies (Maughan *et al.*, 1985b) showed a similar effect from conduct disturbances, as did the Berkeley studies (Caspi *et al.*, in press); the latter also showed how joining the Armed Forces could lead to a prolongation of education (Elder, 1986); and our studies of black school children showed how their greater persistence in education had benefits in the form of higher scholastic achievement (Maughan & Rutter, 1986). In these instances, drop-out from, or persistence in, education closed down or opened up career opportunities that were likely to affect social circumstances in adult life. It is important to appreciate that people's living conditions are in part a consequence of steps that they themselves have taken, steps that serve to shape their later experiences (cf. Scarr & McCartney, 1983).

An equally important factor in shaping the adult environment is the choice of marriage partner. Our study of institution-reared girls (Quinton & Rutter, 1988) showed the strong tendency for them to marry in haste at an early age to escape from what they felt to be an intolerable family situation—a tendency that much increased the likelihood that they would land up with an unsatisfactory marriage that would break down. The same investigation, and the Berkeley study (Clausen, 1986), demonstrated the protective effect of planning, an effect that was associated with a significant increase in marital stability. The studies of Brown *et al.* (1986) have also shown the key role of a premarital pregnancy, and numerous investigations have indicated the greater likelihood of divorce for teenage marriages.

A more continuing shaping of environments stems from the effects of people's behaviour on other people's responses to them. There is much evidence to show that this occurs. For example, experimental investigations have shown how oppositional children elicit different types of adult behaviour than do passive compliant children (Brunk & Henggeler, 1984). Observational studies, too, have demonstrated that aggressive boys tend to elicit negative behaviour from their peers (Dodge, 1980). I mentioned earlier the ECA finding that conduct disturbance in childhood was associated with an increased risk of social rebuffs and job loss in adult life (Robins, 1986).

It should be added that antisocial behaviour also will influence later environments through the societal responses that it induces—such as custodial or correctional actions that may serve both to 'label' and to strengthen antisocial peer group influences, as well as potentially to create more adaptive environments.

On the beneficial side, the available evidence suggests that, insofar as the gains associated with good early educational experiences persist, they do so because they make it more likely that the children will develop a positive approach to schooling that makes them rewarding to teach and *not* because there is a lasting effect on cognitive capacity (Pedersen, Faucher & Eaton, 1978; Berreuta-Clement, Schweinart, Barnett, Epstein & Weikart, 1984).

Of course, too, the fact that a person has children means that they will be exposed to the influence of those children on themselves as adults. The stresses and rewards of parenthood derive from their own behaviour in becoming parents. The circumstances in which they do so (e.g. as a single teenager or a happily married adult) and the number and timing of children are likely to help determine whether the effects are mainly positive or negative.

Cognitive and social skills

The enhancement or reduction of cognitive and/or social skills constitutes a fourth possible mediating mechanism. A variety of studies of children reared in high risk environments have shown that those of higher IQ or better scholastic attainments are less likely to develop later psychiatric disorders (Cohler, 1987; Garmezy, 1983; Rutter, 1979). The reasons why greater cognitive skills are protective remain obscure. Doubtless part of the explanation is that such skills bring their own rewards in terms of enhanced self-esteem and are associated with environmental advantages. But perhaps, too, the skills are protective because they mean that the individuals have a greater repertoire of adaptive strategies to deal with later life challenges and hazards.

However, it is likely that social skills are as important as those in the strictly cognitive domain. Thus, Dodge's work (Dodge, 1983; Dodge, Pettit, McClaskey & Brown, 1986) has shown that aggressive boys lack interpersonal skills and deal ineptly with social interactions. This lack of social skills is likely to play a role in the further perpetuation of their conduct problems. As already noted, social incompetence and poor peer relationships are predictive of later psychopathology (Parker & Asher, 1987).

A major tenet of attachment theory is that early parent–child relationships constitute the basis for all later relationships and that a failure to develop secure attachments in the first few years leads to a relatively lasting impairment in the ability to form close confiding relationships as an adult (Bowlby, 1969, 1988; Bretherton & Waters, 1985; Waters, Hay & Richters, 1986). Early writings, heavily influenced by psychoanalysis, postulated a rather fixed effect on personality organization (Bowlby, 1951). Influences from ethology led to suggestions that parent–child attachment was equivalent to imprinting of the following response seen in certain species of birds (Bowlby, 1969). However, Bowlby's (1988) current views hypothesize a much more fluid process involving developmental pathways that remain open to change throughout life. What remains distinctive, nevertheless, is the notion that the key thread underlying continuities derives from the effect of early relationships as shaping influences on later ones. There is a lack of good data on the extent to which such an association does in fact exist and, insofar as it does, on the mechanisms involved. Nevertheless, the data from Hodges and Tizard's (1989 a,b) follow-up of children who spent their first few years in a residential nursery suggests that there may be something in the proposition. The effects are not as extreme as once suggested but, nevertheless, an early institutional rearing was associated with less intense and less selective relationships in adolescence. It remains to be seen whether this feature will persist into adult life.

Our own follow-up of institution-reared girls also showed that, compared with girls reared in ordinary families, they were more likely to develop disorder when faced with social adversity in adult life (Quinton & Rutter, 1988). Given good social circumstances, their outcome was fairly comparable with controls but they were more likely to succumb when faced with social difficulties. Whether or not this was because they lacked coping skills is not known, but that may have been part of the explanation. Similarly, in the Kauai longitudinal study (Werner & Smith, 1982; Werner, 1985) it was noted that resilience was associated with superior problem-solving skills.

It is often argued that vulnerability of this kind is a consequence of not 'working through', or otherwise coming to terms with, earlier stressful experiences. For example, this is particularly emphasized in relation to grief following bereavement, where it is suggested that there is an increased risk of later psychiatric disorder when grief has not been manifest at the time. It is certainly possible that the ways in which the grieving processes are dealt with psychologically at the time are associated with increased or decreased vulnerabilities to later disorder. However, such evidence as there is shows that an absence of depression following bereavement is not a risk factor; rather the reverse (Wortman & Silver, in press). Similarly, Vaillant's follow-up of the Glueck's inner city sample of deprived children showed that good functioning in adult life tended to have been preceded by the same in childhood—an absence of disturbance is *not* a risk factor (Felsman & Vaillant, 1987). Nevertheless, it could still be the case that the way someone conceptualizes earlier adverse experiences is important in determining later sequelae (Main, Kaplan & Cassidy, 1985; Bowlby, 1988).

Self-esteem and self-efficacy

A related notion is that childhood adversities may create a vulnerability to later psychiatric disorder because they lead to a diminished self-esteem and sense of self-efficacy. For example, this has been postulated as one of the mechanisms mediating the link between lack of affectionate care in childhood and a vulnerability to depression in adult life (Brown *et al.*, 1986). There are findings that are consistent with the hypothesis, but direct longitudinal evidence is so far lacking. However, there is evidence that successful coping and/or positive experiences tend to be protective, and it is plausible that the protection lies in the enhanced self-confidence that derives from the experiences (Rutter, 1987a, in press a). Thus, in the follow-up of institution-reared girls, it was found that positive school experiences were associated with an increased tendency to exert 'planning' in relation to both marriage and careers (Quinton & Rutter, 1988; Rutter *et al.*, in press). It was suggested that this was because the successful coping in one situation—school—increased the likelihood that the girls would feel in control of other aspects of their lives and able to do something about their situation. Similarly, Elder (1974, 1979) found that older children who took on family responsibilities successfully in the Great Depression tended to have better outcomes.

Habits, cognitive sets and coping styles

A sixth mediating mechanism concerns established habits, cognitive sets and coping styles. In a sense, this is the main way that continuities have been conceptualized in the past. The general notion is that through repetition we develop habitual ways of behaving that become both self-reinforcing and reinforced by others. Moreover, these traits become internally organized through the development of cognitive sets about ourselves, our relationships and our environment (Rutter, 1987a, b, c). The notion that this is one way by which personality functions develop and become stabilized is plausible, but we lack knowledge on the processes involved. Research that focused on the associations between cognitions and manifest behaviour, and on the circumstances in which each altered in relation to circumstances, would be helpful. Examples of personality functions conceptualized in this way are provided by 'working models of relationships' (Bretherton & Waters, 1985), styles of coping with stress situations (Moos, 1986; Snyder & Ford, 1987) and the variety of routines and patterns that most people develop in organizing their lives. It is relevant to note that these habits, cognitive sets and coping styles may be important not just—perhaps not even mainly—in the perpetuation of the same behaviours, but also through their effects in leading to other consequences. For example, the use of drugs (such as nicotine, alcohol, opioids or tranquillizers) as a way of dealing with either stress or boredom is likely to predispose to problems from the drugs themselves if their usage increases when stressors increase in later life. Involvement in a satisfying job may be protective in many circumstances but increase vulnerability if the job is lost through redundancy. As with the other mechanisms, it is necessary to consider the ways in which their operation may lead to changes in, as well as stabilization of, behaviour, as both occur.

Links between experiences

The last possible mediating mechanism to mention is the link between experiences. There are many examples of circumstances in which there is a major change of environment, yet nevertheless one bad environment tends to make it likely that another different bad environment will be experienced or, conversely, that one set of advantages predisposes to other advantages. That was evident in our follow-up of institution-reared children (Quinton & Rutter, 1988), as I have indicated. There was a chain of events by which parental mental disorder led to family discord, which was associated with parenting breakdown, which led to institutional admission. On discharge from the institution in adolescence, early parenting breakdown often meant that there was no family home to which the young people could go so that they were largely left to their own resources at a time of vulnerability. In comparable fashion, marital discord may lead to divorce which, in turn, may be followed by disputes over custody and access and then by the additional change brought about by the entry of a step-parent into the family (Hetherington, 1988; Hetherington, Cox & Cox, 1982, 1985). All of this entails several changes of environment, but there is an essential continuity of potentially stressful circumstances. Advantages frequently involve similar mutually reinforcing chains. Children from privileged homes are more likely to go to better quality schools, the experience of good education will make it more likely that the person will go on to higher education, which in turn may open the way to social advantages as well as career success.

Conclusions

In conclusion, it is evident that the limited empirical evidence available on the connections between childhood and adult life emphasizes the need to account for both continuities and discontinuities, and to recognize the multiplicity of pathways across the life-span and the diversity of end points. Life-span transitions have a crucial role in the processes involved, both in strengthening emerging patterns of behaviour and in providing a means by which life trajectories may change direction. Traditionally, such transitions have been thought of in terms of a ladder-like progression through predictable stages, each of which has its own set of tasks—as evident in both Erikson's (1963) and Levinson's (1976) concepts. However, that seems a rather misleadingly rigid way of viewing transitions. Most transitions are not universals—not everyone has a career, not everyone marries, not everyone has children, not everyone outlives their parents and so experiences parental death, some people never retire from work. Moreover, there are hugely important transitions that may be purely individual— as brought about, for example, by migration or by late adoption or by leaving an institutional environment. Transitions need to be considered in personal terms.

Also, however, there is immense individual variability in the number, type and timing of transitions, as is obvious when considering people's experiences of marriage or divorce, retirement, bereavement and physical illness. Equally, there is marked individual variability in the meaning of transitions. There is a world of difference between a much-wanted retirement from a stressful job and involuntary retirement from a rewarding one.

The point that comes over most strongly from longitudinal studies, however, is that the outcome of transitions, and the ways in which they are dealt with, is partially determined by people's past behaviour and experiences. People act in ways that serve to shape their experiences, and there are equally important links between different types of environment. Of course, too, the transitions will be influenced by societal factors. Career progression will be affected by job opportunities; the experience of marriage and childrearing by housing conditions; the choice of jobs and housing by racial or other forms of discrimination. Finally, the negotiation of transitions will similarly be influenced by the past and by societal factors.

The implication, I suggest, is that just as we have learned not to polarize nature and nurture as if they were mutually exclusive alternative explanations, so also we need to get away from the unduly simplified question of whether a person's behaviour

46   M. Rutter

is the result of past or present experiences. Not only will behaviour be shaped by
the biological substrate, genetically and non-genetically determined, as well as by
psychosocial influences, but equally both the past and present are likely to have effects.
Most crucially, however, they are not independent of one another. To an important
extent the past helps to determine the present environment through a variety of different
mechanisms. Chain effects are common and, if we are to understand the developmental
process, we need to analyse each of the links in the chain, to determine how the links
interconnect and to study how changes in life trajectory come about. In this way,
life transitions have to be considered both as end products of past processes and as
instigators of future ones—in data analysis terms as both independent and dependent
variables. It is important to search for unifying principles in the mechanisms underlying
the diversity of pathways from childhood to adult life, but in so doing we must consider
the pathways in personal terms and in the context of possible person–environment
interactions. The elucidation of the processes giving rise to these varied pathways
should provide useful leads for both prevention and treatment through improved
knowledge on how changes take place, for that is what development is all about.

References

Berreuta-Clement, J. R., Schweinart, L. J., Barnett, W. S., Epstein, A. S. & Weikart, D. P. (1984).
    Changed lifes: The effects of the Perry Pre-School Program on youths through age 19. Ypsilanti: High Scope.
Block, J. (1979). Advancing the science of personality: Paradigmatic shift or improving the quality
    of research? In D. Magnusson and M. S. Endler (Eds), *Psychology at the crossroads: Current issues
    and interactional psychology.* Hillsdale, NJ: Erlbaum.
Bowlby, J. (1951). *Maternal care and mental health.* Geneva: World Health Organization.
Bowlby, J. (1969/82). *Attachment and loss:* Vol. 1: *Attachment.* London: Hogarth.
Bowlby, J. (1988). *A secure base: Clinical applications of attachment theory.* London: Routledge.
Bretherton, I. & Waters, E. (Eds) (1985). Growing points of attachment theory and research. *Monographs
    of the Society for Research in Child Development,* Serial No. 209, 50, Nos 1–2.
Bronfenbrenner, U. (1979). *The ecology of human development: Experiments by nature and design.* Cambridge,
    MA: Harvard University Press.
Brown, G. W. (1988). Causal paths, chains and strands. In M. Rutter (Ed.), *Studies of psychosocial risk:
    The power of longitudinal data.* Cambridge: Cambridge University Press.
Brown, G. W., Harris, T. O. & Bifulco, A. (1986). The long term effects of early loss of parent. In
    M. Rutter, C. E. Izard & P. B. Read (Eds), *Depression in young people: Clinical and developmental
    perspectives* (pp. 251–296). New York: Guilford.
Brunk, M. A. & Henggeler, S. W. (1984). Child influences on adult controls. An experimental
    investigation. *Developmental Psychology, 20,* 1074–1081.
Cadoret, R. J., Troughton, E., Moreno, L. & Whitters, A. (in press). Early life psychosocial events
    and adult affective symptoms. In L. N. Robins & M. Rutter (Eds), *Straight and devious pathways
    from childhood to adult life.* Cambridge: Cambridge University Press.
Caspi, A. & Elder, G. H. (1988). Emergent family patterns: The intergenerational construction of
    problem behaviors and relationships. In R. A. Hinde & J. Stevenson-Hinde (Eds), *Relationships
    within families: Mutual influences.* Oxford: Clarendon Press.
Caspi, A., Elder, G. H. & Herbener, E. S. (in press), Childhood personality and the prediction of
    life-course patterns. In L. N. Robins & M. Rutter (Eds), *Straight and devious pathways from childhood
    to adult life.* Cambridge: Cambridge University Press.
Clarke, A. D. B. & Clarke, A. M. (1984). Consistency and change in the growth of human characteristics.
    Journal of Child Psychology and Psychiatry, 25, 191–210.
Clarke, A. D. B. & Tizard, B. (Eds) (1983). *Child development and social policy: The life and work of Jack
    Tizard.* Leicester: British Psychological Society.

Clarke, A. M. & Clarke, A. D. B. (1976). *Early experience: Myth and evidence*. London: Open Books.

Clarke, R. B. G. (1985). Delinquency, environment and intervention. *Journal of Child Psychology and Psychiatry,* **26,** 505–523.

Clausen, J. A. (1986). Early adult choices and the life course. *Zeitschrift fur Sozialisations Forschung und Erzielungsozioligie,* **6,** 313–320.

Cohler, B. J. (1987). Adversity, resilience and the study of lives. In E. J. Anthony & B. J. Cohler (Eds), *The invulnerable child* (pp. 363–424). New York: Guilford.

Dodge, K. A. (1980). Social cognition and children's aggressive behavior. *Child Development,* **51,** 162–172.

Dodge, K. A. (1983). Behavioral antecedents of peer social status. *Child Development,* **54,** 1386–1399.

Dodge, K. A., Pettit, G. S., McClaskey, C. L. & Brown, M. M. (1986). Social competence in children. *Monographs of the Society for Research in Child Development,* Serial No. 213.

Elder, G. H. (1974). *Children of the great depression*. Chicago: University of Chicago Press.

Elder, G. H. (1979). Historical change in life patterns and personality. In P. Baltes & O. G. Brim (Eds), *Life span development and behavior,* Vol. 2. New York: Academic Press.

Elder, G. H. (1986). Military times and turning points in men's lives. *Developmental Psychology,* **22,** 233–245.

Epstein, S. (1979). The stability of behavior: I: On predicting most of the people much of the time. *Journal of Personality and Social Psychology,* **37,** 1097–1126.

Epstein, S. & O'Brien, E. J. (1985). The person-situation debate in historical and current perspectives. *Psychological Bulletin,* **98,** 513–537.

Erikson, E. H. (1963). *Childhood and society* (2nd edn). New York: W. W. Norton.

Farrington, D. P., Loeber, R. & van Kammen, W. B. (in press). Long-term criminal outcomes of hyperactivity–impulsivity–attention deficit and conduct problems in childhood. In L. N. Robins & M. Rutter (Eds), *Straight and devious pathways from childhood to adult life*. Cambridge: Cambridge University Press.

Felsman, J. K. & Vaillant, G. E. (1987). Resiliant children as adults: A 40-year study. In E. J. Anthony & B. J. Cohler (Eds), *The invulnerable child*. (pp. 289–374). New York: Guilford.

Folstein, S. & Rutter, M. (1987). Family aggregation and genetic implications. In E. Schopler & G. Mesibov (Eds), *Neurobiological issues in autism* (pp. 83–105). New York: Plenum.

Folstein, S. E., Franz, M. L., Jensen, B. A., Chase, G. A. & Folstein, M. F. (1983). Conduct disorder and affective disorder among the offspring of patients with Huntington's disease. *Psychological Medicine,* **13,** 45–52.

Garmezy, N. (1983). Stressors of childhood. In N. Garmezy & M. Rutter (Eds), *Stress, coping and development in children* (pp. 43–84). New York: McGraw-Hill.

Goodman, R. (1987). The developmental neurobiology of language. In W. Yule & M. Rutter (Eds), *Language development and disorders: Clinics in developmental medicine, No. 101/102.* London: MacKeith/Blackwell.

Gottesman, I. I. & Shields, J. (1976). A critical review of recent adoption, twin and family studies of schizophrenia: Behavioral genetics perspective. *Schizophrenia Bulletin,* **2,** 360–400.

Graham, P. & Rutter, M. (1985). Adolescent disorders. In M. Rutter & L. Hersov (Eds), *Child and adolescent psychiatry: Modern Approaches* (2nd edn) (pp. 351–367). Oxford: Blackwell Scientific.

Gray, G., Smith, A. & Rutter, M. (1980). School attendance and the first year of employment. In L. Hersov & I. Berg (Eds), *Out of school: Modern perspectives in truancy and school refusal* (pp. 343–370). Chichester: Wiley.

Greenough, W. T., Black, J. E. & Wallace, C. S. (1987). Experience and brain development. *Child Development,* **58,** 539–559.

Harris, T., Brown, G. W. & Bifulco, A. (1986). Loss of parent in childhood and adult psychiatric disorder: The role of lack of adequate parental care. *Psychological Medicine,* **16,** 641–659.

Harris, T., Brown, G. W. & Bifulco, A. (1987). Loss of parent in childhood and adult psychiatric disorder: The role of social class position and premarital pregnancy. *Psychological Medicine,* **17,** 163–183.

Hayes, C. D. (Ed.) (1987). *Preventing adolescent pregnancy: An agenda for America.* Washington DC: National Academy Press.

Hennessy, J. & Levine, S. (1979). Stress, arousal and the pituitary–adrenal system: A psychoendocrine hypothesis. In J. M. Sprague & A. N. Epstein (Eds), *Progress in psychobiology and physiological psychology* (pp. 133–178). New York: Academic Press.

Hertzig, M. E., Birch, H. G., Richardson, S. A. & Tizard, J. (1972). Intellectual levels of school children severely malnurished during the first two years of life. *Pediatrics,* **49,** 814–824.

Hetherington, E. M. (1988). Parents, children and siblings: 6 years after divorce. In R. A. Hinde & J. Stevenson-Hinde (Eds), *Relationships within families: Mutual influences.* Oxford: Clarendon Press.

Hetherington, E. M., Cox, M. & Cox, A. (1982). Effects of divorce on parents and Children. In M. E. Lamb (Ed.), *Nontraditional families* (pp. 223–288). Hillsdale, NJ: Erlbaum.

Hetherington, E. M., Cox, M. & Cox, A. (1985). Long-term effects of divorce and remarriage on the adjustment of children. *Journal of the American Academy of Child Psychiatry,* **24,** 518–530.

Hinde, R. A. (1987). *Individuals, relationships and culture: Links between ethology and the social sciences.* Cambridge: Cambridge University Press.

Hinde, R. A. (1988). Continuities and discontinuities: Conceptual issues and methodological considerations. In M. Rutter (Ed.), *Studies of psychosocial risk: The power of longitudinal data.* Cambridge: Cambridge University Press.

Hinde, R. A. & Bateson, P. A. (1984). Discontinuities versus continuities in behavioural development and the neglect of process. *International Journal of Behavioural Development,* **7,** 129–143.

Hinde, R. A. & Stevenson-Hinde, J. (Eds) (1988). *Relationships within families: Mutual influences.* Oxford: Clarendon Press.

Hodges, J. & Tizard, B. (1989 a). IQ and behavioural adjustment of ex-institutional adolescents. *Journal of Child Psychology and Psychiatry,* **30,** 53–75.

Hodges, J. & Tizard, B. (1989 b). Social and family relationships of ex-institutional adolescents. *Journal of Child Psychology and Psychiatry,* **30,** 77–97.

Hunt, J. McV. (1979). Psychological development: Early experience. *Annual Review of Psychology,* **30,** 103–143.

Kagan, J. (1984). *The nature of the child.* New York: Basic Books.

Kandel, D. B. & Davies, M. (1986). Adult sequelae of adolescent depressive symptoms. *Archives of General Psychiatry,* **43,** 255–262.

Kelly, E. L. (1955). Consistency of the adult personality. *American Psychologist,* **10,** 659–681.

Levinson, D., with Darrow, D. N., Klein, E. B., Levinson, M. H. & McKee, D. (1976). *The seasons of a man's life.* New York: Alfred Knopf.

Lewis, S. W. & Murray, R. M. (1987). Obstetric complications, neurodevelopmental deviance and risk of schizophrenia. *Journal of Psychiatric Research,* **21,** 413–421.

Maccoby, E. E. (1984). Socialization and developmental change. *Child Development,* **55,** 317–328.

Magnusson, D. (1988). *Individual development from an interactional perspective: A longitudinal study.* Hillsdale, NJ: Erlbaum.

Magnusson, D., Stattin, H. & Allen, V. L. (1986). Differential maturation amongst girls and its relation to social adjustment: A longitudinal perspective. In D. Featherman & R. M. Lerner (Eds), *Life span development,* Vol. 7. New York: Academic Press.

Main, M., Kaplan, N. & Cassidy, J. (1985). Security in infancy, childhood, and adulthood: A move to the level of representation. In I. Bretherton & E. Waters, (Eds), Growing points of attachment theory and research. *Monographs of the Society for Research in Child Development,* Serial No. 209, 50, Nos 1–2. (pp. 66–106).

Masten, A. S. & Garmezy, M. (1985). Risk, vulnerability, and protective factors in developmental psychopathology. In B. B. Lahey & A. E. Kazdin (Eds), *Advances in clinical child psychology,* Vol. 8 (pp. 1–52). New York: Plenum.

Maughan, B. & Rutter, M. (1986). Black pupils' progress in secondary schools: II: Examination attainments. *British Journal of Developmental Psychology,* **4,** 19–29.

Maughan, B. M. & Champion, L. (in press). Risk and protective factors in the transition of young adults. In P. B. Baltes & M. M. Baltes (Eds), *Successful aging: Research and theory.* New York: Cambridge University Press.

Maughan, D., Dunn, G. & Rutter, M. (1985a), Black pupils' progress in secondary schools: I: Reading attainment between 10 and 14. *British Journal of Developmental Psychology,* **3,** 113–121.

Maughan, B., Gray, G. & Rutter, M. (1985b). Reading retardation and antisocial behaviour: A follow-up into employment. *Journal of Child Psychology and Psychiatry,* **26,** 741–758.

Mayer-Bahlberg, H. F. L., Ehrhardt, A. A. & Feldman, J. F. (1986). Long-term implications of the prenatal endocrine milieu for sex-dimorphic behavior. In L. Erlenmeyer-Kimling & N. E. Miller (Eds), *Life-span research on the prediction of psychopathology* (pp. 17–30). Hillsdale, NJ: Erlbaum.

McCall, R. B. (1977). Challenges to a science of developmental psychology. *Child Development,* **48,** 333–344.

Mischel, W. (1968). *Personality and assessment.* New York: Wiley.

Mischel, W. (1969). Continuities and change in personality. *American Psychologist,* **24,** 1012–1018.

Moos, R. H. (Ed.) (1986). *Coping with life crises: An integrated approach.* New York: Plenum.

Mortimore, P., Sammons, P., Stoll, L., Lewis, D. & Etob, R. (1988). *School matters: The junior years.* Wells, Somerset: Open Books.

Moss, H. A. & Susman, E. J. (1980). Longitudinal study of personality development. In O. G. Brim & J. Kagan (Eds), *Constancy and change in human development* (pp. 530–595). Cambridge, MA: Harvard University Press.

Murray, R. M., Lewis, S. W., Owen, M. J. & Foerster, A. (in press). The neurodevelopmental origins of demenia precox. In P. McGuffin & P. Bebbington (Eds), *Schizophrenia: The major issues.* London: Heinemann.

Nesselroade, J. (1988). Some implications of the trait–state distinction for the study of development over the life-span: Case of personality. In P. B. Baltes, D. L. Featherman & R. M. Lerner (Eds), *Life span development and behaviour,* Vol. 8 (pp. 163–189). Hillsdale, NJ: Erlbaum.

Nuechterlein, K. H. (1986). Childhood precursors of adult schizophrenia. *Journal of Child Psychology and Psychiatry,* **27,** 133–144.

O'Connor, N. (1956). The evidence for the permanently disturbing effects of mother–child separation. *Acta Psychologica,* **12,** 174–191.

Olweus, D. (1979). Stability of aggressive reaction patterns in males: a review. *Psychological Bulletin,* **86,** 852–875.

Orlansky, H. (1949). Infant care and personality. *Psychological Bulletin,* **46,** 1–48.

Otto, L. B. (1979). Antecedents and consequences of marital timing. In W. R. Burr, R. Hill, F. I. Nye & I. L. Reiss (Eds), *Contemporary theories about the family,* Vol. 1. (pp. 101–126). New York: Free Press.

Parker, J. G. & Asher, S. R. (1987). Peer relations and later personal adjustment: Are low-accepted children at risk? *Psychological Bulletin,* **102,** 357–389.

Parnas, J., Schulsinger, R., Teasdale, T. W., Schulsinger, H., Feldman, P. M. & Mednick, S. A. (1982). Perinatal complications and clinical outcome within the schizophrenia spectrum. *British Journal of Psychiatry,* **140,** 416–420.

Pedersen, E., Faucher, T. A. & Eaton, W. W. (1978). A new perspective on the effects of first grade teachers on children's subsequent adult status. *Harvard Educational Review,* **48,** 1–31.

Petersen, A. C. (1988). Adolescent development. *Annual Review of Psychology,* **39,** 583–607.

Plomin, R. (1986). *Development, genetics and psychology.* Hillsdale, NJ: Erlbaum.

Plomin, R. & Thompson, L. (1988). Life-span developmental behavioral genetics. In P. B. Baltes, D. L. Featherman & R. M. Lerner (Eds), *Life-span development and behavior,* Vol. 8 (pp. 1–31). Hillsdale, NJ: Erlbaum.

Porter, R., O'Conner, M. & Whelan, J. (Eds) (1984). *Alcohol damage in utero.* Ciba Foundation Symposium No. 105. London: Pitman.

Quinton, D. & Rutter, M. (1988). *Parental breakdown: The making and breaking of intergenerational links.* Aldershot: Gower.

Quinton, D., Rutter, M. & Gulliver, L. (in press). Continuities in psychiatric disorders from childhood to adulthood, in the children of psychiatric patients. In L. N. Robins & M. Rutter (Eds), *Straight and devious pathways from childhood to adult life.* Cambridge: Cambridge University Press.

Richman, N., Stevenson, J. & Graham, P. (1982). *Preschool to school: A behavioural study.* London: Academic Press.

Robins, L. (1978). Sturdy childhood predictors of adult antisocial behaviour: Replications from longitudinal studies. *Psychological Medicine,* **8,** 611–622.

Robins, L. N. (1986). The consequences of conduct disorder in girls. In D. Olweus, J. Block & M. Radke-Yarrow (Eds), *Development of antisocial and prosocial behaviour: Research, theories and issues* (pp. 385–408). New York: Academic Press.

Rosenzweig, M. R. & Bennett, E. L. (1977). Effects of environmental enrichment or impoverishment on learning and on brain values in rodents. In A. Oliviero (Ed.), *Genetics, environment and intelligence* (pp. 163–196). Amsterdam: North Holland.

50   M. Rutter

Rutter, M. (1979). Protective factors in children's responses to stress and disadvantage. In M. W. Kent & J. E. Rolf (Eds), *Primary prevention of psychopathology,* Vol. 3: *Social competence in children* (pp. 49–74). Hanover, NH: University Press of New England.

Rutter, M. (1981). *Maternal deprivation reassessed* (2nd edn). Harmondsworth: Penguin.

Rutter, M. (1982). Developmental neuropsychiatry: Concepts, issues and prospects. *Journal of Clinical Neuropsychiatry,* **4,** 91–115.

Rutter, M. (1983). Statistical and personal interactions: Facets and perspectives. In D. Magnusson & V. Allen (Eds), *Human development: An interactional perspective* (pp. 295–319). New York: Academic Press.

Rutter, M. (1984a). Psychopathology and development. I: Childhood antecedents of adult psychiatric disorder. *Australian and New Zealand Journal of Psychiatry,* **18,** 225–234.

Rutter, M. (1984b). Psychopathology and development. II: Childhood experiences and personality development. *Australian and New Zealand Journal of Psychiatry,* **18,** 314–327.

Rutter, M. (1984c). Continuities and discontinuities in socioemotional development: Empirical and conceptual perspectives. In R. Emde & R. Harmon (Eds), *Continuities and discontinuities in development* (pp. 41–68). New York: Plenum.

Rutter, M. (1985a). Family and school influences on cognitive development. *Journal of Child Psychology and Psychiatry,* **26,** 683–704.

Rutter, M. (1985b). Family and school influences on behavioural development. *Journal of Child Psychology and Psychiatry,* **26,** 349–368.

Rutter, M. (1987a). Continuities and discontinuities from infancy. In J. Osofsky (Ed.), *Handbook of infant development* (2nd edn) (pp. 1256–1298). New York: Wiley.

Rutter, M. (1987b). Temperament, personality and personality development. *British Journal of Psychiatry,* **150,** 443–458.

Rutter, M. (1987c). The role of cognition in child development and disorder. *British Journal of Medical Psychology,* **60,** 1–16.

Rutter, M. (1988). Epidemiological approaches to developmental psychopathology. *Archives of General Psychiatry,* **45,** 486–495.

Rutter, M. (in press a). Psychosocial resilience and protective mechanisms. In J. E. Rolf, A. S. Masten, D. Cicchetti, K. Nuechterlein & S. Weintraub (Eds), *Risk and protective factors in the development of psychopathology.* New York: Cambridge University Press.

Rutter, M. (in press b). Age as an ambiguous variable in developmental research. *International Journal of Behavioural Development.*

Rutter, M., Macdonald, H., Le Couteur, A., Harrington, R., Bolton, P. & Bailey, A. (submitted). Genetic factors in child psychiatric disorders: II: Empirical findings.

Rutter, M., Quinton, D. & Hill, J. (in press). Adult outcome of institution-reared children: Males and females compared. In L. N. Robins & M. Rutter (Eds), *Straight and devious pathways from childhood to adult life.* Cambridge: Cambridge University Press.

Rutter, M. & Sandberg, S. (1985). Epidemiology of child psychiatric disorder: Methodological issues and some substantive findings. *Child Psychiatry and Human Development,* **15,** 209–233.

Rutter, M., Tizard, J. & Whitmore, K. (1970). *Education, health and behaviour.* London: Longman.

Rutter, M., Tizard, J., Yule, W., Graham, P. & Whitmore, K. (1976). Isle of Wight Studies 1964–1974. *Psychological Medicine,* **6,** 313–332.

Scarr, S. & MacCartney, K. (1983). How people make their own environments: A theory of genotype-environment effects. *Child Development,* **54,** 424–435.

Smalley, S. L., Asarnow, R. F. & Spence, M. A. (1988). Autism and genetics: A decade of research. *Archives of General Psychiatry,* **45,** 953–961.

Snyder, C. R. & Ford, C. E. (Eds) (1987). *Coping with negative life events: clinical and social psychological perspectives.* New York: Plenum.

Tizard, B. & Hodges, J. (1978). The effect of early institutional rearing on the development of eight-year old children. *Journal of Child Psychology and Psychiatry,* **19,** 99–118.

Tizard, B., Blatchford, D., Burk, J., Farquahar, C. & Plewis, I. (1988). *Young children at school in the inner city.* London: Erlbaum.

Tizard, J. (1975). Three dysfunctional environmental influences in development: malnutrition, non-accidental injury and child minding. In D. Baltrop (Ed.), *Pediatrics and the environment.* Unigate Paediatric Workshops No. 2 (1974) (pp. 19–27). London: Fellowship of Postgraduate Medicine.

Tizard, J. (1976). Psychology and social policy. *British Psychological Society Bulletin,* **29,** 225–234. (Reprinted in A. D. B. Clarke & B. Tizard, 1983. *Child development and social policy: The life and work of Jack Tizard.* Leicester: British Psychological Society.)

Warr, P. (1987). *Work, unemployment and mental health.* Oxford: Clarendon Press.

Waters, E., Hay, D. & Richters, J. (1986). Infant–parent attachment and the origins of prosocial and antisocial behavior. In D. Olweus, J. Block & M. Radke-Yarrow (Eds), *Development of antisocial and prosocial behavior: Research theories and issues* (pp. 97–125). London: Academic Press.

Weinberger, D. R. (1987). Implications of normal brain development for the pathogenesis of schizophrenia. *Archives of General Psychiatry,* **44,** 660–669.

Werner, E. E. (1985). Stress and protective factors in children's life. In A. R. Nicol (Ed.), *Longitudinal studies in child psychology and psychiatry: Practical lessons from research experience* (pp. 335–355). Chichester: Wiley.

Werner, E. E. & Smith, R. S. (1982). *Vulnerable but invincible: A longitudinal study of resilient children and youth.* New York: McGraw-Hill.

Wortman, C. B. & Silver, R. C. (in press). The myths of coping with loss. *Journal of Consulting and Clinical Psychology.*

Yarrow, L. J. (1961). Maternal deprivation: Toward an empirical and conceptual re-evaluation. *Psychological Bulletin,* **58,** 459–490.

Zeitlin, H. (1986). *The natural history of disorder in childhood. Institute of Psychiatry/Maudsley Monograph* No. 29. Oxford: Oxford University Press.

[10]

An ecological approach to social work with children and families

Gordon Jack

Lecturer in Social Work, University of Exeter, Department of Social Work and Probation Studies, Amory Building, Rennes Drive, Exeter EX4 4RJ, UK

Correspondence:
Gordon Jack,
Lecturer in Social Work,
University of Exeter,
Department of Social Work and
Probation Studies,
Amory Building,
Rennes Drive,
Exeter EX4 4RJ

Keywords: child abuse, social support, parenting

Accepted for publication: August 1996

ABSTRACT

This paper examines research into the social ecology of parents and children, with particular reference to the effects of social support on family functioning and outcomes for children. The historical failure of social work in the UK to successfully apply the findings from this area of research to mainstream work with children and families is considered in the light of the prevailing child protection discourse. Challenges to this discourse are now beginning to emerge from developments in both research and practice. The implications of these developments for the construction of a new discourse, which recognizes the wider social and political factors that shape the family environment, are discussed. It is argued that there is sufficient research evidence available to demonstrate the potential of community social work strategies, which enhance the social support networks of families, to significantly reduce the incidence of child abuse. A number of successful action-research projects of this nature are considered.

SOCIAL SUPPORT NETWORKS

'There had always been women like her in this area of London and no doubt there always would be, but who could say whether they created the city or the city created them?' (Ackroyd 1992, p. 134)

The biographer and novelist, Peter Ackroyd, points to the way in which we both shape and are shaped by our environments. This is the domain of human ecology, examining the ways in which people and their habitats shape and influence one another through a process of reciprocal interactions between individuals and groups, and their immediate and wider environments (Bronfenbrenner 1979; Garbarino 1990). In relation to social work with children and families, it is obviously important to understand what factors in the social environment have positive and negative influences on parenting and the development of children. The initial focus of this article will be the ways in which social support networks can influence the quality of family life and outcomes for children.

Throughout the twentieth century there has been interest in the links between social environments and personal well-being (see, for example, Durkheim 1951). However, it was not until the mid-1970s in the USA that empirical studies of social support networks and their influence on health and illness began to emerge (Sarason *et al.* 1990). Cassel's work highlighted the advantages of strengthening personal social supports as a means of preventing illness, rather than trying to reduce an individual's exposure to stressors (Cassel 1976). At the same time, Cobb (1976) pointed out the way in which social support could buffer individuals against the potentially negative effects of crises. This was followed by researchers who used the framework of social network analysis to assess the social ecology of parenting and the possible effects on child development (Cochran & Brassard 1979).

Subsequent research has revealed the extent to which 'social support', like 'child abuse', is an umbrella term that covers a wide range of different factors and variables (Sarason *et al.* 1990). There is a need to distinguish between not only the number and structure of relationships, but also their quality and availability, at different times and in varying social

An ecological approach to social work G Jack

circumstances. There are complex interactions between all of these variables, which lead to different outcomes. Social network relationships are not automatically beneficial. They are often contradictory and they can be stressful as well as supportive (Wellman 1981; Cochran 1993). The potentially contradictory nature of the effects of social support systems on family functioning is graphically illustrated by the ethnographic research which has been undertaken by Korbin (1989, 1991) with mothers convicted of fatal child abuse. These mothers were not found to be socially isolated, but their social networks failed to challenge them when signs of abuse began to emerge. Instead, their friends and relatives sought to minimize the seriousness of the abuse and continued to offer emotional support to the mothers, who they perceived as struggling to raise their children appropriately in very difficult circumstances.

Most models of social support identify a number of different support dimensions. Whilst there is some diversity in the literature, the most important and frequently identified dimensions appear to be emotional support, social integration and practical support (Cutrona & Russell 1990). The evidence available from research, which has been extensively reviewed (see, for example, Cohen & Wills 1985; Kessler & McLeod 1985) indicates that emotional support and perceived availability of support are particularly important in buffering the otherwise potentially harmful effects of stress on health (Newton 1988). For example, the well known work of Brown and his colleagues in London has demonstrated the relatively high incidence of depression amongst working-class women with children. They were found to be four times more likely than similar middle-class women to develop depressive disorders. This difference was attributable to the greater likelihood of working-class women having one or more of four 'vulnerability factors' identified in the study, the most significant of which was the lack of emotional support, through an intimate relationship with a husband or boyfriend (Brown & Harris 1978). A subsequent longitudinal study focused specifically on the influence of perceived intimate relationships ('core support') and their availability at times of stress. It demonstrated that whilst perceived emotional support provided by a close confidant prior to crisis provided no measurable protection against subsequent depression, such support received at the time of crisis did have a significant protective effect. The two groups of women at greatest risk of developing depression were those who either perceived themselves to have the emotional support of a close confidant prior to crisis, which failed to materialize when a crisis occurred, or those who had conflictual marital relationships (Brown *et al.* 1986).

Maternal depression, in turn, has been found to be associated with a variety of child development problems (see Sheppard 1994). For example, in a study comparing urban working-class depressed mothers and their 2-year-old children with a control group of non-depressed but otherwise similar mothers, the children of the depressed mothers generally showed more emotional and behavioural disturbance and expressive language delays than control group children, and this was linked to the social interactions between mothers and children:

> 'In general, depressed mothers were less responsive to their children and less able to sustain social interaction: their children were more often distressed.' (Cox *et al.* 1987, p. 917)

Analysis of the findings suggested that the most significant mechanism operating was maternal depression leading to hostile adult behaviour, which in turn led to child disturbance. The best protector against depression was found to be a good marriage, confirming the findings of Brown's work referred to earlier. All the marriages rated by the participants as poor were found in the depressed group (Pound *et al.* 1985).

In summary, there is now a considerable body of literature which demonstrates that social support is related to both psychological and physical well-being (Gottlieb 1981; Wills 1985; Cohen & Syme 1985). The mechanisms involved can either be *direct*, enhancing health irrespective of stress level, or *buffering*, protecting health in the face of stressful events, depending upon the measure of social support used.

A number of researchers have gone on to consider in more detail the social ecology of parents and children, with particular reference to the effects of social support on the incidence of child abuse or maltreatment, which primarily concerns child physical abuse and neglect (Garbarino 1976; Crittenden 1985). Of central importance is the work of Garbarino and his colleagues in North America, who have conducted a number of studies designed to examine the reasons for varying rates of child maltreatment between different communities. In an early study of three counties in New York State, a substantial proportion of the variance in rates of child maltreatment between different communities was found to be associated with the adequacy or otherwise of social support networks, as well as levels of economic stress

(Garbarino 1976). In a subsequent study, designed to assess the specific influence of social support networks, two socio-economically matched communities, one 'high-risk' and the other 'low-risk' for child maltreatment, were investigated. The former had a higher actual rate of maltreatment than expected, based on the socio-economic indices revealed in the previous study and the latter had a lower than expected rate. The 'high-risk' neighbourhood was found to be an unhelpful environment in which to raise children:

'A family's own problems seem to be compounded rather than ameliorated by the neighbourhood context, dominated as it is by other needy families. Under such circumstances strong support systems are most needed, but least likely to operate... The high-risk area needs outside intervention to increase its capacity to fend for itself and to strengthen families as a way of reducing the demands they place on already tenuous informal helping networks.' (Garbarino & Sherman 1980, p. 195)

They characterized such high-risk areas as 'socially impoverished' environments, which lacked both supportive relationships and protective behaviours. In contrast, the 'socially rich' environment included people who were 'free from drain' and who were able to support others because their resources exceeded their needs. They were also able to provide the sort of protective behaviour towards children lacking in the socially impoverished environment (Emlen 1977). This included keeping an eye on children when they were playing, intervening if a child's safety was threatened and offering help with day-to-day or emergency child care. In the socially impoverished neighbourhood such mutual aid was suppressed, on the one hand by fears of exploitation, and on the other by fears of being a burden. This meant that opportunities for reciprocal social exchange, in which help is both given and received, were either limited or non-existent. Such reciprocal social interactions are an essential component of social bonding (Heller *et al.* 1990).

More recently, Garbarino has attempted to quantify the influence of social support on rates of child maltreatment. In a study of four districts in Chicago, 79% of the variance in rates of child physical abuse and neglect was accounted for by socio-economic and demographic factors. For example, the rates found in the poorest neighbourhoods of Chicago were four times higher than those found in the most affluent areas studied. However, the study demonstrated that just over a fifth of the variation in the rates was attributable to differences in what the researchers

termed the 'climate' of the community. Higher rates of child maltreatment were associated with areas showing little evidence of a supportive social network, whilst lower rates were found in areas demonstrating strong formal and informal social support networks (Garbarino & Kostelny 1993). The association between social support networks and rates of child physical abuse and neglect has also been confirmed in a comprehensive review of the literature, which found an abundance of evidence linking social isolation and limited social ties with higher rates of child maltreatment (Belsky 1993). Finally, this connection has been illustrated by the results of a recent study of 47 lone mothers, which indicates some of the ways in which social support is important in reducing the potential for child abuse. Criticism within the mothers' support networks was found to increase the level of their stress, whereas emotional support from social networks enabled mothers to be more sensitive to their children's needs. Mothers who received adequate emotional support were more likely to feel empathy towards their children and were more able to develop a range of positive discipline strategies, both of which reduced the incidence of conflict-induced physical abuse (Moncher 1995).

Given the considerable volume of research evidence which has demonstrated the significant impact of social support networks and the wider social environment on parenting and outcomes for children's development, one would expect that these issues would be the focus of considerable social work attention and resources:

'There is a strong relationship between individual physical-social-psychological health and social supports and between social isolation and the breakdown in these areas of functioning. In view of the importance of natural support networks, social workers can do no less than explore the linkages between them and professional intervention.' (Meyer 1985, p. 291, in Thompson 1995)

However, any analysis of the development of social work in the UK over the past 20 years will quickly reveal that this is not the case. So why has the apparently logical development of a community approach to social work with children and families failed to materialize and establish itself in the mainstream of services for this group?

COMMUNITY SOCIAL WORK – THE SEEBOHM AND BARCLAY REPORTS

In the UK, official support for a community approach to social work, which aims to harness the positive

An ecological approach to social work G Jack

influence of effective social support networks, has been provided by the two major reviews of the role of social work undertaken during the past 25 years. The Seebohm Report, published in 1968, envisaged a social work service in England and Wales which would be community-based, family orientated and available to all, reaching far beyond the discovery and rescue of 'social casualties':

'It will enable the greatest possible number of individuals to act reciprocally, giving and receiving services for the well-being of the whole community.' (Seebohm 1968, para. 2)

A community approach was seen as fundamental to the success of the new Social Services Departments that the report recommended should be established:

'The notion of a community implies the existence of a network of reciprocal social relationships, which among other things ensure mutual aid and give those who experience it a sense of well-being... *Social work with individuals alone is bound to be of limited effect in an area where the community environment itself is a major impediment to healthy individual development*... If the services are to meet effectively the complex range of individual, family and community problems, the effort devoted to investigating the needs of an area, and to the overall planning and co-ordination of services and resources, both statutory and voluntary, is clearly of the utmost importance.' (Seebohm 1968, paras 476-77, emphasis added)

In order to develop such a service, the report recommended that staff in the new Social Services Departments would need to gain knowledge of their local communities and mobilize voluntary resources. They would also need to develop skills in formal and informal networking and encourage citizen participation, through local forums of community representatives, service users and volunteers (Seebohm 1968, paras. 502 and 506).

Parallel with these recommendations, government policies for tackling social and economic deprivation and inequalities during the 1970s increasingly sought to target help on the most deprived areas and aimed to involve local communities in the development of services (Hadley & McGrath 1980). For example, the Plowden Report on primary school education recommended the establishment of Educational Priority Areas, which would qualify for additional funding. Similar developments occurred in other areas of government policy, including the establishment of Housing Action Areas and the Urban Aid Programme.

In the newly created Social Services Departments, volunteer co-ordinator posts were established and an increasing number of community workers were employed to undertake work designed to help communities to identify their own problems, and to play a part in finding local solutions which tapped into the resources of the community. This was also a period of growing awareness of the role of social workers in providing advice to individuals and groups about their entitlement to welfare benefits, leading to the development of specialist posts for this work.

There was also an increasing interest in some local authorities in the idea of developing integrated services at neighbourhood levels. In the field of social work, these ideas took the form of 'patch-based' social work teams, with varying degrees of delegated authority for financial decisions and staff recruitment and deployment, as well as moves towards the integration of fieldwork, day care, residential and domiciliary services within the 'patch'. Hadley and McGrath (1980) studied seven such patch-based or neighbourhood teams in the late 1970s. Whilst these projects all lacked objective measures of outcomes, an issue that will be considered in more depth later in this paper, they all *claimed* that the community approach to the delivery of social work services 'enhanced their capacity to identify people needing help earlier' and enabled them to 'tap more resources... deal with fewer emergencies and support more people in the community' (Hadley & McGrath 1980).

The National Institute of Social Work (NISW) was asked by the Secretary of State for Social Services, Patrick Jenkins, to undertake an enquiry into the role and tasks of social workers at this time and they too advocated what they termed a community social work approach. This would, they argued, be able to 'tap into, support, enable and underpin the local networks of formal and informal relationships' (NISW 1982, p. xvii). The enquiry identified two major strands of social work – counselling and social care planning. The latter strand, it went on to state, consisted of two aspects:

'It may be related directly to solving or ameliorating an existing social problem which an individual, family or group is experiencing. But social care planning also includes what we call indirect work, to prevent social problems arising by the development and strengthening of various kinds of community groups and associations, and to enable informal as well as formally organized resources to be brought to bear upon them when they do.' (NISW 1982, p. x)

The Barclay Report, as it is commonly referred to, acknowledged that, in recommending a community approach to social work, it was doing little more than reiterating the findings of the Seebohm Committee (NISW 1982, p. 203). The potential benefits of such an approach were illustrated in a comparative study of two similar populations served by social work teams adopting very different policies. Staff in the Normanton team adopted a community approach, with their roles encompassing group and community work as well as individual casework. They recruited and worked alongside volunteers and the team sponsored a number of local community groups. They also strove to establish links with the network of other welfare agencies operating in their area, including health, education and housing staff. By contrast, the Featherstone team adopted a more traditional approach, with their roles largely restricted to individual casework and with fewer links with other agencies and workers in their area. Some significant differences emerged when various outcome measures were considered. For example, the Normanton team had knowledge of a larger proportion of those people considered to be vulnerable living in their area than the Featherstone team. Not only did they have 'formal' contact with about twice the proportion of such people, through referrals and long-term work, but they also had much greater 'informal' contact with other vulnerable individuals through their involvement in various community groups and schemes for children, elderly people and people with disabilities. This was demonstrated by the fact that the Normanton team already knew about 40% of those people formally referred to the team, compared to only 3% in the Featherstone team (Hadley & McGrath 1984).

In a similar but more recent study, Gibbons (1992) compared two demographically similar urban areas served by social work teams with contrasting policies regarding the organization of family support services. 'Newpath' adopted a community social work approach, whereas 'Oldweigh' had a more traditional casework focus. There was evidence that the Newpath service users showed more improvement on measures of social contact and malaise, than similar service users in Oldweigh. Gibbons concluded that the most likely explanations for these differences appeared to be the better developed informal support networks and contact with community resources, particularly day care services, which were enjoyed by service users in Newpath.

However, despite such evidence and the backing of two major official reports, there continues to be little sign that community social work has established itself in the mainstream of social work with children and families. The most significant examples of the implementation of community social work during this period have been the rather isolated examples of neighbourhood social work teams and the development of a relatively small number of family centres, operating on an open-access, neighbourhood basis, mainly within the voluntary sector (see Cannan 1992). In most Social Services Departments, such initiatives have either not survived to the present day or they have never been developed in the first place. As one well known and respected community social worker has observed:

'Family centres are increasingly restricted to child abuse referrals and so closed to the community. Although some patch teams survive, their members are more likely to be regulating and monitoring individual clients than involved with local clubs, food co-ops and community associations. They are not community social workers.' (Holman 1993, p. 7)

There are a number of factors that are significant in understanding why this is the case. Holman identifies three of these factors. First, the political and media focus on child abuse, to the exclusion of other approaches to social work with children and families. Secondly, the British Association of Social Workers' attempts to establish social work as a profession, with a unique body of specialist skills that do not sit well with some aspects of community social work. Thirdly, there is the influence of New Right practices and values on social work management, with its emphasis on identifying 'high-risk' families, who are subjected to decisive state intervention and a policy of minimal intrusion in the lives of the majority (see Jack & Stepney 1995). In addition, the political decision to locate Social Services Departments *within* local authorities, taken at the point of establishing the terms of reference of the Seebohm Committee, has had a very significant effect. This decision has, perhaps inevitably, contributed to the development of a hierarchical and bureaucratically centralized form of organization with procedurally dominated services (see Howe 1992). This has meant that most of the attempts to introduce decentralized services, capable of adopting a community orientation in their work, have been met by strong resistance. This has, in part, been caused by the inherent inertia and rigidity of the organizations themselves and in other respects by the reluctance of their employees, including professionals, managers and administrators, to allow their powers and areas of discretion to be transferred to service users and lay helpers. As a result, those projects which have emerged have tended to be 'bolted-on' to the existing structures that are generally antagonistic to their aims and where any changes introduced have tended to serve organizational and professional agendas, rather than being driven by any fundamental attempt to secure genuine user involvement and participation (Beresford 1993; Beresford & Croft 1993).

In the field of child care, the factors identified by Holman have contributed towards the construction of a discourse around the axis of child protection (Parton 1991) which has been of central importance in shaping public and professional attitudes and current social work services for children and families.

THE INFLUENCE OF THE CHILD PROTECTION DISCOURSE

The child protection discourse, which now dominates all others in social work with children and families, is based on a model which treats child abuse as if it is the product of pathological family interactions, thereby excluding any serious consideration of the effects of such factors as social environment, poverty, race and gender. It relies on the legal system to ensure that a balance is struck between the protection of children from 'significant harm' and the rights of parents to privacy and protection from over-intrusive state intervention. In turn, the imposition of ever tighter and centrally determined regulations are regarded as essential for ensuring that acceptable standards of practice are achieved. The effect of the child protection discourse is to place social workers and the families they are supposed to be helping into clearly demarcated, separate camps, in which fear and suspicion continually undermine individual attempts to develop relationships based on the principles of partnership, common understanding and mutual trust and respect (Jones & Novak 1993; Jack, in press).

The corrosive influence of the child protection discourse on relationships between professional social workers and service users is graphically illustrated by Jordan (in press) who writes about his experiences in a local authority for whom he was undertaking consultancy work. The local authority concerned was something of a pioneer in the field, trying to integrate child protection and family support services for children and families in local family centres. The aim of the consultancy was to promote a partnership approach to practice, management and policy formulation, within the districts in which these integrated centres were being established, consolidating and extending parental participation and the provi-

sion of family support services. Although in some family centres groups of parents were successfully involved in both the provision of mutual support services, including drop-in facilities and holiday care schemes, and were also in dialogue with the local authority about policy issues, there were many other districts in which the child protection social workers and their managers responded to this initiative with a mixture of indifference and open hostility. They appeared to be guarding what they regarded as 'their' territory and were unwilling to commit themselves to the sort of sharing of power and mutual trust and respect necessary for a partnership approach to the provision of family support services to be successful. For their part, the parents in the latter districts perceived child protection social work as 'impermeable'. Rather than attempting to engage with the workers involved and trying to influence their practice and policies, they turned their efforts towards supporting a wider group of parents, entirely separate from the families with which the social workers were engaged in the district teams.

Jordan suggests that, despite protestations to the contrary, many child protection social workers have a stake in the formal, individualized, power-laden role which they have been assigned within the present discourse and organizational structures and that they are therefore resistant to moving towards the more informal, collective, negotiated approaches involved in providing family support services based on principles of partnership. Unfortunately, the degree of polarization which emerged in this local authority between the advocates of the partnership/parents groups approach and the defenders of the child protection perspective, led to major conflict at political and senior managerial levels and ultimately to the termination of the consultancy work (Jordan, in press).

Thus, whilst it can be argued that the Children Act 1989 has provided a legal framework which enables both child protection and family support services to be provided alongside one another, it can be difficult to achieve this in practice within the same agency. The nature of the child protection discourse and its dominant position in social work with children and families means that the family support provisions of the Act are continually squeezed out by the attitudes of professional staff, the procedural requirements of child protection systems and the resources which they consume. Unless and until the child protection discourse can be successfully deconstructed and replaced by a framework which acknowledges the influence of discrimination and structural factors on individual behaviour, and accords more fundamental importance to the views of service recipients (both adults and children), there appears to be little prospect of a robust and lasting community approach to social work with children and families being established. However, some signs are emerging that this process of deconstruction may have begun and it is to some of these signs that we will now turn our attention.

CHALLENGES FROM RESEARCH AND PRACTICE

In 1995, the British Department of Health published the findings of a group of research studies into various aspects of child protection, many of which they had commissioned themselves, as part of the government response to Cleveland and other child abuse inquiries in the late 1980s. The Dartington research team was commissioned to prepare an overview report of these studies (Department of Health 1995). Whilst these studies and particularly the accompanying overview report do not constitute a fundamental challenge to the existing orthodoxy, they do nevertheless move the debate forward in some important respects. A critical appraisal of the research, and particularly the way in which the overview report has been presented to the public and the social work profession, enables a number of important issues to be highlighted (Parton 1996).

First, it is of great welcome that there now exists a range of empirical research upon which to base future directions in policy and practice. This is in marked contrast to the situation which has existed over the past 20 years and more, where policy and practice in this field have been almost exclusively formulated in response to a number of one-off child abuse scandals and the public inquiries that have accompanied them. Whilst the lessons to be learned from such extreme cases have undoubtedly been important in some respects, particularly in relation to inter-agency collaboration, they nevertheless provide a very dubious framework for dealing with the vast majority of cases on a day-to-day basis (Howitt 1992). What the recent research has shown is that the bulk of cases labelled as 'child protection' do not actually involve serious abuse. For example, none of the cases in Cleaver and Freeman's study and only 2% of those in the study undertaken by Thoburn and her colleagues required any medical treatment (Cleaver & Freeman 1995; Thoburn *et al.* 1995).

Secondly, there is a significant, although not total, shift away from the traditional disease model of child abuse, which has underpinned the development of the child protection discourse. Much of the research embraces a phenomenological perspective, in which abusive incidents are understood primarily within the contexts within which they occur, and with an eye towards the longer-term effects which they may have. There is a general acknowledgement that child abuse can have no absolute definition – that it is a socially constructed phenomenon, which varies over time and between different social contexts. Farmer and Owen's study of initial child protection case conferences and the child protection plans formulated, highlights the common failure to take proper account of issues such as housing and social and financial support (Farmer & Owen 1995). Furthermore, the study by Gibbons and her colleagues rightly draws attention to aspects of social disadvantage relevant to child protection (Gibbons *et al.* 1995). Several of the studies also highlight the potentially harmful effects on children of living in what the overview report characterizes as 'low warmth/high criticism' social environments (Department of Health 1995).

Following on from this, one would have hoped that the conclusions contained in the overview report, which is likely to be the only product of the research programme actually read by most social workers and their managers, would have focused attention on the wider social and political factors that help to create and sustain the damaging social environments in which some children are raised. Unfortunately, this is not the case. As Parton has pointed out:

'...poverty...patriarchy, social class, racism and the implications of increasing social divisions in British society...*are never discussed.*' (Parton 1996, p. 9, emphasis added)

Instead, what we get is a concentration on *social work practice* and *management*. The overview report sets out what it calls 'five simple prerequisites of effective practice' to protect children and promote their welfare. In brief, these are as follows:

- Informed and sensitive professional/client relationships.
- Achieving the right balance of power between professionals, parents and children.
- The need for a wider perspective on child protection.
- The effective supervision and training of social workers and other professionals.
- Enhancing children's general quality of life.

In a summary of their overview report the Dartington team conclude that:

> 'The most important condition for success was found always to be the quality of the relationship between a child's family and the responsible professional... Taken as a whole, the findings did not suggest any need for a wholesale restructuring of the child protection process.'
> (Dartington 1996)

Most significantly, for the preservation of the child protection discourse, these sentiments were echoed by the politicians and the media at the launch of the overview report in June 1995. The Junior Health Minister, John Bowis, called for local authority social workers to change their practice by adopting a 'lighter touch' in child protection work and Wendy Rose, Assistant Chief Inspector at the Department of Health, talked about the need for local authorities to achieve 'a better balance' between child protection and family support services, in line with the recommendations of an earlier report prepared by the Audit Commission (Audit Commission 1994).

However, such pronouncements are at odds with the Department of Health's apparent refusal to consider appropriate revisions to the official guidelines for inter-agency child protection work (Department of Health 1991a). In particular, there is no new guidance proposed on the ways in which social workers and their managers are expected to identify less serious cases at an early stage, in order to avoid them getting caught up in the child protection 'net' unnecessarily. What criteria and procedures are supposed to be used, and where will accountability lie for the decisions which are taken? In the present 'blaming culture' which affects all publicly funded services, where is the incentive and support for social workers to take risks in developing less intrusive and more supportive approaches to work with families where there are concerns about the care provided for their children? There are also no signs of the government responding to the calls of many Social Services Directors for additional short-term funding to develop family support services, before expecting any reductions in the number of costly child protection investigations undertaken. Finally, there has been no official response to suggestions that the integrated child protection/family support services model favoured by the Department of Health may contain an inherent incompatability between investigative and supportive functions (Pelton 1989 and 1992; Parton 1995; Jordan, in press).

It is hardly surprising, in these circumstances, that the social work profession in general has reacted to the research, and more particularly its presentation in the public domain, with a mixture of defensiveness and scepticism. However, it would be wrong to suggest that social work practice with children and families is *totally* subordinated to the dominant child protection discourse. There are a number of examples of practitioners and their immediate managers consciously striving to establish and maintain approaches which are based on the principles of community social work, attempting to harness the positive potential of social support networks, and it is to some of these projects that we will now turn our attention.

Garbarino's work in Chicago, discussed earlier, has already alerted us to the significant part played by social support networks in producing different rates of child abuse in otherwise similar communities (Garbarino & Kostelny 1993). A number of intervention strategies, based on the potential of social support for preventing or reducing child abuse and enhancing family functioning in general, have already been introduced and evaluated in North America. These include pre-school, and school-based programmes (Durlak 1995), home visiting schemes (Olds *et al.* 1986; Wasik *et al.* 1990) and intensive family preservation strategies (Wells, in press). Action-research on this scale, into the role of social support in the prevention and reduction of child abuse, has so far not been undertaken in Britain. This is hardly surprising, given the generally hostile political and professional environment already described. Some commentators have even used an alleged vagueness of terminology and objectives of community social work as an apparent justification for blocking the development of such approaches:

> 'Few would argue that prevention or social support should be encouraged, *but the words are dangerous* because they provide a false sense of precision and suggest that there is agreement as to what prevention or social support includes.' (Gough 1993, p. 217, emphasis added)

Whilst there may be problems in trying to apply broad concepts derived from research in practice, this can easily become a self-fulfilling prophecy, since the best way to develop greater precision and agreement lies in attempts to design, implement and evaluate a range of community social work initiatives in practice. The same objections could have been raised in relation to the development of practice and research in the field of child protection, or any other aspect of social work for that matter, with the result that little progress would be made in any area of policy or practice. It would be highly unusual for practitioners in any field of human activity to have all of the information which they required before engaging in any direct intervention. Fortunately, there are a number of practitioners in this country who have not allowed the undoubted problems associated with developing innovative practice of any kind to prevent them from designing appropriate action-research programmes.

For example, the Canklow Estate Project in Rotherham, funded by the local authority, involved a small team of community social workers based in a community centre, taking responsibility for children 'in care', on supervision orders and on the child protection register. The main focus of their work was the development and maintenance of various formal and informal social support networks. The team initiated women's groups, play schemes, adult education classes and youth clubs. Over a 5-year period the effects of the scheme were evaluated. They found that there were marked reductions in the number of children 'in care' and on supervision orders and, most significantly, a drop to almost zero of children on the child protection register.

'No longer feeling stigmatised by approaching social workers, families have come at an early stage of difficulty. Social workers or local groups have been able to reduce environmental stress. Acting together with other community members has improved both the self-image and the coping mechanisms of families.' (Holman 1993)

Along somewhat similar lines, Barnardo's have established an action-research project in Bristol, linked to a family centre in a neighbourhood with high rates of child protection and child care referrals. The project aims to use a social networks approach, supporting and strengthening helpful networks in areas producing high rates of child protection referrals, bringing families together to tackle difficulties and explore ways of protecting children. The project is being evaluated over a 2-year period to examine the effectiveness of this approach (see Gill 1995).

A third example is provided by Newpin, a national organization which was founded in the early 1980s by a former health visitor in South London, as a result of concern about the high levels of child abuse and family distress in the area. Referrals are usually made by health visitors and social workers. About two-thirds of the mothers referred are clinically depressed, a third have been sexually or physically abused and a third have been in local authority care (Barker 1994). Newpin services are based on principles of mutual support and self-help, using trained volunteers, recruited from the same areas and social

backgrounds as the referred families, to provide practical and emotional support. A number of service recipients later go on to become service providers themselves. As one former user of Newpin services has commented:

'It has changed my life completely. I hadn't had much hugging and kissing as a child. It gave me a family.'

This woman has since gone on to become a Newpin co-ordinator, helping to run a centre where isolated parents can meet together and begin to broaden their social networks. However, such centres are more than just social clubs, with both formal and informal training within a 'parent development programme' being central to Newpin's success. Mothers are taught how to play with their children and are also helped to develop greater understanding of their own feelings and those of their children (Barker 1994). Evaluation of the scheme has shown that receivers of Newpin services improved on measures of maternal depression and partner relationships by comparison with families waiting to receive Newpin services (Cox *et al.* 1990; see also Gibbons *et al.* 1990).

Developments like these, carefully designed and targetted, with on-going evaluation of their effectiveness built in from the start, provided within both the statutory and voluntary sectors, can go some of the way towards providing the sort of evidence required to challenge the narrow focus of the existing child protection discourse and to ensure that the family support provisions of the Children Act can develop as originally envisaged. Without this sort of detailed research evidence, it is likely that the vested interests and anxieties of many participants in the present arrangements will continue to provide an effective barrier to the development of community social work within the mainstream of services provided for children and families.

CONCLUSION

It is through the sort of action-research projects outlined in the previous section that the potential of a community social work approach with children and families, utilizing the potential benefits of social support networks for the prevention or reduction of child physical abuse and neglect and contributing to the general well-being of families, can be properly assessed. There is a need to demonstrate what sorts of social support are most effective in ameliorating what sorts of problems. Whilst there is a growing body of research evidence available to assist in this task, a

An ecological approach to social work G Jack

great deal of it originates from the other side of the Atlantic (see Thompson 1995) and requires further practical application in this country before firm conclusions for social work in the UK can be formulated. We have already seen that the existing child protection discourse, with its narrow focus on the identification and investigation of abusive incidents, presents a major obstacle to acceptance of a community social work approach. However, we have also seen the way in which this discourse is beginning to be challenged by evidence emerging from both research and practice and we have, in the Children Act 1989, a legal framework which, for the first time, gives a wide range of family support services an official place within social work.

It is also to be hoped that the findings of the independent National Commission of Inquiry into the Prevention of Child Abuse, established by the NSPCC in 1994, will provide further momentum towards the construction of a more helpful discourse. Like the recently published research studies into the child protection process, this inquiry is not restricted to a retrospective examination of child abuse scandals which have been so instrumental in the development of the existing child protection discourse. Its terms of reference, whilst including an examination of current services, also cover 'external factors which impinge upon child abuse and neglect', and recognize 'that the prevention of abuse involves all sectors of the community' (NSPCC 1994). Importantly, the consultation process has involved not only discussions with professionals and policy makers but also families and children and young people themselves, as well as statutory, voluntary and private organizations representing these groups. It should therefore be possible for the Commission to consider the fundamental issues of how to reduce the incidence of abuse and what other services, if they were available, might prevent abuse from occurring, issues which the Public Inquiries of the 1980s singularly failed to address (Department of Health 1991b).

It is not being suggested that social support strategies and the practice interventions of social workers on their own can provide effective prevention of the circumstances which give rise to child abuse and neglect. However, specific strategies to enhance the social support networks of families with children 'in need' appear, nevertheless, to be capable of producing significant benefits. They can enhance family functioning and parental competence by improving parents' access to information and counselling, providing reinforcement of appropriate par-

enting and integrating family members into wider community networks. These wider networks can help to meet other family needs, including assistance with child care and monitoring of children's safety, increased educational and employment opportunities and welfare benefits advice (Thompson 1995, pp. 122–23). Crucially for the reduction of child abuse and neglect, healthy social support networks help to provide the emotional support which appears to be essential for successful parenting.

The weight of evidence now available clearly suggests that an ecological perspective, leading to interventions designed to enhance personal social support networks, should take its place within the mainstream approaches to social work with children and families. The question of whether or not child protection and family support services can be provided successfully within the same social work agency is still open to debate. This is one aspect of service delivery and organization which would particularly benefit from action-research evaluation. Finally, however, it must be appreciated that social workers will remain impotent to effect real changes in the social environments within which children are raised without the continuing deconstruction of the prevailing child protection discourse and the further development of an alternative discourse, which recognizes the wider social and political factors which help to shape all of our lives.

REFERENCES

Ackroyd, P. (1992) *English Music.* Hamish Hamilton, London.

Audit Commission (1994) *Seen But Not Heard: Coordinating Child Health and Social Services for Children in Need.* Her Majesty's Stationery Office (HMSO), London.

Barker, P. (1994) Learning How to Love Them. *The Guardian,* 21 December.

Belsky, J. (1993) Etiology of child maltreatment: a developmental–ecological analysis. *Psychological Bulletin,* **114,** 413–434.

Beresford, P. (1993) A programme for change: current issues in user involvement and empowerment. In: *A Challenge to Change. Practical Experiences of Building User Led Services* (eds P. Beresford & T. Harding). National Institute for Social Work (NISW), London.

Beresford, P. & Croft, S. (1993) *Citizen Involvement. A Practical Guide for Change.* Macmillan, London.

Bronfenbrenner, U. (1979) *Experiments by Nature and Design.* Harvard University Press, Cambridge, MA.

Brown, G.W., Andrews, B., Harris, T.O., Adler, Z. & Bridge, L. (1986) Social support, self esteem and depression. *Psychological Medicine,* **16,** 813–31.

Brown, G.W. & Harris, T.O. (1978) *Social Origins of Depression.* Tavistock, London.

Cannan, C. (1992) *Changing Families, Changing Welfare,* Wheatsheaf, Hemel Hempstead.

Cassel, J. (1976) The contribution of the social environment to host resistance. *American Journal of Epidemiology,* **102,** 107–123.

Cleaver, H. & Freeman, P. (1995) *Parental Perspectives in Cases of Suspected Child Abuse.* Her Majesty's Stationery Office (HMSO), London.

Cobb, S. (1976) Social support as a moderator of life stress. *Psychosomatic Medicine,* **38,** 300–314.

Cochran, M. (1993) Parenting and personal social networks. In: *Parenting: an ecological perspective* (eds T. Luster & L. Okagaki). Lawrence Erlbaum Associates, Hillsdale, NJ.

Cochran, M. & Brassard, J. (1979) Child development and personal social networks. *Child Development,* **50,** 609–615.

Cohen, S. & Syme, S.L. (1985) 'Issues in the study and application of social support. In: *Social Support and Health* (eds S. Cohen & S. L. Syme), pp. 3–22. Academic Press, Orlando, FL.

Cohen, S. & Wills, T.A. (1985) Stress, social support and the buffering hypothesis. *Psychological Bulletin,* **98,** 310–57.

Cox, A.D., Puckering, C., Pound, A. & Mills, M. (1987) The impact of maternal depression in young children. *Journal of Child Psychology and Psychiatry,* **28,** 917–928.

Cox, A.D., Puckering, C., Pound, A., Mills, M. & Owen, A.L. (1990) *Newpin: the Evaluation of a Home Visiting and Befriending Scheme in South London.* Report to the Department of Health, London.

Crittenden, P.M. (1985) Maltreated infants: vulnerability and resilience. *Journal of Child Psychology and Psychiatry,* **26,** 85–96.

Cutrona, C.E. & Russell, D.W. (1990) Type of social support and specific stress: toward a theory of optimal matching. In: *Social Support: An Interactional View* (eds B.R. Sarason, G.R. Pierce & I.G. Sarason), pp. 319–366. Wiley, New York.

Dartington Social Research Unit (1996) Child protection: messages from research. *Newsletter,* Spring. Dartington Social Research Unit (DSRU), Dartington.

Department of Health, (1991a) *Working Together.* Her Majesty's Stationery Office (HMSO), London.

Department of Health, (1991b) *A Study of Inquiry Reports 1980–89.* Her Majesty's Stationery Office (HMSO), London.

Department of Health, (1995) *Child Protection: Messages from Research.* Her Majesty's Stationery Office (HMSO), London.

Durkheim, E. (1951) *Suicide.* Free Press, New York.

Durlak, J.A. (1995) *School-Based Prevention Programs for Children and Adolescents.* Sage, Thousand Oaks, CA.

Emlen, A. (1977) *If you care about children, then care about parents.* Address to the Tennessee Association for Young Children, November.

Farmer, E. & Owen, M. (1995) *Child Protection Practice: Private Risks and Public Remedies – Decision Making,* *Intervention and Outcome in Child Protection Work.* Her Majesty's Stationery Office (HMSO), London.

Garbarino, J. (1976) A preliminary study of some ecological correlates of child abuse: the impact of socioeconomic stress on mothers. *Child Development,* **47,** 178–85.

Garbarino, J. (1990) The human ecology of early risk. In: *Handbook of Early Childhood Intervention.* (eds S.J. Meisels & J.P. Shonkoff), pp. 78–96. Cambridge University Press, New York.

Garbarino, J. & Kostelny, K. (1993) Neighborhood and community influences on parenting. In: *Parenting: an Ecological Perspective* (eds T. Luster & L. Okagaki), pp. 203–226. Lawrence Erlbaum Associates, Hillsdale, NJ.

Garbarino, J. & Sherman, D. (1980) High-risk neighborhoods and high-risk families: the human ecology of child maltreatment. *Child Development,* **51,** 188–98.

Gibbons, J. (ed.) (1992) *The Children Act 1989 and Family Support: Principles into Practice.* Her Majesty's Stationery Office (HMSO), London.

Gibbons, J., Conroy, S. & Bell, C. (1995) *Operating the Child Protection System: A Study of Child Protection Practices in English Local Authorities.* Her Majesty's Stationery Office (HMSO), London.

Gibbons, J., Thorpe, S. & Wilkinson, P. (1990) *Family Support and Prevention: Studies in Local Areas.* Her Majesty's Stationery Office (HMSO), London.

Gill, O. (1995) Neighbourhood watch. *Community Care,* 8–14 June, pp 30–31.

Gottlieb, B.H. (1981) Social networks and social support in community mental health. In: *Social Networks and Social Support* (ed. B.H. Gottlieb), pp. 11–42. Sage, Beverly Hills, CA.

Gough, D. (1993) The case for and against prevention. In: *Child Abuse and Child Abusers* (ed. L. Waterhouse), pp. 208–232. Jessica Kingsley, London.

Hadley, R. & McGrath, M. (1980) *Going Local. Neighbourhood Social Services.* Bedford Square Press, London.

Hadley, R. & McGrath, M. (1984) *When Social Services Are Local. The Normanton Experience.* National Institute for Social Work (NISW), London.

Heller, K., Price, R.H. & Hogg, J.R. (1990) The role of social support in community and clinical interventions. In: *Social Support: An Interactional View* (eds B. R. Sarason, I. G. Sarason & G. R. Pierce), pp. 482–507. Wiley, New York.

Holman, B. (1993) Pulling together. *The Guardian,* January 20.

Howe, D. (1992) Child abuse and the bureaucratisation of social work. *The Sociological Review,* **40,** 491–508.

Howitt, D. (1992) *Child Abuse Errors.* Harvester Wheatsheaf, Hemel Hempstead.

Jack, G. (in press) Discourses of child protection and child welfare. *British Journal of Social Work.*

Jack, G. & Stepney, P. (1995) The Children Act 1989 – protection or persecution? Family support and child protection in the 1990s. *Critical Social Policy,* **43,** 26–39.

Jones, C. & Novak, T. (1993) Social work today. *British Journal of Social Work,* **23,** 195–212.

An ecological approach to social work G Jack

Jordon, B. (in press) Partnership with service users in child protection and family support.

Kessler, R.C. & McLeod, J.D. (1985) Social support and mental health in community samples In: *Social Support and Health* (eds S. Cohen & S. L. Syme), pp. 219–240. Academic Press, Orlando, Fl.

Korbin, J.E. (1989) Fatal maltreatment by mothers: a proposed framework. *Child Abuse and Neglect*, **13**, 481–89.

Korbin, J.E. (1991) 'Good Mothers', 'Babykillers', and Fatal Child Abuse. Paper presented to the annual meeting of the American Anthropological Association, Chicago, November.

Meyer, C.H. (1985) Social supports and social workers: collaboration or conflict? *Social Work*, **30**, 291.

Moncher, F. (1995) Social Isolation and child-abuse risk. *Families in Society: The Journal of Contemporary Human Services*, September, 421–431.

Newton, J. (1988) *Preventing Mental Illness*. Routledge and Keegan Paul, London.

National Institute of Social Work (1982) *Social Workers: Their Role and Tasks*. (Barclay Report). Bedford Square Press, London.

National Society for the Prevention of Cruelty to Children (1994) *National Commission of Inquiry into the Prevention of Child Abuse: Terms of Reference*. National Society for the Prevention of Cruelty to Children (NSPCC), London.

Olds, D.L., Henderson, C.R., Jr, Chamberlin, R. & Tatelbaum, R. (1986) Preventing child abuse and neglect: A randomized trial of nurse home visitation. *Paediatrics*, **78**, 65–78.

Parton, N. (1991) *Governing the Family: Child Care, Child Protection and the State*. Macmillan, Basingstoke.

Parton, N. (1995) *Current Priorities and Problems in Child Protection*. Paper presented to the conference 'Rethinking Child Protection: Research Leading the Way', Lancaster, January.

Parton, N. (1996) *Child Protection, Family Support and Social Work: a Critical Appraisal of the Department of Health Research Studies in Child Protection*.

Pelton, L.H. (1989) *For Reasons of Poverty: A Critical Analysis of the Public Child Welfare System in the United States*. Praeger, New York.

Pelton, L.H. (1992) A functional approach to reorganizing family and child welfare interventions. *Chidren and Youth Service Review*, **14**, 289–303.

Pound, A., Mills, M. & Cox, T. (1985) A pilot evaluation of Newpin. A home visiting and befriending scheme in South London, MS, summarized in the October *Newsletter of the Association of Child Psychology and Psychiatry*.

Sarason, B.R., Pierce, G.R. & Sarason, I.G. (1990) Social support: the sense of acceptance and the role of relationships. In: *Social Support: An Interactional View* (eds B.R. Sarason, I.G. Sarason & G.R. Pierce), pp. 97–128. Wiley, New York.

Seebohm, F. (1968) *Report of the Committee on Local Authority and Allied Personal Social Services*. Her Majesty's Stationery Office (HMSO), London.

Sheppard, M. (1994) Childcare, social support and maternal depression: a review and application of findings. *The British Journal of Social Work*, **24**, 287–310.

Thoburn, J., Lewis, A. & Shemmings, D. (1995) *Paternalism or Partnership? Family Involvement in the Child Protection Process*. Her Majesty's Stationery Office (HMSO), London.

Thompson, R.A. (1995), *Preventing Child Maltreatment Through Social Support*. Sage, Thousand Oaks, CA.

Wasik, B.H., Bryant, D.M. & Lyon, C.M. (1990) *Home Visiting*. Sage, Newbury Park, CA.

Wellman, B. (1981) Applying network analysis to the study of support. In: *Social Networks and Social Support* (ed. G. H. Gottlieb). Sage, Beverley Hills, CA.

Wells, K. (in press) Family preservation services in context: origins, practices and current issues. In: *Working with troubled children and their families in their own homes: implications for policy-makers and practitioners* (ed. I. Schwartz). University of Nebraska Press, Lincoln.

Wills, T.A. (1985) Supportive functions of interpersonal relationships. In: *Social Support and Health* (eds S. Cohen & S. L. Syme), pp. 61–82. Academic Press, Orlando, Fl.

Part III
Assessing the Needs of
Individual Children

[11]

The Strengths and Difficulties Questionnaire: A Research Note

Robert Goodman

Institute of Psychiatry, London, U.K.

A novel behavioural screening questionnaire, the Strengths and Difficulties Questionnaire (SDQ), was administered along with Rutter questionnaires to parents and teachers of 403 children drawn from dental and psychiatric clinics. Scores derived from the SDQ and Rutter questionnaires were highly correlated; parent–teacher correlations for the two sets of measures were comparable or favoured the SDQ. The two sets of measures did not differ in their ability to discriminate between psychiatric and dental clinic attenders. These preliminary findings suggest that the SDQ functions as well as the Rutter questionnaires while offering the following additional advantages: a focus on strengths as well as difficulties; better coverage of inattention, peer relationships, and prosocial behaviour; a shorter format; and a single form suitable for both parents and teachers, perhaps thereby increasing parent–teacher correlations.

Keywords: Questionnaire, child behaviour, psychopathology, strengths.

Abbreviations: CBCL: Child Behavior Checklist; ROC: Receiver Operating Characteristic; SDQ: Strengths and Difficulties Questionnaire.

Introduction

This paper describes a brief behavioural screening questionnaire that provides balanced coverage of children and young people's behaviours, emotions, and relationships. The value of this novel Strengths and Difficulties Questionnaire (SDQ) is evaluated against the benchmark set by the Rutter parent and teacher questionnaires. The SDQ has been designed to meet the needs of researchers, clinicians, and educationalists.

The Rutter questionnaires are long-established and highly respected behavioural screening questionnaires that have proved valid and reliable in many contexts (Elander & Rutter, 1996). Though substantially shorter and therefore quicker to complete than the Child Behavior Checklist (CBCL; Achenbach, 1991a), the Rutter parent questionnaire seem no less useful for many purposes (Berg, Lucas, & McGuire, 1992; Elander & Rutter, 1995; Fombonne, 1989). Developed three decades ago, the Rutter questionnaires have generally worn well, though they do show their age in some ways. Thus all items are about undesirable traits whereas the recent trend, particularly in education, has been to emphasise children's strengths and not just their deficits. In addition, the range of behavioural items covered by the Rutter questionnaires is now somewhat dated. Thus nail-biting and thumb-sucking are included whereas many areas of contemporary interest—including concentration,

impulsivity-reflectiveness, having friends, being victimised, and acting prosocially—are poorly covered. Finally, whereas one version of the Achenbach questionnaire is designed for completion by young people themselves (Achenbach, 1991b), there is no equivalent Rutter questionnaire for self-completion.

A previous research note (Goodman, 1994) described an expanded Rutter parent questionnaire that incorporated all of the original Rutter items as well as many additional items, mostly on children's strengths. The inclusion of these additional items did not appear to attenuate the valuable properties of the original Rutter questionnaire as a behaviour screening instrument, though the extra items presumably did make the questionnaire somewhat more time-consuming to complete. Factor analyses suggested that among children of normal intelligence the expanded questionnaire was tapping five distinct dimensions: conduct problems, emotional symptoms, hyperactivity, peer problems, and prosocial behaviour.

Using these findings as a guide, the SDQ was designed to meet the following specifications: it should fit easily on one side of paper; it should be applicable to children and young people ranging from 4 to 16 years; the same version should be completed by parents and teachers; a similar version should be available for self-report; both strengths and difficulties should be well represented; and there should be equal numbers of items on each of five relevant dimensions, namely conduct problems, emotional symptoms, hyperactivity, peer relationships, and prosocial behaviour. This paper compares informant-completed SDQs with Rutter parent and teacher questionnaires.

Requests for reprints, or sample questionnaires (available in many languages), to: Dr. R. Goodman, Department of Child and Adolescent Psychiatry, Institute of Psychiatry, De Crespigny Park, London SE5 8AF, U.K.

Materials and Methods

Sampling

Questionnaires were obtained on 403 children aged 4–16 years attending one of two London child psychiatric clinics or the children's department of a London dental hospital. The parents of children attending these clinics were recruited into the study until a planned total of roughly 150–250 children had been attained for both dental and psychiatric samples. In the dental clinic and one of the psychiatric clinics (Clinic A), parents who had given informed consent were asked to complete two behavioural screening questionnaires while awaiting their clinic appointment. Participating parents were subsequently asked for permission for their child's teacher to be approached on a similar basis. The other psychiatric clinic (Clinic B) routinely used questionnaires prior to the first assessment, sending them to all parents and, when permission was obtained, to teachers as well. In this clinic, parents were routinely sent both behavioural screening questionnaires and asked if they would be willing for their answers (and the teacher's answers) to be used not only for clinical purposes but also for research. Some of the parents from Clinic B did not complete questionnaires themselves but did give permission for teacher questionnaires to be used for research. The proportion of refusals was not systematically recorded since, as explained later, the statistical analyses did not require the samples to be representative.

Methods

Respondents were administered a Rutter questionnaire and a Strengths and Difficulties Questionnaire (SDQ) in randomised order. Parents were given the Rutter A(2) Questionnaire and teachers the Rutter B(2) Questionnaire; both were scored in the standard way to generate scores for total deviance, conduct problems, emotional symptoms, and hyperactivity (Rutter, 1967; Rutter, Tizard, & Whitmore, 1970; Schachar, Rutter, & Smith, 1981).

The informant-rated version of the SDQ was administered to both parents and teachers. This version of the SDQ is reproduced in full in Appendix A for information only. The SDQ asks about 25 attributes, 10 of which would generally be thought of as strengths, 14 of which would generally be thought of as difficulties, and one of which—"gets on better with adults than with other children"—is neutral. Though no SDQ item is identically worded to any Rutter item, five items are similarly worded. The initial choice of items was guided by the factor loadings and frequency distributions that had previously been obtained on an expanded Rutter parent questionnaire (Goodman, 1994); items were subsequently modified and amalgamated on the basis of a succession of informal trials as well as advice from colleagues. The 25 SDQ items are divided between 5 scales of 5 items each, as shown below.

Hyperactivity Scale. "Restless, overactive, cannot stay still for long"; "Constantly fidgeting or squirming"; "Easily distracted, concentration wanders"; *"Thinks things out before acting"*; and *"Sees tasks through to the end, good attention span"*.

Emotional Symptoms Scale. "Often complains of headaches, stomach-ache or sickness"; "Many worries, often seems worried"; "Often unhappy, down-hearted or tearful"; "Nervous or clingy in new situations, easily loses confidence"; and "Many fears, easily scared".

Conduct Problems Scale. "Often has temper tantrums or hot tempers"; *"Generally obedient, usually does what adults request"*; "Often fights with other children or bullies them"; "Often lies or cheats"; and "Steals from home, school or elsewhere".

Peer Problems Scale. "Rather solitary, tends to play alone"; *"Has at least one good friend"*; *"Generally liked by other children"*; "Picked on or bullied by other children"; and "Gets on better with adults than with other children".

Prosocial Scale. "Considerate of other people's feelings"; "Shares readily with other children (treats, toys, pencils, etc.)"; "Helpful if someone is hurt, upset or feeling ill"; "Kind to younger children"; and "Often volunteers to help others (parents, teachers, other children)".

Each item can be marked "not true", "somewhat true" or "certainly true". For all of the items except the five printed above in italics, the item is scored 0 for "not true", 1 for "somewhat true", and 2 for "certainly true". For the five items printed above in italics, the item is scored 2 for "not true", 1 for "somewhat true", and 0 for "certainly true". The score for each of the five scales is generated by summing the scores for the five items that make up that scale, thereby generating a scale score ranging from 0 to 10. The scores for hyperactivity, emotional symptoms, conduct problems, and peer problems can be summed to generate a total difficulties score ranging from 0 to 40; the prosocial score is not incorporated in the reverse direction into the total difficulties score since the absence of prosocial behaviours is conceptually different from the presence of psychological difficulties.

The Rutter A(2) and the SDQ were both completed by the parents of 346 children: 158 dental clinic attenders and 188 psychiatric clinic attenders. The Rutter B(2) and the SDQ were both completed by the teachers of 185 children: 39 dental clinic attenders and 146 psychiatric clinic attenders. Most of the teacher reports were on psychiatric clinic attenders because the parents of children attending Child Psychiatric Clinic B generally agreed to the clinic sending questionnaires to teachers for clinical as well as research purposes; parents of children attending the dental clinic or Child Psychiatric Clinic A were less likely to give permission for teacher questionnaires to be obtained solely for research purposes.

Statistical Analysis

As in previous studies comparing the validity of different screening questionnaires (e.g. Berg et al., 1992), analyses of Receiver Operating Characteristic (ROC) curves were used to establish how well each questionnaire was able to distinguish between high- and low-risk samples, determining the area under the curve for each questionnaire (Hanley & McNeil, 1982). For this purpose, the only underlying assumption is that children recruited from the two psychiatric clinics were substantially more likely to have psychiatric disorders than children recruited from the dental clinic. There is no assumption that all subjects recruited from the psychiatric clinics had psychiatric disorders, nor that all subjects recruited from the dental clinic were free from psychiatric disorder. Equally, there is no assumption that the psychiatric sample was representative of all children between 4 and 16 who attend psychiatric clinics, nor that the dental sample was representative of all children attending dental clinics, let alone of all children aged between 4 and 16. Since the ROC curves for the SDQ and Rutter questionnaires were derived from the same set of patients, the statistical comparison of the areas under these ROC curves allowed for the paired nature of the data (Hanley & McNeil, 1982). Comparison of the parent–teacher correlations of the SDQ and Rutter questionnaires also allowed for the paired nature of the data, using structural equation modelling (EQS, BMDP Statistical Software) and examining whether constraining the two correlations to be the same resulted in a significantly poorer fit. Though appropriate for tests of comparative validity and cross-situation correlation, the case-control sampling used in this study does not generate sensitivity or specificity estimates that could securely be generalised to representative epidemiological or clinical samples; such estimates will subsequently be derived from other studies in progress.

Reported correlations are Pearson product-moment correlations, but the pattern of findings was not changed when Spearman correlations were used instead. Intraclass correlations—which are often appropriate for reliability estimates—were not used to measure parent–teacher agreement even though this agreement could be construed as an index of inter-rater reliability. Parents and teachers make ratings based on different sources of information, whereas measures of inter-rater reliability are more appropriately derived from independent ratings based on the same source of information. Furthermore, employing intraclass correlations would have involved mixing parent- and teacher-derived scores, and this would have been inappropriate since mean scores differed systematically between parent and teacher ratings—a difference allowed for when interpreting these scores (Rutter, 1967; Rutter et al., 1970; and see Appendix B).

Results

Age and Gender

The mean age (*SD*) of the dental sample was 10.8 years (3.1) while that of the psychiatric sample was 9.8 years (3.3), a significant difference [t (401) = 3.00, $p < .01$]. As expected, the proportion of males was higher in the psychiatric sample (63 %, 153/244) than in the dental sample (53 %, 85/159) [continuity-adjusted χ^2 (1) = 3.03, $p < .05$, 1-tailed]. The results reported here are for the sample as a whole, though closely similar results were obtained when ROC and correlational analyses were repeated separately for boys and girls, and separately for children aged 4–10 and 11–16.

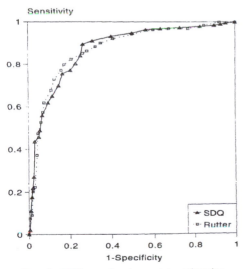

Figure 1.   ROC curves for parent-rated questionnaires.

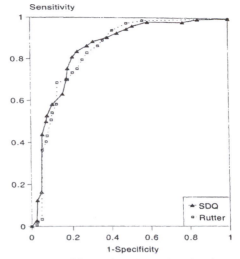

Figure 2.   ROC curves for teacher-rated questionnaires.

Discriminating between Psychiatric and Nonpsychiatric Samples

The ability of the two questionnaires to distinguish between dental and psychiatric cases is reflected in the Receiver Operating Characteristic (ROC) curves shown in Figs. 1 and 2 for parent and teacher reports respectively. The ROC curves for the Rutter questionnaires are based on total deviance scores, whereas the SDQ curves are based on total difficulties scores. The comparable ability of the two measures to discriminate between the two samples is evident from the extent to which the two curves almost superimpose on one another. Quantitatively, this comparability can be judged from the area under each of the curves, which is a measure of how well that measure discriminates between the two samples; the area under the curve would be 1.0 for a measure that discriminated perfectly, and .5 for a measure that discriminated with no better than chance accuracy. For parent reports, the area under the curve (95 % confidence interval) was .87 (.83–.91) for the SDQ as compared with .87 (.83–.91) for the Rutter A(2) parent questionnaire—a nonsignificant difference ($z = .13$, $p = .9$). For teacher reports, the corresponding values were .85 (.78–.93) for the SDQ as compared with .84 (.76–.93) for the Rutter B(2) teacher questionnaire—a nonsignificant difference ($z = .41$, $p = .7$).

SDQ–Rutter Correlations

Table 1 shows the correlations between SDQ and Rutter scores. The correlations were only marginally lower when the analyses were repeated for the dental and psychiatric samples separately. No cross-measure corre-

Table 1
Inter-measure Correlation for Each Type of Rater

	SDQ–Rutter correlation	
	Parent report N = 346	Teacher report N = 185
Total Deviance/Difficulties score	.88	.92
Conduct Problems score	.88	.91
Emotional Symptoms score	.78	.87
Hyperactivity score	.82	.90

Table 2
Inter-rater Correlations for Each Type of Measure

	Parent–Teacher correlation (N = 128)	
	SDQ	Rutter
Total Deviance/Difficulties score	.62*	.52
Conduct Problems score	.65	.57
Emotional Symptoms score	.41	.47
Hyperactivity score	.54	.55
Peer Problems score	.59	—
Prosocial Behaviour score	.37	–

* Correlation significantly higher than the comparable Rutter correlation ($p < .02$): all other comparisons non-significant.

lations can be presented on two SDQ scores—the peer problems score and the prosocial behaviour score—since they have no Rutter counterpart.

Parent–Teacher Correlations

Table 2 presents the correlation coefficients between teacher- and parent-derived scores when both are using the SDQ or when both are using Rutter questionnaires. For comparable scores, the cross-situation correlations of the SDQ and Rutter measures were generally similar, apart from the higher SDQ correlation for total score [χ^2 (1) = 5.90, $p < .02$]. Though the correlations were lower when the analyses were repeated for the dental and psychiatric samples separately, these correlations were generally comparable for the SDQ and Rutter measures, apart from a higher SDQ correlation for total score in the psychiatric sample [χ^2 (1) = 4.05, $p < .05$].

Discussion

Given the well-established validity and reliability of the Rutter questionnaires (Elander & Rutter, 1996), the high correlation between the total scores generated by the SDQ and Rutter questionnaires is evidence for the concurrent validity of the SDQ. Parent–teacher correlations were either equivalent for the two measures or slightly favoured the SDQ, perhaps because the SDQ used identical items for parents and teachers whereas the Rutter questionnaires were somewhat different for parents and teachers. The ROC analyses showed that the two measures had equivalent predictive validity, as judged by their ability to distinguish between psychiatric and nonpsychiatric samples. Of course, discriminating between psychiatric and dental clinic attenders is a relatively easy task, but the high correlation between SDQ and Rutter scores within each clinic group suggests that the two measures are also likely to be comparably discriminating in more demanding screening tasks, such as detecting nonreferred cases of child mental health problems in the community; further empirical studies would be needed to confirm this. Since previous studies have shown that CBCL and Rutter parent questionnaire scores are highly correlated (Berg et al., 1992; Fombonne, 1989), and that these two sets of questionnaires are of comparable predictive validity (Berg et al., 1992), it is likely that the SDQ and CBCL will also be highly correlated and have comparable validity; direct comparisons are currently under way.

The SDQ and Rutter questionnaires can each be used to generate separate scores for conduct problems, emotional symptoms, and hyperactivity. For each of these three scores, there was a high correlation between the SDQ score and the Rutter score; and parent–teacher correlations were comparable for the two sets of measures. Despite its brevity, the SDQ also generated two scores that have no Rutter counterparts: a peer problems score and a prosocial behaviour score.

The performance of the SDQ could potentially have been undermined by three of its design features: inclusion of strengths as well as difficulties; use of an identical questionnaire for both parents and teachers; and a compact presentation on just one side of paper. The equivalence of the SDQ and Rutter scores suggests that these three features have not had an adverse effect. This should encourage researchers and clinicians who are contemplating incorporating similar features into other questionnaires.

Rutter questionnaires are routinely used to categorise children as likely psychiatric "cases" or "non-cases" according to whether their total deviance score is equal to or greater than a standard cut-off: 13 on the Rutter parent questionnaire and 9 on the Rutter teacher questionnaire (Rutter, 1967; Rutter et al., 1970). Using a single cut-off for all studies has both advantages and disadvantages. The advantages are simplicity and equivalence across studies. The main disadvantage is that "caseness" does not have a comparable meaning in different studies simply because those studies have employed the same cut-off. Comparability is particularly likely to be lost when high- and low-risk samples are contrasted. A worked example may be helpful. Study X involves 100 children from a high-risk population with a true rate of psychiatric disorder of 50%; if the screening questionnaire has a sensitivity of .8 and a specificity of .8 when using the standard cut-off, the questionnaire will identify 40 true positives and 10 false positives. Study Y involves 100 children from a low-risk population with a true rate of disorder of 10%; even with the same sensitivity and specificity, the questionnaire will identify 8 true positives and 18 false positives. Despite using the same questionnaire and the same cut-off, a comparison of "cases" from studies X and Y will primarily be a comparison of true positives from study X with false positives from study Y.

Given these problems, the best strategy for researchers may be to choose cut-offs according to the likely disorder rate in the sample being studied, and according to the relative importance for that study of false positives and false negatives. It may also be appropriate to adjust cut-offs for age and gender. Ongoing clinical and epidemiological studies using the SDQ should provide the basis for cut-offs adjusted for these sample characteristics. In addition, planned trials should establish if the predictive validity of the SDQ can further be improved by an algorithm that combines SDQ scores with scores from an additional and even briefer screening instrument that elicits the respondent's view on whether the child has significant emotional or behavioural difficulties, and on the extent to which these difficulties result in social impairment or distress for the child, or burden for others. Until these various studies are completed, SDQ users can use the provisional cut-off scores shown in Appendix B, which are derived partly from the samples used for this study and partly from other ongoing epidemiological surveys using the SDQ. The "borderline" cut-offs can be used for studies of high-risk samples where false positives are not a major concern; the "abnormal" cut-offs can be used for studies of low-risk samples where it is more important to reduce the rate of false positives.

Conclusion

These initial findings suggest that the SDQ may function as well as the Rutter questionnaires (and, by inference, the Achenbach questionnaires) while offering the following additional advantages: a compact format; a focus on strengths as well as difficulties; better coverage of inattention, peer relationships, and prosocial behaviour; and a single form suitable for both parents and teachers, perhaps thereby increasing parent–teacher correlations.

Acknowledgements—I am very grateful for the willing co-operation of parents and teachers, and for the invaluable assistance of Dr. Hilary Richards and the staff of the three London clinics that participated in the study: the Department of Paediatric Dentistry of King's Dental Institute, Camberwell Child Guidance Centre, and the Department of Child and Adolescent Psychiatry, Hounslow.

References

Achenbach, T. M. (1991a). *Manual for the Child Behavior Checklist/4–18 and 1991 Profile.* Burlington, VT: University of Vermont Department of Psychiatry.

Achenbach, T. M. (1991b). *Manual for the Youth Self-Report and 1991 Profile.* Burlington, VT: University of Vermont Department of Psychiatry.

Berg, I., Lucas, C., & McGuire, R. (1992). Measurement of behaviour difficulties in children using standard scales administered to mothers by computer: Reliability and validity. *European Child and Adolescent Psychiatry, 1,* 14–23.

Elander, J., & Rutter, M. (1996). Use and development of the Rutter Parents' and Teachers' Scales. *International Journal of Methods in Psychiatric Research, 6,* 63–78.

Fombonne, E. (1989). The Child Behavior Checklist and the Rutter Parental Questionnaire: A comparison between two screening instruments. *Psychological Medicine, 19,* 777–785.

Goodman, R. (1994). A modified version of the Rutter parent questionnaire including items on children's strengths: A research note. *Journal of Child Psychology and Psychiatry, 35,* 1483–1494.

Hanley, J. A., & McNeil, B. J. (1982). The meaning and use of the area under a receiver operating characteristic (ROC) curve. *Radiology, 143,* 29–36.

Hanley, J. A., & McNeil, B. J. (1983). A method of comparing the areas under receiver operating characteristic curves derived from the same cases. *Radiology, 148,* 839–843.

Rutter, M. (1967). A children's behaviour questionnaire for completion by teachers: Preliminary findings. *Journal of Child Psychology and Psychiatry, 8,* 1–11.

Rutter, M., Tizard, J., & Whitmore, K. (1970). *Education, health and behaviour.* London: Longman.

Schachar, R., Rutter, M., & Smith, A. (1981). The characteristics of situationally and pervasively hyperactive children: Implications for syndrome definition. *Journal of Child Psychology and Psychiatry, 22,* 375–392.

Accepted manuscript received 26 September 1996

To view Appendix A and B please visit www.sdqinfo.com

Classification of Child and Adolescent Psychopathology

Dennis P. Cantwell

UCLA Neuropsychiatric Institute, Los Angeles, California, U.S.A.

This review will consider some of the major issues in the classification of child and adolescent psychopathology. The central issue will be the value of classification systems in child and adolescent psychopathology research. Some comment will also be made on the value of the existing classifications in clinical practice.

Keywords: Classification, nosology, child and adolescent psychopathology, diagnostic assessment

Historical and General Issues in the Classification of Child and Adolescent Psychopathology

The history of classification of mental disorders has very early origins (Cantwell & Baker, 1988; Mattison & Hooper, 1992). The DSM's used in the United States grew out of the 1840 census. Early symptoms were subsequently modified and expanded in the 1880 census culminating in the 1917 National Commission on Mental Hygiene. During World War II, an expanded manual was prepared to deal with psychiatric problems in patients who were in military service and in the Veteran's Administration health care system. ICD 6 (International Classification of Diseases, 6th edition) was the first formal diagnostic version to include mental disorders. DSM I published in 1952, consisted of 106 categories (APA, 1952). DSM II was published in 1968 (APA, 1968). DSM-III-R was meant to be a minor tinkering correction to occur midstream between publication of DSM III in 1980 and DSM IV in 1994 (APA, 1980, 1994). The minor tinkering turned out to be much more of a major modification. DSM-III-R was published in 1987 (APA, 1987) and consisted of 292 categories described in 567 pages. DSM IV published in 1994 consists of 407 number of categories described in 688 pages. Both DSM I and ICD 8 (WHO, 1967) contained a large number of disorders of adult life but very few descriptions of child psychiatric pathology. The first system to focus extensively on the classification of child psychiatric disorders was the developmental profile based on psychoanalytic concepts described by Anna Freud in 1965 (Freud, 1965). The group for the advancement of psychiatry in 1966 published the document "Psychopathological Disorders in Childhood: Theoretical Considerations and a Proposed Classification," Research Report #62 (Group for the Advancement of Psychiatry, 1966). This classification system was developed by a large committee, most of whom

were psychoanalytically oriented. While the document was described as descriptive in nature, it is clear that the categorization was developed primarily with psychoanalytic thinking in mind. A major effort prior to the publication of ICD 9 in 1978 (WHO, 1978) were field trials undertaken to assess the current status of classification of child and adolescent psychopathology. Unfortunately, these field trials showed little agreement among child psychiatrists regarding theoretical conceptualization of child and adolescent psychopathology. However, Rutter and his colleagues in, 1969 (Rutter et al., 1969) suggested that these field trials revealed that child psychiatrists were able to agree fairly well on categories of child and adolescent psychopathology that were phenomenologically described and were rather broad categories, such as those between disruptive behavior disorders or externalizing disorders and those that were emotional disorders or internalizing disorders.

There have been many objections to psychiatric classification in general and to child psychiatric classification in particular (Szasz, 1961, 1978; Hobbs, 1975). Some of the objections are based on the assumption that classification of psychopathology lacks any substance or meaning and produces harmful effects including social deprivation and social stigma. However, it is now recognized that the so called harmful effects of classification of psychopathology result from abuse of the system and not from the classification system per se. There is general agreement among most psychiatrists that the disadvantages of classification are greatly outweighed by the numerous advantages of having a valid and reliable classification system of child and adolescent psychopathology (Weiner, 1982; Kendell, 1975). A major advance in the classification of adult psychopathology was the publication of the Feighner criteria (Feighner et al., 1972). This set of criteria summarized the pioneering work of the Washington University Department of Psychiatry led by Eli Robins and Samuel B. Guze. The publication of the Feighner criteria and subsequent criteria such as the Research Diagnostic Criteria (RDC) has led to the generally accepted view among researchers that classification

Requests for reprints to: Dennis P. Cantwell, M.D., 4490 Poe Avenue, Woodland Hills, CA 91364, U.S.A.

4   D. P. CANTWELL

needs to be based on phenomenology rather than on theories of etiology that lack a sufficient empirical basis. It has been shown in field trials that psychiatrists, and child psychiatrists in particular, may disagree on theoretical concepts, but can agree on phenomenologic description. DSM III was the first official classification scheme to adopt the approach suggested by the Feighner criteria. ICD 10 has adopted a very similar format as have DSM-III-R and DSM IV. ICD 10, however, has separate criteria for research and clinical work whereas DSM IV does not. There is a significant benefit for research purposes in having diagnostic criteria that are used across research studies.

However, it has been pointed elsewhere there are some significant weaknesses in the existent systems— both DSM IV and ICD 10 (Cantwell & Rutter, 1994; Cantwell, 1988; Cantwell & Baker, 1988; Cromwell, Blashfield & Strauss, 1975). The first one concerns the relationship of the diagnostic process to diagnostic classification. There has been only a very limited operation of the diagnostic criteria which specifies which diagnostic instrument is used, what informants are used, and how a rating for presence and severity of the criteria is made absolutely explicit. Thus, one may specify that a certain number and type of symptoms need to be present for a particular diagnosis to be made. Without using the diagnostic process to make the diagnosis using the specific diagnostic criteria the value of the use diagnostic criteria may be suspect.

Since DSM IV and ICD 10 have not used theory as a basis for classification, this has lead at times to the erroneous assumption that cross sectional phenomenology is the sole basis for diagnosis without regard to natural history, biological correlates, psychosocial correlates, familiality, response to treatment and other concepts (Cantwell & Rutter, 1994). Describing diagnostic criteria on a phenomenological basis is not enough for the diagnostic categories to be valid and useful for research. Such diagnoses must differ in areas other than clinical phenomenology. It is clear that individual diagnoses in ICD 10 and DSM IV differ widely in the availability of research evidence to substantiate their external validity. Few psychiatric disorders of childhood and adolescence are fully validated using criteria suggested by Cantwell and others (Cantwell & Rutter, 1994).

Conceptual Issues in the Classification of Child and Adolescent Psychopathology

Some of the important conceptual issues in child and adolescent classification include: (1) whether a dimensional or categorical approach is more appropriate, (2) whether child and adolescent psychopathological disorders can be conceptualized as being quantitatively or qualitatively different from normal, (3) whether categories described in classification schemes such as DSM IV and ICD 10 can be considered to be discrete entities, (4) how is comorbidity handled by a particular system?; (5) how are "subthreshold" clinical conditions considered? (Cantwell & Rutter, 1994).

The distinction between a categorical and a dimensional approach has been discussed by others (Achenbach & Edelbrock, 1978; Quay, 1983; Klein & Riso, 1994; Grayson, 1987; Cantwell & Rutter, 1994). The major official classification systems in use (DSM IV and ICD 10) are categorical in nature. The patient meets or does not meet criteria for a disorder. These categorical classification schemes have a number of advantages over dimensional approaches. A patient is given a diagnosis described by a single term which allows one to summarize a variety of clinical concepts in a discrete fashion to other individuals. In addition, our clinical decisions in child psychiatry are generally based on categorical concepts. Stimulants are given to children with an Attention Deficit Disorder (ADD) diagnosis. Neuroleptics are given to those with a schizophrenic diagnosis. Dimensional approaches such as those developed by Achenbach (Achenbach, 1985) are unlikely to lead to the discovery and description of very rare disorders such as autism. Advantages of the dimensional systems include the ability to describe multiple symptom patterns (anxiety, depression, aggression) present in a particular individual. Dimensional systems are usually more statistically reliable. Categorical diagnoses are at times made on the basis of arbitrary cut off points regarding number and type of symptoms.

Multiple statistical techniques have been used to determine whether psychiatric disorders show continuity or discontinuity with normality. As discussed in Cantwell and Rutter (1994), there are a variety of problems with the statistical approaches that have been used. In addition, the presence of dimensional traits such as a "depressive", "anxiety", or "conduct" factor does not rule out the possibility that there are distinct categorical disorders such as Major Depressive Disorder, Generalized Anxiety Disorder and Conduct Disorder that are biologically and clinically discontinuous with the more "normal" dimensional factors. Discreteness in medicine often assumes that medical conditions are completely discrete from each other and from normality. When a specific single cause can be described for a particular disorder then it is likely that this disorder can be considered discrete in this fashion. However, many diseases in medicine (e.g. hypertension) are multifactorial in nature and may in fact not be that discrete. There is no a priori reason to expect that depression, ADD, and anxiety disorders will necessarily be totally discrete from one another and from normality. What may be more crucial for child psychiatry is whether or not various clinical conditions have a biological outcome, psychosocial outcome, or other correlates that differentiate the conditions from each other and from normality.

Problems with comorbidity in child psychopathology have been reviewed by a variety of authors (Nottelmann & Jensen, 1995 Achenbach, 1990, 1991; Caron & Rutter, 1991; Biederman, Newcorn & Sprich, 1991; Carlson, 1986; Cantwell & Rutter, 1994; Rutter, Shaffer & Shepherd, 1975a; Rutter, Shaffer & Sturge, 1975b). Evidence from epidemiologic studies suggest that comorbidity in child and adolescent psychopathology is quite prevalent. Nottelman and Jensen's review of comorbidity in children and adolescence concentrates primarily on data from epidemiologic studies (Nottelmann & Jensen, 1995). They point out that there are developmental considerations and methodological issues to take into account and that classification and comorbidity are intimately related. It is possible that comorbidity in many studies may be artificially inflated.

Diagnostic criteria for one disorder may not significantly discriminate it from another disorder. Such might be true with depression and anxiety, and ADD and mania which share some symptoms. There may be higher order, broader based patterns (such as externalizing versus internalizing disorders) that may represent more specific single diagnostic entities. Where these higher order disorders are artificially subdivided high patterns of comorbidity result. Thus, it may be that when an overall higher order anxiety disorder is subdivided into multiple anxiety disorders (such as is true of DSM IV and ICD 10) artificial comorbidity among these so called separate anxiety disorders may result. Inappropriate low boundaries between normal variation and pathology can lead to inflated comorbidity. It has been shown in epidemiologic studies that high symptom counts alone lead to high prevalence levels of disorders in the community. Rates are lowered when severity and impairment criteria are added (Weissman, Warner & Fendrich, 1987). The same may be true of comorbidity. Stipulation of severity and impairment may lead to lower prevalence of any particular disorder and lower comorbidities between disorders. Comorbidity may be a problem of the classification system per se when a large number of disorders are broken down into too fine subdivisions that are nonhierarchical and nonexclusionary in nature. Alternatively, comorbidity may reflect a more amorphous early expression of psychopathology in young children that does not begin to crystalize into more definitive psychopathology until later in life. Follow-up data support this idea. General population studies suggest less continuity of disorders from childhood to early adolescence and from early to mid adolescence than from mid to late adolescence (Nottelmann & Jensen, 1995).

Comorbidity is handled quite differently by ICD 10 and DSM IV. ICD 10 makes liberal use of combined categories such as "Hyperkinetic Conduct Disorder" and "Depressive Conduct Disorder". DSM IV encourages the use of multiple diagnoses when criteria for more than one disorder are met. Implicit in the ICD 10 approach is the notion that there is something unique about the co-occurence of depression and conduct disorder that justifies a separate diagnosis. The Harrington studies (Harrington et al., in press) support this uniqueness with regard to the longitudinal course of childhood onset depression. There are family data that support the idea that the co-occurrence of conduct disorder and the hyperkinetic syndrome (Attention Deficit Disorder in DSM IV terms) may be a unique syndrome. Follow-up data suggest the same thing. At this point it is not possible to say with certainty which approach is the preferred one. The best approach may differ for different disorders.

The final conceptual issue to be discussed is subthreshold or subsyndromal psychopathology. When categorical diagnostic schemes are used for classification that require the presence of a certain specific set and/or specific number of symptoms there will be individuals who just miss the cut off score. Likewise, when dimensional measures are used that require a cutoff at a certain level to be considered "clinical" there will again be children as well as adults who fail to meet the specified cut off score. The DSM IV field trials of adults identified (Zinbarg et al., 1994) a substantial number of adults both in psychiatric and primary care settings who did not meet standard DSM IV criteria for any of the depressive or anxiety disorders. However, these individuals had a combination of anxiety and depressive symptomatology that caused a significant degree of functional impairment. In the psychiatric sample, about 20% of patients were so identified and in the primary care sample about 8% were identified whose subsyndromal clinical picture caused functional impairment. It has long been thought by many primary care practitioners that subthreshold disorders in the pediatric age range are more common in their practice than DSM or ICD diagnosable psychiatric conditions. Systematic studies by Costello (Costello, 1990) suggest to a large degree that this is true. Her studies also suggest that individuals in primary care and in psychiatric samples who meet specific criteria for one diagnosis may be subsyndromal for other diagnoses. Subsyndromal conditions are associated with functional impairment, although below the level of functional impairment associated with the presence of definite psychiatric disorders diagnosed by standard DSM or ICD 10 criteria. Thus, any research classification scheme must consider subsyndromal disorders. Both DSM IV and ICD 10 do not adequately address this issue. Both primarily use a "not otherwise specified" grab bag category to lump all disorders that do not meet criteria.

Reliability

For a classification system to be useful for research it must be a reliable system. Researchers of different theoretical persuasions who evaluate a child must be able to make psychiatric diagnoses that are reliable. Thus, if Clinician A sees the patient and makes a diagnosis of Attention Deficit Disorder (ADD) according to a diagnostic scheme, Clinician B evaluating the same child at the same time should make the same diagnosis. In the past 20 years as work proceeded on the development of the DSM and ICD systems, interest in the issue of diagnostic reliability of child and adolescent psychiatric classification has intensified. (Rey, Plapp and Stewart (1989), Cantwell and Rutter (1994)). There is general agreement that most studies show that there is acceptable reliability for major psychiatric disorders (Cantwell & Rutter, 1994).

The creation of structured and semi-structured interviews to be used with parents and children to make specific diagnoses in childhood has led to a series of studies to examine diagnostic reliability (and validity) of the diagnoses. Boyle et al. (1993) evaluated the DICA-R using a test–retest design. Kappas were generally very good in the range of .55–.84. There have been a series of studies using the original DISC and subsequent revisions (presumably improved) (Boyle et al., 1993; Cohen et al., 1987; Fallon & Schwab-Stone, 1994; Jensen et al., 1995; Schwab-Stone et al., 1994; Shaffer et al., 1993; Fisher et al., 1993; Shaffer et al., in press; Shaffer et al., 1995). Test–retest and inter-rater reliability has generally been good and have improved with later versions of the DISC. Schwab-Stone, Shaffer, Dulcan, Jensen, Fisher, Bird, Goodman, Lahey, Lichtman, Canino, Rubio-Stipec, and Rae report good reliability and validity using a complex design when diagnostic information from parents alone is used and when information from parents and child are combined. When a child report alone is used the results are not as good. Certain diagnoses such as ADHD show much less reliability when a child report alone is used. Major depressive disorder, however, has Kappa value of .79 when a child report alone is used.

Some studies have compared diagnoses made when impairment is not required and when impairment is required. Required impairment lowers prevalence rate of some disorders, but does not seem to significantly affect Kappa scores for most disorders. There is variability in Kappa scores that is related to the informant, the algorithm used to synthesize the report of symptoms and design of the comparison studies.

However, more narrowly defined subcategories do not have the same high degree of reliability. For example, a general overall category of "Anxiety Disorder" has a greater degree of reliability than most subtypes of anxiety disorders with the exception of separation anxiety disorder. In some cases a narrow diagnostic set category may be more reliable than the more broad category because the symptom pattern is clear and there is no ambiguity in the diagnostic rules (Cantwell & Rutter, 1994).

However, there are a number of issues with regard to reliability that need to be discussed. Data, for example, show that practicing clinicians are not as reliable using the same diagnostic classification system than researchers who are specifically trained to make diagnoses in a standardized way (Prendergast et al., 1988). At least one reason for this is that data from multiple sources of information in the child assessment process often do not agree with each other. Thus, parents may present one set of data, children another, and teachers yet another. The researcher must sift these various sources of information in some fashion to make an appropriate diagnosis. Those clinicians who rely more on one data source than another are likely to come up with different diagnoses than those who are presented with the same data but arranges them in a different fashion. Precise diagnostic rules will improve reliability. But this is only true if there are precise rules for *how* the symptom is determined to be present, rather than just rules for *what* symptoms need to be present for the diagnosis to be made. For example there is a list of symptoms in DSM IV for several subtypes of ADD: combined, primarily inattentive, and primarily hyperactive and impulsive. The symptoms must be of early onset, persistent over time, and be present in two or more settings. However, there are no precise rules for the researcher to determine whether a symptom is truly present in a particular setting or not. Nor is it clear that the specified number of symptoms that are needed for the diagnosis can come from different sources such as three from a parent, two from a teacher and one from a child (Rutter & Pickles, 1990).

In a major study by Costello (personal communication) using DSM III, the author demonstrated that at an institution known for its attention to psychiatric diagnosis only in a minority of cases did experienced professionals use the data collected in a standardized fashion to make diagnoses according to specific DSM III criteria. Many used a "pattern matching" approach in which the data collected from parents, teachers, child, and others matched what their idea of what a particular diagnosis was.

A recent study of adult psychotic patients as part of the DSM IV field trial demonstrated that despite using specific diagnostic criteria for the various psychotic disorders there was quite a lot of difference in classification or misclassification of patients which arose from variability in the method that the researchers use to assign the diagnostic criteria rather than in the criteria themselves. Although DSM IV criteria were used, four diagnostic procedures were used to determine the *presence* of the criteria. The four were: a diagnostic instrument developed for the DSM IV field trial, the Royal Park Multi-Diagnostic Instrument for Psychosis, the Munich Diagnostic Checklist, and a consensus diagnosis assigned by a team of clinician researchers who were expert in the use of diagnostic criteria. Levels of per cent agreement ranged from 66 to 76% with misclassification rates of 24–34% when pairs of diagnostic procedures were compared with each other, assuming that one procedure was "correct". This type of misclassification will impede all areas of research of a disorder (i.e. genetics, neurobiological correlates, outcome and treatment (McGorry et al., 1995).

For these reasons and others, it is clear that a statement in a research paper that DSM IV criteria or ICD 10 criteria were used to define the population does not tell the reader that the same diagnoses will be made comparably across research centers. The methods used to determine whether the diagnostic criteria were present or not also need to be specified.

Validity

While reliability is a necessary prerequisite for any diagnostic classification system to be useful in research, validity is an even more crucial issue. For a classification system to be useful for researchers, the diagnostic categories must have both internal and external validity. External validity has been discussed by a variety of authors (Feighner et al., 1972; Cantwell, 1975; Rutter, 1978; Kendall, 1982; Rutter & Gould, 1985; Cantwell & Rutter, 1994; Andreasen, 1995). In 1970 Robins and Guze (1970) published a very influential article in which they illustrated a model for the validation of psychiatric disorders. Their model consisted of different stages including clinical description, laboratory studies, exclusion criteria, outcome studies, and studies of familial aggregation. This model was expanded upon by Cantwell (1975) for use in children. The Cantwell model includes the stages of clinical phenomenology, psychosocial factors, demographic factors, biological factors, family genetic factors, family environmental factors, natural history, and response to therapeutic intervention. The starting point for clinical research in this model is clinical phenomenology. Various disorders must be described in terms of their core clinical picture and their common associated features. Subtyping of the disorder and comorbidity also must be considered. Both categorical and dimensional ways of describing clinical symptomatology may be used. Factor and cluster analysis of dimensional measures offer alternative and complimentary ways of describing the psychiatric disorders of childhood and adolescence compared to the categorical model used in DSM IV and ICD 10. Once the clinical phenomenology of a disorder has been clearly defined and subtyped meaningful investigations can be undertaken in other stages of the model to provide evidence of internal and external validity of the disorders. Internal validity is discussed below.

The first external validating stage is the study of demographic factors. Once the clinical picture is described then incidence, prevalence, morbidity risk, and lifetime expectancy rates can be generated. The effects of age, gender, social class, ethnicity and culture on the prevalence and manifestations of the disorder can be documented.

External validation of a disorder can be increased by the presence of certain psychosocial factors correlated with a particular clinical picture. This may include factors such as the level of acute and chronic life stress, early childhood experiences such as separation and attachment difficulties, and physical or sexual abuse.

Biological factors correlated with a particular clinical picture may include the presence of definite brain damage and/or brain dysfunction, physical handicaps and disorders, neurological disorders, and laboratory findings from studies in the areas of neurophysiology, neuroendocrinology, biochemistry, neuropharmacology, brain imaging, and neuropsychology.

The external validating stage of family environmental factors might include such dimensions as discipline styles, and other aspects of parent-child interaction.

Types of family genetic studies factors includes family aggregation, adoption, twin, linkage, segregation, gene mapping, and others.

The study of natural history of the disorder would include true prospective, true retrospective, catch up prospective and anterospective studies to explore continuities and discontinuities between childhood, adolescent and adult disorders and the mechanism for these continuities and discontinuities.

The final external stage of the multistage Cantwell model is response to interventions. If certain clinical syndromes respond differentially to the same type of intervention the first assumption might be that the clinically defined syndrome is heterogeneous in nature (Pliszka, 1989). These validation stages are not independent from one another. Information derived from one stage may inform further studies in another stage. Thus, determining that one disorder may run in close family members may identify familial and nonfamilial subtypes of the disorder. This would allow the original group selected on the basis of a definite clinical picture to be subdivided into two smaller groups. If they are truly different from each other then differences should emerge from other stages of the model as well. Andreasen (1995) has recently noted the growing body of literature

with adult disorders for differential external validity using a variety of biological measures. At this point, child psychiatry lags behind the study of adult psychopathology in this area.

The past decades have seen a substantial increase in the study of diagnostic validation of child and adolescent psychopathology along the lines described above. However, no disorder can be considered to be fully validated and future changes in classification will likely be determined by future advances particularly in the area of neuroscience.

Future studies may determine that certain diagnostic criteria predict one validating criteria while another set might predict another validating criterion. For example, DSM-III-R criteria for ADHD are "tighter" than DSM IV criteria and identify more children who have significant comorbid oppositional defiant and conduct disorder. Thus, DSM-III-R criteria are likely to produce a group more likely to have a natural history including antisocial spectrum disorders than DSM IV criteria, but for family genetic studies, DSM IV criteria might prove to provide a higher heritability estimate and different patterns of psychopathology in the family members. Neither of the criteria may be "right" for other areas of validation. The accumulation of data in all areas of the validating model described above should lead to revisions in the original criteria and subdivisions of the original clinical sample.

However, there is a converging body of evidence that the major psychiatric disorders as described in ICD 10 and DSM IV do have a reasonable external degree of diagnostic validity. That is, that the syndromes described by ICD 10 and DSM IV criteria are known to have a differential association with external validating criteria such as those described in the Cantwell model noted above. Epidemiologic studies using modern diagnostic criteria suggest that the prevalence rate of clinically significant psychiatric disorders between the ages of 4 and 17 in the general population is approximately 20% (Nottelmann & Jensen, 1995). Prevalence rates for individual disorders vary greatly and for the same disorder prevalence rates may change with age and gender. The early onset disorders, such as attention deficit disorder, developmental learning and language disorders and pervasive developmental disorders tend to be more common in boys. The one exception to this is Rett's Syndrome which has been described almost exclusively in girls. Disorders such as Obsessive Compulsive Disorder (OCD) and major depression have equal prevalence rates in males and females in the prepubertal age range. Rates of both disorders increase with puberty, but rates increase much more in females. Studies of psychosocial factors suggest that family dysfunction, discord between the parents and child, and family disruption due to death and divorce tend to be associated more with disruptive behavior disorders than with anxiety and mood disorders. This suggests that it is diagnostically meaningful to separate out the broad class of disruptive behavior disorders from that of anxiety and mood disorders. Whether finer distinctions can be made requires further research. Whether there are *specific* clinical pictures that arise with *specific* psychosocial factors is not clear at the present time.

Biological correlates have begun to be demonstrated with some degree of specificity in clinical syndromes of adult life such as schizophrenia, OCD and others. The study of biological correlates in child and adolescent disorders however has lagged behind their study in adults (Plante, Swisher & Vance, 1991). Some laboratory measures such as the dexamethasone suppression tests, serum cortisol, sleep EEG recordings have revealed different findings in depression in young children as opposed to depression in adults. This may be due to developmental changes in neurobiology with age. Imaging data are beginning to demonstrate abnormalities in some of the developmental problems seen in young children, but replication with larger numbers are needed before we determine that these are specific to certain disorders. Family aggregation studies and high risk studies do suggest that there is familialty to many of the psychiatric disorders of childhood and adolescence. This is true for schizophrenia, mood disorders and to some degree for the anxiety disorders and the disruptive behavior disorders. Further work in the family genetic area will require more significant numbers of adoption, twin, linkage, segregation, and gene mapping studies. This appears to be a fruitful area for further diagnostic validation of our behaviorally defined syndromes and suggests the possibility of ultimately finding familial and nonfamilial (and possibly genetic and nongenetic) subtypes of a disorder.

Natural history studies of child and adolescent psychopathology do suggest continuities over time in a variety of disorders such as ADD, the Pervasive Developmental Disorders, OCD, and probably in mood disorders as well. (Harrington et al., in press) Less data is available on the other anxiety disorders and some of the other forms of psychopathology described in DSM IV and ICD 10. It is reasonable to initially assume that a disorder which begins early in life, is chronic in nature, persisting into adult life may be quite a different condition from a phenomenologically similar condition that is seen only in childhood with no recurrences, relapses, and no chronicity. If these two types of a phenomenologically similar disorder are truly different, then differences in other areas of the model, such as psychosocial factors, biological factors and others should be discovered.

In the area of specificity of response to treatment there is a trend towards more specific methods of both psychosocial and psychopharmacologic intervention with some disorders in adults. For example, the treatment of depression in adults has been enhanced by receptor studies and the demonstration that certain medications have certain effects at specific receptors. This adds to the specificity of selecting an antidepressant drug in adults. Psychosocial manualized therapies such as cognitive behavioral therapy and interpersonal psychotherapy have been developed for some of the adult psychiatric disorders. This trend is just beginning to be demonstrated with childhood and adolescent disorders (Kazdin, 1983). Again, it makes sense to initially assume that a child with ADD at age 7 who has a dramatically positive response to one of the psychostimulants may have an etiologically different condition than a child with phenomenologically defined ADD who

has an adverse response. Adverse and positive responders then should be found to differ in other areas of the models as well.

In summary, ICD 10 and DSM IV contain many child and adolescent disorders for which there is a satisfactory amount of external validation. These would include ADD, Conduct Disorder, Rett's Syndrome, Autistic Disorder, Tourette's Syndrome, OCD, and Anorexia Nervosa.

A complete discussion of the evidence for external validation of each of these disorders is beyond the scope of this paper. There are recent publications that summarize the current evidence (Rutter, Taylor & Hersov, 1994; Kaplan & Sadock, 1995; Lewis, 1995). However, since ICD 10 and DSM IV are classifications that are used in everyday clinical practice, they include many disorders for which the validation is less well developed. Whether one should start with very broad categories or with more narrowly defined sub categories initially in the development of a classification is a question that has been inadequately researched. It is clear that some of the categories that are included in a beginning classification system are bound to have less external validation than others. But, if they are not included they will not be studied. Thus, the separation of ADD into a primarily hyperactive impulsive type and a primarily inattentive type has been done initially on clinical grounds. If further evidence to show differential validation with external criteria of these two subtypes fails to develop, it may be more appropriate to lump them together in some later classification scheme. DSM IV and ICD 10 probably have a stronger founding in the empirical literature than their predecessors. ICD 10 and DSM IV were developed closely together so that the individual child psychiatric diagnostic criteria for most of the disorders are very similar if not identical. For the preparation of DSM IV extensive literature reviews of individual categories were undertaken to determine how well the individual diagnostic categories and their criteria had empirical validation. Any changes in DSM IV from previous editions (DSM III and DSM-III-R) were made on the basis of research evidence available in the current literature or produced in the many field trials that were carried out before DSM IV was published. (Volkmar et al., 1994) The source books which will be published as a companion to DSM IV detail the research base for the DSM IV categories.

Discussion of validation above has concentrated on external validity. Waldman and colleagues (Waldman et al., 1994, Waldman, Lilienfield & Lahey, 1994) have discussed internal validity. They view the process of internal validation as the testing of hypotheses regarding the internal structure of a diagnostic entity. Waldman and colleagues discuss internal consistency analyses, factor analysis, cluster analysis and taxometrical analysis, and latent class analysis in the study of internal validity. Questions to be regarded include: how homogeneous or heterogeneous is the clinically defined disorders; is the disorder categorical or dimensional in nature; how many categories or dimensions underlie its diagnostic indicators; what are the boundaries and reactions among its underlying dimensions or categories? Does a particular diagnostic grouping such as depression have a number of specific subcategories or dimensions in the broader diagnostic category? Is the distinction between major depressive disorder, dysthymic disorder, melancholic depression, psychotic depression, atypical depression, seasonal affective disorder, primary and secondary depression meaningful for research?

Based on their results in the field trials of DSM IV Disruptive Behavior Disorders, (Frick et al., 1994; Lahey et al., 1994, Applegate et al., 1994) they suggest that researchers studying childhood psychopathology need to be more attentive to considerations of construct validity. Among their suggestions include the following: the formulation of specific a priori alternative hypotheses that can be contrasted in terms of their ability to best fit the data; increase the use of latent variable models, a larger number and scope of competing hypotheses; paying greater attention to interval validity as opposed to simply considering external validation of disorders. They suggest that previous studies have concentrated on comparing groups with specific diagnoses that are of unknown *internal* validity to each other on the *external* validating factors described above. If internal validity of a diagnostic category is unknown then results of external validating studies are difficult to interpret.

Directions for Future Research

The above review suggests that we have come a long way in the classification of child and adolescent psychopathology. Earlier views included the view that classification of child and adolescent psychopathology held no value for treatment. Later views included classification schemes that were based heavily on theoretical models such as psychoanalysis. These early attempts at classification have been replaced by classification schemes that are considered to be "theoretical". At times this has lead to the erroneous idea that cross sectional phenomenology is the only basis for classification and a lack of appreciation that the phenomenologic criteria must be shown to have internal as well as external validity. Classification of child and adolescent psychopathology is likely to be an evolving process as we collect more data in a variety of areas. We expect advances in several areas including neuroscience (including the study of genetics), neurophysiology and neurochemistry. We expect advances in studies of response to treatment and to arise from the fact that larger populations of children diagnosed by specific criteria will have been available for follow-up over time to look at continuities and discontinuities between childhood, adolescent and adult disorders (Harrington et al., in press). For all of these reasons, DSM V and ICD 11 should have classification schemes that are based on more than cross sectional phenomenology.

Klein and Riso (1994), Garber and Strassberg (1991), Cantwell and Rutter (1994), Waldman and Lahey (1994) and Waldman et al. (1994) have all pointed out that improved statistical techniques will allow for more specific testing of the adequacy of diagnostic criteria and constructs. Waldman and Lahey (1994) and Waldman et al. (1994) suggest that latent variable models will provide information on internal validity issues including

whether the diagnostic entities are categorical or dimensional, how many of the diagnostic entities there are within the theoretical construct and what are the boundaries and relationships of these various entities. Latent variable models can also provide information on the diagnostic efficiency of specific signs and symptoms. For example, which symptoms provide the greatest degree of prediction of response to psychosocial and/or psychopharmacological intervention. Which symptom combination provides the greatest agreement with some type of biological correlate or with heritability. Finally these latent variable models can address issues of comorbidity, pervasiveness, and the relationship between normality and pathology. Receiver operator curves (Hsiao et al., 1989) are another statistical technique to decide which set of symptoms provide optimal sensitivity and specificity according to an external validating criteria, such as biological correlates, psychosocial correlates, outcome or response to treatment. As Waldman et al. (1994) point out, much more time, energy, and money will be needed in future studies on data analysis rather than data collection in order for these aims to be achieved. Future classification systems will need to take comorbidity into account and assess the impact of comorbidity on such factors as biological and psychosocial correlates, heritability, outcome, and response to treatment. The development of future classification schemes should be accompanied by a multi method approach to measurement of signs and symptoms of the disorder and a multi-measurement approach to the measurement of impairment and other criteria measures. Field trials of DSM IV used a single method of assessing psychopathology and single measures of impairment (Weissman & Warner, 1982; Cicchetti et al., in press). Developmental aspects of classification of child and adolescent psychopathology will have to be given much greater consideration in future classification systems. DSM and ICD 10 essentially say that diagnostic criteria for schizophrenia, mood disorders, and most of the anxiety disorders are essentially the same across the lifespan—preschool, grade school, adolescence and adult life. It is likely that this is not true for some, if not all of the disorders. Some symptoms may be present throughout the lifespan. Others may be more prevalent at certain age ranges than at others. It may be that the diagnosis of depression, for example, will require certain symptoms to be present throughout the course of the lifespan, but that other symptoms will be present in some areas of the lifespan, but not others. For example, a symptom like guilt is much more likely to be prevalent in individuals who have reached the final stages of cognitive development that it is in a preschool or early grade school aged child. DSM IV and ICD 10 are not particularly useful for classification of the psychopathology of infants and very young children. Nor are they as useful for classifying the psychopathology of children (or adults) with severe mental retardation. There have been recent attempts to create alternative classification systems for both of these groups. But these systems have yet to be systematically studied in any great detail (Zero to Three, 1995; Aman, 1991; American Association on Mental Retardation, 1992).

Issues of categorical vs dimensional classification should be tested directly in future developments of classification systems. It may be that some combination of categorical and dimensional approaches may best handle the problems both of comorbidity and of subsyndromal conditions.

It is likely that changing criteria (ICD 9 to ICD 10 and DSM-III-R to DSM IV) will have an effect on epidemiological studies. The recent series of NIMH studies using the DISC as an interview have used DSM-III-R criteria. The DISC is now being revised for DSM IV criteria. The criterion changes may lead to different population prevalence rates for various disorders.

Wolraich (Wolraich, 1994a,b) has recently completed two epidemiologic studies of attention deficit disorder using DSM III, III-R, and IV criteria. One study was in Germany and one was in Tennessee. Teacher information was the sole source of data in both studies. In the German population the prevalence figures for the primarily inattentive subtype, the primarily hyperactive impulse subtype, and the combined subtype were: 9%, 3.9% and 4.8%, respectively.

In the Tennessee population the prevalence figures for the same three subtypes were 4.7%, 3.4% and 4.4%, respectively. The figures in both sites are higher than figures obtained in the same studies using DSM III and DSM III-R criteria. For example, the same German population using DSM III criteria had prevalence rates of 6.4% for ADD with hyperactivity, 3.2% for ADD without hyperactivity and 9.6% total. Using DSM-III-R the prevalence rate for attention deficit hyperactivity disorder was 10.9%. Thus, the application of DSM IV criteria led to a 64% increase in total ADD prevalence rates compared to DSM III and DSM-III-R criteria.

Comparison of the Tennessee and German rates suggest possible cultural, geographical, ethnic differences in prevalence rates. This is a relatively understudied area across cultures with countries and across countries. DSM IV has added a section in the description of each disorder specifically dealing with cultural factors important in each disorder. DSM IV has also added an appendix providing an outline for cultural formulation to address any difficulties that could arise from using DSM IV criteria in a multicultural environment.

It is anticipated that future editions of the DSM and ICD will provide a further advance in the classification of child and adolescent psychopathology. Improvements in classification are in a reciprocal fashion likely to lead to improvements in studies of etiology, outcome, and response to treatment.

References

Achenbach, T. M. (1985). *Assessment and taxonomy of child and adolescent psychopathology*. Beverly Hills: Sage.

Achenbach, T. M. (1990/1991). "Comorbidity" in child and adolescent psychiatry: categorical and quantitative perspectives. *Journal of Child and Adolescent Psychopharmacology, 1*, 1–8.

Achenbach, T. M. & Edelbrock, C. S. (1978). The classification of child psychopathology: a review and analysis of empirical efforts. *Psychological Bulletin, 85*, 1275–1301.

Aman, M. G. (1991). *Assessing psychopathology and behavioral problems in persons with mental retardation: a review of available instrument*. Rockville, MD: U.S. Department of Health and Human Services.

American Association on Mental Retardation (1992). *Mental retardation: definition, classification, and systems of support*. Ed 9. Washington, DC.

American Psychiatric Association (1952). *Diagnostic and statistical manual, mental disorders*. Washington, DC: American Psychiatric Association.

American Psychiatric Association (1968). *Diagnostic and statistical manual, mental disorders*, 2nd edition. Washington, DC: American Psychiatric Association

American Psychiatric Association (1980). *Diagnostic and statistical manual, mental disorders*, 3rd edition, Washington, DC: American Psychiatric Association.

American Psychiatric Association (1987). *Diagnostic and statistical manual, mental disorders*, 3rd edition, revised. Washington, DC: American Psychiatric Association.

American Psychiatric Association (1994). *Diagnostic and statistical manual mental disorders*, 4th edition. Washington, DC: American Psychiatric Association.

Andreasen, N. C. (ed) (1995). Editorial: The validation of psychiatric diagnosis: new models and approaches. *American Journal of Psychiatry, 152*, 2.

Applegate, B., Lahey, B. B., Hart, E. L., Waldman, I., Biederman, J., Hynd, G. W., Barkley, R. A., Ollendick, T., Frick, P. J., Greenhill, L., McBurnett, K., Newcorn, J., Kerdyk, L., & Garfinkel, B. (1994). Age of onset and pervasiveness criteria for DSM–IV attention deficit/hyperactivity disorder: Report of the DSM-IV field trials. (Manuscript in preparation.)

Applegate, B., Waldman, I., Lahey, B. B., Frick, P. J., Ollendick, T., Garfinkel, B., Biederman, J., Hynd, G. W., Barkley R. A., Greenhill, L., McBurnett, K., Newcorn, J., Kerdyk, L., & Hart, E. L. (1994). *DSM-IV field trials for disruptive and attention deficit disorder: Factor analysis of potential symptoms*. (Manuscript in preparation.)

Baumgaertel, A., Wolraich, M. L., & Dietrich, M. (1995). Comparison of diagnostic criteria for attention deficit disorders in a German elementary school sample. *Journal of the American Academy of Child and Adolescent Psychiatry, 34*, 629–638.

Biederman, J., Newcorn, J., & Sprich, S. (1991). Comorbidity of attention deficit hyperactivity disorder with conduct, depressive anxiety, and other disorders. *American Journal of Psychiatry, 148*, 564–577.

Boyle, M. H., Offord, D. R., Racine, Y., Sanford, M., Szatmari, P., Fleming, J. E. & Price-Munn, N. (1993). Evaluation of the Diagnostic Interview for Children and Adolescents for use in general population samples. *Journal of Abnormal Child Psychology, 21*, 663–681.

Cantwell, D. P. (1975). A model for the investigation of psychiatric disorders of childhood: its application in genetic studies of the hyperkinetic syndrome. In: E. J. Anthony, (Ed), *Explorations in child psychiatry*, (pp. 57–59). Plenum Press, New York.

Cantwell, D. (1988). DSM-III studies. In M. Rutter, A. H. Tuma & I. S. Lann (Eds), *Assessment and diagnosis in child psychopathology*, (pp. 3–36). Guilford Press, New York.

Cantwell, D. P. & Baker, L. (1988). Issues in the classification of child and adolescent psychopathology. *Journal of the American Academy of Child and Adolescent Psychiatry, 27*, 521–533.

Cantwell, D. P. & Baker, L. (1991). Psychiatric classification. In R. Michels, A. M. Cooper, S. B. Guze, L. L. Judd, G. L. Klerman, A. J. Solnit, A. J. Stunkard & P. Wilner J. (Eds), *Psychiatry* (revised edition). Philadelphia: J. B. Lippincott.

Carlson, C. L. (1986). Attention deficit disorder without hyperactivity. In *Advances in clinical child psychology*, Vol.

9, B. Lahey & A. Kazdin (Eds), (pp. 153–175). New York: Plenum Press.

Caron, C. & Rutter, M. (1991). Comorbidity in child psychopathology: concepts, issues and research strategies. *Journal of Child Psychology and Psychiatry, 32,* 1064–1080.

Cantwell, D. P. & Rutter, M. (1994). *Classification: conceptual issues and substantive findings in child and adolescent psychiatry.* M. Rutter, E. Taylor & Hersov, L. (Eds).Oxford: Blackwell Scientific Publications.

Cicchetti, D., Volkmar, F., Klin A. & Schowalter, D. (in press). Diagnosing autism using ICD-10 criteria: a comparison of neural networks and standard multivariate procedures. *Journal of Child Neuropsychology.*

Cohen, P., O'Connor, P., Lewis, S., Velez, N., & Malachowski, B. (1987). Comparison of DISC and KSADS-P interviews of an epidemiological sample of children. *Journal of American Academy of Child and Adolescent Psychiatry, 26,* 662–667.

Costello, E. J. (1990). *Sub-threshold psychiatric disorders in pediatric primary care: implications for functional impairment.* Presented at the annual meeting of the American Academy of Child and Adolescent Psychiatry, Chicago, IL. October 1990.

Cromwell, R. L., Blashfield, R. K. & Strauss, J. S. (1975). Criteria for classification systems. In N. Hobbs (Ed), *Issues in the classification of children,* (pp. 4–25). San Francisco: Jossey Bass.

Fallon T. & Schwab-Stone M. (1994). Determinants of reliability in psychiatric surveys of children ages 6 to 12. *Journal of Child Psychology and Psychiatry, 35,* 1391–1408.

Feighner, J., Robins, E., Guze, S. B., Woodruff, R. A., Winokur, G. & Munoz, R. (1972). Diagnostic criteria for use in psychiatric research. *Archives of General Psychiatry, 26,* 57–63.

Fisher, P., Shaffer, D., Piacentini, J. C., Lapkin, J., Kafantaris, V., Leonard, H. & Herzog, D. B. (1993). Sensitivity of the Diagnostic Interview Schedule for Children, 2nd Edition (DISC-2.1) for Specific Diagnoses of Children and Adolescents. *Journal of the American Academy of Child and Adolescent Psychiatry, 32,* 666–673.

Freud, A. (1965). *Normality and pathology in childhood.* New York: International Universities Press.

Frick, P. J., Lahey, B. B., Applegate, B., Kerdyck, L., Ollendick, T., Hynd, G. W., Garfinkel, B., Greenhill, L., Biederman, J., Barkley, R. A., McBurnett, K., Newcorn, J. & Waldman, I. (1994). DSM-IV field trials for the disruptive behavior disorders: symptom utility estimates. *Journal of the American Academy of Child and Adolescent Psychiatry, 33,* 4.

Garber, J. & Strassberg, Z. (1991). Construct validity: history and application to developmental psychopathology. In D. Cicchetti & W. G. Grove (Eds.), *Thinking clearly about psychology: essays in honor of Paul Everett Meehl,* (pp. 219–358). Minneapolis: University of Minnesota Press.

Grayson, D. A. (1987). Can categorical and dimensional views of psychiatric illness be distinguished? *British Journal of Psychiatry, 151,* 335–361.

Group for the Advancement of Psychiatry (1966). *Psychopathological Disorders in Childhood: Theoretical Considerations and a Proposed Classification* (research report no. 62), pp. 229–230. Group for the Advancement of Psychiatry, New York.

Harrington, R., Rudge, H., Rutter, M., Bredenkamp, D., Groothues, C. & Pridham J. (in press). Child and adult depression: a test of continuities with family study data. *British Journal of Psychiatry.*

Hobbs, N. (1975). *Issues in the classification of children.* Jossey-Bass, San Francisco.

Hsiao, J. K., Bartko, J. J. Nand Potter, W. Z. (1989). Diagnosing diagnoses: receiver operating characteristic methods and psychiatry. *Archives of General Psychiatry, 46,* 664–667.

Jensen, P., Roper, M., Fisher, P., Piacentini, J., Canino, G., Richters, J., Rubio-Stipec, M., Dulcan, M., Goodman, S., Davies, M., Rae, D., Shaffer, D., Bird, H., Lahey, B., Schwab-Stone, M. (1995). Test–retest reliability of the Diagnostic Interview Schedule for Children (DISC 2.1). *Archives of General Psychiatry, 52,* 61–71.

Kaplan, H. I. & Sadock, B. J. (1995). *Comprehensive Textbook of Psychiatry VI.* Volume 2. Sixth Edition. Baltimore, MD: Williams and Wilkins.

Kazdin, A. E. (1983). Psychiatric diagnosis, dimensions of dysfunction, and child behavior therapy. *Behavior Therapy, 14,* 73–99.

Kendell, R. E. (1975). The Role of Diagnosis. *Blackwell Scientific Publications,* Oxford. Kendell, R. E. (1982). The choice of diagnostic criteria for biological research. *Archives of General Psychiatry, 39,* 1334–1339.

Klein, D. N. & Riso, L. P. (1994). Psychiatric disorders: problems of boundaries and comorbidity. In C.G. Costello, (Ed), *Basic issues in psychopathology.* New York: Guilford Press.

Lahey, B. B., Applegate, B., Barkley, R. A., Garfinkel, B., McBurnett, K., Kerdyk, L., Greenhill, L., Hynd, G. W., Frick, P. J., Newcorn, J., Biederman, J., Ollendick, T., Hart, E. L., Perex, D., Waldman, I., & Shaffer, D. (1994). DSM-IV field trials for oppositional defiant disorder and conduct disorder in children and adolescents. *American Journal of Psychiatry, 151,* 1163–1171.

Lahey, B. B., Applegate, B., McBurnett, K., Biederman, J., Greenhill, L., Hynd, G. W., Barkley, R. A., Newcorn, J., Johnson, P., Richter, J., Garfinkel, B., Kerdyk, L., Frick, P. J., Ollendick, T., Perex, D., Hart, E. L., Waldman, I. & Shaffer, D. (1994). DSM-IV filed trials for attention deficit hyperactivity disorder in children and adolescents. *American Journal of Psychiatry, 151,* 11.

Lewis, M. (1995). *Comprehensive Textbook of Child Psychiatry,* 2nd Edition. Baltimore, MD: Williams and Wilkins.

Mattison, R. E. & Hooper, S. R. (1992). The history of modern classification of child and adolescent psychiatric disorders: an overview. In S. R. Hooper, G. W. Hynd & R. E. Mattison (Eds), *Assessment and diagnosis of child and adolescent psychiatric disorders. Volume 1. Psychiatric disorders.* Hillsdale, NY: Lawrence Erlbaum Publishers.

McGorry, P. D., Mihalopoulos, C., Henry, L., Dakis, J., Jackson, H. J., Flaum, M., Harrigan, S., McKenzie, D., Kulkarni, J. & Karoly, R. (1995). Spurious precision: procedural validity of diagnostic assessment in psychotic disorders. *American Journal of Psychiatry, 152,* 2.

Nottelmann E. D. & Jensen P. S. (1995). Comorbidity of disorders in children and adolescents: developmental perspectives. *Advances in Clinical Child Psychology, 17,* 109–151.

Plante, E., Swisher, L. & Vance, R. (1991). MRI findings in boys with specific language impairment. *Brain and Language, 41,* 52–66.

Pliszka, S. R. (1989). Effects of anxiety on cognition, behavior, and stimulant response in ADHD. *Journal of the American Academy of Child and Adolescent Psychiatry, 28,* 882–887.

Prendergast, M., Taylor, E., Rapoport, J. L., Bartko, J., Donnelly, M., Zemetkin, A., Aheram, M. B., Dunn, G. & Wieselberg, H. M. (1988). The diagnosis of childhood hyperactivity: a US–UK cross-national study of DSM-III and ICD-9. *Journal of Child Psychology and Psychiatry, 29,* 289–300.

Quay, H. C. (1983). A critical analysis of DSM-III as a

taxonomy of psychopathology in childhood and adolescence. In *Contemporary issues in psychopathology*, T. Millon & G. Klerman (Eds). New York: Guilford.

Rey, J. M., Plapp, J. M. & Stewart, G. W. (1989). Reliability of psychiatric diagnosis in referred adolescents. *Journal of Child Psychology and Psychiatry, 30*, 879–888.

Robins, E. & Guze, S. B. (1970). Establishment of diagnostic validity in psychiatric illness: its application to schizophrenia. *American Journal of Psychiatry, 126*, 983–987.

Rutter, M. & Gould, M. (1985). Classification. In: M. Rutter & L. Hersov (Eds), *Child and adolescent psychiatry: modern approaches*, (2nd ed, pp. 304–431). Oxford: Blackwell Scientific Publications.

Rutter, M. & Pickles, A. (1990). Improving the quality of psychiatric data: classification, cause and course. In D. Magnusson & L. R. Bergman (Eds), *Data quality in longitudinal research*, (pp. 32–57). Cambridge: Cambridge University Press.

Rutter, M. (1978). Diagnostic validity in child psychiatry. *Advances in Biological Psychiatry, 2*, 2–22.

Rutter, M., Kebovici, S., Eisenberg, L., Sneznevskij, A. V., Sadoun, R., Brooke, E. & Lin, T. Y. (1969). A traxial classification of mental disorders in childhood. *Journal of Child Psychology and Psychiatry, 10*, 41–61.

Rutter, M., Shaffer, D. & Shepherd, M. (1975a). *A multiaxial classification of child psychiatric disorders*. Geneva: World Health Organization.

Rutter, M., Shaffer, D. & Sturge, C. (1975b). *A guide to multiaxial classification scheme for psychiatric disorders in childhood and adolescence*. London: Institute of Psychiatry.

Rutter, M., Taylor, E. & Hersov, L. (1994). *Child and adolescent psychiatry: modern approaches*, 3rd Edition. London: Blackwell Scientific Publications.

Schwab-Stone, M., Fallon, T., Briggs, M. & Crowther, B. (1994). Reliability of diagnostic reporting for children aged 6–11 years: a test–retest study of the Diagnostic Interview Schedule for Children-Revised. *American Journal of Psychiatry, 151*, 1048–1054.

Schwab-Stone, M., Shaffer, D., Dulcan, M., Jensen, P., Fisher, P., Bird, H., Goodman, S., Lahey, B., Lichtman, J., Canino, G., Rubio-Stipec, M. & Rae, D. S. (in press). Criterion Validity of the NIMH Diagnostic Interview Schedule for Children Version 2.3 (DISC 2.3). *Journal of American Academy of Child and Adolescent Psychiatry.*

Shaffer, D., Fisher, P., Dulcan, M., Davies, M., Piacentini, J., Schwab-Stone, M., Lahey, B. B., Bourdon, K., Jensen, P., Bird, H., Canino, G. & Regier, D. (in press). The NIMH Diagnostic Interview Schedule for Children (DISC 2.3): description, acceptability, prevalences, and performance in the MECA study. *Journal of American Academy of Child and Adolescent Psychiatry.*

Shaffer, D., Schwab-Stone, Fisher, P., Cohen, P., Piacentini, J., Davies, M., Conners, C. K. & Regier, D. (1993). The Diagnostic Interview Schedule for Children—Revised Version (DISC-R): I. Preparation, field testing, interrater reliability, and acceptability. *Journal of the American Academy of Child and Adolescent Psychiatry, 32*, 643–650.

Szasz, T. S. (1961). *The myth of mental illness*. New York: Harper and Row.

Szasz, T. S. (1978). *The myth of psychotherapy: mental healing as religion, rhetoric, and repression*. New York: Doubleday.

Volkmar, F. R., Klin, A., Siegel, B., Szatmari, P., Lord, C., Campbell, M., Freeman, B. J., Cicchetti, D. V., Rutter, M., Lkine, W., Buitelaar, J., Hattab, Y., Fombonne, E., Furentes, J., Werry, J., Stone, W., Kerbeshian, J., Hoshino, Y., Bregman, J., Loveland, K., Szymanski, L. & Towbin, K. (1994). Field trial for autistic disorder in DSM-IV. *American Journal of Psychiatry, 151*, 1361–1367.

Waldman, I. D. & Lahey, B. B. (1994). Design of the DSM-IV Disruptive Behavior Disorder Field Trials. *Child and Adolescent Psychiatric Clinics of North America, 3*, 1–14.

Waldman, I. D., Lahey, B. B., Applegate, B., Biederman, J., Hynd, G. W., Barkley, R. A., Ollendick, T., Frick, P. J., Kerdyk, L., Garfinkel, B., Greenhill, L., McBurnett, K., Newcorn, J. & Hart, E. L. (1994). *The construct validity of DSM-IV attention-deficit/hyperactivity disorder subtypes: report from the DSM-IV field trials* (Manuscript in preparation).

Waldman I. D., Lilienfeld, S. O. & Lahey, B. B. (1995). Toward construct validity in the childhood disruptive behavior disorders. *Advances in Clinical Child Psychology, 17*, 323–358.

Weiner, I. B. (1982). Classification in developmental psychopathology. In I. B. Weiner (Ed), *Child and adolescent pathology*, (pp. 42-79). New York: Wiley.

Weissman, M., Warner, V. & Fendrich, M. (1987). Applying impairment criteria to children's psychiatric diagnosis. *Journal of the American Academy of Child and Adolescent Psychiatry, 29*, 789–796.

Wolraich, M. L., Hannah, J. N., Pinnock, T. Y., Baumgaertel, A. & Brown, J. (in press). Comparison of diagnostic criteria for attention deficit hyperactivity disorder in a country-wide sample. *Journal of the American Academy of Child and Adolescent Psychiatry.*

World Health Organization (1967). *International Classification of Diseases: Manual of the International Statistical Classification of Diseases, Injuries and Causes of Death, 8th revision.* Geneva: World Health Organization.

World Health Organization (1978). *Mental Disorders: Glossary and Guide to their Classification in Accordance with the Ninth Revision of the International Classification of Diseases*. Geneva: World Health Organization.

World Health Organization (1992). *ICD-10: The ICD-10 Classification of Mental and Behavioral Disorders: Clinical Description and Diagnostic Guidelines*. Geneva: World Health Organization.

World Health Organization (in press). *Multi-axial Version of ICD-10: Prepared for Use by Clinicians Dealing with Child and Adolescent Psychiatric Disorders*. Cambridge: Cambridge University Press.

Zero to Three/National Center for Clinical Infant Programs (1995). Diagnostic Classification of Mental Health and Developmental Disorders of Infancy and Early Childhood. Zero to Three, Arlington, Virginia.

Zinbarg, R. E., Barlow, D. H., Liebowitz, M., Street, L., Broadhead, E., Katon, W., Roy-Byrne, P., Lepine, J. P., Teherani, M., Richards, J., Brantley, P. J. & Kraemer, H. (1994). The DSM-IV field trial for mixed anxiety-depression. *American Journal of Psychiatry, 151*, 8.

Accepted manuscript received 21 July 1995

[13]

Reflections on the Assessment of Outcomes in Child Care

Roy Parker
University of Bristol and
Centre for Social Policy,
Dartington, UK

*Measuring the outcomes of social work interventions with children
raises complex issues. The instability of intermediate outcomes
emphasises the need to undertake regular and carefully timed
assessments. Differences in approach and perspective can obscure
relationships between evaluations of organisational performance and
assessments of outcome for individual children; user perspectives
introduce another point of view. Assessing outcomes of family
support services raises questions of accountability. Aggregate
information about children looked after, collected through the Looking
After Children project, should help to establish the chances of certain
outcomes being realised, although the influence of some factors may
not be easy to explain.*

T he working party that I chaired, and whose report,
Assessing Outcomes in Child Care (1991), led to the
'Looking After Children' scheme, began its deliberations in 1987. It is not too soon, therefore, to reflect upon some
of the issues with which we grappled then and upon others
that have emerged since.

Issues connected with the stability of outcomes over time

Taxing problems surround the question of when an outcome
should be assessed. At certain times there may be a temporary
improvement or an uncharacteristic deterioration. What we
observe may be an enduring condition, but it may also be no
more than a transitional stage. If the latter, there could be
subsequent reversals, further advances or eventual stabilis-
ation. A few examples will illustrate how careful one needs to
be in deciding just when a course of events has reached the
point of being appropriately regarded as an outcome.

Correspondence to: Professor Roy
Parker, Centre for Social Policy,
Warren House, Warren Lane,
Dartington, Totnes,
Devon TQ9 6EG.

A report on Jewish children saved from the concentration
camps and brought to Britain in 1945 described their profoundly disturbed emotional state but also the apparently
miraculous rate of their psychological recovery (Hicklin, 1946).

However, as time passed this recovery often failed to be sustained, although exactly when the setbacks occurred, and how serious or lasting they were, was found to be hard to predict; and no long-term follow up was undertaken.

Other studies, such as that of Cornish and Clarke (1975), long ago drew attention to the fact that although disturbing behaviour could be modified whilst youngsters remained in controlled residential settings the changes did not usually survive once they left and the controls disappeared. Likewise, Bartak and Rutter (1975) showed what progress could be made with autistic children given favourable staff ratios and a well-controlled classroom; but they also noted how difficult it was to maintain the educational improvements when the children returned home, unless there was good collaboration between parents and school.

Such examples draw attention to the fragile and unstable nature of certain kinds of 'progress'; but unexpected improvements may follow changes in context, especially when these occur in the realm of personal relationships. This was demonstrated in Quinton and Rutter's study (1988) of young mothers who had spent considerable periods in children's homes. Despite their unfavourable experiences the majority were providing satisfactory care for their toddlers. What, above all, distinguished these mothers from those who fell short in their child care was the kind of partner they had acquired; ideally someone who was supportive and not a social casualty.

A similar set of issues surrounds what might be called the 'delayed effects' of various types of organised intervention. In my first research on the success and failure of long-term foster care (1966) I found that the peak time for placements to 'fail' was 17 months after the child's arrival, with a rapid increase of such risk from about a year and a steady decline after two. In another study (with Elaine Farmer, 1991) of the return home of children and young people who had been committed to the care of local authorities (but without the court order having expired or been discharged) we found a 25 per cent rate of re-abuse or neglect amongst the children who were in care for their protection. This occurred over a period of two years but did not happen at once, or even during the first year. As we pointed out, the risk to a child may seem to have diminished but may increase again later given new circumstances, new stresses or changed behaviour. Outcomes may be mistakenly considered to be favourable (and then services perhaps withdrawn or wound down) if the assessment is made too soon or, of course, some valuable short-term benefits may be overlooked if it is made too late.

One of the most telling examples of the way in which outcomes may be differently interpreted with the passage of time is provided by the Head-Start initiative in the United States. Significant gains in the IQ scores of the disadvantaged children in the scheme were achieved by the time that they entered mainstream schooling; but these gains were subsequently lost and the programme cut. However, in their late teens the children in the experimental group were found to have fewer difficulties than the controls—but these benefits had occurred in spheres other than their measured intelligence alone (McGuire and others, 1997).

My purpose in offering these few illustrations is to emphasise that a good deal of instability is likely to be found in what, in our report, we termed intermediate outcomes and that, for this reason, we should time the assessment of outcomes with some care. What might this

194   Roy Parker

involve in practice? First, in order to obtain an accurate picture of what has happened it is imperative to know what prevails at a number of stages in a child's career; hence the value of continuing *re*-views that are truly *re*-assessments.

Secondly, it is probably wise to avoid determining an outcome at points of particular stress or crisis, such as starting or changing school, moving home or when a new baby is born into the family. Similarly, the special nature of 'honeymoon' or 'testing out' periods has been recognised for a long time. Over and above such considerations there are also those that take account of ages and stages in child development. For instance, in her study of the consequences of physical abuse Gibbons (1995) note the increased vulnerability of one to two-year olds, suggesting that 'this age might represent a period of particular stress in child rearing' and adding that it was also a time when support from health services declines and when other services are not yet available.

Thirdly, in paying more attention to the timing of outcome assessments it may be necessary to choose differently for different children depending upon their individual circumstances and the kind of help that they or their families are being offered. That may require clearer statements about when specific outcomes are expected to have been achieved.

Finally, one should note how often the research that endeavours to assess outcomes imposes arbitrary points at which that assessment occurs because of the amount of time that the funding will buy. This is certainly a difficulty, but one that may not be insurmountable if the subject groups of the research are more precisely defined and sound arguments advanced for its duration to reflect when it is reasonable to make an assessment of outcome, particularly in the light of the nature of the interventions being made.

Issues arising from the relationship between individual and aggregate outcomes

Our working party identified five perspectives on child care outcomes: public, service, professional, family and that of the child. Although appreciating the importance of each we concentrated upon outcomes from the child's point of view. Since then the assessment of agency performance (that is, service outcomes) has become an increasingly important activity, both routinely and in response to scandals and tragedies. Organisations are anxious to monitor their own performance as well as that of other bodies from whom they may be purchasing services. They are also subject to various kinds of external scrutiny; for example, by the Social Services Inspectorate and the Audit Commission.

These developments raise the question of what exactly the relationship is between the way in which organisational performance is assessed and the manner in which the assessment of outcomes for individual children is approached. Currently, there are notable differences.

In the first place different amounts and types of information are used. Both an organisation's performance targets as well as the indicators employed to monitor their realisation are strongly influenced by the data that are readily available, and then by the ease with which these can be quantified. Hence the emphasis upon such variables as the number of children looked after; the proportion of them in foster care or how many names there are on the child protection register. Above all, of course, there is constant reference to details of expenditure and cost. Coupled with this is the fact that when it comes to the interpretation of this type of performance data (how good or bad are we?) considerable reliance is placed upon comparisons with other 'similar' organisations as well as with previous performance. These are the conventional bench marks.

By contrast, the assessment of outcomes for individual children involves a great deal more information, and information of a personalised nature. Furthermore, there is little systematic comparison with other children, either with those who have been exposed to similar misfortunes or with 'control' groups of one kind or another. Indeed, there is a common conviction that the children with whom social workers are engaged (especially those with the most complex problems) defy the classification that permits this to be done. On the other hand, aggregate performance data rely upon the creation of categories; but these rarely give an idea of the extent of the individual variations that they encompass. The aggregation of data is a process of simplification and generalisation and as such is prone to obscure the reality of mixed performances (some good, some not so good) in particular authorities.

The 'Looking After Children' project offers an opportunity to build a bridge between the assessment of individual and organisational outcomes. The information that it generates can be assembled to provide more sensitive indicators of how well an authority is attending to the welfare of those children for whom it carries some responsibility. Certainly, it would still be necessary to take account of the kinds of items (such as unit costs, the rates of provision of this or that service, or social workers' case loads) that are to be found in the Department of Health's list of 'key indicators' (1994) or in the Audit Commission's review of services for children (1994); but these are essentially input variables and are not based upon what is actually done (or not done) on behalf of specific children, and to what effect. Were these more child-centred types of aggregated data included a rather different style of social accountancy would be introduced, and one that was likely to give a more accurate picture of overall performance. Indeed, the groundwork for such a development is already being laid in the research that Harriet Ward describes in her companion article.

The categories of children for whom outcomes are assessed

The 'Looking After Children' scheme of outcome assessment was conceived mainly in relationship to 'looked-after' children; that is, children living away from home for whom a local authority was acting *in loco parentis*. However, since the working party was engaged in its deliberations the work of 'child care' has become more diverse and more complicated. Fewer children are being looked after in ways that impose parent-like responsibilities upon authorities and more are being sustained in situations in which there is a mixed pattern of responsibility, and hence of accountability.

We adopted a straightforward criterion for what an authority should do in order to give the best chance of favourable outcomes for the children for whom it was directly responsible; namely, they should ensure that those matters were attended to which it could reasonably be expected would be the concern of ordinary parents. There is not a similar

196　Roy Parker

criterion that helps to decide what an authority should be expected to do when working 'in partnership' with parents to promote the well-being of children in their own homes. How far, in this situation, should authorities be expected to go; for example, in improving the health or education of the children? And do answers to questions like these depend upon the extent to which the parents' collaboration in such endeavours can be enlisted?

Of course, the change in the balance of the child care work of social services departments does not affect the desirability of monitoring outcomes with respect to vulnerable children, but it may well alter the degree to which agencies (and thereby the state) are held responsible for what happens as well as those matters for which they are considered to have *some* responsibility. Take, for example, the question of meeting the needs of parents. If they are to provide better care for their children then, in many instances, they will need to be helped to do so. Should authorities be held accountable for providing such help if a favourable outcome for the child appears to depend upon it?

The second volume in the 'Looking After Children' series, *Research into Practice* (Ward and others, 1995) showed that the materials that were devised could be used successfully with a group of children in families *not* in contact with social services departments, and that they could highlight difficulties and alert parents to matters that needed their attention. However, the participation of this control group was voluntary and no social services department had any current responsibility for the children's well-being. The assessment of outcomes for children at home (or in brief respite care) for whom there *was* some such responsibility would seem to be a different proposition and poses the question of just what kind of instrument would be most appropriate for the purpose.

A practical way forward might be to investigate (on an exploratory basis at first) how far the 'Looking After Children' schedules could be used as part of the agenda for work with children in need and their families in the community; elsewhere in this journal Harriet Ward describes such an initiative being undertaken by one local authority. Certainly, social workers have reported that using the schedules has helped them to confront difficult issues with older children, with foster carers and, in some cases, with parents as well. Furthermore, they have helped to settle just who is to be responsible for which actions (and by when) and this approach could certainly be used in working with families and children in their own homes.

Nevertheless, the situation of the looked-after child *is* different from that of the vulnerable child who remains at home or who is returned home, as is the position of the engaged authority; and although some features of the 'Looking After Children' initiative are applicable in both contexts the questions of how the outcomes of welfare interventions should be determined for different groups of children for whom local authorities and others have different degrees of responsibility remains to be answered.

Matters relating to the problem of how narrow or broad-sweeping selected outcomes should be

The 'Looking After Children' project identifies seven dimensions upon which children's outcomes should be considered: health; education; emotional and behavioural development; family and peer relationships; self-care and competence; identity, and social presentation. It was agreed that this reflected the need to disaggregate the notion of 'an' outcome, since progress was likely to be different in different components of a child's life. However, it was not proposed that outcomes in these separate areas should be re-assembled into an overall 'score'. This was partly because such a process of homogen-isation was likely to mask potentially important variations (for instance, that between an improvement in education and a persistence in confusion about identity) but also because of the practical problems of deciding what weight should be attached to outcomes on one dimension in comparison with those on another. Furthermore, how was any cancelling out effect of combining the positives with the negatives to be dealt with or the consequences of disproportionate reinforcement reflected?

Despite our decision not to try to resolve these difficulties, the concept of different dimensions of outcome seemed a useful advance from the one-dimensional approach to the assessment of outcomes that has been seen in much research in the past. Indeed, it hardly needs to be said that there are many types of outcomes, in many spheres and these are associated with a variety of interventions and life events. But how do these combine and to what effect and, in any case, are they actually as mixed (in terms of the good and the bad) as our working party was pleased to assume? One example will serve to emphasise the complexity of the issue. In our study of children returned home from care 'on trial' Elaine Farmer and I found that 44 per cent of the teenage girls became pregnant over the two years of the study, as against a national rate for the 16–19 age group of three per cent. Indisputably, a poor outcome some would conclude; but only one of their babies was taken into care and their relations with their families (especially their mothers) appeared to improve.

Just how specific should we be in the outcomes that we choose to assess? If the kind of disaggregation that is to be found in the 'Looking After Children' scheme is the preferred pattern is there not also a strong case for making some general assessment of how a child's welfare has improved or deteriorated? In my view there is, but I have to admit that I am unsure how it is best to be done. Life satisfaction scales might help, as might the exercise of informed judgement or autobiographical reflection.

Both adults and children do differentiate between outcomes (he's doing well at school but I'm worried about ...); but they also weigh up the pros and cons to convey a view of their lives overall. I was struck by this in reading Albert Facey's moving autobiography *A Fortunate Life* (1981). After an Australian childhood of harsh treatment and emotional deprivation, the absence of schooling, slave-like employment, and suffering serious wounds at Gallipoli he concluded his story by writing: 'I have lived a very good life, it has been very rich and full. I have been very fortunate and I am thrilled by it when I look back'. By contrast, one of the men quoted in Harrison's collection of the life stories of people sent to Canada from Britain as children (1979) tells her that he wonders "what I might have been if I had had a normal childhood. Actually I ceased to be a child at the age of ten. No one can understand my feelings of loneliness and despair ..."

The message from these two extracts is not only that different people view the quality of their lives in different ways and for different reasons, but that what happens later (in Facey's case his marriage in particular) can offset the effect of what occurred earlier or simply confirm it. Yet we are still uncertain how the multiplicity and succession of particular 'intermediate' outcomes are or should be assembled in order to provide the

198   Roy Parker

more comprehensive assessment that, in the end, will most accurately reflect children's sense of their own well-being.

The evaluation of outcomes

Most research that seeks to identify the influences upon outcomes also endeavours to evaluate them, often by incorporating at the outset a definition of what will be regarded as a good or a bad result. Yet the favourable or unfavourable nature of many outcomes is actually quite hard to decide; except, of course, in extreme cases. This is true for both individual outcomes and organisational performance. Let me illustrate the point by drawing yet another example from our 'home on trial' study. We employed an essentially 'overall' assessment of outcomes, constructed in part from our own judgements and in part from those of a mixed panel of professionals; children who had been in care; parents of children in care, and a grandparent. On this basis the placements of 30 per cent of the children over the age of criminal responsibility who offended during the two years of the research were classed as 'positive'. Similarly, once placed at home the school attendance of nearly three-fifths of the older children who should have been at school was poor or non-existent; but the outcomes of a quarter of their placements were also considered to have been positive.

Had special significance been attached to offending or to the failure to attend school the overall rate of successful placements would have been considerably lower; and there were grounds for according these factors greater prominence, since many of the offenders had originally been committed to care because of their earlier offences and many of those not going to school had been committed for non-attendance. Had we evaluated the outcomes against the ostensible reason for these children's removal from home (certainly a defensible position) a rather disheartening picture of their return home would have been reported.

Indeed, one of the problems of evaluating aggregate outcomes lies in knowing what 'levels' are to be regarded as good, good enough, indifferent, or quite unsatisfactory practice and policy. Again, in the same study, as noted earlier, a quarter of the younger children were abused or neglected whilst back at home; but three-quarters were not, despite the fact that the reasons for most of them being in care sprang from their previous abuse or neglect. How is such an aggregate outcome to be evaluated, and against what criteria?

Do we pitch our expectations too often at an unreasonably high level and hence virtually ensure poor rates of success? Or, on the other hand, do we set them too unambitiously, thereby being content with mediocre outcomes? The lesson may be that more attention needs to be paid to what would constitute a good outcome (or indeed a poor one) on a child-by-child basis rather than by the application of blanket formulae. Again, the 'Looking After Children' approach goes a considerable way to making this possible, although it may be necessary to give rather more emphasis to the children's evaluations of the services that they have received. Several studies (for example, Thoburn, 1980 and Triseliotis and others, 1996) have discovered that the recipients' views of the help that they have been offered were more favourable than those of the social workers who were responsible for providing it.

In their study of teenagers and social work services Triseliotis and his colleagues found that two-thirds of the young people thought that their lives were better at the end than at the beginning of the one-year inquiry, although not always as a result of social work help. Nevertheless, nearly half said that their expectations of such help had been met. By contrast, only 30 per cent of the social workers were equally satisfied with what had been achieved and parents were more likely than their children to consider the interventions as ineffective. Results such as these underline the fact that even those closely involved can reach different conclusions about the value of the same intervention; they also warn us against attaching exclusive importance to any one interpretation.

Attribution, prediction and explanation

It goes without saying that many factors contribute to shaping an 'outcome'. Sophisticated statistical techniques and the power of computing allow us to identify significant associations, take account of overlapping influences and different combinations, as well as discern those sets of factors that best discriminate between one outcome and another. But the scope of such analyses is circumscribed by the extent and nature of the data to which they are applied and those data, in their turn, are largely the product of what is already believed to be important, together with what it is considered possible to collect.

Although it is necessary to be aware of such limitations and difficulties we should not be deterred by the task of sifting out what has contributed to a particular outcome and then using the results to inform child care practice and policy. Even with 'gold standard' research employing randomised controlled trials we are unlikely to be able to say with complete confidence that a particular outcome is attributable to this or that form of intervention or set of factors. However, with aggregate data about enough cases it is feasible to establish the chances of an outcome being realised (or not realised) given the existence or absence of certain intervening variables. In short, the prediction of outcomes from known past regularities can furnish the kind of informed guidance that is often sadly lacking in child care and for which practitioners are often heard to ask.

Of course, none of this removes the need for the exercise of judgement; even if it is established that there is, say, an 80 per cent probability of a successful outcome with these kinds of children, in these circumstances and with this type of intervention it remains to be decided whether the case in question conforms with the great majority or whether it promises to be one of the exceptions. There are, indeed, certain intangible aspects of any social situation that are not amenable to statistical treatment but which may need to be taken into account. Likewise, knowing that there is an 80 per cent chance of 'success' if certain steps are taken in these circumstances cannot indicate what is an *acceptable* level of risk. This will be determined by considerations of policy, prevailing expectations and aspirations, and the availability of alternatives and *their* presumed risk.

Hence well-founded prediction, based upon the examination and recording of past outcomes, offers relevant information in a condensed and usable form. It also serves to broaden the range of experience upon which practitioners can call as well as providing them with a yardstick against which they can assess and reflect upon their own assessments. In these ways such an approach can counteract or compensate for the uniqueness of each worker's experience.

200   Roy Parker

Over and above these benefits the prediction of outcomes may have an important contribution to make to the more appropriate deployment of scarce resources. For instance, if, having made a decision, we know that the likelihood of success is fairly low, more attention and support may be required or special precautions taken. Similarly, knowledge of prevailing probabilities may assist in the conservation of resources. For example, there are key decisions in social work which, if inappropriately made, commit the agency to years of expensive and unrewarding work. Just how much work social services agencies actually create for themselves in this way is hard to tell, but if well-calculated probabilities can forewarn of such risks they may more often be avoided.

There are, of course, several notes of caution that should also be sounded. One at least ought to be mentioned. As in all assessments of outcome there is the danger that we learn more about one alternative than others. The evaluation of outcomes rarely, if ever, proceeds as an evenly paced scrutiny of all the options. We are likely to know more about the probable consequences of one course of action than of others and for that reason come either to regard it too pessimistically or too optimistically.

Thus, I would argue that the use of statistical prediction based upon good initial data is one important means of dealing with the complicated business of sorting out just which factors contribute just how much to identified outcomes. The 'Looking After Children' project offers an excellent prospect that the kind of information needed for such developments will be forthcoming.

Even so, however well we untangle the problem of attributing outcomes to key influences we do not necessarily *explain* what we discover. For instance, in foster care placement, as Wolkind and Rushton (1994) have noted, "the finding that the presence of an own child of similar age constitutes a risk factor has been replicated ... and must be regarded as one of the few items of secure knowledge with clear practice implications."

But what exactly are the processes involved? We can construct theories about jealousy and rivalry, about the tensions created by the need for foster carers to choose between the needs of their own child and those of the foster child, or about the disappointed expectations of happy childhood companionship; but we are still not sure about why things seem to go wrong. Plausible explanations of other established relationships between influence and outcome are often even more difficult to provide. The point is that attribution should not be confused with explanation, although the one may take us a good way towards understanding the other; and it is undoubtedly helpful to know what 'works' or does not work even though the precise reasons remain unclear.

Conclusion

Let me return to where I began—with the 'Looking After Children' initiative. It is not a panacea for all the problems that beset us in child care, and there are conceptual and practical matters that still need to be resolved. But it is a notable step forward, with many potentialities for ensuring that what is done in the name of child welfare is as effective as possible in actually securing that welfare. Its rationale was captured 200 years ago by the Marquis de Laplace (1951) who wrote that it was essential 'to keep in each branch of public administration an exact register of the results which the various means used have produced ...'. We can hardly do less today.

References

Audit Commission (1994) *Seen but not Heard: Co-ordinating Community Child Health and Social Services for Children in Need*, HMSO

Bartak, L and Rutter, M (1975) 'The measurement of staff-child interaction in three units for autistic children', in Tizard, J and others *eds* (1975) *Varieties of Residential Experience*, Routledge & Kegan Paul

Cornish, D.B. and Clarke, R.V.G. (1975) *Residential Treatment and its Effects upon Delinquency*, HMSO

de Laplace, M (1951) *Essays on Probabilities*, Dover Books

Department of Health (1994) *Key Indicators of Local Authority Social Services*

Facey, A.B. (1981) *A Fortunate Life*, Australia: Penguin

Farmer, E and Parker, R (1991) *Trials and Tribulations: Returning Children from Local Authority Care to their Families*, HMSO

Gibbons, J (and others) (1995) *Development After Physical Abuse in Early Childhood*, HMSO

Harrison, P *ed.* (1979) *The Home Children*, Winnipeg: Watson & Dwyer

Hicklin, M (1946) *War-Damaged Children*, Association of Psychiatric Social Workers

McGuire, J and others (1997) 'Evidence-based medicine and child mental health services', *Children and Society*, **11**, 2, 89–96

Parker, R.A. and others *eds* (1991) *Assessing Outcomes in Child Care*, HMSO

Parker, R.A. (1966) *Decision in Child Care*, Allen & Unwin

Quinton, D and Rutter, M (1988) *Parenting Breakdown*, Aldershot: Avebury

Thoburn, J (1980) *Captive Clients: Social Work with Families of Children Home on Trial*, Routledge, Kegan Paul

Triseliotis, J and others (1996) *Teenagers and the Social Work Services*, HMSO

Ward, H *ed.* (1995) *Looking After Children: Research into Practice*, HMSO

Wolkind, S and Rushton, A (1994) 'Residential and foster family care', in Rutter, M and others, *Child and Adolescent Psychiatry*, Blackwell

Contributor's details

Roy Parker is Professor Emeritus of Social Policy, University of Bristol and Fellow, Centre for Social Policy, Dartington. Professor Parker has had a long-standing involvement in child care research stretching over some 40 years and covering issues of foster and residential care, adoption, child disability, migration and history.

[14]

Single Case Evaluation Methods: Review and Prospects

Brian Sheldon

THE CASE FOR A STRUCTURED APPROACH TO CASE EVALUATIONS

Anyone who digs to any depth into the pre-1974 social work effectiveness literature is likely to come across a paradoxical set of findings; favourable expectations and impressions of the participants in research programmes, and dismal final results. Several of the experimental studies [1] [2] note this phenomenon and the effect is also quite well known in psychological research [3] [4]. Here is Fischer [5] commenting on it in the Cambridge-Somerville study:

> 'Throughout the programme, counsellors were asked on several occasions to list all the treatment group boys they thought had "substantially benefitted" from the services offered by the project. Roughly two thirds of the boys were so listed. Further, at the end of treatment over half the boys volunteered that they had been helped by their caseworkers. Similarly, in a follow-up of treatment-group boys (N=254) ratings suggested that two thirds were adjusting satisfactorily ...'

The problem with these apparently reassuring findings is that no significant differences were found between experimental and control group subjects in this study!

Variations on this effect are also to be found in consumer-opinion research [6] [7] [8] where there are profound differences of interpretation between workers and clients as to what has happened, what its value is, and who is deserving of praise or blame. An analysis of reports from dissatisfied clients by Mayer and Timms concludes [6]:

> 'There is an almost Kafkaesque quality about these worker-client transactions. To exaggerate only slightly, each of the parties assumed that the other

> shared certain of his underlying conceptions about behaviour and the ways in which it might be altered. Then, unaware of the inappropriateness of his extrapolations, each found special reasons to account for the other's conduct.'

A larger, later study produced similar findings [9]:

> 'While they expressed their gratification in having the worker listen to them, they were puzzled as to how this was supposed to help. Another recurring theme was the client's expectation that the worker play a more active role in the helping process through expressed opinions, giving advice, and suggestions. This was evident among respondents from both the middle and lower socio-economic groups.'

These results, frequently repeated in consumer-studies, albeit alongside more positive outcomes, suggest that miscommunication and the misattribution of change are endemic to social work. Perhaps it would be surprising if this were not so in a profession so heavily reliant upon verbal interaction as its main medium of influence. The important questions, however, remain:

(i)   how does this effect (which seems to rob social workers of accurate feedback on their ideas and actions) operate?
(ii) what can be done to lessen its influence?

My own short-list of the answers to question (i) is:

(a) Social workers especially, but clients too, develop their own implicit theories as to the nature and aetiology of the difficulties before them; for example, that an in-depth discussion has powerful behaviour-changing properties in its own right; or, in the case of clients, that problems of child behaviour have their origins almost exclusively in genetic factors. Sometimes these implicit assumptions are so fundamental as to escape detection altogether. It was not until the clients were independently interviewed in the Mayer and Timms study [6] that they articulated their views: that, for example, the historical/development of attitude of workers to their problems was at odds with their own experience of these difficulties as contemporary and practical.

(b) It is in the nature of the human perceptual apparatus to go well beyond the available evidence [10]. Contrary to how it often seems to the busy social worker, even the most intensively-visited clients live 98% of their lives outside the influence of professional helpers. There is, therefore, often a mass of complicated material to

42

make sense of and relate to one or two key themes. In such circumstances, it is impossible not to jump to some conclusions to try to impose (not always accurately) some pattern on events.

(c) Why do clients not correct these misperceptions when they spot them? Some do, of course, and some social workers listen carefully when this happens. But even to ask this question is to ignore firstly, the tremendous power differences between anxious, verbally-unsophisticated, working class clients and their predominantly middle-class, relatively unanxious, verbally sophisticated helpers and, secondly, the established practices of a profession which is only now beginning to kick its long-established habit of regarding the testimony of clients as so much raw material thinly salted through with clues as to 'underlying pathology'. This pathology was once viewed through individual, stage-developmental, fixation-related propositions [11] [12]; today, there is a good chance that it will be viewed in terms of patterns of disordered family functioning [13] [14] or through a set of socio-political assumptions [15]. With one or two important differences [16] [17] the same could be said of the increasingly influential behavioural approaches.

This discussion is not a plea for less explicit theorising or less interpretation. Implicit theorising is far more dangerous because it is rarely available for public scrutiny and criticism. The point is that we cannot not interpret the evidence of our senses, but we could try harder to control our use of theory and interpretation so that the client has a chance to share in and to influence this process.

(d) Finally there are 'demand effects', the unaccountable tendency of subjects without very strong feelings (and sometimes with) to give their questioners the information they think they would like to hear. As psychologists, psychotherapy researchers [18] [19] and market researchers know to their cost, great care and considerable artifice is required to extract uncoloured information from respondents.

In answer to question (ii) the arguments so far suggest that social work's acceptance of subjectivity, unbridled eclecticism, exclusively verbal and qualitative assessment and evaluation, and 'open-plan' (unstructured, blank-sheet) case recording, is very questionable. If we are to begin to square up to some of the distorting influences ranged against us, we must develop a more critical approach to questions of evidence, and a more robust set of evaluation practices.

Fortunately, much of the groudwork has already been done. In Single Case Experimental Designs and the assessment approaches that go with them, there is on offer an evaluation technology which is both rigorous, flexible, and well-attuned to the relatively small-scale individual and family problems which remain the main focus of social work.

ORIGINS AND HISTORY OF SINGLE CASE EXPERIMENTATION

The application of Single Case Experimental Designs to clinical work stems from the work of a British psychologist [20] [21] [22] who used prototype A B A design (pre-intervention fixing of the rate of a piece of problematic behaviour – followed by intervention – followed by a withdrawal of intervention) in a range of cases including one involving paranoid delusions [23]. Shapiro's achievement was to bring together the traditional concern in psychology and psychiatry for the unique individual and his problems, and the idea of careful experimentation to determine outcome, which was at this time the exclusive province of group-comparison research.

The next phase of rapid development took place as a result of the work of Chassan [24] and the explosive growth of the various clinical approaches based upon operant learning theory [25] known collectively as Behaviour Modification. Key features of this approach are the systematic introduction and removal of therapeutic or situational factors while the monitoring of behaviour continues in respect of a number of key variables.

Such measurement techniques are now in widespread use not only in clinic-based programmes, but also in field settings [17] [26]. The social work literature has thrown up spasmodic contributions on this theme, in general suggesting that these approaches show considerable promise for at least part of our work, describing the main methods, and giving one or two examples.

However, these examples present some problems. Firstly the numbers of actual instances of their use is low. Secondly, the approach is made to seem rather 'pat' in some, as if there were no inherent difficulties apart from the question of the knowledge and skill of the practioner. Thirdly, there is a tendency to choose problems which seem rather nicely discrete, or well-circumscribed. However, this is not true of all the contributions [27] [28] [29] [30] [31] [32] [33] [34].

For me these methods are the most important contribution of Behaviour Modification approaches to social work. Moreover, as the reader will see, they do not actually require adherence to any particular therapeutic approach.

44

GOAL-SETTING, OBSERVATION AND ASSESSMENT METHODS

My experience of using and teaching single case evaluation designs (S.C.E.Ds) [17] [35] convinces me that the main difficulties of the approach lie not in persuading clients to co-operate, not in the production of graphs, but in the early stages of choosing and defining the parameters to be measured. The social work literature on S.C.E.Ds is not as helpful as it might be here. Successful use of S.C.E.Ds depends upon a number of prior assessment stages. These are as follows:

(i)   Negotiations have to take place about what the various definitions which surround referrals mean in terms of actual behaviour or specific influence. We need to know what an 'inadequate personality' [36] or a 'paranoid reaction' means in respect of who does what, where, how often, and with what apparent consequences? One cannot measure 'an inferiority complex'; we have to decide what someone who is supposed to have one of these does too much, or too little of, to so earn themselves the title. All this is necessary for technical reasons but it has other consequences, as when a careful analysis of 'disturbed behaviour' on the part of a schoolchild, maps out as: interfering with the work of other pupils, making unexpected noises, leaving his desk without permission, and occasionally hitting classmates without apparent provocation [17]. The problem is still serious, but the negative impact of the psychopathological 'labelling' of the earlier definition is reduced.

(ii)   Two or three key elements or reliable indicators of the problem(s) have to be selected: clearly distinguishable behaviours, or patterns of interaction which, though not sufficient to encompass the whole, are nevertheless necessary conditions of it, and co-vary reliably with the presence and magnitude of it. This is not as easy in field or residential work as it can be elsewhere in the helping professions. Social work problems tend to be broad in scope and ill-defined, or, conversely, over-defined by other would-be helpers prior to referral. They may also be well-immunised against change by previous abortive attempts at solution; made up of many different interacting elements, and are sometimes problems of relationships between people, not just the problems *of* people. So the difficulties of this stage should not be underestimated. Nevertheless, it is possible in some cases to decide that, for example, references to surveillance, or messages coming through the TV, are the essence of 'paranoid reaction', failure to initiate conversations and to maintain short periods of eye contact are at the centre of Mr X's 'social inadequacy', and Mr Y's outbursts of temper are related to Mrs Y's anxious withdrawal, and vice versa. Readers must judge for themselves the validity of such indicators, but should bear in mind that such exercises are always to some extent arbitrary – they are educated guesses which are tested out later.

(iii) This process of convergence and specification requires practice simply because it runs counter to many of the established methods of the profession. Students tend to receive praise for the complexity of their case-formulations. Yet what is required here is not a long series of flexible, multi-purpose goals, but a few inflexible, and discrete-as-possible goals, based upon hypotheses about what is wrong in the situation and how it might be put right. These ideas are consistent with certain practices in the natural sciences, where the hallmark of good practice is the construction of tests which could easily fail; which in Popper's terms [27] are as 'risky' as possible. Only in this way do we obtain clear feedback on our case-experiments. Protean goals and indicators, capable of endless re-interpretation and re-appraisal in the light of threatening evidence, though easier to live with in the short term, are ultimately self-defeating. In using them we rob ourselves of clear feedback on progress, and therefore of an opportunity to substitute new and more relevant objectives for old. Dealing in behaviour, or clearly distinguishable events, substantially reduces the risk of the 'Kafkaesque' effect referred to earlier in the context of consumer-opinion research.

(iv) Single Case Designs introduce a quantitative element into case evaluation. This is not to say that qualitative variables, such as how people feel about their situation, should or can be ignored. An increased level of contact between natural parents and foster child may look nice on a graph, but if all concerned continue to dislike it, then is this the most relevant assessment point? The sensible approach is to use quantitative alongside qualitative assessment so that each reinforces the other. Thus, reports of a 'better atmosphere' in the hostel may need closer investigation (they may be due to demand-effects) if the amount of time residents spend in communal activities is in sharp decline. Alternatively, the problem could be reassessed in terms of a need for more personal space or for freedom from communal pressures. The main characteristic of qualitative assessment based on experimental principles is that end-states, which are as closely defined as possible, should be pre-decided. This can be done by asking clients and other interested parties to typify the present features of their problems, and then to typify what would be happening if there were a substantial improvement. In my experience, clients do this readily: 'We'd talk to each other, and consult each other more, and wouldn't be so afraid to say how we felt about things for fear of bringing on a row or a sulking session ...'.

This last statement contains four potentially quantifiable elements.

(v)   Having selected representative indicators, the next step is to produce a sample of the relevant pre-intervention behaviour, that is, pre-specific, problem-countering, pre-assessment intervention: sometimes just assessing a problem alters

46

it – normally for the better. This is known as a baseline, or base-rate measure, and is the standard against which progress is measured. The aim here is to produce a representative sequence, that is a typical range or pattern, continuing long enough for odd fluctuations to iron out or be seen in context. Therefore, length of recording will vary according to the frequency of the behaviour. Periods of rumination in a case of clinical depression, or obsessive-cumpulsive rituals from a severely neurotic client, being high-frequency, will yield representative samples in a short time. Enuresis and stealing will usually be low in frequency and will need a much longer period of observation. Having some yardstick against which to measure improvement is an advance on traditional methods where often there is only a hazy impression of the status quo ante.

(vi) Space here is too limited to allow a full discussion of recording methods [27] [38]. In essence, success in persuading clients or mediators to co-operate depends on clear, matter-of-fact explanations about the purpose and the advantages of so doing, clear and well-produced proforma (clients need not be troubled with graphs; diaries are better and can be used to record both occurrences and reflections), rehearsal of any likely difficulties, and the social worker actually using the results in front of the clients. Observation and recording can be carried out by a wide range of people in different parts of the client's environment, or by clients themselves. If no basis for co-operation emerges, then this approach to evaluation cannot proceed, but then therapeutic gains would be likely to be minimal anyway.

DIFFERENT TYPES OF S.C.E.D.

A.B. Methods

The simplest design is the A.B. 'before and after' comparison (see Fig. 1). This is the one most often used in social work settings and can give much useful correlational information. It is, however, quasi-experimental only, as will become clear later.

This example is an extract from a three month project to maintain a disruptive (or as the head teacher preferred 'disturbed') schoolboy in the normal school provision rather than a specialised unit. The scheme has much in common with modern delinquency-prevention and de-labelling schemes.

The main methods used were:

(i)   encouraging teachers to respond to reasonable behaviour and ignore most of the bad (the opposite contingencies applied previously);

Fig 1.   Data from a classroom management scheme for a 'disturbed' nine year old boy.

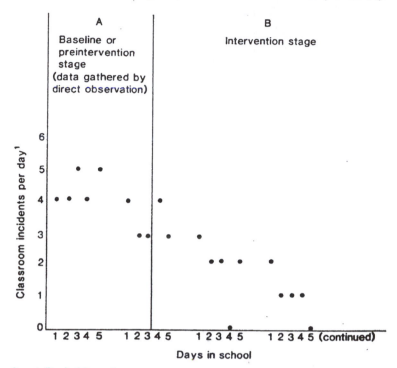

¹Predefined with teachers as any combination of: Interfacing with the work of others, causing physical pain to others; leaving his seat and failing to return within one minute of first being asked; making loud noises, or noises continuing long enough to distract other pupils.

(Source: Sheldon [17])

(ii)   a time-out scheme for episodes of violence to replace heavy 'psychological' sessions with well-intentioned staff – who were (unwittingly) positively reinforcing this bad behaviour;

(iii) a points scheme linking home and school [17].

On follow-up at fourteen weeks and six months the disruptive behaviour was well under control and the child continued to be taught at his ordinary school.

Fig. 2 presents a piece of work by a probation student to check out his withdrawn client's responsiveness to social skills training. The gains are modest but worthwhile, and gave a considerable boost of confidence to a client who tended to see his inhibited behaviour as unalterable. Note the incorporation of a follow-up period. There are one or two problems with the graph, not least the rising and rather

48

Fig 2. AB Design with follow up: Social Skill Training with a Withdrawn Client.

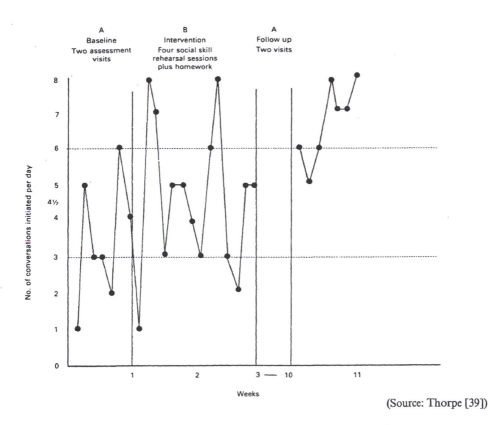

(Source: Thorpe [39])

unstable baseline, but field studies are seldom as tidy as one might wish. Ideally, the student should have continued to monitor for a longer period to see if the marked fluctuations would moderate, but then clients who stoically cope with problems for years often get suddenly impatient when help seems at hand.

I have given considerable space to the least sophisticated designs for the simple reason that these correlational studies are likely to have most relevance to routine social work for some time to come. However, they do present problems as Fig. 3 illustrates.

The hypothetical relationship in Fig. 3 demonstrates that in A.B. designs the social worker may be intervening at a fortuitous moment in the natural course of a problem. We have known for many years that certain problems and conditions

Fig 3. Hypothetical natural course of problems encountered on discharge from psychiatric hospital.

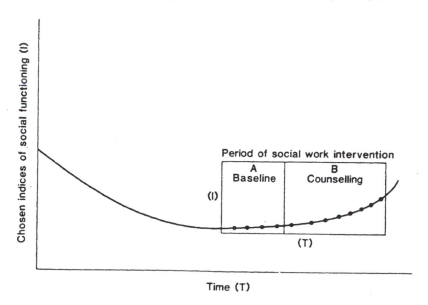

(Source: Sheldon [17])

'spontaneously remit' [40] [41] and although the misattribution of good news may not worry the busy social worker much, there remains the question of replication and a set of wider disciplinary concerns to do with the improvement of our methods.

In order to check whether a particular approach is responsible for a given effect, further phases have to be added.

A.B.A. Designs

The inclusion of a return-to-baseline phase gives two points of comparison:- between A[1] and B and B and A[2] and considerable levels of coincidence are necessary if a behaviour first alters one way as the intervention scheme is applied, then another, as the scheme is suspended or reversed. In some cases, where rapid learning effects are expected, the second A phase can be used as a check on progress and if rates remain favourable, then the scheme can be terminated pending later follow-up. In Fig. 4, as in most cases of its type, the aim is to see whether the controlling variables (in this case, the incidence of parental attention and over-harsh

50

Fig 4.   ABA Design: Behaviour Problems in a 7 year old Mentally Retarded Child at Home.

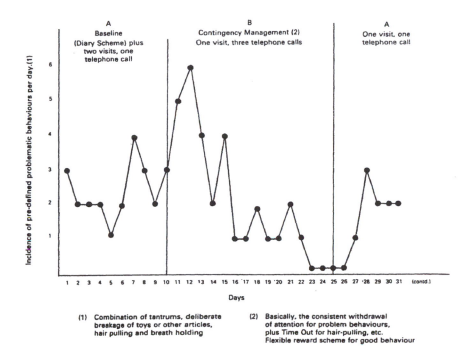

(1) Combination of tantrums, deliberate breakage of toys or other articles, hair pulling and breath holding

(2) Basically, the consistent withdrawal of attention for problem behaviours, plus Time Out for hair-pulling, etc. Flexible reward scheme for good behaviour

disciplinary practices) are as hypothesised. The fact that, following the typical period of testing-out, the problematic behaviours fall in the B phase (parents could not remember a day free of it in the previous six months), and then increase as the scheme is halted, is strong evidence in favour of this proposition. In this case a further B phase (contingency management) was instituted, to very good effect.

B.A.B. Intervention First Designs

In certain cases it is inadvisable to wait before attempting to make changes and it is perfectly possible to intervene and monitor at the same time; suspend the scheme once it appears to be producing clear effects, and then restart it again. Such designs suit operant behavioural techniques or forms of environmental manipulation. In Fig. 5 the 'urgency' in the case stems from the fact that the child subject was beginning to attract quasi-psychiatric descriptions such as 'withdrawn'. In fact he was a shy, rather under-socialised West Indian boy in a predominantly white nursery school. With the co-operation of two junior members of staff his behaviour was gently shaped away from tearful isolation towards co-operative play.

Fig 5.   Withdrawn behaviour in a four year old nursery school child.

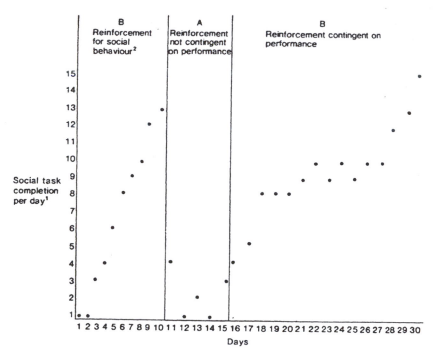

¹ Predefined tasks (behaviour shaping, ranging from showing interest in play of others, to solitary play nearby, to participatory play).
² Approval plus sweets (given by nursery staff).

(Source: Sheldon [17])

A.B.A.B. Designs

The most satisfactory design from a case-research point of view poses the greatest practical and ethical difficulties. In this approach a 'therapeutic' influence is first compared to a baseline measure of key indicators, withdrawn or deliberately reversed, and then reintroduced. Fig. 6 is an example featuring an attempt to reduce the overstimulation at the hands of her parents of a young woman suffering from schizophrenia. Their habit was to enquire into, discuss and attempt to refute her delusional preoccupations regarding electronic and other forms of surveillance. The family were advised to ignore delusional references, but to respond encouragingly to other patterns of conversation. This study is simply one part of the attempt to help this client and is concerned with the management of a problem which family members found very difficult to cope with and which, it was hypothesised, was tied up with periodic requests for her removal to hospital.

52

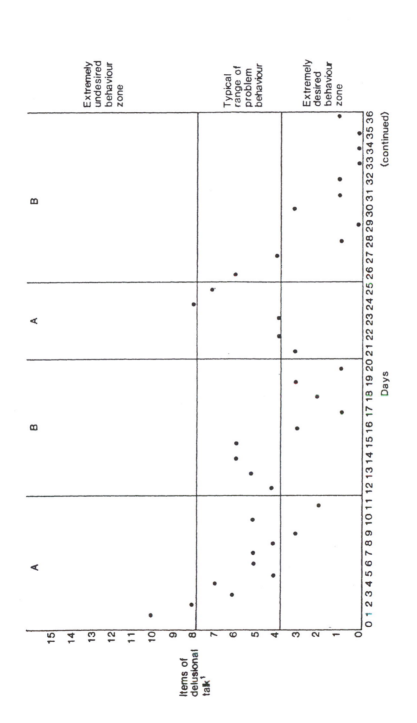

Fig 6. Contingency management scheme for reducing delusional talk in twenty four year old psychiatric out-patient.

[1] Operationally defined with relatives.

(Source: Sheldon [17])

Fig 7. Multiple baseline design: Disciplining problems in a single parent family.

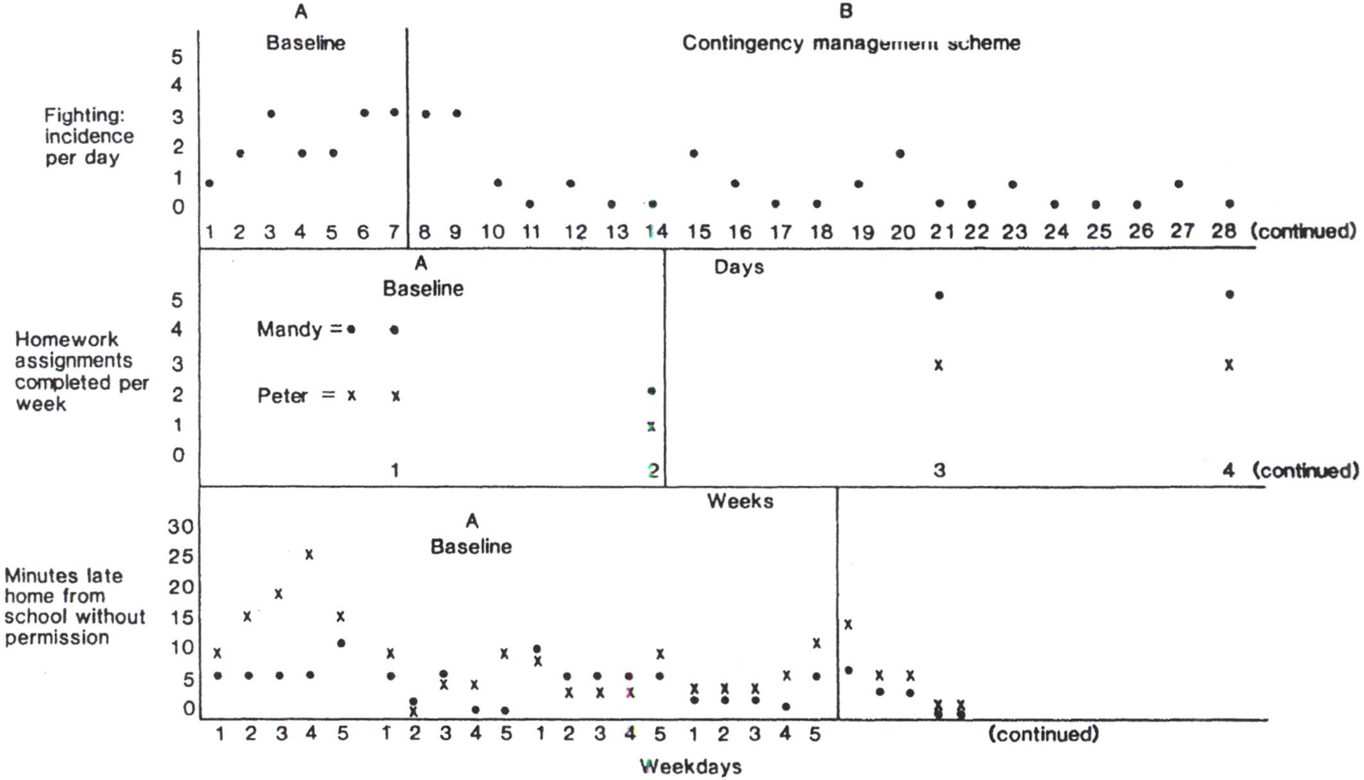

[1] Programme equals: reinforcement of cooperative behaviour with star chart, sweets, models, comics, plus extra TV time and bonus outings with social worker, determined on a sliding scale. Also agreed rates for deprivation of privileges.

(Source: Sheldon [17])

54

Multiple Baselines and Baselines Across Settings Designs

Social problems rarely come in tidy single units. Often it is necessary to deal with a number of problems at once. The multiple baseline approach allows this. Problems are baselined one at a time, and the method and incidence decided upon is then applied. The point of observation here is between the B phase of problem one and the A phase of problem two, therefore it is necessary that problems are fairly discrete, and do not co-vary when work begins on the first of them. Methods are thus applied in sequence, as Fig. 7 demonstrates.

'Baselines across settings' designs may be applied where a given sequence of problematic behaviour, or problems arising from a lack of certain skills, occur in a range of substantially different circumstances. For example, it might have been possible to handle the case outlined in Fig. 1 along these lines. Disruptive behaviour of a kind also occurred at home and, had it been sufficiently similar in character, could have been used to provide a control sample as the methods described above were first applied to the school setting. If monitoring at home revealed a stable baserate of disruption, while similar behaviours in school were coming under the influence of the new contingencies, then this would add weight to the view that any behavioural changes were due to the newly introduced influences.

PROBLEMS ARISING FROM THE USE OF SINGLE CASE EXPERIMENTAL DESIGNS

I have already put forward the view that most of the problems which might defeat the application of the principles discussed in this paper, occur at the problem-definition stage. Aside from these, the following obstacles may need to be overcome:

1. It is only sensible to acknowledge that sometimes therapeutic objectives, and the goals of careful outcome-evaluation are at odds, and that some kind of compromise between rigour and relevance must be attempted. Studies exist which show that when student psychologists are evaluating clients on clinical outcome-measures they tend to hunt for snake phobics to work with and avoid multi-problem families like the plague. Needless to say, this would be particularly senseless in the case of social work. The methods must serve our interests, and not the reverse. Often this problem can be handled by using S.C.E.Ds to evaluate one part of a programme and rigorous qualitative procedures to supplement these. There exists now a continuum of evaluation procedures and we should respond accordingly [34].

2. Suspending and reversing therapeutic inputs causes some problems for social workers and I can think of cases of my own where I might have pursued these rather too enthusiastically. However, there is a powerful demonstration-effect to be had, for example when parents see that their behaviour and that of the children is closely related.

3. Strictly speaking, the changes that occur and do not occur in S.C.E.Ds can tell us nothing for sure about how to handle other cases that appear to be similar. This is the issue of representativeness, or external validity. In practice human beings do tend to generalise from specific situations to a range of apparently similar circumstances, but our feelings about the applicability of certain of the methods we have tested in two or three cases must be put to the test in each successive encounter.

CONCLUSIONS

Social workers have the opportunity with these methods to have the best of both worlds – to test out the theoretical propositions they obtain from others, and to follow through on their own hunches about what might work; to use rigorous evaluation devices, and yet take full account of individual differences and idiosyncracies in their application. These experimental and quasi-experimental approaches can be used in conjunction with other, more familiar (but sadly, rarely spelled-out) qualitative methods – and in fact are better for being used in combination. Moreover, there is nothing to suggest that these approaches need be applied in an excessively 'mechanical' way, or that they are the sole preserve of behaviourists. The position is simply that few other kinds of therapists make use of them. To the extent that this is because they cannot accommodate tangible, pre-set indicators of outcome into their methods (the only pre-requisite) our suspicions should be aroused.

References

1. Powers, E. & Witmer, H. An Experiment in the Prevention of Delinquency – the Cambridge Somerville Youth Study. Columbia University Press, New York, 1951.

2. Meyer, H., Borgatta, E. & Jones, W. Girls at Vocational High. Russell Sage Foundation, New York, 1965.

3. Bergin, A.E. 'The Evaluation of Therapeutic Outcomes' in Bergin, A.E. & Garfield S.L. (Eds.) Handbook of Psychotherapy and Behaviour Change. Wiley, New York, 1971.

4. Rachman, S.J. & Wilson, G.T. The Effects of Psychological Therapy. Oxford University Press, 1980 (2nd edition).

56

5. Fischer, J. The Effectiveness of Social Casework. Charles C. Thomas, Springfield, Illinois, 1976.

6. Mayer, J.E. & Timms, N. The Client Speaks. Routledge & Kegan Paul, London, 1970.

7. Rees, S.J. 'No More than Contact: An Outcome of Social Work' British Journal of Social Work. 4, 3, 1974, 255-79.

8. Rees, S.J. & Wallace, A. Verdicts on Social Work. Edward Arnold, London, 1982.

9. Maluccio, A.N. Learning from Clients. Free Press, London, 1979.

10. Gregory, R. Eye and Brain. Weidenfeld & Nicolson, London, 1979.

11. Erikson, E. Childhood and Society. Pelican, 1967.

12. Hollis, F. Casework: A Psychosocial Therapy. Random House, New York, 1968.

13. Satir, V. Conjoint Family Therapy. Science and Behaviour Books, New York, 1964.

14. Selvini-Palazzoli, M., Bascolo, L., Cechin, G & Prata, G. Paradox and Counter Paradox. Aronson, New York, 1978.

15. Corrigan, P. & Leonard, P. Social Work Practice under Capitalism. Macmillan, London, 1978.

16. Sheldon, B. 'Theory and Practice in Social Work: A Re-examination of a Tenuous Relationship' British Journal of Social Work. 8, 11, 1978.

17. Sheldon B. Behaviour Modification: Theory, Practice and Philosophy. Tavistock, London, 1982.

18. Heine, R. 'A Comparison of Patients' Reports on Psychotherapeutic Experience with Psychoanalytic, Non-Directive and Adlerian Therapists' American Journal of Psychotherapy. 7, 1953.

19. Bandura, A. Principles of Behaviour Modification. Holt Rinehart, New York, 1969.

20. Shapiro, M.B. & Ravenette, A.T. 'A Preliminary Experiment on Paranoid Delusions' Journal of Mental Science. 105, 1959, 295-312.

21. Shapiro, M.B. 'The Single Case in Clinical-Psychological Research' Journal of General Psychology. 74, 1966, 3-23.

22. Shapiro, M. 'The Single Case in Fundamental Clinical Psychological Research' British Journal of Medical Psychology. 34.1961, 255-263.

23. Hersen, M. & Barlow, D.H. Single Case Experimental Designs. Pergamon, Oxford, 1976.

24. Chassan, J.B. Research Design in Clinical Psychology and Psychiatry. Appleton Crafts, New York, 1967.

25. Skinner, B.F. Science and Human Behaviour. Collier-Macmillan, London, 1953.

26. Oliver, J. 'The Behavioural Treatment of a Case of Obsessional House Cleaning in a Personality Disordered Client' International Journal of Behavioural Social Work. 1, 1, 1981, 39-54.

27. Bloom, M. The Paradox of Helping. Wiley, New York, 1975.

28. Fischer, J. & Gochros, H. Planned Behaviour Change. Free Press, New York, 1976.

29. Green, J.K. & Morrow, W.R. 'Precision Social Work : General Model and Illustrative Student Projects with Clients' Education for Social Work. 1972, 19-29.

30. Howe, M.W. 'Using Clients' Observations in Research' Social Work. 21, 1, 1976.

31. Man Keung Ho 'Evaluation as a Means of Treatment' Social Work. 21, 1, 1976, 24-27.

32. Jayaratne, S. 'Single Subject and Group Designs in Treatment Evaluation' Social Work Research & Abstracts. 1977, 35-42.

33. Bloom, M. & Block, S.R. 'Evaluating One's Own Effectiveness and Efficiency' Social Work. 22, 1977, 130-136.

34. Gambrill, E. & Barth, R. 'Single Case Study Desings Revisited' Social Work Research and Abstracts. 16, 3, 1980, 15-20.

35. Sheldon, B. 'The Use of Single Case Experimental Designs in the Evaluation of Social Work' British Journal of Social Work. 13, 1983, 477-500.

36. Hudson, B. 'An Inadequate Personality' Social Work Today. 6, 16, 1975.

37. Popper, K. Conjectures and Refutations. Routledge & Kegan Paul, London, 1963.

38. Sheldon, B. Evaluation-Oriented Case Recording. Scottish Office, 1984.

39. Thorpe, N. Unpublished Student Report. University of Birmingham, 1983.

40. Eysenck, H.J. 'The Effects of Psychotherapy: An Evaluation' Journal of Consulting Psychology. 16, 1952, 319-24.

41. Eysenck, H.J. The Effects of Psychotherapy, Handbook of Abnormal Psychology. Pitman Medical, London, 1960.

Part IV
Measuring the Needs of
Child Populations

[15]

WHY DO LEVELS OF HUMAN WELFARE
VARY AMONG NATIONS?

Ian Gough and Theo Thomas

This article investigates what factors explain the wide differences in human welfare among nations. Applying the theory of human need developed by Doyal and Gough, the authors construct a series of indicators of need satisfaction and use these to map contemporary national levels of welfare. They criticize past cross-national studies of welfare outcomes for using a single index of welfare, usually the Physical Quality of Life Index. A comprehensive model of national differences in need satisfaction is then developed. Seven theories are deployed and are tested against the evidence using path analysis, which permits different causal patterns to be simultaneously considered. The authors conclude that per capita incomes are only one of several factors explaining cross-national variations in need satisfaction: the degree of economic and political independence, the extent of democracy and human rights, the capacity and dispositions of the state, and relative gender equality all positively and independently affect a nation's level of welfare. Economic development alone cannot guarantee social development.

This article reports our attempt to answer a central question in comparative political economy: what are the determinants of national variations in levels of human welfare? It is well established that on balance, richer countries do better according to certain measures of human welfare than poorer ones; yet some rich nations, such as the United States, do relatively badly while some poorer ones, such as Costa Rica, do relatively well. What explains these discrepancies? Some claim that socialist states perform better than capitalist ones at any given level of economic development, whilst others argue that the communist system hinders both economic and social development. Again, is democracy or a good record in human rights conducive to, or competitive with, social welfare? With the demise of the centrally planned economies and the global dominance of capitalism, these questions do not disappear. Rather, it becomes still more urgent to understand why different capitalist systems vary so much in their impact on the lives and welfare of ordinary people. Many of the dominant international agencies now recognize that levels of welfare ("investment in human capital") can also improve economic

International Journal of Health Services, Volume 24, Number 4, Pages 715–748, 1994 performance in a virtuous circle, and for this reason, if no other, are showing a novel interest in the global level and spread of the quality of life.

Research into these questions is long-standing and has been addressed by some contributors to this journal (1, 2). What, then, do we offer that is new? Two things. First, a theory of universal need developed by Len Doyal and Ian Gough (3) that provides a justification for using human need satisfaction as a measure of human welfare, whilst avoiding the criticisms often leveled at past attempts to do this. This theory generates a set of need measures, which avoids the reliance on one crude measure (usually the Physical Quality of Life Index) typical of previous studies. Second, we attempt to go beyond simple correlation and multiple regression analysis, both of which encounter severe problems of multicollinearity, and develop a complex causal model linking our system variables and several indicators of basic and intermediate need satisfaction. The applied model appears robust and generates some interesting results. These show that level of economic development, national dependency and world position, historic paths of societal development, state capacities and dispositions, democracy and human rights, and gender equality all have significant and independent but linked effects on cross-national differences in need satisfaction.

THEORIZING HUMAN NEED

Our measures of welfare stem from the Doyal–Gough theory of human need, and we begin with an extremely brief summary of it here. Our intention is to develop a rigorous concept of human need that is both objective and universal. This is essential if human welfare is to be comparable over time and space—if we are to be able to say that this group of people has a higher objective level of welfare than that group. If the very concept of need varies between cultural groups or social formations, then such comparison is impossible. Unfortunately, a relativistic perspective on these issues is dominant today, and one of our goals is to critique that position. Figure 1 presents a pictorial summary of the five levels of the theory (3, Parts 2 and 3).

To begin with we define need as some goal that, if not achieved, will result in serious *harm* of some objective and specified kind. We equate harm with fundamental impairment in the capacity to engage in social *participation*. Whatever our goals, they must always be achieved on the basis of past, present, or future interaction with others. We build a self-conception of our own personal capacities through learning from others. *Thus objective basic needs are, at the very least, those universalizable preconditions that enable sustained participation in one's form of life.*

We identify these basic human needs as *physical health* and *autonomy*. Both can be assessed negatively by their absence. Physical health can be assessed through measures of mortality and cross-cultural measures of disability. Autonomy of agency comprises three things: mental health, cognitive skills, and

Differences in Human Welfare among Nations / 717

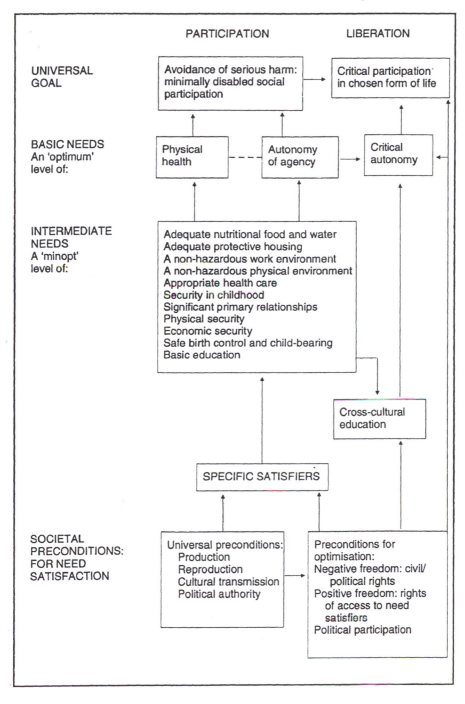

Figure 1. Outline of Doyal and Gough's theory of human need.

opportunities to engage in social participation. A deficit in autonomy of agency can thus be assessed through measures of mental ill-health, cognitive deprivation, and social barriers to participation. We argue against the relativist view that such ideas are intrinsically internal to particular cultures. In a separate argument, an "optimum" standard of physical health and autonomy is advocated with which to evaluate present achievements and alternative policies. This refers not to the abstract notion in economic theory but to "the best feasible level" within a particular culture.

Thus far we have specified the general preconditions for successful participation in any social form of life and referred only to the left-hand side of Figure 1. However, some forms of life are extremely oppressive to their members, and all existing forms harm some of their members. Successful participation in a cruel or exploitative system is hardly a recipe for objective welfare. Beyond the goal of successful participation lies the goal of *critical* participation in a social life form that is, as far as possible, of one's own choosing. Similarly, beyond autonomy of agency lies critical autonomy—the ability to situate, criticize, and if necessary challenge the rules and practices of the culture one is born into, or presently lives in. Critical autonomy entails the same levels of physical and mental health as autonomy of agency but with extra increments of cognitive skills and social opportunities—in particular, some knowledge of other cultures and political freedom. Using these concepts we can go on to specify a set of cross-cultural indicators of basic need satisfaction (3, Table 9.2).

However, basic needs can be met in numerous different ways. Common needs do not imply uniform satisfiers. There is an almost infinite variety of goods, services, activities, and relationships that, to a greater or lesser extent, meet basic needs. To deal with this problem we identify a set of "universal satisfier characteristics," referring to all those properties of goods, services, activities, and relationships that enhance physical health and autonomy in all societies and cultures. For example, provision of energy and/or protein is (or should be) a common property of foodstuffs, protection from the elements is (or should be) a common property of dwellings, and so on. These universal satisfier characteristics we refer to as "intermediate needs."

We distinguish 11 categories of intermediate need (Figure 1). Like all taxonomies these groupings are in one sense arbitrary. The crucial thing is that all the characteristics gathered under these headings are universally and positively associated with one or more of the components of physical health and autonomy, according to the best available natural and social scientific knowledge. Nine of these categories apply to all people, one refers to the specific needs of children, and one refers to the specific needs of women for safe child bearing, reflecting the one salient biological difference within the human species. Again, the level of satisfaction in each of these categories can be monitored using social indicators. The appropriate evaluative standard here is the minimum level of intermediate need satisfaction necessary to achieve optimum levels of basic need satisfaction.

At a further stage of our analysis we face the problem of subjective disagreements over the best satisfiers and economic/social programs for improving need satisfaction, and over priorities to be accorded to different groups or different needs in a situation of scarcity. This last set of problems raised by relativist critics requires that the *substantive* theory of need outlined above must be complemented by a *procedural* theory which sets out the social framework wherein such disputes can be resolved in the most rational way possible. These societal preconditions divide into procedural ones, concerned with what are commonly labeled "negative" freedoms, and material ones, concerned with "positive" freedoms (Figure 1, lower right).

Civil and political rights are necessary preconditions for critical autonomy and enable people to engage in open and rational debate and thus to improve decision-making about how to better meet needs. Alongside standard civil and political rights, the ability to participate actively in political processes is another index of procedural preconditions. Positive freedoms entail socioeconomic rights to optimum need satisfaction, as defined and operationalized above. However, because the potential gap between de facto and de jure rights is so much greater in the welfare field, the simple codification of such rights is an inadequate indicator of their satisfaction. Instead, to operationalize socioeconomic rights we utilize a cross-cultural model of production developed by Stewart (4, Chapt. 2). On this basis four material preconditions for optimum need satisfaction are identified:

1. production: the quantity, composition and quality of need satisfiers produced;
2. distribution: the distribution of these satisfiers among households and other units of consumption;
3. need transformation: the effectiveness with which these satisfiers are converted into individual needs satisfactions (which reflects in part the distribution of satisfiers within households and the status of women);
4. material reproduction: the rate of depletion/accumulation of capital goods, the natural resource base, and human resources.

Again we contend that these procedural and material preconditions can be monitored in a cross-cultural way using appropriate indicators.

Many complex issues are raised by this short summary that cannot be discussed here (3, Parts 2 and 3; 5). But the upshot, we argue, is that universal and objective human needs exist and are knowable. At any point in time there is a body of best knowledge about what they are and how best to meet them. Such knowledge is dynamic and open-ended, and specific social arrangements are required to enable such continual exploration of their nature to continue. Needs are not reducible to subjective wants or preferences best understood by sovereign individuals (though they will on many occasions overlap). Nor are they reducible to static essences best understood by planners, professionals, or experts (though some of these will also have much to contribute). Notwithstanding the raids and reconstructions of relativists, human needs provide the common metric for comparing the welfare of groups of people.

We end up with three sets of indicators: of basic needs, intermediate needs, and the societal preconditions for improving levels of welfare. These provide external and independent standards with which to evaluate the performance of very different social, economic, and political systems. They thus permit objective human welfare to be assessed independent of the cultural values of any single social grouping. Of course, in practice we must rely on whatever valid and reliable indicators are compiled by international agencies. However, the theory of need does contribute something to the exercise by forcing us to select only those that have (some degree of) cross-cultural validity. It enables us to reject some commonly used indicators and to identify the many gaps in present social reporting. Valid and comparative indicators are lacking in many areas; for example, morbidity rates and the prevalence of disability; syndromes of mental illness; the extent of child neglect, abuse, and ill treatment; the presence or absence of primary support groups; and economic insecurity. We must now consider what valid, reliable, and universally available indicators exist to map levels of basic and intermediate need satisfactions.

MEASURES OF NEED SATISFACTION

Basic Needs

To measure *survival*, we follow common practice and use life expectancy at birth. It applies to mortality throughout the lifespan, and it is more closely correlated than other measures, such as the infant mortality rate, with the "health intermediate" needs discussed below. However, survival chances simply cannot provide a valid measure of *health*, though they are undoubtedly correlated over large populations. Here, however, the available data, even in high-income countries, fall far short of what is desirable. For example, no reliable information exists on the prevalence of disabilities or of those suffering from severe pain. The only area where some light can be thrown concerns children suffering from developmental deficiencies. The World Health Organization and United Nations have information on low birth weight babies, underweight babies, and infants suffering from "wasting" and "stunting." The data we use are derived from the U.N. Development Program's 1992 Human Development Report (6) augmented by Sivard (7) and UNICEF (8). The percentage of low birth weight babies (under 2,500 grams) is a standard index of the risks facing the newborn; the indicators of wasting, stunting, and underweight refer to children of under five years, 12 to 23 months, and 24 to 59 months, respectively, and so cover different aspects of a child's early development. These indicators face problems of erratic coverage within countries, and of a bias in coverage toward the developing world where the problems are most acute. They exhibit a high degree of multicollinearity, except for the incidence of wasting, and little can be gained from using the indicators individually. After experimenting with Borda rankings we decided to use low birth weight as a proxy for all these indicators of child health, on the grounds of its greater coverage and reliability.

When we turn to the other basic need of *autonomy*, we encounter more intractable methodological and measurement problems. Ideally we require, as argued earlier, measures of mental disorder, cognitive deprivation, and lack of opportunities for participation in socially significant activities. In practice, the development of valid and reliable social indicators is sparse in even the most socially aware and resource-rich nations; for most of the world there is virtually nothing. The only exceptions are UNESCO indicators of adult literacy, also broken down by sex. Our theory regards literacy as a critical indicator of cross-cultural autonomy, but notes that it taps only one aspect of one component of autonomy of agency (not to speak of critical autonomy). International data on adult literacy are based on UNESCO sources and definitions: the percentage of those aged 15 years and above who can, with understanding, both read and write a short simple statement on their everyday life. These data are augmented with the U.N. Development Program's own estimates contained in the 1992 Human Development Report (6, Table 1).

Intermediate Needs

It is clear that reliable indicators tapping the 11 groups of intermediate needs shown in Figure 1 are simply not available for all the major nations. The ones we are left with are considered below.

For *nutritional status* we can use the Food and Agriculture Organization/WHO calculations of daily per capita calorie supply as a percentage of the "average" requirements of moderately active men and women. There are numerous problems with these figures, both conceptual and practical. It is argued that the caloric requirements of different people vary with their group characteristics and their environment; hence using an average requirement does not accurately measure the welfare, or "functionings" to use Sen's (9) terminology, generated by the food (3, pp. 194–195). The FAO's data mainly derive from estimates of food production, imports, storage losses, and wastage, and cannot readily be used to identify areas or population groups in special need, except very roughly (10). Nonetheless, we must perforce use such data—for 1988 (11).

Access to *safe water* and *sanitation* is regularly calculated by WHO on the basis of national survey statistics. "Access" is defined differently for urban areas (a source of water or sanitation within approximately 200 meters) and rural areas (a reasonable daily time spent in fetching and carrying water so that alternative economic activities are not seriously inhibited). "Safe" is defined to include standardized water purity tests and sanitary means of excreta and waste disposal including latrines, composting, and sanitary wells (12). Interpreting access rights, ownership, and distribution entitlements to water and sanitation is complicated, but most social scientists find both measures reliable enough (13, p. 5). These indicators can also be regarded as measuring one aspect of the intermediate need for safe housing.

The next intermediate need for which cross-national data are reasonably abundant is *health care services*, though this area too is fraught with conceptual and methodological problems discussed elsewhere. WHO estimates of the ratios of population to doctors, nurses, and hospital beds have been extensively criticized for their implicit bias toward urban and middle-income groups and for ignoring distribution and efficiency concerns, especially in many less developed countries (10). A second indicator constructed by UNICEF defines "access to health services" as the percentage of the population that can reach appropriate local health services by local means of transport in less than one hour. It is open to wide variation in interpretation. Better than measures of medical inputs are direct measures of health care utilization, such as the numbers immunized against specific diseases. WHO calculates average vaccination coverage for children under 1 year of age for the four antigens used in the Universal Child Immunization Program (6). Its point-of-delivery recording makes it a more reliable statistic than those services that are assessed pre- or post-administration and require more qualitative elements of perception and recall. Faced with such a variety of indicators of access to health services each of which taps something different, we calculate a composite indicator using an equally weighted Borda ranking of population per doctor, the percentage of births attended by trained personnel, and the proportion immunized. A Borda ranking simply sums the rank scores of nations on the individual indicators and expresses the result as an aggregate score (5, p. 8).

One aspect of *economic security* can be crudely approximated by using the U.N.'s calculation of the numbers of people in absolute poverty. This is defined as the percentage of the population who live on an income below a recognized income poverty line below which minimum nutritional and essential nonfood requirements are not met. These figures are calculated by the World Bank and are taken from the U.N. Development Program (6). The numerous problems with "poverty lines" are well known and are discussed at length in the World Bank's 1990 Report (14; see also 15). The most pressing problem for the purposes of this cross-national study is lack of coverage and comparability. One measure of *physical insecurity* is national homicide rates assembled by both WHO and Interpol. For our purposes, however, their usefulness is limited due to poor coverage and a bias toward developed nations. Another relevant indicator is the incidence of war and war-related deaths throughout the world: Sivard (7) calculates total military and civilian deaths through war and its related causes for the period 1945–1989.

Turning to *education*, there is a relative wealth of international data compiled by UNESCO. The problems confronting the use of this material are similar to those discussed for literacy rates (16). We shall use the following. To tap the total stock of formal educational experience of a population, we use the mean years of schooling of adults aged 25 and over. This has the problem that it says nothing about the quality and appropriateness of the education received. It has been used because of its superior coverage (all 128 countries in our survey) and because it is separately available for men and women. Second, to tap the flow of children receiving formal education we include the percentage of the population who have successfully completed primary education level (6). Completion rates are superior to enrolment rates in that they take account of pupil drop-out. Primary education is more appropriate than secondary and tertiary levels, which frequently monitor access to an elitist and technologically inappropriate level of functional education (8). Completed primary education taps opportunities to acquire basic functional skills and as such the platform on which an extended basic and critical autonomy can be built.

Our last intermediate need, for *safe birth control and child-rearing*, can draw on some regularly assembled U.N. data. The first can use indicators of contraceptive use, though these may underestimate total contraceptive practice and will not take into account the relative safety of the techniques available. The second can draw on indicators of births attended by recognized health personnel and, as an indirect measure, the maternal mortality rate. The data are derived from the U.N. Development Program's 1992 Human Development Report (6).

In Table 1 we summarize the range of human need indicators that we consider reasonably valid and reliable and for which sufficient data exist.

CHARTING HUMAN WELFARE

The indicators listed in Table 1, together with other measures of societal preconditions discussed below, can be used to audit the welfare performance of countries. We have space here only to summarize Doyal and Gough's audit of global needs in the mid-1980s (3, pp. 269–272, 289–290).

Low-income Countries, Including China and India

Setting aside China and India for the moment, we find that levels of need satisfaction are lowest in the low-income countries in every domain of substantive need satisfaction for which we have records. Moreover, procedural and material preconditions for improved need satisfaction are extremely underdeveloped. Women in particular are most disadvantaged in the poorest countries, though there are some significant differences between nations. On all counts the blocks to human flourishing are daunting in the poorest sector of the third world. Yet the much better record of countries such as Sri Lanka (at least until recent years) upholds the view of those who argue that the relationship between need satisfaction and income per head is certainly not simple or linear. It is also logically

724 / Gough and Thomas

Table 1

Human need indicators

Basic needs		
Survival	LIFEXP	Life expectancy at birth
Health	MATMORT	Maternal mortality rate, per 100,000 live births
	LOWBWT	Low birth weight babies (%)
Cognitive skills	LIT	Adult (15+) literacy rate
	FEMLIT	Female adult literacy rate
Intermediate needs		
Nutrition	CAL	Average daily calorie supply as percent of requirements
Housing	WATER	Population with access to safe water (%)
	SAN	Population with access to sanitation (%)
Health care and health services	HLTHSERV	Borda ranking of POPDOC, IMMUN, BIRTHAT
	POPDOC	Population per doctor
	IMMUN	One year olds immunized against Universal Child Immunization Program diseases (%)
Economic security	POV	Population below poverty line (%)
Physical security	WARVIC	War and war-related deaths 1945–1989 (% 1990 population)
Education	PRIMCOM	Primary school completion rate
	YRSED	Mean years of schooling of adults
	FEMED	Mean years of schooling of women
Safe reproduction/ child-bearing	CONCEP	Use of contraception by married women (%)
	BIRTHAT	Births attended by health personnel (%)

possible that in those domains for which there is little or no information, for example child care, standards are better (relatively or absolutely) in the third world. But in the absence of hard data it would be foolish to contend that this invalidates the overwhelming import of such knowledge as we have.

China remains one of the star performers among the low-income nations in meeting basic needs, and performs relatively well in many measures of gender inequality. On the other hand, it is one of the worst abusers of human rights and other procedural needs. Though India does better in terms of access to certain universal satisfier characteristics than other poor countries, such as clean water, health services, and education, its record in other areas is equally poor. The general level of welfare among women in India is among the very worst. On the other hand, its record in upholding civil and political rights is relatively good.

Middle-income Countries

The middle-income countries exhibit a wide variation in income per head and in need satisfaction, but generally speaking, levels of need satisfaction lie between those of the West and of the low-income countries, though usually closer to the latter. Survival chances are more akin to those in the poorest countries, and in most, people are worse off than in China, though average health status may be better than mortality rates suggest. An average calorie consumption of 110 percent of requirements suggests that undernutrition is avoidable, but the still-high incidence of absolute poverty indicates that maldistribution generates malnutrition on a wide scale. Access to water and health services remains poor in most of these countries, and the housing conditions of the masses are very low—much closer to poor third world than to first world standards. Physical and economic insecurity are also rife, particularly in certain Latin American countries where human rights are in general poorly protected. Indicators of access to education and literacy are intermediate between the poorest and richest nations. Access to birth control and safe child-bearing is often little better than in the low-income nations. However, women's access to education and literacy, and average autonomy levels according to some other indicators, are better on average (except in the Middle East). Our data suggest that some countries in this group achieve high levels of overall welfare, for example Costa Rica.

State Socialist Countries

Despite their lower per capita income, the state socialist countries appear to achieve levels of substantive need satisfaction comparable to those of the first world for nutrition, physical and economic security, and most notably, education opportunities. They do less well, however, in terms of physical health, and notably less well in providing adequate housing. Women enjoy good educational access, but suffer from the same deprivations as Western women plus possibly others besides, such as heavier dual burden on their time. For the period up to the mid-1980s, of course, respect for civil and political rights was minimal and achievements in all other aspects of our social preconditions were equally poor.

The Advanced Capitalist World

Levels of substantive need satisfaction are highest in the West in almost all domains for which we have data, and it is here where material/procedural preconditions for improved performance in meeting needs are most securely in place. Many (but not all) aspects of women's welfare for which we have information are highest in these nations, despite the entrenched gender-based disadvantages that persist. However, the advanced capitalist world (and the state socialist bloc to a lesser extent) lays claim to a disparate share of planetary resources, in a fashion that is neither generalizable over space nor sustainable through time. In this sense its performance in the domain of material reproduction is inferior.

Despite their high average scores, there are notable differences in objective well-being among advanced capitalist countries. For example, the United States

726 / Gough and Thomas

exhibits low scores for many domains, Sweden very high scores, and the United Kingdom often lies somewhere in between. The United States records high levels in some domains of welfare: notably, housing, opportunities for higher education, and female participation in education and paid employment. However, levels of substantive need satisfaction are among the lowest across a wide range of other needs, including health, access to health services, income security, and physical security. In some domains standards are at or below those found in middle-income countries. For example, a black child born in Washington, D.C., has less chance of surviving to her or his first birthday than one born in Kingston, Jamaica, and physical insecurity as measured by the risk of homicide is one of the highest in the world. Hunger and malnutrition, poverty and homelessness are also spreading. Moreover, the United States exhibits relatively low standards of procedural need satisfaction (respect for human rights, economic equality, and political participation) and is the second most wasteful nation in terms of energy consumption. Its record in meeting women's needs is more mixed, though women are more at risk from poverty and more excluded from political participation, than in most other Western countries. Its failure is therefore rather comprehensive and, given its economic wealth, initially puzzling. Sweden provides a polar contrast—indeed it emerges as the global leader, the country most closely approximating optimum need satisfaction at the present time.

Since this audit of the mid-1980s was prepared much has changed. Since 1989 a catastrophic decline in need satisfaction has occurred in Eastern Europe, especially Russia. To cite just one figure: mortality in Russia has risen by 33 percent, taking two years off the life expectancy of middle-aged men and one year off that of middle-aged women. The result, according to a UNICEF report, is a "demographic catastrophe," a process of "social disintegration." Unfortunately, our research is unaffected by these developments since it refers to the situation in 1989–1990.

CROSS-NATIONAL RESEARCH ON
WELFARE OUTCOMES

How do previous studies explain these findings? Certain common features emerge. For example, all researchers find a strong link between per capita gross national product (GNP) and various measures of welfare or human development: according to Stewart (4, p. 62) about 70 percent of national variation in life expectancy can be explained by differences in average per capita incomes. Despite this, it is also widely observed that nations at similar stages of economic development differ widely in their basic need achievements. The U.N. Development Program (6, p. 14) claims that its Human Development Index ranks countries very differently than does GNP per capita. The central issue is, then, what other factors account for these discrepancies from level of development? Cross-national analysis to answer this question has mushroomed over the last 15 years, and this article does not pretend to survey or summarize that research. Rather, we consider the ways that need satisfaction is treated in such research and summarize the important analysis by Moon (17), which can act as a benchmark of cross-national research to date.

The dependent variable(s) that are used to measure need satisfaction are inevitably constrained by the availability of valid and reliable international data. Those commonly used include life expectancy at birth (4, 5, 18), the infant mortality rate (19–21), and the literacy rate (5). More commonly, a composite index of all three—the Physical Quality of Life Index, or PQLI—is used (15, 22, 23). This ranges each of the variables between a minimum defined by the worst national level recorded since 1950 and a maximum defined as the present "best conceivable" national level, and takes the unweighted average of all three scores. The PQLI has been criticized by Hicks and Streeten (24) and Streeten (25) on conceptual and methodological grounds. Conceptually, they argue that different components of need satisfaction contribute independently to human well-being, that these components cannot morally or logically be traded off against each other, and that they should not therefore be aggregated into a single measure. Methodologically, PQLI is rejected as redundant due to the significant correlations between it and all three of its components. Against this, defenders contend on practical grounds that an index reduces the impact of the idiosyncrasies of any of its components and that it greatly eases the burden of analysis (17, pp. 24–31).

A second composite index is the Human Development Index (HDI) developed by the U.N. Development Program since 1990. Human development is conceived as the formation of human capabilities combined with the use people make of them. The HDI proposed to measure this combines longevity, knowledge, and income. In the first, 1990 version, these are computed from life expectancy at birth; percentage adult literacy; and the log of income per head at purchasing power parties (26, pp. 91–104). The HDI has also been criticized on the grounds of redundancy (27) and because it, like PQLI, has little relevance for the developed nations that all score close to the maximum (28, p. 318). This last criticism has been moderated by the inclusion of years of schooling in the 1992 index (6), which is the one we use.

The link between our theory of need and these two indicators is mixed. We have already outlined how our theory requires three sets of indicators: basic needs, intermediate needs, and societal preconditions. Some of these are common to PQLI and HDI. It will be apparent that life expectancy and literacy find substantial support in our theory as measures of survival chances and cognitive autonomy, so there is some justification for using PQLI. The HDI adds to this a measure of income, which could stand as a proxy for what we would call the material preconditions for need satisfaction. Nevertheless, the gap between what our theory requires and what these two indices provide is immense.

Cross-national research on variations in human welfare, mainly using PQLI, is extensive. Quite frequently, however, each study tests a few, discrete explanatory factors, as when Cereseto and Waitzkin (1) examine the effect of just two: level of economic development and political-economic system. Such partial analysis is not cumulative—it does not simultaneously test for other variables found to be significant elsewhere (2). In terms of method, some, such as Stewart (4), have looked at nations deviating from the value of PQLI predicted by their income per capita. In this way "good" and "poor" performers are singled out for explanation. However, it is difficult to integrate this approach into a more general one that can consider the full range of explanations for different countries' performances.

The most substantial cross-national study, taking into account a full range of theories and hypothesized determinants of basic human need satisfaction, is that by Moon (17, 29). He undertakes a multiple regression analysis of all nations for which there are adequate data—a maximum of 120 countries—including advanced market economies and state socialist economies as well as developing nations. The method is cross-sectional and the bulk of the data refer to the "early 1970s" (though some hark back to the early 1960s). He uses only one dependent variable—PQLI.

As Moon points out, cross-sectional designs are dogged by two related problems (17, pp. 31–38). First, the dependent variable may not have fully adjusted to changes in the independent variable, casting doubt on the customary interpretation that the relationships discovered represent a long-term equilibrium condition. Second, cross-section designs cannot of themselves establish the causal direction of the relationship. However, he rehearses the argument that these problems are less salient where the theoretical foundations for ascribing causal priority are strong, and/or where the temporal priority of variables is clear and the adjustment times are sufficient to take into account their effects. To cope with multicollinearity among independent variables he develops a hierarchical design in which variables are introduced in an explicit order. Cross-sectional analysis, he concludes, is most appropriate where both exogenous and dependent variables are relatively stable and slow-changing and where confidence in the causal relationships is high (17, pp. 264–265).

Running a sequence of regressions and then a stepwise regression of the full model, Moon arrives at the following conclusions on the determinants of national differences in the level of PQLI:

1. The most powerful predictor is level of economic development, as measured by the inverse of the share of labor in agriculture rather than per capita GNP.

2. Economic structure is important: development centered around the factory and, surprisingly, plantation agriculture produces more effective need satisfaction levels than development centered around mining or subsistence agriculture.

3. State socialist nations exhibit higher PQLI scores than capitalist nations, but only at lower levels of development.

4. State capacities, measured by central government expenditure as proportion of gross domestic product (GDP) and in other ways, are of no importance or have a negative impact. On the other hand, military personnel levels have a positive

effect on PQLI (though when these are included military expenditures have a negative effect).

5. Some sociopolitical factors are significant. Democracy, as measured by Bollen's (30) index, is a significant predictor of enhanced need satisfaction, but so is (more weakly) an interactive measure of military regimes. Blondel's (31) classification of regime ideology is not significant (leftwards or rightwards) in isolation. Yet taking state capacities and sociopolitical factors together as influences on state dispositions, Moon finds a significant interlinkage: "At higher levels of state expenditures, the left achieves the best results and the right the worst; at very low levels the reverse is true" (17, p. 142, footnote 30; 29).

6. A nation's position in the world system is linked in ways that are rather variable and weak.

7. A variety of historical and "distal" influences are significant: PQLI is associated positively with a history of plantation agriculture, with colonization by the British, and with Buddhism. It is negatively associated with late national independence (i.e., colonization), with Islam, and with an African regional factor.

Overall, Moon's model has an adjusted R^2 of .94. The results are unusually robust over different samples of nations produced by the addition and deletion of variables where there are missing data. Thus a variety of politicoeconomic and historical/world system factors can explain the bulk of cross-national differences in need satisfaction. Moon's study is important in the depth and range of the theories that he explores and then operationalizes. However, many of his data were 20 years out of date when published. Our first task is thus to update his analysis.

RESEARCH DESIGN

We decided broadly to replicate Moon's approach, but with three major differences. First, of course, we want to update the analysis by using data for 1990 or thereabouts. For the old Soviet Union and Eastern bloc countries, the data are prior to the economic reforms and the collapse of some of the constituent nation states. Second, the Doyal–Gough theory of human need dictates that we use a greater variety of more specific measures of need satisfaction than in previous research. Third, it also requires that we consider the interrelation between need indicators, including the possibility that some act as intermediate determinants of others, which leads us to explore alternatives to multivariate regression analysis, including path analysis. The problems of multicollinearity in global cross-national analysis of basic needs are well known and pose methodological problems that require alternative solutions.

Apart from these differences, the research design is similar to that of Moon. We adopt a quantitative, static approach, looking for associations across a large number of nations at one point in time. Two alternatives were available: a qualitative comparative historical investigation, or a quantitative time-series analysis of trends. A splendid recent example of the former is the study of the development of democracy by Rueschemeyer, Stephens, and Stephens (32). It exhibits research resources and skills beyond our capacity, though our study has sought to mix a variety of "qualitative" and "quantitative" variables to produce insight into the longer-term structural factors that affect need levels. A time-series approach has several merits, but is not appropriate or feasible for our goal because it taps many more short-term phenomena and can misrepresent longer-lasting causally lagged structures. The limitations of cross-national analysis have been touched on above but, we believe, are not a threat given the theoretical basis of this work.

Given this basic design, we have chosen to investigate all nation states in the world, rather than a selection of them or various subsets of nations. There is a case for and a tradition of investigating welfare outcomes separately within affluent nations of the "North" and the developing nations of the "South." This strategy enables more specific questions to be answered and permits different and more socially relevant indicators of welfare outcomes to be used in each country grouping. However, it directly flouts a central tenet of our theory of need that we wish to utilize: that needs are objective and universal, and that indicators of need satisfaction should be explicitly cross-cultural.

Our goal of global coverage was tempered in practice by the existence of numerous small countries and micro-states. It is a central tenet of comparative research that each nation is treated equally whatever its population—that Nepal counts for the same as China. However, on the grounds of practicality we follow a common practice and exclude all nations with a population of less than one million from our data set. All other countries are included, data permitting, including such "unusual" countries as oil-rich Middle-Eastern states with high income levels but traditionally rather poor welfare levels. This leaves us with a maximum of 128 countries, and all tables refer to this number unless otherwise stated. Our desire to secure as good a coverage as possible means that, in practice, good indicators with poor coverage are sometimes rejected in favor of less satisfactory but more available indicators. The individual measures and their sources are discussed in the next two sections.

DETERMINANTS OF NEED SATISFACTION: THEORIES AND MEASURES

There is no single accepted explanation of national differences in welfare, so there is no alternative but to consider all the major theoretical contenders in turn. We shall consider those theories that focus on the following seven factors:

- economic development
- dependency and position in the international order
- paths of development

- socioeconomic system
- state capacities and dispositions
- democracy, human rights, and other sociopolitical factors
- women's status and gender equality

Economic Development and Income per Head

The importance of a nation's level of economic development in explaining its aggregate level of need satisfaction is widely accepted, whether explicitly as in the modernization and "stages of growth" theories or implicitly as a welfare-facilitator. It is also widespread in accounts of the development of welfare states and some welfare outcomes within the developed world. For example, industrialization and modernization theories regard the general imperatives of economic growth and the varying availability of resources as key determinants of national social policies. Some forms of structural Marxist theories echo this, but emphasize the general imperatives of capital accumulation (33).

We experiment with several measures and in the end favor GNP per capita at purchasing power parity. The measure of national differences in per capita GNP at current exchange rates suffers from well-known conceptual problems. Official exchange rates may be very different from hypothetical market-clearing rates that would prevail in the absence of restrictions, and abrupt devaluations or revelations shift countries' relative incomes in an unrealistic way. GNP at purchasing power parity is a better indicator of the quantum of productive resources in a society, which is the focus of our attention. We use the log of the World Bank's ICP estimates for 1990 (34), which is highly correlated with both PQLI (.86) and HDI (.93).

Of course, income per head ignores the distribution of that income, which will also have an impact on aggregate need satisfaction. To combine the two we propose a new index: the "real income of the worst off" (3, p. 238). The U.N. Development Program now calculates the absolute GNP per capita of the lowest 40 percent of households in a country, which can serve as a reasonable approximation of this (6, Table 17). Interestingly, this measure exhibits the highest correlation with PQLI (.86) and HDI (.93) of any of our system variables. It suggests that combining the efficiency and equity of an economy in this way provides a most powerful predictor of welfare outcomes. Unfortunately there are data for only 45 countries at present, so we are not able to pursue this line of inquiry here.

Dependency and Position in the International Order

In opposition to modernization theories of economic development stand the dependency school (35, 36) and world systems theories (37, 38). These claim that the interpenetration of poor countries by external actors, whether states or powerful private organizations, generates paths of development that are different in kind from those followed by the advanced Western economies (33, p. 785 ff). Generally speaking, it is supposed that welfare is lower (than other factors would warrant) in peripheral nations, is higher in the core nations, and is indeterminate in the semiperiphery. The mechanisms by which these dependency relations operate can vary and are disputed. They can embrace economic dependency—such as reliance on single commodities, inward investment by multinationals, or trade dependency—geopolitical dependency, and combinations of the two. Consequently, many different measures have been developed, including trade reliance, export revenue fluctuations, primary product specialization, and penetration by multinational companies. For example, London and Williams (39) use a measure of investment dependency, or the penetration of a nation's economy by multinational corporations around 1967, and find that this is associated with lower PQLI levels, controlling for level of economic development. Moon subjects many of these measures to a typically searching theoretical and empirical analysis. When these factors are entered into his comprehensive model he finds that none of them are powerfully related to welfare outcomes. He concludes: "While the periphery is not a category of analysis in which we have a great deal of confidence, it does appear to serve us reasonably well as a general summary for a series of attributes that are neither strongly related to one another nor powerfully associated with basic needs levels" (17, p. 209).

In the light of this we do not enter any of these single-factor variables into our model. Instead we follow others and use Snyder and Kick's (40) synthetic index of the structural position of nations in the world economy for the 1960s. This revealed the highest correlation coefficient (.68) with PQLI and HDI of all the measures we tried.

Paths of Development

Both conventional and dependency theories of development imply a temporal aspect that we now need to consider more explicitly. Present geographical differences between world regions cannot be logically separated from different historical paths of development. This insight is a particular feature of world systems theories (17, Part IV; 37, 38). The institutional residues of historical experience and their importance in explaining welfare outcomes is also a feature of state-centered theories considered below. One distinction in the modern world to which all such theories accord importance is that between colonized and colonizing nations. Hypothesizing that nations with a more recent colonial experience should manifest a lower PQLI than other factors would warrant, Moon distinguishes between countries that were and were not independent by 1945; we also use this index, which is significantly associated with PQLI (.63) and HDI (.68).

More recently, Therborn (41) has developed a novel perspective on "paths to modernity" which, although arising from within the sociological problematic of modernity, provides an alternative way of conceptualizing the place of different states within the world system. He distinguishes four routes to modernity: (*a*) the route pioneered in Europe, including, he claims, Russia and East-Central and South-Eastern Europe; (*b*) the settler societies of the New Worlds, including both North and South America; (*c*) the colonial zone of Africa and much of Asia; and (*d*) externally induced modernization, where nominally independent states, in response to external pressures, undertake autonomous strategies of development (including such nations as Egypt, Turkey, Japan, and China). When we allocate each country to one of these four paths, we find that countries in the first two paths have significantly higher levels of welfare, those in the third path have lower levels, and there is no significant association for those in the fourth.

Socioeconomic System

The respective contribution of capitalism and socialism to human welfare is the subject of an important debate with a long lineage (42). The claims of free-market capitalism are that its efficiency and dynamism create need satisfiers in large quantity and of high quality, sufficient numbers of which trickle down to improve the need satisfactions of the worst-off. Moreover, the historically observed development of democratic institutions alongside capitalism ensures that need-claims can be voiced and public policies modified. State socialism, on the other hand, is credited with an ability to collectively identify and target the meeting of basic needs as the fundamental goal of national policy, and to plan to produce appropriate need satisfiers and to distribute them equitably. There are also powerful arguments against both systems. Unregulated capitalism suffers from well-established market failures, maldistribution, and the threat to democracy posed by economic inequality and the pursuit of individual gain. State socialism suffers from a lack of democratic representation that results in a "dictatorship over needs" as well as profound information and incentive problems that result in shortages of even basic need satisfiers.

Some studies have tried to test these predictions. Cereseto and Waitzkin (1) find that at any particular stage of development, socialist systems yield higher levels of PQLI than capitalist ones, but they do not take other explanatory variables into account (2). Moon (17, Chapt. 4) concludes that the 11 countries he identifies as socialist do have higher PQLI levels than would be predicted by GNP per capita, for example China and Cuba. However, when all other variables are included, the association remains significant only for nations at lower levels of development.

Others have claimed that both systems are fundamentally flawed as socio-economic frameworks within which to improve need satisfaction, and have argued the merits of various forms of mixed economic system. Students of corporatism in Europe and elsewhere have claimed that this represents another variant of modern

734 / Gough and Thomas

capitalism, and that a third coordination mechanism should be recognized: negotiation between interest groups within a public framework. Gough (42) has generalized this to generate three variants of contemporary capitalism: neoliberal, statist, and corporatist. He hypothesizes that corporatist capitalism will do relatively well in meeting human needs and neoliberal relatively poorly, and that statist capitalism is indeterminate in the absence of information about the goals that state economic and social intervention will pursue. Thus a variety of theories exist predicting different linkages between economic system and human welfare.

Unfortunately, there is no widely acceptable index available that identifies such differences in socioeconomic systems. We have had recourse to Gastil's (43) categorization of countries into five groups: capitalist, state capitalist, mixed capitalist, mixed socialist, and state socialist. However, the derivation of his categories is unclear and an inspection suggests that not all of his allocations are plausible; for example, Germany is characterized as a "pure" capitalist system. None of the systems has any significant association with good or poor levels of PQLI or HDI, except for (weakly) the mixed capitalist group. This finding supports the mixed economy theories and questions the role of both pure capitalism and pure state socialism as frameworks for human welfare. But to get at more subtle measures of differences in economic systems we must consider the role of the state.

State Capacities and Dispositions

A broad range of neoinstitutional theories regard the capacities and dispositions of different states as crucial in determining economic and social outcomes (29; 44, Chapt. 3). For our purposes, two features are of major importance (45). The first comprises the resources available to a state to pursue its goals. Skocpol (46, p. 17) persuasively argues that "a state's means of raising and deploying financial resources tell us more than could any other single factor about its existing (and immediate potential) capacities to create or strengthen state organisations, to employ personnel, to coopt political support, to subsidise economic enterprises and to fund social systems." An effective tax state is the most general precondition for an effective welfare state, and when we calculate the share of taxation in GDP we find a significant association with both PQLI (.56) and HDI (.52).

Government expenditures, on the other hand, are better regarded as indicators of state dispositions. The most useful here is the "social priority ratio" constructed by the U.N. Development Program (29, Chapt. 3), which calculates the share of social expenditure allocated to priority concerns, such as primary education and health care. Unfortunately, this is only available for a minority of nations at present. Using instead the share of total health and social expenditure in GNP (7), we find it to be significantly correlated with PQLI (.58) and HDI (.59).

Unlike Moon, we do not find military expenditures to be significantly associated either way.

Democracy, Rights, and Other Sociopolitical Factors

Two sociopolitical factors are frequently regarded as significant predictors of welfare outcomes. The first is the existence and extent of democracy in a country. What Hewitt (47) calls the "simple democratic hypothesis" contends that the degree and extent of democratic institutions generates egalitarian policies, since the equal distribution of the vote countervails the unequal distribution of property. However, this can be criticized on the grounds that it does not predict what particular political coalitions will be formed to press what interests. More general is the argument that extensive civil and political liberties and the broadest range of democratic decision-making in a society are a necessary prerequisite for rational programs to improve collective human welfare (3, Chapt. 11).

To take these theories into account requires indices of both civil and political rights. The former have been expertly and comprehensively monitored by Humana (48) who has devised an index based on various international Human Rights treaties, which is now recognized by the latest U.N. Development Program Report. The cross-national operationalization of democracy has improved greatly in recent years (40) and provides us with several alternative measures, which we have subjected to scrutiny and statistical testing. Of the up-to-date indices perhaps the most sophisticated is that devised by Hadenius (50); unfortunately, however, he calculates it only for third world countries. In the end we have had recourse to Gastil's frequently cited and annually updated index of political liberties, using his 1989 index (43). It is closely correlated with PQLI (.60) and HDI (.61). The use of the 1989 index may, however, overestimate the impact of democracy on need satisfaction given the wave of democratization that swept the world in the 1980s (6, p. 28).

The second sociopolitical factor hypothesized to affect the disposition of state policy-making and thus welfare outcomes is the class balance of forces in society. This theory has both a social democratic and neo-Marxist provenance and has been advocated for both the first and third worlds. Korpi (51) and others argue that collective action in trade unions and/or left political parties enables the working class to exert leverage on both state policies and private institutions in advanced capitalist societies. They are likely to use that leverage to pursue welfare-related policies of various kinds. Moon and Dixon (29) and Evans and Stephens (30) argue that in developing nations too, relative class power is a crucial variable intermediate between democracy and socioeconomic development. There is, however, disagreement over the respective roles of the working class, agrarian classes, and the middle classes in pressing for welfare reforms. Unfortunately, despite the theoretical case for its inclusion, we know of no conceptually sound and up-to-date data on regime ideology or the class balance of forces in societies, and must therefore omit this factor from our analysis.

736 / Gough and Thomas

Gender Differences and Households

The above theories all tend to "stop at the front door" and to be gender-blind (52). They assume that the family or household is the basic unit of society and do not inquire about the distribution of income and welfare within the family, between women and men, adults and children, and between other household members. A growing body of theory and evidence has revealed the importance of intra-household power, wealth, and status for welfare outcomes. In particular, the position of women and gender inequalities are very relevant to the need transformation process identified above (4, Chapt. 5; 11, 14). This has been recognized in the 1992 U.N. Development Program report (6) in the form of a "gender sensitive HDI" that measures the gender ratios of its constituents, although it is presently available for only 33 (mainly developed) countries. After experimenting with a variety of available measures to tap gender inequalities and the status of women, we use the composite index of the "status of women" calculated for 127 of the countries by the Population Crisis Committee (53). More especially, we favor and use the separate subindex of women's social equality, which combines measures of women's political and legal equality, gender differences in economic equality, and equality in marriage and the family. This records very high rank correlation coefficients with both PQLI (.72) and HDI (.66).

Summary

We find that almost all of these factors exhibit a significant association with PQLI and HDI in the late 1980s. Only types of economic system appear not to be linked to welfare outcomes: socialist societies are not more likely to exhibit higher levels of basic need satisfaction than capitalist ones, and only the mixed capitalist systems show any significant positive correlation. Of the remaining system variables we attach especial importance to those listed in Table 2. These constitute our independent system variables in the following analysis.

CORRELATES OF BASIC AND INTERMEDIATE
NEED SATISFACTION

We are now in a position to inquire about simple associations between our more sophisticated measures of need satisfaction and our basic independent variables. Table 3 shows the correlation coefficients with five basic need indicators, and Table 4 with six intermediate need indicators.

These tables suggest the following conclusions. First, GDP per capita at purchasing power parities continues to prove a powerful predictor of cross-national variations in need satisfaction. Second, national economic dependency, as measured by the Snyder index, is significantly associated with poorer need satisfaction levels, except for nutrition where the association is not significant. Third,

Differences in Human Welfare among Nations / 737

Table 2

Independent system indicators

Economic development	GDP	GDP per head (International Comparison Program estimates)
	LOWINC	Real income of the poorest 40%
Dependency and world position	DEPEND	Dependency index (negative) (Snyder and Kick) (40)
	DEBTEX	Debt-export ratio, 1990 (negative)
Paths of development	INDEP	Independence by 1945
	PATH1	European
	PATH2	Settler societies
	PATH3	Colonial zone (negative)
Economic system	MIXEDCAP	Mixed capitalist system
State capacities/ dispositions	TAX	Tax/GDP
	SOCEXP	Social expenditure/GDP
Sociopolitical factors	RIGHTS	Human rights index
	POLLIB	Political liberties (Gastil) (43)
Status of women	GENDEQ	Women's social equality index

Table 3

Spearman correlation coefficients between basic need indicators and independent variables[a]

	LIFEXP	MATMORT	LOWBWT	LIT	FEMLIT
GDP	0.83** (N = 128)	−0.82** (N = 128)	−0.73** (N = 119)	0.75** (N = 128)	0.59** (N = 82)
DEPEND	−0.64** (N = 104)	0.62** (N = 104)	0.51** (N = 98)	−0.63** (N = 104)	−0.31 (N = 65)
INDEP	0.49** (N = 128)	−0.48** (N = 128)	−0.44** (N = 119)	0.54** (N = 128)	0.42** (N = 82)
MIXEDCAP	0.27** (N = 128)	−0.27** (N = 128)	−0.20 (N = 119)	0.2 (N = 128)	0.02 (N = 82)
TAX	0.50** (N = 103)	−0.54** (N = 103)	−0.40** (N = 98)	0.58** (N = 103)	0.27 (N = 61)
SOCEXP	0.58** (N = 117)	−0.59** (N = 117)	−0.54** (N = 111)	0.52** (N = 117)	0.19 (N = 75)
RIGHTS	0.53** (N = 127)	−0.52** (N = 127)	−0.39** (N = 119)	0.52** (N = 127)	0.42** (N = 82)
GENDEQ	0.64** (N = 95)	−0.62** (N = 95)	−0.41** (N = 91)	0.74** (N = 95)	0.54** (N = 56)

[a]N = number of countries for which data used.
One-tailed significance: * = .01; ** = .001.

738 / Gough and Thomas

Table 4

Spearman correlation coefficients between selected intermediate need indicators
and independent variables[a]

	CAL	WATER	HLTHSERV	YRSED	FEMED	CONCEP
GDP	0.74**	0.74**	0.87**	0.77**	0.76**	0.87**
	(N = 94)	(N = 126)	(N = 101)	(N = 128)	(N = 128)	(N = 101)
DEPEND	–0.22	–0.55**	–0.70**	–0.62**	–0.61**	–0.64**
	(N = 73)	(N = 103)	(N = 83)	(N = 104)	(N = 104)	(N = 82)
INDEP	0.25	0.45**	0.48**	0.55**	0.56**	0.55**
	(N = 94)	(N = 126)	(N = 101)	(N = 128)	(N = 128)	(N = 101)
MIXEDCAP	0.01	0.25*	0.27*	0.19	0.20	0.20
	(N = 94)	(N = 126)	(N = 101)	(N = 128)	(N = 128)	(N = 101)
TAX	0.22	0.46**	0.60**	0.49**	0.50**	0.54**
	(N = 72)	(N = 102)	(N = 84)	(N = 103)	(N = 103)	(N = 88)
SOCEXP	0.34**	0.53**	0.64**	0.50**	0.50**	0.51**
	(N = 85)	(N = 115)	(N = 95)	(N = 117)	(N = 117)	(N = 97)
RIGHTS	0.01	0.42**	0.50**	0.50**	0.53**	0.56**
	(N = 94)	(N = 126)	(N = 101)	(N = 127)	(N = 127)	(N = 101)
GENDEQ	0.16	0.41**	0.65**	0.67**	0.69**	0.67**
	(N = 65)	(N = 94)	(N = 78)	(N = 95)	(N = 95)	(N = 83)

[a]N = number of countries for which data used.
One-tailed significance: * = .01; ** = .001.

political independence by 1945 is positively linked to all the dimensions of welfare covered in these tables. Fourth, of the types of economic system only the mixed capitalist system reveals any association with need satisfaction, and this is erratic and weak, though positive. Fifth, the level of government taxation, a measure of state capacity, is a significant predictor of health status and of most measures of intermediate need satisfaction. However, it is not significantly associated with literacy levels or nutrition. Social expenditure, a measure of state dispositions, on the other hand, is strongly linked to all the indicators covered in these tables. Sixth, human rights (and political liberties, not shown) are strong predictors of high levels of need satisfaction in all dimensions. Seventh, gender equality is positively associated with all need indicators except for nutrition.

Of the dependent variables, the least supported by our explanatory hypotheses are literacy and nutrition. Our indicators of physical and economic insecurity— "war victims" and "poverty" (not shown in the tables)—also do not reveal significant associations. These aberrant findings warrant further investigation, but they may be due to the relatively small number of countries for which we have data on these dimensions of need satisfaction.

Differences in Human Welfare among Nations / 739

Nevertheless, there is prima facie evidence supporting six of the seven theories we are seeking to test. However, the overwhelming problem remains that the degree of intercorrelation between many of these independent variables (not to speak of the dependent variables) is so high that few firm conclusions can be drawn from simple correlation analysis.

A PATH ANALYSIS OF THE DETERMINANTS OF NEED SATISFACTION

One of the main problems with global cross-national data of this kind is multicollinearity: the high linear correlation between the regressor variables that can lead to serious problems in identifying the underlying causal linkages. For example, Gastil's political liberties index (POLLIB) is highly correlated to the status of women (WOMSTAT) and logged GDP (LOGGDP) and more loosely to most of the other explanatory variables. Indeed, almost every independent variable is closely correlated with almost every other. Many previous studies have relied on traditional methods of multivariate regression analysis to overcome this. For example, Moon develops a "hierarchical" design whereby additional regressor variables are added stage by stage using Ordinary Least Squares principles. He points out that he chose this method in order to highlight rather than deemphasize this causal complexity. We too experimented with multiple regression analysis but found that it is unable to overcome the problems associated with multicollinearity between the regressor variables. We next turned to Principal Components Analysis to attempt to group the system variables into a smaller number of related categories that could be justifiably used in a fuller regression analysis. However, we again encountered problems since only two principal components were identified between which there was a substantial overlap (54).

What we require is a method of statistical analysis that can (*a*) cope with several intercorrelated independent variables, (*b*) handle more than one dependent variable (in order to take account of the range of indicators of basic and intermediate needs), and (*c*) test simultaneously for direct and indirect causation. This last prerequisite is necessary to handle more complex transmission mechanisms from system variables to both basic and intermediate need variables, and to allow for other causal relations between our dimensions of welfare discovered in past analysis—for example, the impact of literacy on health. Path analysis meets all these conditions.

Path analysis is a method for testing a postulated linear causal model for internal consistency and can display the results in the form of path diagrams. It enables complex systems of direct and indirect causation to be tested simultaneously in a recursive system. Simple regression and interdependent system techniques are normally nonrecursive. Path analysis entails ordering a set of jointly dependent or effect variables regressed on the independent or cause variables. We use a single causal model using covariance structure analysis in the LISREL computer

740   /   Gough and Thomas

program. (For further details of the methods used together with diagnostic tests for our final model, see 54, Appendix 3.)

The first task is to specify the hypothesized causal linkages between our variables, and these are shown in Figure 2. We begin by commenting on each of the causal arrows shown, and leave discussion of the results till later. In the interests of clarity we have had to omit several system and need variables; even so, the final model is rather complex. It is divided into four stages, shown as columns in Figure 2. These are, from left to right: first, the two temporally prior system variables; second, the remaining system variables; third, four indicators of intermediate needs; and fourth, three basic need indicators. All the linkages are hypothesized to be positive, except for those from DEPEND to all other variables and those from other variables to LOWBWT. In the remainder of this section we justify the causal assumptions of this model.

A major reason for singling out Snyder and Kick's measure of economic dependency in the 1960s and Moon's measure of political independence by 1945 as causally prior is that they are temporally prior to all the other variables. However, there is also theoretical argument and statistical evidence for this. Several studies find that dependency partially determines the level of economic development, whether using a broad-based measure of economic dependency

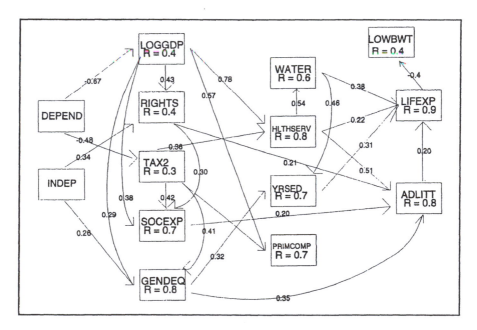

Figure 2. Path diagram of the determinants of need satisfaction, showing maximum likelihood estimates. Diagnostics: chi-square with 36 degrees of freedom = 70.95 (P = .000); goodness of fit index = 0.860; adjusted goodness of fit index = 0.590; root mean square residual = 0.053.

such as we do or a more specific measure of penetration by multinational corporations (55, 56). Bollen (57), using a modified version of the Snyder and Kick index, finds that both peripheral and semiperipheral countries are less democratic than core countries, holding level of economic development constant. Dependency also affects both our measures of state strength, according to Rubinson (58) and Delacroix and Ragin (59). There is also evidence linking economic dependency to at least one of our measures of gender equality: gender differences in labor force participation (60, 61).

Hard evidence linking political independence by 1945 to the other system variables is less systematic. Moon (17, pp. 234–239) presents an argument why former colonies have a poorer level of economic development than nations with a longer history of statehood. Therborn's (41) analysis of the effects of different paths to modernity on the development of universal suffrage clearly demonstrates the relative backwardness of the colonial zone. The association between his "path 3" and independence by 1945 is highly significant and negative. Besides its long temporal priority, we feel confident in defining political independence along with economic independence as a causally prior explanatory variable.

Next we turn to the causal relationships between the variables in the second column of Figure 2. From the remaining system variables we select five, representing per capita income, democracy and human rights (for which, taken together, we prefer the more systematic Humana index as a measure), state capacities, state dispositions, and gender equality. First, our model hypothesizes that per capita GDP affects positively all the remaining components. The impact of economic development on democracy has been the subject of numerous studies that posit different and conflicting mechanisms to explain the link (32, 62). But whatever the mechanism, the link is well established in cross-national research (57). Comparative analysis shows that economic development affects the share of state expenditure in GNP in a curvilinear way, increasing from low to middle per capita incomes and then declining (63), although the association is rather weak. If state revenues and expenditures are assumed to covary, then a similar impact of GNP per capita on state capacity as measured by share of tax revenue may be assumed. Comparative research has also consistently demonstrated that per capita income partially determines social expenditures on health, education, and social security (64, Chaps. 4, 5; 65; 66). A link between democratic pressures and state social expenditure is implied by Hewitt's (47) "simple democratic hypothesis" and is demonstrated in the case of social security programs by Cutright (67).

In the third column of Figure 2 we introduce four indicators, representing just three of our intermediate needs, for which reasonably reliable and comprehensive data exist: access to water supplies, access to health services, primary school completion rates, and mean years of schooling of adults. We assume that per capita incomes, level of political and human rights, state capacities, and state social expenditure will all act positively on all four intermediate need variables. This is a commonplace of much cross-national research and will not be separately

742 / Gough and Thomas

argued here. Gender equality is assumed to affect the education variables but not access to water and health services. More extensive rights for women are likely to enhance the schooling of girls and thus the aggregate schooling ratio and the mean years of education of women and the whole population.

In the fourth column of Figure 2 we introduce three indicators for our basic needs: low birth weight, life expectancy, and literacy. The first is used by default as the only proxy indicator of infant health available for a sufficient number of countries. These three indicators are hypothesized as lying at the end of our causal tree: they are the final variables that we wish to explain. In specifying their determinants we begin by assuming, following the Doyal–Gough theory, that they are affected by the level of satisfaction of our four intermediate need variables. However, we also assume that literacy is directly determined by the level of democracy, state social expenditure, and gender equality. Lastly, we allow for causal relations between basic needs; notably the evidence from many studies that literacy (and in particular, female literacy) affects health standards (68, Chapt. 3; 69).

RESULTS: EXPLAINING CROSS-NATIONAL VARIATIONS IN NEED SATISFACTION

Figure 2 also presents the results of our analysis.[1] Let us summarize the results of the model from right to left starting at the top of our causal hierarchy with *survival/health*, as measured by life expectancy and low birth weight. The low birth weight measure performs poorly and appears to be unrelated to other variables, except life expectancy, casting doubt upon the validity and/or the reliability of this indicator. However, intercountry variations in life expectancy are significantly affected by the extent of adult literacy, confirming findings of other studies. It also shows that three of our intermediate needs—access to safe water, utilization of health services, and mean years of schooling of adults—all significantly affect final health status as measured by the life expectancy. Overall these factors contribute to a high R^2 of 0.9.

---

[1] Again, for further details and diagnostic tests, see Gough and Thomas (54). The latter show that the model performs well on all three of the tests advocated for those using the LISREL technique: overall goodness of fit of the whole model, detailed diagnostic tests of fit, and an examination of the overall solution. These findings give us confidence that the model accurately represents and measures the causal relations between our variables. One note of caution concerns the sample size, here reduced to 70 countries, which will always tend to introduce an element of bias if, as is normally observed, the missing data are distributed nonrandomly. To test this we removed the TAX variable, which accounts for the bulk of the missing countries and is less readily available for less developed nations, but found that this made no significant difference to the results. Moreover, surprisingly little systematic bias appears to have been introduced by listwise case deletion, although developed nations obviously have better data.

Differences in Human Welfare among Nations / 743

The extent of adult *literacy* plays an important role in our model. It is influenced significantly by only one of the intermediate need indicators—our composite measure of health services. The absence of a significant linkage running from mean years of schooling to literacy rates may reflect the fact that the former only relates to 1980, or to differences in the groups included (those over 25 years and 15 years, respectively). On the other hand, this absence may be because years of schooling is really another and broader measure of educational outcomes. Literacy *is* directly and positively affected by the respect a country accords to civil and political rights, by the share of government social expenditure in GNP, and by the degree of gender equality. Here there is direct support for theories linking democracy, state welfare effort, and women's rights to levels of human welfare.

Turning to our intermediate need indicators we find that both *health services* and *primary school completion* rates are influenced by national income per head and tax shares. The extent of *adult education* is influenced by gender equality and by access to safe water, which may serve as an indicator of housing conditions. The R^2 values for these three intermediate needs are reasonably high, but the model offers no significant explanations of access to water. By this stage we find evidence linking all five of our system variables with welfare outcomes, both intermediate and final.

When we consider the system variables themselves, the most striking aspect is perhaps the relatively small part played independently by GDP per head in the direct explanation of welfare outcomes. It does however indirectly promote welfare through its influence on the rights accorded to women, human and political rights, and a state's social expenditure share in GDP. These findings replicate those of previous studies, but they elaborate on their interconnections. Lastly, the temporally prior system variables capturing national economic and political dependence/independence are both found to be significant. The former is negatively associated with contemporary income per head, as would be predicted, and with low tax shares. Political independence by 1945 is positively associated with human rights levels and gender equality, supporting the independent importance of paths of development for universal citizenship rights.

Taken as a whole, the model provides confirmation for six of the seven theories with which we began. Aggregate levels of need satisfaction are explained by a range of interdependent factors and not simply by income per head as the outcome of a unilinear process of development. Paths of politicoeconomic development, position in the world economy, state capacities and dispositions, political and civil liberties, and gender equality all play a role. The influence of these other factors is often disguised when simple regression techniques are used.

Disaggregating measures of need satisfaction, as we have done, also reveals the interconnections between different dimensions of welfare. In particular, the role of literacy is revealed as crucial in influencing health status. Human needs are not passive "requirements"; they indicate the capacities people have to act—and to act critically to change their environment. No doubt further feedback loops could and should be introduced into our model to reflect this—for example, between literacy and income per head and human rights.

CONCLUSION

This project is premised on the theory of need developed by Doyal and Gough and has two goals. The first is to evaluate, as far as is possible in a study such as this, the validity of the general model of human need depicted in Figure 1. The second aim is to test various theories advanced to explain cross-national differences in need satisfaction in the contemporary world.

The first task is most closely approximated in the final model shown in Figure 2. It tentatively confirms two of the linkages advanced by the Doyal–Gough theory. Variations in levels of intermediate need satisfaction affect variations in levels of basic need satisfaction in significant ways. The concept of universal satisfier characteristics that in all cultures and social settings contribute to final levels of welfare is supported, insofar as we can model these relations with the data at our disposal. The system variables in the second column of Figure 2 can stand as proxy measures for some of the procedural and material preconditions in the Doyal–Gough theory: production of satisfiers (LOGGDP), the prioritization of need satisfiers together with their production and distribution (SOCEXP), the need transformation process (GENDEQ), and respect for civil and political rights and political participation (RIGHTS). The model shows that all of these preconditions are significantly and positively associated with levels of satisfaction of at least one of our intermediate needs. There is support in all this for the concept of universal, cross-cultural societal preconditions for enhanced need satisfaction.

The results of the second task are also best illustrated in Figure 2. Of the seven theories we tested for, six receive support from our analysis. *We may conclude that level of economic development, (lower levels of) national economic dependency, early political independence, state capacity, democracy and human rights, and relative gender equality all contribute positively to need satisfaction and human welfare.* And since state capacity captures some of the aspects of different socioeconomic system discussed above, our model does not necessarily rule out support for this seventh theory. These effects are both direct and, in the case of income per head and human rights, indirect. Put another way, income per head and, more generally, level of economic development does not by any means explain all cross-national variation in need satisfaction. The form of economic development, the extent of political dependence, and the presence or absence of our procedural preconditions (civil, democratic, and women's rights) all play an independent causal role.

These are encouraging findings. They suggest that social rights and levels of human welfare are best guaranteed by forms of economic development guided by an effective public authority that guarantees civil and political rights to all and is thus open to pressure by effective political mobilization in civil society.

Acknowledgments — We wish to thank Diane Elson, Bruce Moon, Frances Stewart, and Robin Stryker for advice on the initial research design; staff at the United Nations Development Program for help with data sources; and Bruce Moon and Alex Hicks for helpful comments on an earlier draft of the final report.

REFERENCES

1. Cereseto, S., and Waitzkin, H. Capitalism, socialism and the physical quality of life. *Int. J. Health Serv.* 16(4): 643–658, 1986.
2. Lena, H. F., and London, B. The political and economic determinants of health outcomes. *Int. J. Health Serv.* 23(3): 585–602, 1993.
3. Doyal, L., and Gough, I. *A Theory of Human Needs.* Macmillan, New York, 1991.
4. Stewart, F. *Planning to Meet Basic Needs.* Macmillan, New York, 1985.
5. Dasgupta, P. Well-being and the extent of its realisation in poor countries. *Econ. J.,* 1990, Conference Papers, pp. 1–32.
6. United Nations Development Program. *Human Development Report, 1992.* United Nations, New York, 1992.
7. Sivard, R. *World Military and Social Expenditures 1989,* Ed. 13. World Priorities Inc., 1989.
8. UNICEF. *The State of the Worlds Children 1990.* Oxford University Press, New York, 1990.
9. Sen, A. *Resources, Values and Development.* Blackwell, Oxford, 1984.
10. United Nations Research Institute for Social Development. *Qualitative Indicators of Development.* Discussion Paper 15. Paris, 1992.
11. United Nations Development Program. *Human Development Report, 1988.* United Nations, New York, 1988.
12. World Bank. *World Bank Development Report.* Oxford University Press, New York, 1988.
13. United Nations Educational, Scientific, and Cultural Organisation. *Statistical Yearbook.* Paris, 1991.
14. World Bank. *World Bank Development Report.* Oxford University Press, New York, 1990.
15. Kanbur, R. *Poverty and the Social Dimensions of Structural Adjustment in Côte d'Ivoire.* Social Dimensions of Adjustment Working Paper 2. World Bank, Washington, D.C., 1990.
16. Spearitt, D. Evaluation of national comparisons. In *The International Encyclopaedia of Educational Evaluation,* edited by H. Walberg and G. Haertel. Pergamon Press, Oxford, 1990.
17. Moon, B. *The Political Economy of Basic Human Needs.* Cornell University Press, Ithaca, N.Y., 1991.
18. Hicks, N. Sector priorities in meeting basic needs: Some statistical evidence. *World Dev.* 10(6): 489–499, 1982.
19. Goldstein, J. Basic human needs: The plateau curve. *World Dev.* 13(5), 1985.
20. Cumper, G. *Determinants of Health Levels in Developing Countries.* Research Studies Press, Letchworth, 1984.

746 / Gough and Thomas

21. Pampel, F., and Williamson, J. B. *Age, Class, Politics and the Welfare State.* Cambridge University Press, Cambridge, England, 1989.
22. Morris, M. D. *Measuring the Condition of the World's Poor.* Pergamon Press, Oxford, 1979.
23. Rosh, R. Militarisation, human rights and basic needs in the third world. In *Human Rights: Theory and Measurement,* edited by D. Cingranelli. Macmillan, New York, 1988.
24. Hicks, N., and Streeten, P. Indicators of development: The search for a basic human needs yardstick. *World Dev.* 7(6), 1979.
25. Streeten, P. *Development Perspectives.* Macmillan, New York, 1981.
26. United Nations Development Program. *Human Development Report, 1990.* United Nations, New York, 1990.
27. McGillivray, M. The Human Development Index: Yet another redundant composite development indicator. *World Dev.* 19(10): 1461–1468, 1991.
28. Kelley, A. The Human Development Index: "Handle with care." *Pop. Dev. Rev.* 17(2): 315–324, 1991.
29. Moon, B., and Dixon, W. Politics, the state and basic human needs: A cross-national study. *Am. J. Polit. Sci.* 29(4): 661–694, 1985.
30. Bollen, K. A. Issues in the comparative measurement of political democracy. *Am. Sociol. Rev.* 45: 370–390, 1980.
31. Blondel, J. *An Introduction to Comparative Government* Praeger, New York, 1969.
32. Rueschemeyer, D., Stephens, E. H., and Stephens, J. D. *Capitalist Development and Democracy.* Polity Press, Cambridge, England, 1992.
33. Evans, P., and Stephens, J. Development and the world economy. In *Handbook of Sociology,* edited by N. J. Smelser. Sage, Beverly Hills, Calif., 1988.
34. World Bank. *World Bank Development Report.* Oxford University Press, New York, 1992.
35. Cardoso, F., and Faletto, F. *Dependency and Development in Latin America.* University of California Press, Berkeley, 1979.
36. Evans, P. *Dependent Development: The Alliance of Multi-National, State and Local Capital in Brazil.* Princeton University Press, Princeton, N.J., 1979.
37. Wallerstein, I. *The Modern World System.* Academic Press, New York, 1974.
38. Chase-Dunn, C. Interstate system and capitalist world-economy: One logic or two? *Int. Stud. Q.* 25: 19–42, 1981.
39. London, B., and Williams, B. A. National policies, international investment, and basic needs provision: A cross-national analysis. *Soc. Forces* 69: 565–584, 1990.
40. Snyder, D., and Kick, E. Structural position in the world system and economic growth 1955–70: A multiple network analysis of transnational interactions. *Am. J. Sociol.* 84(5): 1096–1126, 1979.
41. Therborn, G. The right to vote and the four world routes to/through modernity. In *State Theory and State History,* edited by R. Torstendahl. Sage, Beverly Hills, Calif., 1992.
42. Gough, I. Economic institutions and the satisfaction of human needs. *J. Econ. Issues* 28(1), 1994.
43. Gastil, R. D. *Freedom in the World: Political Rights and Civil Liberties, 1988–89.* Freedom House, Boston, 1989.
44. United Nations Development Program. *Human Development Report, 1991.* United Nations, New York, 1991.
45. Rueschemeyer, D., and Evans, P. The state and economic transformation. In *Bringing the State Back In,* edited by P. Evans et al. Cambridge University Press, Cambridge, England, 1985.

46. Skocpol, T. Bringing the state back in: Strategies of analysis in current research. In *Bringing the State Back In*, edited by P. Evans et al. Cambridge University Press, Cambridge, England, 1985.

47. Hewitt, C. The effects of political democracy and social democracy on equality in industrial societies. *Am. Sociol. Rev.* 42: 450–464, 1977.

48. Humana, C. *World Human Rights Guide*. Oxford University Press, New York, 1992 [1986].

49. Bollen, K. A. Political democracy: Conceptual and measurement traps. In *On Measuring Democracy*, edited by A. Inkeles. Transaction Publishers, London, 1991.

50. Hadenius, A. *Democracy and Development*. Cambridge University Press, Cambridge, England, 1992.

51. Korpi, W. *The Democratic Class Struggle*. Routledge & Kegan Paul, London, 1983.

52. Elson, D. Male bias in macroeconomics: The case of structural adjustment. In *Male Bias in the Development Process*, edited by D. Elson. Manchester University Press, Manchester, 1991.

53. Population Crisis Committee. *Country Ranking on the Status of Women: Poor, Powerless and Pregnant*. Population Briefing Paper No. 20. Washington, D.C., 1988.

54. Gough, I., and Thomas, T. Explanations of Cross-National Variations in Need Satisfaction. Final Report of a Research Project, Department of Social Policy and Social Work, Manchester University, 1993.

55. Chase-Dunn, C. The effects of international dependence on development and inequality: A cross-national study. *Am. Sociol. Rev.* 40: 720–738, 1975.

56. Bornschier, V., Chase-Dunn, C., and Rubinson, R. Cross-national evidence of the effects of foreign investment and aid on economic growth and inequality: A survey of findings and a reanalysis. *Am. J. Sociol.* 84(3): 651–684, 1978.

57. Bollen, K. A. World system position, dependency, and democracy: The cross-national evidence. *Am. Sociol. Rev.* 48: 468–479, 1983.

58. Rubinson, R. Dependence, government revenue, and economic growth, 1955–1970. *Stud. Comp. Int. Dev.* 12: 3–28, 1977.

59. Delacroix, J., and Ragin, C. Structural blockage: A cross-national study of economic dependency, state efficacy and underdevelopment. *Am. J. Sociol.* 86: 1311–1347, 1981.

60. Marshall, S. Development, dependence and gender inequality in the Third World. *Int. Stud. Q.* 29: 217–240, 1985.

61. Clark, R. Economic dependency and gender differences in labor force sectoral change in non-core nations. *Sociol. Q.* 33(1): 83–98, 1992.

62. Lipset, S. M. *Political Man*. Anchor Books, Garden City, N.Y., 1960.

63. Chenery, H., and Syrquin, M. *Patterns of Development 1950–1970*. Oxford University Press, New York, 1975.

64. Pryor, F. *Public Expenditures in Communist and Capitalist Nations*. Allen and Unwin, 1968.

65. Wilensky, H. *The Welfare State and Equality*. University of California Press, Berkeley, 1975.

66. Schmidt, M. Social Policy in Rich and Poor Countries: Socioeconomic Trends and Political-institutional Determinants. Paper presented to the conference on The Welfare State in Transition, Bergen, August 24–27, 1989.

67. Cutright, P. Political structure, economic development and social security programs. *Am. J. Sociol.* 70: 537–550, 1965.

748   /   Gough and Thomas

68. World Bank. *World Bank Development Report*. Oxford University Press, New York, 1991.
69. King, E., and Hill, M. A. *Women's Education in Developing Countries*. Johns Hopkins University Press, Baltimore, 1993.

Direct reprint requests to:

Professor Ian Gough
School of Social Policy
Manchester University
Manchester M13 9PL
England

[16]

AUDITING SOCIAL NEEDS

Janie Percy-Smith

The idea of social auditing has attracted considerable interest in recent years. This paper outlines a model of a social audit that has at its heart the concept of social needs as both a basis for policy formulation and a criterion for policy evaluation. The author presents the arguments in favour of regular social audits, describes the processes involved in conducting a social audit and, finally, outlines a practical example of an audit of health and welfare needs. While the auditing of social needs is not without its difficulties, the author concludes that, nevertheless, it is a vital component in the policy process.

Introduction

The aim of this paper is to propose a particular kind of social audit which has as its focus the assessment of the impact of policy on social needs and which can act as a vital counter-weight to narrower techniques of policy evaluation.

The paper begins with an account of what is meant by the terms 'social audit' and 'social needs' before looking at the following questions: Why audit policy? What are the advantages of social audits over other evaluative techniques? Having presented the case for social audits the paper goes on to consider practical issues such as what kinds of information need to be collected and how, in order to carry out a social audit; which policy areas are amenable to social auditing techniques; who should conduct the audit; how often audits should be carried out; and what the resource implications are.

The ideas contained in this paper derive from two main sources: firstly the practical work over a period of three years of the Leeds Urban Audit which, through a process of experimentation, resulted in the development of a workable model for social auditing. Secondly, I have benefited from discussions with Ian Gough about the concept of needs and much of what follows is influenced by his ideas and our collaborative attempt to operationalise both those ideas and the model of social auditing mentioned earlier in relation to health and welfare needs in a study described later in this paper.

What is a social audit?

The idea and practice of social auditing or social accounting is now quite widespread and both terms are used to refer to a range of techniques which are related but not identical. The focus of this paper is social audit not social accounting. The latter term is more usually used in connection with the private sector when companies are examined in terms of the effects of their activities on the local community. In other words there is an attempt to extend the accounting process beyond purely financial or economic issues to include such things as the environmental impact or social effects of companies' activities or their employment practices. Such social accounts have been carried out both by companies themselves concerned to improve their corporate image and by community or pressure groups wanting to demonstrate the likely effects of corporate policies (e.g. factory closures) on the locality.

This form of corporate accounting shares with social auditing a concern to demonstrate the effects of policy on people and a broadening of normal accounting methods in order to go beyond purely financial or economic costs and benefits. However the form of social audit that I wish to propose is different in that, firstly, it takes primarily public sector policy as its focus; secondly, it is argued that the social audit should become an integral part of the policy process; and thirdly, the main criterion for evaluation is the impact of policy on social need. The latter point arises from an explicit assumption that meeting social need is, or ought to be, what public policy is about. Such an assumption, however, immediately raises the question of what constitutes social need. Indeed the concept of need is frequently treated (especially by economists) as so problematic in terms of both definition and operationalisation that it should be abandoned for all practical purposes. Such arguments are well known and focus on the assumption that needs are necessarily subjective, relative and therefore not assessment, and difficult to value because they do not have a price attached to them.

However the concept of need is not necessarily any more difficult to work with than the equally slippery concepts of demand or, indeed, the three 'Es' which the Audit Commission uses as the standard by which to judge the performance of the public sector — economy, efficiency and effectiveness. But what is important to recognise is that it may be necessary to utilise a definition of need that contains a number of different dimensions. For this I draw on the work of Bradshaw (1972) who argues for a 'taxonomy' of need based, essentially, on who is doing the defining. (I have collapsed together Bradshaw's categories of 'felt' and 'expressed' needs since the latter is essentially a sub-category of the former.)

> *Normative need* — need as determined by 'experts' or professionals
> *'Felt' need* — individuals' subjective assessment of their own needs
> *'Comparative' need* — need as defined in relation to a particular standard, e.g. an agreed minimum or a local, national or international average.

These three perceptions of need are likely to be different. However this is not an argument for rejecting the whole concept of need as too difficult to work with nor for opting for one measure of need rather than another. Rather it suggests that we should try to incorporate all three dimensions of need into a composite category. How this might be achieved is discussed later.

In order to elaborate further on the concept of need we must turn to the work of Doyal and Gough (1991) who argue that well-being can be defined as 'the ability of people to participate in life'. In order for well-being to be achieved certain attributes are necessary which can be termed *basic needs*. These consist of *health* and *autonomy*. In turn, for these basic needs to be fulfilled, it is necessary to meet a set of *intermediate needs* which they list as follows:

> * Clean water/adequate nutrition
> * Adequate protective housing
> * Non-hazardous occupation
> * Appropriate health care
> * Non-hazardous physical environment
> * Secure and loving childhood
> * Significant primary relationships
> * Significant social role(s)
> * Security — physical, economic and normative
> * Appropriate education
> * Safe birth control and child-bearing

The aim of a needs audit is to find out the extent to which these intermediate needs (and the elements that go to make them up) are being fulfilled among the target population or in relation to the area of policy under review.

Why audit needs?

The question of why we should audit needs is related to a broader question of what policy evaluation ought to be about. To the extent that social auditing is, in part, about monitoring and evaluation of policy then it should be able to fulfil the same purposes as any other good technique of policy evaluation. These should include the following:

1. To assess the extent to which a set of principles or values are promoted.
2. To assess the extent to which a set of objectives has been achieved.
3. To assess the cost of achieving those objectives.
4. To examine the impact on other policies/policy areas.
5. To provide information to inform future policy development.
6. To provide a means of accountability — both financial and political.

While a number of different techniques may be quite effective in achieving the first five of these aims, social audits have the potential for achieving the accountability (especially political accountability) referred to in the final objective. However, as Stewart (1984) observes, there is a 'ladder of accountability' which includes the following rungs:

1. *Accountability for probity and legality:* to ensure that monies are used properly and in the manner intended and that legal powers are not exceeded.
2. *Process accountability:* to ensure that there is no maladministration and that 'procedural justice' is achieved.
3. *Performance accountability:* to ensure that performance reaches the required standards.
4. *Programme accountability:* to ensure that a particular agency or department or policy team is meeting its objectives.
5. *Policy accountability:* to ensure that agencies are held accountable for the totality of both activities and also non-activities, i.e. agencies should be held accountable not only for those programmes which they introduce but also for areas for which they have responsibility in which they fail to take action.
6. *Political accountability:* to ensure accountability for the overall direction of policy. Political

accountability relies crucially on information, evaluation of that information, the attribution of praise or blame, and, if necessary, the renewal or withdrawal of a mandate (Stewart, 1984, p. 14).

Clearly, the type of information that the policy evaluation process releases will determine how far up that 'ladder of accountability' it is possible to go. Social auditing has far greater potential in this regard than other techniques of policy evaluation although it may also incorporate within it techniques such as cost-benefit analysis or aspects of the 'value-for-money' audit. However, these techniques are, on their own, too narrow in their focus to provide the information necessary for either policy accountability or political accountability. Indeed, the widespread enthusiasm for social auditing can be seen, in part, as a reaction to the tendency to try to apply narrowly defined accounting criteria to the evaluation of policy. Criticisms of conventional techniques of evaluation have focused not only on their technical limitations but also on their normative bases, in particular the idea that a narrowly economic focus is objective, scientific or non-political. To choose one set of objectives (e.g. short term financial savings) as the sole criterion for determining policy success or failure is to make a very important policy, if not political, choice. And to hold agencies accountable only in terms of economy and efficiency or financial probity and legality will inevitably influence the shape, if not the substance of policy.

Social auditing not only releases information of crucial importance to policy evaluation, it also provides the basis for ongoing monitoring of policy and for policy formulation. One of the essential purposes behind auditing social needs is to measure the shortfall between needs and resources. Clearly this information is necessary, especially in an environment of scarce resources, if those resources are to be utilised most effectively.

While social auditing has clear advantages over other techniques in relation to policy evaluation and formulation it is important to recognise that what it cannot do is provide a ready-made formula for making the hard decisions in a technocratic manner (e.g. whose needs should be met and at what level?) Choices will still have to be made and priorities set. Those are necessarily *political* choices and are properly made by fully accountable politicans. However there is the possibility that they will be in a position to make better choices based on the fuller information that the social auditing process releases while at the same time, that same information provides the bench-mark against which citizens can assess politicians' achievements and failures.

Practical considerations

Ideally the social audit process should generate three kinds of information drawn from three different sources. Firstly information is required on the needs of the 'target' population in relation to a particular area of policy. Secondly, information is required on existing services and provision and also on the *form* that provision takes. And finally, information is required on best practice and alternative strategies.

Given different perceptions of needs this information should ideally be collected from three different sources. Firstly, comparative information is required to enable judgements to be made about the level of needs satisfaction or resource allocation in relation to that of other groups or geographical areas. This may entail collection, compilation and collation of existing data. Secondly, the opinions of experts and professionals should be sought and, thirdly, information needs to be obtained from the target population themselves. Thus a 'matrix' of information can be arrived at as follows:

Type of information

		Needs	Resources	Alternative strategies
Source of information	Comparative			
	Normative			
	Felt			

It is, of course, highly likely that the three different sources of information will result in different views in relation to all three types of information. For example the needs as expressed by the target population will be different to the view of needs held by the 'experts', which in turn will differ from what comparison with other groups or areas might indicate. It is therefore important to reconcile these three different perspectives with the intention of trying to achieve a degree of consensus. This might be done by producing a consultation document summarising the three different views of needs which could then be presented to, and discussed at, a public meeting or series of public meetings with the aim of arriving at a common position.

The social audit process has clear application to all areas of policy where needs already play some part in resource allocation, in particular housing, health and social services. But there seems no reason why it could not just as easily be applied to other areas of policy where need is not currently a relevant or dominant consideration, such as transport, training and local economic development.

The issue of who should be the auditors is an important consideration and there are a number of possible candidates. Firstly it could be argued that those with responsibility for provision should have a responsibility for periodically auditing their own work. The problem here is the obvious one, of whether people responsible for formulating, administering or implementing policy could be sufficiently detached to monitor and evaluate it as well. An example of this kind of audit is perhaps the work undertaken by the Policy Unit of Newcastle City Council in order to identify priority areas of the City (Newcastle City Council, 1985).

The second possibility is that those directly affected by policy (consumers, users or communities) could be enabled to undertake their own social audits. There have been a number of such audits carried out recently. In particular it is worth mentioning the work of a number of Church of England groups which have undertaken parish audits in inner city areas. However the problem here is that they frequently fall short of the mark because community or user groups may not have the necessary expertise to carry out an audit which has sufficient validity. They also run the risk of being ignored by the very policy makers whom they are seeking to influence because the latter feel threatened by what is perceived as oppositional grassroots criticism. Nevertheless social audits can be a valuable tool for groups involved in campaigns of various kinds and, perhaps more importantly, the process of carrying out a social audit can be an important

element in empowering a local community. A particularly good example of this kind of audit is the report produced by a group of local authority tenants to counter the work of government appointed consultants charged with examining the case for a Housing Action Trust (Halton Moor Tenants, 1989). Whether or not they initiate it, any social audit must provide some avenue for the articulation of the consumers', users' or target populations' views and, where possible, directly involve them in the social audit process.

A third possibility is that agencies with a responsibility for provision should also have a statutory responsibility for carrying out periodic social audits but that they should be obliged to employ approved researchers to carry out the work in accordance with a tightly drawn brief.

A fourth possibility might be that the Audit Commission widens its scope from 'value-for-money' auditing to include social auditing and carries out this work periodically.

The final practical issue that needs to be addressed is how often needs audits ought to be carried out. A full-scale needs audit of a particular area of policy is obviously not a tool that can be employed too often. Ideally one would want to be able to continuously monitor and update the information collected from the initial audit. It is therefore important to carry out a full needs audit along the lines already suggested and, in so doing, identify changes to the systems for routinely gathering information that would enable monitoring to continue between audits. If this was the case then, once the initial audit had been carried out, a further audit should not be necessary for several years (depending on the policy area).

Applying the social audit model

An example of how the model of needs auditing outlined above might be applied in practice can be found in the audit of health and welfare needs commissioned by the Institute of Public Policy Research and carried out by the Policy Research Unit (Percy-Smith and Sanderson, 1991). The aim of this study was to 'test' a model similar to that described above in relation to the health and welfare needs of people living in one inner city ward in Leeds. In line with the multi-faceted approach to needs assessment, this study incorporated a number of different elements.

Firstly all the available information about the ward — its population, mortality, morbidity, employment status, existing services — was collated and, where appropriate, these indicators were compared with both city or regional, and national figures. Secondly, information about the project was sent to statutory and voluntary agencies working in the fields of health and welfare, and community organisations in the area in order to seek their cooperation and active participation.

In the next phase of the project the researchers sought to find out the views of the local population about their own health and welfare needs. On the basis of the list of intermediate needs developed by Doyal and Gough, a questionnaire was drafted which asked questions about respondents' own state of health, factors affecting their health and well-being such as environment, housing, employment, social contacts and income, and their experience of a wide range of health and welfare services. The questionnaire was sent to a one in three sample of the adult population, derived from the electoral register. This postal survey was used to obtain extensive information from a broadly representative sample of the population. More in-depth and qualitative information on the needs of particular groups (older people, women with children and ethnic minorities) was obtained through a series of interviews. The postal survey and interview stages of the project were intended to provide information on the 'felt' needs of the population. Information on 'normative' needs, i.e. the needs of the population as perceived by 'experts' and professionals working in the area, was obtained through a series of semi-structured interviews with those responsible for delivering health, welfare and related services — GPs, health visitors, social workers, home helps, housing managers and so on.

Once this stage of the research had been completed, a draft report was written summarising the information so far collected and highlighting areas and issues on which it appeared there was little consensus between the views of the various groups. In order to try to reconcile these differing perspectives a series of public meetings were organised to which were invited representatives of statutory and voluntary agencies, user groups, community organisations and members of the public. The intention of these meetings was to increase understanding of the issues by both local people and professionals and to try to forge some kind of consensus as to what were the most important health and welfare needs in the area, how they should be met, by whom, at what level and so on. The final element of the audit was the

writing of a report that incorporated all the information from the survey, interviews and meetings which in turn provided the basis for a series of policy recommendations.

This audit (still in progress at the time of writing) fulfils two functions of importance to the policy process. In the first place it will provide information on health and welfare needs and priorities drawn from both 'experts' and those who experience need and use health and welfare services. Such information is of relevance not only to this particular area of Leeds but also to other similar areas. Secondly the audit will provide a set of publicly available data which can be used as a base-line against which to assess the effectiveness of health and welfare policy in the future. The importance of such base-line studies (and periodic follow-up audits) is only too apparent given current changes in the delivery of health and welfare services as a result of care in the community and the shift towards a more market-based health service.

Conclusions

Needs auditing using the social audit process outlined here offers the possibility of evaluating policy in terms of criteria that are broader than those offered by most other techniques. In so doing there is also the opportunity to provide information essential to policy formulation. Needs audits will, in addition, release information that will enable those responsible for public provision to be held properly accountable.

To undertake needs audits along the lines described here is not easy. A commitment of resources in terms of people and money is required which may be difficult to justify when resources are scarce. The clearest justification for such expenditure is that it will result in 'better' policy and 'better' services in the sense that policy objectives relate more closely to people's actual needs, and that those needs are met more fully and in a manner that is most acceptable to people.

A further problem is that, as with most survey-based means of collecting information, those whom one can assume are in the most need are least likely to respond. This problem can, in part, be overcome by soliciting the views of those who work with such people (GPs, social workers and home helps) or who claim to represent their interests (self-help and campaigning groups) although this is in no sense a perfect solution. However, just because it may not be possible to get perfect 'bottom-up' information is not a reason for continuing to use only 'top-down' information. Rather it is an argument for continuing to try to improve information-gathering techniques.

One final point should be made in relation to needs auditing namely that 'need does not entail rights'. In other words it does not necessarily follow that simply because a set of needs has been articulated there is any absolute duty on the part of policy makers to allocate resources in such a way that those needs are met. In an environment of scarce resources hard choices will still have to be made. However, social auditing does at least offer the prospect that rationing of public goods takes place on the basis of the fullest information about social needs rather than on the basis of demand.

REFERENCES

Ball, M. (1979)· 'Cost-benefit analysis: a critique' in Green and Nore (eds), *Issues in political economy*, Macmillan.

Bradshaw, J. (1972) 'The concept of need', *New Society*, 30 March.

Carley, M. (1980) *Rational techniques in policy analysis*, Policy Studies Institute/Heinemann.

Doyal, L. and Gough, I. (1991) *A theory of human need*, Macmillan

Garrett, J. (1986) 'Developing state audit in Britain', *Public Administration*, 64.

Geddes, M. (1988a) 'Social audits and social accounting in the UK: a review', *Regional Studies*, 22, 1, February.

Geddes, M. (1988b) *Social audits and social accounting: an annotated bibliography and commentary*, Applied Economics and Social Studies Working Paper 8/87, South Bank Polytechnic.

Green, F. and Nore, P. (eds) (1979) *Issues in political economy*, Macmillan.

Halton Moor Tenants (1989) *A Housing Action Trust: the tenants' view*, Policy Research Unit, Leeds Polytechnic.

Harte, G. (1986) 'Social accounting in the local economy', *Local Economy*, 1.

Hogwood, B. W. and Gunn, L. A. (1984) *Policy analysis for the real world*, Oxford University Press.

Hopwood, A. (1984) 'Accounting and the pursuit of efficiency' in Hopwood and Tomkins (eds), *Issues in public sector accounting*, Philip Alan.

Hopwood, A. and Burchell, S. (1980) 'Social accounting', *Public Finance and Accountancy*, September.

Hopwood, A. and Tomkins, C. (eds) (1984) *Issues in public sector accounting*, Philip Alan.

Kline, R. and Mallaber, J. (1986) *Whose value? Whose money? How to assess the real value of council services*, Birmingham TURC/LGIU.

Leeds Urban Audit (1988) *Children in Leeds*, Policy Research Unit, Leeds Polytechnic.

Leeds Urban Audit (1989) *Where does all the money go?*, Policy Research Unit, Leeds Polytechnic.

Leeds Urban Audit (1990) *Finding out about your community: how to do a social audit*, Policy Research Unit, Leeds Polytechnic.

McSweeney, Brendan (1988) 'Accounting for the Audit Commission', *The Political Quarterly*, 59, 1 March.

Metcalfe, L. and Richards, S. (1984) 'Raynerism and efficiency in government' in Hopwood and Tomkins (eds) (1984), *op. cit.*

Newcastle City Council (1985) *Newcastle upon Tyne: a social audit 1979–84*, Newcastle City Council.

Percy-Smith, J. and Sanderson, I. (1991 forthcoming) *Auditing Health and Welfare Needs*, Institute for Public Policy Research.

Stewart, J. D. (1984) 'The role of information in public accountability' in Hopwood and Tomkins (eds) (1984), *op. cit.*

Janie Percy-Smith
Senior Lecturer in Policy Studies
Policy Research Unit
Leeds Polytechnic

[17]

Mapping the Needs of Children in Need

Michael Preston-Shoot and Veronica Wigley

Michael Preston-Shoot is Professor of Social Work and Head of the Department of Applied Social Studies at the University of Luton. Veronica Wigley is an independent research project manager in Sheffield.

Correspondence to Professor Michael Preston-Shoot, Department of Applied Social Studies, University of Luton, Park Square, Luton LU1 3JU. E-mail: *michael.preston-shoot@luton.ac.uk*

Summary

This paper reviews the literature on mapping needs, with particular reference to children in need, and locates this within the legal mandate for children's services planning and New Labour's modernization policies for social care work. The paper surveys possible approaches to mapping needs and highlights the challenges involved. One research project, which collected information on children in need from a variety of different agencies within one geographical location, is then used to question mapping's contribution to the achievement of quality, co-ordination and responsiveness in modernized child care services. The paper includes a critical review of the extent to which mapping research informs practice, of the contested nature of need, and of an approach that rests on identifying those in greatest need and targeting available resources at those most at risk.

Keywords: planning, mapping, need and unmet need, research, service development.

Introduction

A duty exists under the 1989 Children Act to promote and safeguard the welfare of children in need and their families. Local authorities must also take reasonable steps to identify the extent to which there are children in need in their area, and to prevent their ill-treatment and neglect. To effectively discharge these duties requires, *inter alia*, that social services departments and other agencies with a contribution to make know who these children are, where they are located and what services might be effective in meeting their needs (Green *et al.*, 2001). Questions revolve around whether available services are reaching appropriate groups and meeting their needs, and around the degree to which indicators of need correspond with patterns of utilization of services. Put another way, identification of needs, and the nature of required services, demand accurate and reliable information (Hare *et al.*, 2002).

In its review of children's services as a backcloth to modernization proposals, the Department of Health (1998) concluded that many social services departments did not identify trends in need or demand, and were unable to adequately assess and prioritize need and target services on the most serious problems. Subsequently, planning has become a core feature of the modernization agenda.

The legal framework

The Children Act 1989 (Amendment) (Children's Services Planning) Order 1996 requires local authorities to plan children's services and to consult with a wide range of agencies, including voluntary organizations and the private sector. As in community care, plans should be strategic and collaborative, agreed between local, health and education authorities, inter-agency working documents that contain clearly agreed definitions of need, information about levels of local need, and statements of long-term aims to meet need, priorities and monitoring mechanisms. This approach reflects an acknowledgement that disadvantage arises from a multiplicity of interlocking factors, for which the response must be located in partnership work and joined-up policy making (Green *et al.*, 2001) if young people's needs are to be met. Plans should be derived from information that includes:

* the child population in an area;
* looked after children by age, reason, time;
* children on the child protection register;
* the range of placements available;
* staffing information;
* the range of support services available to families;
* young people's requirements for education and housing services;
* targets for vulnerable children against national and local objectives, with action plans set for local agencies.

The Quality Protects programme (Department of Health, 2000*a*) prioritizes, *inter alia*, the participation of young people and families in planning and service delivery, and the enhancement of information systems. Its goal is to make local planning for vulnerable children more effective and coherent. One objective here focuses on referral and assessment systems discriminating effectively between different types and levels of need. Another refers to departments having a complete picture of the numbers and circumstances of disabled children, which requires information sharing between social services departments, health authorities and education departments.

Later guidance (LASSL, 2000, 3) envisages planning services for vulnerable children as a corporate activity, with full participation of NHS bodies, to secure better services and outcomes for young people. *Vulnerable children*, defined more broadly than *children in need*, are seen as those who have acquired or encountered some difficulty that requires additional help if their life chances are to be optimized or the risk of social exclusion averted. The guidance advocates bringing together national and local objectives and targets for vulnerable children and engaging service users and other stakeholders in order to discover people's needs. The culmination should be detailed action to be taken to support vulnerable children.

Planning: the research evidence

The aim of planning is fivefold—to secure better services, to obtain better outcomes for service users, to focus business planning, to use finite resources effectively and to provide information to the public. However, what is the evidence that planning is achieving these aims?

Reports on the first children's services plans (LAC, 1996, 10) found that few contained strategic statements or action plans for the future. There were variations surrounding, for example, the inclusion of targets, needs assessment, financial information, inter-agency plans, and identified service priorities linked to resources (SSI, 1994). Consultation with minority ethnic groups had proved variable, and difficulties establishing joint registers between health authorities, education departments and social services departments had restricted their usefulness for planning in respect of disabled children (AMA, 1994). Most authorities were reported as being unclear concerning whom these plans were for (SSI, 1995). Mapping of needs was variable. Few plans adequately addressed implementation and many were considered too vague to be useful.

More recently, the SSI (1999) found that the process of planning and review, underpinning children's services plans, was not an effective driver of real change in outcomes for vulnerable children. This may, in part, be the result of too many plans, with insufficient coherence between them. There is no single, unified plan for young people and it is doubtful whether planning processes are now better co-ordinated or more coherent. However, social services authorities had significant gaps in information and were failing to involve other agencies fully in setting up children's services plans. None of the authorities surveyed had identified their children in need population and unmet need was rarely analysed systematically.

Similarly, Little (1999) found that most agencies did not understand the pattern of need and were therefore struggling to quantify the volume of services required and the extent to which provision overlapped. Janzon and Sinclair (2002) criticized local authorities for wasting opportunities to use information sources already available to underpin a more evidence-based approach to planning children's services. Huber (1999) reported that joint reviews had concluded that social services departments held only a patchy understanding of the demand for services. Their strategic planning when working with other agencies had been weak. There had been a lack of planning between social services departments and voluntary organizations, which was attributed to cash-constrained local authorities cutting back on funds for information-technology systems, strategic management and financial analysis, in order to protect front line services. Hare and colleagues (2002) found that quality protect plans were weak on references to services for children from minority ethnic groups.

These issues suggest the presence of other obstacles, particularly variable record keeping, concerns about confidentiality, and territorial boundary guarding by health and welfare organizations. Guidance (LASSL, 2000, 3) which proposes co-ordinated planning for vulnerable children to jointly address levels of need, to articulate shared objectives and to agree targets therefore misses the mark, since it does not explicitly challenge familiar blocks to inter-agency work.

In summary, research findings about local authority planning processes and needs assessments suggest that plans vary in quality and are often not strategic documents. There are gaps in information, for example population surveys on unmet need, whilst user and community consultation are rare. Social Services Departments are struggling to involve other agencies and sectors, whilst the absence of clear statements of roles, accountability and reporting lines results in inadequate commitment from partner agencies.

Methods of mapping

Service planning requires good information about individuals and whole populations (Huber, 1999). What factors precipitate people's contact with services or their identification of need? Guidance (LASSL, 2000, 3) identifies key questions to which mapping might contribute answers, namely: what outcomes are achieved now and must be attained in the future? What services are required to bridge any gaps derived from this opening analysis? Given the range and level of need, what targets and shared objectives should be set? What contributions from each agency should be planned to meet these targets? The guidance proposes that mapping should include health and social care needs and the impact of projected changes in population levels. It refers to mapping need geographically, with comparisons to socio-demographic data to see how demand coincides with expected need and to identify pockets of social exclusion. It suggests that data are analysed by ethnicity and disability. It also envisages mapping as covering the volume of services being provided by different outlets, and pinpointing formal and informal assets in communities in order to assess the actual and latent capacity of neighbourhoods to promote well-being. From these data, gaps at need (no or inadequate services) and outcome (services missing targets or objectives) levels can be highlighted, facilitating priority setting and action planning.

Green and colleagues (2001) conceptualize mapping as a process of quantifying the population characteristics of young people and how these characteristics relate to each other. Within an inter-agency framework, it can also measure the overlap between different 'caseloads' of young people and describe how services offered by different agencies do (not) link together. May (1997) argues that surveys are a rapid and relatively inexpensive way of discovering a population's characteristics and beliefs, and that they can provide factual and attitudinal information. How issues such as representativeness of samples and questionnaire design are resolved will influence whether a population's characteristics are understood as well as measured, and whether relationships between variables can be established.

Green (2000) lists a number of community needs profiling methods, which can challenge stereotypical views and act as a basis for change. These include interviews, surveys, focus group discussions, observation and the use of secondary data (statistics, census, service take-up rates). Census data can provide a back-cloth—age structure, unemployment levels, educational attainment, residential stability, age and volume of public housing, which are possible indicators of socio-economic stress. Hawtin *et al.* (1994) distinguish between needs assessment, community consultation, social audits and community needs profile. They further distinguish these methods by purpose, who is responsible for initiating the research, the extent of community involvement, and the scope of the exercise. These distinctions take the policy planner and the researcher into questions of partnership—the degree to which individuals and communities are involved in decision-making about the research. Janzon and Sinclair (2002) advocate that routinely collected data can be used to understand the changing relationship between needs and services. Planning service provision can then take into account patterns, trends and likely demand, drawing upon the most significant factors that appear to influence entry of young people and their families into welfare agencies, such as long-term illness, housing conditions and reliance on income support.

Percy-Smith (1996) cautions that a service-led approach is conservative and likely to result in only marginal improvements to existing services. She suggests that this approach is unlikely to generate information about needs for different types of services. To inform decision-making about appropriate and responsive services, and definition of desired outcomes, research on needs assessment should start with engaging people in defining categories of needs. Everitt *et al.* (1992) criticize traditional needs assessment for being an expert model of service development where practitioners and policy makers construct definitions of needs. This is not a reciprocal process but one where practitioner values and routine agency practices define boundaries. They urge, instead, an emancipatory research process, which locates 'clients' and communities as 'knowers' and involves them in all stages, from problem definition, through data collection and analysis, to dissemination and involvement in the political process, so that people can act on their (new) understanding. Similarly, Barber (1991) argues that community analysis must involve a redistribution of power and consideration of the forces opposed to change. He distinguishes between locality development (participation in community change), social planning (problem solving) and social action (redistributing power, community education), and uses community forums and key informant groups to sample opinion.

All research, including mapping, reflects the values and political stance of the researchers. One question, therefore, to resolve is how power is distributed in the research process, irrespective of the methods actually adopted to obtain data. These methods can include key informants (community leaders, residents), community forums (meetings), treatment rates (referrals, open cases), social indicators (records) and surveys (questionnaires and interviews) (Berger and Patchner, 1988).

Percy-Smith (1996), discussing population needs assessment, identifies four stages:

1   A population profile (primary research; secondary sources).

2   Development of strategic plans, which define relative levels of need, priorities and preferred options, which are costed against the population profile to estimate the level of service required and the budget implications.

3   Individual needs assessment, which refines the overall population profiles.

4   Review of the strategic plan.

The approach combines quantitative and qualitative methods, allowing both numerical analysis and an in-depth understanding of people's experience and needs. Mixing quantitative and qualitative data provides a comprehensive picture, with the latter illuminating details of experiences that are obscured in the former. In an earlier paper, Percy-Smith (1992) grasps the complex nature of need and develops a matrix for planning and audit (outcome measurement) purposes. She recognizes the distinction between normative need (determined by experts), felt need (an individual's subjective assessment) and comparative need (defined against a standard). She suggests that information can be collected from three sources—professional definitions of need in relation to the target population; information from existing services and 'clients'; and data on best practice. Needs, resources and alternative strategies can then be mapped against comparative, normative and felt needs as sources of information. This provides information on, for example, health and welfare needs and priorities, drawn from 'experts' and those who experience those needs.

The research–practice interface

Various studies identify blocks or challenges that contribute to poor understanding and planning for (changes in) need (Green *et al.*, 2001; Hare *et al.*, 2002; Janzon and Sinclair, 2002). These are now reviewed against the experience of one project, which focused on children and young people in need on a Crown Dependency island. While maintaining its own legislative framework, in relation to children, this closely mirrors that pertaining in England. The project aimed to provide a snapshot of the needs of children and the services that they received at a particular point in time, which could then be used as a basis for ongoing information gathering. It aimed to identify the location, age and gender of children and young people with social care, educational or health needs, the nature of those needs and the services being provided to meet them. The project's scope also included views on the effectiveness of services provided, reasons for lack of effectiveness, professionals' perspectives on resources needed or for which children had to wait, and needs outside the remit of the agency and whether services were provided to meet them. Professionals completed a pro forma for each child on their case list during a selected month.

Staff attitudes

Staff may prove reluctant to engage because research does not form part of their daily work culture or because of cynicism about organizational change (Qureshi and Nicholas, 2001). Meetings with team leaders and social workers to explain the purposes of the research were held but collecting information from a minority of social workers posed problems, mainly because of genuine pressure of work but sometimes because they did not value the outcomes of the project. Some were concerned that data might reinforce prejudices about particular geographic locations; others were uncertain about the slippery concept 'need'. Eventually, some forms were completed in face-to-face interviews, following a letter from the Director and discussion with the researchers, but the project reinforced the importance of considering the research commissioner's relationships with their own staff. The interview was seen as a positive experience by a number of these informants who valued the overview of their caseload which it offered.

Teachers with responsibility for special educational needs (SENCOs) were based in schools spread over the island rather than centrally, making it difficult to meet them to introduce the project. There were also concerns about asking a group of professionals who consider themselves overburdened with forms to complete yet more, for what many would have considered non-educational purposes. It was therefore decided to conduct telephone interviews with SEN-COs, or the head in schools which were too small to have a SENCO in post, following a letter from the Department of Education introducing the project to all heads and to staff. While we had initially considered telephone interviews to be time consuming, it became apparent that they were effective, both in terms of the quality of the data collected and the time involved (from three to twelve minutes per case). Missing data only occurred where there was no information and not because it had been unintentionally omitted. Again, a number of teachers reported that they had enjoyed the experience of being interviewed.

The ability of the researcher to understand the issues that were being addressed in the face-to-face, or phone, interviews may have been an important factor in this. Interviews with teachers were conducted by ex-teachers of children with special educational needs and of social workers by interviewers who were known to have worked in social services departments. Face-to-face interviews were not carried out with health workers. The relevant manager felt that staff should return the forms as requested, and it may be significant in terms of the difficulties experienced that no one on the research team had any experience of working within health, or any particular expertise in this field.

Inter-agency collaboration

The project included children in need known to health, education and/or the police, and information about all children living in families in receipt of benefits. This was because many referrals of social care needs come via health practitioners and/or teachers and education welfare officers (Little *et al.*, 2003). However, the commissioning department rather than an inter-agency forum was the driver behind the project. Reflecting the commissioning agency's relationships with other organizations, this impacted on the research process in several ways.

Confidentiality

Divergent protocols complicated the nature of the information that it was possible to gather from the health service. Health professionals were unwilling to give children's initials or, less understandably, the limited postcode information required for matching children involved with different agencies. There did not seem to be any agency guidance about confidentiality, with health workers appearing to make their own decisions about what they felt comfortable with in terms of sharing information with other agencies and with researchers.

Contrasting agency remits or targets

Agencies may adopt divergent definitions when determining which children and families to assist. As Hamer (2003) notes, challenges and barriers to joint planning include different priorities and targets. Agencies may categorize children's needs in different ways and hold data-sets that do not easily facilitate cross-checking of information and activity, either because of differences in the level of detail in recording, or the efficiency with which it is done. This, of course, reduces the utility of information held about the experiences, circumstances, needs and context of young people.

In this project, decisions about which children should be included caused some problems. Social workers were familiar with guidance from the Department of Health on assessing children in need and their families and working around the threshold of significant harm (Department of Health, 2000*b*). Equally, the criteria for education were clear; in collaboration with the Education department, it was agreed that information would be collected about all pupils within schools or units who had special educational needs at level 4+ or 5 during the selected month.

Health visitors and school health advisers provide a universal service and selecting the children who should be included as in health need was seen as complex by them. Department of Health definitions of need led to difficulties, as some health workers concerned were unclear about which children to include. While the researchers asked health workers to include only what they saw as significant needs, there were some who included needs which were indicative more of *vulnerable children* rather than *children in need* (LASSL, 2000, 3). Hare *et al.* (2002) found that the number of children actually known to services was significantly lower than the number of children estimated as vulnerable. Mapping the broader category of *vulnerable children* may prove more helpful if seeking to target service development and provision on preventing members of this group becoming *children in need*.

Contrasting perspectives on need

Different remits or targets are underpinned by diverse, even competitive, philosophical approaches to need. Health and education professionals may emphasize collective entitlement to their services, whilst social workers may prioritize individual well-being (Tisdall *et al.*, 2000). Similarly, operationalizing prevention and family support may rely on wide-ranging or more restrictive definitions of need. The former includes support services targeted on the early emergence of difficulties and the ability to benefit from provision. The latter focuses down on risk, working with families in which problems are severe and established (McCrystal, 2000; Percy, 2000). Difficulties in this project, especially for health practitioners, in knowing which young people to include, are indicative of definitional confusions and inadequacies (Colton *et al.*, 1995) in policy and practice surrounding prevention, family support and need. Inter-agency co-operation must reconcile the competing and contrasting imperatives in the 1989 Children Act, and agree priorities and targets, if joint planning is to identify the numbers, location and needs of children who may require services throughout childhood, others at various transitional life points, and others at times of crisis. This, however, is easier to pronounce (Hamer, 2003) than achieve.

Balancing cost with benefit

Guidance (LASSL, 2000, 3) suggests that mapping should not be so time or resource consuming that it becomes unsustainable. Deriving codes for needs based on the needs actually identified by informants, interpreting the language of 'need' when it was unclear what practitioners were identifying, for instance when referring to 'support', entering and then organizing the data, were indeed time intensive.

Although the Department of Health recognizes the importance of mapping needs and resources (LASSL, 2000, 3), there is little information available about the specifics of doing so. Ideally, a format for data is selected that is appropriate for a particular purpose. In the real world of imperfect knowledge, this is not always the case. Decisions about which tools are used or designed in research projects are made in the context of researcher knowledge and skills. We suspect that a similar situation obtains in local authorities, where the tools selected are likely to be those that staff feel confident about using. We originally decided that an Access database would be appropriate. Computer staff were familiar with it and its use would therefore enable us to pass on the information gathered in a format accessible to staff. Moreover, the database needed to be able to handle limited amounts of text, which Access can do. Finally, someone who could set up an Access database was available. However, the database was designed with the aim of facilitating input and reducing input errors, which are not necessarily directly compatible with analysis requirements. Following initial analysis using the Access database, it became apparent that using Statistical Package for the Social Sciences (SPSS) would have facilitated the kind of analysis we were interested in. SPSS, although not designed to do so, could also cope with text in small amounts. This is not to say that Access could not have met our requirements, but that to do so required entries in specific query language that were time consuming compared with the ease of querying and recoding the data using SPSS. However, using SPSS would have made it difficult for staff to access our information as the programme is expensive and no staff members were familiar with it.

Information gathering

Little (1999) identifies three methods. The first involves gathering information on each child in a community and testing the effect of different children in need thresholds. The second looks at referrals to different agencies and, whilst a partial picture of all children in a community, reveals patterns. The third tests professionals' judgements about 'in need'. The approach we adopted essentially combined the second and third methods. It used agency information systems to locate and map current 'clients', the reasons for referral, the resources allocated, and patterns of overlap or mismatch between need and provision.

It would have been possible to conduct a survey of a sample of children, using a sampling frame of all children on the island derived from information on all those receiving child benefit held by the Department of Social Security. Parents and children would have been the informants. Such a survey would have empowered service users to formulate their needs and the outcomes they saw as desirable, assuming that the interview had been developed in collaboration with users and did not therefore use professional definitions of need.

While recognizing that such a survey could provide information about need not already known to agencies, and information about vulnerable children as differentiated from children in need, we decided not to use survey methods. While this method may be appropriate for gathering information about the needs of older people, for example, it is less appropriate for mapping children in need where the incidence of need is likely to be low. If an assumption is made that the number of children in need on the island is likely to be comparable to levels in the UK, with estimates of 2.7 per cent (LASSL, 2000, 3), a random sample would produce a great deal of redundant information. Additionally, it was felt that families under stress were less likely to respond and that even if a high response rate was achieved, we could not be certain that families under stress had been included. Finally, we sought a wide range of information which would have required a long and complicated questionnaire. This would have been very time consuming for parents of children with multiple and/or complex needs, making it unlikely that an acceptable response rate would have been achieved, particularly from families under stress. However, the approach taken meant that children in need but unsupported in the community would be missed—what Percy (2000) refers to as hidden need—with mapping unable to answer why they and their families had not come to the notice of health and welfare organizations.

Accordingly, information was gathered from agencies about children in need and about children who were waiting to be allocated to a worker in a specific period (one calendar month). The data collected from key informants relating to children known to each agency were entered into one main database using Access. The total count of all children identified therefore provided information about the number of cases known, which gave an estimate of resources being used and needed. However, as some children would be known to more than one agency and would therefore be included twice or more, the number of cases was not equivalent to the number of children in need. To reach that figure, it was necessary to identify children known to more than one agency by merging the information gathered from different organizations so that those who were identified by more than one agency could be recognized. For this purpose, date of birth, the first two numbers of the child's postcode, gender and initials for matching were used. The primary matching criteria used were the date of birth and gender. No child was counted as a match of any kind unless these factors matched. Having sorted children by date of birth and gender, a 'matching' score was then allocated to each case to identify children whom we could be sure were the same, within the criteria established, with a score of 5–6, and those who were likely to be the same with a score of 4–5. Where very limited information was available (less than four criteria), the child was excluded from the matching process. Within the limitations described above, by matching where information was available, it was possible to identify children who were known to more than one agency.

Initially, we also considered using secondary analysis of agency data sets, assuming successful negotiation for access, acknowledging that no single approach will provide comprehensive and reliable measures of a population's needs for services (Percy, 2000). However, the range of information held by

Social Services, the main focus of the project, was too limited for our purposes. Although there was information about case type, age, gender and location, there was insufficient information about services being provided and no information about the extent to which these were seen as meeting needs, or about other needs which had been identified. There may be legal issues where services are thought by the provider not to be meeting needs. Mapping need and services from such databases results in the omission of important aspects of services that would provide information to planners and policy formulators about services which are effective in meeting needs, and about services which are required to meet needs that are not currently provided for. This limits their ability to re-evaluate the role of services that are not thought to meet the needs for which they are provided. While recognizing that there are impairments which are extremely resistant to change (Little *et al.*, 2003), databases providing the range of information that we gathered could contribute to the information base about what works.

This project's findings could also have been compared with proxy indicators of need, for example reliance on benefits and deprivation indices, and with community profiling data, in order to recognize that indicators of need may (not) correlate with actual or required use of social and other services.

Mapping and modernization

The modernization agenda (Department of Health, 1998) aims to ensure provision for those who need support. It requires an information and research based approach to commissioning and purchasing services, which has analysed the needs of the population served, has mapped current provision, and has evaluated with relevant stakeholders the effectiveness of current arrangements. Mapping provides, then, a theoretical framework to underpin service provision and can prove a source of new ideas. It can provide data as justification or argument for particular policy decisions (Barnardos, 2000). However, how does the approach to mapping taken in the project reported here respond to the principles within the modernization agenda?

Flexibility and responsiveness

This principle requires services to meet people's specific and changing needs. The project obtained professional and inter-agency perspectives on needs and the degree to which they were being met. However, it was one resource intensive snapshot, which omitted the service user and family/community perspective. The categories of need did not preclude inclusion of structural issues when recognizing risk factors limiting young people's life chances—low income, poor housing and unemployment. To date, though, planning in response to these factors, and to family conflict, low educational attainment, poor health and behavioural problems, has tended to personalize services.

Co-ordination between agencies

This principle aims to secure an integrated system of care. Some problems concerning collaboration encountered by the project were discussed earlier, reinforcing again that the experience of partnership between service sectors has not been uniformly positive or straightforward. Co-ordination has been patchy, especially at the policy planning level (Audit Commission, 1994; Bull *et al.*, 1994). Indeed, Laming (2003) is not alone in concluding that patterns of need and risk have been obscured by different agencies holding fragments of a jigsaw rather than a complete picture, and in recommending that effective communication and safeguarding requires intra- and inter-agency systems that, through handling and transferring information, highlight risk, urgency and details of harm to children. Currently, collaborative working between agencies at the macro level of strategic planning, and at the micro level of practice, appears too often to operate in a vacuum of shared information resources.

On the island, there were no shared databases of information, although each agency had computer-based information about their own service users, patients and pupils. The use of different language for those an agency works with may be indicative of the gulfs that remain between professionals, which are exacerbated by concerns about confidentiality, and lack of clarity about the boundaries of practice expertise. None of the information sources was available to other agencies—a situation that, in our experience, also pertains in many UK local authorities. Hamer (2003), indeed, has identified overcoming collection of incompatible data and use of information in different ways as one barrier to joint planning. As Hare and colleagues (2002) have suggested, agencies need to think about how they share information at the local level to identify children as early as possible; they require agreements on confidentiality and on common data sets.

Further complexity arose when, on querying the data, cases emerged where a match had not appeared but where one agency had identified that another was also involved. These challenges, arguably underplayed in the literature, renew the questions about inter-agency collaboration—here in relation to how the research was commissioned and generally about how information is shared. Extending the preventive and protective circles around children requires that data be exchanged so that they are brought within a co-ordinated system of assessment, planning and intervention. The inquiry into the death of Victoria Climbié (Laming, 2003) is not the first to recommend improvements on how information is exchanged within and between agencies if children are to be safeguarded.

Services of consistent quality

Although it had been hoped to collect data for six months, in order to track changes in needs and services, this proved difficult in terms of the burden of frequent form filling imposed on professionals, and impossible within the project budget. Nonetheless, the scope was rather wider than that used in the Children in Need Data Collection (CINDC) exercise, introduced in February 2000, and the Children in Need Surveys which followed this (Department of Health, 2003), both in the number of agencies involved and in the breadth of information sought. While the CINDC exercise focused on Social Services and aimed to link needs, services and costs of services, the island study collected detailed demographic data for each child and information about social care, educational and health needs. Up to four needs were identified by each professional. Information about services provided by the agency, identifying the need, the extent to which the provision of services was thought to meet need and reasons if it did not do so, were related to specific needs. Professionals were also asked to identify needs which were outside the remit of their own agency and to indicate whether or not services were provided to meet these needs, but not to make a judgement about the extent to which such needs were met because of the difficulty of doing so. Additional information was collected about whether a child was waiting for a service and, if so, for what, and professionals' views on resources needed to meet the needs that they had identified.

Thus, the project provided an evaluation of what was proving effective but this was in the context of a narrowing, more procedural and instrumental interpretation of the social work role. Data produced then can be used either to promote a comprehensive framework or to construct narrower provision. The competing orientations within the legal and policy frameworks return.

Like Janzon and Sinclair (2002), we found that the information which was available was not being utilized to its full potential. Our experience indicates that there are a number of factors which contribute to this situation. First, information systems need to be multi-purpose, to avoid duplication, so that systems used for producing the statistics necessary for government returns are also designed to provide information relevant for local planning. Secondly, managers and/or those responsible for planning need to be familiar with the system and knowledgeable about what sort of information it can produce. They also need to see this as a significant rather than a peripheral aspect of their role. On the island, there was a lack of awareness on the part of senior managers about the potential of the information system, and lack of time to explore and develop this. Thirdly, there needs to be access to technical expertise to interrogate the system to obtain the information required. While those who had set up the system and/or operated it on the island were skilled in these techniques, they were not planners or researchers and were not able to identify appropriate questions; nor did they have sufficient status within the organization to raise these issues.

User involvement

People should have a voice in what services are provided and how. A sample of parents and children who were already receiving services were to be interviewed about the extent to which services met needs and about what services should be provided to meet current needs. Consultation groups, conferences and youth councils could also have been considered (Tisdall *et al.*, 2000). Because of the time involved in the initial mapping exercise and analysis of the data, and the changing priorities of the funder, it was not possible to gather information on and analyse user views about services. As Fisher (2002) has noted, when service users are not involved in defining the problem, deciding categories for and analysing data collection, the way that issues are framed will reflect power structures that exclude other conceptualizations. The failure to collect data from parents and from children themselves means that the research provided information about needs and the extent to which they were met from a professional perspective only. While information from a range of professional perspectives was collected, this is, nevertheless, a serious limitation in terms of identifying needs and the services required to meet them. Can need be said to have been mapped and understood when felt need (individual self-assessment) is excluded? Indeed, personal accounts from parents and young people can act as a restraint on using needs assessment as a tool for targeting and obscuring the existence of diminishing resources (Percy-Smith, 1996). They can dispel any notion of family as a single entity, revealing individuals who may disagree, yet have unequal opportunities to express their views. Relying solely on professional judgements of need is dangerous when practice is vulnerable to managerial agendas, and to collusion between managers and practitioners to conceal unlawful decisions and inappropriate or under-resourced interventions (Preston-Shoot, 2001).

Informing policy and practice

Information about the percentage of cases in the population with any given need or range of needs provides opportunities to question differences between reported levels and what would be expected in comparable areas. Reasons for the differences, for example different eligibility criteria or different interpretations of eligibility criteria, can then be explored. The percentage of the child population of the island identified by Social Services was 2.4 per cent compared with 2.7–3.6 per cent for the UK (LASSL, 2000, 3). The percentage of cases identified by Education was similar, at 2.3 per cent, and is again in line with expectations. However, the percentage identified by health professionals was 3.6 per cent. This may be accounted for by the difficulty that health professionals had in deciding whether a child was a *child in need* in health terms.

This information confirmed that the levels of need with which agencies were working on the island were very similar to what would be expected in the UK. This was an important finding in an island with pockets of poverty and need amidst affluence, and one with political implications for the resourcing of services within the locality. While information about overall levels of need at any given time can provide broad indications of the need for resources, its usefulness is limited for predictive purposes. Estimates of population change by age group are readily available. However, such information is only useful for planning social care services if there are reliable estimates of other factors, such as poverty levels, alcoholism and housing need, which factors, among many others, are likely to affect the numbers of people with social care needs (Little *et al.*, 2003). In general, only short-term estimations can be made of need, as the effects of current and future policies in these areas are as yet unknown.

The usefulness to practitioners and policy formulators of the research reported here, and, arguably, of much mapping work, lies in the questions that it raises. These are questions about identifying the number of children in need, numbers of children known to more than one agency, levels and types of needs, current identification of need, and the identification of resources that are needed. There are also questions about the equitable allocation of resources in terms of gender, age, ethnic minority group membership and location.

Identifying the numbers of children in need and those known to more than one agency was made more difficult by the lack of information from health services, which severely affected the credibility of the matched data. To identify the number of children in need known to more than one agency, we identified duplicate cases and then calculated how many children these cases represented. To calculate the number of children in need on the island, we took the number of cases on the complete inter-agency database and deducted the cases that we identified as duplicates, giving us the number of cases and therefore children known to only one agency. To obtain the total number of children in need, we then added the number of children represented by the cases identified as duplicates. This figure included children living in families in receipt of benefits and, while the majority of these would have been children at risk of living in poverty, not all would have been children living in poverty. Similar calculations were carried out excluding all cases identified by Social Security and this produced a figure of 1,079 children in need, or 6.7 per cent of the child population. This figure may either reflect the lack of validity of the matching process or a high number of children with difficulties unique to one agency, or the complexity of distinguishing between *vulnerable children* and *children in need*. The difficulty of obtaining reliable figures relating to basic data underlines the desirability of one inter-agency database to inform planning and service development.

With regard to equitable allocation of resources, an analysis of the gender breakdown for each agency showed that of the cases identified by Social Services, 58 per cent were male and 42 per cent female. A small part of this difference is attributable to the greater number of males in contact with the police, but, because only small numbers were reported by the police (thirty-four) compared with Social Services cases (three hundred and eighty-one), the difference is not solely due to this factor. Similarly, a comparison of those identified as beyond control or with no carer showed little difference related to gender (twenty-four female, twenty-nine male).

There were similar gender differences in the data provided by Health to those shown by Social Services. The difference in gender was particularly striking in the case of Education, where 69 per cent of those identified were boys. This may well reflect widely documented evidence in the UK that teachers are more likely to identify boys as having difficulties than girls, but the issue of whether girls are receiving an equitable share of resources remains. There were only slight differences between the percentage of male and female children who were identified by Social Security (51 and 49 per cent, respectively), suggesting that poverty on the island was not gender related, as might be expected, but that access to social care services was. The figures for the police were small, with fourteen females and nineteen males.

Analysis of the identification of need and services by age group ($N = 3814$, age known) indicated that there were clear differences between agencies in terms of the age groups with whom they were in contact. Excluding Social Security, cases aged under five were predominantly identified by Health (83 per cent of those under five and 57 per cent of all identified by Health). In contrast, cases in the age group eight to twelve were identified predominantly by Education (49 per cent of all cases aged eight to twelve, 47 per cent of all Education cases), with Social Services identifying only a quarter of the cases in this age group (26 per cent). Social Services had proportionately more cases in the over-thirteen age group (40 per cent of all cases, and 40 per cent of all Social Services cases). Differences between agencies and within agencies, in terms of the age groups that they work with, raise issues about working practices and about unrecognized need. Differences between agencies may reflect an agreed pattern of working between agencies. For example, in this study, the role played by health in work with under-fives appeared to reflect an explicit practice agreement between professionals, although whether this had been agreed through formal policies or had simply emerged as a pattern of working was less clear. However, where this type of agreement is not in place, considerable differences within an agency may indicate that the needs of children in a particular age group are being neither identified nor addressed.

No children from minority ethnic groups were identified as children in need. This raises issues about possible discrimination and the accessibility of services but should be seen in the context of a very low population of people from ethnic minority groups.

Analysis of the location of cases showed predictable clusters—nearly one in three cases was located in just five postcode areas, with one in five located in three of these postcode areas. These areas were characterized by social housing and high numbers of parents in receipt of benefits. Such cases accounted for 10 per cent of all Social Services cases, 8 per cent of those identified by Education, but only 2 per cent of those identified by Health. These happened to be areas where health workers did not provide adequate data and consequent under-reporting may account for the differences. The Social Exclusion Unit has suggested that it is often the case that '... the poorest neighbourhoods get the poorest services' (Social Exclusion Unit, 2000). While this is certainly what we expected to find, there appeared to be few differences between professionals' views of the effectiveness of services in poorer areas compared with their evaluation of the effectiveness of services in more affluent areas. It is possible that professional expectations were lower for poorer areas, so that the effectiveness of services was rated more highly in poorer areas than it would have been elsewhere. It is also possible that a different view would have emerged if service users had been consulted or if the formal and informal assets in these communities were mapped. Mapping this geography would identify the latent and actual capacity in these areas to promote children's well-being. Mapping households in these areas might identify those children with needs but unsupported by agencies and their communities. It would also respond to Laming's recommendation (2003) that local authorities should more closely engage with their local communities in defining needs and responses to them. Priority setting and action planning could then follow.

In order to identify resource needs, agencies were asked about services for which children had to wait and those that they thought were needed but which, currently, were not provided at all. Resource needs were analysed by location and where a child had more than one resource need, these were listed as separate resource needs. Social Services staff identified very few children who were waiting for services, and very few resource needs. Education professionals identified needs for more staff, including more Nursery Nursing Education Board (NNEB) staff, more one-to-one time and access to speech therapy services. Overall, no clear pattern of resource needs emerged from health service data, in part because of the ambiguity of many returns.

Participants were asked to indicate reasons where services did not meet needs, using five pre-selected categories. These were—lack of time, lack of motivation on the part of the child or family, services in the wrong location, services not provided at the right time (for example weekends), lack of collaboration between agencies, and other. There were clear differences between professional attributions. Lack of motivation was the reason given most frequently by social workers (55 per cent of all their reasons) and by health service staff (33 per cent of all their reasons), but only 14 per cent of the reasons that teachers gave related to motivation. The cause most frequently cited by teachers was lack of time (46 per cent of all their reasons) but this accounted for only 4 per cent of reasons given by social workers and 13 per cent of reasons given by health workers.

The focus on motivation by Social Services staff in particular may be related to lack of motivation associated with the income and housing difficulties faced by a high proportion of service users. There is, however, the possibility that some social workers did not accept responsibility for working with lack of motivation as an issue.

Conclusion

Attempts to integrate research into practice and management have only been partially successful (Barnardos, 2000). Obstacles include:

1 under-resourcing of dissemination and failure to follow up data publication with change strategies;

2 organizational culture, where managers are so preoccupied with operational demands (Balloch *et al.*, 1999) that their capacity to respond strategically is deteriorating;

3 the lived experience of work, with the sector overwhelmed by targets, insufficient resources and unmanageable workloads (Audit Commission, 2002).

Such obstacles challenge a rational planning model where outcomes are supposed to follow from researched–informed change goals. Thus, this project illustrated types and levels of (unmet) need but researchers were not involved in subsequent policy development. Moreover, managing change itself requires a commitment at political, strategic and operational levels to unfreeze existing systems of interests and relationships (Hadley and Hugman, 1991/92), coupled with support and involvement from key stakeholders for developing collaborative planning practice (Hamer, 2003). This project documented aspects of family life but for such data to achieve organizational and social change would require greater co-ordination and integration of planning, commissioning and delivery of services (Hamer, 2003). This level of integration of vision and priorities, characterized by a corporate approach to children's services, genuine inter-agency collaboration and joint planning relationships (Tisdall *et al.*, 2000) remained aspirational rather than actual.

UK government guidance on planning for children's services directs attention away from a concentration on needs and services. It proposes 'a fundamental shift of focus by making working to shared objectives and the pursuit of beneficial outcomes for children and their families the primary driver for the co-operation necessary for successful planning and coherent provision of services' (LASSL, 2000, 3, bold omitted). However, the need for detailed information on needs and services is still seen as an essential prerequisite for planning. Plans should be written with a statistical summary which sets out 'all the resources currently available for meeting the needs of vulnerable children and children in need. The geographic distribution of service outlets should be represented in such a way that it can be matched with the distribution of need and demand' (LASSL, 2000, 3).

The approach taken in the project reported herein provided some answers to the question of whether health and welfare agencies were providing children with the services that they needed. It enabled an analysis of professional inputs and, to the extent that practitioners could comment on the degree to which needs had been met, outcomes. It enabled some mapping of gaps in services but it illustrated once again the fragility of the inter-agency co-operation, and the cost and complexities involved in attempting to capture the concept 'need'.

Accepted: December 2003

References

Association of Metropolitan Authorities (AMA) (1994) *Special Child: Special Needs. Services for Children with Disabilities*, London, Association of Metropolitan Authorities, Child Care Services No. 4.

Audit Commission (1994) *Seen But Not Heard*, London, HMSO.

Audit Commission (2002) *Recruitment and Retention: A Public Service Workforce for the 21st Century*, London, The Stationery Office.

Balloch, S., McLean, J. and Fisher, M. (eds) (1999) *Social Services: Working under Pressure*, Bristol, The Policy Press.

Barber, J. (1991) *Beyond Casework*, London, Macmillan.

Barnardos (2000) *Linking Research and Practice*, York, Joseph Rowntree Foundation.

Berger, R. and Patchner, M. (1988) *Planning for Research: A Guide for the Helping Professions*, London, Sage.

Bull, J., Cameron, C., Candappa, M., Moss, P., Owen, C. and Statham, J. (1994) *Implementing the Children Act for Children Under 8*, London, HMSO.

Colton, M., Drury, C. and Williams, M. (1995) 'Children in need: definition, identification and support', *British Journal of Social Work*, **25**(6), pp. 711–28.

Department of Health (1998) *Modernising Social Services*, London, The Stationery Office.

Department of Health (2000a) *The Quality Protects Programme: Transforming Children's Services 2001–02 (LAC (2000) 22)*, London, Department of Health.

Department of Health (2000b) *Framework for the Assessment of Children in Need and their Families*, London, The Stationery Office.

Department of Health (2003) *Guidance for the Children in Need National Collection*, London, Department of Health.

Everitt, A., Hardiker, P., Littlewood, J. and Mullender, A. (1992) *Applied Research for Better Practice*, London, Macmillan.

Fisher, M. (2002) 'The role of service users in problem formulation and technical aspects of social research', *Social Work Education*, **21**(3), pp. 305–12.

Green, R. (2000) 'Applying a community needs profiling approach to tackling service user poverty', *British Journal of Social Work*, **30**(3), pp. 287–303.

Green, A., Maguire, M. and Canny, A. (2001) *Keeping Track: Mapping and Tracking Vulnerable Young People*, Bristol, Policy Press.

Hadley, R. and Hugman, R. (1991/92) 'Managing change in a turbulent climate: the experience of a Social Services Department', *Social Work and Social Sciences Review*, **3**(3), pp. 204–26.

Hamer, L. (2003) *Planning with a Purpose*, London, Health Development Agency, Local Government Association and the NHS Confederation.

Hare, P., Baxter, M. and Newbronner, E. (2002) 'Taking a count of vulnerable children', *Community Care*, **24–30 January**, pp. 40–41.

Hawtin, M., Hughes, G. and Percy-Smith, J. (1994) *Community Profiling: Auditing Social Needs*, Buckingham, Open University Press.

Huber, N. (1999) 'Children's services suffer from variable performance', *Community Care*, **21–27 October**, pp. 10–11.

Janzon, K. and Sinclair, R. (2002) 'Needs, numbers, resources: informed planning for looked after children', *Research Policy and Planning*, **20**(2), pp. 1–7.

Local Authority Circular (LAC) (1996) 10. *Children's Services Planning*, London, Department of Health.

Laming, H. (2003) *Inquiry into the Death of Victoria Climbié*, London, The Stationery Office.

Local Authority Social Service Letter (LASSL) (2000) 3. *New Guidance on Planning Children's Services*, London, Department of Health.

Little, M. (1999) 'Prevention and early intervention with children in need: definitions, principles and examples of good practice', *Children and Society*, **13**, pp. 304–16.

Little, M., Axford, N. and Morpeth, L. (2003) 'Children's services in the UK 1997–2003: problems, developments and challenges for the future', *Children and Society*, **17**, pp. 205–14.

May, T. (1997) *Social Research: Issues, Methods and Process*, 2nd edition, Buckingham, Open University Press.

McCrystal, P. (2000) 'Operationalising the definition of children in need from UK child care legislation', in D. Iwaniec and M. Hill (eds), *Child Welfare Policy and Practice*, London, Jessica Kingsley Publishers.

Percy, A. (2000) 'Needs-based planning for family and child care services in Northern Ireland: problems and possibilities', in D. Iwaniec and M. Hill (eds), *Child Welfare Policy and Practice*, London, Jessica Kingsley Publishers.

Percy-Smith, J. (1992) 'Auditing social needs', *Policy and Politics*, **20**(1), pp. 29–34.

Percy-Smith, J. (ed) (1996) *Needs Assessments in Public Policy*, Buckingham, Open University Press.

Preston-Shoot, M. (2001) 'Regulating the road of good intentions: observations on the relationship between policy, regulations and practice in social work', *Practice*, **13**(4), pp. 5–20.

Qureshi, H. and Nicholas, E. (2001) 'A new conception of social care outcomes and its practical use in assessment with older people', *Research Policy and Planning*, **19**(2), pp. 11–25.

Social Exclusion Unit (2000) *National Strategy for Neighbourhood Renewal: A Framework for Consultation*, London, Social Exclusion Unit.

Social Services Inspectorate (SSI) (1994) *Report on the National Survey of Children's Services Plans*, London, Department of Health.

Social Services Inspectorate (SSI) (1995) *Children's Services Plans. An Analysis of Children's Services Plans*, London, Department of Health.

Social Services Inspectorate (SSI) (1999) *Planning to Deliver*, London, Department of Health.

Tisdall, K., Monaghan, B. and Hill, M. (2000) 'Communication, co-operation or collaboration? The involvement of voluntary organisations in the first Scottish Children's Services Plans', in D. Iwaniec and M. Hill (eds), *Child Welfare Policy and Practice*, London, Jessica Kingsley Publishers.

[18]

The Background of Children who enter Local Authority Care

ANDREW BEBBINGTON AND JOHN MILES

Andrew Bebbington is a Senior Research Fellow and Assistant Director of the Personal Social Services Research Unit at the University of Kent at Canterbury. John Miles is a Research Associate at the PSSRU.

SUMMARY

The family backgrounds of 2500 children admitted to care in England were investigated, to quantify the association between indicators of material and social deprivation and entry to care. These indicators are more closely associated than in Packman's national survey of 1962. Broken family is the most significant factor, though there are several alternative explanations for this, which have quite different policy implications. When allowance is made for other social factors, children from particular ethnic minorities do not seem specially vulnerable, though children of mixed race are. The study confirms that many children who come into care after an offence have experienced similar deprivations to non-offenders. There remain great variations between authorities in children's routes into care, but less so in the circumstances of the children themselves.

This article reports the findings of a survey which investigated the family circumstances of children who entered care in 1987, and draws comparisons with the situation twenty-five years ago when Packman (1968) undertook the last national survey of this type, *Child Care: Needs and Numbers*. Three research questions are investigated. Firstly, to compare the family backgrounds of children who come into care with those of other children and to quantify the predictive power of indicators. Secondly, to compare the children who come into care today with those in Packman's survey: a pragmatic test of the effect of the many changes in policy as well as of changes in social conditions since the early 1960s. Thirdly, to explain differences between areas in the family circumstances of children coming into care.

Address for correspondence: Andrew Bebbington, PSSRU, Cornwallis Building, The University, Canterbury, Kent, CT2 7NF.

BACKGROUND

Children may be taken into the care of local authorities in a number of ways. In the majority of cases it is at the parents' voluntary request under section 2 of the 1980 Child Care Act, often as a temporary arrangement. Most of the remainder are taken in compulsorily through a court committal under the 1969 Children and Young Person's Act, either because the child is in danger or inadequately cared for, or as a result of a criminal offence by the child.

After the 1948 child care legislation there was a steady rise in the number of children in care in England up to a peak of 96,000 in 1977, followed by a rapid decline so that by 1986 numbers had fallen to 67,000, not far above the level they had been in the mid 1960s. These changes are not simply due to fluctuations in the numbers or age structure of children. The rates per 1000 children under 18 have gone from 5.3 in the mid 1960s to 7.6 at the peak and back to 6.0 in 1986. The rate of entry into care has declined throughout, from 4.1 in 1966 to 3.5 at the peak and 2.8 in 1986, per 1000 children under 18. This implies an increase in the average length of stay in care since the mid 1960s.

Child care policy has been surrounded by persistent disquiet. In the last twenty-five years three major Acts (1963, 1969, 1975) and a consolidating Act have been introduced, and another is proposed shortly. There has been much public attention, most notably the investigations of a series of child abuse incidents from the Maria Colwell case of 1974 to the Butler-Sloss inquiry of 1988.

Underlying this concern has been a series of controversies about the causes of need and hence the circumstances under which interventions are appropriate. One of the most fundamental is about the origins of deprivation. Twenty years ago sociologists associated deprivation with social malaise. Some children seemed 'born to fail' as a result of poverty, lack of opportunity, and an alienating environment (Wedge and Prosser, 1978). Thus the focus of intervention should be to support the natural family, with an emphasis on casework, welfare rights, support services such as day care, as well as broader approaches such as the Community Development Programmes, designed to tackle the root causes of social malaise. But since then behavioural explanations of deprivation have been sought. Isaac *et al.* (1986) associate entry into care with parents' personal problems and mental health. It has been suggested that deprived children grow up to be inadequate or mentally disturbed parents who in turn cause their own children to be deprived—the 'cycle of deprivation' (Rutter and Madge, 1976. Evidence for this has been sought from cross-generational studies but so far is not conclusive: see Quinton and Rutter, 1984). As deprivation has been associated with personal inadequacy, so the emphasis in intervention has shifted away from a preventative approach towards improved methods of creating substitute families.

There has been a second, equally fundamental debate about personal responsibility and social forces concerning the delinquent child. Is he 'a miniature adult with free will . . . if necessary dealt with by control and discipline'; or '. . . a dependent victim of circumstance whose offence was a cry for help and who therefore needed care and treatment'? (Packman, 1975, pp. 111–13). A very substantial research literature now roots delinquency and behaviour problems in the social environment. Rutter and Giller (1983) identify parental criminality and social maladjustment, family discord, weak family relationships, harsh or ineffective parental discipline, and peer group pressure, as the main influences on delinquency. Even so, the question remains of whether the forces of deprivation are the same for the 'villain' as for the 'victim', and so whether it is appropriate to use similar means of treating their adverse effects.

A third fundamental question concerns the importance of the bonds between the child and his or her parents. What is more in the long-term interests of the child: to preserve natural family links wherever possible, as Bowlby's (1952) work on maternal deprivation implied; or to be removed from situations where there is any possibility that he or she is at risk? This dilemma, when to stand aside and when to intervene, has been highlighted in the 1987/8 period by the contrasting reports on Jasmine Beckford, Tyra Henry, and Kimberley Carlile on the one hand and the 'Cleveland' children on the other.

But it is not only child care policies which have been of concern. There have been long-standing criticisms of how they are put into practice. Packman (1968) and Davies *et al.* (1972) both demonstrated that variations between local authorities in the numbers in care could not be attributed to local needs or to explicit local policies, so implying that they are '. . . the consequences of varying degrees of inadequacy in the stocks of human and physical capital' (Davies *et al.*, p. 122). As a result, much attention has been focused on the processes of decision making, including: the identification of need; the use of preventative measures; decisions about when and how to take children into care; their placement and treatment in care; and the length of stay in care (DHSS, 1971; Parker, 1971; Rowe and Lambert, 1973; Bacon and Rowe, 1978; Cooper, 1978; Fruin and Vernon, 1983; Millham *et al.*, 1986; Packman *et al.*, 1986; House of Commons Committee on Social Services, 1987; Butler-Sloss, 1988; Rowe *et al.*, 1988.) Criticisms have been made repeatedly that too many children come into care, and that insufficient use is made of foster care and adoption. Many reports and inquiries by individual local authorities echo these concerns. But while the problems have been repeatedly identified, solutions have proved much more elusive. Research studies like that of Packman *et al.* (1986) which have investigated how decisions are made for individual children have found it hard to pin-point the root cause of these problems.

These issues and debates provide a context against which to place evidence about the family backgrounds of children who come into care.

THE 1987 SURVEY

The 1987 survey was based in thirteen of the 108 social services authorities in England. These were chosen so as to contain two Inner London authorities, two Outer London authorities, four Metropolitan Districts and five Shire Counties. Within each stratum authorities were approached which would represent a broad spectrum of social conditions and geographical locations, while ensuring that collectively they would be nationally representative both in respect of numbers of children entering care and a number of key social indicators. The only significant departure was that the chosen local authorities, particularly the shire counties, turned out to be larger than average.

Each local authority agreed to collect information from social workers on the family backgrounds of all children formally taken into care between 1 June and 30 November 1987. This excludes children on place-of-safety orders only. At the same time these authorities undertook a survey of all foster families, which will be reported in a later article. The information collected concerned the circumstances of the parental family as it had been in the month preceding entry into care, prior to family breakup. It should be noted that the expression 'broken family' is used loosely throughout this article to describe any situation in which a child is not living with both natural parents, or with two adoptive parents, or with one natural parent and that parent's marital partner. Cohabitation is distinguished from marriage though in practice some long-standing cohabitations may have been described as marriages.

Of the thirteen authorities, complete records for six months were successfully obtained from ten. In the case of one particularly large county with a high rate of entry it was agreed in advance to run the survey for a shorter period. The two remaining authorities each collected only one half of the expected returns, due to union problems in one and to the difficulties of data collection in a large rural area in the other. In all, information was returned on 2528 children out of about 32,000 nationally who entered care during 1987. The sample was divided into 151 from Inner London, 129 from Outer London, 548 from metropolitan districts and 1700 from shire counties. This roughly represents the national distribution though with some bias towards shire counties which provided sixty-seven per cent of the total sample compared with sixty per cent of all children in care. For 356 (fourteen per cent) of children information on the parental family was unavailable. Usually this was because the child had not been living with either parent for some considerable time before coming into care. This group also includes newborn children who were to be placed for adoption direct from hospital, and also runaways and foundlings. The effective sample size for much of the analysis is therefore 2165.

WHO ENTERS CARE?

Children who come into care come from atypical families. The most striking findings about such children are:

— only one quarter were living with both parents;
— almost three-quarters of their families received income support;
— only one in five lived in owner-occupied housing;
— over one half were living in poor neighbourhoods (wards).

In order to investigate these circumstances in greater detail, the circumstances of children who enter care have been compared with a sample of 5407 children not in care aged sixteen or under in England and Wales, drawn from the 1985 General Household Survey (OPCS, 1988). These are the children found in a nationally representative sample of 12,000 households in Great Britain, excluding a small number who were being fostered. (Children who live in institutions, hotels or very temporary accommodation are omitted.)

Children can enter care at any age: but two age groups are particularly vulnerable. Children under one comprised eleven per cent and those aged fourteen to fifteen were twenty-three per cent of all children entering care. The lowest rate of entry occurs between ages five and twelve. Thirty-eight per cent of children came into care in a family group, that is with at least one sibling.

The family factors which were chosen as the basis of comparison are those which have been found significant by Packman (1968), or in a number of local studies since (Ward, 1974; Davies and Plank, 1975; Grampian, 1978; Bradford, 1979; Boldy and Howell, 1980; Lambeth, 1981; Kensington and Chelsea, 1981; Tower Hamlets, 1981 and 1982; Packman *et al.*, 1986), or have been widely associated with being 'in need'. For a list of the main factors used in the comparison, see Table 1.

(Table 1 shows the features of each variable that proved to be of greatest interest. The actual information collected was considerably more detailed.)

To establish the importance of each factor, we have determined its effect on the probability of admission. These factors are mostly highly inter-correlated and for this reason a logistic regression analysis has been used. This analysis is more complicated than a simple comparison of percentages, but it has three major advantages. First, it disentangles the effect of each factor and thus enables us to say, for example, what are the influence of broken homes and poverty independently of one another. Second, it enables an estimate of the odds ratio associated with each factor. For example an odds ratio of three signifies that a child in given circumstances is three times as likely to enter care as other children. This both allows comparisons of the significance of each factor, and facilitates comparisons with other studies. Third, it provides a predictive formula which can be used subsequently to predict the probability that a child will enter care, given his or her personal and family circumstances.

The same approach has been used by Plewis (1979) in a study of day nursery need and Knapp *et al.* (1988) in an investigation of placement decisions in a local authority. Knapp and his colleagues provide an account of the method and the way of estimating probabilities, which will not be repeated here.

Table 1 shows the proportions of each of the two samples living in particular circumstances as well as the results of the logistic regression analysis. From this formula it is possible to predict the probability that a child will enter care during the course of a year, given both their own characteristics and the circumstances of their families. The following examples illustrate these probabilities for two children who are in very different circumstances:

Child 'A'.	*Child 'B'.*
Aged 5 to 9	Aged 5 to 9
No supplementary benefit	Household head receives SB.
Two parent family	Single adult household
Three or fewer children	Four or more children
White	Mixed ethnic origin
Owner occupied home	Private rented home
More rooms than people	One or more persons per room
Odds are 1 in 7,000	*Odds are 1 in 10*

The significance of individual factors to entry into care are as follows.

Broken Families. Living with one adult only is the single greatest risk factor amongst those investigated here. Nearly one half of all children

TABLE 1. *Family circumstances of children in the General Household Survey and the Children Entering Care Surveys compared*

	Samples		Logit Analysis		
	Care %	GHS %	Coef.	Std. Err.	Odds Ratio
Benefits					
Housing (but not SB)	9	9	−0.09	(0.12)	0.9
Supplementary benefit	66	15	1.16*	(0.09)	3.2
Mother under 21	5	1	0.77*	(0.22)	2.1
Single parent family					
With 2 or more adults	12	4	1.06*	(0.12)	2.9
With one adult only	45	7	2.07*	(0.10)	7.9
Four plus children in family	24	9	0.27*	(0.10)	1.3
Ethnic group					
Afro-Caribbean	3	2	0.34	(0.22)	1.4
Asian	3	3	−0.06	(0.19)	0.9
Mixed race	6	1	0.92*	(0.21)	2.5
Tenure					
Council renting	66	25	0.96*	(0.12)	2.6
Private renting	14	8	1.06*	(0.09)	2.9
Overcrowded (1+ person per room)	28	7	1.27*	(0.08)	3.6
Child's age					
5 to 9	20	28	−0.30	(0.10)	0.7
10 and over	46	41	0.67*	(0.08)	2.0
Constant			−8.31	(0.10)	0.0
Sample size	(2016)	(4996)			

The percentages shown in columns 1 and 2 are the proportion of children in each of the two samples coming from households of the type described.

The logistic regression was run using GLIM (Baker and Nelder, 1985). Coefficients shown with an asterisk are statistically significantly greater than zero (1 per cent level), and so assuming that the fixed biases and design effects are small, correspond to factors which are independently associated with entry into care.

The constant term has been adjusted to allow for the different sampling fractions of the two surveys (see McCullagh and Nelder, 1983, p. 78).

It should be noted in this and all subsequent tables that the circumstances of children *entering* care is not necessarily an accurate reflection of the children *in* care at any time, due to the wide variations in length of stay in care.

entering care were living with one adult only, compared with just seven per cent of other children. Such children are nearly eight times as likely to enter care compared with two-parent families. Children in single parent families with more than one adult in the household—typically the child's mother and a cohabitee or grandparent—are also at risk of coming into care but the odds are only three times as great as for two-parent families.

Housing Conditions. Living in crowded accommodation is the next most significant indicator. Children living in such homes are three-and-a-half times more likely to enter care than children living in homes with more rooms than people (a crowded home has one or more persons for every room). Closely related is the fact that one half of the children who came into care were living in homes with four or less rooms. Tenure is also related to risk, with a child from rented accommodation three times, and from council accommodation twice as likely to enter care as a similar child from an owner-occupied home.

Receipt of Benefits. Children from homes where the head of household received supplementary benefit were three times more likely to come into care (supplementary benefit is now replaced by income support). Almost all these households also receive housing benefit. Housing benefit on its own did not appear to be an indicator of need.

Ethnic Origin. Single-race children from ethnic minorities are not over-represented amongst the children entering care, especially when allowance is made for other factors. Table 1 shows that from the samples Afro-Caribbean and African children are a little more likely to come into care than white children, but the differences are not statistically significant. On the other hand, a child of mixed race is two-and-a-half times as likely to enter care as a white child, all else being equal.

Mother Under Twenty-one. This doubles the odds that a child will enter care. However, our data did not record mother's age for children taken into care directly from hospital after birth. Almost certainly this group has a disproportionate number of young mothers. If in *all* such cases the mother had been under twenty-one, it would imply that having a mother under twenty-one quadruples the odds.

Large Family. Coming from a family of four or more children has a comparatively small effect on the risk of entry, though it is associated with many factors that do raise the risk, like overcrowding. (A similar conclusion is drawn by Rutter, 1985, on the association between family size and delinquency.)

Poor Neighbourhood. In addition to these family circumstances, some evidence is available about the type of neighbourhood that children admitted into care come from. However, as this information is not available in the General Household Survey, this factor could not be included in the analysis of Table 1. Instead, an analysis has been made from the 1981 Census of all wards in England, to identify those which have a preponderance of children living in the family circumstances described above. This analysis is explained in the appendix, and leads to the identification of the worst twenty per cent of wards on a combined index. These are referred to as 'poor' wards for a child to live in. They occur particularly in inner cities, which are often also materially poor, though in London some of the 'poor' wards occur in the wealthiest areas of the West End. Table 2 shows that more than one half of all children admitted to care came from poor wards, compared with a third of all children in 1981.

TABLE 2. *Children living in poor wards in the 13 local authorities in the survey*

	Entering Care %	1981 Census %	Odds Ratio
Proportion from poor wards	56	33	2.6

For the definition of a poor ward, see Appendix. The proportion in the 1987 children entering care sample is based on 2197 children whose ward of origin is known. The 1981 Census figure is based on 1.6m children under 16 in the 13 local authorities in the study.

The analysis of Table 2 does not separate the effect of living in a poor ward from other factors. To a considerable extent children from these areas come into care because they are themselves deprived, rather than because they live in proximity with other deprived children. However, Bebbington and Miles (1988) show that the rate of entry into care in areas with many poor wards is higher than would be predicted from family related social indicators alone, implying that coming from a poor ward has an independent effect on the probability of entry.

VOLUNTARY AND COMPULSORY ADMISSIONS

Three main routes into care were identified above: voluntary admissions, offenders, and children taken into care compulsorily in the interests of their welfare.

The children who come into care by each of these routes are rather different in certain obvious respects. Children who come into care following a criminal offence were almost all aged twelve or over and ninety-six per cent were boys. Children taken into care compulsorily were slightly younger than average and over half were girls.

TABLE 3. *Family characteristics of children by legal category on entering care,*
compared with all children

	Children Entering Care			General Population (GHS)
	Voluntary	Court Orders		
		Offenders	Others	
	%	%	%	%
Broken (Single Parent) Family	76	57	69	15
Household head gets income support (SB or unemployment benefit)	71	48	76	26
Not owner occupied home	80	68	85	28
Crowded home (one or more persons per room)	55	50	67	21
Mixed ethnic origin	6	5	5	1
(Sample size)	(1659)	(174)	(593)	(5274)

Figures shown are the proportion of children who come from particular family backgrounds, in the Children Entering Care survey and the 1985 General Household Survey. Sample sizes on which these proportions are based are shown at the bottom, though some proportions are based on slightly smaller numbers due to missing information.

Nevertheless, Table 3 shows that the same problematic circumstances appear in the family backgrounds of all children entering care. Our results confirm that deprivation is a common factor among all types of children who enter care. There are however, some differences: for example poverty and adverse housing conditions are particularly common among children taken into care compulsorily. It is also apparent from Table 3 that family deprivation factors are less significant for offenders than for other children who come into care. Indeed ten per cent of this group were not affected by any of the factors listed in Table 3. Though the majority of delinquent children do come from deprived backgrounds, deprivation is not an invariable explanation of why children offend.

COMPARISONS WITH CHILDREN IN NEED IN 1962

Packman's (1968) survey of 1962 included all children for whom, during a six month period, an application for admission to care was made, or who were subjects of a court order, in a representative sample of local authorities across England and Wales, but excluding London. This provided about 4500 cases, of whom around 2800 were subject to court orders or admitted to care.

CHILDREN WHO ENTER LOCAL AUTHORITY CARE 359

Since Packman's survey there have been major legislative changes. The 1963 Children and Young Persons Act gave local authorities the power to take preventative action to stop children coming into care. The 1969 Children and Young Persons Act was designed to reduce the distinction between offenders and non-offenders. The system of 'approved schools' was abolished so many offenders who would have previously been treated separately were subsequently brought in under the same care system as non-offenders. The combined effect of these legislative changes has been to try to prevent less problematic children coming into care at all, while bringing in more delinquent and disturbed children. In addition, the 1969 Children and Young Persons Act sought to avoid juvenile court appearances when possible. In practice this could mean that social workers and police would co-operate to bring children into care voluntarily rather than invoke court proceedings. So the distinction between voluntary and other admissions is blurred.

As a result, the administrative reasons why children come into care have changed considerably. Both Packman's survey and our own investigated this by expanding on the classification of reason for entry used by the Home Office and the Department of Health and Social Security respectively. After simplifying these reasons to the major groups used by Packman (1968), Table 4 shows how they compare. It is impossible to achieve precise comparability due to legal changes, shifts of meaning, and shortage of exact details. Even so, Table 4 shows there have been major changes, with a far higher proportion of children now admitted primarily for behaviour problems and offences. A concomitant is that more older children are now coming into care. The proportion aged under five on admission has fallen from fifty-six per cent in 1962 to thirty per cent in the 1987 survey, while those aged over fourteen has increased from three per cent to twenty-five per cent.

Bearing in mind these changes, but also the evidence given above that the backgrounds of children are similar whatever the reason for entry, Table 5 compares the families of children admitted to care in the two surveys. Three features of this table should be noticed.

— The odds ratios of most factors have increased, indicating that entry into care is even more closely associated with 'deprived' families than it was in 1962. This is all the more noteworthy since the number of behaviourally disturbed and delinquent children has increased, groups which we identified as having lower than average levels of deprivation.
— The factor most highly correlated with entry has changed from unemployment in 1962 to broken (or 'non-nuclear') family in 1987.
— In the population at large, there has been some increase since 1962 in

TABLE 4. *Reasons for entry into care, 1962 and 1987*

	1962 survey %	1987 survey %
Voluntary admission:		
Incomplete family (Parental death, desertion, illegitimacy etc.)	21	18
Ill health of parents	56	19
Poor home conditions (including homeless and parents unable to cope)	9	12
Child's behaviour difficulties	1	12
Miscellaneous, unclassifiable, unknown	3	8
Court Orders:		
Offenders	3	7[a]
Non-offenders	7	24[b]
	100	100
(n)	(2819)	(2490)

The 1962 figures are from Packman (1968) Tables III and IV, combining prime reason for court orders, long- and short-term admissions. Comparability between the two surveys is very approximate, for reasons described in the text.
[a] Including children on remand, committed or detained, and children admitted under CYP Act 1969 Sections 7(7) and 15(1).
[b] Includes children on interim care orders, CYP Act 1969 Section 1, and various matrimonial proceedings Acts.

the proportion of children living in broken homes. Housing has improved dramatically but unemployment has worsened. On balance, the number of children in care relative to the level of deprivation is probably similar now to twenty-five years ago, even though the type of children entering care has changed.

DIFFERENCES BETWEEN AREAS IN THE CIRCUMSTANCES OF CHILDREN

It is well known that there are striking differences between local authorities in the numbers of children who come into care. In 1986 the number of children in care (per 1000 aged under eighteen) ranged from two in the Outer London boroughs of Barnet and Harrow up to fourteen in Manchester and sixteen in the Inner London borough of Hackney.

CHILDREN WHO ENTER LOCAL AUTHORITY CARE 361

TABLE 5. *Family circumstances associated with entry into care, 1962 and 1987*

	1962			1987		
	Enter Care %	General Pop. %	Odds Ratio	Enter Care %	General Pop. %	Odds Ratio
Broken (Single Parent) Family	48	12[a]	7	72	15	14
Four plus dependent children	35	8[b]	6	18	4	5
Mother under 21	7	1[b]	7	7[c]	1	7
Unemployed father	23	2[d]	14	47[c]	9[c]	9
Not owner-occupier tenure	88	58[b]	5	79	30	8
Home has under 5 rooms	55	45[b]	1	51	11	8

The 1962 figures for children entering care are from Packman (1968) Tables VI, VII, X, XII, XV, and XVI, combining percentages for court orders, long and short admissions, and eliminating 'not known' categories. The 1987 figures are adapted from the Children entering care survey and a reanalysis of the 1985 General Household Survey. Figures show estimates of the percentage of *families* possessing the given characteristic. As definitions are not exactly comparable through time odds ratios are shown to the nearest whole number only.
[a] Packman's estimate, p. 45 footnote 2. This figure seems a little higher than other contemporary estimates.
[b] From 1961 Census, families with children.
[c] Omitting newborn children taken into care, so probably an underestimate.
[d] Packman's estimate, p. 52.
[e] This is the percentage of heads of household receiving supplementary benefit or unemployment benefit among families with fathers.

Analysis of these variations in relation to need indicators is considered elsewhere (Bebbington and Miles, 1988).

As well as these variations in rates of entry and length of stay there are also significant differences in the characteristics of children entering. In particular there is variation between authorities in reasons for entry into care. This is shown in Table 6. For example the proportion of children who enter care on remand ranges from zero up to fourteen per cent. We think there are three potential explanations for these differences.

— Reasons for entry are associated with a child's circumstances. There are differences between areas in the circumstances of children generally, and this is reflected in the circumstances of the children who come into care.
— Local authorities have different strategies—they may be particularly sensitive to certain needs—which mean that children in certain circumstances are more readily taken into care in some areas than others.
— Authorities adopt different strategies in their interpretation of the 1969 Children and Young Persons Act. The result is that although children with certain problems will always come into care wherever

TABLE 6. *Authority variations in the legal status of children admitted to care*

Local authority	Voluntary	Court Orders		Sample
		Offender	Others	Size
	%	%	%	
East-End Inner London borough	87	0	23	(82)
West-End Inner London borough	73	0	27	(66)
Southern Outer London borough	58	7	35	(80)
Northern Outer London borough	85	6	8	(48)
Yorkshire metropolitan district (1)	45	14	41	(222)
Yorkshire metropolitan district (2)	62	5	33	(115)
Lancashire metropolitan district	82	6	12	(101)
Midlands metropolitan district	75	4	21	(89)
North-east county	64	11	25	(492)
North-west county	80	8	22	(552)
Home county	71	6	14	(198)
Southern county	47	3	26	(347)
West-country county		1	52	(73)
Overall	68	7	25	(2465)

The figures show the proportion of children in each major legal category for each of the 13 local authorities in the 1987 survey. Voluntary admissions are under section 2 of 1980 CYP Act. Offenders are children on remand or admitted under sections 7(7) or 15(1) of the 1969 CYP Act.

they live, the legislation which is used to take them into care will reflect local practice.

It appears that all three of these explanations are true in some measure. As evidence of this, we contrast children admitted into care in the two inner London authorities with those admitted elsewhere.

The two inner London authorities are strikingly different from other areas in certain respects. Both have halved the number of children in care since the start of the decade. (Several other London authorities have made similar reductions but some have not changed at all.) The children they take into care are particularly prone to the adverse conditions of 'need' identified above. A high proportion come from broken homes, where the family receives income support, from rented housing, from overcrowded homes, and are of mixed race. But all these circumstances are particularly common among children who live in inner London (see Table 7). So the high incidence of adverse conditions among children admitted in these two areas is simply because these circumstances occur more frequently in the general population of these localities. We have tested formally the differences between area types in the odds ratios of

CHILDREN WHO ENTER LOCAL AUTHORITY CARE 363

entry into care, for broken family, receipt of income support, owner occupation, overcrowding and ethnic group. Four area types were used for this purpose: Inner London, Outer London, Metropolitan Districts and Shire Counties (not shown in Table 7). The tests are complicated by small sample sizes and large design effects, but overall there is little evidence of statistically significant differences between areas.

TABLE 7. *Family circumstances of children in Inner London and elsewhere: children entering care and all children*

| | Inner London | | Elsewhere | |
	Enter care %	General pop. %	Enter care %	General pop. %
Broken (Single Parent) Family	80	26	73	14
Household head gets income support (SB or employment benefit)	75	26	70	16
Not owner occupied home	97	80	67	30
Crowded home (one or more persons per room)	66	57	45	24
Mixed ethnicity	20	8	5	1
Non-white single race ethnic group	24	19	6	5
Aged under 5	47	33	32	29
(Sample size)	(148)	(264)	(2327)	(5010)

Figures shown are the proportion of children who come from given family backgrounds, in the Children Entering Care survey and the 1985 General Household Survey. Sample sizes on which these proportions are based are shown at the bottom, though some proportions are based on slightly smaller numbers due to missing information.

Inportant: The Inner London samples are based on two local authorities only in the Children Entering Care survey and on a small number of areas in the General Household survey, so figures must be interpreted with caution.

Concern has been expressed about the high proportion of children from ethnic minorities being admitted to care in London: indeed in one of our authorities more than half the children admitted were non-white. But on our evidence, as shown in Table 7, this is little more than a reflection of the local ethnic composition.

So differences between areas among children entering care can be mainly attributed to the circumstances of children locally. There is, however, one conspicuous exception shown in Table 7. The two Inner London authorities were admitting far more young children into care than other authorities in the study. The average age on entry was under six compared with eight and a half elsewhere. The reason for this is not known and it is only possible to speculate, but an impression we formed during the course of the field-work was that the London authorities were particularly sensitive to the risks of child abuse in the wake of the Jasmine Beckford, Tyra Henry and Kimberley Carlile inquiries, each relating to incidents which occurred in London and which were receiving much publicity shortly before and during our survey. Osmond (1988) indicates that the number of children on Lambeth's child abuse register rose by sixty-three per cent in the three years after Tyra Henry died.

A third explanation of the differences between authorities is that the actual reason for entry may have more to do with administrative practices than with the child's needs or behaviour. We have already seen how similar are the backgrounds of children who come into care, whatever the reason for admission. During the field-work for this research, in many areas we were made aware of the efforts some social work teams make to bring children into care voluntarily rather than compulsorily. But much depends on local co-operation between police, magistrates and social services, as well as the social services department's own policy and perceptions. In some areas co-operation was good: in others the distrust which Packman (1975) describes as having accompanied the 1969 Children and Young Persons Act was still in evidence. It is worth noting that the high variation in entry routes reported in Table 6 occurs just as much between local teams within authorities as it does between authorities.

DISCUSSION

It must be stressed that our findings are associative and do not lead to simple conclusions about prevention. For example, though children living in council accommodation have above average probability of entering care, this does not mean that their risk could be reduced simply by moving their families to other accommodation.

Nevertheless, the link between certain adverse family circumstances and entry into care is noteworthy. That single-parent families are associated with entry has been shown many times, though the magnitude of the correlation is a surprise. Those concerned with prevention will wish to understand what it is about these families that is so significant to admission. Our results do imply that it is not simply because single parent families are often poor, because the correlation persists even when allowance is made for indicators of poverty.

An alternative explanation is that single parents lack not only partners but find it difficult to maintain other social networks which would enable them to cope during times of adversity, and in general with the tensions of raising a family (see, for example, Brown and Harris, 1978). If family breakdown and lack of social support is the prime cause of entry, this highlights the salience of family support strategies to prevention. But not all would agree. As was discussed above, at one time both family breakdown and entry into care were seen as symptoms of anomie resulting for social forces beyond the control of individuals. Our own evidence offers limited support for this by showing the effect of living in a deprived community, and West (1982) has shown that delinquency tended to diminish when boys were moved outside London.

But generally explanations in terms of social malaise are out of fashion: Rutter *et al.* (1975) having shown that the relationship between family circumstances and child disorder was very similar in both Inner London and a deeply rural area. Rutter (1985) has yet another explanation for the link. It is not marital breakdown *per se* that causes behaviour problems among children, but the child's previous exposure to family discord. However, it is hard to attribute this explanation to the children who are admitted for reasons not linked to behaviour. In the final analysis, it may be that although children who are admitted to care for different reasons come from similar family backgrounds, the dynamics of the situation that creates their problems may be very different.

It is even possible that the causal link between family breakdown and entry is sometimes in the other direction. Bell and Harper (1977) provide a review of child effects on family and Quine and Pahl (1986) report evidence that a behaviourally disturbed handicapped child is a major cause of marital tension and breakdown.

A final explanation of why the correlation may have increased is that children in broken families are now likely to receive much professional attention, and the connection with admission may partly reflect the way in which resources and social work activity are targeted. Indeed, two of the authorities in the study were proposing to allocate social work resources on the basis of needs indicators similar to those we have found significant. The system of rate support grant introduced in 1980 has undoubtedly put local authorities under pressure to match provision to expenditure needs assessments.

Two of the other main findings of this article are that provision is more closely linked to deprivation than at the time of Packman's 1962 survey; and that variations between areas in the circumstances of children entering care reflect local social conditions. These findings, supported by our other work on the relationship between levels of provision and need indicators draw us to the conclusion that although significant anomalies continue to exist, variations in practice are more explicable now than they were twenty-five years ago.

366   ANDREW BEBBINGTON AND JOHN MILES

ACKNOWLEDGEMENTS

We would like to thank all the participating authorities, and in particular the liaison officers and team administration officers who provided us with the information on children entering care; Hazel Green (OPCS) for permission to use data from the 1985 General Household Survey; and members of the DHSS and Local Authorities Associations research steering group. The project was funded by a grant from the Department of Health and Social Security.

REFERENCES

A Child in Trust: The report of the panel of enquiry into the circumstances surrounding the death of Jasmine Beckford (1987), London Borough of Brent.

A Child in Mind: Report of the inquiry into the circumstances of the death of Kimberley Carlile (1987), London Borough of Greenwich.

Baker, R. J. and Nelder, J. A. (1985) *GLIM 3 Manual*, London, Royal Statistical Society.

Bacon, R. and Rowe, J. (1978) *Substitute Family Care*, London, Association of British Adoption and Fostering Agencies.

Bebbington, A. C. and Miles, J. B. (1988) 'A need indicator of in care services for children', *PSSRU Discussion Paper 574*, University of Kent.

Bell, R. W. and Harper, L. V. (eds.) (1977) *Child Effects on Adults*, New Jersey, Erlbaum.

Boldy, D. and Howell, N. (1980) 'Forecasting the number of children in local authority care and their placement requirements', *Social Policy and Administration*, 14, pp. 124–50.

Bone, E. (1977) *Preschool Children and the Need for Day Care*, London, HMSO.

Bowlby, J. (1952) *Maternal Care and Mental Health*, Geneva, World Health Organisation.

Bradford SSD (1979) 'Forecasting numbers of children in care subject to care orders', *Clearing House for Local Authorities Social Services Research*, 4, pp. 53–95.

Brown, G. W. and Harris, T. (1978) *Social Origins of Depression*, London, Tavistock.

Butler-Sloss Inquiry *Report of the Inquiry into Child Abuse in Cleveland 1987* (1988), London, HMSO.

Cooper, J. (1978) *Patterns of Family Placement*, London, National Childrens Bureau.

Davies, B. P., Barton, A. and McMillan, I. (1972) *Variations in Children's Services among British Urban Authorities*, London, G. Bell and Sons.

Davies, H. and Plank, D. (1975) *Children in care of the London Boroughs*, London, GLC Intelligence Unit.

Department of Health and Social Security (1971) *Begone Dull Care*, Report no.1. Advisory Council on Child Care, Community Homes Design Guide, London, HMSO.

Fruin, D. and Vernon, J. (1983) *Social work decision making and its effects on length of time children spend in care*, London, National Children's Bureau.

Grampian Regional Council (1978) *Study of admissions of children into care*, Internal report.

House of Commons Committee on Social Services (1987) *1st Special Report, Children in Care*, London, HMSO.

Holtermann, S. (1975) 'Areas of Urban Deprivation in Great Britain—an analysis of 1971 Census data', *Social Trends*, 6, 33–47.

Isaac, B. C., Minty, E. B. and Morrison, R. M. (1986) 'Children in Care—The Association With Mental Disorder in Parents', *British Journal of Social Work*, 16, pp. 325–9.

Kensington and Chelsea SSD (1981) *A study of decisions to receive children into care*, Internal report (ed. T. Mellings).

Knapp, M., Baines, B. and Fenyo, A. (1988) 'Consistencies and Inconsistencies in Child Care Placements', *British Journal of Social Work*, 18, (supp.), pp. 107–30.

Lambeth SSD (1981) *Why do children come into care?* Internal report.

McCullagh, P. and Nelder, J. A. (1983) *Generalized Linear Models*, London, Chapman and Hall.

Millham, S., Bullock, R., Hosie, K. and Haak, M. (1986) *Lost in Care*, Aldershot, Gower.

Office of Population Censuses and Surveys (1987) *General Household Survey 1985*, London, HMSO.

Osmond, R. (1988) 'Difficult Social Task', *Social Work Today*, 19, no.50, p. 20.

Packman, J. (1968) *Child Care: Needs and Numbers*, London, Allen and Unwin.

Packman, J. (1975) *The Child's Generation*, Oxford, Blackwell.

Packman, J., Randall, J. and Jacques, N. (1986) *Who Needs Care?* Oxford, Blackwell.

Parker, R. A. (1971) *Planning for Deprived Children*, London, National Childrens Home.

Plewis, I. (1979) 'Desire for and use of day care nurseries: a socio-demographic analysis', *Clearing House for Local Authority Social Services Research*, 3, pp. 71–98.

Quine, L. and Pahl, J. (1986) 'Parents with severely handicapped children: marriage and the stress of caring', in Chester, R. and Divall, P., *Mental Health, Illness and Handicap in·Marriage*, NMGC Research Report 5.

Quinton, D. and Rutter, M. (1984) 'Parents with children in care 1: Current circumstances and parenting', *J. Child Psychology and Psychiatry*, 25, pp. 211–29.

Report of Committee of Inquiry into Care and Supervision in relation to Maria Colwell (1974), London, HMSO.

Rowe, J., Hundleby, M. and Garnett, L. (1988) *Child Care Placements Patterns and Outcomes*, Report to the DHSS, London.

Rowe, J. and Lambert, L. (1973) *Children Who Wait*, London, Association of British Adoption Agencies.

Rutter, M. (1985) 'Family and School Influences: Meanings, Mechanisms and Implications', in Nichol, A. R. (ed.) *Longitudinal Studies in Child Psychology and Psychiatry*, New York, John Wiley.

Rutter, M. and Giller, H. (1983) *Juvenile Delinquency: Trends and Perspectives*, London, Penguin Press.

Rutter, M. and Madge, N. (1976) *Cycles of Disadvantage*, London, Heinemann Educational.

Rutter, M., Yule, B., Quinton, D., Rowlands, O., Yule, W., and Berger, M. (1975) 'Attainment and adjustment in two geographical areas III: Some factors accounting for area differences', *British Journal of Psychiatry*, 126, pp. 520–33.

Tower Hamlets SSD (1981) *Why does Tower Hamlets have so many children in care?* Internal report.

Tower Hamlets SSD (1982) *Children who come into care in Tower Hamlets*, Internal report.

Ward, D. F. (1974) *Child Care in South Hampshire*, Hampshire SSD Internal report.

Wedge, P. and Prosser, H. (1978) *Born to Fail*, London, Arrow.

West, D. J. (1982) *Delinquency: Its Roots, Careers and Prospects*, London, Heinemann Educational.

Whose Child: Report of inquiry into the death of Tyra Henry (1987), London Borough of Lambeth.

APPENDIX: AN INDEX OF POOR WARDS

An analysis was carried out on all wards in England from the 1981 census to construct an index of adverse social conditions for children. The method is similar to that of Holtermann (1975), though with a focus on indicators relating specifically to children from the 1981 Census Ward Library. The following indicators were included:

Population density (persons per hectare);
Proportion of children in households not self contained;

368   ANDREW BEBBINGTON AND JOHN MILES

Proportion of children in households lacking basic amenities;
Proportion of children in crowded households (1+ persons per room);
Proportion of children in single parent households;
Proportion of children where the household head was born in the New Commonwealth of Pakistan.

Firstly, principle components analysis was used to check the scalability of these six indicators over the 8443 wards in England with eighty or more resident children. The first principle component accounts for fifty-two per cent of the total variance, and there is no other large component. This is consistent with the hypothesis that these items form a single factor.

Secondly, each of the indicators is standardized, and the index is constructed by adding together the standardized scores. The worst 1689 (twenty per cent) of wards are identified as 'poor' wards. The index clearly illustrates the concentration of adverse social conditions in inner city areas. The very worst wards are in Inner London: St Mary's (Tower Hamlets), Brownswood (Hackney) and Chamberlayne (Brent). Elsewhere Manchester, Wolverhampton and Hull have the worst wards.

[19]

Child Poverty and Needs Based Budget Allocation

D. Gordon
Research Fellow, School for Policy Studies, University of Bristol.
F. Loughran
Planning Officer for Children's Services, Planning and Evaluation Group, Somerset Social Services.

Abstract: Many local authorities allocate their childcare resources on the basis of the distribution of the child population. However, this method does not take account of the variation in the levels of need between areas and is likely to disadvantage those areas with the greatest need. The advantages of different needs based allocation methods are discussed and two new indices of child poverty are developed: the Modified Low Cost Budget index which is most suitable for use in rural areas and the Children's Breadline Britain Index which can be used by Urban and Sub-urban authorities. In addition to their use for resource allocation purposes, the child poverty indices have considerable potential for other planning purposes, especially the development of Children and Family Services Plans, the siting of specific child care units and services and the drawing/redrawing of administrative boundaries.

Introduction

The initiative to develop an index of child need arose from Somerset Social Services department's wish to have a fair means of dividing the child care budget between its eight child care teams. Resources had been allocated on the basis of the distribution of the child population but, as this method did not take account of the variation in levels of need between the teams, it was likely to be disadvantaging those areas with the greatest need.

Before adopting the need index approach, other methods that could be used for resource allocation were considered. Formulae could be produced based on:

(i) the level of current service provided (for example, the number of children Looked After, or on the child protection register), or

(ii) measures of demand for service (for example, number of requests for help received from families, referrals from other agencies).

Both of these approaches have limitations. It is very difficult to disentangle the level of current services provided by a child care team from the resources it has available. The level of services is not independent of the amount of resources. For example, if a child care team is given additional social work time, it is likely to 'find' more families in need of services. This is particularly true at a time when financial restrictions have reduced the level of services below that which would otherwise be desirable.

Measures of demand are beset by problems of definition. For example, what constitutes a referral? What is a new referral as opposed to a re-referral of the same family? The number of referrals needs to be treated with some caution since they are not entirely independent of current levels of service provision. Gibbons, Conroy and Bell (1995) found in their study of six local authorities that referrals came from a wide range of sources; teachers, school nurses and education welfare staff contributed 23%; health staff (health visitors, hospitals and GPs) 17%; lay people 17%; police and probation 12% and anonymous callers 6%. However, 13% of all referrals were contributed by other sections of the social services department so referrals are largely, but not entirely, service independent.

Requests for help from families are certainly a direct measure of demand but it cannot be assumed that those who request the most necessarily have the greatest need. Also, some families who may require social services intervention may not seek it or will deliberately avoid contact.

In comparison with other possible methods of resource allocation, an index of need has the advantage of being relatively independent of service-based measures and definitions. Instead, a measure of need in the population of families would be used on the assumption that child care clients predominantly originate from families living in poverty. This is a fair assumption: there is a wealth of research studies showing strong associations between measures of poverty and, for example, the likelihood of being Looked After, juvenile offending and childhood disability (Creighton, 1992; Gordon and

Research, Policy and Practice (1997) Vol. 15 No. 3

Gibbons, 1997).

The need to commission a new index arose from two limitations of existing needs indices. Firstly, Somerset is a predominantly rural county and all the existing national indices inevitably had an urban bias as it is in the major urban centres that the greatest concentrations of poverty are located. Secondly, no specific index of need for children and families was available. It was felt particularly important to avoid the use of a general measure of deprivation as, within Somerset, the two major groupings of 'poor' households, the elderly and families with children, have very different geographical distributions. Poor families are clustered in the main towns whereas there are concentrations of poor elderly households in the popular retirement areas along the coast.

Needs based budgeting and child poverty

The Children Act, 1989, made it a statutory requirement for local authorities to assess the numbers of children in need (including poor/deprived children) in their area. Schedule 2 of the Act, which came into force in October 1991, required local authorities to identify the extent to which there are children in need living in their area. Social services departments in local authorities do not have to seek out and identify every individual child in need but they should use information on the extent of need in their area to inform the planning of children's services. Children in need are defined as (Children Act, 1989, Section 17, (10):

- children who are unlikely to achieve or maintain a reasonable standard of health or development without the provision of local authority services;
- children whose health or development is likely to be significantly or further impaired without the provision of local authority services;
- children with disabilities.

Local authorities were asked to provide statistics on the following categories of children to the Department of Health, which were based on the categories in the Guidance (DoH, 1991) for senior child care managers in Part 111 of the Children Act (our emphasis):

- children with disabilities;
- children at risk of abuse or neglect;
- children who are delinquent or at risk of becoming so;
- children separated from their parents;
- children with serious family problems;
- children whose home conditions are unsatisfactory;
- children living in poverty;

- children leaving care.

Unfortunately, few authorities were able to provide statistics on any of these categories, except children at risk of neglect or abuse (Colton *et al.,* 1995). Research in Wales has found that child care managers in social service departments are currently having to concentrate their efforts on children at risk of physical or sexual abuse or neglect. However, as Table 1 demonstrates, most managers would like to give a higher priority to problems of child poverty, disability, children with severe family problems and unsatisfactory home conditions (Colton *et al.,* 1995).

Table 1: Priority given to categories of children in need by Welsh child care managers.

Need Category	Actual Priority	Ideal Priority
Sexual abuse	1.50	2.75
Other abuse/neglect	1.88	3.00
Delinquency	4.31	5.94
Leaving Care	4.38	4.56
Disabilities	5.88	5.75
Separated from parents	6.13	6.81
Severe family problems	6.38	4.63
Unsatisfactory home conditions	6.94	6.00
Poverty	7.81	5.56

(source: Colton, et al., 1995, p719)

The nine groups of children in need listed in Table 1 are not mutually exclusive and there are considerable overlaps between them. For example, the two largest groups are usually children with disabilities and children in poverty. Analysis of the 1985 OPCS disability surveys by Berthoud, Lakey and McKay (1993) indicated that 45% of all disabled adults were living in poverty and that poverty rates were likely to be even higher amongst families with disabled children. This finding has been recently confirmed by Gordon, Parker and Loughran (1996) who showed almost 55% of families with disabled children were living in or on the margins of poverty.

Similarly, there is a considerable degree of overlap between poor families and 'referred' families. A recent study of six local authorities by Gibbons, Conroy and Bell found that 54% of all referred families were in receipt of Income Support and that 'the overall picture was of deprived families living in poverty' (1995: 43)[1]. There are also obvious overlaps between children in poverty and children living in families with severe problems and/or unsatisfactory home conditions.

Research, Policy and Planning (1997) Vol. 15 No. 3

The 1991 Census can provide some data on the two largest categories of children in need: children living in poverty and children with disabilities, at small area level. Administrative data can be used to provide statistics on the numbers at risk of abuse, leaving care and delinquency. However, at present, there is no easy way of estimating the numbers of children separated from their parents, with severe family problems or with unsatisfactory home conditions.

Methodology and problems of measuring child poverty in rural areas

The release of the 1991 Census data saw a plethora of new deprivation indices produced. None of the questions in the 1991 Census was specifically designed to measure either poverty or deprivation. Therefore, any Census based index must comprise variables that are, at best, proxy indicators of deprivation rather than direct measures. It is, therefore, unsurprising that a bewildering array of indices has been proposed, using different combinations of variables and different statistical methods.

An evaluation of the ten most widely used indices was recently undertaken on behalf of the Joseph Rowntree Foundation (Lee *et al.*, 1995) and they concluded that the *Breadline Britain* index of Gordon and Forrest (1995) was the most representative of deprivation nationally. However none of 1991 Census based deprivation indices are designed to measure either children's poverty or poverty in rural areas. The only index of children's deprivation so far produced is based on 1981 Census results (Bebbington and Miles, 1987) and is a children's version of the 1981 DOE Z-Scores. It was constructed from six 1981 Census variables:

- population density;
- children in non self-contained accommodation;
- children in households lacking basic amenities;
- children in overcrowded households;
- single parent households;
- children in households where the head was born in the New Commonwealth/Pakistan.

However, the Z-Score methodology has now been superseded by the *Index of Local Conditions* and the DoE no longer recommends it as an adequate measure of deprivation (Robson *et al.*, 1995). Therefore, it would not be appropriate to use this index for measuring the present level of child deprivation.

A number of local authorities have used the *Young Persons' Support Index* as a planning tool for children's services. This used 1991 Census results and is based on research by Bebbington and Miles (1988, 1989) into the differences between the family circumstances of children entering care and children in the general population. Unfortunately, Bebbington and Miles did not analyse their results with a view to producing a Census based index and the attempts to produce such an index have resulted in a number statistical errors that mean it is of only very limited value. It would be very unwise to use the Young Persons' Support Index for resource allocation purposes.

What is Poverty?

In order to measure deprivation/poverty accurately, it is necessary to be precise about the meaning of these terms. Poverty, like 'evolution' or 'health' is both a scientific and a moral concept. Many of the problems of measuring poverty arise because the moral and scientific concepts are often confused.

There are two basic concepts of poverty in social science: the 'absolute' and the 'relative'. The 'absolute' concept of poverty is dominated by the individual's requirements for physiological efficiency. However, this is a very limited conceptualisation of human needs, especially when considering the roles that men and women play in society. People are not just physical beings. They are social beings with obligations as workers, parents, neighbours, friends and citizens that they are expected to meet and which they themselves want to meet. Studies of people's behaviour after they have experienced a drastic cut in resources show that they sometimes act to fulfil their social obligations before they act to satisfy their physical wants. They require income to fulfil their various roles and participate in the social customs and associations to which they have become habituated and not only to satisfy their physical wants (Townsend and Gordon, 1989).

Poverty can be defined as the point at which resources are so seriously below those commanded by the average individual or family that the poor are, in effect, excluded from ordinary living patterns, customs and activities. As resources for any individual or family are diminished, there is a point at which there occurs a sudden withdrawal from participation in the customs and activities sanctioned by the culture. The point at which withdrawal escalates disproportionately to falling resources can be defined as the poverty line or threshold (Townsend, 1979; 1993).

In scientific terms a person or household in Britain is 'poor' when they have both a low standard of living and a low income (Gordon and Pantazis, 1997). They are not poor if they have a low income and a reasonable standard of living or if they have a low standard of living but a high income. Both low income and low standard of living

Research, Policy and Practice (1997) Vol. 15 No. 3

can only be accurately measured relative to the norms of the person's or household's society. This 'relative' concept of poverty is now widely accepted (Piachaud, 1987). However it is not easy measure poverty directly (Atkinson, 1985a; 1985b; Lewis and Ulph, 1988) although it is possible to obtain measures of 'deprivation'. These two concepts are tightly linked and there is general agreement that the concept of deprivation covers the various conditions, independent of income, experienced by people who are poor. The concept of poverty refers to the lack of income and other resources which make those conditions inescapable or at least highly likely (Townsend, 1987).

Put simply, a low standard of living is often measured by using a deprivation index (high deprivation equals a low standard of living) or by consumption expenditure (low consumption expenditure equals a low standard of living). Of these two methods, deprivation indices are more accurate since consumption expenditure is often only measured over a brief period and is obviously not independent of available income.

The measurement of poverty and deprivation

From these definitions it is clear that, in order to measure poverty or deprivation accurately, surveys or censuses must be used that establish both the 'normal' or 'average' standard of living of the majority in a society/culture as well as any 'enforced' reductions in this standard due to lack of resources.

Social scientists have been using deprivation surveys to study poverty in Britain for over a hundred years. All these surveys have shown that certain groups are more likely to suffer from multiple deprivation than others (i.e. lone parents and unemployed people are not equally likely to be living in poverty and indices that consider them to be are probably wrong). Therefore, Census based deprivation indices that give equal weight to their component variables are likely to yield inaccurate results.

Since all Census based deprivation indices are generally composed of surrogate or proxy measures of deprivation rather than direct measures, there are two basic requirements they should fulfil to ensure accuracy (Gordon, 1995):

(i) the components of the index should be weighted to reflect the different probability that each group has of suffering from deprivation;

(ii) the components of the index must be additive, eg if an index is composed of two variables, unemployment and lone parenthood, then researchers must be confident that unemployed lone parents are likely to be poorer than either lone

parents in employment or unemployed people who are not lone parents.

Weighted indices also have the advantage that their results are often much easier to understand. For example, saying that, in West Somerset, 17% of households are living in poverty has a much greater intuitive meaning than saying that Somerset has a Townsend Z-score of -1.3 or a Department of Environment Index of Local Conditions signed Chi squared score of 2.46.

Obtaining weightings for census based poverty indices

The easiest method of obtaining weightings for component variables in Census based poverty indices is to use a survey (conducted at or around the same time as the Census) that was specifically designed to measure poverty and deprivation. However, there were only two nationally representative surveys of poverty conducted during the 1980s. The 1983 and 1990 surveys undertaken by MORI for the two *Breadline Britain* television series made for London Weekend Television. These are the only special national surveys of poverty to be produced since the Royal Commission on the Distribution of Income and Wealth reported in 1978 (Gordon and Pantazis, 1997).

The 1983 *Breadline Britain* study pioneered what has been termed the 'consensual' or 'perceived deprivation' approach to measuring poverty. This methodology has since been widely adopted by other studies both in Britain and abroad (Saunders and Matheson, 1992; Halleröd, 1995; Nolan and Whelan, 1996). The consensual or perceived deprivation approach sets out to determine whether there are some people whose standard of living is below the minimum acceptable to society. It defines 'poverty' from the viewpoint of the public's perception of minimum need:

> This study tackles the questions 'how poor is too poor?' by identifying the minimum acceptable way of life for Britain in the 1980s. Those who have no choice but to fall below this minimum level can be said to be 'in poverty'. This concept is developed in terms of those who have an enforced lack of **socially perceived** necessities. This means that the 'necessities' of life are identified by public opinion and not by, on the one hand, the views of experts or, on the other hand, the norms of behaviour *per se* (Mack and Lansley, 1985:175).

The 1983 *Breadline Britain* study used a relative criterion to define the 'poor'. It assumed that:

Research, Policy and Planning (1997) Vol. 15 No. 3

poverty is a situation where such deprivation has a multiple impact on a household's way of life affecting several aspects of living thus, a family which just about manages but to do so does without an annual holiday, is deprived by today's standards; in our judgement, however, it is not in poverty. Deprivation has to have a more pervasive impact to become poverty.

Two criteria were identified for determining at what point multiple deprivation was likely to be causing poverty:

(i)   the poverty line should be drawn where the overwhelming majority of those who lacked necessities[2] have low incomes in the bottom half of the income range;

(ii) their overall spending pattern should reflect financial difficulty rather than high spending on other goods.

By carefully examining a large number of tables, Mack and Lansley decided that: 'A level of lack of one or two necessities is largely enforced though not overwhelmingly...a level of lack of three or more necessities is, by contrast, overwhelmingly enforced' (1985: 176).

The 'three or more necessities lacked' poverty line was later confirmed by regression analysis (Desai and Shah, 1985; Desai, 1986). Using this poverty threshold, Mack and Lansley showed that 14% of British households could be shown to be living in poverty in 1983 and, by 1990, the numbers in poverty had increased to 20% of British households (Frayman, 1991; Gordon and Pantazis, 1997).

A national measure of child poverty using the 1991 Census

It is possible to obtain weightings for the best subset of deprivation indicator variables that were measured in both the 1991 Census and the *Breadline Britain* survey using a multivariate statistical technique of logistic regression[3] (Gordon and Forrest, 1995; Gordon, 1995). Initially ten variables were selected that have been shown to be reasonable proxy indicators of child poverty by other studies and were measured in similar ways in both the *Breadline Britain* survey and the 1991 Census. These were:

(i)   **no earners:** households with dependent children with no adult in employment;
(ii)   **low social class:** households with dependent children with the head in social class IV or V;
(iii) **lone parents:** with dependent children and one adult;
(iv)   **large families:** households with four or more dependent children;

(v)   **no bath:** households with dependent children sharing or lacking a bath or shower;
(vi)   **no toilet:** households with dependent children with just an outside or shared toilet;
(vii)   **not self-contained:** households with dependent children in not self-contained accommodation;
(viii) **no car:** households with dependent children and no access to a car;
(ix)   **renting:** households with dependent children in rented accommodation (LA and private);
(x)   **disability:** household with dependent children with either an adult or a child with a limiting long-term illness.

The step-wise logistic regression analysis allowed the best subset of variables to be selected that were proxies of poverty (as defined by the *Breadline Britain* survey) and provided weightings for each variable after allowing for the overlaps between variables (i.e. lone parent households may also be low social class or no earner households).

The number of poor households with dependent children
=

36.2% of no car households +
30.6% of low social class households +
25% of renting households +
15.7% of no earner households +
15.2% of disabled households.

The highest rates of child poverty in the eight Somerset child care team areas are found in Minehead (26%) and Bridgwater (23%) and the lowest in Burnham (16.3%). However, for a needs-based budgeting exercise, absolute numbers of poor households are more important than rates of poverty, since there is a considerable variation in the population sizes of the eight Somerset child care areas.

The estimates of the numbers of poor households with dependent children produced by Children's *Breadline Britain* index are reliable and nationally representative. However, Somerset is a rural county and has a population that differs in a number of significant ways from the national average. A number of studies have demonstrated that the probability that a particular type of household is poor is different in rural and urban Britain. For example, car ownership which is often used in poverty indices is a far greater necessity for families with children in remoter rural areas than it is in the centre of a major city.

Similarly, Payne *et al.,* (1996) have shown that lone parents in rural and semi-rural areas have a 15 to 1 chance of being in the lowest income group. This compares with only a 10 to 1 chance for lone parents in the UK as a whole. Conversely, both council and private tenants and households with an unemployed head are less likely to be in the lowest income group in rural and semi-

Research, Policy and Practice (1997) Vol. 15 No. 3

rural areas than they are in the rest of the UK. This is probably because council estates have not suffered from the same degree of residualisation (the concentration of the poorest in council accommodation) in rural areas that has occurred in the cities. It is also likely that, although there is a lot of unemployment in many rural areas, it is often of short duration because of the availability of seasonal jobs. Therefore, households with unemployed heads in rural areas may sometimes avoid sinking as deeply into poverty as similar households in the cities.

Therefore, although the estimates of the number of poor households with dependent children produced by the Children's *Breadline Britain* index are nationally representative, they are unlikely to be very accurate in a rural and semi-rural county like Somerset as poverty in the countryside and in small towns differs from poverty in large metropolises. Unfortunately, the *Breadline Britain* survey did not have a large enough sample to produce reliable estimates of poverty for just rural and semi-rural areas. Therefore, an alternative method (and survey) must be used to produce estimates of poverty that more closely reflect the situation in Somerset.

A rural children's poverty index

The annual *Family Expenditure Surveys* (FES) contain a relatively crude indicator of rurality, which allows the identification of households that live in local authority districts with population densities below 220 people per square kilometre (all the districts in Somerset are in this category). Although, the FES is not specifically designed to measure poverty, it does provide a great deal of detail on the expenditure and income of households and people. It has been used extensively to study the characteristics of people in the lowest income groups (usually the bottom 20% of disposable income). However, the actual disposable income of a household is not always the best measure of standard of living. It is self-evident that, the larger the household, the more income will be needed to maintain the same standard of living. It is also clear that economies of scale exist within a household, i.e. it does not cost a family of four twice as much as a family of two to maintain the same standard of living. It is not self-evident, though, how much extra is needed by larger households in order to have the same standard of living as smaller households. When comparing households of different sizes and structures the government equivalises their incomes using the *McClements' equivalisation scale* (McClements, 1977).

However, the McClements' scale has been heavily criticised, both on methodological grounds and because it makes a lower allowance for the additional costs of children than any of the other widely used equivalisation scales (Muellbauer, 1979; 1980). It is also unfair to rural

areas like Somerset because it makes no allowance for the additional costs of going to work (transport, clothes, etc.) or for the extra costs of disability, which are important for families with children with a disabled adult or child. Townsend (1979) has produced an equivalence scale that allows for both these additional costs but it is based on a survey carried out in 1968/69 so it is now rather old.

The budget standards approach can be used to produce estimates of the amount of child poverty using the Family Expenditure Survey and this approach avoids most of the pitfalls of just using crude equivalised income figures as a proxy for poverty. A budget standard is a specified basket of goods and services which, when priced, can represent a particular standard of living. Budgets can be devised to represent any living standard (Bradshaw, 1993).

Budget standards are probably the oldest method of exploring living standards, pioneered by Rowntree (1901) in his famous study of poverty in York. They were used by Beveridge (1942) in the setting of the National Assistance scales and then they went into the doldrums and have not been used much in Britain since the Second World War (with the exception of Piachaud's study in the late 1970s). A budget standard estimates what families *ought* to spend rather than what they actually *do* (or think they need to) spend. A characteristic of this approach is that the judgements of 'experts' are used to create a basket of goods and services which represents the type of commodities, quantities and quality of family consumption (Oldfield and Yu, 1993).

Producing budget standards is expensive and extremely time consuming since it requires a team of 'experts' first to decide on the contents of the budget (housing, transport, food, clothing, etc.) and then for this budget to be priced for different types of household in different circumstances. Fortunately, the Joseph Rowntree Foundation financed a large two year research project by the Family Budget Unit at the University of York and they produced two budgets at 1991 prices. The 'moderate but adequate' budget and the 'low cost' budget (Bradshaw, 1993). Neither of these budgets was designed to be subsistence budgets and families that had sufficient income to afford these budgets would not be living in poverty.

In order to use these budget standards to produce estimates of child poverty, the low cost budget was modified so that a family with this standard of living would have just slipped over the poverty threshold and be living in poverty as defined in the 1990 *Breadline Britain* survey. Table 2 shows the type of things that are included and excluded from this modified low cost budget.

Research, Policy and Planning (1997) Vol. 15 No. 3

Table 2: Example of Budget Items Included and Excluded by the Modified Low Cost Budget for Families with Children (Budget adapted from Bradshaw, 1993)

Examples of items included	Examples of items excluded
Basic furniture, textiles and hardware, carpets only in living rooms and bedrooms	Antiques, handmade or precious household durables, carpets throughout the house
Adequate basic food for children and adults (cheapest 'own-brand' supermarket prices)	Eating out or luxury foods, alcohol, tobacco
Heating temperature in winter in living rooms at 20°C and 18°C in bedrooms	'Normal' household heating temperature in winter of 21°C
First aid kit and basic medicine	Prescription, dental work, sight tests, glasses
Bath, cooker, fridge, washing machine, lawn mower and vacuum cleaner	Freezer, tumble dryer, shower, electric blanket, microwave, food-mixer, sewing machine
Basic clothing (cheapest prices at C&A and BHS)	Second-hand, designer fashion clothing or footwear
Telephone	Television, video, radio-cassette, camera, music system, compact discs
One return local bus journey a week, children's bikes	National coach or train fares, car adults' bikes, taxi fares, more than one local bus journey a week
Clocks and watches	Jewellery
Tooth brush, scissors, haircuts for adults	Cosmetics, haircuts for children
Visit to cinema twice a year	Annual day trip to the seaside or any type of annual holiday away from home
Swimming for children, walking, cycling for children, and other free activities organised locally	School trips, out of school activities that cost money, scouts/guides or youth clubs, tumble-tots classes, panto, football matches, or visits to museums that charge
Low cost toys for children	Childcare costs, household services (eg window cleaning, etc)

A family living on this 'modified low budget' would be considered by the majority of the population to just be living in poverty and probably consider itself to be poor. Although it can afford to adequately feed and clothe itself and keep warm, it cannot afford to save money or to have any hobbies or leisure activities that cost money, or for the children to participate in out of school activities. It cannot afford a television (or a television licence) or money for outings or trips of any kind other than two annual visits to the cinema. Using the *Breadline Britain* definition of poverty, a family was likely to be living in or on the margins of poverty if it cannot afford to have

three or more items that were considered to be necessities by the majority of the population. Table 3 shows that a family living on this 'modified low cost budget' would not be able to afford four of these items and could therefore be considered to be living in poverty by current standards.

It must be emphasised that no family would actually live in the way specified by this budget. Many studies have demonstrated that parents will go without meals or adequate warm clothing in order to protect their children from shame. Many, ordinarily law abiding, poor families will also risk fines and imprisonment by keeping a television after their income has been reduced so far that they can no longer afford a television licence since they feel that television provides a source both of entertainment and education for their children, particularly in circumstances where they can no longer afford to pay for educational or other outings.

However, the important point is that the 'modified low cost budget' is constructed in such a way that the family does not have enough money to pay for anything extra, so if it wants to pay for a school outing it could only do so by cutting down on food or some other essential item of' expenditure. Table 4 shows the average amount of weekly disposable income needed by different types of household to have a standard of living equivalent to the 'modified low cost budget'. A number of assumptions have also been made about the families' circumstances; for example that it has modern efficient central heating. If it possesses any other type of heating it will require additional money adequately to heat its accommodation.

Constructing the modified low cost budget child poverty index for rural and semi-rural areas

The levels of income shown in Table 4 were used to divide the rural and semi-rural households with children in the Family Expenditure Survey into two groups. These groups comprise the 'poor' with incomes at or below this level, and those with incomes above this level who were considered not to be poor. Logistic regression analysis was used to obtain weightings for the best subset of poverty indicator variables that were measured in both the 1991 Census and the Family Expenditure Survey (FES).

Research, Policy and Practice (1997) Vol. 15 No. 3

Table 3: Percentage of People in 1990 Considering Standard of Living Item to be a Necessity and the Number of These Items a Household with Children Living on the Modified Low Cost Budget Could Afford

Standard-of-living items in rank order	% claiming item as necessity	items that the Household could Afford
A damp-free home	98	✓
Heating to warm living areas in the home of it's cold	97	✓
An inside toilet (not shared with another household)	97	✓
Bath, not shared with another household	95	✓
Beds for everyone in the household	95	✓
A decent state of decoration in the home	92	✓
Fridge	92	✓
Warm waterproof coat	91	✓
Three meals a day for children	90	✓
Two meals a day (for adults)	90	✓
Insurance of contents of dwelling	88	✓
Daily fresh fruit and vegetables	88	✓
Toys for children e.g. dolls or models	84	✓
Bedrooms for every child over 10 of different sexes	82	✓
Carpets in living rooms and bedrooms	78	✓
Meat/fish (or vegetarian equivalent) every other day	77	✓
Two pairs all-weather shoes	74	✓
Celebrations on special occasions	74	✓
Washing machine	73	✓
Presents for friends or family once a year	69	✓
Child's participation in out-of-school activities	69	✗
Regular savings of £10 a month for "rainy days" or retirement	68	✗
Hobby or leisure activity	67	?
New, not second hand, clothes	65	✓
Weekly roast/vegetarian equivalent	64	✓
Leisure equipment for children e.g. sports equipment or bicycle	61	✓
A television	58	✗
A telephone	56	✓
An annual week's holiday away, not with relatives	54	✗
A "best outfit" for special occasions	54	✓
An outing for children once a week	53	?
Children's friends round for tea/snack fortnightly	52	✓
A dressing gown	42	✓
A night out fortnightly	42	✗
Child's music/dance/sport lessons	39	✗
Fares to visit friends in other parts of the country 4 times a year	39	✗
Friends/family for a meal monthly	37	✗
A car	26	✗
Pack of cigarettes every other day	18	✗
Holidays abroad annually	17	✗
Restaurant meal monthly	17	✗
A video	13	✗
A home computer	5	✗
A dishwasher	4	✗

✓   can afford item
✗   can't afford item
?   can only have item if it is free or very low cost

(source: adaptation from Gordon and Pantazis (1997) Table 3.1, page 73).

Research, Policy and Planning (1997) Vol. 15 No. 3

Table 4: Average Normal Weekly Disposable Income Required for Different Types of Household with Children to be Able to Afford the Modified Low Cost Budget at 1991 Prices.

household composition	normal weekly disposable income required £
1 adult 1 child	85.14
1 adult 2+children	125.75
2 adults 1 child	115.12
2 adults 2 children	139.59
2 adults 3 children	173.04
2 adults 4 children	203.35
3 adults 1 child	153.44
3 adults 2 children	186.79
3 adults 3 children	219.34

(Source: 1991 F@ly Expenditure Survey, data supplied by ESRC Data Archive)

Initially nine variables were selected that have been shown to be reasonable proxy indicators of child poverty by other studies and were measured in similar ways in both the FES and the 1991 Census (some of these variables are different to those used in the *Breadline Britain* survey). These were:

(i) **no earners:** households with dependent children with no adult in employment;

(ii) **low social class:** households with dependent children with the head in social class IV or V;

(iii) **lone parents:** households with dependent children and one adult;

(iv) **large families:** households with four or more dependent children;

(v) **overcrowding:** households with dependent children and more than one person per room;

(vi) **no heat:** households with dependent children and no central heating;

(vii) **not self-contained:** households with dependent children in not self contained accommodation;

(viii) **no car:** households with dependent children and no access to a car;

(ix) **renting:** households with dependent children in rented accommodation (LA and private).

The step-wise logistic regression analysis allowed the best subset of variables to be selected that were proxies of poverty (defined as those households with incomes below the 'modified low cost budget' level) and provided weightings for each variable after allowing for the overlaps between variables:

The number of poor households with dependent children
=

39.5% of no earner households +
21.4% of renting households +
18.1% of overcrowded households +

6.9% of lone parent households+
6.7% of no car households+
6.4% of no heat households.

The 'modified low cost budget' method estimates of the number of poor households with children in Somerset is less than those using the Children's *Breadline Britain* index (MLCB = 6,567 households *and Breadline Britain* = 10,547 households). The areas with the highest rates of child poverty were again found to be Minehead (14.6%) and Bridgwater (14.1%) and the lowest in Burnham (9.5%). These results are unsurprising considering that the *Breadline* method estimates those both living in poverty and on the margins of poverty, while the modified low cost budget method' only estimates the numbers living in poverty. Despite the many differences between these two methods, Table 5 shows that the results they produce on the distribution of poverty in Somerset are remarkably similar, which is indicative of the reliability of these methods.

Yeovil and Taunton are the areas with the greatest amounts of need on all the indicators. This is unsurprising since these two areas contain the greatest population. The child poverty figures for each area, on average, differ by less than 1%. The exception is Taunton, which the 'low cost budget' method estimates contains 22% of all poor households with children in Somerset and the *Breadline Britain* method estimates contains 20.5% of poor households with children (a difference of 1.5%). This difference is due to the relatively large numbers of lone parent households in Taunton and the greater emphasis that the 'low cost budget' method places on poor lone parent households compared with the *Breadline Britain* method.

Conclusions

Allocating resources on the basis of need is preferable to allocation on the basis of population distribution, if the areas of greatest need are not to be disadvantaged. The Children's *Breadline Britain* index and the 'modified low cost budget index' can be used as a basis for a more equitable distribution of childcare resources within local authority areas. While they produce comparable results, the Children's *Breadline Britain* index is most suitable for measuring child poverty in urban and sub-urban authorities, whereas the 'modified low cost budget' index is of greatest use in rural areas.

In addition to their use for resource allocation purposes, the child poverty indices have considerable potential for other planning purposes, especially the development of authorities' Children and Family Services Plans.

Research, Policy and Practice (1997) Vol. 15 No. 3

Table 5: The distribution of child poverty, disability, referrals and population between the eight child care areas of Somerset

Child Care Area	Poor Households with Children (LCB Method) (N=6,377)	Poor Households with Children (Breadline Britain Method) (N= 10,547)	Disabled Children 0-15 (N=1,635)	Referrals (N=10,022)	Child Population (0-17) (N=99,737)
	%	%	%	%	%
Frome	12	12.5	11	13	13.2
Glastonbury	7	7.5	10	6	8.9
Bridgwater	16	15	14	18	13.5
Burnham	7	7	9	6	8.2
Chard	7	7.5	8	4	7.5
Yeovil	23	23	23	21	23.3
Taunton	22	20.5	20	26	20.2
Minehead	6	7	5	6	5.2
Somerset	**100**	**100**	**100**	**100**	**100**

Mapping exercises at different geographical levels (E.D., postcode sector, electoral ward and service defined areas) can inform decisions on the need for and location of specific child care units and services or on the drawing/redrawing of administrative boundaries.

Acknowledgments

We are grateful to the staff in the Social Services Department of Somerset County Council and in particular to Chris Smith and Jon Gray for their helpful comments. We would like to thank Helen Anderson for her help with editing. Somerset County Council funded this work. The *Breadline Britain in the 1990s* Survey was funded by London Weekend Television (LWT) with additional funding from the Joseph Rowntree Foundation, and was carried out by Marketing and Opinion Research International (MORI). It was conceived and designed by Joanna Mack and Stewart Lansley for Domino Films, with the help of Brian Gosschalk of MORI. We acknowledge the help of the ESRC Data Archive in providing the Family Expenditure Survey data.

Notes

[1]   It must be noted that this study also showed that although poor families had a high risk of referral, poverty was not a causal factor in the placement of children on the Child Protection Register or in the instigation of an initial case conference, once referral had taken place.

[2]   Lack of necessities refers to households that stated they did not have a necessity because they could not afford it and not to those households who lacked a necessity because they did not want it.

[3]   Note: the actual amounts of money required are dependent on where the family lives, since the cost of living is greater in

London (7%) and in rural areas (2.6%) than it is in the rest of the country. The greater cost of living in these areas has been allowed for in the calculations.

[4]   Households from the 1990, 1991 and 1992 Family Expenditure Surveys were combined in order to obtain a large enough sample of households. The Modified Low Cost Budget was deflated using the Retail Price Index.

References

Atkinson, A. B. (1985a) *How Should we Measure Poverty? Some Conceptual Issues.* Discussion Paper No. 82, ESRC Programme on Taxation, Incentives and Distribution of Income. London School of Economics: London.

Atkinson, A. B., (1985b) *On the Measurement of Poverty.* Discussion Paper No. 90, ESRC Programme on Taxation, Incentives and the Distribution of Income. London School of Economics: London.

Bebbington, A. and Miles, J. (1 987) An Index of Children's Deprivation Applied to English Local Authority Electoral Wards. *PSSRU Discussion Paper No. 53412.*

Bebbington, A. and Miles J. (1988) Children's GRE Research: Children Entering Care. A Need Indicator for In-care Services for Children. *PSSRU Discussion Paper No. 5741A.*

Bebbington, A. and Miles, J. (1989) The Background of Children who Enter Local Authority Care. *British Journal of Social Work,* 19, 349-68.

Berthoud, R., Lakey, J. & McKay, S. (1993) *The Economic Problems of Disabled People.* Policy Studies Institute: London.

Beveridge, W. (1942) Cmd. 6404, *Social Insurance and Allied Services.* HMSO: London.

Bradshaw, J. (ed), 1993, *Budget Standards for the United Kingdom.* Avebury: Aldershot.

Colton, M., Drury, C. and Williams, M. (1995) 'Children in Need: Definition, Identification and Support'. *British Journal of Social Work,* 25, 711-728.

Creighton, S. J. (1 992) *Child Abuse Trends in England and Wales 1988-1990 and an Overview from 1973-1990.* NSPCC: London.

Desai, M. (1986) Drawing the Line: On Defining the Poverty Threshold, in *Excluding the Poor* (Golding, P., ed). Child Poverty Action Group: London.

Desai, M. and Shah, A. (1985) *An Econometric Approach to the Measurement of Poverty,* Suntory-Toyota International Centre for Economics and Related Disciplines, WSP/2. London School of Economics: London.

Frayman, H. (1991) *Breadline Britain -1990s: The Findings of the Television Series.* Domino Films and London Weekend Television: London.

Gibbons, J., Conroy, S. and Bell, C., (1995) *Operating the Child

Research, Policy and Planning (1997) Vol. 15 No. 3

Protection System. Studies in Child Protection, HMSO: London.

Gordon, D. (1995) 'Census Based Deprivation Indices: Their Weighting and Validation'. *Journal of Epidemiology and Community Health*. 49 (Suppl 2), 39-44.

Gordon, D. and Forrest, R.(1995) *People and Places Volume II: Social and Economic Distinctions in England - A 1991 Census Atlas*. SAUS and the Statistical Monitoring Unit: Bristol.

Gordon, D., Parker, R. and Loughran, F. (1996) *Children with Disabilities in Private Households: A Re-analysis of the Office of Population Censuses and Surveys' Investigation*. Report to the Department of Health. University of Bristol: Bristol.

Gordon, D. and Gibbons, J.S. (1997) Placing Children on Child Protection Registers: Risk Indicators and Local Authority Differences. *British Journal of Social Work*, (in press).

Gordon, D. and Pantazis, C. (eds) *(1997) Breadline Britain in the 1990s*. Ashgate: Aldershot.

Halleröd, B. (1995) 'The Truly Poor: Indirect and Direct Measurement of Consensual Poverty in Sweden', *Journal of European Social Policy. 5(2):* 111-29.

Lee, P., Murie, A. and Gordon, D. (1995) *Area Measures of Deprivation. A study of Current Methods and Best Practices in Identification of Poor Areas in Great Britain*. University of Birmingham: Birmingham.

Lewis, G. W. and Ulph, D. T. (1988) 'Poverty, Inequality and Welfare'. *The Economic Journal* 98 (Conference 1988): 11 7-131.

Mack, J. and Lansley, S. (1985) *Poor Britain*. Allen and Unwin: London.

McClements, L. D. (1977) 'Equivalence Scales for Children.' *Journal of Public Economics 8:* 197-210.

Muellbauer, J. (1979) 'McClements on Equivalence Scales for Children'. *Journal of Public Economics* 12: 221-231.

Muellbauer, J. (1980) 'The Estimation of the Prais-Houthakker Model of Equivalence Scales'. *Econometrica 48(1):* 153-17(6.

Nolan, B. and Whelan, C. T. (19516) 'Measuring Poverty Using Income and Deprivation Indicators: Alternative Approaches'. *Journal of European Social Policy,* 6(3), 225-240.

Oldfield, N. and Yu, A. S. (1993) *The Cost of a Child: Living Standards for the 1990s*. CPAG: London.

Pantazis, C. and Gordon, D. (1997) 'Television Licence Evasion and the Criminalisation of Female Poverty.' *Howard Journal,* 36, 2, 170-186.

Payne, S., Henson, B., Gordon, D). and Forrest, R. (1996) *Poverty and Deprivation in West Cornwall in the 1990s.* A Report to the West Cornwall Initiative: Bristol.

Piachaud, D. (1998) 'Problems in the Definition and Measurement of Poverty' *Journal of Social Policy* 16(2): 125-146.

Robson, B., Bradford, M. and Tye, R. (1995) 1991 *Deprivation Index: A Review of Approaches and a Matrix of Results*. HMSO: London.

Rowntree, B. S. (1901) *Poverty: A Study of Town Life*. Macmillan: London.

Saunders, P. and Matheson, G. (1992) *Perceptions of poverty, income adequacy and living standards in Australia,* Social Policy Research Centre, University of New South Wales (Reports and Proceedings No 99): Sydney.

Townsend, P. (1979) *Poverty in the United Kingdom*. Allen Lane and Penguin Books: Harmondsworth, Middlesex and Berkeley.

Townsend, P (1987) 'Deprivation'. *Journal of Social Policy* 16(2): 125- 46.

Townsend, P. (1 993) *The International Analysis of Poverty,* Harvester Wheatsheaf: Milton Keynes.

Townsend, P. and Gordon, D. (1989) Low Income Households, *Memorandum of Evidence to the House of Commons Social Services Committee,* 579, 45-73.

[20]

Mapping the Data Needed to Plan Integrated Services: A Case Study of Children's Services in one Locality

Nick Axford

Jill Madge

Louise Morpeth
DARTINGTON SOCIAL RESEARCH UNIT

Jo Pring
TEIGNBRIDGE PRIMARY CARE TRUST

ABSTRACT

Children's services agencies in England are increasingly expected to work together to plan needs-led interventions in their locality. Such planning requires good information on local need and service take-up, yet this is often lacking. Connecting data from single agency, multi-agency and community studies in one district shows how the severity of need overlaps with different service and administrative categories. The findings point to the value of such mapping exercises, while the pattern that emerges highlights the importance of planning provision for *all* children and of linking intervention to thresholds of severity of need. The approach will have relevance to other care groups.

KEYWORDS: CHILDREN'S SERVICES; NEEDS-LED; PLANNING; REFOCUSING

Contact details: 01803 862231, unit@dartington.org.uk

Introduction

This article aims to give an overview of the severity of children's needs and the pattern of service take-up in an administrative district in England, and to make recommendations for service planning action by the local planning and implementation group (LPIG). The district, Teignbridge, is in Devon and has a population of 121,000, including 23,000 children aged 0-17. The Office for National Statistics classification places Teignbridge in the 'resort and retirement' category (Wallace & Denham, 1996) and it is ranked 248th on the Townsend Deprivation Index (out of 366 districts) (Gordon & Forrest, 1995). The main town in the district is Newton Abbot, which in the 2001 census recorded a population of 23,600. Some of the work that informs this research was conducted on the Buckland estate on the edge of the town, which has a population of approximately 3,600. The ethnic profile of the population is predominantly white British.

Several new policy initiatives in England, including the Green Paper *Every Child Matters* (DfES, 2003) and the emerging National Service

Framework for children, have combined to set the context in which LPIGs operate. The focus on implementing local preventative strategies, on needs-based service planning and on inter-agency working is part of this and is developed further in *Next Steps* (DfES, 2004) and the Children Bill. Much is written about what needs to be done to improve the planning of children's services, for example the need for closer inter-agency working and for focusing more on children's needs when determining provision. There is less on how to do it.

Part of the 'how' involves collating and analysing local data on need and service take-up, yet this is done less often than one would expect (Audit Commission, 1996; Carr-Hill *et al*, 1997). In particular, there are few succinct visual representations in which the work of agencies can be sited and potential new areas of development planned for. The exercise reported in this article sought to address this deficit and so contribute to efforts to respond to national requirements. The data are summarised in *Figure 1*, opposite. Although the broad pattern will be right, it is important to note here that weaknesses in the methods are likely to have affected the accuracy of *Figure 1*, both in terms of the numbers of children in the assigned categories and also in relation to the positioning, proportionate size and overlap of the rectangles. These difficulties relate more to the basis on which the numbers are estimated or extrapolated than to the methods used in the research and development studies themselves.

Local data on need and service take-up

Since 1997, the Dartington Social Research Unit has maintained a research and practice relationship with Teignbridge – first in a formal partnership with the social services department and then, from 2002, in a partnership with the local NHS primary care trust (PCT). Research work carried out locally by the Research Unit has enabled the accumulation of a series of datasets on patterns of need and service take-up among local children and their families. In each study information on need was recorded on five dimensions (living situation, family and social relationships, social and anti-social behaviour, physical and psychological health, and education and employment).

It is important to note that service take-up refers to services to meet a social need. Social need is defined here as a health or developmental difficulty, the origins of which are at least partly social in nature - that is, relating to housing, environment, relationships, family income and so on. When a service to meet social need is provided by universal services such as health or education, the focus is on services **over and above** the baseline mainstream provision. For example, in relation to education it would refer to special psychological help or measures to address truancy rather than to attendance at school *per se*.

Broadly, the various datasets can be grouped according to whether the data were gained from a cross-agency sample of cases, from a single agency or directly from families in the community regardless of their contact with children's services agencies. Brief descriptions of the sources follow.

Cross-agency

A) A study of referrals to health, education, social services and the police in Teignbridge in 1997 (Little & Madge, 1998). In a sample of 807 cases, professionals and researchers collected data on children's needs from agency files using the Matching Needs and Services method (Little *et al*, 2001).

B) An audit of community health professional activity in May/June 2003 (Madge *et al*, 2003). Health visitors, community nursery nurses and school nurses kept detailed records of all professional activity in one week, using a specially designed form. Thus, a picture of all indirect and direct work was formed, the latter being a sample of 912 instances of professional contact with individual children or their parent/carer.

C) The work of three action learning sets in which two groups of child care social workers and one group of health visitors discussed the question 'what can we do

Mapping the Data Needed to Plan Integrated Services: A Case Study of Children's Services in one Locality

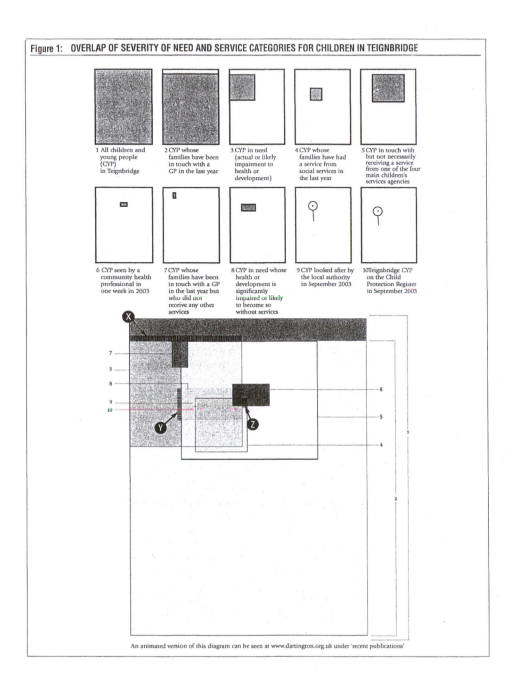

Figure 1: OVERLAP OF SEVERITY OF NEED AND SERVICE CATEGORIES FOR CHILDREN IN TEIGNBRIDGE

1 All children and young people (CYP) in Teignbridge

2 CYP whose families have been in touch with a GP in the last year

3 CYP in need (actual or likely impairment to health or development)

4 CYP whose families have had a service from social services in the last year

5 CYP in touch with but not necessarily receiving a service from one of the four main children's services agencies

6 CYP seen by a community health professional in one week in 2003

7 CYP whose families have been in touch with a GP in the last year but who did not receive any other services

8 CYP in need whose health or development is significantly impaired or likely to become so without services

9 CYP looked after by the local authority in September 2003

10 Teignbridge CYP on the Child Protection Register in September 2003

An animated version of this diagram can be seen at www.dartington.org.uk under 'recent publications' about the things that get in the way of effective practice?' (Randall *et al*, 2000).

Single agency

D) The number of children and young people looked after by the local authority in September 2003 (DSSD, 2003). Adoption cases are not included.

E) The number of children on the child protection register in September 2003 (DSSD, 2003).

F) A study of social work effectiveness that drew on the results of study (A) above and that also examined consecutive data in files from four social services departments, one of which was Teignbridge (Bullock *et al*, 2001).

Community

G) The number of children and young people aged 0-17 in Teignbridge PCT area in June 2003 (Teignbridge PCT, 2003).

H) A community survey on the Buckland estate, involving detailed information on need, service take-up and coping strategies gathered by one-hour semi-structured interviews of parents/carers in their homes, producing a sample of 500 children (Axford *et al*, 2003).

Connecting data from the different sources

These data were used to construct a visual representation of need and service take-up in Teignbridge. A starting point was the Assessment Framework (DoH, 2000) in which a diagram of overlapping circles was used to represent the number of children in England and the numbers and proportions of children designated as vulnerable, 'in need', 'looked after' and on the child protection register (p3). In order to capture the more complex picture that emerges from the work in Teignbridge, which includes service take-up data, this article uses a diagram comprising a series of inter-locking rectangles (*Figure 1*).

The size of the rectangles reflects the number of children represented. In some places, it was necessary to make informed estimates based on data collected from one area in the district. Usually this involved extrapolating findings from the Buckland estate into figures for the whole of Teignbridge. Primarily, these calculations were required in relation to need, as the population on the estate is disproportionately deprived compared with the district. As a rule of thumb, percentages from Buckland were halved for Teignbridge on the grounds that levels of deprivation on the estate were approximately double those for the district, although there are slight variations because information from all datasets and from other research was brought to bear on each calculation. No adjustments were made in relation to the level of service take-up. This was because the service data reported in the article that were gathered for the Buckland estate related primarily to contact with the GP. This is known to be high universally, and there was no indication that the problems dealt with by the GP were specifically related to poverty.

The positioning of the rectangles was decided by following a logical procedure, starting with data on all children in Teignbridge and working from large to small numbers, ending in the tiny group of children on the local child protection register. In most cases it was clear where the different groups of children should be located, although some pragmatic decisions were required. For example, some children with 'actual or likely significant impairment' (represented by rectangle 8) will only have had a service from their GP; in that sense, technically there should be at least some overlap with rectangle 7.

Patterns of need and service take-up

The findings set out below are based on *Figure 1*. Numbers 1 to 10 refer to the label on each rectangle on *Figure 1*. Source headings A to H refer to those studies listed in the method section above. Studies C and F are not included here as source materials, but served to

Mapping the Data Needed to Plan Integrated Services: A Case Study of Children's Services in one Locality

assist in understanding the broader context in which the local pattern of service take-up is located.

1) 23,000 – The number of children and young people aged 0-17 in Teignbridge PCT area in June 2003.
Source: (G)

2) 20,930 – An estimate of the number of children and young people living in a household where they or a family member had been in touch with a GP in the previous 12 months. The figure is an estimate based on a community survey of parents/carers living on the Buckland estate, where 91% of children and young people lived in such a household.
Source: (H)

3) 4,600 – An estimate of the number of children in need in Teignbridge. The community survey on the Buckland estate showed that over one third (38%) of the children were 'in need' using the definition in the *Children Act 1989*, namely actual or likely impairment to the child's health or development. Since Buckland is the most deprived ward in Teignbridge, an informed estimate suggests that 20% of children in the district are in need.
Source: (H)

4) 920 – An estimate of the number of children and young people living in a household where they or a family member have received a service from social services in the previous 12 months. The figure is an estimate based on the results of the community survey of parents/carers living on the Buckland estate, where eight per cent of children lived in such a household. This figure has been halved to reflect the less disadvantaged profile of the district of Teignbridge (ie four per cent).
Source: (H)

5) 7,670 – An estimate of the number of children and young people in touch with but not necessarily receiving a service from one of the four main children's services agencies (health, police, education and social services). This figure comes from a study of referrals to

these agencies in Teignbridge in 1997.
Source: (A)

6) 1,000 – The approximate number of children and young people seen by a community health professional (school nurse, health visitor or community nursery nurse) in one week in Teignbridge. This figure is derived from an audit of community health professional activity in May/June 2003.
Source: (B)

7) 506 – An estimate of the number of children in need living in a household where one or more family members received a service in the previous 12 months from the GP but no-one else. This figure is an estimate based on the finding from the community survey that 11% of children in need on the Buckland estate were in this situation. This figure was not adjusted, as there is no clear reason to assume that these proportions would be different in less deprived areas.
Source: (H)

8) 1,150 – An estimate of the number of children and young people in need whose health or development is significantly impaired or likely to become so without the provision of remedial services. This figure is based on the community study, which shows that eight per cent of children and young people on the Buckland estate were in this situation. Since this is likely to be an overestimate for the Teignbridge district as a whole (owing to the more disadvantaged profile of the population on the estate), a figure of five per cent was used as an informed estimate.
Source: (H)

9) 93 – The number of children and young people looked after by the local authority in September 2003 (0.4% of all children, two per cent of children in need). This figure excludes adoption cases.
Source: (D)

10) 14 – The number of children on the child protection register in September 2003 (0.06% of all children, 0.3% of children in need).
Source: (E)

Mapping the Data Needed to Plan Integrated Services: A Case Study of Children's Services in one Locality

Implications for policy and practice

There is often considerable focus in prevention work on small, discrete groups of children. The identification of potentially useful need groupings for service planning purposes has been undertaken as separate pieces of work in two of the research studies cited here (studies A and H). Work on tracking the progress of referrals to and between different agencies, undertaken in study (A), has highlighted the potential benefits of planning more co-ordinated inter-agency responses to need.

Frequently missing in present prevention work, however, is the 'big picture' that enables prevention activity to be located and planned for within a coherent overview of need and service take-up. A strength of the somewhat 'rough and ready' estimations outlined in this article, therefore, is the way that they allow researchers to make some clear and simple recommendations about the dilemmas facing service planners.

With these caveats in mind, at least four points from *Figure 1* merit reflection in relation to policy and practice in children's services. First, service planners need to decide which children in their locality they are currently most concerned about and then communicate this clearly to service users and actual or potential service providers. For example, there are children in need who have not been in contact with any agency (even their GP) in the past year (shaded area X). There are also children in need who have had a service from their GP but no-one else (rectangle 7). How should services respond to such patterns?

Second, *Figure 1* shows that the importance of organisations other than the four main agencies needs to be recognised when planning services. It is known that a sizable proportion of the children in need who are not in contact with the main agencies do have contact with a range of other organisations, including the Citizen's Advice Bureaux, other voluntary organisations and solicitors (Axford *et al*, 2003). This includes some children (shaded area Y) with actual or likely significant impairment to their

---

Box 1:	DARTINGTON PRACTICE TOOLS

The practice tools fall into two groups. First are those related to clinical decision-making.

- *Paperwork* is a clinical assessment tool
- *Prediction* encourages practitioners to make and use prognoses
- *Threshold* offers a framework for determining the extent of impairment to children's development
- *Going Home?* assists practitioners in deciding when and how to re-unite separated children with their families

The second group of practice tools is geared towards management planning.

- *Aggregating Data* helps with collecting and analysing management information
- *Matching Needs and Services* is a method for designing needs-led services
- *Structure Culture Outcome* is used to improve residential services for children

Details of all tools can be found at www.dartington-i.org/practicetools.shtml.

---

health and development who will not be in contact with the four main agencies.

Third, some children (shaded area Z) who are not in need are in contact with more than one agency, including health, education, police or social services. Whether this is appropriate will depend on a range of factors but, arguably, the issue should be debated in a forum such as an LPIG, given the demand that this makes on scarce resources.

Fourth, it is noticeable from *Figure 1* that children who receive much agency attention - those looked after and those whose names are on the child protection register (rectangles 9 and 10) - represent a very small part of a much larger group of children for whom the LPIG has a responsibility to plan provision. Without diminishing the importance of recognising and meeting the often serious needs of children in such administrative categories, this does raise further questions about the appropriate amount and distribution of resources.

Conclusions

This article has outlined the method and findings from an exercise aimed at summarising the pattern of need and service take-up in a district in England with a child population of 23,000. It has set out the numbers of children in different need, service and administrative categories and highlighted particular issues for consideration by service planners. There is no obvious reason why the broad pattern should be significantly different in similar areas elsewhere, that is, in districts in the resort and retirement category with a comparable level of deprivation.

Figure 1 enables LPIG participants and others involved locally in planning children's services to consider provision in the context of the overall number of children in the area and the current proportion of children in need. While many participants will work with specific client groups, if the function of the LPIG is to plan for **all** children in the area, then this basic shared understanding of the scale of the task is needed. The data therefore point clearly to the need to map existing services, to the requirement to consider decommissioning ineffective or unnecessary services and to the value of designing and evaluating new services to meet identified local need (DSRU, 2004). Issues that frequently inhibit such development, such as the often short-term funding of voluntary services, can be addressed within this more coherent overview.

Figure 1 also provokes several questions for any LPIG member in relation to their own particular service for local children. Is the service currently serving mainly children in need and those with actual or likely **significant** impairment to their health or development or are a substantial proportion of the users **not** in need? Is this what the service should be doing, and why? If there is a plan to change the mix, what is the best way to do it? The article does not attempt to answer such questions; rather it makes explicit that they must be considered as part of the efforts of local authorities

to formulate preventative strategies and to refocus children's services in line with *Every Child Matters* and the National Service Framework for children.

Taking this work forward requires practical methods for analysing local need and service data, linking these data to evidence and then using the information to inform planning and clinical decisions. With this in mind, a series of practice tools developed at Dartington is currently being tested with agencies in various locations in the UK and abroad (*Box 1*, below). The tools seek to assist local practitioners and planners in their efforts to improve child development outcomes for children, at both aggregate and individual case levels. It is hoped that this combination of local evidence and practical methods will help agencies to respond to themes of the new central policy initiatives, including needs-based service planning and inter-agency working.

References

Audit Commission (1996) *Seen But Not Heard: Coordinating Community Health and Social Services for Children in Need.* London: Audit Commission Publications.

Axford N, Little M & Morpeth L (2003) *A Study of Children Supported and Unsupported in the Community.* Report submitted to the Department of Health. Dartington Social Research Unit.

Bullock R, Randall J & Weyts A (2001) *The Contribution of Social Workers to Interventions with Children in Need and their Families.* Report submitted to the Department of Health. Dartington Social Research Unit.

Carr-Hill R, Dixon P, Mannion R et al (1997) *A Model of the Determinants of Expenditure on Children's Personal Social Services.* York: University of York.

Department for Education and Skills (2003) *Every Child Matters.* Cm 5860. London: The Stationery Office.

Department for Education and Skills (2004) *Every Child Matters: Next Steps.* Nottingham: DfES Publications.

Department of Health (2000) *Framework for the Assessment of Children in Need and their Families.* London: The Stationery Office.

Mapping the Data Needed to Plan Integrated Services: A Case Study of Children's Services in one Locality

Department of Health (2001) *The Children Act Now: Messages from Research*. London: The Stationery Office.

DSRU (Dartington Social Research Unit) (2004) *Refocusing Children's Services Towards Prevention: Lessons from the Literature*. Research Report 510. Nottingham.

DfES Publications. DSSD (Devon Social Services Directorate) (2003) Verbal communication, September.

Gordon D & Forrest R (1995) *People and Places 2: Social and Economic Distinctions in England*. Bristol: SAUS.

Little M & Madge J (1998) *Inter-agency Assessment of Need in Child Protection*. Report submitted to the NHS Executive S&W. Dartington Social Research Unit.

Little M, Madge J, Mount K *et al* (2001) *Matching Needs and Services*, 2nd edn. Dartington: Dartington Academic Press.

Madge J, Morpeth L & Pring J (2003) *An Audit of Community Health Professional Activity in Teignbridge, Devon*. Report submitted to Teignbridge Primary Care Trust. Dartington Social Research Unit.

Randall J, Cowley P & Tomlinson P (2000) Overcoming barriers to effective practice in child care. *Child and Family Social Work* 5 (4) 343-52.

Teignbridge PCT (2003) Verbal communication, September.

Wallace M & Denham C (1996) *The ONS Classification of Local and Health Authorities of Great Britain*. London: HMSO.

Part V
Towards Meeting
Children's Needs

[21]

Needs, Numbers, Resources: Informed planning for looked after children

Karin Janzon, Director, Care Equation Ltd
Dr Ruth Sinclair. Director of Research. National Children's Bureau

Abstract
This case study illustrates how analysis of basic published and internally collected routine data on looked after children can be used to achieve a better understanding of patterns and trends over time within an authority, produce comparisons and benchmarking in relation to similar authorities, expose data quality issues, challenge mis-conceptions and myths and help organisations to plan pro-actively based on evidence. Whilst the case study is time and location specific, the findings raise questions about potentially wasted opportunities to use the information sources already available to local authorities to underpin a more evidenced based approach to planning for children's services.

Introduction

The obligation on Local Authorities to collect and collate information is greater than ever. Effective information systems are now required to routinely collect information, most often quantitative data, on a new range of performance and outcome indicators through the Performance Assessment Framework and, for children, to draw up relevant Quality Protects Management Action Plans and report on Quality Protects specific indicators. Over time, this will greatly assist in the task of monitoring performance in delivering better outcomes for service users. Similarly, Best Value and other reviews collate a wide range of data (likely to be both routine quantitative and one-off qualitative) in their task of reviewing the effectiveness of particular services. However, the very range of this routinely collected data, and the fragmented way in which it is often collected, increases the complexity of the task of bringing statistical information from different sources together to get a true sense of how the service is responding to demands upon it. This paper looks at the example of services to children looked after by local authorities. It illustrates from a case study how routinely collected data can be used to understand the changing relationship between needs and services to support more informed strategic service planning.

Predicting the Looked After Children (LAC) Population

In trying to plan service provision local authorities will want to take into account, among other things, the likely demands upon its resources. In children's services the most significant factor is the number of children being looked after by the authority. However, predicting trends in the need for children to be looked after, and the associated costs, is far from a precise science. Given that decisions to take a child into care will be based on a wide ranging assessment of individual circumstances, there are no easy answers to the question how many children it is appropriate for a local authority to be looking after at any one time, or where they are best placed.

Nonetheless, study of LAC populations reveals some clear patterns – in both size and characteristics of the population and over time and between and within authorities. A reasonable benchmark for local authorities is a comparison between looked after populations in similar local authorities. Research by Bebbington and Miles (1989) suggests differences and similarities between local authorities can be explained by three factors:

- The needs of the child population.;
- Differences in local policy and practices through different interpretations of legislation;
- Differences in policies relating to resource allocation and service provision.

The needs factors found by Bebbington and Miles to be most significant in relation to entry into care include:

- Children in one parent, and especially one adult, households;
- Children in overcrowded accommodation;
- Children in poor households, especially dependent on benefit;
- Children of mixed ethnic parentage.

More recent research (Carr-Hill et al, 1997) relating the needs of local populations to their use of children's personal social services has identified the importance of the following factors:

paper one

- Children living in lone parent families;
- Children living in flats;
- Children in families on income support;
- Children living in densely populated areas;
- Children with a limiting long term illness.

Over time, the size and characteristics of the looked after children population are also likely to change in response to national legislative and policy changes. Two current examples are the implementation of the Children (Leaving Care) Act 2000 and the Adoption White Paper (Department of Health, 2000).

Whatever the reason for changing patterns of demand, local authorities need to be able to respond to the impact of such changes on their services and budgets if the life chances of children are not to be compromised. Being aware of changing patterns and trends is a pre-requisite for responsive planning; understanding the reasons for change may even allow for pro-active action.

Experience gained through consultancy work in several authorities indicates that authorities often do not possess the overview necessary for informed strategic planning for looked after children.

The Case Study

The overall aim of the study was to assist a Social Services Department to understand the changes over time in the composition of its looked after children (LAC) population, and how this could help predict possible future changes, especially in resources for placements. The authority was particularly concerned that numbers seemed to be going up and that, in spite of efforts to control placement budgets, there was a continuing gap between budget and actual spending for this group of children.

While the details of the case study presented here are time and location specific, the methods have a general applicability and the messages are likely to be relevant to others struggling to develop a more evidence-based approach to planning children's services.

Method

The main elements of the study were:

- *Inter-borough comparisons*: Five authorities were selected on the basis of the Audit Commission family groupings and discussion with staff. It was agreed that they represented those local authorities that most closely match the circumstances of the study authority. As this was a London Borough, comparisons were also made with London as a whole.
- *Ten year perspective*: A reasonable time span was required to allow an examination of underlying trends and to understand the 'bigger picture'.
- *Published data*: Analysis of routinely collected and published statistics from the Department of Health, CIPFA and the Office for National Statistics (ONS) formed the main part of the study.
- *Local information*: The consultants also drew on additional local management information and discussions with staff. In particular, discussions with staff helped to provide background information that was useful in exploring changing or unusual local trends that did not seem to follow the wider pattern.
- *National policy*: Knowledge of past, current and likely future developments in national policy which impact on children and children's services was used to inform the analysis and predictions for the future.

In drawing conclusions from analysis of such data one is making assumptions about the accuracy and reliability of local authority information. There is much evidence from researchers and inspectors to suggest these assumptions may be ill-founded; that was also the case in this study. Nonetheless the principle still applies of drawing on all available evidence to inform service planning.

Findings

Poor use information
Although the methodology for the study was fairly simple, something we felt that authorities should easily be able to manage themselves, most of the findings were surprising and, sometimes, a revelation, to senior staff in the authority. The

study as a whole highlighted the lack of focus and time that staff were able to give to using and understanding their own data. This in turn resulted in a poor understanding of activity within the care system among front-line and senior managers, and a lack of understanding of and planning for changes in need in the population among commissioning and finance managers. It also challenged a number of misconceptions held by senior staff.

Relative deprivation and children in need
The DETR Index of Local Conditions, which includes two of the factors specifically related to entry into care, ranked the study authority as one of the most deprived authorities in the country. Other factors were examined through census data. Although some of this information may now be out of date, the overall picture suggested that, on the particular factors that may affect entry into care, the scores of this authority were high seen in the Greater London context, and average within the comparator borough group.

Children looked after make up only a proportion of 'children in need' (CIN) as defined by the Children Act. In turn, 'children in need' are only a small proportion of children who may be 'vulnerable' – that is children whose life chances may be compromised or who are at risk of social exclusion. The boundaries between these groups are very loose and children will move between them. Whilst it is difficult to quantify the number of vulnerable children, comparative information (even if still imperfect) on 'children in need' (CIN) is now available from the Department of Health CIN census. The census requires local authorities to record the number of children who are on their caseload, those whose cases are 'open' and those who receive a service in the census week.

We compared the rate per population under 18 of CIN, children on child protection registers and looked after children (LAC), and the ratio of LAC to CIN, in the comparator boroughs and found that variations were considerable. Given that the comparator boroughs were chosen for their similarity in terms of socio-economic factors, the implications are that the boroughs apply different thresholds for responding to children in need of support and/or protection. The study authority

occupied a 'middle of the road' position both with regard to comparator boroughs and the Greater London average, which would not have been predicted from the high level of deprivation in the borough. This suggested the need to look at other local factors.

Child population and numbers of LAC
Trends in the child population by five year age bands were analysed using ONS mid year estimates 1991 to 2000. This revealed a substantial rise overall (22%) in the 0-17 year age group over the period, with some levelling off in the younger age bands in the last two years.

Table 1. Increases in population of 0 – 17 year olds in the study authority

Numbers aged 0-17 1991/2	Numbers aged 0-17 1999/0	Total increase (No's)	Total increase (%)
58,870	71,660	12,790	22%

Source: ONS Mid year estimates; KIGS

Inter-borough comparisons showed a similar pattern, though the study authority stood out as having the steepest increase and the highest proportion of under 18s in the population.

The total rise in numbers of LAC over the period was consistent with this overall trend, though numbers of LAC did not start to rise until 1996.

Table 2. Increases in number of looked after children in the study authority

Numbers aged 0-17 31/3/1992	Numbers aged 0-17 31/3/2000	Total increase (No's)	Total increase (%)
384	486	102	26%

Source: KIGS

The percent increase in looked after children was slightly higher than the population increase (26% compared to 22%). This had resulted in a very modest rise in the rate of LAC per population under 18, which was not generally mirrored in the comparator boroughs, several of which already had rates of LAC considerably above that of the study authority. Local information indicated that unaccompanied asylum seeking children supported under Section 20, although making up only a small proportion (7 percent) of total numbers of LAC, would have contributed about a third of the rise in the *rate* of LAC in recent years.

Figure 1: Numbers of LAC at 31 March in study authority

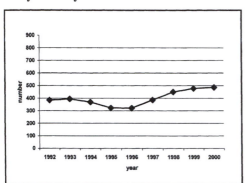

Overall there was no evidence to suggest that the rate of looked after children was higher than would be expected for a borough exhibiting the levels of deprivation that characterised the study authority; if anything the rate appeared relatively low. The authority was, of course, still faced with the problem of coping with the absolute increase in numbers. The analysis put into sharp relief the need to plan for consequences of increasing child populations and indeed the lack of attention paid to this basic factor. The results raised questions as to whether the pressures to control numbers of children coming into care were reasonable, or in the interest of children in need. It also highlighted the limited use of such evidence in the formulation of local policy to reduce the numbers in public care.

Entrants and leavers
End of year snapshots, although useful for examining overall trends, only give a limited picture of pressures on the care system. In this example the trends for entrants to and leavers from care indicated a *substantial rise in activity* during the nineties. The numbers of children entering and leaving the care system were closely aligned in any one year, though they fluctuated between years.

For example, the statistics showed exceptionally high numbers of entrants and leavers in 1997/8 and 1998/9 - the number of children starting to be looked after in 97/8 rose from 221 to 328, and the number of children leaving care from 246 to 361. The numbers stayed at a similar level in 98/9, dropping back to previous levels in the following year. Thus, the relatively steady numbers in public care on set days seemed to camouflage other changes. Managers appear not to have been aware of the scale of this rise in activity until demonstrated by the present analysis. Local explanations highlighted effects of changes in the authority's policies, practice and organisation during this period, including a more interventionist approach from senior management, restructuring of child protection services resulting in a more pro-active mode of operation and the changed remit of the children's planning and review centre. Account must also be taken of the possibility of inaccurate data.

This part of the study demonstrates the importance of monitoring activity throughout the year in order to identify and question what could be effects of changing practices that may otherwise go unnoticed. Changes in the rates of entrants and leavers, if closely aligned, may have little effect on overall numbers and only limited impact on direct placement budgets, but will significantly affect the workloads of front-line social workers. A large number of entrants in one year may pose pressures in the future if the number of leavers drop in subsequent years; this will also be dependent on the age profile of new entrants and leavers.

Budgets and Expenditure
The analysis of expenditure data raised questions about availability, quality and transparency of financial information and about budget planning. However, both financial data sets (CIPFA and RO3 returns to DETR) demonstrated a substantial ongoing gap, averaging £3.6m per year, between the total amount spent and the amount budgeted for children and families services.

While there may be issues of insufficient resources to meet demand in many SSDs this does not negate the need to base budget planning on calculated estimates of need. This did not appear to be happening.

Figure 2: PSS actual and estimated expenditure on children and families 1996/97 - 2000/01 in the study authority (source: CIPFA returns)

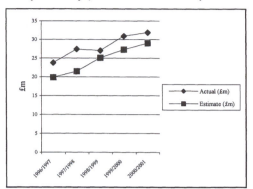

Figure 3: Expenditure on different components of services for children and families in the study

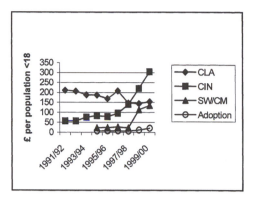

In this authority the gap between budget and expenditure was largely due to overspending on placements: more money had been spent on placements than had been budgeted for in all but one of the last five years. The Social Services Department was therefore under pressure from the Treasurer to 'control' placement expenditure. However, looked at over the recent five year period, it appeared that the percentage rise in expenditure on LAC was considerably lower than the percentage rise in numbers of LAC and that the budgeted rise was substantially lower again. This indicated to us that there was no link between budget planning and any estimate of the likely need/ demand, for example for the placement of LAC, and that, as a consequence, LAC services continued to be under funded in relation to changing levels of need.

This picture was reinforced when we compared the changes in rates of expenditure per population under 18 for different types of children's services. Whilst the rate of expenditure on Children in Need and Social Work / Care Management had risen dramatically, the rate of expenditure on LAC had declined over the ten year period. Although this pattern would be in line with national policy direction, there was no indication that the authority was aware of, or had made use of this information and hence it raises questions about the quality of their needs based planning

Placement patterns and costs
The proportion of children looked after in family placements in the study authority had increased substantially over the nineties from just under fifty per cent in 1992 to over seventy-seven per cent in March 2000 and was the highest among the comparator boroughs. There had been a corresponding decline in proportions of residential placements, though the *numbers* of residential placements had not changed substantially in the last 5 years.

As was expected, the difference between the cost of different types of placements appeared to be very large, though the absence of true unit costs for in-house fostering made like for like comparisons difficult. For the purposes of this study placements were grouped into four cost bands: low, moderate, high, very high. Most children were in low / moderate cost placements, while most of the total expenditure was incurred by high/very high cost placements. At one end of the spectrum half of LAC accounted for 16 percent of total placement costs, while at the other end 10 percent of LAC accounted for one third of placement costs. This is illustrated in Figure 4.

Table 3. Placement patterns in the study authority

	Foster Placements		Residential Placements		Other Placements	
	No. of	% of	No. of	% of	No. of	% of
	Children		Children		Children	
31/3/92	189	49%	89	23%	106	28%
31/3/95	222	69%	46	14%	53	17%
31/3/00	376	77%	42	9%	68	14%

Source: KIGS

Local feedback suggests that placement costs may have been adversely affected over the last few years by limited management control over placement decisions, and poor resourcing of the family placement team, with consequent decline in the recruitment of in-house foster carers.

Figure 4: Proportion of CLA and expenditure in different cost bands - study authority 2001

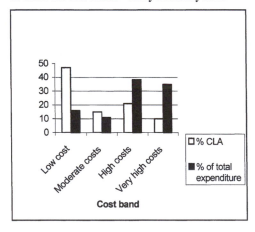

Although the authority had access to substantial data on placement demands and costs, there was little evidence that this was used for determining operational objectives or pro-active resource allocation.

Discussion

The study raised a number of general issues about use of data to inform understanding of and planning for children's services. Although it is not possible for us to say how far these issues are reflected in other areas, consultancy undertaken by the authors across several authorities suggests that social services departments are not exploiting the opportunity to use their own basic data collection to gain an overview of need and demand and to make a link between need and budget planning.

A comment often made is that data is not reliable. But data will only be improved if it is used regularly and there is a feedback loop, which ensures continual improvement of data. This is particularly true of financial data and unit costs. Another frequent comment concerns lack of software systems to assist data analysis. Whilst it is acknowledged that implementation of new information systems is a major task for authorities, the analysis in this project was undertaken on core data that all authorities collect and with basic software packages, which most authorities possess.

Even where data is monitored on a regular basis, authorities often fail to see developments in a wider perspective. This case study demonstrated the value of seeing the 'bigger picture' by comparing with other similar boroughs, and over a longer time period. The Best Value process has encouraged councils to undertake this kind of analysis, but to have an ongoing impact it needs to be an integral part of the management process, not just a series of 'one-offs'.

Conclusion

Local authorities have substantial information sources at their disposal, both from their own recording systems and from published statistical data covering all authorities, and a lot of time and effort is expended by staff at all levels recording data. There is considerable potential for using this information for more informed strategic planning and, in particular, to link financial planning more coherently to an understanding of service activity and operational realities. Using comparative data across time and/or across authorities can also help managers to detect trends and to benchmark themselves against other similar authorities. This case study has illustrated the benefit that may be derived from regular analysis of even very basic data, and the wasted opportunity to develop a more evidence based approach to planning for children's services of not using such information to underpin decision-making.

References

Bebbington, A. and Miles (1989) 'The background of children who enter local authority care', *British Journal of Social Work,* 19(5): 349-368.

Carr-Hill et al (1997) *A Model of the Determinants of Expenditure on Children's Personal Social Services,* York: University of York.

Children (Leaving Care) Act 2000.

CIPFA (annual) *PSS Actual and Estimated Expenditure on Children and Families,* www.ipf.co.uk/sis/

Department of Environment and Transport (1998) *Index of Local Conditions,* www.statistics.gov.uk

Department of Health (annual) *Social Services Performance in The Personal Social Services Performance Assessment Framework indicators,* London: Government Statistical Service

Department of Health (annual) *Children Looked After by Local Authorities,* www.doh.gov.uk/HPSSS/index.htm

Department of Health (annual) *Key Indicators Graphical System (KIGS),* London.

Department of Health (2000) *Children in Need in England,* www.doh.gov.uk/public/stats1.htm

Department of Health (2000) *Adoption: a new approach: a white paper,* London: TSO (Cm.5017).

Department of Health (1999) *The Government's Objectives for Children's Social Services,* London: Department of Health.

Office of National Statistics (annual) *Mid-Year Estimates,* www.statistics.gov.uk

[22]

A developmental and clinical model for the prevention of conduct disorder: The FAST Track Program

CONDUCT PROBLEMS PREVENTION RESEARCH GROUP

Abstract

This paper presents a developmental and a clinical model for the treatment of conduct disorder through the strategy of preventive intervention. The theoretical principles and clinical strategies utilized in the FAST Track (Families and Schools Together) Program are described. We indicate how the clinical model is derived from both our developmental model and previous findings from prevention trials. The FAST Track Program integrates five intervention components designed to promote competence in the family, child, and school and thus prevent conduct problems, poor social relations, and school failure. It is our belief that testing the effects of such a comprehensive approach is a necessary step in developing new intervention models for this population.

This article presents a developmental and a clinical model for the treatment of conduct disorder through the strategy of preventive intervention. The theoretical principles and clinical strategies utilized in the FAST Track (Families and Schools Together) Program will be described to illustrate one research-based model of preventive intervention for families with children showing early aggression and peer difficulties.

The primary aims of the FAST Track Program are to develop, implement, and evaluate a comprehensive intervention to prevent severe and chronic conduct problems in a sample of children selected at high risk when they first enter school. The intervention is guided by a developmental theory positing the interaction of multiple influences on antisocial behavioral development.

The article is organized as follows. First, the problem of conduct disorder and the difficulties inherent in its prevention will be summarized. Second, a developmental model of the disorder will be presented. Third, the clinical model that is based on this developmental model will be presented. Finally, the issues and implications of the clinical model for the prevention of such disorders are explored.

The Problem

Conduct disorder defined

Conduct disorder (CD) is one of the most intractable mental health problems of childhood and adolescence. Its prevalence is estimated to range from approximately 4 to 10%, with higher rates in boys than in girls. CD comprises a cluster of oppositional and

Support for this research was provided by National Institute of Mental Health grant R18-MH48043. We gratefully acknowledge the support and advice of Doreen Spilton Koretz, numerous consultants, and the FAST Track National Advisory Board.

Members of the CPPRG (in alphabetical order) are Karen L. Bierman (Pennsylvania State University), John D. Coie (Duke University), Kenneth A. Dodge (Vanderbilt University), Mark T. Greenberg (University of Washington), John E. Lochman (Duke University), and Robert J. McMahon (University of Washington).

Address correspondence and reprint requests to: Mark Greenberg, PhD, Department of Psychology, University of Washington, Seattle, WA 98195.

antisocial behaviors, including excessive noncompliance, stealing, lying, running away, physical violence, cruelty, and sexually coercive behavior (Loeber & Schmalling, 1985). This disorder is characterized by constant conflict with others (parents, teachers, and peer group), and in adolescence it often causes physical injury, pain, and property damage to others (Kazdin, 1985).

CD commonly begins in early to middle childhood (in the form of oppositional defiant disorder) (Loeber, Lahey, & Thomas, 1991). Although up to half of the cases of childhood CD remit by adolescence, rarely do adolescent cases of CD or adult cases of antisocial personality disorder begin without warning signs in early childhood (Patterson, 1982; Robins, 1966). Thus, adolescent CD can be predicted reliably from early childhood behavior and related risk factors with relatively low false-negative predictions (Loeber, 1991). Early forms of CD are also known to be predictive of other psychological disorders, delinquency, drug abuse, school dropout, suicide, and criminality in adolescence and adulthood (Loeber & Dishion, 1983; Robins, 1978; West & Farrington, 1973). With advancing age, CD becomes increasingly resistant to change, in spite of extraordinary efforts in treatment (Kazdin, 1985, 1987). In addition to the consequences of CD for the children and their families and the costs of remediation, CD children have a continuing disruptive impact on the school system and undermine the quality of education for other children. In light of the serious consequences of adolescent CD and the difficulty in treating it at this age, the focus of concern is the development of prevention models for use with young children (and their families) who are at risk by virtue of showing early aggression and poor peer relations.

Previous prevention efforts with CD children

Numerous short-term prevention efforts have been directed at young children who show high rates of aggressive or impulsive behavior and/or problems with peer relationships. Interventions have been based on a variety of theoretical models (behavioral, social-cognitive, sociological) and have used both universal delivery systems and directed interventions with targeted, high-risk children. In general, the results of such efforts have been disappointing, showing limited effectiveness (Kazdin, 1985, 1987; Lytton, 1990). Often, some posttest change is evident, but little success has been documented in the maintenance of this change across time and in cross-setting generalization. No known study to date has been successful in the long-term prevention of CD.

The problems with past efforts are as follows. First, some past interventions have failed to articulate and to evaluate a developmental hypothesis of how intervention aimed at a short-term, proximal goal will lead to long-term prevention of CD. To be successful, intervention efforts must be based on a comprehensive theory of the developmental psychopathology of CD. Second, most past interventions have lacked a developmental focus that is attentive to age-related stressors and the need for continued intervention over long periods (Cicchetti, 1984). CD can be considered a chronic disorder (Kazdin, 1985; Patterson, 1982) in need of monitoring and focused intervention at high-stress times (such as school entry and transition to middle school). Thus, preventive intervention must continue across developmental periods. Third, many past intervention efforts have been directed at just a single component of CD (such as the child's social-cognitive skills deficits, behavioral deficits, or parental discipline practices), often because of the researcher's theoretical interest in that component with limited attention given to other aspects of the disorder. Given that CD usually develops in a context of multiple determinants (family stress, parenting deficits, alienation between school and family, child social skill deficits, academic failure, etc.), it is not surprising that limited-focus interventions have limited effects. Thus, preventive intervention should be comprehensive and attentive to the social fields of the peer group, classroom, and family as well as the connections between the family and the school (Comer, 1980; Hawkins & Weis, 1985).

Fourth, many interventions have been inflexible and inattentive to the heterogeneity of the population of high-risk children (Dodge, 1986). Just as the determinants of CD are multiple (Greenberg, Speltz, & De-Klyen, in press), the needs and treatment responsivities of high-risk children and their families are variable (Miller & Prinz, 1990; Prinz & Miller, 1991). Researchers must either develop preventive models that apply to multiple groups (e.g., persons of diverse ethnicity and cultural background, gender differences, subtypes of behavioral difficulty) or evaluate which interventions are successful with particular groups.

Developmental Model

To understand CD, a developmental model of its defining features and correlates is required. Such a model is necessary to determine the appropriate loci and timing for preventive intervention. The interventions should not only focus on building behavioral and cognitive skills in the school and family environments, but also focus specifically on changing the patterns of interaction among members of the child's social fields (family, school, and peer) to promote consistent expectations for the child's performance.

Preschool years

A growing body of research suggests that CD has early beginnings and that signs of the disorder can be seen in the preschool years (Campbell, 1990; Patterson, DeBaryshe, & Ramsey, 1989; Richman, Stevenson, & Graham, 1982). As early as ages 2 and 3, child characteristics such as irritability and discipline problems (Bates & Bayles, 1988; Bates, Bayles, Bennett, Ridge, & Brown, 1991) and inattentiveness and impulsivity (Campbell, Breaux, Ewing, & Szumowski, 1986) are associated with conduct problems in later childhood. Not sur-

prisingly, children with these problems often come from families characterized by a pattern of high stress and instability, parental psychopathology, and punitive discipline (Dodge, Bates, & Pettit, 1990; Maziade, Cote, Bernier, Boutin, & Thivierge, 1989; McGee, Silva, & Williams, 1984; Richman et al., 1982; Werner & Smith, 1977). Although debate continues about the relative importance of genetic and environmental factors in determining CD (Dodge, 1990; Lytton, 1990), the dominant perspective (e.g., Offord, 1989; Rutter & Giller, 1983) is that individual characteristics interact with family and environmental conditions to place some children at identifiable high risk for CD by the time they enter school.

The most influential short-term developmental model for describing the family dynamics underlying early childhood conduct problems is Patterson's (1982, 1986) theory of coercive family process. According to Patterson (1982), stressful conditions in families (such as financial difficulties, marital conflict and instability, parental disorder, or unpreparedness for parenting) make it difficult for parents to set limits consistently for their children or to provide effective support for them, especially when the children themselves have characteristics such as irritability or hyperactivity. Without effective guidance, children can become increasingly noncompliant, aggressive, and impulsive. An escalating cycle of aversive exchanges with parents may emerge in which the children learn to respond to requests for compliance with negative, resistant verbalizations and behavior. When beleaguered parents give in to such behavior, they promote the likelihood of increasingly aversive and hostile child behavior on future occasions. In this way, children develop the skilled use of aversive behavior in social interactions. Increasing parental demoralization may accompany this cycle, and parents may withdraw from or alienate their outside sources of social support (Dumas & Wahler, 1983; Patterson, 1983; Webster-Stratton, 1990), thus adding stress to the family system. Consistent with this model, a significant component of the predictability of CD comes from family variables. High-risk children come from families marked by a combination of factors that include marital discord (Offord, 1982; Rutter & Giller, 1983), socioeconomic stress (Offord, Alder, & Boyle, 1986), criminal record or psychopathology on the part of parents (Robins, West, & Herjanic, 1975; West & Farrington, 1973), insecure attachments (Greenberg, Speltz, DeKlyen, & Endriga, 1991), and punitive and inconsistent discipline methods (Campbell et al., 1986; Patterson, 1982).

Coercive parent–child interactions may be accompanied by low levels of parental stimulation and support for the development of emotional control, social skills, and academic readiness. For example, Greenberg, Kusche, and Speltz (1991) postulated that the development of emotional control requires an integration of affect, language, cognition, and action. Young children need to learn to recognize internal cues of affect, to label them with appropriate terms, and to develop cognitive skills for self-monitoring in order to translate strong negative feelings into socially adaptive behavior. Parents who react to negative expressions of child affect as being intolerable or frightening may not only involve their children in coercive cycles of aversive interpersonal control, but also fail to assist them in developing internalized forms of control or appropriate expressions of these emotions (Cook, Greenberg, & Kusche, 1992).

Escalating and aversive parent–child interactions may also impede the development of adaptive social-cognitive skills. It is clear that elementary school children with conduct problems are deficient in critical social-cognitive skills and that these skills deficits are related directly to their aggressive tendencies (Dodge et al., 1990; Dodge, Pettit, McClaskey, & Brown, 1986). Specifically, aggressive children, relative to their peers, fail to attend to relevant social cues (Dodge et al., 1990), inaccurately interpret peers' intentions (Dodge, Murphy, & Buchsbaum, 1984), and are biased toward presuming hostile intent (Dodge & Frame, 1982; Lochman, 1987). They are unskilled in social problem solving, displaying an impoverished repertoire of competent verbally assertive strategies and a tendency instead to access action-oriented and aggressive responses (Asarnow & Callan, 1985; Lochman, Lampron, & Rabiner, 1989). They evaluate aggression as leading to positive interpersonal and instrumental outcomes (Dodge et al., 1986; Perry, Perry, & Rasmussen, 1986). Dodge et al. (1990) found that these deficits and biases are predictable from early family experiences, such as overly harsh discipline practices, and they predict the later development of social and behavioral difficulties in school. Moreover, these biases and deficits mediate the effect of early family experiences on later conduct problems. Thus, a social-information-processing perspective on the development of CD emphasizes the mediating role of acquired skills deficits and social-cognitive biases in linking early family experience with later CD (Parke, MacDonald, Beitel, & Bhavnagri, 1988).

Finally, children with CD often receive poor cognitive stimulation and support from their parents, which may contribute to low levels of academic readiness at school entry. Concurrent child problems of inattentiveness (Moffitt & Silva, 1988) and hyperactivity (Richman et al., 1982; Satterfield, Hoppe, & Schell, 1982) may impede learning at school (Meltzer, Levine, Karniski, Palfreg, & Clarke, 1984; Moffitt, 1990). In addition, families often provide poor support for academic performance and good behavior in school, leading to a lack of synchrony between the socialization activities of home and school and low levels of child readiness at school entry (Comer, 1980; Rutter & Giller, 1983). More often than not, high-risk children attend schools in which there is a high density of other high-risk children (Rutter, Maughan, Mortimore, Ouston, & Smith, 1979), creating an atmosphere less conducive to learning and more evocative of conduct problems. This, in turn, makes teaching more difficult and, for inexperienced or highly stressed teachers, can lead to a reenactment of the coercive and inconsistent home situation.

Middle childhood years

During the grade school years, negative school and social experiences further exacerbate the adjustment difficulties of children with conduct problems. Children who are aggressive and disruptive with peers quickly become rejected by their peers (Ladd, Price, & Hart, 1990). Across time peers become increasingly mistrustful of these children (Dodge, 1989) and respond to them in ways that increase the likelihood of even greater reactive aggression on the part of these high-risk children (Dodge & Coie, 1987; Hymel, Wagner & Butler, 1990; Li, 1985). Because of their noncompliant and disruptive behavior, high-risk children develop poor relations with their teachers and are less supported and nurtured in the school setting (Campbell, 1991; Dodge, Coie, & Brakke, 1982). In addition to this pattern of rejection by peers and teachers, another pattern, that of rejection by parents, has been described by Patterson (Patterson & Bank, 1989; Patterson et al., 1989). Parents' negative encounters with teachers, coupled with continued and escalating aversive interactions with their children in the home, lead some parents to reject their own highly aggressive children and show less interest in them as they enter adolescence. Several consequences follow from this spiraling pattern of aversive behavior, rejection, and reactivity. One is that high-risk children perform more poorly in school and become alienated from the goals and values of this major socializing institution (Hawkins & Weis, 1985). A second consequence is that some of these children become depressed and develop negative self-concepts in the cognitive, social, and behavioral domains. A third consequence is that rejected, aggressive children drift into deviant peer groups in early adolescence (Coie, 1990).

Early adolescence

By early adolescence, alienation from the mainstream culture and association with deviant peers may play a particularly critical role in promoting adolescent delinquency. Peer rejection and aggression in fourth grade are predictive of deviant group membership in early adolescence, about the time of transition from elementary school to middle school (Dishion, Patterson, & Skinner, 1989). Peer rejection and aggression in third and fourth grade are also significantly predictive of CD in the first year of middle school (Coie, Lochman, Terry, & Hyman, in press). It is the deviant peer group in adolescence that appears to be a major training ground for delinquency and substance abuse (Dishion & Loeber, 1985; Elliott, Huizinga, & Ageton, 1985; Hirschi, 1969; Kandel, 1973; Loeber & Baicker-McKee, 1990). Parents of high-risk adolescents are relatively unlikely to monitor their children's activities adequately (Patterson et al., 1989), and teachers at this level cannot consistently monitor contact with adolescents (Eccles, Midgley, & Adler, 1984). In fact, dropping out of school seems to be predictable from deviant peer group membership in middle school (Cairns, Cairns, & Neckerman, 1989).

Although a developmental model is a critical feature of the analysis of pathways to CD, it is quite clear that a sociological frame is also necessary for a more complete understanding (Kellam & Ensminger, 1980). Bronfenbrenner (1979) elucidated the importance of not only the interactions that children have in their growing social fields of the family, peer, and student–teacher interactions (i.e., microsystem), but also the connections among these social fields (i.e., exosystem). The child's "bonding" to social institutions (both family and school) and the family's positive bonding to both the child and school (as well as other social institutions) are believed to be critical features for the prevention of deviant behavior and delinquency during the early adolescent period (Hawkins & Weis, 1985; Hirschi, 1969). As such, a preventive model requires not only the development of appropriate social-cognitive and behavioral skills in the child and parent, but also the development of a healthy bond between the family and school, child and family, and child and school. Hawkins and Weis articulated three components of bonding: attachment, commitment, and positive beliefs. A critical point of bonding occurs between the parent and school in the early years. We believe that it is critical that parents develop a positive bond to the school and that they be seen as important partners in the process of education (Comer, 1980). Through this process, healthy microsystem connections develop that transmit to the child a tone of positive expectations, interest, and support in the child's social and academic performance. Other exosystem connections such as those typified by effective parental monitoring (Patterson & Bank, 1989) become increasingly important across the elementary years.

Implications of the developmental model for intervention

This comprehensive model suggests two strategic points in development for preventive intervention. By school entry there is an identifiable constellation of child and family variables that mark some children at high risk for CD and major adjustment difficulties in later life. Because school entry is a significant developmental transition, families are under more stress and their patterns of coping are more subject to redefinition (Alexander & Entwisle, 1988). It is at such times that families are most open to reorganization and responsive to the kind of proactive intervention proposed here (Minuchin, 1974). The goals for intervention at this point in development also follow from the model. First, high-risk children need help in learning to control anger, in developing social-cognitive skills, and in generating more socially acceptable and effective alternatives to aggression and oppositional behavior. Many high-risk children need concentrated assistance in getting ready for the academic tasks of school. Second, their parents need to acquire more consistent, more positive, and less punitive discipline methods. Parents also need to learn how to provide support for their children's cognitive growth. Many parents need support in learning to relate to teachers and to provide

support at home for the goals of the school for their children. Third, teachers may need help in preparing their classrooms for these high-risk children, especially classrooms with a high concentration of high-risk children. Finally, a case management approach may be necessary to assist highly stressed and disorganized families in providing a more stable and supportive atmosphere for child-rearing.

A second logical point for intervention is at the transition into middle school. High-risk children are clearly identifiable at this age. The key issues for these children seem to be the control of aggressive behavior, the acquisition and use of prosocial skills for integrating themselves into the mainstream peer culture, and concentrated assistance with academic skills. They may also profit from individual competency-enhancing experiences to maintain or restore self-esteem and positive affect. Parents of these preadolescents need to establish effective and nonpunitive disciplinary control of their children and to maintain or regain an active interest in their activities so that reasonable monitoring of adolescent behavior can occur. Furthermore, some active partnership between parents and the schools must take place if the monitoring of homework, school attendance, and resistance to deviant peer group involvement is to take place.

Summary

The developmental model of CD presented suggests a prevention strategy that encompasses the first 6 or 7 years of schooling for high-risk children, with particularly intensive interventions during the transitions at school entry and from the elementary grades to middle school. In light of the many and pervasive factors operating to promote antisocial tendencies among high-risk children, it seems reasonable to expect that only a comprehensive, long-term, and multistage prevention design could have a pronounced effect on the incidence of delinquency and related problems in this population. The remainder of this article focuses on the FAST Track Program clinical model that we have developed and are currently implementing during the first few years of formal schooling (beginning in first grade).

Clinical Model

Design and selection process

Consistent with our developmental model, evaluation and intervention begin at school entry. Given the treatment focus of this article, only a brief overview of the experimental model, assessment measures for screening, and criteria for candidacy for intervention in the FAST Track Program will be given here. Our current intervention trial involves a multistage screening of all children attending kindergarten in selected schools in four regions of the U.S. (Durham, NC; Nashville, TN; Seattle, WA; and rural central Pennsylvania). These regions were selected to assess the effectiveness of our intervention model with children varying in gender, ethnicity, urban versus rural living conditions, social class, and family composition. Children meet criteria for intervention by showing disruptive behavior and poor peer relations both at home and in school. Screening involved a multistage process. In the first stage, all children in kindergarten were screened through teacher interviews using a revised version of the Teacher Observation of Classroom Adaptation–Revised (Werthamer-Larsson, Kellam, & Wheeler, 1991). In the second stage, parent phone interviews were conducted for children who scored in the top 40% on the teacher rating of disruptive behavior. The parent interview assessed noncompliance and aggression in the home and was developed for this project. Scores from the teacher and the parent were then summed and the top 10% of all children were selected (this percentage varied somewhat by site). Schools at each site were selected for participation on the basis of their relatively high prevalence rates of conduct problems in their neighborhoods. Schools were approached for participation, and, *after* they agreed, they were randomly assigned to intervention or control status.

Goals of intervention at school entry

The intervention proposed at school entry targets proximal changes in six domains, attempting to promote (a) reductions in the child's display of disruptive behaviors (e.g., noncompliance, aggression, impulsive, and immature behaviors) in the home setting, with corresponding improvements in the quality of the parent–child relationship; (b) reductions in the child's aggressive, disruptive, and off-task behaviors in school settings; (c) increases in the social-cognitive skills facilitating child affect regulation and interpersonal problem solving; (d) improvements in the quality of peer relations; (e) gains in academic skills, particularly reading; and (f) improvements in the quality of the family–school relationship. The hypothesis will be tested that improvements in these six domains will lead to the long-term prevention of CD. To accomplish these goals, intervention will be multifaceted, involving multiple agents who have an impact on child socialization (i.e., parents, teachers, and peers), and will be cross-situational, targeting improvements in home and school contexts and augmenting the synchrony between these two contexts.

Components

Five integrated intervention programs provide the central components of the FAST Track model: (a) parent training; (b) home visiting/case management; (c) social skills training; (d) academic tutoring; and (e) teacher-based, classroom intervention. Each of these components will be reviewed, followed by a discussion of their integration and staffing pattern.

Parent training. Social learning-based parent training and behavioral family therapy models of intervention with children with conduct problems are predicated on the assumption that parenting skills deficits, especially in the domain of discipline practices, are key factors in the development and maintenance of child conduct problems (McMahon & Wells, 1989; Patterson, 1982).

Several recent reviews have documented the efficacy of this approach to intervening with children with conduct problems and their families (Kazdin, 1990; McMahon & Wells, 1989; Miller & Prinz, 1990).

The parent training intervention during first grade, which is taught in a group format, consists of a 22-session curriculum that covers two very broad content areas: (a) the development of positive family-school relationships, and (b) teaching social learning-based parenting skills to encourage positive parent-child interactions and to decrease child conduct problem behaviors.

As already noted, a primary goal of the FAST Track Program is to help parents help their children succeed in school. The sessions in the first part of the school year (Sessions 1-6) focus explicitly on ways in which the parents can foster their children's learning and develop positive family-school relationships. Topics addressed in these sessions include setting up a structured learning environment at home, parental involvement in and encouragement of the child's learning (especially reading), parental communication with the child about school, and establishing a positive relationship with the child's teacher. Much of the material included in these sessions has been adapted from programs developed by Hawkins and Catalano at the University of Washington (e.g., Burgoyne, Hawkins, & Catalano, 1991). In addition to the obvious timeliness of focusing on these school-related issues early in the school year, we also hope that the material in this part of the curriculum will facilitate parental involvement in, and commitment to, FAST Track and that we will be less likely to encounter resistance when the focus of the weekly meetings shifts to parenting skills later in the year. In a conscious attempt to develop cross-linkages with the social skills training and PATHS (Promoting Alternative Thinking Strategies) components of the intervention, parents are then taught (Sessions 7-9) how to help their children implement the anger control and problem-solving strategies that the children are learning in the classroom. Parents are also taught to use a similar method to increase their *own* self-control.

The remaining sessions in first grade (Sessions 10-22) are concerned with teaching appropriate parenting skills to facilitate the development of positive parent-child interactions and to decrease the occurrence of conduct problem behaviors. The content of the parenting skills portion of the FAST Track parent training program is adapted primarily from the well-validated program developed by Forehand and his colleagues (Forehand & McMahon, 1981; McMahon & Forehand, 1984). The focus of these sessions is on teaching appropriate play skills to foster and enhance positive parent-child interaction, differential attention procedures using praise and ignoring, training in giving clear instructions to increase child compliance, time out, and establishing rules.

In terms of structure, the parenting skills portion of the parent training program combines the group-based approach developed by Webster-Stratton (1989) and the more individualized approach taken by Forehand and McMahon (1981). Fortunately, both programs evolved from earlier work by Hanf (1969), so the approach to parent training and the skills that are taught overlap considerably. The group context for training was chosen not only because of its obvious advantage in enabling us to work with more families, but also because of the potential for the group to serve an ongoing social support function for the families. The Webster-Stratton (1989) program makes extensive use of videotaped vignettes and group discussion to teach parenting skills. A subset of the vignettes employed by Webster-Stratton was selected for inclusion in the FAST Track parent training program. A focus of future iterations of our parent training program will be the development of additional videotaped vignettes that are more representative of our families in terms of socioeconomic status and ethnicity. The Forehand and McMahon (1981) program, which is based on a therapist working with a single family, emphasizes extensive demonstration and modeling by the therapist, behavioral rehearsal of skills with the parent, and guided practice with the child. Our expectation is that this focus on actual *performance* of the skills with the children will increase the likelihood of generalization to the home setting and facilitate maintenance over time. Demonstration, behavioral rehearsal, and guided practice with the child occur in the parent group, during the subsequent parent–child activity time, and/or during home visits with the families.

Following the hour-long parent group, the parents and children come together for a 30-min parent–child learning activity session. The purpose of these sessions is to facilitate the development of more positive parent–child interactions. The content of the sessions varies, but it is generally tied to the content of the parent group session. For example, in the first part of the school year, a number of parent–child activities involve parents and children sharing books. Not only do such activities follow from the parent group discussions on learning and school success, but they also complement the reading tutoring component, which is primarily phonics-based, by employing a whole-language approach to reading. It is also during the parent–child activity time that much of the behavioral rehearsal and practice activities occur that are thought to be necessary to increase the likelihood of generalization of the parenting skills to the home. Throughout the year, games that are tied to material covered in the parent group, children's friendship group, and/or PATHS are also presented.

Home visiting. The skill training that occurs during the weekly parent group is supplemented with biweekly home visits (or telephone contacts) in order to practice skills, apply concepts to family contexts, and respond to individual resistance in implementing skills.

There are three other major goals of the home visiting program as well, based on the formulations that parents of high-risk children often lack: (a) competence in solving the problems of life management (Rutter, 1990; Shure & Spivack, 1978), (b) feelings of empowerment and confidence to achieve positive outcomes for their children (Dunst, Trivette, & Deal, 1989), and (c) sufficient organization to provide a safe and supportive environment for their children (Wasik,

Bryant, & Lyons, 1990). Thus, the goals of home visiting are to teach parental problem-solving skills, to promote feelings of empowerment and efficacy, and to enhance family organization.

The strategies implemented by the family coordinators (FCs) to achieve these outcomes are *not* traditional social work efforts to take over parenting functions on behalf of, or in place of, parents. Rather, FCs take a problem-solving approach (Haley, 1978; Shure & Spivack, 1978; Wasik et al., 1990) in their work with families, in which they ask questions of parents and work jointly with parents to solve specific current problems. The questions are designed to help parents process problem-related information and feelings in ways that lead to competent solutions to real-life problems. Even more important than the proximal goal of solving immediate problems is the FC's latent goal of enhancing the parent's skills and sense of self-efficacy.

After broaching a specific problem (such as how to arrange after-school care, what to do about an overly intrusive grandmother, or how to avoid contact with a former physically abusive boyfriend), FCs ask questions of the parent such as, "How does this make you feel?" "What would you like to see happen?" "What are the solutions you could try?" and "What would be the consequences if you tried a particular solution?" These questions follow the information-processing and problem-solving sequence that has been identified as crucial to competent responding (Dodge et al., 1986; Shure & Spivack, 1978).

The skills training and empowerment component of the home visiting is necessarily individually paced. Some parents respond immediately with enthusiastic interest, whereas other parents require slower pacing and greater attention to barriers such as parent psychopathology, substance abuse, family disorganization, and reticent family members. The FC's perspective is one that envisions change as occurring over a multiyear period (i.e., from the beginning of first grade until sometime in middle school), so she (all FCs are female) moves slowly and attends first to issues of trust, common ground, and the interpersonal relationship with the family.

Social skills training. A third component of the intervention package is social skills training that is designed to improve the child's social-cognitive skills and peer social adjustment. Impaired peer relations are a central feature of CD (McMahon & Wells, 1989), and it predicts later school maladjustment, juvenile delinquency, and referral for mental health services (Kupersmidt, Coie, & Dodge, 1990; Parker & Asher, 1987). Furthermore, although aggressive behavior is one primary cause of poor peer relations (cf. Coie, Dodge, & Kupersmidt, 1990), teacher or parent training programs that promote reductions in child aggression often fail to improve peer relations (cf. Bierman, 1989). To be more effective, interventions may need to address problems that contribute to interpersonal difficulties, such as social anxiety and withdrawal, insensitive and immature behavior, and aggression (French & Waas, 1985; Pope, Bierman, & Mumma, 1991). Interventions also may need to address deficits in social cognitive skills, such as asocial goals or orientations, negatively biased social perceptions, impulsive direct-action tendencies, and poor problem-solving skills (cf. Dodge, 1989; Lochman & Curry, 1986; Lochman & Lampron, 1986). Furthermore, intervention may need to create opportunities for positive peer interactions in naturalistic interactions, providing high-risk children with the multiple benefits of peer instruction and camaraderie (cf. Hartup, 1983) and fostering positive attitude changes and supportive responses from peers (cf. Bierman, 1989).

With these considerations in mind, the FAST Track intervention combines features of previously tested social skills training programs focused on friendship and play skills (Bierman, Miller, & Staub, 1987; Ladd, 1981; Oden & Asher, 1977) with features of programs focused on self-control skills, anger coping strategies, and interpersonal problem-solving skills (Coie & Krehbiel, 1990; Lochman, Burch, Curry, &

Lampron, 1984). These skills are arranged in a developmental sequence. For example, the first-grade program begins with an emphasis on participation, communication, and emotional expression—skills designed to foster the identification of common ground and friendship initiation among members. Then, behavioral inhibition, anger management, and cooperative play skills (e.g., helping, sharing) are introduced to strengthen the ability of group members to associate cooperatively with each other. The third phase of the program focuses on the understanding of reciprocity in relationships. Fair play concepts are introduced (e.g., taking turns, following rules, refraining from teasing) along with basic negotiation skills. Finally, the concluding part of the first-grade program focuses on skills to maintain friendships, including attending to feedback, giving feedback, and using interpersonal problem-solving skills to work through conflicts.

Following a standard format for coaching programs, each session begins with a presentation of a specific skill concept (Ladd, 1985). To foster children's interest and comprehension, multiple media are used to present skills concepts, including modeling videotapes, stories, puppet shows, and coach role-plays. Skills are practiced in the context of both structured activities (e.g., child role-plays and puppet shows, focused board games, guided peer interactions) and naturalistic peer interactions (e.g., dramatic play, group games). Coaches cue skilled performance and provide feedback to group members in order to increase children's recognition of cause–effect relations linking their behavior to peer responses and to foster increasingly child-generated (self-regulated) use of targeted skills in peer interactions.

In addition to these group social skills training sessions, additional strategies have been added to foster the generalization of skillful behavior to the classroom setting and to promote positive responsivity of classroom peers to improved target child behaviors (cf. Bierman, 1989). In a peer-pairing program that runs parallel to the group social skills training program, each target child has a weekly 30-min guided play session during the school day with a classroom peer. (Classmate partners rotate during the course of the school year.) In these sessions, the dyad completes activities (games, art, and crafts activities) designed to allow the target child to display improved social skills to the classroom peer and to foster mutually rewarding exchanges between the target child and a variety of classmates.

Although previous social skills training programs have been unable to document stable long-term improvements in teacher, parent, and peer ratings (cf. Coie & Krehbiel, 1990), it is hypothesized that by extending the scope and duration of this program and by embedding this training within a multifaceted intervention, more pervasive and long-term effects will be attained.

Academic tutoring. The fourth component of the proposed intervention is academic tutoring in reading skills. Learning difficulties and academic failure frequently accompany CD and may contribute to social maladaptation; likewise, CD can interfere with academic skills development (Kohlberg, La-Crosse, & Ricks, 1972; Moffitt, 1990). Programs that foster behavioral control in the classroom do not necessarily promote achievement; however, programs that enhance academic performance may facilitate behavioral improvements. Coie and Krehbiel (1984) found that academic tutoring with low-achieving, socially rejected children produced improvements in achievement scores, classroom behavior, and sociometric ratings. Their interpretation was that, by reducing frustration and increasing skills, academic tutoring promoted increases in attentive classroom behavior and reductions in disruptiveness. The latter, in turn, enhanced peer social adjustment. A phonics-oriented program developed by Wallach and Wallach (1976) was adopted for this intervention. This program is suitable for use by paraprofessionals and has been demonstrated to bring low-readiness children from poor, urban backgrounds up

to reading skill levels comparable to high-readiness children in the first year of school.

The Wallachs' program is phonics-based and designed to promote phonemic awareness skills in young children who might otherwise have difficulty learning to read because of deficits in this area. Pennington (1991) built a convincing case for the importance of phonemic awareness skills for all readers, but particularly for those who have reading disabilities. Tutors work individually with children three times a week, and one of these sessions (usually on Saturday) is conducted with the parent present both so that parents can develop a feeling for a child-paced approach to helping their children and to have them experience the regular progress their child is demonstrating. The parent's ability to participate is used as a guide to the extent to which they are actively included in tutoring exercises. Classroom teachers also sit in on these Saturday sessions, occasionally, and are encouraged to take some of this time to talk with parents about the things they have observed. This is one way that a collaboration between parent and teacher is encouraged early on in the program.

Classroom intervention. Although the emergence of child conduct problems at school may be fostered by coercive family processes (Patterson, 1982), characteristics of the classroom context (particularly teacher and peer responding) may facilitate the maintenance of these negative child behaviors. Observations suggest that teacher reinforcement for positive behavior is infrequent and reprimands given to problematic students are often noncontingent upon student behavior (Strain, Lambert, Kerr, Stagg, & Lenkner, 1983). Furthermore, students often do not acquire affective, social-cognitive, and behavioral skills that promote social and peer competence. Teachers are trained by the FAST Track staff in the implementation of the PATHS Curriculum (Kusche & Greenberg, in press), a multiyear (first through fifth grade) classroom prevention program designed to facilitate the development of self-control, a positive peer climate, emotional awareness, and interpersonal problem-solving skills of children in the primary grades (Greenberg & Kusche, in press; Greenberg, Kusche, & Cook, 1991). The curriculum is taught by teachers approximately three times each week. The lessons serve the purpose of didactic presentation, discussion, modeling, and role-playing of such skills as gaining or keeping behavioral control when upset, recognizing and communicating feelings effectively, building and maintaining friendships, problem prevention, and problem solving.

An essential part of PATHS is generalization across the classroom day and to other settings of the school. To promote generalization, a variety of techniques are utilized to promote the recognition of feelings and the performance of self-control and problem solving as real problems occur. The curriculum also includes frequent parent updates on curriculum content and suggestions for ways parents can promote their children's growing competence. There are also regular home activities in which children engage their parents in cooperatively completing drawings or stories related to curriculum components.

Additionally, teachers are taught strategies for the effective management of disruptive behavior (e.g., establishing clear rules and directions; providing positive and corrective feedback for appropriate behavior; applying reprimands, time out, or response cost procedures contingent upon the occurrence of problematic behaviors). Field trials have revealed stable behavioral improvements for children involved in programs using these teacher management strategies (Hops et al., 1978; McMahon & Wells, 1989). Whereas behavior management procedures may facilitate the control of specific behavior problems of targeted risk children, the provision of the PATHS Curriculum to all children is intended to foster social-emotional development and promote supportive changes in the classroom atmosphere, including greater compliance and on-task behavior of all children (reducing the distractions that may stimulate inappropriate behavior of risk children) and increasing support for the display of self-control and nonaggressive solutions to peer problems. Educational coordinators observe PATHS lessons on a weekly basis and have a weekly consultation time with each teacher to discuss both PATHS and more general issues in classroom management.

A context for integrating program components. Although the five types of programs that provide the components of FAST Track were originally developed and implemented as distinct and free-standing programs, there were several compelling reasons for integrating these components into one multifaceted program. The contexts and agents on which these programs focus (e.g., parents, teachers, peers) each exert unique influences on the developmental trajectories of high-risk children (Loeber, 1990), suggesting that treatment directed at more than one of these contexts/agents should promote complementary (and not redundant) improvements in target child behavior and adjustment (Kazdin, 1987). Furthermore, from a systems perspective, the participation of both parents and school personnel in the intervention facilitates the development of supportive cross-situational communication networks. We believe that this coordinated involvement is critical to the long-term maintenance of treatment gains. As described in more detail later, the format of the intervention is designed to maximize the integration of the five component programs.

Schedule of intervention components. The intervention program at school-entry begins in the fall of the first-grade year and continues through the end of the second grade. A central feature of the program during each school year is a weekly 2-hr Saturday or evening/after school "extracurricular enrichment program" that is attended by high-risk children and their parents and program staff (teachers occasionally attend these Saturday sessions). During the first hour of this enrichment program, the children participate in the social skill/friendship sessions. During this time, parents meet in small groups with staff for the parent training sessions. During the second hour, each parent–child pair spends 30 min together in the parent–child learning activity. Then, the parent joins the child and reading tutor for 30 min of reading tutoring. The model enrichment program contains five risk children and their parents or caregivers. The weekly sessions are held for 22 weeks (from October to April) of each school year.

Several additional intervention procedures take place during each week. First, to promote parent skill development, regularly scheduled biweekly home visits and weekly telephone calls are conducted to monitor parent progress and to provide individualized consultation regarding home-based, parent–child problems. Second, teachers have regular meetings with a consultant to facilitate their implementation of PATHS, keep informed on progress in reading tutoring and social skills development, and consult on behavior management strategies for individual children. Third, to foster the generalization of social skills to the classroom context and to foster acceptance by classmates, program children participate in a supplementary 30-min dyadic skill training "peer-pairing" session once each week during school that has been described above. Finally, program children receive two supplementary 30-min academic tutoring sessions each week during school hours. All of the in-school activities are arranged with each teacher to minimize disruption to ongoing school activities.

During the summer after first grade, case managers (family coordinators) continue to contact and to monitor the families with monthly home visits and weekly phone calls. This periodic contact enables staff to help parents apply the parenting principles presented during the first year of the program and provide support and case management to related family issues. In the second year of intervention, parents and children again attend the enrichment program on a biweekly basis and a second year curriculum is provided in both the parent and social skills groups, which builds on the skills learned during the first year. Second-grade teachers are trained in the implementation of the PATHS Curriculum and the behavior management procedures during

the second year of the intervention program, and midweek academic tutoring or peer-pairing is continued in second grade on an "as needed" basis.

Across the various intervention contexts, similar goals are fostered by complementary procedures. For example, the PATHS (classroom), anger-coping (enrichment program), parent training (enrichment program and home), and friendship skills (enrichment program and school) programs are integrated so that similar strategies of self-control, communication, and behavioral management are implemented in the teacher, parent, and child training sessions. Similarly, the principles of interpersonal awareness and consideration, negotiation and reciprocity, communication and interpersonal support, and interpersonal problem solving are introduced in the PATHS Curriculum and the multicontext social skills training programs. Parents are taught to implement these skills in their own interactions with their children and also are taught how to prompt and to reinforce these behaviors when supervising their children's peer interactions. This cross-situational consistency of behavioral management and prosocial support is intended to promote generalized and sustained improvements in child adaptation.

Staffing and supervision. Two central professional staff positions provide the direct services discussed above. The FC works directly with families and is responsible for school–family communication, parent training and support, home visits, assistance to the family as needed, and promoting communication between parents and teachers. The FC conducts the parenting sessions in the enrichment program. The FC is also responsible for general case management and referral. The educational coordinator (EC) is responsible for supervision of the reading tutoring program and the peer-pairing program, consultation and training with teachers using PATHS in the classroom, and liaison with building principals and other educational support staff. The EC conducts the social skills training in the enrichment program and provides ongoing training to teachers and tutors. Tutors are responsible for conducting both the thrice-weekly reading and weekly peer-pairing sessions.

The participants of FAST Track include families experiencing high levels of stress and disorganization, some of whom are experiencing serious problems involving family violence and parental psychopathology, and child abuse or neglect. In recognition of the skills required, both the FC and EC positions require mature individuals with appropriate education and experience. FC staff members are required to have prior experience in working with families at risk (either at schools or social service agencies) and are likely to have an MSW or partial social work training and significant on-the-job experience. EC staff members are required to have teaching experience at the elementary school level, and many have significant experience with at-risk or severe behavior-disordered children. Most ECs have received Masters degrees in counseling, psychology, or special education. EC and FC staff receive weekly supervision from an experienced PhD-level clinical, counseling, or school psychologist. There are no formal educational requirements for tutoring other than a high school education and tutors are recruited from neighborhoods surrounding the schools whenever possible. Tutor characteristics include experience in working with children in some capacity, a desire for long-term involvement with risk children, the ability to relate in a warm but professional manner with children, and the ability to closely follow the scripts and procedures for the reading and peer-pairing programs. Tutors receive weekly supervision from their EC.

Prevention

Issues regarding the induction to participation

Two critical features of the FAST Track clinical model are the involvement of parents in the enrichment program and home visiting and their increased positive involvement with school personnel. As such, it is important to provide the appropriate atmosphere and inducements for parent participation. Furthermore, because this is a prevention model, it is important to approach parents as participants, not as parents of "identified cases."

Given these requirements, parents are approached as collaborators and potential staff members to assist their children. The FC approaches each parent through a home visit at the beginning of the school year. Parents are told that first grade presents numerous new challenges to both children and families. Furthermore, how children do in the first few grades often sets the tone for their achievement as they grow older. FAST Track is a new program in their school to help every child get off to a great start in the early years of schooling. Thus, we approach them to join us as staff members to help their child succeed, and parents are treated as an "expert member" of the program team. To gain the interest of parents, as well as to treat them as "professionals," they are paid as staff members for their participation in the enrichment program. Thus, in addition to providing a setting for child tutoring and social skills training, the enrichment program has the intended benefits of teaching parents new skills, providing a support group atmosphere for parents in high-risk situations, assisting parents in learning the role of tutor and homework helper with their children, and providing a positive and supportive atmosphere in which the parents, project staff, and teachers can develop trusting relationships. This latter circumstance is quite contrary to the usual interactions between high-risk parents and school personnel where contacts are few and usually due to child behavior or learning problems. To overcome other obstacles to parent participation, the program provides child care for other members of the family during the enrichment program as well as transportation to and from the enrichment program.

Fitting the intervention to community contexts

An important consideration for implementing a demonstration project such as this is to make it fit with the community in which it is implemented. The four community sites in which FAST Track is being field-tested differ from each other in significant ways. The rural Pennsylvania site comprises small towns with almost exclusively white populations. Family mobility is relatively low compared to the other three urban settings. Schools vary in size, but the teachers are often familiar with families before the children begin school. The Nashville program is located in large city schools that serve a mixed-race population that is achieved by busing. In many ways it is similar to the Durham site, except that the Durham families are 90% African American owing to a white, middle-class exodus to newer suburban housing. The Seattle program is located in low-income urban areas, with schools serving African-American, Asian-American, and white families. To maintain the fidelity and integrity of each intervention component across different sites, staff members follow detailed manuals of intervention procedures, and cross-site as well as within-site supervision is conducted on a weekly basis.

The differences in community context have led to small modifications in the way the program is structured to adjust for such things as school priorities, activities that fit child interests, and travel constraints. A more important issue has been staff recruitment. As much as possible, staff members have been recruited to match the ethnic identity of the families served. This is especially critical for the FC positions, because FCs provide training to parents as well as conduct regular home visiting.

Taking a long-range approach to intervention

In a design such as ours, which features both a universal and a targeted intervention (Gordon, 1983), the goal is to reduce conduct problems in the large school population as well as in the high-risk sample. The presumed virtue of this combined approach is that there will be reciprocal benefits to both samples over the long run. As the classrooms change because of the skills and

orientation introduced by the PATHS Curriculum and teacher consultation, the high-risk children will be attending schools that function better and thus facilitate more appropriate behavior. Conversely, because the targeted program has its effects on the high-risk group, these children will be less disruptive in the classroom and less aggressive on the playground. This change will enhance the learning and social opportunities of the nontarget children. These processes take time, and the time frame for our intervention is not just 1 or 2 years, but through the end of elementary school and into middle school. After the first 2 years of the program in first and second grade, both PATHS and home visiting will continue. Home visiting and services to the child, such as academic tutoring, will be criterion-based, with the goal of helping children and families function at a normative level in the domains specified by our developmental risk model.

One methodological problem of a targeted intervention with control and experimental groups is the need to deal with attrition and selection bias. Once we identify children as high risk for later problems, they become part of the intervention cohort, whether or not they stay in these schools or agree to participate in all of the program's components. While respecting the right of families to decline to participate, our staff has developed a long-range perspective on full recruitment of some families. Taking this long-range view allows continuous accessibility of the program to families, taking them where they are and responding to shifts in openness to participation. Thus, as some children have struggled to adjust to first grade, nonparticipating families have slowly moved into the program. This is not to say that once families begin to participate that they all stay faithfully involved. Some families are faced with difficult life stresses and often find it difficult to follow through with commitments to the program. In part, the home visit component is designed to accommodate for these absences. The same problem of inconsistent involvement has been true for some teachers. Across the first year of the program, we have seen some teachers shift from wariness, or even open hostility, to continuous but often unenthusiastic participation, to confident and enthusiastic implementation of the PATHS Curriculum.

Because of the variations in program implementation, we have developed detailed process measures that record both the fact of participation and the level of quality of implementation. These records will become important as the yearly progress measures and outcome measures are analyzed in terms of "dosage" effects.

Summary

In this article, we have discussed both our developmental model and parallel clinical strategies for the prevention of serious conduct problems in children and adolescents. Past interventions at a single developmental stage or with a single focus have been unsuccessful in preventing these problems and the pain and suffering that violence, substance abuse, and serious delinquency incur. Additional steps are necessary given the intractability and seriousness of this problem to society.

We believe that there are six innovations that will contribute to improved outcomes.

First, the FAST Track intervention model is built on a clear developmental conceptualization of the problem of early aggression and its developmental trajectory, and its clinical procedures and targets are derived from this model. Second, FAST Track is based on the belief that combining universal and target interventions at the same time will lead to reciprocal effects. Third, the choice of periods of intensive prevention efforts are defined by important transitions or choice points in which children are at most risk and we believe families are most receptive. Fourth, the program takes a multisystemic focus. We not only attempt to build appropriate skills, attitudes, and expectancies in each system (family, school, peer), but also focus on building positive relations among these systems. Fifth, the intervention is structured in a manner that recognizes that this is a developmental problem, one that is unlikely to be solved in a single developmental period. Finally, we treat parents and other family members as collaborative partners in the process of helping their children succeed. We believe that carefully testing the effects of such a comprehensive approach is a necessary step in developing improved service models for this population.

References

Alexander, K. L., & Entwisle, D. R. (1988). Achievement in the first two years of school: Patterns and processes. *Monographs of the Society for Research in Child Development, 53*(2, Serial No. 218).

Asarnow, J. R., & Callan, J. W. (1985). Boys with peer adjustment problems: Social cognitive processes. *Journal of Consulting and Clinical Psychology, 53*, 80–87.

Bates, J., & Bayles, K. (1988). Attachment and the development of behavior problems. In J. Belsky & T. Nezworski (Eds.), *Clinical implications of attachment*. Hillsdale, NJ: Erlbaum.

Bates, J. E., Bayles, K., Bennett, D. S., Ridge, B., & Brown, M. M. (1991). Origins of externalizing behavior problems at eight years of age. In D. J. Pepler & K. H. Rubin (Eds.), *The development and treatment of childhood aggression* (pp. 93–120). Hillsdale, NJ: Erlbaum.

Bierman, K. L. (1989). Improving the peer relationship of rejected children. In B. B. Lahey & A. E. Kazdin (Eds.), *Advances in clinical child psychology* (Vol. 12, pp. 53–84). New York: Plenum.

Bierman, K. L., Miller, C. M., & Staub, S. (1987). Improving the social behavior and peer acceptance of

rejected boys: Effects of social skill training with instructions and prohibitions. *Journal of Consulting and Clinical Psychology, 55*, 194–200.

Bronfenbrenner, U. (1979). *The ecology of human development*. Cambridge, MA: Harvard University Press.

Burgoyne, K., Hawkins, D., & Catalano, R. (1991). *How to help your child succeed in school*. Seattle, WA: Developmental Research and Programs.

Cairns, R. B., Cairns, B. D., & Neckerman, H. J. (1989). Early school dropout: Configurations and determinants. *Child Development, 60*, 1437–1452.

Campbell, S. B. (1990). *Behavior problems in preschool children: Clinical and developmental issues*. New York: Guilford.

Campbell, S. B. (1991). Longitudinal studies of active and aggressive preschoolers: Individual differences in early behavior and outcome. In D. Cicchetti & S. L. Toth (Eds.), *Rochester Symposium on Developmental Psychopathology, Vol. 2: Internalizing and externalizing expressions of dysfunction* (pp. 57–90). Hillsdale, NJ: Erlbaum.

Campbell, S. B., Breaux, A. M., Ewing, L. J., & Szumowski, E. K. (1986). Correlates and prediction of hyperactivity and aggression: A longitudinal study of parent-referred problem preschoolers. *Journal of Abnormal Child Psychology, 14*, 217–234.

Cicchetti, D. (1984). The emergence of developmental psychopathology. *Child Development, 55*, 1–7.

Coie, J. (1990). Toward a theory of peer rejection. In S. R. Asher & J. D. Coie (Eds.), *Peer rejection in childhood* (pp. 365–402). New York: Cambridge University Press.

Coie, J. D., Dodge, K. A., & Kupersmidt, J. (1990). Peer group behavior and social status. In S. R. Asher & J. D. Coie (Eds.), *Peer rejection in childhood* (pp. 17–59). New York: Cambridge University Press.

Coie, J. D., & Krehbiel, G. (1984). Effects of academic tutoring on the social status of low-achieving, socially rejected children. *Child Development, 55*, 1465–1478.

Coie, J. D., & Krehbiel, G. K. (1990). Adapting intervention to the problems of aggressive and disruptive rejected children. In S. R. Asher & J. D. Coie (Eds.), *Peer rejection in childhood* (pp. 309–337). New York: Cambridge University Press.

Coie, J. D., Lochman, J. E., Terry, R., & Hyman, C. (1992). Predicting early adolescent disorder from childhood aggression and peer rejection. *Journal of Consulting and Clinical Psychology, 60*, 783–792.

Comer, J. P. (1980). *School power*. New York: Free Press.

Cook, E. T., Greenberg, M. T., & Kusche, C. A. (1992). *The relations between emotional understanding, intellectual functioning, and disruptive behavior problems in elementary school aged children*. Unpublished manuscript.

Dishion, T. J., & Loeber, R. (1985). Adolescent marijuana and alcohol use: The role of parents and peers revisited. *American Journal of Drug and Alcohol Abuse, 11*, 11–15.

Dishion, T. J., Patterson, G. R., & Skinner, M. S. (1989, April). *A process model for the role of peers in adolescent social adjustment*. Paper presented at the biennial meeting of the Society for Research in Child Development, Kansas City, MO.

Dodge, K. A. (1986). A social information processing model of social competence in children. In M. Perlmutter (Ed.), *Minnesota Symposium in Child Psychology* (pp. 7–125). Hillsdale, NJ: Erlbaum.

Dodge, K. A. (1989). Enhancing social relationships. In E. J. Mash & R. J. Barkley (Eds.), *Behavioral treatment of childhood disorders* (pp. 222–244). New York: Guilford.

Dodge, K. A. (1990). Nature versus nurture in childhood conduct disorder: Is it time to ask a different question. *Developmental Psychology, 26*, 698–701.

Dodge, K. A., Bates, J. E., & Pettit, G. S. (1990). Mechanisms in the cycle of violence. *Science, 250*, 1678–1683.

Dodge, K. A., & Coie, J. D. (1987). Social information processing factors in reactive and proactive aggression in children's peer groups. *Journal of Personality and Social Psychology, 53*, 1146–1158.

Dodge, K. A., Coie, J. D., & Brakke, N. P. (1982). Behavior patterns of socially rejected and neglected preadolescents: The roles of social approach and aggression. *Journal of Abnormal Child Psychology, 18*, 389–409.

Dodge, K. A., & Frame, C. L. (1982). Social cognitive biases and deficits in aggressive boys. *Child Development, 53*, 620–635.

Dodge, K. A., Murphy, R. R., & Buchsbaum, K. (1984). The assessment of intention-cue detection skills in children: Implications for developmental psychopathology. *Child Development, 55*, 163–173.

Dodge, K. A., Pettit, G. S., McClaskey, C. L., & Brown, M. (1986). Social competence in children. *Monographs of the Society for Research in Child Development, 51*(2, Serial No. 213).

Dumas, J. E., & Wahler, R. G. (1983). Predictors of treatment outcome in parent training: Mother insularity and socioeconomic disadvantage. *Behavioral Assessment, 5*, 301–313.

Dunst, C. J., Trivette, C. M., & Deal, A. (1989). *Enabling and empowering families: Principles and guidelines for practice*. Cambridge, MA: Brookline Book.

Eccles, J. E., Midgley, C. M., & Adler, T. F. (1984). Age-related changes in the school environment: Effects on achievement motivation. In J. P. Nicholls (Ed.), *The development of achievement motivation* (pp. 283–331). Greenwood, CT: JAI Press.

Elliott, D. S., Huizinga, D., & Ageton, S. S. (1985). *Explaining delinquency and drug use*. Beverly Hills, CA: Sage.

Forehand, R., & McMahon, R. J. (1981). *Helping the noncompliant child: A clinician's guide to parent training*. New York: Guilford.

French, D. L., & Waas, G. A. (1985). Behavior problems of peer-rejected elementary-age children: Parent and teacher perspectives. *Child Development, 56*, 246–252.

Gordon, R. (1983). An operational definition of prevention. *Public Health Reports, 98*, 107–109.

Greenberg, M. T., & Kusche, C. A. (in press). *Promoting social and emotional development in deaf children: The PATHS Project*. Seattle: University of Washington Press.

Greenberg, M. T., Kusche, C. A., & Cook, E. T. (1991, April). *Improving children's understanding of emotions: The effects of the PATHS Curriculum*. Paper presented at the Society for Research in Child Development, Seattle, WA.

Greenberg, M. T., Kusche, C. A., & Speltz, M. (1991). Emotional regulation, self-control and psychopathology: The role of relationships in early childhood. In D. Cicchetti & S. Toth (Eds.), *Rochester Symposium on Developmental Psychopathology* (Vol. 2, pp. 21–66). New York: Cambridge University Press.

Greenberg, M. T., Speltz, M. L., & DeKlyen, M. (in press). Toward a conceptual model for understanding the early development of disruptive behavior problems. *Development and Psychopathology*.

Greenberg, M. T., Speltz, M. L., DeKlyen, M., & Endriga, M. C. (1991). Attachment security in preschoolers with and without externalizing problems: A replication. *Development and Psychopathology, 3*, 413–430.

Haley, J. (1978). *Problem solving therapy*. San Francisco: Jossey-Bass.

Hanf, C. (1969). *A two-stage program for modifying maternal controlling during mother–child (M-C) interaction*. Paper presented at the meeting of the Western Psychological Association, Vancouver, BC.

Hartup, W. W. (1983). Peer relations. In E. M. Hetherington (Ed.) & P. H. Mussen (Series Ed.), *Hand-*

book of child psychology: Vol. 4. Socialization, personality and social development (pp. 103–196). New York: Wiley.

Hawkins, J. D., & Weis, J. G. (1985). The social development model: An integrated approach to delinquency prevention. *Journal of Primary Prevention, 6*, 73–95.

Hirschi, T. (1969). *Causes of delinquency.* Berkeley: University of California Press.

Hops, H., Walker, H. M., Fleischman, D. H., Nagoshi, J. T., Omura, R. T., Skindrud, K., & Taylor, J. (1978). CLASS: A standardized in-class program for acting-out children. II. Field test evaluations. *Journal of Educational Psychology, 70*, 636–644.

Hymel, S., Wagner, E., & Butler, L. J. (1990). Reputational bias: View from the peer group. In S. R. Asher & J. D. Coie (Eds.), *Peer rejection in childhood* (pp. 156–186). New York: Cambridge University Press.

Kandel, D. B. (1973). Adolescent marijuana use: Role of parents and peers. *Science, 181*, 1067–1081.

Kazdin, A. E. (1985). *Treatment of antisocial behavior in children and adolescents.* Homewood, IL: Dorsey.

Kazdin, A. E. (1987). Treatment of antisocial behavior in children: Current status and future directions. *Psychological Bulletin, 102*, 187–203.

Kazdin, A. E. (1990, June). *Prevention of conduct disorder.* Paper presented at the National Conference on Prevention Research, National Institute of Mental Health, Bethesda, MD.

Kellam, S. G., & Ensminger, M. E. (1980). Theory and method in child psychiatric epidemiology. In F. Earls (Ed.), *Studies of children.* New York: Prodist.

Kohlberg, L. A., LaCrosse, J., & Ricks, D. (1972). The predictability of adult mental health from childhood behavior. In B. Wolman (Ed.), *Manual of child psychopathology* (pp. 1217–1283). New York: McGraw-Hill.

Kupersmidt, J. B., Coie, J. D., & Dodge, K. A. (1990). The role of poor peer relationships in the development of disorder. In S. R. Asher & J. D. Coie (Eds.), *Peer rejection in childhood* (pp. 274–308). New York: Cambridge University Press.

Kusche, C. A., & Greenberg, M. T. (in press). *The PATHS Curriculum.* Seattle, WA: EXCEL.

Ladd, G. (1981). Effectiveness of a social learning method for enhancing children's social interaction and peer acceptance. *Child Development, 52*, 171–178.

Ladd, G. W. (1985). Documenting the effects of social skill training with children: Process and outcome assessment. In B. H. Schneider, K. H. Rubin, & J. E. Ledingham (Eds.), *Children's peer relations: Issues in assessment and intervention* (pp. 243–269). New York: Springer-Verlag.

Ladd, G. W., Price, J. M., & Hart, C. H. (1990). Preschoolers' behavioral orientations and patterns of peer contact: Predictive of peer status? In S. R. Asher & J. E. Coie (Eds.), *Peer rejection in childhood* (pp. 90–115). New York: Cambridge University Press.

Li, A. K. F. (1985). Early rejected status and later social adjustment: A 3-year follow-up. *Journal of Abnormal Child Psychology, 13*, 567–577.

Lochman, J. E. (1987). Self and peer perceptions and

attributional biases of aggressive and nonaggressive boys in dyadic interactions. *Journal of Consulting and Clinical Psychology, 55*, 404–410.

Lochman, J. E., Burch, P. R., Curry, J. F., & Lampron, L. B. (1984). Treatment and generalization effects of cognitive-behavioral and goal-setting interventions with aggressive boys. *Journal of Consulting and Clinical Psychology, 52*, 915–916.

Lochman, J. E., & Curry, J. F. (1986). Effects of social problem-solving training and self-instruction training with aggressive boys. *Journal of Clinical Child Psychology, 15*, 159–164.

Lochman, J. E., & Lampron, L. B. (1986). Situational social problem solving skills and self-esteem of aggressive and nonaggressive boys. *Journal of Abnormal Child Psychology, 14*, 605–617.

Lochman, J. E., Lampron, L. B., & Rabiner, D. L. (1989). Format differences and salience effects in assessment of social problem-solving skills of aggressive and nonaggressive boys. *Journal of Clinical Child Psychology, 18*, 230–236.

Loeber, R. (1990). Development and risk factors of juvenile antisocial behavior and delinquency. *Clinical Psychology Review, 10*, 1–41.

Loeber, R. (1991). Antisocial behavior: More enduring than changeable? *Journal of the American Academy of Child and Adolescent Psychiatry, 30*, 393–397.

Loeber, R., & Baicker-McKee, C. (1990). *The changing manifestations of disruption/antisocial behavior from childhood to early adulthood: Evolution or tautology?* Unpublished manuscript.

Loeber, R., & Dishion, T. J. (1983). Early predictors of male delinquency: A review. *Psychological Bulletin, 74*, 68–99.

Loeber, R., Lahey, B. B., & Thomas, C. (1991). Diagnostic conundrum of oppositional defiant disorder and conduct disorder. *Journal of Abnormal Psychology, 100*, 379–390.

Loeber, R., & Schmalling, K. B. (1985). The utility of differentiating between mixed and pure forms of antisocial child behavior. *Journal of Abnormal Child Psychology, 13*, 315–336.

Lytton, H. (1990). Child and parent effects in boys' conduct disorder: A re-interpretation. *Developmental Psychology, 26*, 683–697.

Maziade, M., Cote, R., Bernier, H., Boutin, P., & Thivierge, J. (1989). Significance of extreme temperament in infancy for clinical status in pre-school years II. *British Journal of Psychiatry, 14*, 544–551.

McGee, R., Silva, P. A., & Williams, S. (1984). Perinatal, neurological, environmental, and developmental characteristics of seven-year-old children with stable behavioral problems. *Journal of Child Psychology and Psychiatry, 25*, 573–586.

McMahon, R. J., & Forehand, R. (1984). Parent training for the noncompliant child: Treatment outcome, generalization, and adjunctive therapy processes. In R. F. Dangel & R. A. Polster (Eds.), *Parent training: Foundations of research and practice* (pp. 298–378). New York: Guilford.

McMahon, R. J., & Wells, K. C. (1989). Conduct disorders. In E. J. Mash & R. A. Barkley (Eds.), *Treatment of childhood disorders* (pp. 73–134). New York: Guilford.

Meltzer, L. J., Levine, M. D., Karniski, W., Palfreg, J. S., & Clarke, S. (1984). An analysis of the learning style of adolescent delinquents. *Journal of Learning Disabilities, 17,* 600–608.

Miller, G. E., & Prinz, R. J. (1990). Enhancements of social learning family interventions for childhood conduct disorder. *Psychological Bulletin, 108,* 291–307.

Minuchin, S. (1974). *Families and family therapy.* Cambridge, MA: Harvard University Press.

Moffitt, T. E. (1990). Juvenile delinquency and attention deficit disorder: Boy's developmental trajectories from age 3 to age 15. *Child Development, 61,* 893–910.

Moffitt, T. E., & Silva, P. A. (1988). Self-reported delinquency, neuropsychological deficit, and history of attention deficit disorder. *Journal of Abnormal Child Psychology, 16,* 553–569.

Oden, S., & Asher, S. R. (1977). Coaching children in social skills. *Child Development, 48,* 495–506.

Offord, D. R. (1982). Family backgrounds of male and female delinquents. In J. Gunn & D. P. Farrington (Eds.), *Delinquency and the criminal justice system.* New York: Wiley.

Offord, D. R. (1989). Conduct disorder: Risk factors and prevention. In D. Shaffer, I. Philip, & N. B. Enzer (Eds.), *Prevention of mental disorders, alcohol and other drug use in children and adolescents.* Rockville, MD: Office for Substance Abuse Prevention.

Offord, D. R., Alder, R. J., & Boyle, M. H. (1986). Prevalence and sociodemographic correlates of conduct disorder. *American Journal of Social Psychiatry, 6,* 272–278.

Parke, R. D., MacDonald, K., Beitel, A., & Bhavnagri, N. (1988). The interrelationships among families, fathers, and peers. In R. Peters & R. J. McMahon (Eds.), *Social learning and systems approaches to marriage and the family* (pp. 17–44). New York: Bruner/Mazel.

Parker, J. G., & Asher, S. R. (1987). Peer relations and later personal adjustment: Are low-accepted children at risk? *Psychological Bulletin, 102,* 357–389.

Patterson, G. R. (1982). *Coercive family process.* Eugene, OR: Castalia.

Patterson, G. R. (1983). Stress: A change agent for family process. In N. Garmezy & M. Rutter (Eds.), *Stress, coping and development in children* (pp. 235–264). New York: McGraw-Hill.

Patterson, G. R. (1986). Performance models for antisocial boys. *American Psychologist, 41,* 432–444.

Patterson, G. R., & Bank, C. L. (1989). Some amplifying mechanisms for pathologic processes in families. In M. Gunnar & E. Thelen (Eds.), *Systems and development: Symposia on Child Psychology* (pp. 167–210). Hillsdale, NJ: Erlbaum.

Patterson, G. R., DeBaryshe, B. D., & Ramsey, E. (1989). A developmental perspective on antisocial behavior. *American Psychologist, 44,* 329–335.

Pennington, B. F. (1991). *Diagnosing learning disorders.* New York: Guilford.

Perry, D. G., Perry, L. C., & Rasmussen, P. (1986). Cognitive social learning mediators of aggression. *Child Development, 57,* 700–711.

Pope, A. W., Bierman, K. L., & Mumma, G. H. (1989). Relations between hyperactive and aggressive behaviors and peer relations at three elemen-

tary grade levels. *Journal of Abnormal Child Psychology, 17,* 253–267.

Prinz, R. J., & Miller, G. E. (1991). Issues in understanding and treating childhood conduct problems in disadvantaged populations. *Journal of Clinical Child Psychology, 20,* 379–385.

Richman, N., Stevenson, J., & Graham, P. J. (1982). *Preschool to school: A behavioral study.* London: Academic.

Robins, L. N. (1966). *Deviant children grown up: A sociological and psychiatric study of sociopathic personality.* Baltimore, MD: Williams & Wilkins.

Robins, L. (1978). Sturdy childhood predictors of adult antisocial behavior: Replications from longitudinal studies. *Psychological Medicine, 8,* 611–622.

Robins, L., West, P. A., & Herjanic, B. (1975). Arrests and delinquency on two generations: A study of Black urban families and their children. *Journal of Child Psychology and Psychiatry, 16,* 125–140.

Rutter, M. (1990). Intergenerational continuities and discontinuities in serious parenting difficulties. In D. Cicchetti & V. Carlson (Eds.), *Child maltreatment: Theory and research on the causes and consequences of child abuse and neglect* (pp. 317–348). New York: Cambridge University Press.

Rutter, M., & Giller, H. (1983). *Juvenile delinquency: Trends and perspectives.* New York: Penguin.

Rutter, M., Maughan, B., Mortimore, P., Ouston, J., & Smith, A. (1979). *Fifteen thousand hours: Secondary schools and their effects on children.* Cambridge, MA: Harvard University Press.

Satterfield, J. K., Hoppe, C. M., & Schell, A. M. (1982). A prospective study of delinquency in 110 adolescent boys with attention deficit disorder and 88 normal adolescent boys. *American Journal of Psychiatry, 139,* 795–798.

Shure, M. B., & Spivack, G. (1978). *Problem-solving techniques in child rearing.* San Francisco: Jossey-Bass.

Strain, P. S., Lambert, D. L., Kerr, M. M., Stagg, V., & Lenkner, D. A. (1983). Naturalistic assessment of children's compliance to teacher's requests and consequences for compliance. *Journal of Applied Behavior Analysis, 16,* 243–249.

Wallach, M. A., & Wallach, L. (1976). *Teaching all children to read.* Chicago: University of Chicago Press.

Wasik, B. H., Bryant, D. M., & Lyons, C. M. (1990). *Home visiting: Procedures for helping families.* Newbury Park, CA: Sage.

Webster-Stratton, C. (1989). *The parents and children series.* Eugene, OR: Castalia.

Webster-Stratton, C. (1990). Stress: A potential disrupter of parent perceptions and family interactions. *Journal of Clinical Child Psychology, 19,* 302–312.

Werner, E., & Smith, S. (1977). *Kauai's children come of age.* Honolulu: University of Hawaii Press.

Werthamer-Larsson, L., Kellam, S., & Wheeler, L. (1991). Effects of first-grade classroom environment on shy behavior, aggressive behavior, and concentration problems. *American Journal of Community Psychology, 19,* 585–602.

West, D. J., & Farrington, D. P. (1973). *Who becomes delinquent?* London: Heinemann Educational.

[23]

Prevention and Early Intervention with Children in Need: Definitions, Principles and Examples of Good Practice

Michael Little
Dartington Social
Research Unit

Prevention and early intervention for children in need has considerable appeal to policy makers and professionals operating from health, education and social services contexts. This paper sets out definitions intended to inform the development of ideas in this area. It summarises principles of effective prevention and early intervention based on an extensive review of the literature. It then sets out examples of good practice, one from previous North American attempts to give vulnerable children a better start in life, the other a contemporary illustration from England which seeks to build on some of the principles of good practice. Copyright © 1999 John Wiley & Sons, Ltd.

The idea of prevention has much appeal to any profession. Why spend so much time and effort dealing with difficult problems—often ineffectively—when the problem could be stopped from happening in the first place? This article is about children in need as defined by the *Children Act* 1989 and is aimed at professionals in health, education, social services and police settings; but the opening sentiments and observations that follow hold true in just about any professional context.

Despite its generic appeal, there will be periods when prevention is used more frequently in the vocabulary of policy makers and practitioners than others. At certain times there will be requests for overviews of the evidence and new prevention initiatives will be launched. Occasionally they will be carefully evaluated and professionals will become more attuned to prevention opportunities. Since, however, so little is usually known about the nature of the problems being prevented and the volume and type of activity marshalled in response to them, it is difficult to decide whether modifications to professional vocabulary offer any indication of change in professional behaviour.

Correspondence to: Michael Little, Dartington Social Research Unit, Warren House, Warren Lane, Dartington, Totnes, Devon TQ9 6EG.

Much of this article is an argument for a clearer set of ground rules to be used in respect to preventative activity. This is certainly not the first word on the subject (much of what follows relies on the experience of others who have thought more deeply about the issue) nor will it be the last, but it might encourage more widespread interest in a common use of terms, ideas and principles. A good place to start is with definitions in respect of children in need.

Definitions

(i) Children in need

The concept of children in need is one of the foundation stones of the *Children Act* 1989 in England and Wales (with adaptations in Scotland and Northern Ireland). It is a definition that has relevance to all children since all potentially have needs. It is a definition which should interest professionals in health, education, social services and police since it encompasses all aspects of children's lives, not just their need for protection from maltreatment, for a safe place to live or for the other commonly specified aims of child welfare legislation.

In legal terms, the *Children Act* 1989 defines as in need any child whose health or development is impaired or is at risk of impairment. This is helpful but not entirely sufficient. It acts as a guide to clinical judgement (although more work is required to help professionals make consistent judgements), but has proved difficult for local or health authorities to apply as a threshold to an entire population.

Work at the Dartington Research Unit is currently testing different applications of thresholds at the clinical level and for general populations. These take three tracks, the first two of which are most relevant here. First, by looking at an entire community and gathering information on every resident child it has been possible to test the effect of different thresholds used to define need in the local population. It is too early to report the findings of this work, except to say that it does seem possible to construct an empirically based definition of children in need built, as it were, from the ground up (Axford, Little and Morpeth, 1999).

A second route has been to look at all referrals to health, education, social services and police in selected geographical areas (Little and Madge, 1998). This is a partial view of need since it is based on those that come forward for help. It nonetheless reveals more about the pattern of need than had previously been understood. For example, one in four children in one of the selected localities was referred as being in potential need each calendar year. It shows that the majority of referrals were to education and health services but that for the long-term cases social services often became the provider. To this type of evidence it is possible to add several other studies whose empirical base is referrals to social services departments (Aldgate and Tunstill, 1995; Tunnard, 1999; Aldgate, Bradley and Hawley, 1999).

A third route has been to test the consistency of professionals' judgement about whether or not a child is in need and, if he or she is, the seriousness of that need (Little and Ryan, 1999). The results are at the same time both discouraging and encouraging. With very little guidance, only about 40 per cent of professionals (even when all are members of the same

306   Michael Little

professional group) agree on where thresholds should be placed with respect to individual cases. After some discussion about uncertainties and initial disagreement, the proportion rises to about 80 per cent, meaning that for one in five cases it is extremely difficult to get a common view.

This tentative empirical evidence is reported to support the proposition that the first task intrinsic to solid progress is for professionals within local and health authorities to work together (and where possible involve children, families and community representatives in the process) to agree an empirical definition of children in need. Ideally, this should take two routes: the first beginning with some assessment of all children in the community, the second encouraging professionals to discuss how they can make consistent judgements about the cases that are referred.

Wise local and health authorities will also use the opportunity of working together better to define the nature and pattern of children's needs, a practical consideration that will also contribute to academic requirements for precision and rigour, which in turn will contribute to better practice.

(ii) Children's services

With or without the evidence, most localities will recognise that few children have needs that can be fully met by single agency. In England and Wales, children's social needs are referred to health, education, social and police services, and where these needs are met an intervention comprising a combination of professional contributions is likely to be applied. Much of the input comes from local government agencies with a proportion—probably about 10 per cent—being purchased from the voluntary and private sectors. The term 'health, education, social and police services on behalf of children in need' is a little long winded and so, for the sake of brevity and to avoid repetition, the shorter description of children's services will be used from here.

In the United Kingdom and for health services in most other developed nations, it is now common to grade an intervention according to its place in the development of the problem being addressed. In England, for example, child and adolescent mental health services use the terms tier one, tier two, tier three and tier four services (NHS HEA, 1995). The first tier is concerned with problems in the early stage of their development, the second requires more specialist help and the third refers to the more serious and complex cases. The fourth tier focuses on cases who have failed to respond to activity in the three previous tiers.

Unfortunately, whatever the grading system employed, what these agencies actually do on behalf of children has become unclear. Certain functions, usually undertaken on behalf of the most difficult cases, for example the provision of special education, some child and adolescent mental health services and foster care, are relatively clear. But, too often functions become blurred so that social workers, to select a case in point, often describe their contribution during the assessment or review process as part of the intervention itself.

As true as these claims may be (there is no evidence for or against) the lack of clarity is a handicap when trying to classify the nature of activities into various forms of prevention and intervention. It also makes evaluation problematic since it is difficult to pinpoint what has worked, for whom, when and why.

Most of the examples of effective prevention and early intervention on behalf of children in need rely on well-defined activity on behalf of well-defined groups of children. Some examples are given here. They may appear alien to some readers but they are probably a pre-requisite for more effective children's services.

(iii) Prevention, early intervention, treatment and social prevention

There are mountains of books setting out different classifications of professional and voluntary activity on behalf of different categories of people (Albee and Gullotta, 1997). In the context of children's services, it has been common to distinguish between primary, secondary and tertiary prevention where the first stage is to stop the problem happening at all and the third is to ensure that a well established condition improves (Hardiker, Exton and Barker, 1991; Sinclair, Hearn and Pugh, 1997).

In a recently published overview of research on prevention, a slightly different formulation was assembled reflecting some changes in thinking about prevention activity (Little and Mount, 1999). It has four categories:

- Prevention to intervene with an entire population to stop potential problems from emerging. Universal pre- and post-natal care to reduce infant mortality is an illustration of such activity.
- Early intervention with people who show the first indications of an identified problem and who are known to be at unusually high risk of succumbing to that problem. Special classroom help with children who are exceptionally active in primary school would be one illustration, inoculation against childhood diseases is another.
- Treatment or intervention to focus on the particular circumstances of individuals who have developed most of the symptoms of the identified problem. Notwithstanding the aforementioned criticisms about lack of specificity, most established children's services fit into this category.
- Social prevention to minimise the damage that those who have developed an identified condition can do to others with whom they come in contact. Encouraging people not to leave their property unattended as a mechanism for reducing opportunities for crime provides an illustration of social prevention in the context of children's services.

(iv) Preventing a need not a service

One reason for eschewing the primary, secondary, tertiary formulation was its association, in the 1960s in particular, with the idea of preventing a service. This was particularly the case in respect to social services interventions (Barclay, 1982). A typical example would be the introduction of services intermediate between a child's home and residential care (intermediate treatment as it became known) in order to reduce the overall numbers of children placed in residence (Thorpe and others, 1980).

This was a popular and in many ways successful formulation. But, the emergence of the concept of a continuum of services to meet the identified needs of children, a perspective implicit in the *Children Act* 1989, required a different approach. It is now recognised that over time complex needs may require several services from several agencies. It does not help, therefore, to place health services in opposition to social services or day care against residential care since all may be a necessary part of a child's recovery.

308   Michael Little

In the context of children's services, therefore, a modern definition of prevention emphasises the notions of preventing a need from arising and highlighting those services most likely to achieve the best results.

Principles of effective prevention and early intervention with children in need

So far, this article has been concerned with questions of definition. Although it has not defined children in need, services to meet those needs or the special nature of preventative activity, hopefully it has offered some useful insights that highlight the value of working towards a common language on these issues. As might be expected from an empirical researcher, much of the language used has either built upon what has gone before or invites more evidence (or both) about children. It has also often been implicit that the production of useful data should not be the sole preserve of researchers. Indeed, there is much to be said for encouraging communities to build and learn from their own evidence base.

For many policy makers and practitioners these suggestions will appear inconvenient. It may seem much more expedient to work from a set of principles setting out what is known about effective prevention and early intervention. Dartington's recently published review of evidence on the subject ends, reluctantly, with such a set of principles. The hesitation reflected doubts about whether good practice would emerge from the application of the principles; more likely that the principles will be reaffirmed by good practice, especially if it is evidence based.

Nonetheless, the principles are set out again here, with greater brevity. A summary allows space to discuss selected ones in more depth. This approach enables us to provide two examples of good practice, one historical, the other contemporary. The first two principles are:

1. Prevention and early intervention tend to be more effective when they are a response to clear evidence on the needs of children in any location. It is better to start from empirical evidence about the nature of a problem than from professionals' or managers' perceptions. (Such evidence can be rapidly assembled and need not rely only on published research studies.)
2. Prevention and early intervention are more effective when they are designed in response to clear evidence about the likely causes of children's problems. Most authoritative evidence expresses these potential causal links as 'chains of effects' in children's lives.

Discussion around the second principle

The causes of the various problems experienced by children in need are still a matter of speculation. There is plenty of evidence of proven associations between one variable and another, but this is not the same as identifying cause (Wadsworth, 1991; Rutter, 1979). Hence, it is known that children with needs for warm and supportive relationships at home are more likely to be growing up in poverty despite the fact that most poor parents provide a close and loving environment for their children (Department of Health, 1995). There is some possible association between a child's genotype and his or her likelihood of later conduct disorder (Rutter, Giller and Hagell, 1998). But, as yet none of these results add up to a clear indication of what causes different types of childhood difficulty.

This difficulty should not lead us to abandon efforts to connect interventions (early or late) and potential explanations of cause. The nearest approximation to cause in the children's services field are the hypotheses about chains of effects forwarded by researchers mainly working in the field of psycho-social development (Rutter and Smith, 1995; Sampson and Laub, 1993). Here, the concern is not so much how what happens today influences what occurs tomorrow or even how a single event can lead to a subsequent occurrence. Chains of effects suggest the interplay of several risk factors interacting over time, sometimes being mediated by protective factors operating in a child's life.

The longitudinal studies following birth cohorts in the 1940s, '50s and '60s are the best source of information on potential chains of effects (even if the studies do not always use the chain metaphor) (Essen and Wedge, 1978; Kolvin and others, 1990; West and Farrington, 1973, Farrington, 1990 and 1995). For example, Wadsworth found that poor diet and unsatisfactory environment predisposes children to infection and the inhibition of growth or biochemical development. In the longer term, poor child health correlates with poor adult health, particularly respiratory and cardiovascular illness.

These data give health, education, police and social services the best clues about where to place their scare resources. This way of thinking also provides an opportunity for children's services to plan interventions that may be evaluated and so contribute to the existing stock of knowledge about chains of effects for children in need. There is greater scope for policy makers, managers and practitioners to learn from research but, under the right conditions, so too is there an opportunity for researchers to learn from careful evaluations undertaken by professionals in a practice setting. One of the examples of potentially good prevention and early intervention practice set out below illustrates the possible overlap.

Principles continued

3.   Since chains of effects intersect all areas of children's lives, prevention and early intervention require the cooperation of health, education, social and police services as well as voluntary agencies.
4.   Better diagnosis is a prerequisite of improved understanding of the balance between prevention and intervention early and late in children's services. The goal should be consistency between one professional and another about the nature of children's needs, their seriousness, the likely prognosis and conclusions about what works.
5.   Since children's social and psychological problems are frequently a manifestation of difficulty in several areas of life, an accurate diagnosis requires information about all aspects of the child's situation from birth to the point of referral.
6.   Prevention should complement early intervention, treatment and social prevention as they are defined earlier. Professionals should regard these activities as complementary and not in competition.

Discussion about the sixth principle

Because prevention has such an obvious appeal to professionals, there has been a tendency to place it against other activity design to tackle the problem in hand. Stop the problem

310   Michael Little

occurring in the first place and there will be neither need for intervention, early or late, nor a requirement for social prevention. On the back of such discussions are built arguments about cost. Spending a little more earlier on in the development of an identified problem may save much more money later on. Unfortunately, the logic in each case is not supported by empirical evidence.

John Snow was a pioneer in medical prevention. Without being able to explain the causal chains, he hypothesised that drinking water was a probable carrier of cholera, which, in the mid-1800s was a major cause of death in London and other major cities. His theory was widely derided and it is said that he removed the handle from a water pump thought to be a source for the disease and, in so doing, prevented several cholera deaths (Porter, 1997). His work led eventually to the treatment of water, a major and successful prevention strategy that has greatly reduced the incidence of the disease, in the economically developed world at least.

But people still die of cholera today. The disease has not been eradicated and nor has any other (except smallpox) been stopped as a result of a prevention strategy. Several other mechanisms help keep the disease to a minimum. Those in or travelling to infected areas are given inoculations so they build up resistance to the disease, a successful early intervention strategy. Those who develop the condition are treated by rehydration therapy, an intervention that has greatly reduced the mortality rate. Those who treat or live with cholera sufferers use social prevention strategies which means they are unlikely to contract the disease.

Hence the appeal to look to combinations of prevention, early intervention, treatment and social prevention when trying to change the pattern of children's problems. Note that it is the pattern that changes not necessarily the volume. To use the cholera comparison again, the combined forces of prevention and other interventions have reduced the incidence of that disease (cholera) but have not eradicated disease as a whole. For this reason, it is probably folly to imagine that more prevention will reduce overall expenditure on children's services. In his review of the cost-effectiveness of various prevention programmes, Welsh (1999) shows the results to be at best mixed with some experiments increasing not decreasing the burden on the public purse. These findings are not arguments against prevention but they do offer counsel on its effective use and realistic expectations about outcomes.

Principles continued

7. The object of the exercise is to prevent the development of problems. It is counter-productive to think in terms of preventing a service. Services should be provided only when there is evidence that they benefit some children at some point in their development.
8. Professionals in agencies should work to a common definition of prevention and agree on how this activity differs from other forms of intervention, early and late.
9. Effective early intervention and prevention involve sharing knowledge and with it the burden of developing new knowledge separately or in combinations in different locations. No location will develop all the answers alone and all will have some contribution to make.

10. Early intervention need not mean early in a child's life. 'Early' refers to early in the development of any social or psychological problem and so can apply as accurately to a 16-year old exhibiting the first signs of mental health problems as to a three-year old whose difficulties in school may prefigure later behavioural problems.

11. Since the majority of support for children in need comes from within the state infrastructure of health, education and social services, effective prevention and early intervention will be delivered within or with the expressed cooperation of these agencies.

12. There is evidence for and against universal and targeted modes of prevention and early intervention activity (Rose, 1992). Targeted prevention is a better strategy since it can be used to assemble better knowledge about the development of children's needs.

13. A proportion of all expenditure of services for children in need should be devoted to evaluating the effectiveness of that service. The principle applies as much to interventions as it does to prevention and as much to the activity of local and health authorities as it does to the voluntary and private sector, and as much to existing responses as the innovative.

14. Many ideas for better prevention and early intervention are unproven. New initiatives should incorporate evaluation designed to explain the nature of the problems being addressed as well as the effectiveness of individual responses. A consistent and systematic approach to new initiatives would ensure effective sharing of results nationally and internationally.

15. The effects of good prevention and early intervention activity may be delayed for several years, for example, when effective parenting support for pre-school children reduces later antisocial behaviour. Evaluations have to allow for the measurement of such delayed effects.

16. Since nearly all children in need live with their families and nearly all separated children eventually return home, effective prevention and early intervention must take account of the ordinary features of family life and incorporate their strengths.

17. Much of the expertise concerning the solution of children's problems rests with children and families themselves. Effective prevention and early intervention begin with professionals asking how children and families cope with specific problems.

18. Effective prevention and early intervention strategies may depend on a sophisticated understanding of causal mechanisms, but they are likely to take the form of simple practical help for the practical problems experienced by children and their families.

19. There are considerable strengths in current arrangements for children in need as well as many identified weaknesses. Effective prevention and early intervention build upon agencies' known strengths and set clear targets to overcome identified weaknesses. Good prevention work is not a matter of starting from scratch.

20. Effective inter-agency work does not necessarily require or imply that work is done from the same geographical or bureaucratic location. The ability to work across conventional boundaries is a particularly important component of effective prevention and early intervention activity.

Examples of good practice

(1) High Scope

Probably the most referenced prevention and early intervention programme is the High Scope Perry pre-school established in Ypsilanti, a university town near Detroit, North

312   Michael Little

America in 1962. It sought to evaluate the benefits of good pre-school programmes on poor working class children. Its claims about being highly cost-effective in the long-term have elicited many counter claims and doubts about the methodology. That said the design is rigorous although the numbers involved were small.

High Scope aimed to help poor children make a better start in the transition from home to community through pre-school programmes. The initiative emerged from Headstart, a cross US initiative that by the autumn of 1965 had served half a million children in 13 000 centres supported by 41 000 teachers and a third of a million other helpers. The long-term goal of High Scope became the self-sufficiency of the children as adults.

Given its initial size, High Scope is incredibly well known. It was offered to 58 children aged three and four years. They were at high risk of psycho-social difficulty in adulthood and came from areas of low socio-economic well-being where children had traditionally performed badly in school. Two fifths came from families where no adult was employed; nearly half were from lone parent households; and, even by 1960's standards, exceptionally low proportions of the parents (11 per cent of the fathers and 21 per cent of the mothers) had finished their own schooling.

Teachers were employed to engage the children in a high quality, active learning programme in the two years prior to mainstream school. The half-day sessions were offered during school term times, every working day. Teachers worked with the children individually as well as in groups. The goal was to enhance cognitive and social skills. In addition, the teacher visited the child's home once a week and encouraged parents to take an active role in their child's education.

High Scope was rigorously evaluated (Schweinhart and Weikart, 1980; Schweinhart and others, 1993). The 58 children on the programme were matched with 65 deprived children who did not receive any special intervention. All 123 children, 72 boys and 51 girls were assessed every year between the ages of three and 11 years and then again at 15, 19 and 27 years. The results have been published in several papers and are best summarised in Weikhart and Schweinhart (1997). Initially, the High Scope children did not fare any better. The encouraging results came later in later follow-ups and extended to nearly all dimensions of the children's lives.

At 15 years, the High Scope children were reporting lower levels of involvement in crime than their matched cases and at 19 and 27 years they had experienced significantly fewer arrests. Most notably, the proportion of chronic offenders (defined as those arrested five or more times) was seven per cent for the High Scope graduates compared with 35 per cent for the controls. This outcome was no doubt encouraged by the higher income, home ownership rates and second car ownership of the High Scope children, which in turn probably bore some relationship to their higher rates of school completion. The economic cost-benefit analysis of the Ypsilanti scheme estimates that it saved seven dollars for every dollar spent on each individual involved, an extraordinarily high return for a scheme of its type.

(2) A contemporary and speculative example

Earlier in this article, research to help local and health authorities identify patterns of need in the children referred to help in a selected geographical location was considered

Prevention and Early Intervention with Children in Need   313

(Little and Madge, 1998). The methods used in this study have allowed health, education, social services and police to work together to design new services for specified groups of children in need. Several service designs have emerged in 12 international sites experimenting with this approach: one is offered here as an illustration.

In one mainly rural location with a total population of 100 000, 700 children each year referred to children's services because of their relatively minor social, emotional or learning needs have been targeted. These children had needs described as an acute form of adolescent unhappiness, which, left unattended, were thought by professionals as likely to be manifest in school exclusion, youth crime and strained family and social relationships.

The method used for service design in this context requires professionals jointly to examine quantitative and qualitative evidence on the needs of children in that category. The evidence comes from children referred for help in the previous calendar year. It extends to all aspects of children's lives. Professionals are next asked to specify the outcomes they think are achievable within a specified time period. They are asked to consult the relevant research evidence along the way. Having agreed potential outcomes, professionals are asked to set out services likely to achieve those outcomes. Next they turn to thresholds, specifying both the level of impairment to health and development required for a child to qualify for the specified service and other characteristics that can be used by professionals to select children for the intervention. Each new service has an evaluation built in, usually a randomised control trial or quasi-experimental design.

For the children with low-level emotional health problems just described, the desired outcomes were pretty clear cut. Professionals sought to help the child remain at home with relatives for at least a 12-month period. There was also a goal for the parent and child to be happy (if relationships were judged to be satisfactory at referral) or happier (if they were troubled at referral) six months after the intervention began. The programme intended that 95 per cent of referrals would not be convicted of a criminal offence within six months and that there would be some measured improvement in self-esteem in 75 per cent of cases. Fundamental to these outcomes, an objective was outlined to return all children in this group to school (if they were away) or to maintain them in full-time education with at least 90 per cent attendance.

To achieve these goals, an enhanced preventative programme is being established in the largest town in the area experimenting with the methodology. This encompasses an advice and information service covering such things as leisure and contraception and is thought of as a kind of Citizen's Advice Bureau for children. Those children meeting the thresholds for inclusion in the group and picked up by health, education, social or police services are then referred on to a designated youth coordinator funded by all the agencies. The coordinator ensures that all children get one of two services: (a) youth education support which involves mentoring by a volunteer working with the young person outside of and, where appropriate, inside school; (b) youth health support comprising specialist advice from an expert with 'street credibility'. Young people accepted onto the programme are offered up to 35 hours of education or health support over a three-month period as agreed with the coordinator.

Cases referred to the coordinator are being randomly assigned to the new service or to existing provision. Both groups are being followed up at six months with comparisons

314   Michael Little

concentrating on stability of living situations, self-esteem, participation in education, family and social relationships and criminality. It is too early to say whether the intervention is having its desired effects.

Conclusions

Interest in prevention and early intervention is, like much else in the children's services world, subject to change. But each time it comes into fashion, the focus is different and new insights and understandings emerge. In the current cycle, it is the potential coincidence between new resources for prevention activity and the concern to use and build an evidence base for children's services that excites.

There are many potential difficulties to overcome if this opportunity is to be seized. The knowledge base in children's services is extremely weak. Most agencies do not understand the pattern of need and many are struggling to quantify the volume of children and families being served and the way in which their business overlaps with that of other agencies. The amount being invested in understanding and producing evidence is pitiful; the contribution of all social services departments in England and Wales adds up to less than one pound for every thousand spent (compared with one in a hundred for the National Health Service dealing with medical matters). Local health authorities are better, but not much better. When the British government announced its SureStart programme to emulate the 1960s Headstart, it devoted less than one quarter of one per cent to researching its effects (Department for Education and Employment, 1999).

The bulk of the evaluation should be taking place within the infrastructure of children's services and should focus on the benefits, side effects and drawbacks of existing approaches. The low interest expressed in evidence can lead the uninformed observer to believe that social and health services in particular, are less concerned with prevention than are the smaller voluntary organisations operating outside of the central bureaucracy. (This perception is not helped by the fact that small voluntary organisations seem more anxious to evaluate outcomes.) From what little is known this is a misperception; the bulk of a social worker's, health visitor's and possibly a general practitioner or police person's day is likely spent on some form of activity engaging early on in the development of childhood difficulties.

As important as building a reliable knowledge base are some realistic expectations about what better prevention and early intervention can achieve for young people. Prevention is no more an alternative to early intervention than early intervention is to treatment or social prevention. It is the combination of these activities that can make a difference to children's lives. But, even then, the ultimate balance between the four parts of the professional contribution will never eradicate a need. The best that can be hoped for is to change the pattern of childhood disturbance in a community and that along the way, something can be learned about how that change was achieved. Those waiting for prevention to bring an end to or even significantly reduce levels of delinquency, child abuse or mental health problems will require a patience that endures beyond their lifetime.

Much of this speaks to a desire for some common language to help ease communication between those who seek to support children in need; from the top of each agency to the

Prevention and Early Intervention with Children in Need   315

bottom, from one agency to another and even between countries. Such a task is immense but agreeing what is meant by prevention and how this differs from early intervention and other activity on behalf of vulnerable children could make a valuable start. If nothing else is achievable in the context of the current preoccupation with all things preventative, this much should be possible.

References

Albee, G and Gullotta, T eds (1997) *Primary Prevention Works*. Thousand Oaks, Sage

Aldgate, J, Bradley, M and Hawley, D (1999) *Supporting Families Through Short-term Foster Care*, Stationery Office

Aldgate, J and Tunstill, J (1995) *Making Sense of Section 17*, HMSO

Axford, N, Little, M and Morpeth, L (1999) *Patterns and Thresholds of Need in an Ordinary Community*, Dartington Social Research Unit

Barclay, P (1982) *Social Workers: Their Roles and Tasks*, NISW

Department for Education and Employment (1999) *SureStart: A Guide for Trailblazers*, DfEE Publications

Department of Health (1995) *Child Protection: Messages from Research*, HMSO

Essen, J and Wedge, P (1978) *Continuities in Childhood Disadvantage*, Heinemann

Farrington, D (1990) 'Implications of criminal career research for the prevention of offending', *Journal of Adolescence*, **XIII**, 93–113

Farrington, D (1995) 'The development of offending and antisocial behaviour from childhood: key findings from the Cambridge study in delinquent development', *Journal of Child Psychology and Psychiatry*, **CCCLX**, 929–964

Hardiker, P, Exton, K and Barker, M (1991) 'The Social Policy Contexts of Prevention in Child Care', *British Journal of Social Work*, **XXI**, 341–359

Kolvin, I, Miller, F, Scott, D, Gatzanis, S and Fleeting, M (1990) *Continuities of Deprivation? The Newcastle 1000 Family Study*, Aldershot: Avebury

Little, M and Madge, J (1998) *Inter-Agency Assessment of Need in Child Protection*. Report to NHS Executive. Dartington Social Research Unit

Little, M and Mount, K (1999) *Prevention and Early Intervention with Children in Need*, Ashgate

Little, M and Ryan, M (1999) *Making Sense of Significant Harm*, Dartington Social Research Unit

Porter, R (1997) *The Greatest Benefit to Mankind: a medical history of humanity from antiquity to the present*, Harper Collins

Rose, G (1992) *The Strategy of Preventative Medicine*, Oxford Medical Publications

Rutter, M (1979) *Changing Youth in a Changing Society*, Nuffield Provisional Hospitals Trust

Rutter, M, Giller, H and Hagell, A (1998) *Anti-Social Behavior by Young People*, Cambridge University Press

Rutter, M and Smith, D eds (1995) *Psycho-social Disorders in Young People: Time Trends and Their Causes*, John Wiley

Sampson, R and Laub, J (1993) *Crime in the Making: Pathways and Turning Points Through Life*, Harvard University Press

Schweinhart, I and Weikart, D (1980) *Young Children Grow Up: The Effects of the Perry Pre-school Program on Youths Through Age 15*, Monographs of the High/Scope Educational Research Foundation, Number Seven

Schweinhart, I, Barnes, H and Weikart, D (1993) *Significant Benefits: The High-Scope Perry Pre-school Study Through Age 27*, Ypsilanti, Monograph of the High/Scope Educational Resource Foundation Number Ten

Sinclair, R, Hearn, B and Pugh, G (1997) *Preventive Work with Families*, National Children's Bureau

Thorpe, D and others (1980) *Out of Care: The Community Support of Juvenile Offenders*, Allen and Unwin

316   Michael Little

Tunnard, J 'Matching needs and services: emerging themes from its application in different local authority settings', *in* Ward, H *ed.* (1999) *Approaches to Needs Assessment in Children's Services*, HMSO

Wadsworth, M (1991) *The Imprint of Time: Childhood, History and Adult Life*, Clarendon Press

Weikart, D and Schweinhart, L 'High/Scope Perry Pre-school Program', *in* Albee, G and Gullotta, T *eds* (1997) *Primary Prevention Works*, Thousand Oaks, Sage

Welsh, B 'Economic Costs and Benefits of Primary Prevention of Delinquency and Later Offender', *in* Farrington, D and Coid, J *eds* (forthcoming 1999) *Early Prevention of Adult Anti-Social Behaviour*, University Press

West, D and Farrington, D (1973) *Who Becomes Delinquent?*, London, Heinemann

Contributor's details

Michael Little is Co-director, Dartington Social Research Unit, and Visiting Fellow at the Chapin Hall Center for Children at the University of Chicago. He is a career researcher on children in need.

[24]

Measuring Outcomes in the 'New' Children's Services

Nick Axford
Vashti Berry
DARTINGTON SOCIAL RESEARCH UNIT

ABSTRACT

This article seeks to help senior local policy-makers, managers and practitioners in children's services to develop robust but realistic and manageable strategies for measuring outcomes in a multi-disciplinary context. Drawing on orthodox research methods, it sets out strategies for measuring outcomes in children's services at individual child, service and community levels. It is intended to show how, in a given local jurisdiction, different approaches to measuring outcomes could fit together logically and within a reasonable budget, so creating an outcome culture and contributing to the development and integration of services. The principles outlined would also apply to adult services.

KEYWORDS: CHILD WELL-BEING; CHILDREN'S SERVICES; EVALUATION; INTEGRATION; MULTI-DISCIPLINARY; OUTCOMES; OUTCOME MEASUREMENT

Contact details: naxford@dartington.org.uk

Introduction

Under the *Children Act 2004* children's services agencies are required to work towards improving outcomes for children in the areas of health, safety, economic well-being, achievement, and enjoyment and contribution to society. They also need to provide evidence of progress in achieving these outcomes. This requirement forms part of a far wider movement towards accountable public services; indeed there is much valuable work relevant to this area. Major and established initiatives exist at international and national levels to monitor child well-being, notably the United Nations annual *State of the World's Children* reports and the *Kids Count* project to track the status of children in US states, while recent years have seen a growing emphasis on identifying trends at the community level (Ben-Arieh *et al*, 2001). In the UK there has been important conceptual and methodological work on measurement of outcomes, particularly in relation to children cared for away from home (Parker *et al*, 1991). Even so, a regular comprehensive analysis of the well-being of children in the UK is still long overdue (Bradshaw & Mayhew, 2005) and necessary changes to local practice and measurement strategies have been slow, agencies often admitting that they struggle to provide meaningful figures. Why is this?

Reasons can be found at several levels. Conceptually, there continues to be confusion about the definition of 'outcome'. Methodologically, there has been uncertainty about the meaning and techniques of evaluation and, arguably, a stronger focus on process than effectiveness – born in part of hostility in some quarters towards experimental approaches to determining service effectiveness. Practically, professionals are often distracted by competing demands (including the need to supply agency-specific performance data), nervous about statistics, constrained by funding and generally overwhelmed by public and government expectations. Organisationally, different agencies have tended to

Measuring Outcomes in the 'New' Children's Services

pursue different priorities from one another or, at best, to work in partnership on an *ad hoc* basis. The *Children Act 2004* requires a leap of imagination in the shape of 'whole systems working' where emphasis is given to co-operation to meet the five outcomes identified above (Hudson, 2005).

This article seeks to help senior local policy-makers, managers and practitioners in children's services to develop robust but realistic and manageable strategies for measuring child outcomes in this multi-disciplinary context. After a brief discussion of the definition and measurement of 'outcome', the article draws on orthodox research methods to set out strategies for evaluating outcomes in children's services at individual child, service and community levels. It is intended to show how, in a given local jurisdiction, different approaches to measuring outcomes could fit together logically and within a reasonable budget, so creating an outcome culture and contributing to the development and integration of services. Many readers will be familiar with the research terms used here but others may wish to consult a complementary article (Axford *et al*, 2005a) or any good text on evaluation. Given its aims, the article does not discuss concepts or methods in any detail, but instead deliberately makes extensive reference to useful sources on outcome measurement.

Measuring outcomes

Outcomes in children's services may be viewed from the perspectives of different stakeholders, including parents, professionals, the public and children (Parker *et al*, 1991). In the present context they refer to changes in a child's well-being that are the product of a policy or practice input. They are different from outputs, which refer to the effects of a process, such as a service, on an administrative indicator. Thus the number of children in residential or foster care, receiving special educational help or arrested in a specified period all concern outputs; they say little about whether life for those children is good or bad relative either to the norm or to what might reasonably be expected

by experts given the children's previous experiences. In contrast, having good physical health, being safe from abuse, showing good behavioural development and achieving one's potential at school all refer to well-being; life is better for these children than it would have been otherwise, irrespective of where they live or where they figure in the health, education, social care or youth justice systems. When linked to a service input they can be used as measures of outcome. A useful rule of thumb is that the things that we are concerned with for our own children invariably relate to outcomes not outputs.

The *Children Act 2004* is concerned with outcomes in all areas of children's lives, hence its five categories. There are other possible divisions, of course, including the seven life dimensions under the 'child development' heading of the *Assessment Framework* (DoH *et al*, 2000). The detail is less important than the principle, namely to acknowledge that there is a spread of outcomes; no single agency should focus exclusively on one area – indeed integrated services are encouraged to achieve common outcomes. The outcomes are to be pursued by children's services, defined here as a series of activities organised but not necessarily provided by health, education, social and police services as well as voluntary agencies on behalf of children with the intention of addressing an identified social need. Thus, for example, GPs and hospitals (working with social workers and teachers) need to contribute towards children's safety and achievement as well as to child health.

Given the significance of the *Children Act 2004* it makes sense for the selected local measures of outcome to relate directly to the five outcomes in the legislation. Care is required to ensure that they do actually capture outcomes, not outputs. Even the government outcomes framework falls short on this count when, for example, it advocates the number of re-registrations on the Child Protection Register as an indicator of child safety and counts access to children and adolescent mental health services as evidence of good mental health (DfES,

Measuring Outcomes in the 'New' Children's Services

2004). It is also widely acknowledged that children's services agencies typically collect too much information and do too little with it. Standard research procedures help to avoid such errors and involve specifying some dimensions of the concept in question, deciding on some measures to capture the dimension and, finally, developing a methodology to apply them. Thus, the flow of activity is:

Concept → Dimensions → Measures → Method.

Table 1, below, illustrates what this might mean in relation to three of the outcomes in the *Children Act 2004* and for children of different ages. Three observations are worth making about the nature of the data collected, their source and the methods by which they are collected. First, there are benefits to having a mix of quantitative and qualitative information. Second, it helps to have inputs from different sources and perspectives. Third, information can be gathered in various ways, including by observation and standardised self-completion instruments as well as from sifting through agency files. The sections that follow elaborate how such methods can be used to measure outcomes at the three levels already mentioned, namely the individual child, an agency/discrete service and the community.

(1) Individual (child) level

One approach to measuring outcomes at the first level is to encourage reflective practice among practitioners on individual cases. From a qualitative perspective, there is reflective learning (Gould & Taylor, 1996), although empirical accounts of its application in children's services are scarce. A more quantitative approach, known as single case experimental designs (SCED), involves systematically introducing and withdrawing therapeutic and situational factors while monitoring the subject's well-being (Kazi & Wilson, 1996; Dillenburger, 1998). The simplest design is the 'before and after' comparison. For instance, Sheldon (1984) describes a project to maintain a disruptive pupil in mainstream school. The number of classroom incidents (such as causing physical pain to others) per day were monitored both at the initial stage (pre-intervention) and while the intervention was applied (which included a time-out scheme for episodes of violence and a points scheme). This approach is used rarely in social care, partly because it is seen to conflict with therapeutic objectives, but practitioners report its usefulness, not least in the powerful demonstration effect for parents (Slonim-Nevo & Ziv, 1998).

The practices described in the previous paragraph can be developed through professional supervision and by ensuring that clinical

Concept (outcome) →	Dimensions →	Measures →	Method
Healthy → (0-5 years)	Physical health → Psychological health…	Weight → Motor skills →	Scales + chart Observation/tests
Enjoying life → (6-11 years)	Happy → Lack of stress …	Quality of life scale →	Self-completion in class
Contributing to → society (12-16 years)	Engaged in education → Altruistic activity …	Truancy rates → Behaviour →	School records SDQ (teacher version)

Table 1: EXAMPLES OF DEVELOPING METHODS TO MEASURE OUTCOMES*

* *The table should be read from left to right on each row, that is from concept through dimensions and measures to method. This is a simplification; for example each dimension listed could be sub-divided into further dimensions.*

assessment forms have space on them for the systematic recording of outcomes. This need only be in relatively simple terms, for example whether the child's needs have been met and if the child is at risk of maltreatment when the case closes. Clinical practice tools such as *Paperwork* can assist here, particularly when used in consultation with colleagues and supervisors (Little, 2002; Little & Mount, 2003).

A different approach at the individual child level involves applying screening instruments to identify children who are likely to develop specified difficulties. They can usually be administered quickly, and not necessarily by expensive, clinically trained professionals. (If they are being used for practice purposes they may need following up in a clinical interview.) The Strengths and Difficulties Questionnaire (SDQ), for instance, is suitable for detecting emotional, behavioural and social problems among children aged 3-16 years (Goodman, 1997). It takes as little as two minutes to complete – there are versions for parents, teachers and children – and generates a score that can be compared with normative data in order to give an idea of the seriousness of need and to help discriminate between normal and clinical cases. Numerous similar generic screening questionnaires for assessing psychopathology exist and cover similar content, are user-friendly and have evidence of validity and reliability; the choice of scale will depend on purpose and resources (for an overview see Verhulst & Van der Ende, 2002).

Initial assessment instruments can be adopted for the same purpose; for example the Bolton Child Concern model helps practitioners to categorise children according to the severity of their needs (Jones & O'Loughlin, n.d.). Similarly, the Dartington practice tool *Threshold* generates a global judgement of actual and likely impairment against a three-fold categorisation of seriousness, so indicating whether a child needs remedial intervention to ensure healthy development, and also identifies the type of impairment (physical, behavioural, emotional, etc) (Little *et al*, 2003).

When applied at the beginning and end of service episodes, such instruments – as with rating scales – provide a useful estimate of outcome. This is not to undermine the importance of disaggregating the notion of outcome to reveal differential development in different areas of children's lives, but there is a case for a general assessment (Parker, 1998).

(2) Agency and service level

The audit of agency files provides one method for measuring outcomes at agency level. Quantitative and qualitative methods exist to gather and then aggregate key data from agency files in order to identify broad patterns. For example, when applied to a representative sample of social services cases, it would give an indication of the type and severity of the children's needs, the services that the children and their families have used and the outcomes of any services (again in relatively simple terms, such as 'needs met?' and 'child at risk of maltreatment?'). Repeated periodically and over a sustained period to provide time-series data, such cross-sectional analyses indicate aggregate trends, although care is required to ensure that the data are comparable across different years (Tarls, 2000). Alternatively, a cohort of children can be tracked over time. Whichever approach is used, in order to translate what is effectively the **monitoring of well-being** to the **measurement of outcomes** it is necessary to link identified trends in well-being to developments in policy and practice. To give an example from a different field, it was such analysis that made it possible to attribute with confidence the sudden and dramatic fall in road accident deaths in the UK to the introduction of compulsory seat-belt-wearing in the *Road Traffic Act 1967* (Davies, 2003).

The *Looking After Children* materials are relevant under this heading. For example, one cohort study examined LAC records for a representative sample of 249 children placed away from home for 12 months or more in six English local authorities (Ward *et al*, 2003). It followed up the children for three years, gathering data on factors such as health

Measuring Outcomes in the 'New' Children's Services

and educational achievement as well as safety and placement stability. A similar study reinforced the message about the potential for aggregating individual LAC assessments in order to trace trends in the well-being of a group of children (Bailey *et al*, 2002). In Canada an alternative system for children in long-term care generated good-quality data using cross-sectional analyses, showing for example the proportion of children year-on-year who participate in team sports (relevant to the outcome of enjoyment) (Flynn *et al*, 2003), while a major collaboration in the US between researchers and providers uses administrative data to track children's well-being over time and study and plan service reforms (Goerge *et al*, 2001). Other systems such as *Matching Needs and Services* exist for children supported at home, and rely on a mixed group of professionals and researchers aggregating data from agency case files on all dimensions of children's lives (Little *et al*, 2001, 2002a).

A different approach to measuring outcomes involves evaluating discrete services provided by agencies. Here, evaluation refers to the use of social research procedures to investigate systematically the effectiveness of social intervention programmes with a view to improving policy and practice (Rossi *et al*, 1999). This distinguishes evaluation from longitudinal research, which measures what happens to children over time. The former must include the latter, but is distinct because something has been done to alter a child's life trajectory. Evaluation measures the success of that 'something'.

Non-experimental evaluations of services usually entail comparing measures applied pre- and post-intervention. Good measures are critical, and many standardised instruments are available (Hough, 2003; RMC Corporation, 2003; Montes Marqués, 2004) to complement bespoke questions designed for the evaluation in hand. Non-experimental methods can be strengthened in various ways. For instance, comparing actual outcomes with 'shadow controls' – that is, predictions about what would happen to the child

without any intervention – provides some indication of service efficacy and, therefore, whether actual outcomes are 'good' (Rossi *et al*, 1999; Axford & Berry, forthcoming). Confidence should be greatest for results that show a stronger effect when more intervention is received (the 'dose-response relationship') or where the logic of the service as set out in the plan is realised in practice (Rutter *et al*, 1998; Reynolds, 1998). This is to simplify, but much has been written in this area in recent years (Shaw & Shaw, 1997; Kazi, 2000; Shaw, 2004), and universities or independent research centres can advise on or implement the appropriate methodology.

Matching method to purpose is important, and experimental methods of evaluation are vital to establish with a high degree of certainty whether an intervention is effective (Macdonald, 1996). Random allocation studies are often costly and labour-intensive, and ethical concerns need to be dealt with properly. In the UK they are generally more common in child health (Eisen *et al*, 1992; Oakley *et al*, 2003) and, to a lesser extent, youth justice (Little *et al*, 2004; Shapland *et al*, 2004) than in social care for children, although studies do exist in the field, for example in relation to residential care, parenting support and therapy for sexual abuse victims (Cornish & Clarke, 1975; Scott & Sylva, 2004; Monck *et al*, 1996). Matched control (quasi-experimental) designs are lower in the hierarchy of evidence but also valuable and, as with RCTs, require expert assistance.

(3) Community level

By no means all children are in contact with services at any given time, even though some of those not served by agencies have levels of well-being similar to those of children who are receiving help. Another important approach to obtaining and analysing measures of outcome, therefore, operates at the community level and involves collecting epidemiological data on children resident in a given area using population survey methodologies. This approach is common in medicine and has been used extensively to chart the extent and nature of emotional and conduct problems among young people. One study, for example, analysed data on 15-16 year olds from national surveys undertaken between 1974 and 1999, and showed an increase in depression, anxiety and non-aggressive behavioural problems such as disobedience and stealing (Collishaw *et al*, 2004). Large national surveys like this are difficult to interpret at local level, so various methods of 'need profiling' populations in discrete geographical areas have also been developed (Percy-Smith, 1996). These provide reasonably robust baseline data on the well-being of local residents. For instance, Percy-Smith and Sanderson (1992) surveyed a sample of randomly selected adults from a district of a large UK city and asked them to assess their needs in areas such as health, housing and education.

Some progress has been made in adapting the epidemiological and community-profiling approaches for use with representative samples of families with children, involving semi-structured interviews with parents or carers in their home (eg Axford *et al*, 2004a). The survey sample might be selected from all children living in a particular electoral ward or conurbation, or from those of a given age in the area – children starting school, perhaps. In addition to providing hard data about children's health and development, surveys like these can include softer measures, such as how helpful families found particular services. Repeated periodically, and conditional on the use of appropriate techniques, they can indicate trends in child well-being; if data on services received are also collected, it is possible to estimate the impact on those trends of local interventions.

Connecting the parts

What should happen to all this information? The approaches described can be connected together as shown in *Figure 1*, overleaf. Results obtained at clinical (individual child) level through reflective practice (1a) and from screening instruments (1b) may be aggregated in agency need audits (2a).

Findings about patterns and levels of need from such audits may be used together with epidemiological data (3) to inform the design of new services (and, in some cases, the de-commissioning of unnecessary or ineffective provision). Such design work is best undertaken by a dedicated team of creative and analytic people, drawing on other evidence; this might include summarising the main messages from other audits of local need or reviewing an international database of proven programmes, including those maintained by Child Trends (2005) and this research centre. The emerging services can be evaluated (2b/c) and the findings fed into the design process. Periodically the outcome data contained in reports from 1–3 may be summarised in expert reviews. It is worth bearing in mind that in England the inspection of children's services will increasingly focus on the five outcomes from the *Children Act 2004* and, as far as possible, exploit existing data and documentation (CSCI *et al*, 2004).

The remainder of this section describes moves towards this approach to outcome measurement in a local children's services context in the UK. It is based on research and development work undertaken by the Dartington centre in collaboration with agencies in a district in South-West England with a child population of 21,600 (described more fully in Axford *et al*, 2004b). The district is classed as a rural area with coast and country and is not particularly deprived, ranking at the time 248th out of 366 districts on Townsend's index of deprivation (Gordon & Forrest, 1995). What follows is designed to give those responsible for planning and managing local children's services a sense of what is possible. Since the work mostly took place in the period 1996-2002 and was not designed to focus on outcome measurement, some additional comments are made about subsequent developments aimed at building on the approaches described.

Reflective practice (element 1a) was encouraged in the district through a partnership between Dartington and the social services department,

Measuring Outcomes in the 'New' Children's Services

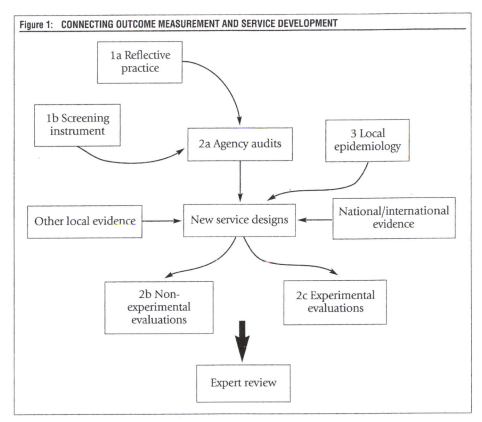

Figure 1: CONNECTING OUTCOME MEASUREMENT AND SERVICE DEVELOPMENT

involving regular expert lectures, an enhanced library facility for practitioners and assistance with identifying and applying evidence in individual cases (Randall, 2002; Thistlethwaite, 2000). Early prototypes of the *Threshold* and *Paperwork* practice tools – which have screening and review functions (1b) – were tested in the district but their implementation has been more extensive elsewhere.

A multi-agency need audit (element 2a) was conducted, involving a representative sample of 719 children referred with a social need to health, police, education and social services (Little & Madge, 1998). The *Matching Needs and Services*

method developed at Dartington was used. This involved completing a summary for each child of their situation on the day of referral in all areas of their life (this covers *de facto* the child's health, safety, achievement, enjoyment, economic well-being and contribution to society). A mixed group of professionals and researchers then grouped cases together according to the similarity of the children's needs, so forming 13 'need groups'. They included, for example, groups where the primary need was for 'simple practical assistance', for 'protection from deficient care', for 'help to overcome trauma' and for 'parenting support' (see also Little *et al*, 2002b). Since the groups varied in

Measuring Outcomes in the 'New' Children's Services

size, it would be possible to repeat the exercise in the same area but at a later stage to see whether and how the pattern has changed.

Moving to element (2b) in *Figure 1*, non-experimental evaluations were conducted of services designed for three of the need groups. These were selected for group size, the priorities of the local authority and the inclusion of children from all four stakeholder agencies mentioned above. For example, local findings about the need for better parenting support were used together with national and local evidence to design a new service. Again, the *Matching Needs and Services* method was followed. This involves five steps:

• identifying a group with similar need profiles
• agreeing on desired outcomes
• designing services that will logically achieve those outcomes
• developing threshold criteria to ensure that the right children receive the service
• deciding how to measure actual outcomes.

The evaluation of the new parenting support service found signs of improvement in perceived control and skills among parents, although the small numbers involved and the use of non-experimental methods made it difficult to draw firm conclusions about service efficacy (Madge & Morpeth, 2002).

Work at community level (element 3) involved a survey of families with children in one ward in the district, comprising 225 interviews with parents or carers in their homes and providing data on 500 children, a sample that was broadly representative in terms of the number and ages of children in each household (Axford *et al*, 2003). Data were collected via a semi-structured interview that covered child well-being on the dimensions referred to above. As well as employing a quantitative classification technique known as 'cluster analysis' the work used a prototype of the Dartington *Threshold* practice tool to estimate the level of actual and likely impairment to the children's health and development. The need data fed into the development of a local project under

the auspices of the Children's Fund, and a follow-up survey could examine changes in the proportion of children fitting into the 'few or no unmet needs' group or showing evidence of impaired health or development.

Several areas for development emerged from this work. The following points emphasise those that have greatest resonance with progress elsewhere in the field of outcome measurement.

First, there is a need for better training for practitioners on using specially-designed instruments and rating scales (Walter *et al*, 2004). Otherwise it is easy for aspects to be ignored or completed inaccurately, as happened in this instance with critical sections in the practice tools on reviewing outcomes. Experience suggests that coaching may help, at least in the initial stages of implementation. Assuming that information gathered at the individual child level is aggregated for the agency/service level, this approach offers efficiencies for busy practitioners by obviating the need to collect extra data.

Second, efforts should be made to capture children's insights and experiences directly. This shift is prompted largely by the view that children are social actors in their own right rather than passive objects to be acted on by adults (James & Prout, 1990). Among various methods for doing this are versions of rating scales adapted for completion by children. Connected with this is the value of going beyond the basic needs of development and a traditional focus on deficiencies in health, behaviour, achievement and so on, to include indicators of children's assets and positive well-being (Ben-Arieh *et al*, 2001). Because intermediate outcomes are often quite unstable, there is also a strong case for looking at what prevails at a number of points in a child's career in order to obtain an accurate picture of what happens (Parker, 1998).

A third point concerns the benefits of robust preparatory work aimed at making a service amenable to evaluation. The parenting support service evaluation discussed above suffered because some of the early clarity about target group criteria, service components and how the evaluation dovetailed with the process of service delivery became diluted in the nitty-gritty of practice. Real-world evaluation always meets obstacles, including the resistance of suspicious or hard-pressed agency staff, but they can be minimised by following a few set procedures (Axford *et al*, 2005b).

Fourth, the administrative data collected by professionals in the normal conduct of business to support the organisation's functions and stored internally could be exploited more fully. In the above example, follow-ups to the inter-agency audit would have enabled some analysis of change in child well-being over time. Moving beyond the descriptive, they would have allowed an assessment of the impact of policy and practice. Determining the net effect of policies and services invariably requires systematically relating inputs to indicators of child well-being, and while sophisticated statistical techniques and the power of computing make it easier to identify those factors that discriminate between one outcome and another, it is acknowledged generally that more such work is needed (Ben-Arieh *et al*, 2001).

A fifth consideration for service providers is the appropriate use of external expertise. Outcome measurement is arguably most effective when it involves collaboration between professionals and researchers (Maluccio *et al*, 2000). The above case study and previous examples have demonstrated the value of involving practitioners in collecting and analysing data at different levels and their critical role in helping service evaluations to run smoothly. However, professionals need not and cannot be expected to be expert in particular methods. For example, the appropriate sample size and sampling technique for community surveys depend on various factors and some of the statistical tests required to establish trends and service-effectiveness are complex. Arguably it is more important that local managers and policy-makers grasp the broad principles, know where to seek advice – be it from research textbooks (such as

Bryman, 2004) or statisticians based in universities – and are able to articulate their requirements to researchers clearly where necessary (SRA, 2002). This may also make the task seem less daunting.

The sixth point concerns the management and application of work to measure child outcomes. There are two parts to this. One is the need for a sustained planning commitment and investment of future resources. Establishing macro trends in well-being and linking them to services requires repeated measurement of the same indicators over time (though not necessarily every year). The other aspect is finding appropriate mechanisms for using evidence about the successes and failures of policies and programmes to plan services and allocate resources. The case study was more successful on the latter front, but recent experience suggests that both parts would benefit considerably from an over-arching strategy based on 'logic modelling' – an approach to strategic planning that enables the relevant agencies to come together and agree common and specific outcomes towards which services must work and the set of activities required to achieve these outcomes (Morpeth & Kemp, forthcoming). It is reasonable to hypothesise that this would also see outcome measurement acting as a catalyst for the fuller integration of services required by the *Children Act 2004*.

Conclusions

This article has outlined approaches for agencies that make up the 'new' children's services to monitor child outcomes as defined in the *Children Act 2004*. It has shown how the methods can fit together logically to chart general trends in aspects of child well-being, to inform service development and to measure the contribution of local services to any improvement. As well as addressing some of the conceptual and methodological issues raised at the outset, it is hoped that the suggestions begin to tackle the practical and organisational obstacles encountered by agencies when seeking to measure outcomes.

Measuring Outcomes in the 'New' Children's Services

Is the approach possible within a reasonable budget though? It depends, of course, on the definition of 'reasonable budget'. The pharmaceutical company GlaxoSmithKline spends about 15% of its turnover on research and development (Annual Report 2004). A large English county with a child population of 170,000 has an annual budget of approximately £650 million for children's services. In any given year a considerable amount of high-quality work to measure child outcomes could take place at individual child, agency/service and community levels for as little 0.1% of this amount. Of course, £650,000 is a lot of money viewed in the context of staff shortages, increasing levels of adolescent psychopathology, family centres threatened with closure and so forth, and the maths will be different for smaller authorities (the point is more important than the figures). The other way of looking at it, though, is to reflect on the likely benefits of better outcome measurement for children's services and vulnerable children and then to ask 'Can we afford not to spend 0.1%?'.

Acknowledgements

We would like to thank our colleagues Roger Bullock, Roy Parker and Emma Sherriff for helpful comments on an earlier draft of this article.

References

Axford N & Berry V (forthcoming) Exploring the potential of shadow controls in the evaluation of children's services. *International Journal of Social Research Methodology*.

Axford N, Berry V & Little M (2005b) *Enhancing Programme Evaluability: A Research Note*. Working Paper 6. Dartington Social Research Unit.

Axford N, Little M, Duffy L *et al* (2004a) *How Are Our Kids?* Working Paper. Tallaght West Childhood Development Initiative.

Axford N, Little M & Morpeth L (2003) *A Study of Children Supported and Unsupported in the Community*. Report submitted to the Department of Health. Dartington Social Research Unit.

Axford N, Little M, Morpeth L & Weyts A (2005a) Evaluating children's services: recent conceptual and methodological developments. *British Journal of Social Work* 35 (1) 73–88. See also www.dartington-i/evaluation.

Axford N, Madge J, Morpeth L & Pring J (2004b) Mapping the data needed to plan integrated services: a case study of children's services in one locality. *Journal of Integrated Care* 12 (3) 3–10.

Bailey S, Thoburn J & Wakeham H (2002) Using the 'Looking After Children' dimensions to collect aggregate data on well-being. *Child and Family Social Work* 7 (3) 189–201.

Ben-Arieh A, Hevener-Kaufman N, Bowers Andrews A *et al* (2001) *Measuring and Monitoring Children's Well-being*. Dordrecht: Kluwer Academic Publishers.

Bradshaw J & Mayhew E (Eds) (2005) *The Well-being of Children in the UK* (second edition). London: Save the Children.

Bryman A (2004) *Social Research Methods* (second edition). Oxford: Oxford University Press.

Child Trends (2005) *Lifecourse Model: Guide to Effective Programs for Children and Youth*. www.childtrends.org 'Projects and research' [Accessed 20th May 2005].

Collishaw S, Maughan B, Goodman R & Pickles A (2004) Time trends in adolescent mental health. *Journal of Child Psychology and Psychiatry* 45 (8) 1350–62.

Cornish D & Clarke R (1975) *Residential Care and its Effects on Juvenile Delinquency*. London: HMSO.

CSCI (Commission for Social Care Inspection) *et al* (2004) *Every Child Matters – The Framework for Inspection of Children's Services: Draft for Consultation*. www.everychildmatters.gov.uk. [21/3/05]

Davies P (2003) *Social Experiments: Organisation and application*. Social Research Association Conference on Social Experiments, London, 19th June.

DfES (Department for Education and Skills) (2004) *Every Child Matters: Change for Children*. www.everychildmatters.gov.uk. [21/3/05]

Department of Health, Department for Education and Employment and Home Office (2000) *Framework for the Assessment of Children in Need and their Families*. London: The Stationery Office.

Measuring Outcomes in the 'New' Children's Services

Dillenburger K (1998) Evidencing effectiveness: the use of single-case designs in child care work. In: D Iwaniec & J Pinkerton (Eds) *Making Research Work: Research Policy and Practice in Child Care*. Chichester: John Wiley and Sons.

Eisen M, Zellman G & McAlister AL (1992) A health belief's model social learning theory approach to adolescents' fertility control: findings from a controlled field trial. *Health Education Quarterly* 19 (2) 229–62.

Flynn R, Lemay R, Ghazal H & Hébert S (2003) P3M: a performance measurement, monitoring and management system for child welfare organisations. In: B McKenzie & K Kufeldt (Eds) *Child Welfare: Connecting Research, Policy and Practice*. Ontario: Wilfrid Laurier University Press.

Goerge RM, Lee BJ, Mackey Bilaver L *et al* (2001) *The State of the Child in Illinois 2000*. Chicago: Chapin Hall Center for Children.

Goodman R (1997) The Strengths and Difficulties Questionnaire: a research note. *Journal of Child Psychology and Psychiatry* 38 (5) 581–6.

Gordon D & Forrest R (1995) *People and Places 2: Social and Economic Distinctions in England*. Bristol: SAUS.

Gould N & Taylor I (Eds) (1996) *Reflective Learning for Social Work*. Aldershot: Ashgate.

Hough H (2003) *Tests and Measures in the Social Sciences: Tests Available in Compilation Volumes*. www.libraries.uta.edu/helen/Test&meas/Allkeywords.htm#D.

Hudson B (2005) Partnership working and the children's service agenda: is it feasible? *Journal of Integrated Care* 13 (2).

James A & Prout A (Eds) (1990) *Constructing and Reconstructing Childhood: Contemporary Issues in the Sociological Study of Childhood*. London: The Falmer Press.

Jones L & O'Loughlin T (n.d.) *Developing a Child Concern Model to Embrace the Framework*. Bolton: Area Child Protection Committee.

Kazi MAF (2000) Contemporary perspectives in the evaluation of practice. *British Journal of Social Work* 30 (6) 755–68.

Kazi MAF & Wilson J (1996) Applying single-case evaluation in social work. *British Journal of Social Work* 26 (5) 699–717.

Little M (2002) *Prediction: Perspectives on Diagnosis, Prognosis and Interventions for Children in Need*. Dartington: Warren House Press.

Little M, Axford N & Morpeth L (2002a) *Aggregating Data: Better Management Information and Planning in Children's Services*. Dartington: Warren House Press.

Little M, Axford N & Morpeth L (2003) *Threshold: Determining the Extent of Impairment to Children's Development*. Dartington: Warren House Press.

Little M, Bullock R, Madge J & Arruabarrena I (2002b) How to develop needs-led, evidence-based services. *MCC Building Knowledge for Integrated Care* 10 (3) 28–32.

Little M, Kogan J, Bullock R & Van der Laan P (2004) ISSP: an experiment in multi-systemic responses to persistent young offenders known to children's services. *British Journal of Criminology* 44 (2) 225–40.

Little M & Madge J (1998) *Inter-agency Assessment of Need in Child Protection*. Report submitted to the NHS Executive S&W. Dartington Social Research Unit.

Little M, Madge J, Mount K *et al* (2001) *Matching Needs and Services* (second edition). Dartington: Dartington Academic Press.

Little M & Mount K (2003) *Paperwork: The Clinical Assessment of Children in Need*. Dartington: Warren House Press.

Macdonald G (1996) Evaluating the effectiveness of social interventions. In: A Oakley & H Roberts (Eds) *Evaluating Social Interventions*. Ilford: Barnardo's.

Madge J & Morpeth L (2002) *Report of a Development Exercise to Evaluate a Service Designed to Meet the Need for Parenting Support*. Working Paper 3, Dartington Social Research Unit.

Maluccio AN, Ainsworth F & Thoburn J (2000) *Child Welfare Outcome Research in the United States, the United Kingdom, and Australia*. Washington DC: CWLA Press.

Monck E, Sharland E, Bentovim A *et al* (1996) *Child Sexual Abuse: A Descriptive and Treatment Study*. London: The Stationery Office.

Montes Marqués MP (2004) *Index of Instruments: Child Development in the Context of Residential Education*

Outcomes Study. Chicago: Chapin Hall Center for Children.

Morpeth L & Kemp F (forthcoming) Integrating children's services: a logical approach? *Journal of Integrated Care*.

Oakley A, Strange V, Toroyan T *et al* (2003) Using random allocation to evaluate social interventions: three recent UK examples. *Annals of the American Academy of Political and Social Science* **589** (1) 170–89.

Parker R (1998) Reflections on the assessment of outcomes in child care. *Children & Society* **12** (3) 192–201.

Parker R, Ward H, Jackson S *et al* (Eds) (1991) *Looking After Children: Assessing Outcomes in Childcare*. London: HMSO.

Percy-Smith J (Ed) (1996) *Needs Assessments in Public Policy*. Buckingham: Open University Press.

Percy-Smith J & Sanderson I (1992) *Understanding Local Needs*. London: IPPR. .

Randall J (2002) The practice-research relationship: a case of ambivalent attachment? *Journal of Social Work* **2** (1) 105–22.

Reynolds AJ (1998) Confirmatory program evaluation: a method for strengthening causal inference. *American Journal of Evaluation* **19** (2) 203–21.

RMC Corporation (2003) *Compendium of Assessment and Research Tools for Measuring Education and Youth Development Outcomes*. cart.rmcdenver.com.

Rossi P, Freeman H & Lipsey M (1999) *Evaluation: a Systematic Approach* (sixth edition). Thousand Oaks: Sage.

Rutter M, Giller H & Hagell A (1998) *Antisocial Behaviour by Young People*. Cambridge: Cambridge University Press.

Scott S & Sylva K (2004) The SPOKES Project: supporting parents on kids' education. In: D Quinton (Ed) *Supporting Parents: Messages from Research*. London: Jessica Kingsley Publishers.

Shapland J, Atkinson A, Colledge E *et al* (2004) *Implementing Restorative Justice Schemes (Crime Reduction Programme): a Report on the First Year*. Online Report 32/04. London: Home Office.

Shaw C (2004) *NIFTY Evaluation: an Introductory Handbook for Social Care Staff*. Research in Practice/National Children's Bureau.

Shaw I & Shaw A (1997) Keeping social work honest: evaluating as profession and practice. *British Journal of Social Work* **27** (6) 847–69.

Sheldon B (1984) Single case evaluation methods: review and prospects. In: J Lishman (Ed) *Evaluation* (second edition). London: Jessica Kingsley Publishers.

Slonim-Nevo V & Ziv E (1998) Training social workers to evaluate practice. *International Social Work* **41** (4) 431–42.

SRA (Social Research Association) (2002) *Commissioning Social Research: A Good Practice Guide* (second edition). London: Social Research Association. www.the-sra.org.uk/commissioning.pdf [20th May 2005].

Taris TW (2000) *A Primer in Longitudinal Data Analysis*. London: Sage Publications.

Thistlethwaite P (2000) *Evidence and Ethical Practice: An Evaluation of the DATAR Project for Devon Social Services*. Dartington Social Research Unit.

Verhulst F & Van der Ende J (2002) Rating scales. In: M Rutter & E Taylor (Eds) *Child and Adolescent Psychology and Psychiatry* (fourth edition). Oxford: Blackwell.

Walter I, Nutley S, Percy-Smith J *et al* (2004) *Improving the Use of Social Care Research*. SCIE Knowledge Review 7. Bristol: The Policy Press.

Ward H, Macdonald I, Pinnock M & Skuse T (2003) Monitoring and improving outcomes for children in out-of-home care. In: B McKenzie & K Kufeldt (Eds) *Child Welfare: Connecting Research, Policy and Practice*. Ontario: Wilfrid Laurier University Press.

Name Index